Volume II
Since 1560

WESTERN CIVILIZATION

The Continuing Experiment

BRIEF EDITION

Thomas F. X. Noble
University of Virginia

Barry S. Strauss
Cornell University

Duane J. Osheim
University of Virginia

Kristen B. Neuschel
Duke University

William B. Cohen
Indiana University

David D. Roberts
University of Georgia

Jennifer Michael Hecht
Nassau Community College

Houghton Mifflin Company   Boston   New York

Editor in Chief: Jean L. Woy
Sponsoring Editor: Andrea Shaw
Basic Book Editor: Elizabeth M. Welch/Jennifer E. Sutherland
Senior Project Editor: Christina M. Horn
Editorial Assistant: Leah Y. Mehl
Senior Production/Design Coordinator: Sarah Ambrose
Senior Manufacturing Coordinator: Priscilla J. Abreu
Senior Marketing Manager: Sandra McGuire

Volume II Cover Image: Jules Adler, *Le Grève au Creusot.* AKG Photo.

Cover Designer: Diana Coe

Printed in the U.S.A.

Library of Congress Catalog Card Number: 98-72224

ISBN: 0-395-88550-7

1 2 3 4 5 6 7 8 9-VH-02 01 00 99 98

Brief Contents

Contents

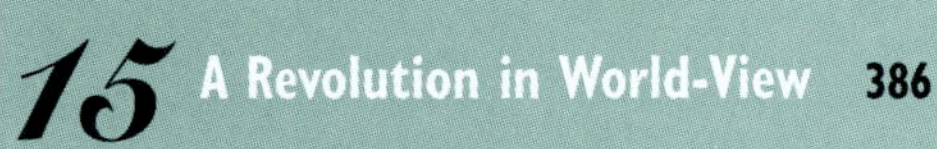

Maps

Documents

Preface

In 1994 Thomas F. X. Noble, Barry S. Strauss, Duane J. Osheim, Kristen B. Neuschel, William B. Cohen, and David D. Roberts published *Western Civilization: The Continuing Experiment*. Our goal was to create a book that was balanced and coherent; that addressed the full range of subjects a Western civilization book needs to address; that provided the student reader with interesting, timely material; that was up-to-date in terms of scholarship and approach—in short, a book that helped the instructor to teach and the student to learn. In 1998 the Second Edition appeared, revised on the basis of what colleagues told us of their experience in using the book.

Some instructors said that they liked our book but there was just too much of it: To cover the course in a single term or to assign extensive supplementary readings, they had to have a shorter text. The Brief Edition, based on the Second Edition, is designed to meet their needs. With four hundred fewer pages, it is 40 percent shorter than the original book. Prepared by Jennifer Michael Hecht of Nassau Community College, the Brief Edition retains the conceptual and analytical strengths of the original text. It continues to develop large themes, providing carefully chosen illustrative details. Instructors and students will still find the important and long-captivating stories of Western history. In addition, Professor Hecht has drawn on her own research and teaching to provide new content and features for students of the survey course. For example, she has brought the book up to the present by adding a new discussion of postmodernism and by updating the coverage of NATO expansion and the European monetary union.

CENTRAL THEMES AND APPROACH

The Brief Edition retains a strong chronological narrative and the traditional division of Western civilization into ancient, medieval, early modern, and modern periods. By focusing on the most important people and developments, we highlight the most enduring aspects of the story.

To enhance the narrative line, we continue to examine power in all its senses: public and private; economic, social, political, and cultural; symbolic and real: Who had power and who did not? How was power gained, lost, and exercised in a given time and place? How did people talk about power? What kinds of rituals and ceremonies displayed power? In addition, the Brief Edition has further developed the treatment of gender and gender relations to reflect new scholarship, adding, for example, a new section on the women's movement in the nineteenth century.

The Brief Edition also shares its parent's distinctive vision of the West as extending far beyond Western Europe. The Celtic world, Scandinavia, and the Slavic world are integral parts of the story. We look often at the lands that border the West—Anatolia/Turkey, western Asia, North Africa, the Eurasian steppes—in order to show the to-and-fro of peoples, ideas, technologies, and products. And we consistently situate the West in its global context, in recognition of the fact that just as the West has influenced the rest of the world, the rest of the world has influenced the West.

DISTINCTIVE FEATURES

To make the book as accessible as possible to teachers and students, the Brief Edition includes several new features. As with the full edition, each chapter begins with a thematic introduction to engage the reader's interest and point to the major issues that will follow. But, new for the Brief Edition, the introduction is followed right away by a list of "Questions and Ideas to Consider," to focus student attention on the major themes to think about while reading. In addition, a new "Chapter Chronology" at the beginning of every chapter organizes and conveniently reviews major events and developments. At the end of each chapter a "Summary" draws together the major topics and themes, and an annotated list of "Suggested Reading" alerts students to scholarly classics and exciting new works.

To give students an opportunity to work with primary sources, each chapter contains two or three boxed documents, including one called "Encounters with the West." To advance the book's goal of situating the West in its global context, these boxes show Western people commenting on the non-Western world and non-Western people commenting on the West.

The Brief Edition provides a generous selection of maps illustrating key political and social developments. Each chapter is also enhanced by a number of illustrations, including several new photographs selected to accompany new discussions in the last two chapters.

To meet the varying needs of instructors, *Western Civilization: The Continuing Experiment*, Brief Edition, is available in the following formats: a complete version (Chapters 1–27); Volume I: To 1715 (Chapters 1–15); and Volume II: Since 1560 (Chapters 13–27).

THE CONTINUING EXPERIMENT

We ask, finally, that you note the subtitle of the book: *The Continuing Experiment.* It was carefully chosen to convey our resolve to avoid a deterministic approach. We always try to give individual actors, moments, and movements the sense of drama, possibility, and contingency that they actually possessed. We, with faultless hindsight, always know how things turned out. Contemporaries often hadn't a clue. We respect them. Indeed, much of the fascination, and the reward, of studying Western civilization lies in its richness, diversity, changeability, and unpredictability. As you read and study our book, we hope that you will send us your own thoughts on how we might improve it. You can reach us at this e-mail address: college_history@hmco.com.

SUPPLEMENTS

We have thoroughly revised our array of text supplements provided to aid students in learning and instructors in teaching. These supplements include a *Study Guide*, an *Instructor's Resource Manual with Test Items*, a *Computerized Test Bank*, *Map Transparencies*, a *Videodisc Guide*, and a new multimedia supplement: a CD-ROM of interactive maps. Together, these items provide a tightly integrated program of teaching and learning.

The *Study Guide*, written by Miriam Shadi of Ohio University, includes an introductory essay on how to make the best use of your Western civilization course. Each chapter of the *Study Guide* contains learning objectives, an annotated outline of the chapter, multiple-choice questions keyed to the text, essay questions with guidelines, analytical questions, and map exercises.

The *Instructor's Resource Manual with Test Items*, prepared by Janice Liedl of Laurentian University, contains useful teaching strategies and tips for getting the most out of the text. Each chapter includes a summary and outline, learning objectives, lecture suggestions, discussion questions, recommended outside reading and writing assignments, and paper topics. For this edition, we have also expanded the *Instructor's Resource Manual* to include test questions and exercises that will help test the student's comprehension of the book.

An exciting addition to our map program is *GeoQuest*™, a CD-ROM of thirty interactive historical maps, available to both instructors and students. We also offer *The Western Civilization Videodisc/Videotape/Slid*e program, a multimedia collection of visual images, as well as a set of *Map Transparencie*s of all the maps in the text.

Finally, we are proud to announce the creation of our on-line primary-source collection, *BiblioBase*™*: Custom Coursepacks in Western Civilization.* This resource will allow instructors to elect from over six hundred primary-source documents to create their own customized reader.

ACKNOWLEDGMENTS

Jennifer Michael Hecht would like to thank her colleagues at Nassau Community College, particularly Professors Paul Devendittis, Gil Schrank, and Glenn Whaley, for their helpful comments and advice. She also thanks Mary Keller and the whole Hecht clan of traveling doctorates and showmen: Amy, Carolyn, Darla, Gene, and Jamey. She would also like to express warm thanks to the six original authors of *Western Civilization: The Continuing Experiment* for welcoming yet another voice into their midst and allowing the brief version to take on a character and shape of its own.

Much thanks are due to our former editor, Elizabeth Welch, whose enthusiasm and insight influenced the book's trajectory even after she had moved off the project, and to Jennifer Sutherland for ably helping to carry the project to its conclusion. We are grateful to Christina Horn, our Senior Project Editor, for her cheerful assistance and good judgment, and to Jean Woy, Editor in Chief for History and Political Science, for her confidence in the project.

Thomas F. X. Noble
Barry S. Strauss
Duane J. Osheim
Kristen B. Neuschel
William B. Cohen
David D. Roberts
Jennifer Michael Hecht

About the Authors

Thomas F. X. Noble Since receiving his Ph.D. from Michigan State University, Thomas Noble has taught at Albion College, Michigan State University, Texas Tech University, and since 1980 at the University of Virginia. He is the author of *The Republic of St. Peter: The Birth of the Papal State, 680–825; Religion, Culture and Society in the Early Middle Ages;* and *Soldiers of Christ: Saints and Saints' Lives from Late Antiquity and the Early Middle Ages.* Noble's articles and reviews have appeared in many leading journals, and he has contributed chapters to several books and articles to three encyclopedias. Noble, who was a member of the Institute for Advanced Study in 1994, has been awarded fellowships by the National Endowment for the Humanities (twice) and the American Philosophical Society.

Barry S. Strauss Professor of history and classics at Cornell University, where he is also director of the Peace Studies Program, Barry S. Strauss holds a Ph.D. from Yale University. He has received several academic fellowships, including one from the National Endowment for the Humanities and a Rockefeller Visiting Fellowship. He is the recipient of the Clark Award for excellence in teaching from Cornell. His many publications include *Athens After the Peloponnesian War, Fathers and Sons in Athens, The Anatomy of Error: Ancient Military Disasters and Their Lessons for Modern Strategists* (with Josiah Ober), and *Hegemonic Rivalries from Thucydides to the Nuclear Age* (with R. N. Lebow).

Duane J. Osheim A Fellow of the American Academy in Rome with a Ph.D. in history from the University of California, Davis, Duane Osheim is professor of history and associate dean of the Graduate School of Arts and Sciences at the University of Virginia. He is the author of *A Tuscan Monastery and Its Social World* and *An Italian Lordship: The Bishopric of Lucca in the Late Middle Ages*, as well as numerous papers and articles on rural life, religious experience, and medieval plagues.

Kristen B. Neuschel Associate professor of history at Duke University, Kristen B. Neuschel received her Ph.D. from Brown University. She is the author of *Word of Honor: Interpreting Noble Culture in Sixteenth-Century France* and articles on French social history and European women's history. In 1988 she received the Alumni Distinguished Undergraduate Teaching Award for excellence in teaching at Duke.

William B. Cohen Since receiving his Ph.D. at Stanford University, William Cohen has taught at Northwestern University and Indiana University, where he is now professor of history. A previous president of the Society for French Historical Studies, Cohen has received several academic fellowships, among them a National Endowment for the Humanities and a Fulbright fellowship. Among his many publications are *Rulers of Empire, The French Encounter with Africans, European Empire Building, Robert Delavignette and the French Empire, The Transformation of Modern France,* and *Urban Government and the Rise of the French City.*

David D. Roberts After taking his Ph.D. in modern European history at the University of California, Berkeley, David Roberts taught at the Universities of Virginia and Rochester before becoming professor of history at the University of Georgia in 1988. A recipient of Woodrow Wilson and Rockefeller Foundation fellowships, he is the author of *The Syndicalist Tradition and Italian Fascism, Benedetto Croce and the Uses of Historicism,* and *Nothing but History: Reconstruction and Extremity after Metaphysics,* as well as numerous articles and reviews.

Jennifer Michael Hecht Since earning her Ph.D. from Columbia University in 1995, Jennifer Michael Hecht has taught European history and the history of science at Nassau Community College. Her studies of nineteenth-century French anthropology and philosophy have appeared in *French Historical Studies, The Journal of the History of the Behavioral Sciences,* and *Isis* (forthcoming). She has also written for *The Partisan Review, The Denver Quarterly, The Antioch Review,* and other journals.

CHAPTER 13

Europe in the Age of Religious War, 1555–1648

In the early hours of August 24, 1572, armed noblemen accompanied by the personal guard of the king of France hunted out about one hundred other nobles, asleep in their lodgings in and around the royal palace in Paris, and murdered them in cold blood. The attackers were Catholic, their victims were Protestant—but all were French nobles, many of them related to one another. The king and his counselors had planned the murders as a preemptive strike because they feared that other Protestant noblemen were gathering an army outside of Paris. But when ordinary Parisians joined in, the calculated strike became a general massacre. About three thousand Protestants were murdered in Paris over the next three days.

This massacre came to be called the Saint Bartholomew's Day Massacre for the Catholic saint on whose feast day it began. Though particularly horrible in its scope (indeed, thousands more people were murdered in the French provinces as word of events in Paris spread), the massacres were not unusual in the deadly combination of religious and political antagonisms they reflected. Throughout Europe ordinary people took religious conflict into their own hands as rulers, for their part, tried to enforce religious uniformity, or at least religious peace.

Existing political tensions contributed to instability and violence, especially when reinforced by religious difference. Royal governments continued to consolidate authority, but resistance to royal power by provinces, nobles, or towns accustomed to independence now might have religious sanction. In several conflicts between Spain and the Netherlands, for example, religious issues were inseparable from political struggles. Tensions everywhere were also worsened by the rise of prices and unemployment as the sixteenth century wore on. These economic problems affected the rich as well as the poor and created particular hardship for working women. Economic stress was heightened because changes in military technology and tactics made warfare itself more destructive than ever before.

The late sixteenth and early seventeenth centuries were a period of extraordinary violence, but they were also distinguished by great innovation in statecraft. Queen Elizabeth transformed England through inspired diplomacy, aggressive development of the country's talent and resources, and strong leadership in military and religious conflicts. This was also a period of innovation in the arts. The plays of Shakespeare, for example, mirrored the passions but also reflected on the tensions of the day and helped to analyze Europeans' circumstances with a new degree of sophistication.

Questions and Ideas to Consider

- In what ways did economic distress affect men and women differently?
- What was "iconoclastic fury"? What did it suggest about the relations between Spain and the Netherlands? What did Margaret of Parma do about the situation?
- Queen Elizabeth of England was widely recognized as an extraordinarily intelligent and able ruler. What were the chief accomplishments of her reign? How did she negotiate the difficulties of being a female ruler in a patriarchal society?
- What was the Defenestration of Prague? Why was it significant?
- When printing and literacy were first becoming widespread, cultures of drama and oral expression were still vibrant. Using specific examples from Montaigne, Shakespeare, and Cervantes, discuss this phenomenon.

SOCIETY AND THE STATE

Religious strife, warfare, and economic change disrupted the lives of whole communities in the late sixteenth and early seventeenth centuries. The sixteenth century, especially, saw profound economic transformation that, by the end of the century, altered power relations in cities, in the countryside, and in the relationship of both to central governments.

The most obvious economic change was a steady rise in prices, which resulted in the concentration of wealth in fewer hands. Economic change did not spawn all of this era's social and political change: States made war for religious and dynastic reasons more than for calculated economic advantage. Nevertheless, the movements of the economy and the effects of war together created notable shifts in centers of wealth and power.

Economic Transformation and the New Elites

Sixteenth-century observers attributed rising prices to the inflationary effects of the influx of precious metals from Spanish territories in the New World. Historians now believe that there were also European causes for this "price revolution." Steady population growth caused a relative shortage of goods, particularly food, and the result was a rise in prices. Both the amount and the effect of price changes were highly localized, depending on factors such as the structure of local economies and the success of harvests. Between 1550 and 1600, however, the price of grain may have risen between 50 and 100 percent, and sometimes more, in cities throughout Europe—including eastern Europe, the breadbasket for growing urban areas to the west. Where we have data about wages, we can estimate that wages lost between one-tenth and one-fourth of their value by the end of the century. The political and religious struggles of the era thus took place against a background of increasing want.

These economic changes affected the wealthy as well as the poor. During this period, monarchs were making new accommodations with the hereditary aristocracy—with the Crown usually emerging stronger, if only by making concessions to aristocrats' economic interests. Underlying this new symbiosis of monarchy and traditional warrior-nobles were the effects of economic

CHAPTER CHRONOLOGY

1559	Peace of Cateau-Cambrésis; Act of Supremacy (England)
1565	Netherlands city councils and nobility ignore Philip's law against heresy
1566	Calvinist "iconoclastic fury" begins
1567	Duke of Alba arrives in the Netherlands; Margaret of Parma resigns her duties as governor-general
1571	Defeat of Turkish navy at Lepanto
1576	Sack of Antwerp
1579	Union of Utrecht
1588	Defeat of Spanish Armada
1598	Edict of Nantes
1603	Death of Elizabeth I
1609	Truce is declared between Spain and the Netherlands
1618	Bohemian revolt against Habsburg rule Defenestration of Prague
1619	Ferdinand II is elected Holy Roman emperor
1619	Frederick, elector of the Palatinate, is elected king of Bohemia
1620	Catholic victory at Battle of White Mountain
1621	Truce between Spain and the Netherlands expires; war between Spain and the Netherlands begins
1626	Imperial forces defeat armies of Christian IV of Denmark
1629	Peace of Alais
1631	Swedes under Gustav Adolf defeat imperial forces
1632	Death of Gustav Adolf
1635	Peace of Prague
1640–1653	The "Long Parliament" is in session
1648	Peace of Westphalia

changes that would eventually blur the lines between these noble families and new elites and simplify power relationships within the state.

Conditions in the countryside, where there were fewer resources to feed more mouths, grew less favorable. But at the same time expanded production and trade delivered more capital to wealthy families to invest in the countryside. As a result, a stratum of wealthy, educated, and socially ambitious "new gentry," as these families were called in England, began to appear. Many of the men of these families were royal officeholders. Many bought titles or were granted nobility as a benefit of their offices. They often lent money to royal governments, as the monumental expense of wars made becoming a lender to the government an attractive way to live off one's capital. Monarchs deliberately favored these new gentry as counterweights to independent aristocrats.

City governments also changed character as wealth accumulated in the hands of formerly commercial families. By 1600 traditional guild control of government had been subverted in many places. Town councils came to be dominated by successive generations of privileged families, and towns became more closely tied to royal interests by means of the mutual interests of the Crown and town elites. The long medieval tradition of towns serving as independent corporate bodies had come to an end.

Economic Change and the Common People

The growth of markets in Europe and Spanish possessions overseas had a profound effect on urban producers in western Europe. Production of cloth on a large scale for export, for example, now required huge amounts of capital—much more than a typical guild craftsman could amass. In many regions, guild members lost political power, and the guild structure itself began to break down. Master artisans began to treat apprentices virtually as wage laborers, at times letting them go when there was not enough work.

The effect on women workers was particularly dramatic. One of the first reflections of the dire circumstances faced by artisans was an attempt to lessen competition at the expense of the artisans' own mothers, sisters, daughters, and sons. Increasingly, widows were forbidden to continue practicing their husbands' trades, though they headed from 10 to 15 percent of households in many trades. Women had traditionally learned and practiced many trades but rarely followed the formal progress from apprenticeship to master status. A woman usually combined work of this kind with household production, with selling her products and those of her husband, and with bearing and nursing children. Exclusion of women from guild organization appears as early as the thirteenth century but now began regularly to appear in guild statutes. In addition, town governments tried to restrict women's participation in work such as selling in markets, which they had long dominated. Even midwives had to defend their practices, even though as part of housewifery women were expected to know about herbal remedies and practical medicine. (See the box "A Woman Defends Her Right to Practice Healing.") Single women and widows experienced increasing difficulty supporting themselves and their children.

Many women found work in cloth production, for spinning was a life skill that women learned as a matter of course. Cloth production was changing, too; it became increasingly controlled by new investor-producers with significant capital and access to distant markets. These entrepreneurs bought up large amounts of wool and hired it out to be cleaned, spun into thread, and woven into cloth by wage laborers in urban workshops or by pieceworkers in their homes. In the countryside, thousands of women and men helped to support themselves and families in this way.

In western Europe, countless peasants lost their lands to wealthy elites, "rentiers," who lent them money and claimed the land when the money was not repaid. Other peasants were unable to rent land as rents rose. To survive, some sought work as day laborers. Many found their way to cities, where they swelled the ranks of the poor. Others became part of the expanding network of cloth production, combining spinning and weaving with subsistence farming. One bad harvest might send them out on the roads begging or odd-jobbing; many did not long survive such a life.

In eastern Europe, peasants faced other dilemmas. The more densely urbanized and wealthy western Europe sought grain, from eastern Germany, Poland, and Lithuania. Thus, there was an economic incentive for landowners in eastern Europe to bind peasants to the land just as the desire of their rulers for greater cooperation had granted the landlords more power. Serfdom now spread in eastern Europe at the same time that it was gradually disappearing in the West.

Coping with Poverty and Violence

The common people of Europe did not submit passively either to economic difficulties or to the religious and political crises of their day. Whether Catholic or Protestant, common people took the initiative in attacking members of the other faith. At the community level, heretics were considered to be spiritual pollution that might provoke God's wrath. Thus, ordinary citizens believed that they had to eliminate heretics if the state failed to do so.

Townspeople and country people participated in riots and rebellions to protest their circumstances when the situation was particularly dire. The devastation of civil war in France, for example, led to a number of peasant rebellions and urban uprisings. Former soldiers, prosperous farmers, or even noble landlords whose economic fortunes were tied to peasant profits might lead rural revolts. If they succeeded, it would be only to relieve a local problem, such as a local tax burden. Urban protests often

A Woman Defends Her Right to Practice Healing

In this document, Katharine Carberiner testifies to the city council of Munich that she does not deliberately compete with male doctors but has skills that might lead other women to choose her rather than male medical practitioners.

I use my feminine skills, given by the grace of God, only when someone entreats me earnestly, and never advertise myself, but only when someone has been left for lost. . . . I do whatever I can possibly do . . . using only simple and allowable means that should not be forbidden or proscribed in the least. Not one person who has come under my care has a complaint or grievance against me. If the doctors, apothecaries or barber-surgeons have claimed this, it is solely out of spite.

At all times, as is natural, women have more trust in other women to discover their secrets, problems and illnesses, than they have in men—but perhaps this jealousy came from that. Undoubtedly as well, husbands who love and cherish their wives will seek any help and assistance they can, even that from women, if the wives have been given up (by the doctors) or otherwise come into great danger.

Because I know that I can help in my own small way, I will do all I can, even, as according to the Gospel, we should help pull an ox out of a well it has fallen into on Sunday.

Source: Merry Wiesner, "Women's Defense of Their Public Role," in Mary Beth Rose, ed., *Women in the Middle Ages and the Renaissance* (Syracuse: Syracuse University Press, 1986), p. 9.

began spontaneously when new grievances worsened existing problems. In Naples, in 1585, food riots were provoked not simply by a shortage of grain but by a government decision to raise the price of bread during the shortage. The property of the privileged was sometimes seized and city leaders were sometimes killed, but these protests rarely generated lasting political change.

Governments tried to cope with the increasing problem of poverty by changing the administration and scale of poor relief. In both Catholic and Protestant Europe, caring for the poor became more institutionalized and removed from religious impulses. In the second half of the sixteenth century, public almshouses to distribute food or to care for orphans sprang up in towns throughout Europe. These institutions reflected an optimistic vision, drawn from humanism, of an ideal Christian community. But by the end of the century, the distribution of food was accompanied by attempts to distinguish "deserving" from "undeserving" poor, by an insistence that the poor be forced to work to receive their ration of food, and even by an effort to compel the poor to live in almshouses and poorhouses. European elites were beginning to view the poor as a social problem, in need of collective control and institutional discipline.

The Hunt for Witches and the Illusion of Order

Between approximately 1550 and 1650, Europe saw a dramatic increase in the persecution of women and men for alleged witchcraft. Approximately a hundred thousand people were tried and about sixty thousand executed. The surge in witch-hunting was closely linked to the aftermath of the Protestant Reformation.

Food and Clothing Distributed by Government Officials In this rendering, a poor woman receives bread, and a destitute man clothing. Wealthy citizens' wills began to reflect the new definition of charity: Bequests to institutions increased and personal donations to the poor dwindled. *(The British Library)*

Certain kinds of witchcraft had long existed in Europe. So-called black magic of various kinds—one peasant casting a spell on another peasant's cow—had been common since the Middle Ages. What began to make black magic seem menacing to authorities were theories linking black magic to Devil worship. Religious leaders and legal scholars first began to advance such theories in the fifteenth century. By the late sixteenth century, both Catholic and Protestant elites viewed a witch not only as someone who might cast harmful spells but also as a heretic. Persecution for witchcraft rose dramatically after the initial phases of the Reformation ended, reflecting a continuation of reforming zeal directed at the traditional forms of folk religion and magic.

As far as we can tell, no proof that an accused person ever attended a Devil-worshiping "black" Sabbath was ever produced in any witch trial. Nevertheless, authorities were certain that Devil worship occurred, so convinced were they that Satan was in their midst and that the folkways of common people were somehow threatening.

Contemporary legal procedures allowed the use of torture to extract confessions. Torture or the threat of torture led most of those accused of witchcraft to "confess." Probably willing to say what they thought their captors wanted to hear, many named accomplices. In this way, a single initial accusation could lead to dozens of prosecutions. In regions where procedures for appealing convictions and sentences were fragile or nonexistent, prosecutions were pursued with zeal. They were widespread, for example, in the small principalities and imperial cities of the Holy Roman Empire, which were virtually independent of all higher authority.

Prosecutions numbered in the thousands in Switzerland, Poland, France, and Scotland. The majority—perhaps 80 percent—of those convicted and executed in all areas of Europe were women, many of them poor. The marked increase in poverty during the late sixteenth and early seventeenth centuries made poor women particularly vulnerable to accusations of witchcraft. It was easier to find such a person menacing—and to accuse her of something—than to feel guilty because of her evident need. The modern stereotype of the witch as an ugly old crone dates from this period.

Christian dogma and classically inspired humanistic writing portrayed women as morally weaker than men and thus as more susceptible to the Devil's enticements. Devil worship was described in sexual terms, and the prosecution of witches had a voyeuristic, sexual dimension. The bodies of accused witches were searched for the "Devil's mark"—a blemish thought to be the imprint of the Devil. Both Protestantism and Catholicism taught that sexual lust was evil. One theory has found the roots of witch-hunting in the guilt elite men suffered over their own sexual longings.

The witch-hunts virtually ended by the late seventeenth century, as intellectual energies shifted from religious to scientific thought. Reflecting religious fear and guilt and class divisions, the witch-hunts are central to an understanding of European life in this period.

IMPERIAL SPAIN AND THE LIMITS OF POWER

To contemporary observers, no political fact of the late sixteenth century was more obvious than the ascendancy of Spain. Philip II (r. 1556–1598) presided over the greatest empire since the time of Rome. Yet imperial Spain did not escape the turmoil of the era. An explosive combination of religious dissent and political disaffection led to revolt against Spain in the Netherlands. This conflict reflected the tensions of sixteenth-century political life: towns, provinces, and nobles trying to safeguard medieval liberties against efforts at greater centralization, with the added complications of economic strain and religious division. The revolt also demonstrated the material limits of royal power, since even with gold and silver from the American colonies pouring in, Philip could at times barely afford to keep armies in the field.

The Revolt of the Netherlands

Philip II's power stemmed in part from the far-flung territories he inherited from his father, the Habsburg Holy Roman emperor Charles V: Spain, the Low Countries (the Netherlands), the duchy of Milan, the kingdom of Naples, and the conquered lands in the Americas (see Map 13.2). Treasure fleets bearing precious metals from the New World began to reach Spain regularly during Philip's reign. In addition, Spain now belonged to an expanding trading economy unlike any that had existed in Europe before. To supply its colonies, Spain needed timber and other shipbuilding materials from the hinterlands of the Baltic Sea. Grain from the Baltic region fed the urban population of Spain (where wool was the principal cash crop) and the Netherlands, while the Netherlands, in turn, was a source of finished goods, such as cloth. The major exchange point for all these goods was the city of Antwerp in the Netherlands, the leading trading center of all of Europe.

Thus, Spain's expanding trading network necessitated tight links with the Netherlands, the real jewel among Philip's European possessions. These seventeen provinces (corresponding roughly to the modern nations of Belgium and the Netherlands; Map 13.1) had been centers of trade and manufacture since the twelfth century. Each province had a representative assembly (Estates) that controlled taxation, but each also acknowledged a governing council sitting in Brussels as the central administrative authority. Heading the principal council of state was a governor-general, typically, like Philip, a member of the Habsburg family. Yet political power, here and elsewhere, was still highly decentralized, and Philip, like other rulers, could rule effectively only with the cooperation of local elites. Philip's clumsy efforts to adjust this distribution of power in his favor pushed his subjects in the Netherlands into revolt.

Map 13.1 The Netherlands, 1559–1609 The seventeen provinces of the Netherlands were strikingly diverse politically, economically, and culturally. Like his father, Philip was, technically, the ruler of each province separately: He was count of Flanders, duke of Brabant, and so forth.

Tensions arose partly over taxation and partly over Spanish insistence on maintaining tight control. When the Peace of Cateau-Cambrésis of 1559 brought an end to the fighting between the Habsburgs and the Valois kings of France, the people of the Netherlands hoped for lower taxes and reduced levels of Spanish control.

Philip, born and raised in Spain, had little real familiarity with the densely populated, linguistically diverse Netherlands and never visited there after 1559. He appointed as governor-general his half-sister, Margaret of Parma, who presided over a council made up exclusively of Spaniards and men with close ties to the Spanish court. These arrangements affronted local nobles who were accustomed to positions of influence in the council of state.

To economic and political tensions were added severe religious problems created by Philip's aggressive pursuit of Protestant "heretics." Unlike his father, Philip directed the hunt for heretics not just at lower-class dissenters but also at well-to-do Calvinists, who now existed in increasing numbers. Punishment for heresy now included confiscation of family property as well as execution of the individual. By 1565, municipal councils in the Netherlands were routinely refusing to enforce Philip's religious decrees, believing that urban prosperity—as well as their personal security—depended on relative restraint in the prosecution of heresy.

During the spring and summer of 1566, religious dissension in the Netherlands grew dramatically. Encouraged by greater tolerance, Protestants began to hold open-air meetings, and in many towns ordinary people began to embrace Protestantism for the first time. In a series of actions called the "iconoclastic fury," townsfolk stripped Catholic churches of the relics and statues deemed idolatrous by Calvinist doctrine. Food riots also occurred. Both Spanish authorities and local elites feared the outbreak of general unrest.

By early 1567, Calvinist insurgents had seized two towns in the southern Netherlands, hoping to spark a general revolt that would secure freedom of worship. Although some nobles also supported a widening rebellion, Margaret of Parma successfully quelled the uprisings by rallying city governments and loyal nobles, now alarmed for their own power and property. But she then learned that far away in Spain a decision had been made to send the Spanish duke of Alba with an army of ten thousand men.

Alba arrived in August 1567 and acted more like a conqueror than a peacemaker. He billeted troops in friendly cities, established new courts to try rebels, arrested thousands of people, executed about a thousand rebels (including Catholics as well as prominent Protestants), and imposed new taxes to support his army. Thus, Alba repeated every mistake of Spanish policy that had triggered rebellion in the first place.

Margaret of Parma resigned in disgust and left the Netherlands. Protestants escaped into exile and were joined by nobles who had been declared treasonous for minor lapses of loyalty. The most important of these was William of Nassau, prince of Orange (1533–1584), whose lands outside of the Netherlands, in France and the empire, lay out of Spanish reach and so could be used to finance continued warfare against Spain. Thus, a significant community with military capability began to grow in exile.

In 1572 ships of exiled Calvinist privateers known as the "Sea Beggars" captured some fifty towns in the northern provinces. The towns' impoverished inhabitants—eager to strike a blow at expensive Spanish rule—welcomed the exiles. For the rest of the century, the northern provinces became increasingly Calvinist strongholds and were the center of opposition to the Spanish, who concentrated their efforts against rebellion in the wealthier southern provinces. Occasionally the French and English lent aid to the rebels. The Spanish never had the resources to crush the rebellion.

Some northern cities improved their fortifications by constructing new defensive works known as "bastions"; such cities could not be taken by storm but had to be besieged for long periods. Military campaigns in the Netherlands now consisted of grueling sieges, skirmishes in a city's surrounding area for control of villages' supplies, and occasional pitched battles between besiegers and forces attempting to break the siege. Inevitably, the army put a great strain on the countryside, and both soldiers and civilians suffered great privations. On occasion, Spanish troops reacted violently to difficult conditions and to delayed pay (American treasure dwindled badly between 1572 and 1578). In 1576, Spanish troops sacked the hitherto loyal southern city of Antwerp and massacred about eight thousand people, an event long remembered as the "Spanish Fury."

In 1579 the northern provinces concluded a defensive alliance, the Union of Utrecht, against

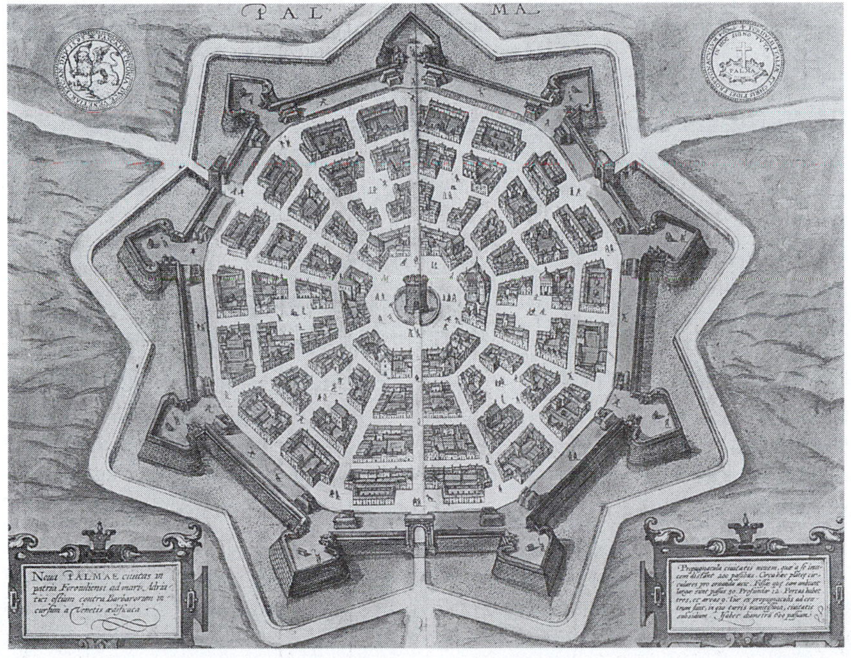

The Bastion Seen here in an example from an Italian fortress, the bastion was the triangular projection from the fortress wall. It enabled defenders to fire on the flanks of besieging forces; lower than medieval fortress walls and reinforced with earth, walls built in this manner were also less vulnerable to artillery blasts. *(Universitäts und Stadtbibliothek Cologne)*

the Spanish-controlled south, now governed by Margaret's son, Alexander, duke of Parma. Parma met with losses and faced declining resources as Spain diverted money to conflicts with England and with France. In 1609 a twelve-year truce was finally concluded between Spain and the northern provinces. This truce did not formally recognize the "United Provinces" as an independent entity, though in fact they were.

The independent United Provinces (usually called the Netherlands) was a fragile state, an accident of warfare. But commercial prosperity had begun to emerge as its greatest strength. Much of the economic activity of Antwerp had shifted north to Amsterdam in the province of Holland because of fighting in the south. Philip's policies had created a new enemy nation and had enriched it at his expense.

The Failure of the Invincible Armada

The political and economic importance of the Netherlands lured Spain into wider strategic involvement, most notably against England. England and Spain had long maintained cordial relations. They had a common foe in France and common economic interests. Philip's marriage to Mary Tudor, the Catholic queen of England (r. 1553–1558), had been a logical step in that relationship. Even after the accession of the Protestant queen Elizabeth (r. 1558–1603), Spanish-English relations initially remained cordial.

Relations started to sour, however, when Elizabeth began tolerating the use of English ports by the rebel Sea Beggars and authorizing English attacks on Spanish treasure fleets. In response, Spain supported Catholic resistance to Elizabeth within England, including a series of plots to replace Elizabeth on the throne with Mary, Queen of Scots. Greater Spanish success in the Netherlands, raids by the Spanish and English on each other's shipping, and Elizabeth's execution of Mary in 1587 prompted Philip to order an invasion of England. A fleet (armada) of Spanish warships sailed in 1588.

"The enterprise of England," as the plan was called in Spain, represented an astounding logistical effort. The Spanish Armada was supposed to clear the English Channel of English ships in order to permit an invading force—troops under Parma in the Netherlands—to cross the Channel on barges. The fleet of about 130 ships also carried troops from Spain, as well as large quantities of supplies. The sheer number of ships required meant that some, inevitably, were slower supply ships, or naval vessels designed for the more protected waters of the Mediterranean. The fleet as a whole was slower and less maneuverable than the English force it faced. The English also had the advantage in arms, since they had better long-range artillery and better-trained gunners.

When the Armada entered the Channel on July 29, the English fleet fell in behind them. They could harass the Spanish with artillery from a distance without sustaining much damage themselves. On the night of August 7, the English launched eight fireships into the anchored Spanish fleet; at dawn on August 8, they attacked the disorganized enemy off Gravelines, and their advantage in arms was decisive (see Map 13.2).

The Battle at Gravelines was the first major gun battle by sailing ships and helped set the future course of naval warfare. For the Spanish, it was a disaster. Many ships were sunk or forced into hostile harbors as the Spanish rounded the northern tip of the British Isles and sailed for home. Fifteen thousand sailors and soldiers died in battle or on the return journey. Less than half of Philip's great fleet made it back to Spain.

Successes at Home and Around the Mediterranean

Many of Philip's interests still centered on the Mediterranean, despite the new overseas empire and his preoccupation with the Netherlands. Spain and the kingdom of Naples had exchanged trade for centuries. Newer ties had been forged with the duchy of Milan and the city-state of Genoa, whose bankers were financiers to the Spanish monarchy. Charles V had tried to secure the western Mediterranean against the Turks and their client states along the African coast, but it was under Philip that the Turkish threat in the western Mediterranean receded.

The years of the greatest Turkish threat coincided with the beginning of the Netherlands' revolt. To Philip and his advisers, the Turks represented a potential internal threat to Spain as well. Philip thus inaugurated a new wave of persecution of his Muslim subjects, eventually provoking a major rebellion in Granada between 1568 and 1571. After this revolt was crushed, the Muslim inhabitants of Granada were forcibly exiled farther north in Spain. The Spanish allied temporarily with the papacy and Venice—both were concerned with the Turkish advances in the Mediterranean—and their combined navies inflicted a massive defeat on the Turkish navy at Lepanto, off the coast of Greece, in October 1571. The Turks remained a power in the eastern Mediterranean, but their ability to threaten Spain was over.

Philip's powers in each of his Spanish kingdoms were circumscribed by the traditional privileges of towns, nobility, and clergy. In Aragon, for example, he could raise revenues only by appealing to local assemblies, the Cortes. In Castile, the king was able to levy taxes with greater ease. Philip established his permanent capital, Madrid, and his principal residence, the Escorial, there. The Spanish Empire became more and more Castilian as the reign progressed.

Philip made significant inroads into Aragonese independence by the end of his reign. Noble feuds and peasant rebellions had combined to create virtual anarchy in some areas of Aragon by the 1580s, and in 1591 Philip sent in veteran troops from the Netherlands campaigns to establish firmer royal control. Philip was successful in Aragon because he used adequate force, followed by constitutional changes that were cleverly moderate. Finally, he cemented the peace by doing what he had failed to do in the Netherlands. He appeared in Aragon in person, in the words of a contemporary, "like a rainbow at the end of a storm."[1]

Philip also invaded and annexed Portugal in 1580, completing the unification of the Iberian Peninsula. The annexation was assured by armed force but had been preceded by careful negotiation to guarantee that Philip's claim to

Philip II in 1583 Dressed in the austere black in fashion at the Spanish court, Philip holds a rosary and wears the Order of the Golden Fleece, an order of knighthood, around his neck. At age 56 Philip had outlived four wives and most of his children. *(Museo del Prado, Madrid)*

the throne—through his mother—would find some support within the country. This was old-fashioned dynastic politics at its best. When Philip died in 1598, he was old and ill, a man for whom daily life had become a painful burden. His Armada had been crushed; he had never quelled the Netherlands' revolt. Yet he had been more successful, by his own standards, in other regions that he ruled.

Spain in Decline

Spain steadily lost ground economically and strategically after the turn of the century. Imports of silver declined. The American mines were depleted, and the natives forced to work in them were decimated by European diseases and brutal treatment. Spain's economic health was further threatened by the very success of its colonies: Local industries in the Americas began to produce goods formerly obtained from Spain. The increasing presence of English, French, and Dutch shipping in the Americas provided colonists with rival sources for the goods they needed. Often, these competitors could offer their goods more cheaply than Spaniards could.

Spain renewed hostilities with the United Provinces in 1621, after the truce of 1609 had expired. Philip IV (r. 1621–1645) also aided his Habsburg cousins in the Thirty Years' War in the Holy Roman Empire (see page 348). Squeezed for troops and revenue for these commitments, other Spanish territories revolted. The uprisings reflected both economic distress and unresolved issues of regional autonomy.

In Portugal, a war of independence began in 1640, also with a popular revolt. The Spanish government tried to restore order with troops under the command of a leading Portuguese prince, John, duke of Braganza. The duke, however, was the nearest living relative to the last king of Portugal, and he seized this opportunity to claim the crown of Portugal for himself. Although war dragged on until 1668, the Portuguese under John IV (r. 1640–1656) succeeded in winning independence from Spain. In 1647 there would also be upheaval in Spain's Italian possessions of Sicily and Naples. By midcentury, Spain had lost its position as the pre-eminent state in Europe.

RELIGIOUS AND POLITICAL CRISIS IN FRANCE AND ENGLAND

Civil war wracked France from 1562 until 1598. As in the Netherlands, the conflicts in France had religious and political origins as well as international implications. Though a temporary resolution was achieved by 1598, religious division persisted. England, however, was spared dramatic political and religious upheaval in the second half of the sixteenth century, in part because of the talents—and long life—of its ruler. In the seventeenth century, constitutional and religious dissent began to reinforce each other in new and dramatic ways and threaten the stability of the realm.

The French Religious Wars

The king of France, Henry II (r. 1547–1559), had concluded the Peace of Cateau-Cambrésis with Philip II in 1559, ending the Habsburg-Valois Wars, but Henry died in July of that year from wounds suffered at a tournament held to celebrate the new treaty. His death was a political disaster. Nobles from the Guise and Bourbon families vied for influence over his 15-year-old son, Francis II (r. 1559–1560). The queen mother, Catherine de' Medici (1519–1589), worked carefully and intelligently to balance their interests. She gained greater authority when, in late 1560, the sickly Francis died and was succeeded by his brother, Charles IX—a 10-year-old for whom Catherine was officially the regent. But keeping the conflicts among the great courtiers from boiling over into civil war proved impossible.

Noble conflict invariably had a violent component. Noble men went about armed and accompanied by armed entourages. Although they relied on army commands from the Crown, the Crown depended on their services. Provincial nobles had the resources for private warfare and assumed a right to wage it.

Religious tension was rising throughout France. Public preaching and secret meetings of Protestants (known as "Huguenots" in France) were causing unrest in towns. At court, members of the Bourbon family and other leading nobles had converted to Protestantism and worshiped openly in their rooms in the palace. In 1561, Catherine convened a national religious council to reconcile the two faiths. When it failed, she decided that the only practical course was at least provisional religious toleration, so she issued a limited edict of toleration in the name of the king in January 1562. Protestants, however, ignored the edict's restrictions and armed themselves. Townspeople of both faiths attacked one another at worship sites and religious festivals. Then in March, the duke of Guise's men killed a few dozen Protestants gathered in worship near the duke's estate at Vassy.

The killing at Vassy began the first of eight civil wars because it brought together the military power of the nobility with the broader problem of religious division. In some ways the initial conflict was decisive. The Protestant army lost the principal pitched battle of the war, near Dreux, west of Paris, in December. This defeat ultimately checked the growth of the Protestant movement, but the turning point most obvious to contemporaries came a decade later. In 1572, the Protestant nobleman Gaspard de Coligny was pressing for a war against Spain to aid Protestant rebels in the Netherlands. Alarmed by this pressure and by rumors of Protestant armies outside of Paris, Charles IX (r. 1560–1574) and his mother authorized royal guards to murder Coligny and other Protestant leaders on August 24, 1572—Saint Bartholomew's Day. Coligny's murder touched off a massacre of Protestants throughout the kingdom.

The Saint Bartholomew's Day Massacre revealed the degree to which religious differences had strained the fabric of community life. Neighbor murdered neighbor, and bodies of the dead, including Coligny's, were torn apart. When a truce was finally called, members of both Huguenot and Catholic forces refused to stop fighting—against the wishes of the Crown.

Another impetus to the breakdown of royal authority by the 1580s was the accession to the throne of Charles's brother, Henry III (r. 1574–1589), another king of limited abilities. Middle-aged, Henry had no children. The heir to his throne was the Protestant Henry of Navarre, and the assumption of the throne by a Protestant was unimaginable to the Catholics. By the end of Henry III's reign, the king had almost no royal authority left to wield. In December 1588, he resorted to murdering two members of the Guise family who led the ultra-Catholic faction, and, in turn, he was murdered by a priest in early 1589.

Henry of Navarre, who became Henry IV (r. 1589–1610), was able to force acceptance of his rule only after agreeing to return to Catholicism. After his conversion in 1593, the wars continued for a time, but after thirty years of civil war many of his subjects realized that only rallying to the monarchy could save France from chaos. The civil wars had demonstrated the power of the warrior-nobility to disrupt the state. But now nobles grew increasingly disposed, for both psychological and practical reasons, to cooperate with the Crown. The civil war period thus proved to be an important phase in the accommodation of the nobility to the power of the state.

In April 1598, Henry granted toleration for the Huguenot minority in a royal edict proclaimed in the city of Nantes. Nobles were allowed to practice the Protestant faith on their estates; townspeople were granted more limited rights to worship in selected towns in each region. Protestants were guaranteed access to schools, hospitals, royal appointments, and separate judicial institutions to ensure fair treatment. They were also guaranteed rights of self-defense—specifically, the right to maintain garrisons in about two hundred towns. About half of these garrisons would be paid for by the Crown.

The problem was that the Edict of Nantes, like any royal edict, could be revoked by the king at any time. Moreover, the provision allowing Protestants to keep garrisoned towns meant that living peacefully with religious diversity was not yet thought to be possible. Henry IV successfully ended the French religious wars, but the problem of religious and political division within France had not been solved.

The Consolidation of Royal Authority in France, 1610–1643

During Henry IV's reign, France recovered from the long years of civil war. Population and productivity began to grow; the Crown encouraged internal improvements to facilitate commerce. Yet Henry's regime was stable only in comparison with the preceding years of civil war.

The power of the great nobility had not been definitively broken. Several leading nobles plotted with foreign powers, including Spain, to influence French policy and gain materially themselves. Moreover, to raise revenue after decades of civil war, the king had agreed to a provision, known as the *paulette* (named for the functionary who first administered it), that allowed royal officeholders not merely to own their offices but also to bequeath those offices to their heirs in return for the payment of an annual fee. Although the paulette helped cement the loyalty of royal bureaucrats, their privileged position made them largely immune from royal control. A position in the royal bureaucracy now became property, like the landed property of the traditional nobility.

Henry IV was assassinated by a fanatical Catholic in 1610, when his son, Louis XIII (r. 1610–1643), was only 9 years old. Louis's mother, Marie de' Medici, acted ably as regent but soon after Louis took control of government from her, he faced a major Huguenot rebellion in southwestern France. Huguenots felt threatened by the recent marriage of the king to a Spanish princess and by Louis's reintroduction of Catholic institutions in nearby Navarre, an independent border territory he had inherited from his father (see Map 13.2). Huguenot nobles initiated fighting in 1621 as a show of force against the king. These religious wars persisted, on and off, until 1629. They reflected the continuing military might of great nobles and the importance of fortifications in warfare: The Crown had difficulty successfully besieging even small fortress towns. In the end, the Peace of Alais (1629) was a political triumph for the Crown because it broke the connection between religious dissent and political upheaval. The treaty reaffirmed the policy of religious toleration but rescinded the Protestants' military and political privileges. Most of the remaining great noble leaders began to convert to Catholicism.

The Peace of Alais was also a personal triumph for the king's leading minister, who crafted the treaty: Armand-Jean du Plessis (1585–1642), Cardinal Richelieu. From a provincial noble family, Richelieu had risen in the service of the queen mother. At court he was admired and feared for his skill in the political game of seeking and bestowing patronage. His control of many lucrative church offices gave him the resources to build up a large network of clients.

Richelieu favored an aggressive foreign policy to counter what he believed to be the greatest threat to the French crown: the Spanish Habsburgs. War had resumed between the Netherlands and Spain when the truce expired in 1621; since then, Richelieu had used his power to direct limited military campaigns against Spanish power in Italy. After 1630, with the king's full confidence, he superintended large-scale fighting against Spain in the Netherlands itself, as well as in Italy, and subsidized armies fighting the Spanish and Austrian Habsburgs in Germany as part of the Thirty Years' War (see page 348).

By 1640, Richelieu's expensive policies had caused taxes to triple. Courtiers and provincial elites' own power was also directly threatened by Richelieu's monopoly of patronage and by his creation of new mechanisms of government that bypassed their offices. The French had won territory along their northern and eastern borders by their successes against Habsburg forces. But when Richelieu and Louis XIII died within five months of each other, in December 1642 and May 1643, Richelieu's legacy was tested. Louis XIII was succeeded by his 5-year-old son, and the warrior-nobility as well as royal bureaucrats would dramatically challenge the Crown's authority.

England: Precarious Stability, 1558–1603

England experienced no civil wars during the second half of the sixteenth century, but religious dissent challenged the power of the monarchy. In Elizabeth I (r. 1558–1603), England—in stark contrast to France—possessed an able and long-lived ruler. Elizabeth was well educated in the humanistic tradition and was already an astute politician when she acceded to the throne at the age of 25. Religious, political, and constitutional disputes existed in England as elsewhere, but they did not provoke violence on anything like the continental scale.

Elizabeth came to the throne at the death of her Catholic half-sister, Mary Tudor (r. 1553–1558), wife of Philip II. Elizabeth faced the urgent problem of crafting a consensus in religious matters—a consensus that could embrace the two extremes of the Catholic-like doctrine and practice of Anglicanism and Calvinist-inspired Protestantism.

Elizabeth quickly issued a new Act of Supremacy (1559), intended to restore the monarch as head of the Church of England. She was willing to accept some difference of belief, but church liturgy, clerical vestments, and, above all, the hierarchical structure of the clergy closely resembled Catholicism. Elizabeth handled resistance to the Act of Supremacy with resolute firmness: She arrested the bishops and lords whose votes would have blocked its passage by Parliament.

The problem of religious dissent, however, was not definitively solved. Catholicism continued to be practiced. Loyal nobility and gentry in the north of England practiced it with discretion. But priests returning from exile, beginning in the 1570s, practiced it more visibly. In the last twenty years of Elizabeth's reign, approximately 180 Catholics were executed for treason; two-thirds of them were priests.

In the long run, the greater threat to the English crown came from growing tensions with the most radical Protestants in the realm, known (by their enemies initially) as Puritans. Puritanism was a movement for reform of church practice along familiar Protestant lines: Puritans emphasized Bible reading, preaching, and private scrutiny of conscience and wanted to simplify church ritual and reduce clerical authority. A significant Presbyterian underground movement began to form among them. Presbyterians wanted to dismantle the episcopacy, the hierarchy of bishops and archbishops, and govern the church with councils, called "presbyterys," that included lay members of the congregation. Laws were passed late in the reign to enable the Crown more easily to prosecute, and even force into exile, anyone who attended "nonconformist" (non-Anglican) services.

The greatest challenge Elizabeth faced from Puritans came in Parliament, where they were well represented by many literate gentry. Parliament met only when called by the monarch and in theory could merely voice opinions; it could not initiate legislation or demand changes in royal policy. However, only Parliament could vote taxes. During Elizabeth's reign, Puritans used meetings of Parliament to press their cause of further religious reform. In 1586 they went so far as to introduce bills calling for an end to the episcopacy and the Anglican prayer book. Elizabeth had to resort to imprisoning one Puritan leader to end Parliament's right to address the issue.

Elizabeth's reign saw the beginnings of English expansion overseas, but great interest in overseas possessions lay in the future; Elizabeth, like all her forebears, felt her interests tightly linked to affairs on the European continent. Her prime concern lay in safeguarding the independence of the Netherlands. Philip II's policy in the Netherlands increasingly alarmed her. She began to send small sums of money to the rebels and allowed their ships access to southern English ports, from which they could raid Spanish-held towns on the Netherlands coast. In 1585 she committed troops to help the rebels.

Her decision represented a reaction not only to the threat of a single continental power dominating the Netherlands but also to the threat of Catholicism. Spain had threatened her interests, and even her throne, in other ways. From 1579 to 1583, the Spanish had helped the Irish to resist English domination and were involved in several plots to replace Elizabeth with her Catholic cousin, Mary, Queen of Scots. Eventually, in 1588, the English faced the Spanish Armada and the threat of invasion that it brought. The English victory ended any Catholic threat to Elizabeth's rule. In the wake of victory, a mythology quickly began that portrayed Spain as an aggressive Goliath confronting the tiny David of England.

The defeat of the Armada has tended to overshadow other aspects of Elizabeth's foreign policy, such as the struggle over Ireland. Since the twelfth century, an Anglo-Irish state had been loosely supervised from England, but most of Ireland remained under the control of Gaelic chieftains.

Elizabeth I: The Armada Portrait Both serene and resolute, Elizabeth is flanked by "before" and "after" glimpses of the Spanish fleet; her hand rests on the globe in a gesture of dominion that also memorializes the circumnavigation of the globe by her famous captain, Sir Francis Drake, some years before. See the discussion of Elizabeth's image on page 355. *(By kind permission of Marquess of Tavistock and Trustees of Bedford Estate)*

Henry VIII's minister, Thomas Cromwell, had proposed that the whole of Ireland be brought under English control by making the Irish chieftains vassals of the king of England.

Under Elizabeth, this legalistic approach gave way to virtual conquest. Elizabeth's governor, Sir Henry Sidney, inaugurated a policy whereby Gaelic lords could be entirely dispossessed of their land. Any Englishman capable of raising a private force could help enforce these dispossessions and settle his conquered lands. Eventually, the Irish, with Spanish assistance, mounted a major rebellion, consciously Catholic and aimed against the "heretic" queen. The rebellion gave the English an excuse for brutal suppression and massive transfers of land to English control. To Elizabeth and her English subjects the conquests in Ireland seemed as successful as the victory over the Spanish Armada. Overall, the English enjoyed remarkable peace at home during Elizabeth's reign.

Rising Tensions in England, 1603–1642

In 1603, Queen Elizabeth died. Her successor to the throne, James I (r. 1603–1625), was the son of Mary, Queen of Scots, and his ascension began a period of severe financial problems for the monarchy. James's leanings toward extravagance were partly to blame for his financial problems, but so were pressures for patronage from elites. There were considerable debts left from the Irish conflicts and wars with Spain.

To raise revenue without Parliament's consent, James relied on sources of revenue that the Crown had enjoyed since medieval times: customs duties granted to the monarch for life, wardship (the right to manage and borrow liberally from the estates of minor nobles), and the sale of monopolies, which conveyed the right to be sole agent for a particular kind of goods. James increased the number of monopolies sold and added other measures, such as the sale of noble titles. These financial expedients were resented: Merchants opposed monopolies' arbitrary restriction of production and trade; common people found that the prices of certain ordinary commodities, like soap, rose prohibitively.

Under James's son, Charles I (r. 1625–1649), tensions between Crown and Parliament increased. Charles declared war on Spain and supplied costly support to the Huguenots in France. Wealthy merchants opposed this foreign policy because it disrupted trade. In 1626, Parliament was dissolved without granting any monies in order to stifle its objections to royal policies. The Crown's reliance on unpopular financial expedients continued. Above all, Charles's religious policies were a source of controversy. Charles was personally inclined toward "high church" practices: an emphasis on ceremony and sacrament reminiscent of Catholic ritual. In time he clashed with gentry who leaned toward Puritanism.

Charles was an intensely private man whose cold style of rule worsened religious, political, and economic tensions. When Charles again summoned Parliament in 1628 to get funds for his foreign policy, the members presented him with a document called the Petition of Right, which protested his financial policies as well as arbitrary imprisonment. (Seventeen members of Parliament had been imprisoned for refusing loans to the Crown.) Charles dissolved the Parliament in March 1629, having decided that the money he might extract was not worth the risk. For eleven years, he ruled without Parliament. In 1639, Charles started a war against his rebellious Scottish subjects but, lacking men and money, he was forced to agree to a peace treaty. Intent on renewing the war, he summoned Parliament in 1640 to obtain funds. By now royal finances were in desperate straits and religious tension had risen markedly.

Instead of voting Charles the funds he wanted, Parliament questioned the war with the Scots and other royal policies. Frustrated, Charles dissolved what is now known as the "Short Parliament" after just three weeks. But another humiliating defeat at the hands of the Scots later in 1640 made summoning another Parliament imperative. Members of Parliament could now exploit the king's predicament. This Parliament is known as the "Long Parliament" because it sat from 1640 to 1653. Charles was forced to agree not to dissolve Parliament without the members' consent and to summon Parliament at least every three years. Parliament abolished many of his unorthodox and traditional sources of revenue and removed his leading ministers from office. The royal commander deemed responsible for the Scottish fiasco, Thomas Wentworth, earl of Strafford, was executed without trial in May 1641.

Meanwhile, Parliament began debating the religious question. A bare majority of members favored abolition of Anglican bishops as a first step in thoroughgoing religious reform. Working people in London, kept apprised of the issues by the regular publication of parliamentary debates, demonstrated in support of that majority. Moderate members of Parliament, in contrast, favored checking the king's power but not upsetting the Elizabethan religious compromise.

Another revolt in Ireland in October 1641 brought matters to a head. Few trusted the king with the troops necessary to quash the rebellion, and Parliament demanded control of the army to put down the rebellion. In November the Puritan majority introduced a document known as the "Grand Remonstrance," a long catalog of grievances against the king. By a narrow margin, it was passed, further setting public opinion against Charles. The king's remaining support in Parliament eroded in January 1642, when he attempted to arrest five leading members on charges of treason. When the attempt failed, the king withdrew from London and began to raise an army. In mid-1642 the kingdom stood at the brink of civil war.

THE HOLY ROMAN EMPIRE AND THE THIRTY YEARS' WAR

The Holy Roman Empire enjoyed a period of comparative quiet after the Peace of Augsburg halted religious and political wars in 1555. By the early seventeenth century, however, fresh causes of instability brought about renewed fighting. Especially destabilizing was the drive by the Habsburgs, as emperors and territorial princes, to reverse the successes of Protestantism both in their own lands and in the empire at large and to consolidate their rule.

In the Thirty Years' War (1618–1648), as it is now called, we can see the continuation of conflicts from the sixteenth century—religious tensions, regionalism versus centralizing forces, rivalries between rulers. The war was particularly destructive because of the size of the armies and the degree to which army commanders evaded control by the states for which they fought. Some areas of the empire suffered catastrophic losses in population and productive capacity. As a result of the war, the empire was eclipsed as a political unit by the regional powers within it.

Peace Through Diversity, 1555–ca. 1618

The Habsburgs ruled over a diverse group of territories. Most lay within the boundaries of the empire, but many were not German. Though largely contiguous, the territories comprised independent duchies and kingdoms, each with its own institutional structure. Habsburg lands included speakers of Italian, German, and Czech, as well as other languages. The non-German lands of Bohemia and Hungary had been distinct kingdoms since the High Middle Ages. Most of Hungary was now under Ottoman domination, but Bohemia, with its rich capital, Prague, was a wealthy center of population and culture in central Europe.

Unlike the Netherlands, these linguistically and culturally diverse lands were still governed by highly decentralized institutions. The Habsburg family often divided rule of the various territories among themselves. For example, during the lifetime of Holy Roman Emperor Charles V, his brother Ferdinand (d. 1564) was more active than he in governing these family lands. At Ferdinand's death, rule of the various provinces and kingdoms was split among his three sons. One member of the family was routinely elected Holy Roman emperor. Unlike most of their contemporaries, the Habsburgs made no attempt to impose religious uniformity in this period. Ferdinand was firmly Catholic but tolerant of diverse reform efforts within the church, including clerical marriage. His son, Emperor Maximilian II (r. 1564–1576), granted limited rights of worship to Protestant subjects within his lands and kept his distance from policies pursued by Catholic rulers elsewhere—most notably, those of his cousin, Philip II, in the Netherlands. During Maximilian's reign a variety of faiths flourished side by side. In this tolerant atmosphere, education, printing, and humanistic intellectual life flourished.

Given the course of events elsewhere in Europe, this late Renaissance was unlikely to last. Members of the Jesuit order had begun to appear in Habsburg lands in the reign of Maximilian. During the reign of Maximilian's son, Rudolf II (r. 1576–1612), they established Catholic schools and became confessors and preachers to the upper classes. Self-confident Catholicism emerged as one form of cultural identity among the German-speaking ruling classes and thus as a religious impetus to further political consolidation of all these Habsburg territories.

The Thirty Years' War, 1618–1648

In the seventeenth century, tensions between Catholic and Protestant states (and among Protestants, for Calvinists and Lutherans were not necessarily allies) were heightened by a succession crisis: The childless emperor Rudolf II was aging.

Bohemia (the core of the modern Czech Republic) had a large Protestant population. Rudolf II had set up his court in Prague, its bustling capital. Although Catholicism was reclaiming lost ground, Protestants had been confirmed in their rights to worship in the early seventeenth century both by Rudolf and by his younger brother, Matthias, who hoped to succeed Rudolf as king of Bohemia and as Holy Roman emperor. Since the crown of Bohemia was bestowed by election, rival claimants to this wealthy throne needed the acquiescence of the ruling elites, both Protestant and Catholic.

When Matthias did become king of Bohemia and Holy Roman emperor (r. 1612–1619), he reneged on his promise to the Protestants. The Habsburg succession to the Bohemian throne seemed secure, and concessions to Protestant elites seemed less necessary. As in the Netherlands, there was in Bohemia a delicate balance between regional integrity and Bohemia's expectation of sharing its ruler with other regions. As Philip II had done, Matthias appointed a council of regents that enforced unpopular policies. The right to build new Protestant churches was denied, and Bohemian crown lands were given to the Catholic church.

On May 23, 1618, delegates to a Protestant assembly that had unsuccessfully petitioned Matthias to end these policies marched to the palace in Prague where the hated royal officials met. After a confrontation over their demands, the delegates "tried" the officials on the spot for treason and, literally, threw them out the window. The incident became known as the Defenestration of Prague (from the Latin, *fenestra*, "window"). The officials' lives were saved only because they fell into a pile of manure. The rebels proceeded to set up their own government.

The new Bohemian government deposed Matthias's successor as king, his Catholic cousin, the Holy Roman emperor Ferdinand II. Instead they elected Frederick, a Calvinist prince whose territories in west central Germany carried with them the right to be one of the seven electors who chose the emperor.

This new success seemed to threaten the religious balance of power in the empire. Other Protestant princes saw their chance to make political gains. Rival claimants to Habsburg rule in Hungary took up arms. The Protestant king of Denmark, Christian IV (r. 1588–1648), who was also duke of Holstein in northern Germany, sought to take advantage of the situation and conquer more German territory. Powers outside the empire were also interested in these events. England practiced a pro-Protestant foreign policy, and the English king, James I, was Frederick's father-in-law. Spain's supply routes north from Italy to the Netherlands passed next to Frederick's lands in western Germany. France's first interest was its rivalry with Spain. In addition, it was in France's interest, much to the disgust of the devout Catholic faction at the French court, to keep Protestant as well as Catholic rulers in the empire strong enough to thwart Austrian Habsburg ambitions.

The revolt in Bohemia thus triggered a widespread war not only because it challenged Habsburg control but because other princes felt their interests to be involved. From the outset, the war was over the balance of power in the empire and in Europe (Map 13.2).

After the Protestant king Frederick was defeated by Ferdinand's forces at the Battle of White Mountain in Prague in the fall of 1620, fighting became widespread. The truce between Spain and the Netherlands, established in 1609, expired in 1621. At this point, Christian IV, the Danish king, decided to seize more territory. Christian received little help from Protestant allies, however; the Dutch were busy with Spain, the English were still wary of continental entanglements, and Denmark's regional rivals, the Swedish, were uninterested in furthering Danish ambitions. Imperial forces defeated Christian's armies in 1626. Yet, alarmed at the possibility of greater imperial control in northern Germany, Catholic princes arranged a truce that led to Denmark's withdrawal from the fighting on relatively generous terms.

Christian's rival, Gustav Adolf, king of Sweden (r. 1611–1632), then assumed the role of Protestant champion. Gustav Adolf was a brilliant and innovative military leader. When he was killed at the Battle of Lützen in late 1632, the tide turned in the favor of imperial forces. A decisive imperial victory over a combined Swedish and German Protestant army led to a peace treaty favorable to the Catholics: the Peace of Prague (1635).

The Peace of Prague brought only a temporary peace, however, because French involvement increased now that other anti-Habsburg forces had been eclipsed. France tried to seize imperial territory along its eastern border and generously subsidized Protestant mercenaries fighting within the empire. Fighting dragged on. The Swedes re-entered the war, hoping to obtain

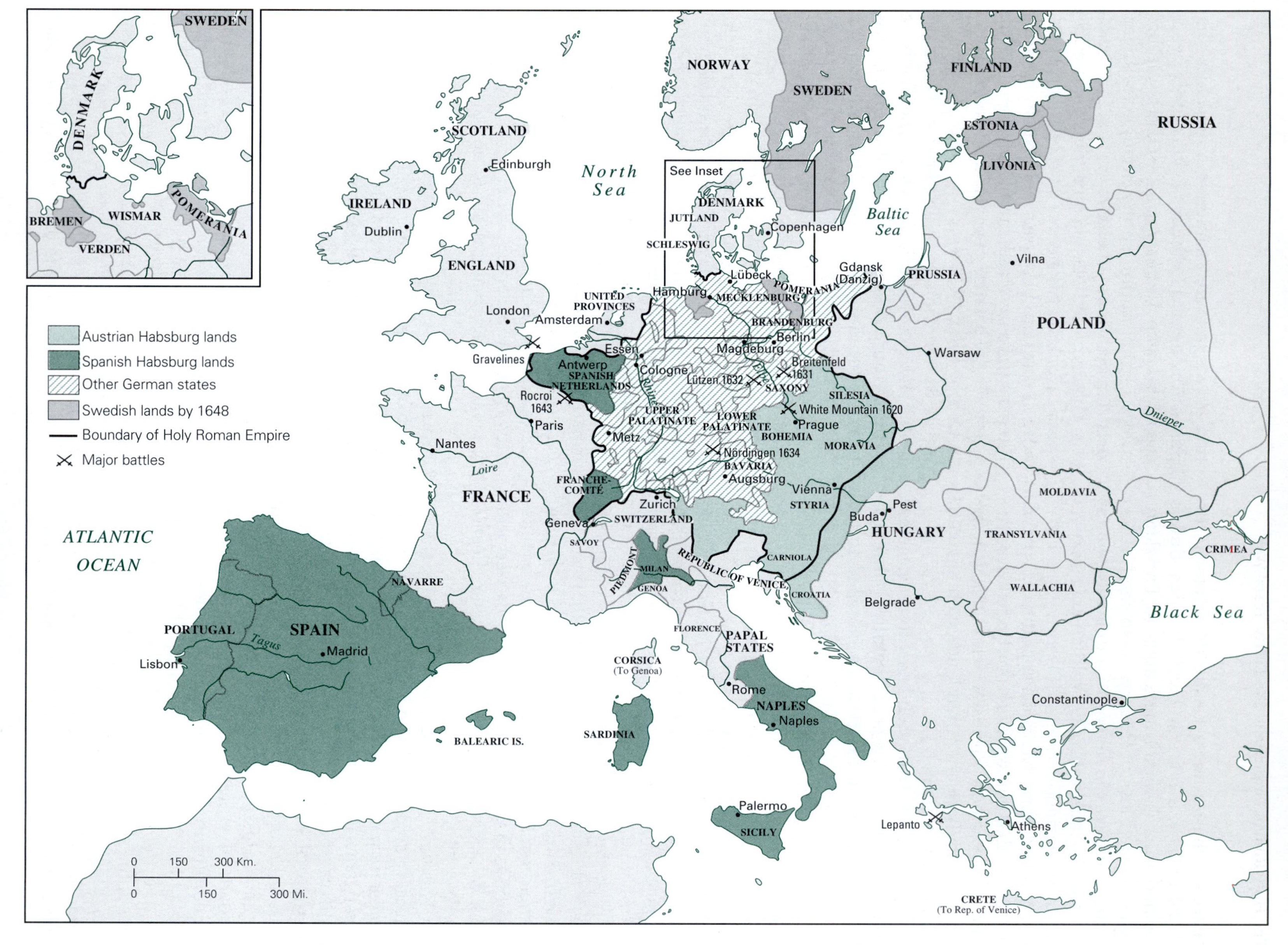
SWEDEN
DENMARK
BREMEN
WISMAR
POMERANIA
VERDEN
Austrian Habsburg lands
Spanish Habsburg lands
Other German states
Swedish lands by 1648
Boundary of Holy Roman Empire
Major battles
NORWAY
SWEDEN
FINLAND
ESTONIA
LIVONIA
RUSSIA
SCOTLAND
Edinburgh
North Sea
See Inset
DENMARK
JUTLAND
SCHLESWIG
Copenhagen
Baltic Sea
IRELAND
Dublin
ENGLAND
London
Gravelines
UNITED PROVINCES
Amsterdam
Hamburg
Lübeck
MECKLENBURG
POMERANIA
BRANDENBURG
Berlin
Gdansk (Danzig)
PRUSSIA
Vilna
POLAND
Warsaw
Essen
Antwerp
SPANISH NETHERLANDS
Cologne
Rhine
Magdeburg
Elbe
Breitenfeld 1631
Lützen 1632
SAXONY
SILESIA
White Mountain 1620
Prague
BOHEMIA
MORAVIA
Rocroi 1643
Paris
UPPER PALATINATE
LOWER PALATINATE
Metz
Nördingen 1634
BAVARIA
Augsburg
Vienna
STYRIA
Nantes
Loire
FRANCE
FRANCHE-COMTÉ
Zurich
SWITZERLAND
Geneva
SAVOY
Pest
Buda
HUNGARY
MOLDAVIA
TRANSYLVANIA
WALLACHIA
CRIMEA
Dnieper
ATLANTIC OCEAN
NAVARRE
PIEDMONT
MILAN
GENOA
REPUBLIC OF VENICE
CARNIOLA
CROATIA
Belgrade
Black Sea
PORTUGAL
SPAIN
Tagus
Madrid
Lisbon
FLORENCE
PAPAL STATES
CORSICA (To Genoa)
Rome
NAPLES
Naples
Constantinople
BALEARIC IS.
SARDINIA
Palermo
SICILY
Lepanto
Athens
CRETE (To Rep. of Venice)
0 150 300 Km.
0 150 300 Mi.

territory on the northern coast. In the south, rivals to the Habsburgs in Hungary tried to seize territory. By the end of the war, order had disintegrated so completely in the wake of the marauding armies that both Catholic and Protestant rulers made alliances with religious enemies to safeguard their states.

A comprehensive peace treaty did not become possible until France withdrew its sponsorship of continued fighting. There were domestic reasons for France's withdrawal. Louis XIII (r. 1610–1643), the king of France, had died, leaving a child to rule and face the burden of war debt. France wanted only a workable balance of power in the empire, but territorial rivalry continued with the Spanish Habsburgs. Fighting between them continued until 1659.

The Effects of the War

The Thirty Years' War caused economic devastation and population decline in many parts of the empire and had long-term political consequences for the empire as a whole. One reason for the war's devastation was the heightened application of firepower. The new development was volley fire: Foot soldiers were arranged in parallel lines so that one line of men could fire while another reloaded. Gustav Adolf refined this new tactic, amassing large numbers of troops and increasing the rate of fire to create a virtually continuous barrage. This increased both the size of armies and their deadly force in battle.

Although armies of all the major states adopted these new offensive tactics, defensive tactics—such as holding fortresses—remained important, and pitched battles still tended to be part of sieges. The costs in resources and human life of this kind of warfare reached unheard-of dimensions. Popular printed literature and court drama both condemned the irrationality of the war.

Map 13.2 Europe in the Thirty Years' War The Thirty Years' War was fought largely within the borders of the Holy Roman Empire. It was the result of conflicts within the empire as well as the meddling of neighbors for their own strategic advantage.

Where fighting had been concentrated, such as in parts of Saxony, between a third and half of the inhabitants of villages and major towns may have disappeared. Many starved, were caught in the fighting, or were killed by marauding soldiers. The most notorious atrocity occurred in the aftermath of the siege of Magdeburg in 1631. After the city surrendered to besieging Catholic forces, soldiers ate and drank themselves into a frenzy, raped and killed indiscriminately, and set fires that destroyed the town (killing some of their own ranks in the process).

Compounding the misery of war were the actions of armies hired by enterprising mercenary generals. The generals contracted to provide, supply, and lead troops and thus were more willing than the princes would have been to allow troops to live on plunder.

A series of treaties known as the Peace of Westphalia (1648) finally ended fighting in the empire. The treaties recognized Calvinism as a tolerated religion within the empire. The requirement that all subjects must follow their rulers' faith was retained, but some leeway was allowed for those who found themselves under new rulers. The property of those who decided to move elsewhere for religious reasons was protected. In its recognition of religious plurality, the Peace of Westphalia effectively put an end to religious war in the empire. The rights of states, however, were still enforced over the desires of individuals.

The treaties reflected some of the recent successes of the Swedish by granting them Baltic coast territory. France gained important towns on its eastern border. The United Provinces (the Netherlands) and Switzerland were recognized as independent states. Most of the major Catholic and Protestant rulers in the empire extended their territories at the expense of smaller principalities. From this point forward, each major state of the empire would conduct its own foreign policy; the Holy Roman Empire was no longer a meaningful political entity. Though weakened as emperors, the Habsburgs were strengthened as rulers of their own hereditary lands on the eastern fringes of the empire. They moved their capital from Prague to Vienna, and the government of Habsburg lands gained in importance as administration of the empire waned.

SOCIETY AND CULTURE

In the late sixteenth and early seventeenth centuries, both literature and political speculation often addressed questions of the legitimacy of rulers and divine authority—an urgent problem in an age of religious division. The form as well as the content of thought reflected its context. Authors and rulers alike often relied on still-prevalent oral modes of communication. Indeed, some of the greatest literature of the period and some of the most effective political statements were presented as drama and not conveyed in print. Nevertheless, literacy continued to spread and led to greater opportunities for knowledge and reflection. In the visual arts, the dramatic impulse was wedded to religious purposes to create works of great power and emotion.

Literacy and Literature

Traditional oral culture changed slowly under the impact of the spread of printing, education, and literacy. Works of literature from the late sixteenth and early seventeenth centuries incorporate material from traditional folktales, consciously reflecting the coexistence of oral and literature culture. In *Don Quixote*, by Spain's Miguel de Cervantes (1547–1616), the title character and his companion, Sancho Panza, have a long discussion about this subject. The squire Panza speaks in the style that was customary in oral culture—a rather roundabout and repetitive style, by our standards, that enabled the speaker and listener to remember what was said. Much of the richness of *Don Quixote* is due to the interweaving of prose styles and topical concerns from throughout Cervantes' culture—from the oral world of peasants to the world of court life.

The spread of education and literacy in the late sixteenth century had a dramatic impact on attitudes toward literature and on literature itself. The value of education—particularly of the continuing humanist recovery of ancient wisdom—was reflected in much of the literature of the period. Writers found in humanistic education a vision of what it meant to be cultivated and disciplined. This vision provided the beginnings of a new self-image for members of the warrior class.

Certain elite women who were able to secure a humanistic education were moved to reflect on their own situation in society. The French poet Louise Labé (1526–1566), writing in 1555, described the benefits of education for women but exaggerated its availability:

> Since the time has come . . . when the severe laws of men no longer prevent women from applying themselves to the sciences and other disciplines, it seems to me that those of us who can should use this long-craved freedom to study and let men see how greatly they wronged us when depriving us of its honor and advantages.[2]

As for men, it is customary to regard the French author Michel de Montaigne (1533–1592) as the epitome of the reflective and—most important—self-reflective gentleman. Montaigne had been a judge in the parlement of Bordeaux; in 1570 he resigned and retired to his small château, where he wrote his *Essais* (from which we derive the word *essays*), a collection of short reflections that were revolutionary in form and content. Montaigne invented writing in the form of a sketch, a "try" (the literal meaning of *essai*), which enabled him to combine self-reflection with formal analysis.

Montaigne's reflections ranged from the destructiveness of the French civil wars to the consequences of European exploration of the New World. Toward all of these events, Montaigne was able to achieve an analytic detachment remarkable for his day. For example, he noted the irony in Europeans labeling New World peoples "savage," given Europeans' seemingly endless violence against those "savages" and against each other. (See the box "Encounters with the West: Montaigne Discusses Barbarity in the New World and the Old.")

Montaigne's greatest achievement was the deep exploration of his own private moral and

ENCOUNTERS WITH THE WEST

Montaigne Discusses Barbarity in the New World and the Old

In one of his most famous essays, Michel de Montaigne ironically compares the customs of Native Americans, about whom he has heard, with the customs of his own society.

They have their wars with [other] nations, to which they go quite naked, with no other arms than bows or wooden spears. . . . It is astonishing that firmness they show in their combats, which never end but in slaughter and bloodshed; for, as to routs and terror, they know nothing of either.

Each man brings back as his trophy the head of the enemy he has killed. . . . After they have treated their prisoners well for a long time with all the hospitality they can think of . . . they kill him with their swords. This done, they roast him and eat him in common and send some pieces to their absent friends.

I am not sorry that we notice the barbarous horror of such acts, but am heartily sorry that . . . we should be so blind to our own. I think there is more barbarity . . . in tearing by tortures and the rack a body still full of feeling, in roasting a man bit by bit, having him bitten and mangled by dogs (as we have not only read but seen within fresh memory . . . among neighbors and fellow citizens, and what is worse, on the pretext of piety and religion).

Three of these men (were brought to France) . . . and [someone] wanted to know what they had found most amazing. . . . They said that in the first place they thought it very strange that so many grown men, bearded, strong and armed who were around the king . . . should submit to obey a child. . . . Second (they have a way in their language of speaking of men as halves of one another), they had noticed that there were among us men full and gorged with all sorts of good things, and that their other halves were beggars at their doors, emaciated with hunger and poverty; and they thought it strange that these needy halves could endure such injustice.

Source: Donald M. Frame, trans., *The Complete Essays of Montaigne* (Stanford, Calif.: Stanford University Press, 1948), pp. 153, 155–159. Reprinted by permission of the publisher.

intellectual life, detached from any vocation or social role. Thanks to the spread of printing and literacy, Montaigne had a virtually unparalleled opportunity to juxtapose different events, values, and cultures. His writings thus reflect a distancing from his own society and a tolerance of others. His essays also reveal a distancing from himself, and this distancing is another result of literacy—the ability to enjoy long periods of solitude and reflection in the company of other solitary voices contained in books. Montaigne's works mark the beginning of what we know as the "invention" of private life, in which an individual is known more by internal character and personality traits than by social role and past behavior.

Dramatists, poets, and prose writers like Montaigne ask profound and in some ways timeless questions about the meaning of human experience; however, the kinds of questions thought important change as society changes. The works of the great English poet and playwright William Shakespeare (1564–1616) are still compelling to us because of the profundity of the questions he asked about love, honor, and political legitimacy, though he posed these questions in terms appropriate to his own day. One of his favorite themes—evident in *Hamlet* and *Macbeth*—is the legitimacy of rulers. He also explored the contradictions in values between the growing commercial world he saw around him and the older, seemingly more stable world of feudal society. Subtle political commentary distinguishes Shakespeare's later plays, written near and shortly after the death of Queen Elizabeth in 1603, when political problems were becoming increasingly visible. Shakespeare explored not only the duties of rulers but also the rights of their subjects.

Shakespeare, Cervantes, and other writers of their day were also representatives of what were starting to be self-consciously distinct national literatures. The spread of humanism added a historical dimension to their awareness of their own languages and to their subject matter: their own society and its past. This kind of self-consciousness is evident in Shakespeare's play *Richard II*:

This royal throne of kings, this sceptred isle,
This earth of majesty, this seat of Mars,
This other Eden, demi-paradise,
This fortress built by Nature for herself
Against infection and the hand of war,
This happy breed of men, this little world,
This precious stone set in the silver sea,
Which serves it in the office of a wall,
Or as [a] moat defensive to a house,
Against the envy of less happier lands;
This blessed plot, this earth, this realm, this England . . .
(*Richard II*, act 2, sc. 1, lines 40–50)[3]

The Great Age of Theater

Shakespeare's career was possible because his life coincided with the rise of professional theater. In the capitals of England and Spain, professional theaters first opened in the 1570s. Some drama was produced at court or in aristocratic households, but most public theaters drew large and very mixed audiences, including the poorest city dwellers. Playwrights, including Shakespeare, often wrote in teams under great pressure to keep acting companies supplied with material. The best-known dramatist in Spain in this period, Lope de Vega (1562–1635), wrote more than fifteen hundred works on a wide range of topics.

Over time, theater became increasingly restricted to aristocratic circles. In England, Puritan criticism of the "immorality" of public performance drove actors and playwrights to seek royal patronage. The first professional theater to open in Paris, in 1629, was dependent on Cardinal Richelieu's patronage. As court patronage grew in importance, the subject matter treated in plays began to narrow to topics of aristocratic concern, such as family honor and martial glory. These themes were depicted in the work of the Frenchman Pierre Corneille (1606–1684), whose great tragedy of aristocratic life, *Le Cid*, was one of the early successes of the seventeenth-century French theater.

That drama was one of the most important art forms of the late sixteenth and early seventeenth centuries is reflected in its impact on the development of music: The opera, which weds drama to music, was invented in Italy in the early seventeenth century. The first great work in this genre is generally acknowledged to be *Orfeo* (*Orpheus*, 1607) by Claudio Monteverdi (1567–1643). The practice of music itself changed. Monteverdi was the first master of a new style known as monody. Monodic music was inherently dramatic, creating a sense of expectation and resolution through the progression of chords.

Sovereignty in Ceremony, Image, and Word

Whether produced formally on stage or in some less-structured setting, drama was a favored method of communication in this era because people responded to and made extensive use of oral communication. Dramatic gesture and storytelling to get a message across were commonplace and were even important components of politics.

When great noble governors entered major towns, such as when Margaret of Parma entered Brussels, a solemn yet ostentatious formal "entry" was often staged. The dignitary would ride into the town through its main gate, usually beneath a canopy made of luxurious cloth. The event might include costumed townspeople acting in brief symbolic dramas and end with an elaborate banquet. A remnant of these proceedings survives today in the ceremony by which distinguished visitors are given "the keys to the city," which, in the sixteenth century, really were useful.

Royalty began to make deliberate and careful use of dramatic ceremony for royal entries into towns, at royal funerals, and on other occasions. In France, for example, the ritual entry of the king into Paris had originally stressed the participation of elites such as the leading guild members, judges, and administrators. But in the last half of the sixteenth century, the procession began to glorify the king alone.

Queen Elizabeth had the particular burden of assuming the throne in a period of instability. Hence, she paid a great deal of attention to the image of herself that she fashioned in words and authorized to be fashioned in painting. Elizabeth styled herself variously as mother to her people and as a warrior-queen. Having refused to marry (despite the wishes of Parliament and the resultant absence of an heir), Elizabeth made artful use of the image of her virginity. Avoiding the status of wife, with all its connotations of dependence and submission, she adopted an image of self-contained purity, sanctity, and inviolability. In this way, she presented herself as the wholly devoted, chaste mother (which, of course, had religious tradition behind it) and as an androgynous, aggressive ruler. (See the box "Elizabeth I Addresses Her Troops.")

More formal speculation about constitutional matters also resulted from the tumult of the sixteenth and seventeenth centuries. In France, the Huguenot party advanced an argument for the limitation of royal power, particularly after the Saint Bartholomew's Day Massacre. The best-known Huguenot tract (probably authored by the well-educated nobleman Philippe Duplessis-Mornay), *Defense of Liberty Against Tyrants* (1579), advanced the notion of a contract between the king and the people. Under the terms of this contract, obedience to the king was conditional, dependent on his acting for the common good—above all, maintaining and protecting God's true church.

Alternative theories enhancing royal authority were offered, principally in support of the Catholic position though also simply to buttress the beleaguered monarchy itself. The most famous of these appeared in *The Six Books of the Republic* (1576), by the French legal scholar Jean Bodin (1530–1596). Bodin was a Catholic but offered a fundamentally secular perspective on the source of power within a state—namely, that there is a final sovereign authority, which, for Bodin, was the king. Bodin's theory of sovereignty was immediately echoed in other theoretical works, most notably that of Hugo Grotius (1583–1645). A Dutch jurist and diplomat, Grotius developed the first principles of modern international law. His major work, *De Jure Belli ac Pacis* (*On the Law of War and Peace*) (1625), was written in response to the turmoil of the Thirty Years' War. Grotius argued that relations between sovereign states could be based on respect for treaties and that war must be justified. He developed criteria to distinguish just wars.

Baroque Art and Architecture

Speculation about and celebration of power, as well as of dramatic emotion, also occurred in the visual arts—most notably in painting and architecture, in the style now known as "baroque." The word *baroque* comes from the Portuguese *barroco*, used to describe irregularly shaped pearls; the term as applied to the arts was initially derogatory, describing illogic and irregularity. Baroque architecture modified the precision, symmetry, and orderliness of Renaissance architecture to produce a sense of greater dynamism in space. Façades and interiors were both massive and, through clever use of architectural and decorative components, suggestive of movement. Baroque churches were impressively grand and emotionally engaging at the same time. Baroque techniques were pioneered in Italy in the late sixteenth century and spread slowly,

Elizabeth I Addresses Her Troops

The day after English ships dispersed the Spanish Armada in 1588, Elizabeth addressed a contingent of her troops. She used the opportunity to fashion an image of herself as a warrior above all but also as the beloved familiar of her people, unafraid of potential plots against her.

My loving people, we have been persuaded by some that are careful of our safety, to take heed how we commit ourselves to armed multitudes, for fear of treachery. But I assure you, I do not desire to live to distrust my faithful and loving people. Let tyrants fear. I have always so behaved myself that, under God, I have placed my chiefest strength in the loyal hearts and good will of my subjects; and therefore I am come amongst you, as you see, at this time, not for my reaction or disport, but being resolved, in the midst and heat of the battle, to live or die amongst you all, to lay down for my God, and for my kingdom, and for my people, my honor and my blood, even in the dust. I know I have the body of a weak and feeble woman, but I have the heart and the stomach of a king, and of a king of England too, and think foul scorn that Parma or Spain, or any prince of Europe should dare to invade the borders of my realm; to which, rather than any dishonor shall grow by me, I myself will take up arms, I myself will be your general, judge, and rewarder of every one of your virtues in the field.

Source: J. E. Neale, *Queen Elizabeth I* (New York: Anchor, 1957), pp. 308–309.

with many regional variations, throughout Catholic Europe especially, during the seventeenth century.

The most influential baroque painter in northern Europe was Peter Paul Rubens (1577–1640), a native of Flanders in the southern Netherlands. His early career in Italy, from 1600 to 1608, was profoundly important both in shaping him as an artist and in establishing his secondary career as a diplomat, trusted by his princely patrons. Throughout his life, he undertook diplomatic missions on behalf of the viceroys in the Spanish Netherlands, to Spain, France, and England, where he also gained artistic commissions. He simultaneously maintained a large studio in Antwerp where he could train students. Rubens's subject matter varied widely. It included church design and decoration as well as portraiture and landscapes. His technique was distinguished by the brilliant use of color and by the dynamic energy of his figures, often executed on a very large scale.

SUMMARY

The late sixteenth and early seventeenth centuries were an era of intense struggle over political and religious authority. Rulers everywhere tried to buttress and expand royal power. They were resisted by traditional centers of power, such as independent-minded nobles. But they were also resisted by the novel challenge of religious dissent, which empowered subjects to claim a greater right to question authority and risk more in their attempts to oppose it. In some areas of Europe, such as the Holy Roman Empire, the struggles reached some resolution. In other countries, such as England, decades of bloody conflict still lay ahead.

On the whole, these conflicts did not result in victories for ordinary people, since for the most part it was victorious elites who decided matters of religion and governance in their own interests. In addition, the difficult economic circumstances of these decades meant that working people, desperate for a secure livelihood, rioted or took up arms out of economic as well as religious concern.

Yet however grim the circumstances people faced, the technology of print and the spread of literacy helped spur speculative and creative works by providing the means for reflection and the audiences to receive it. Ironically, the increased importance of court life, although a cause of political strain, was also a source of patronage for art, literature, and drama. Some of the works, such as Rubens's paintings, portray the splendor and power of court life. Other works, such as Shakespeare's plays, reflect the tensions and contradictions in the society of the day: for example, the importance of the stability provided by royal authority and the dignity and wisdom of ordinary people, who had no claim to power at all.

NOTES

1. Quoted in A. W. Lovett, *Early Habsburg Spain, 1517–1598* (Oxford, England: Oxford University Press, 1986), p. 212.
2. Quoted in Ann Rosalind Jones, "City Women and Their Audiences: Louise Labé and Veronica Franco," in Margaret W. Ferguson et al., *Rewriting the Renaissance: The Discourses of Sexual Difference in Early Modern Europe* (Chicago: University of Chicago Press, 1986), p. 307.
3. From *The Riverside Shakespeare*, 2d ed. (Boston: Houghton Mifflin, 1997), p. 855.

SUGGESTED READING

Bonney, Richard. *The European Dynastic States, 1494–1660*. 1991. A recent, rich survey of the period. Good on eastern as well as western Europe but does not consider England as part of Europe.

Braudel, Fernand. *The Perspective of the World*. Vol. 3, *Civilization and Capitalism, 15th to 18th Century*. Translated by S. Reynolds. 1984. A particularly useful volume by this celebrated author of economic history concerning overall patterns in the European and international economies.

Davis, Natalie Zemon. *Society and Culture in Early Modern France*. 1975. Essays on social and cultural changes of the period, including important studies of women's participation in Protestantism.

Diefendorf, Barbara. *Beneath the Cross: Catholics and Huguenots in Sixteenth-Century Paris*. 1991. Traces the intersection of political and religious conflict in the French capital during the religious wars. Excellent bibliography.

Eagleton, Terry. *William Shakespeare*. 1986. A brief and highly readable interpretation of Shakespeare that emphasizes the tensions in the plays caused by language and by ideas from the new world of bourgeois, commercial life.

Elliott, J. H. *Europe Divided, 1559–1598*. 1968. An older but still reliable and readable survey by a leading scholar of Spanish history.

Evans, R. J. W. *The Making of the Hapsburg Monarchy*. 1979. A thorough survey of the rise of the Austrian Habsburg state from the breakup of Charles V's empire, emphasizing the importance of the ideology and institutions of Catholicism in shaping the identity and guaranteeing the coherence of the Habsburg state.

Greenblatt, Stephen. *Renaissance Self-Fashioning*. 1979. An interpretation of sixteenth-century literature and culture that emphasizes the "invention" of interior self-reflection and self-awareness.

Holt, Mack P. *The French Wars of Religion, 1562–1629*. 1995. An up-to-date synthesis that evaluates social and political context while not slighting the importance of religion.

Huppert, George. *After the Black Death: A Social History of Early Modern Europe*. 1986. A survey of developments in social and economic history throughout Europe from the fifteenth through the seventeenth centuries. A brief but very usable bibliography will guide further reading.

Jütte, Robert. *Poverty and Deviance in Early Modern Europe*. 1994. Discusses poverty, poor relief, and peasant rebellion.

Kelley, Donald R. *The Beginnings of Ideology: Consciousness and Society in the French Reformation*. 1981. A study of political thought, including but not limited to formal theory, as inspired by the experience of the wars of religion.

Klaits, Joseph. *Servants of Satan*. 1985; and Levack, Brian P. *The Witch-Hunt in Early Modern Europe*. 1987. Two surveys of witch-hunting in the sixteenth and seventeenth centuries. Levack synthesizes the work of various historians with particular care; Klaits's work is more interpretive.

Lynch, John. *Spain, 1516–1598: From Nation-State to World Empire*. 1991. An excellent survey.

Mattingly, Garret. *The Armada*. 1959. A well-crafted and gripping narrative of the sailing of the Armada and all the interrelated events in France, the Netherlands, England, and Spain, told from an English perspective.

Ong, Walter J. *Orality and Literacy: The Technologizing of the Word*. 1982. A synthesis of scholarship that concentrates on the psychological and cultural impact of literacy.

Parker, Geoffrey. *The Dutch Revolt*. 2d ed. 1985. The best survey of the revolt available in English.

———. *The Military Revolution*. 1988; and Black, Jeremy. *A Military Revolution?* 1991. Two works that disagree about the nature and extent of the changes in military practices and their significance for military, political, and social history.

———. *The Thirty Years' War*. 2d ed. 1987. A readable general history by one of the best-known military historians.

Patterson, Annabel. *Shakespeare and the Popular Voice*. 1989. An interpretation of Shakespeare's work that emphasizes his connection to the complex political and social milieu of his day.

Regosin, J. *The Matter of My Book: Montaigne's "Essais" as the Book of the Self*. 1977. One of the leading scholarly treatments of Montaigne's work.

Smith, A. G. R. *The Emergence of a Nation-State: The Commonwealth of England, 1529–1660*. 1984. A good place to start through the immense bibliography on the Elizabethan period.

Wiesner, Merry. *Women and Gender in Early Modern Europe*. 1993. Discusses all aspects of women's experience, including their working lives.

CHAPTER 14

Europe in the Age of Louis XIV, ca. 1610–1715

Toward the end of his reign, the subjects of Louis XIV of France began to grumble that he had lived too long. Indeed, he outlived his own son and grandson and was followed on the throne by a great-grandson when he died in 1715. In his prime, Louis symbolized the success of royal power in surmounting the challenges of warrior-nobles, in suppressing religious dissent, in tapping the wealth of the nation's population, and in waging war. A period of cultural brilliance early in his reign and the spectacle of an elaborate court life crowned his achievements. By the end of his reign, however, France was struggling under economic distress brought on by the many wars fought for his glory. Although Louis outlived his welcome, he was then, and is for us now, a central symbol of the age that ended with his death.

In England, by contrast, the Crown was not as successful in overcoming political and religious challenges to its authority. Resistance to the king, led by Parliament, resulted in a revolutionary overturning of royal authority that was temporary but had long-term consequences. In central and eastern Europe, a period of state building in the aftermath of the Thirty Years' War led to the dominance in the region of Austria, Brandenburg-Prussia, and Russia. The power of these rulers derived, in part, from the economic relationship of their lands to the wider European economy.

The seventeenth century also witnessed a dynamic phase of European overseas expansion, following on the successes of the Portuguese and the Spanish in the fifteenth and sixteenth centuries. Eager migrants settled in the Americas in ever increasing numbers, while forced migrants—enslaved Africans—were transported by the thousands to work on the profitable plantations of European colonizers. Aristocrats, merchants, and peasants back in Europe jockeyed to take advantage of—or to mitigate the effects of—the local political and economic impact of Europe's expansion.

Questions and Ideas to Consider

- The seventeenth-century courtier relied on ceremony, etiquette, and conversational skills to exert influence and secure favor. Why? How did this experience differ for men and women?
- If Louis XIV was so effective at streamlining government and bringing revenues into the treasury, why did he experience desperate financial difficulties toward the end of his reign? What effect did this have on government?
- What was the Glorious Revolution?
- After the Thirty Years' War, what three powers came to dominate central and eastern Europe? How did Peter the Great pull his country into interaction with the rest of Europe?
- Why was slavery set up in the New World?

FRANCE IN THE AGE OF ABSOLUTISM

Absolutism describes the power achieved by monarchs, most notably Louis XIV (r. 1643–1715), in the seventeenth century. Louis continued the expansion of state power begun by his father's minister, Cardinal Richelieu. The extension of royal power, under Louis as well as his predecessor, was driven by the desire to sustain an expensive foreign policy. The policy itself was a traditional one: fighting the Habsburg enemy and generally seeking military glory. Louis XIV's successes in these undertakings made him both envied and emulated by other rulers; the French court became a model of culture and refinement. But increased royal authority was not accepted without protest.

The Last Challenge to Absolutism

Louis came to the throne as a 5-year-old child in 1643. As regent, his mother, Anne of Austria (1601–1666), had to defuse a serious challenge to royal authority during her son's minority. Together with her chief minister and personal friend, Cardinal Jules Mazarin (1602–1666), she faced opposition from royal bureaucrats and the traditional nobility as well as the common people.

Revolts against the concentration of power in royal hands and against the high taxation that had prevailed under Louis's father began immediately. Several provincial parlements tried to abolish the special ranks of officials created by Richelieu. In 1648, after a few more years of foreign war and the financial expedients to sustain it, the most serious revolt began, led by the Parlement and the other sovereign law courts in Paris.

The source of the Parlement's leverage over the monarchy was its traditional right to register laws and edicts, which amounted to a right of judicial review. Now, the Parlement attempted to extend this power by debating and even initiating government policy. The courts sitting together drew up a reform program abolishing most of the machinery of government established under Richelieu and calling for consent to future taxation. The citizens of Paris rose to defend the courts when royal troops were sent against them. In the countryside, the machinery of government, particularly tax collection, virtually ceased to function.

Mazarin was forced to accept the proposed reform of government, at least in theory. He also had to avert challenges by great nobles for control of the young king's council. Civil war waxed and waned around France from 1648 until 1653. These revolts, derisively termed the "Fronde" after a children's game of the time, posed a serious challenge to the legacy of royal government as it had developed under Richelieu. It ended without a noteworthy impact on the growth of royal power for several reasons. First, Mazarin methodically regained control of the kingdom through armed force and by making concessions to win the loyalty of individual aristocrats eager for the fruits of royal service. In addition, when civil war threatened starvation as well as political unrest, the Parlement of Paris and many citizens of the capital welcomed a return to royal authority.

Unlike in England, there was in France no single institutional focus for resistance to royal power. A strong-willed and able ruler, such as Louis XIV proved to be, could face down challenges to royal power, particularly when he satisfied the ambitions of aristocrats and those bureaucrats who profited from the expansion of royal authority.

CHAPTER CHRONOLOGY

1643	Louis XIV comes to the French throne
1648	Peace of Westphalia
1648–1653	"Fronde" revolts in France
1649	Execution of King Charles I
1659	Peace of the Pyrenees
1660	Monarchy restored in England
1661	Louis XIV assumes full control of government
1664	East India Company and the West India Company established
1682	Peter the Great takes the Russian throne
1683	Death of Colbert
1685	Revocation of the Edict of Nantes
1688	The Glorious Revolution
1713	The Peace of Utrecht
1715	Death of Louis XIV

France Under Louis XIV, 1661–1715

Louis XIV assumed full control of government at Mazarin's death in 1661. It was a propitious moment. The Peace of the Pyrenees in 1659 had ended—in France's favor—the wars with Spain that had dragged on since the end of the Thirty Years' War. As part of the peace agreement, Louis married a Spanish princess, Maria Theresa. Louis was physically attractive and extremely vigorous. He had been lovingly coached in his duties by Mazarin and his mother, Queen Anne, and he proved a diligent king. He worked consistently at the affairs of state while sustaining the ceremonial life of the court with its elaborate hunts, balls, and public events.

In the first ten years of his active reign, Louis achieved a degree of control over the mechanisms of government unparalleled in the history of France or anywhere else in Europe. He did not invent any new bureaucratic devices but rather used existing ranks of officials in new ways that increased government efficiency and the centralization of control. He radically reduced the number of men in his High Council, the advisory body closest to the king, to only three or four great ministers of state affairs. This intimate group, with Louis's active participation, handled all policymaking. The ministers of state, war, and finance were chosen exclusively from men of modest backgrounds whose training and experience fitted them for such positions. Jean-Baptiste Colbert (1619–1683), perhaps the greatest of them, served as minister of finance and of most domestic policy from 1665 until his death; he was from a merchant family and had served for years under Mazarin.

Several dozen other officials, picked from the ranks of up-and-coming lawyers and administrators, drew up laws and regulations for execution at the provincial level. These officials at the center were often sent to the provinces on special supervisory missions. The effect of this system was largely to bypass many entrenched provincial officials, particularly many responsible for tax collecting. The money saved by the more efficient collection of taxes enabled the government to streamline the bureaucracy: Dozens of the offices created to bring cash to the Crown were bought back by the Crown from their owners.

The system still relied on the bonds of patronage and personal service, however. Officials rose through the ranks by means of service to the great, and family connection and personal loyalty were still essential. Of the seventeen men who were part of Louis XIV's High Council in the course of his reign, five were members of the Colbert family, for example.

Some of the benefits of centralized administration can be seen in certain achievements of the early years of Louis's regime. Colbert encouraged France's economic development by reducing internal tolls and customs barriers and promoting industry with state subsidies and protective tariffs. He also set up state-sponsored trading companies, including the East India Company and the West India Company, both established in 1664.

Mercantilism, the philosophy behind Colbert's efforts, stressed self-sufficiency in manufactured goods, tight control of trade to foster the domestic economy, and the absolute value of bullion. Capital for development—bullion—was presumed to be limited in quantity. Protectionist policies were believed necessary to guarantee a favorable balance of payments. Although this static model did not wholly fit the reality of growing international trade in the seventeenth century, mercantilist philosophy was helpful to France. France became self-sufficient in the all-important production of woolen cloth, and French industry expanded notably in other sectors. Colbert's greatest success was the expansion of the navy and merchant marine. By 1677 the size of the navy had increased almost six times, to 144 ships. By the end of Louis XIV's reign, the French navy was virtually the equal of the English navy.

A general determination to manage national resources distinguished Louis's regime. Colbert and other ministers began to develop the kind of planned government policymaking we now take for granted. They tried to formulate policy based on carefully collected information. How many men of military age were available? How abundant was the harvest? Answers to such questions enabled them to formulate economic policy and manage production and services effectively—especially the recruitment and supply of the king's vast armies.

Beginning in 1673, Louis also tried to bring the religious life of the realm more fully under royal control by claiming for himself some of the church revenues and powers of appointment in France that still remained to the pope. Partly to bolster his position with the pope, he also began to attack the Huguenot community in France. He offered financial inducements for conversions to Catholicism, then quartered troops in Huguenot households to force them to convert. In 1685 he declared that there was no longer any Protestant community and revoked the Edict of Nantes (see page 343). A hundred thousand Protestant subjects who refused even nominal conversion to Catholicism chose to emigrate.

Despite Louis's achievement of unprecedented centralized control, "absolutism" overstates the situation. By modern standards, the power of the Crown was still greatly limited. Louis was not above the law. Louis's foremost apologist, Bishop Jacques Bossuet (1627–1704), asserted that although the king was guided only by fear of God and his own reason in his application and interpretation of law, he was obligated to act within the law. The "divine right" of kingship did not mean unlimited power to rule; rather it meant that hereditary monarchy was the divinely ordained form of government.

Absolutism meant not iron-fisted control but rather the successful focusing of energy and loyalties on the Crown, in the absence of alternative institutions. Much of the glue holding the absolutist state together lay in informal mechanisms such as patronage and court life, as well as in the traditional hunt for military glory—all of which Louis amply supplied.

The Life of the Court

An observer comparing the lives of prominent noble families in the mid-sixteenth and mid-seventeenth centuries would have noticed striking differences. By the second half of the seventeenth century, most sovereigns had the power to crush revolts. The nobility had relinquished its former independence but retained economic and social supremacy and, as a consequence, considerable political clout. Nobles also developed new ways to safeguard their privilege by means of cultural distinctions. This process was particularly dramatic in France as a strong Crown won out over a powerful nobility.

Louis maintained a brilliant court life. No longer able to wield independent political power, aristocrats lived at court whenever they could, in order to participate in the endless jostling for patronage and prestige—for commands in the royal army and for offices and honorific positions at court. Instead of safeguarding one's status with a code of honor backed up by force of arms, the seventeenth-century courtier relied on elegant ceremony, precise etiquette, and clever conversation.

As literacy became more widespread and the power of educated bureaucrats of humble origin became more obvious, more and more nobles from the traditional aristocracy began to use reading and writing as a means to think critically about their behavior—in the case of men, to reimagine themselves as gentlemen rather than warriors. Noble women and men alike began to reflect on their new roles—in letters, memoirs, and the first novels. The most influential early French novel was

Louis at Versailles Louis XIV (center, on horseback) is pictured among a throng of courtiers at a grotto in the gardens of Versailles. The symbol of the sun appeared throughout the palace; the image of Louis as the "Sun King" further enhanced his authority. *(Château de Versailles/Art Resource, NY)*

The Princess of Cleves by Marie-Madeleine Pioche de la Vergne (1634–1693), known by her title, Madame de Lafayette. Mme. de Lafayette's novel treats the particular difficulties faced by aristocratic women who, without military careers to buttress their honor, were more vulnerable than men to gossip and slander at court.

Louis XIV's court is usually associated with the palace he built at Versailles, southwest of Paris. Some of the greatest talent of the day worked on the design and construction of Versailles from 1670 through the 1680s. The palace was a masterpiece of luxury, and yet it symbolized order in its restrained, geometrical, baroque styling. Life there was sumptuous and grand. And yet, the great conglomeration of people in a building without much technology for the removal of waste or the maintenance of heat suggests that amid all the gaiety, comfort was unlikely. Still, nobles wore gorgeous clothes; meals and entertainments were extravagant. Ritual and ceremony surrounded the king, and his attention was sought constantly. Both women and men struggled to secure royal favor for themselves, their relations, and their clients. (See the box "Politics and Ritual at the Court of Louis XIV.")

The early years of Louis's personal reign were the heyday of French drama. The comedian Jean-Baptiste Poquelin, known as Molière (1622–1673), impressed the young Louis with his productions in the late 1650s and was rewarded with the use of a theater in the main royal palace in Paris. Like Shakespeare earlier in the century, Molière explored the social and political tensions of his day. He satirized the pretensions of the aristocracy, the social climbing of the bourgeoisie, the self-righteous piety of clerics. Some of his plays were banned, but most were not only tolerated but extremely popular with the elite audiences they mocked—their popularity is testimony to the confidence of Louis's regime in its early days.

Also popular at court were the tragedies of Jean Racine (1639–1699), a master of the poetic use of language. His plays, which treated familiar classical stories, focused on the emotional and psychological life of the characters and tended to stress the limits that fate places even on royal persons. The pessimism in Racine foreshadowed the less successful second half of Louis's reign.

Louis XIV and a Half-Century of War

Wars initiated by Louis XIV dominated the attention of most European states in the second half of the seventeenth century. Louis's wars sprang from traditional causes: the importance of the glory and dynastic aggrandizement of the king and the preoccupation of the aristocracy with military life. But they were more demanding on state resources than any previous wars.

In France and elsewhere, the size of armies grew markedly. The new offensive tactics developed during the Thirty Years' War changed the character of armies and increased the burden on governments to provide for them (see page 348). A higher proportion of soldiers became gunners, whose effectiveness lay in how well they operated as a unit. Since drill and discipline were vital to success, armies began to train seriously off the field of battle. The number of men on the battlefield increased somewhat, while the total numbers of men in arms supported by the state at any one time increased dramatically.

Louis's first war reflected the continuing French preoccupation with Spanish power. The goal was territory along France's eastern border to add to the land recently gained by the Peace of Westphalia (1648) and the Peace of the Pyrenees (1659). Louis invoked rather dubious dynastic claims to demand, from Spain, lands in the Spanish Netherlands and the large independent county on France's eastern border called the Franche-Comté.

War began in 1667. French troops first seized a wedge of territory in the Spanish Netherlands without difficulty and then, in early 1668, occupied the Franche-Comté. When the brief conflict ended later that year, the French retained only some towns in the Spanish Netherlands. Louis had already begun to negotiate with the Austrian Habsburgs over the eventual division of Spanish Habsburg lands, for it seemed likely that the Spanish king, Charles II (r. 1665–1700), would die without heirs. For the moment, Louis was content

Politics and Ritual at the Court of Louis XIV

This document is from the memoirs of Louis de Rouvroy, duke of Saint-Simon (1675–1755), a favored courtier but one critical of Louis's power over the nobility. Notice his descriptions of court ceremony focusing on the most private moments of the king—an example of Louis's deliberate and exaggerated use of tradition, in this case of personal familiarity among warriors.

The frequent fetes, the . . . promenades at Versailles, the journeys, were means on which the king seized in order to distinguish or mortify courtiers, and thus render them more assiduous in pleasing him. He felt that of real favors he had not enough to bestow. . . . He therefore unceasingly invented all sorts of ideal ones, little preferences and petty distinctions, which answered his purpose as well.

He was exceedingly jealous of the attention paid him. . . . He looked to the right and to the left, not only upon rising but upon going to bed, at his meals, in passing through his apartments, or his gardens of Versailles . . . ; not one escaped him, not even those who hoped to remain unnoticed. He marked well all absences from court. . . .

At eight o'clock [every morning] the chief valet . . . woke the king. At the quarter [hour] the grand chamberlain was called, and those who had what was called the *grandes entrées.* The chamberlain or chief gentleman drew back the [bed] curtains and presented holy water from the vase. . . . The same officer gave [the king] his dressing gown; immediately after, other privileged courtiers entered, and then everybody, in time to find the king putting on his shoes and stockings. . . . Every other day we saw him shave himself; . . . he often spoke of [hunting] and sometimes said a word to somebody.

Source: Bayle St. John, trans., *The Memoirs of the Duke of Saint-Simon on the Reign of Louis XIV and the Regency,* 8th ed. (London: George Allen, 1913); quoted in Merry Wiesner et al., eds., *Discovering the Western Past,* 3d ed., vol. 2 (Boston: Houghton Mifflin, 1997), pp. 37–38.

to return the Franche-Comté, confident that he would get it back, and much more, in the future.

Louis's focus then shifted from Spain to a new enemy: the Dutch. The Dutch had been allied with France since the beginning of their existence as provinces in rebellion against Spain. The French now turned against the Dutch for reasons that reflected the growth of the international trading economy—specifically, the Dutch dominance of seaborne trade. "It is impossible that his Majesty should tolerate any longer the insolence and arrogance of that nation," asserted the pragmatic Colbert in 1670.[1] The Dutch War began in 1672, with Louis personally leading one of the largest armies ever fielded in Europe—perhaps 120,000 men. At the same time, the Dutch were challenged at sea by England. The English had fought the Dutch over trading issues since the 1650s; now Louis secretly sent the English king a pension to ensure his alliance with the French.

At first, the French were spectacularly successful against the tiny Dutch army. Louis, however, presumptuously overrode a plan to move decisively on Amsterdam so that he could preside at the solemn reinstatement of Catholic worship in one of the Dutch provincial cathedrals. The Dutch opened dikes and flooded the countryside to protect their capital, and what had begun as a French rout became a stalemate. Moreover, the Dutch were beating the combined English and

French forces at sea and gathering allies who felt threatened by Louis's aggression. The French soon faced German and Austrian forces, and in 1674 the English made a separate peace with the Dutch and withdrew from the fighting. Nonetheless, the French managed to hold their own, and the Peace of Nijmegen, in 1678, gave the illusion of a French victory. From Spain France received further border areas in the Spanish Netherlands as well as the Franche-Comté.

Ensconced at Versailles since 1682, Louis seemed to be at the height of his power. Yet the Dutch War had cost him more than he had gained. Internal reforms ended under the pressure of paying for war, as the old financial expedients of borrowing money and selling privileges were revived. Colbert's death in 1683 dramatically symbolized the end of an era of innovation in French government.

Louis's unforgiving Dutch opponent, William of Orange, king of England from 1689 to 1702 (see page 370), renewed former alliances against him. The war, known as the Nine Years' War, or King William's War, was touched off late in 1688 by French aggression—an invasion of Germany to claim an inheritance. In his ongoing dispute with the pope, Louis seized the papal territory of Avignon in southern France. Boldest of all, he helped the exiled Catholic claimant to the English crown mount an invasion to reclaim his throne.

A widespread war began with all the major powers—Spain, the Netherlands, England, Austria, the major German states—ranged against France. This time there was no illusion of victory for Louis. In the Treaty of Ryswick (1697), Louis had to give up most of the territories in Germany, the Spanish Netherlands, and northern Spain that he had managed to occupy by war's end. Avignon went back to the pope. The terrible burden of taxes to pay for the wars combined with crop failures in 1693 and 1694 caused widespread starvation in the countryside. French courtiers began to criticize Louis openly.

The final major war of Louis's reign, now called the War of Spanish Succession, broke out in 1701. Both Louis and Holy Roman Emperor Leopold I (r. 1657–1705) hoped to claim for their heirs the throne of Spain, left open at the death in 1700 of the Spanish king, Charles II. The Dutch and the English responded to the prospect of a Frenchman on the throne of Spain by joining the emperor in a Grand Alliance in 1701.

Again the French fought a major war on several fronts on land and at sea. Again the people of France felt the cost in crushing taxes worsened by harvest failures. Major revolts inside France forced Louis to divert troops from the war. For a time it seemed that the French would be soundly defeated, but they were saved by a dynastic accident: Unexpected deaths in the Habsburg family meant that the Austrian claimant to the Spanish throne suddenly was poised to inherit rule of Austria and the empire as well. The English were more afraid of a revival of unified Habsburg control of Spain and Austria than of French domination of Spain, so they opened peace negotiations with France. The Peace of Utrecht in 1713 helped to set the agenda of European politics for the eighteenth century. Louis XIV's grandson, Philip of Anjou, became Philip V of Spain, on condition that the Spanish and French crowns would never be worn by the same monarch. To maintain the balance of power against French interests, the Spanish Netherlands and Spanish territories in Italy were ceded to Austria, which for many decades would be France's major continental rival. The Peace of Utrecht also marked the beginning of England's dominance of overseas trade and colonization. The French gave to England lands in Canada and the Caribbean and renounced any privileged relationship with Spanish colonies. England was allowed to control the highly profitable slave trade with Spanish colonies.

Louis XIV had added small amounts of strategically valuable territory along France's eastern border, and a Bourbon ruled in Spain. But the costs in human life and resources were great for the slim results achieved. Moreover, the army and navy had swallowed up capital for investment and trade, and strategic opportunities overseas were lost, never to be regained. Louis's government had been innovative in its early years but remained constrained by traditional ways of imagining the interests of the state.

THE ENGLISH REVOLUTION

In England, unlike in France, a representative institution—Parliament—became an effective, permanent brake on royal authority. The process by which Parliament gained a secure role in governing the kingdom was neither easy nor peaceful, however. As we saw in Chapter 13, conflicts between the English crown and its subjects centered on control of taxation and the direction of religious reform. Beginning in 1642, England was beset by civil war between royal and parliamentary forces. The king was eventually defeated and executed, and there followed a period when the monarchy was abolished altogether. The monarchy was restored in 1660, but Parliament retained a crucial role in governing the kingdom, a role that was confirmed when, in 1688, it again deposed a monarch whose fiscal and religious policies became unacceptable to its members.

Civil War and Revolution, 1642–1649

Fighting broke out between Charles I and parliamentary armies in the late summer of 1642. The Long Parliament (see page 347) continued to represent a broad coalition of critics and opponents of the monarchy, ranging from aristocrats concerned primarily with the abuses of royal prerogative to radical Puritans eager for thorough religious reform and determined to defeat the king. Fighting was halfhearted initially, and the tide of war at first favored Charles.

In 1643, however, the scope of the war broadened. Charles made peace with the Irish rebels and brought Irish troops to England to help his cause. Parliament, in turn, sought military aid from the Scots in exchange for a promise that Presbyterianism would become the religion of England. Meanwhile, Oliver Cromwell (1599–1658), a Puritan member of the Long Parliament and a cavalry officer, helped reorganize parliamentary forces in order to defeat the king's forces. The eleven-hundred-man cavalry trained by Cromwell, known as the "Ironsides," helped parliamentary and Scottish infantry defeat the king's troops in July 1644. The victory made Cromwell famous.

Shortly afterward, Parliament reorganized its forces to create the New Model Army, rigorously trained like Cromwell's Ironsides. Upper-class control of the army was reduced by barring sitting members of Parliament from commanding troops. The New Model Army won a convincing victory in 1645, and in the spring of 1646, Charles surrendered to a Scottish army in the north. In January 1647, Parliament paid the Scots for their services in the war and took the king into custody. In the negotiations that followed, Charles tried to play his opponents off each other, and, as he hoped, divisions among them widened.

Most members of Parliament were Presbyterians, Puritans who favored a strongly unified and controlled state church along Calvinist lines. They wanted peace with the king in return for acceptance of the new church structure and parliamentary control of standing militias for a specified period. They did not favor expanding the right to vote or other dramatic constitutional or legal changes. These men were increasingly alarmed by the rise of sectarian differences and the actual religious freedom that many ordinary people were claiming for themselves. With civil war and the weakening of royal authority, censorship was relaxed and public preaching by ordinary women and men who felt a religious inspiration was becoming commonplace.

Above all, Presbyterian gentry in Parliament feared more radical groups in the army and in London. Most officers of the New Model Army were Independents, Puritans who favored a decentralized church, a degree of religious toleration, and a wider sharing of political power among men of property, not just among the very wealthy gentry. In London, a well-organized artisans' movement known as the Levellers favored universal manhood suffrage, reform of law, and better access to education in addition to decentralized churches—in short, the separation of political power from wealth and virtual freedom of religion. Many of the rank and file of the army were deeply influenced by Leveller ideas.

In May 1647 the majority in Parliament voted to offer terms to the king and to disband the New Model Army without first paying most of the soldiers' back wages. This move provoked the first direct intervention by the army in politics. Representatives of the soldiers were chosen to present grievances to Parliament but, when this failed, the army seized the king and, in August, occupied the palace of Westminster, where Parliament met.

However, in November, Charles escaped from his captors and raised a new army among his erstwhile enemies, the Scots, who were also alarmed by the growing radicalism in England. Civil war began again in early 1648. Although it ended quickly with a victory by Cromwell and the New Model Army in August, the renewed war hardened political divisions and enhanced the power of the army. The king was widely blamed for the renewed bloodshed, and the army did not trust him to keep any agreement he might now sign. When Parliament, still dominated by Presbyterians, once again voted to negotiate with the king, army troops under a Colonel Thomas Pride prevented members who favored Presbyterianism or the king from attending sessions. The "Rump" Parliament that remained after "Pride's Purge" voted to try the king. Charles I was executed for "treason, tyranny and bloodshed" against his people on January 30, 1649.

The Interregnum, 1649–1660

A Commonwealth—a republic—was declared. Executive power resided in a council of state. Legislative power resided in a one-chamber Parliament, the Rump Parliament (the House of Lords was abolished). Declaring a republic proved far easier than running one. The execution of the king shocked most English and Scots people and alienated many elites from the new regime. The legitimacy of the Commonwealth government would always be in question.

The tasks of making and implementing policy were made difficult by the narrow political base on which the government now rested. The majority of the reformist gentry had been purged from Parliament. Also excluded were the more radical Levellers. Within a few years, many disillusioned Levellers would join a new religious movement called the Society of Friends, or Quakers, which espoused complete religious autonomy. Quakers refused all oaths or service to the state and refused to acknowledge social rank. New religious sects tended to promote gender equality as well, and many Quaker women became popular preachers.

Above all, the new government was vulnerable to the power of the army, which had created it. In 1649 and 1650, Cromwell led expeditions to Ireland and Scotland, partly for revenge and partly to put down resistance to the new English government. In Ireland, Cromwell's forces acted with great ruthlessness. English control there was furthered by more dispossession of Irish landholders, which also helped pay off the army's wages. Meanwhile, Parliament could not agree on systematic reforms, particularly the one reform Independents in the army insisted on: more broadly based elections for a new Parliament. Fresh from his victories in the north, Cromwell led his armies to London and dissolved Parliament in the spring of 1652.

In 1653 some army officers drew up the "Instrument of Government," England's first and only written constitution. It provided for an executive, the Lord Protector, and a Parliament to be based on somewhat wider male suffrage. Cromwell was the natural choice for Lord Protector, and whatever success the government of the Protectorate had was largely due to him.

Cromwell was an extremely able leader who was not averse to compromise. Although he had used the army against Parliament in 1648, he had worked hard to reconcile the Rump Parliament and the army before marching on London in 1652. He believed in a state church, but one that allowed for local control by congregations. He also believed in toleration for other Protestant sects, as well as for Catholics and Jews, as long as no one disturbed the peace.

As Lord Protector, Cromwell oversaw impressive reforms in law that testify to his belief in the limits of governing authority. For example, contrary to the practice of his day, he opposed

Popular Preaching in England Many women took advantage of the collapse of royal authority to preach in public—a radical activity for women at the time. This print satirizes the Quakers, a religious movement that attracted many women. *(Mary Evans Picture Library)*

capital punishment for petty crimes. The government of the Protectorate, however, accomplished little because Parliament remained internally divided and opposed to Cromwell's initiatives. For example, Cromwell was challenged by radical republicans in Parliament who thought the Protectorate represented a step backward, away from republican government. Yet in the population at large, there were still royalist sympathizers, and a royalist uprising in 1655 forced the temporary division of England into military districts administered by generals.

Cromwell died of a sudden illness in September 1658, and the Protectorate did not long survive him. In February 1660, the decisive action of one army general seeking a solution to the chaos enabled all the surviving members of the Long Parliament to rejoin the Rump. The Parliament summarily dissolved itself and called for new elections. The newly elected Parliament recalled Charles II, son of Charles I, from exile abroad and restored the monarchy. The chaos and radicalism of the late civil war and *interregnum*—the period between reigns, as the years from 1649 to 1660 came to be called—had provoked a conservative reaction.

The Restoration, 1660–1685

Charles II (r. 1660–1685) claimed his throne at the age of 30. He had learned from his years of uncertain exile and the fate of his father. He did not seek retribution but rather offered a general pardon to all but a few rebels (mostly those who had signed his father's death warrant), and he suggested to Parliament a relatively tolerant religious settlement that would include Anglicans as well as Presbyterians. He was far more politically adept than his father and much more willing to compromise.

That the re-established royal government was not more tolerant than it turned out to be was not Charles's doing but Parliament's. Anglican orthodoxy was reimposed, including the reestablishment of bishops and the Anglican *Book of Common Prayer*. All officeholders and clergy were required to swear oaths of obedience to the king and the established church. As a result, hundreds of them were forced out of office. Holding nonconformist religious services became illegal, and Parliament passed a "five-mile" act preventing dissenting ministers from visiting or even traveling near their former congregations. Property laws were strengthened and the criminal codes made more severe.

The king's attitudes began to mimic prerevolutionary royalist positions. Charles II began to flirt with Catholicism, and his brother and heir, James, openly converted. Charles promulgated a declaration of tolerance that would have included Catholics as well as nonconformist Protestants, but Parliament would not accept it. When Parliament moved to exclude James from succession to the throne, Charles dissolved it. A subsequent Parliament, cowed by fears of a new civil war, backed down. By the end of his reign, Charles was financially independent of Parliament due to more revenue from overseas trade and to secret subsidies from France, his recent ally against Dutch trading rivals (see page 365).

But it was impossible to silence dissent. After two decades of religious pluralism and broadly based political activity, there were well-established communities of various sects and a self-confidence that bred vigorous resistance. Also, anti-Catholic feeling still united all Protestants. Parliament focused its attention on anti-Catholicism, passing an act barring all but Anglicans from Parliament itself.

The clearest reflection of the regime's revolutionary background was Parliament's ability to assert its policies against the desires of the king. And yet Charles retained a great deal of power. If he had been followed by an able successor, Parliament might have lost a good measure of its independence.

The Glorious Revolution, 1688

When James II (r. 1685–1689) succeeded Charles, Parliament initially cooperated, granting him customs duties for life and funds to suppress a rebellion by one of Charles's illegitimate sons. James did not try to impose Catholicism on England, but he did try to achieve toleration for Catholics in two declarations of indulgence in 1687 and 1688. His efforts were undermined by his heavy-handed tactics. When several Anglican bishops refused to read the declarations from their pulpits, he had them imprisoned and tried for seditious libel. The jury acquitted them.

James also failed because of the coincidence of other events. In 1685, at the outset of James's reign, Louis XIV of France had revoked the Edict of Nantes. The possibility that subjects and their monarch could be of different faiths seemed increasingly unlikely. Popular fears of James's Catholicism were thus heightened early in his reign, and his later declarations of tolerance, though also benefiting Protestant dissenters, were viewed with suspicion. In 1688 the king's second wife, who was Catholic, gave birth to a son, raising the specter of a Catholic succession.

In June 1688, seven leading members of Parliament invited William of Orange, the husband of James's Protestant daughter Mary, to come to England. William mounted an invasion that became a rout when James refused to defend his throne and fled to France. William called Parliament, which declared James to have abdicated and offered the throne to him and to Mary. James eventually invaded Ireland in 1690 with French support but was defeated by William at the Battle of the Boyne that year.

The substitution of William (r. 1689–1702) and Mary (r. 1689–1694) for James, known as the "Glorious Revolution," was engineered by Parliament and confirmed its power. Parliament presented the new sovereigns with a Bill of Rights that defended freedom of speech, called for frequent Parliaments, and stipulated that no

Catholic could ever succeed to the throne. The effectiveness of these documents was reinforced by Parliament's power of the purse.

The issues that had faced the English since the beginning of the century were common to all European states: religious division and elite power, fiscal strains and resistance to taxation. Yet events in England were unusual in that the assumption of authority by a well-established institution, Parliament, made challenge of the monarchy more legitimate and more effective. Political participation also developed more broadly in England than in other states. In the long run, the strength of Parliament would make easier the task of broadening participation in government.

NEW POWERS IN CENTRAL AND EASTERN EUROPE

By the end of the seventeenth century, central and eastern Europe were dominated by three states: Austria, Brandenburg-Prussia, and Russia. After the Thirty Years' War, the Habsburgs' power as emperors waned, and their interest in the coherence of their own territories, centered on Austria, grew. Brandenburg-Prussia, in northeastern Germany, grew to a position of power rivaling that of the Habsburg state. The rulers of Brandenburg-Prussia had gained lands in the Peace of Westphalia, and astute management transformed their relatively small and scattered holdings into one of the most powerful states in Europe. Russia's new stature in eastern Europe resulted in part from the weakness of its greatest rival, Poland, and the determination of one leader, Peter the Great, to assume a major role in European affairs. Sweden controlled valuable Baltic territory through much of the century but by the end of the century it, too, was eclipsed by Russia as a power in the region.

The development of states in central and eastern Europe was closely linked to developments in western Europe. This was true politically and strategically as well as economically. One of the most important factors influencing the internal political development of these states was their relationship to the wider European economy: They were sources of grain and raw materials for the more densely urbanized west.

The Consolidation of Austria

In 1648 the main Habsburg lands were a collection of principalities comprising modern Austria, the kingdom of Hungary (largely in Turkish hands), and the kingdom of Bohemia (Map 14.1). In 1713 the Peace of Utrecht ceded to Austria the Spanish Netherlands, renamed the "Austrian Netherlands," and substantial territories in Italy. Although language and ethnic differences prevented the establishment of an absolutist state along French lines, Leopold I (r. 1657–1705) instituted political and institutional changes that enabled the Habsburg state to become one of the most powerful in Europe in the eighteenth century.

Much of the coherence that already existed in Leopold's lands had been achieved by his predecessors in the wake of the Thirty Years' War. The lands of rebels in Bohemia had been confiscated and redistributed among loyal, mostly Austrian, families. In return for political and military support for the emperor, these families were given the right to exploit their newly acquired land and the peasants who worked it. The desire to recover population and productivity after the destruction of the Thirty Years' War gave landlords an incentive to curtail peasants' autonomy sharply, particularly in devastated Bohemia. Austrian landlords throughout the Habsburg domains provided grain and timber for the export market, and elite families provided the army with officers. This political-economic arrangement provoked numerous serious peasant revolts, but the peasants were not able to force changes in a system that suited both the elites and the central authority.

The institutions of the imperial government still functioned in Leopold's capital, Vienna, but Leopold worked to extricate the government of his own lands from the imperial offices, which were staffed largely by Germans more loyal to imperial than to Habsburg interests. In addition,

Map 14.1 New Powers in Central and Eastern Europe The balance of power in central and eastern Europe shifted with the strengthening of Austria, the rise of Brandenburg-Prussia, and the expansion of Russia at the expense of Poland and Sweden.

Leopold used the Catholic church as an institutional and ideological support for the Habsburg monarchy.

Leopold's personal preoccupation was the reestablishment of zealous Catholicism throughout his territories. Acceptance of Catholicism became the litmus test of loyalty to the Habsburg regime, and Protestantism vanished among elites. Leopold encouraged the work of Jesuit teachers and members of other Catholic orders. These men and women helped staff his government and administered religious life down to the most local levels.

Leopold's most dramatic success, as a Habsburg and an ardent Catholic, was his reconquest of Hungary from the Ottoman Empire. Since the mid-sixteenth century, the Habsburgs had controlled only a narrow strip of the kingdom. Preoccupied with countering Louis XIV's aggression, Leopold did not himself choose to begin a reconquest. His centralizing policies, however, alienated nobles and townspeople in the portion of Hungary he did control, as did his repression of Protestantism, which had flourished in Hungary. Hungarian nobles began a revolt, aided by the Turks, aiming for a fully united Hungary under Ottoman protection.

The Habsburgs emerged victorious in part because they received help from the talented Polish king Jan Sobieski, whose own lands in Ukraine were also threatened by the Turks. The Turks overreached their supply lines to besiege Vienna in 1683. After the siege failed, Habsburg armies slowly pressed east and south, recovering Buda, the ancient capital of Hungary, in 1686 and Belgrade in 1688. The Danube basin was once again in Christian hands.

Leopold gave land in the reclaimed kingdom to Austrian officers whom he believed were loyal to him. The traditions of Hungarian separatism, however, were strong, and the great magnates retained their independence. The peasantry, as elsewhere, suffered a decline in status as a result of the Crown's efforts to ensure the loyalty of elites. In the long run, Hungarian independence weakened the Habsburg state, but in the short run Leopold's victory over the Turks and the recovery of Hungary were momentous events, confirming the Habsburgs as the pre-eminent power in central Europe.

The Rise of Brandenburg-Prussia

In addition to Austria, three German states gained territory and stature after the Thirty Years' War: Bavaria, Saxony, and Brandenburg-Prussia. By the end of the seventeenth century, the strongest was Brandenburg-Prussia, a conglomeration of small territories held, by dynastic accident, by the Hohenzollern family. The two principal territories were electoral Brandenburg, in northeastern Germany, with its capital, Berlin, and the duchy of Prussia, a fief of the Polish crown along the Baltic coast east of Poland proper (see Map 14.1). In addition there was a handful of small principalities near the Netherlands. The manipulation of resources and power that enabled these unpromising lands to become a powerful state was primarily the work of Frederick William, known as "the Great Elector" (r. 1640–1688).

Frederick William took advantage of a war between Poland and its rivals, Sweden and Russia, to win independence for the duchy of Prussia from Polish overlordship. When his involvement in the war ended in 1657, he kept the general war commissariat intact and bypassed traditional civilian councils and representative bodies. He also used the standing army to force the payment of high taxes. Most significantly, he established a relationship with the *Junkers*, hereditary landholders, which assured him both revenue and loyalty. He agreed to allow the Junkers virtually total control of their own lands in return for their agreement to support his government—in short, to surrender their accustomed political independence.

Peasants and townspeople were taxed, but nobles were not. The freedom to control their estates led many nobles to invest in profitable agriculture for the export market. The peasants were serfs who received no benefits from the increased productivity of the land. Frederick William further enhanced his state's power by sponsoring state industries. These industries did not have to fear competition from urban producers because the towns had been frozen out of the political process and saddled with heavy taxes. Although an oppressive place for many Germans, Brandenburg-Prussia attracted many skilled refugees, such as Huguenot artisans fleeing Louis XIV.

In contrast to Brandenburg-Prussia, Bavaria and Saxony had vibrant towns, largely free peasantries, and weak aristocracies, but they were less powerful in international affairs. Power on the European stage depended on military force. Such power, whether in a large state like France or in a small one like Brandenburg-Prussia, usually came at the expense of the state's inhabitants.

Competition Around the Baltic: The Demise of the Polish State and the Zenith of Swedish Power

The rivers and port cities of the Baltic coast were conduits for the growing trade between the Baltic hinterland as well as its coastline and the rest of Europe; transit tolls on timber, grain, and naval stores were an important source of local income, and the commodities themselves brought profits to their producers. This trading system had profound consequences for all of the states bordering the Baltic Sea in the seventeenth century.

First, it was a spur to war. Through the sixteenth and seventeenth centuries, Sweden, Denmark, and Russia fought over access to and control of the Baltic trade, and in the seventeenth century, Poland and Russia fought over grain- and timber-producing lands. Second, profits from grain exports reinforced the power of large landholders, particularly in Poland, where most of the grain was produced.

In 1600 a large portion of the Baltic hinterland, as well as its coastline, lay under the control of Poland-Lithuania, a dual kingdom at the height of its power. A marriage in 1386 had brought the duchy of Lithuania under a joint ruler with Poland; earlier in the fourteenth century, Lithuania had conquered Belarus and Ukraine. Like the neighboring Habsburg lands, Poland-Lithuania was a multi-ethnic state, particularly in the huge duchy of Lithuania, where Russian-speakers predominated. Poland was Catholic but had a large minority of Protestants and Jews. Lithuanians were mostly Catholic, while Russian-speakers were Orthodox.

Internal strains and external challenges began to mount in Poland-Lithuania in the late sixteenth century. The economic power of Polish landlords gave them political clout; the king was forced to grant concessions that bound peasants to the nobles' estates. The spread of the Counter-Reformation, encouraged by the Crown, created problems for both Protestant and Orthodox subjects. In Ukraine, communities of Cossacks, nomadic farmer-warriors, grew as Polish and Lithuanian peasants fled harsh conditions to join them. The Cossacks had long been tolerated because they were a military buffer against the Ottoman Turks, but now Polish landlords wanted to reincorporate the Cossacks into the profitable political-economic system that they controlled.

In 1648 the Cossacks staged a major revolt, defeated Polish armies, and established an independent state. In 1654 they transferred their allegiance to Moscow and became part of a Russian invasion of Poland that, by the next year, had engulfed much of the eastern half of the kingdom. At the same time, the Swedes seized central Poland and competed with the Russians for control elsewhere; the Swedes were helped by Polish and Lithuanian aristocrats acting like independent warlords.

Often called the First Great Northern War, this war is remembered in Poland as "the Deluge." The population of Poland may have declined by as much as 40 percent, and vital urban economies were in ruins. The religious tolerance that had distinguished the Polish kingdom and had been mandated in its constitution was thereafter abandoned. Polish royal armies managed to recover much territory, but much of this was only nominal. In parts of Lithuania inhabited by Russian-speaking peoples, the Russian presence during the wars had achieved local transfers of power from Lithuanian to Russian landlords loyal to Moscow.

The elective Polish crown passed in 1674 to the brilliant military commander Jan Sobieski (r. 1674–1696), who would become known as "Vanquisher of the Turks" for his victory in raising the siege of Vienna. Given Poland's internal weakness, Sobieski's victories helped the Austrian and Russian rivals of the Turks more than the Poles. His successor, Augustus II of Saxony (r. 1697–1704, 1709–1733), dragged Poland back into war, from which Russia would emerge the obvious winner in eastern Europe.

On the Baltic coast, however, Sweden remained the dominant power through most of the seventeenth century. Swedish efforts to control Baltic territory began in the sixteenth century, first to counter the power of its perennial rival, Denmark, in the western Baltic. It then competed with Poland to control Livonia (modern Latvia), whose principal city, Riga, was an important trading center for goods from Lithuania and Russia. Swedish intervention in the Thirty Years' War came when imperial successes against Denmark both threatened the Baltic coast and created an opportunity to strike at Sweden's old enemy. The treaty of Westphalia (1648) confirmed Sweden's earlier gains and added control of further coastal territory, mostly at Denmark's expense.

The port cities held by Sweden were profitable though their revenue mostly went to pay for the wars necessary to seize and defend them. All of these efforts to hold Baltic territory were driven by dynastic and strategic needs as much as economic rationales. For example, Sigismund Vasa, son of the king of Sweden, had been elected king of Poland in 1587 but also inherited the Swedish throne in 1592. The one permanent gain Sweden realized from its aggression in the First Great Northern War was the renunciation of the Polish Vasa line to any claim to the Swedish crown. Owing to its earlier gains, Sweden remained the dominant power on the Baltic coast until the end of the seventeenth century, when it was supplanted by Russia.

The Expansion of Russia: From Ivan "the Terrible" Through Peter "the Great"

The Russian state expanded dramatically in the sixteenth century. Ivan IV (r. 1533–1584) was proclaimed "Tsar [Russian for "Caesar"] of All the Russias" in 1547. This act was the culmination of the accumulation of land and authority by the princes of Moscow through the late Middle Ages, when Moscow had vied for pre-eminence with other Russian principalities. Ivan IV's grandfather, Ivan III (r. 1462–1505), the first to use the title *tsar*, had absorbed neighboring Russian principalities and ended Moscow's subservience to Mongol overlords.

Ivan IV is also known as Ivan "the Terrible" ("awe-inspiring" is a better translation of the Russian). He was the first actually to be crowned tsar and routinely to use the title. His use of the title aptly reflected his imperial intentions, as he continued Moscow's push westward and, especially, eastward against the Mongol states of central Asia. The Russians pushed eastward over the Ural Mountains to Siberia for the first time. Within this expanding empire, Ivan IV used ruthless methods, including the torture and murder of thousands of subjects, to enforce his will. The practice of gathering tribute for Mongol overlords had put many resources in the hands of Muscovite princes, but Ivan IV was able to bypass noble participation and intensify the centralization of government by creating ranks of officials, known as the service gentry, loyal only to him.

A period of disputed succession known as the Time of Troubles followed Ivan's death in 1584. Aristocratic factions fought among themselves as well as against armies of Cossacks and other common people who wanted a less oppressive government. Nonetheless, the foundations laid by Ivan enabled Michael Romanov to rebuild autocratic government after being chosen tsar in 1613. The Romanovs were an aristocratic family related to Ivan's. Michael (r. 1613–1645) was chosen by an assembly of aristocrats, gentry, and commoners more alarmed by civil wars than by the prospect of a return to strong tsarist rule. Michael was succeeded by his son, Alexis (r. 1645–1676), who presided over the extension of Russian control to Ukraine in 1654 and developed interest in further relationships with the West. Shifting the balance of power in eastern Europe and the Baltic in Russia's favor was also the work of Alexis's son, Peter I, "the Great" (r. 1682–1725). Peter accomplished this by military successes against his enemies and by forcibly reorienting Russian government and society.

Peter was almost literally larger than life. Nearly 7 feet tall, he towered over most of his contemporaries and had physical and mental energy to match his size. He set himself to learning trades and studied soldiering by rising in the ranks of the military like any common soldier. He traveled abroad to learn as much as he could about other states' economies and government. He wanted the revenue, manufacturing, technology and trade, and, above all, the up-to-date army and navy that other rulers enjoyed.

Peter initiated a bold and even brutal series of changes in Russian society upon his accession to power. Peasants already bore the brunt of taxation, but their tax burdens increased. Peter noticed that European monarchs coexisted with a privileged but educated aristocracy and that a brilliant court life symbolized and reinforced the rulers' authority. So he set out to refashion Russian society in what amounted to an enforced cultural revolution. (See the box "Peter the Great Changes Russia.") He provoked confrontations with Russia's traditional aristocracy over everything from education to matters of dress. He elevated new families to the ranks of gentry and created an official ranking system for the nobility, to encourage service to the government.

Peter's effort to reorient his nation toward Europe was most apparent in the construction of the city of St. Petersburg on the Gulf of Finland, which provided access to the Baltic Sea. In stark contrast to Moscow, dominated by the medieval fortress of the Kremlin and churches in the traditional Russian style, St. Petersburg was a modern European city with wide avenues and palaces designed for a sophisticated court life. But although Peter was intelligent, practical, and determined to create a more productive society, he was also cruel and authoritarian. The building of St. Petersburg cost staggering sums in money and in workers' lives. Peter's entire reform system was carried out autocratically; resistance was brutally suppressed. Victims of Peter's oppression included his son, Alexis, who died after torture while awaiting execution for questioning his father's policies.

The primary reason for the high cost of Peter's government to the Russian people was his ambition for territorial gain and for an improved army and navy. Working side by side with workers and technicians, many of whom he had recruited while abroad, Peter created the Russian navy from scratch. Peter also modernized the Russian army by employing tactics and training he had observed in the West. By 1709, Russia was able to manufacture most of the up-to-date firearms it needed. He also introduced military conscription.

Russia waged war virtually throughout Peter's reign. Initially, he struck at the Ottomans and their client state in the Crimea, with some success. But later phases of these conflicts brought reverses. Peter had his greatest success against Sweden in contests for control of the weakened Polish state and the Baltic Sea. The conflicts between Sweden and Russia, known as the Second Great Northern War, raged from 1700 to 1709 and, in a less intense phase, lasted until 1721. The acquisitions of this war made Russia the pre-eminent Baltic power at Sweden's and Poland's expense (see Map 14.1).

THE RISE OF OVERSEAS TRADE

During the seventeenth century, European trade and colonization expanded and changed dramatically. The Dutch not only became masters of the spice trade but led the expansion of trade to include many other commodities. In the Americas, the expansion of sugar and tobacco production created a new trading system linking Europe, Africa, and the New World. French and English colonists began settling in North America in increasing numbers. Overseas trade had a dramatic impact on life within Europe: on patterns of production and consumption, social stratification, and the distribution of wealth.

Peter the Great Changes Russia

Peter the Great's reforms included not only monumental building and a new relationship with elites but also practical changes in education, technology, and administration. Writing about a hundred years after the end of Peter's reign, the Russian historian Mikhail Pogodin (1800–1875) reflected on all the changes Peter had introduced, perhaps exaggerating only the respect Peter earned in foreign eyes in his lifetime.

Yes, Peter the Great did much for Russia. . . . One keeps adding and one cannot reach the sum. We cannot open our eyes, cannot make a move, cannot turn in any direction without encountering him everywhere, at home, in the streets, in church, in school, in court, in the regiment. . . .

We wake up. What day is it today? . . . Peter ordered us to count the years from the birth of Christ; Peter ordered us to count the months from January.

It is time to dress—our clothing is made according to the fashion established by Peter the First, our uniform according to his model. The cloth is woven in a factory which he created. . . .

Newspapers are brought in—Peter the Great introduced them.

You must buy different things—they all, from the silk neckerchief to the sole of your shoe, will remind you of Peter. . . . Some were ordered by him . . . or improved by him, carried on his ships, into his harbors, on his canals, on his roads.

Let us go to the university—the first secular school was founded by Peter the Great.

You decide to travel abroad—following [his] example; you will be received well—Peter the Great placed Russia among the European states and began to instill respect for her; and so on and so on.

Source: Nicholas V. Riasanovsky, *A History of Russia,* 2d ed. (London: Oxford University Press, 1969), pp. 266–267.

The Growth of Trading Empires: The Success of the Dutch

By the end of the sixteenth century, the Dutch and the English were trying to make incursions into the Portuguese-controlled spice trade with areas of India, Ceylon, and the East Indies. Spain had annexed Portugal in 1580, but the drain on Spain's resources from its wars with the Dutch and the French prevented Spain from adequately defending its enlarged trading empire in Asia. The Dutch and, to a lesser degree, the English rapidly supplanted the Portuguese in this lucrative trade.

The Dutch were particularly well placed to be successful competitors in overseas trade. They already dominated seaborne trade within Europe, including the most important long-distance trade, which linked Spain and Portugal—with their wine and salt, as well as spices, hides, and gold from abroad—with the Baltic coast, where these products were sold for grain and timber produced in Germany, Poland-Lithuania, and Scandinavia. The geographic position of the Netherlands and the fact that the Dutch consumed more Baltic grain than any other area because of their densely urbanized economy help to explain their dominance of this trade. In addition, the Dutch had improved the design of their merchant ships to enhance their profits.

The Dutch were successful in Asia because of institutional as well as technical innovations. In 1602 the Dutch East India Company was formed. The company combined the government management of trade, typical of the period, with both public and private investment. In the past, groups of investors had funded single voyages or small numbers of ships on a one-time basis. The formation of the Dutch East India Company created a permanent pool of capital to sustain trade. The risks and delays of longer voyages could be spread among larger numbers of investors. The English East India Company, founded in 1607, also supported trade, but it had one-tenth the capital of the Dutch company. The Bank of Amsterdam, founded in 1609, became the depository for the bullion that flowed into the Netherlands with trade. The bank established currency-exchange rates and issued paper money and instruments of credit to facilitate commerce.

A dramatic expansion of trade with Asia resulted from the Dutch innovations, so much so that by 1650 the European market for spices was glutted and traders' profits had begun to fall. To control the supply of spices, the Dutch seized some of the areas where they were produced. Control of supply helped prop up prices, but these gains were somewhat offset by greater military and administrative costs.

The Dutch and English further responded to the oversupply of spices by diversifying their trade. The proportion of spices in cargoes from the East fell from about 70 percent at midcentury to just over 20 percent by the century's end. New consumer goods such as tea, coffee, silks, and cotton fabrics took their place. Eventually, the Dutch and the English even entered the local carrying trade among Asian states. Doing so enabled them to make profits without purchasing goods, and it slowed the drain of hard currency from Europe—currency in increasingly short supply as the silver mines in the Americas were worked out. (See the box "Encounters with the West: Agents of the Dutch East India Company Confront Asian Powers.")

The "Golden Age" of the Netherlands

The prosperity occasioned by the Netherlands' "mother trade" within Europe and its burgeoning overseas commerce helped foster social and political conditions unique within Europe. The concentration of trade and shipping sustained a large merchant oligarchy as well as an extensive and prosperous artisanal sector. Disparities of wealth were smaller than anywhere else in Europe. The shipbuilding and fishing trades, among others, supported large numbers of workers with a high standard of living for the age.

Political decentralization in the Netherlands persisted: Each of the seven provinces retained considerable autonomy. However, merchant oligarchs in the Estates of the province of Holland in fact constituted the government for the whole for long periods because of Holland's economic dominance. The head of government was the *pensionary* (executive secretary) of Holland's Estates. An Estates-General existed but had no independent powers of taxation.

The only competition in the running of affairs came from the House of Orange, aristocratic leaders of the revolt against Spain. They exercised what control they had by means of the office of *stadholder*—a kind of military governorship. They continued to lead the defense of the Netherlands against Spanish attempts at reconquest until the Peace of Westphalia confirmed Dutch independence in 1648. Their power also came from the fact that they represented the only counterweight within the Netherlands to the dominance of Amsterdam merchant interests. Small towns dependent on land-based trade or rural areas dominated by farmers and gentry looked to the stadholders of the Orange family to defend their interests.

As elsewhere, religion was a source of political conflict. The stadholders favored rigid Calvinism. The pensionaries and regents of Holland (as the leading families were known) were more relaxed, reflecting the needs of the diverse mercantile communities of Holland, where thousands of Jews as well as Catholics and various kinds of Protestants lived. Foreign policy also turned on Holland's desire for peace in order to foster commerce versus the stadholder's greater willingness to engage in warfare for territory and dynastic advantage.

These differences notwithstanding, Dutch commercial dominance drew them into costly

ENCOUNTERS WITH THE WEST

Agents of the Dutch East India Company Confront Asian Powers

This 1655 letter from a local agent of the Dutch East India Company to its board of directors (the "Seventeen") shows that the Dutch had to maintain good working relationships with local powers in Asia—in this case, with the king of Siam (modern Thailand). The letter discusses the Dutch blockade of Tennasserim, a major port under Siamese control, and the promises of help the Dutch, via their local agents, had made the king for some of his military ventures.

It appears that the merchant Hendrich Craijer Zalr had promised, so they [the Siamese] say, 20 ships, which was a very rash proceeding on his part, and thereupon they made the abovementioned expedition, which they said, if our support did not appear, would be obliged to return unsuccessful and with shame and dishonor to the crown, as was actually the case. Moreover, it happened that a writing had come unexpectedly from the governor of Tennasserim that two Dutch ships had held the harbor there for 2 months, and had prevented the entrance and departure of foreign traders, which caused great annoyance in Siam, especially at Court, and embittered everyone against us. This gave the [English] Companies very favorable opportunity to blacken us and to make us odious to everyone, and to change the King's feeble opposition into open enmity, the more so since the news has from time to time been confirmed and assured, and no one there doubts it any longer.

Wherefore the resident Westerwolt, who was convinced of the contrary, since he would certainly have been informed before any such action was taken, finally found himself obliged to ask that certain persons, on the King's behalf and on his own, should be deputed and sent overland to Tennasserim, in order to discover on the spot the truth of the case, which request was granted by the King, and on our behalf the junior merchant, Hugo van Crujlenburgh was sent.

Meanwhile the aforementioned resident Westerwolt had on various occasions made complaint of the bad and unreasonable treatment received, . . . so that the resident was in very great embarrassment and did not know whether even his life was any longer safe. These questions were for the most part on the subject of the help asked for against Singgora, the Siamese professing to have gone to war with the Spanish on our account, and to have suffered much damage in the same, and that we now refused to assist his Majesty against the rebels with ships and men; whereas the beforementioned merchant, Hendrich Craijer, had definitely made him such promises.

Source: Records of the Relations Between Siam and Foreign Countries in the Seventeenth Century (Bangkok: Council of theVajiranana National Library, 1916), vol. 2. Quoted in Alfred J. Andrea and James H. Overfield, *The Human Record: Sources of Global History*, 2d ed., vol. 2: *Since 1500* (Boston: Houghton Mifflin, 1994), pp. 134–135.

wars throughout the second half of the century. Between 1657 and 1660 the Dutch defended Denmark against Swedish ambitions in order to safeguard the sea-lanes and port cities of the Baltic. Other, more costly conflicts arose from rivalries with other states, notably England and France. Owing largely to the land war with France, the Estates in Holland lost control of policy to William of Nassau (d. 1702), who was prince of Orange after 1672. William drew the Netherlands

Rembrandt: The Syndics of the Cloth Drapers' Guild (1662) In this painting, the last group portrait of his career, Rembrandt depicts the guild members with artful, stylized simplicity. It was Rembrandt's genius also to be able to convey a sense of personality and drama in such commissioned portraits. *(Rijksmuseum-Stichting, Amsterdam)*

into his family's long-standing close relationship with England. Like other members of his family before him, William had married into the English royal family: His wife was Mary, daughter of James II.

Ironically, after he and Mary assumed the English throne in 1689, Dutch commerce suffered more in alliance with England than in its previous rivalry. William used Dutch resources for the land war against Louis XIV and used the English navy for the fight at sea. Dutch maritime strength was being eclipsed by English seapower by the end of the century.

To contemporaries, the Netherlands appeared to be an astonishing exception to the normal structures of politics. In France and most other states in Europe, political life was dominated by a court where aristocrats and ministers mingled and conspired and an elaborate ritual of honor and deference glorified the king. The princes of Orange surrounded themselves with splendid trappings, but their court was not the sole focus of political life in the Netherlands. The portraits of the Dutch painter Rembrandt van Rijn (1606–1667) portray the austerity of the merchant oligarchs; theirs was a novel kind of power that could be symbolized with ostentatious simplicity.

The Growth of Atlantic Colonies and Commerce

In the seventeenth century, the Dutch, English, and French joined the Spanish as colonial and commercial powers in the Americas. The Spanish colonial empire, in theory a trading system closed to outsiders, was in fact vulnerable to incursion by other European traders. In 1628, for example, a Dutch captain seized the entire Spanish treasure fleet. But by then Spain's goals and those of its competitors had begun to shift, due largely to the declining output of the Spanish silver mines during the 1620s. The Spanish and their Dutch, French, and English competitors expanded the production of the cash crops of sugar and tobacco.

The European demand for sugar and tobacco grew steadily in the seventeenth century. European entrepreneurs had developed the *plantation system*—the use of forced labor to work large tracts of land—on Mediterranean islands during the Middle Ages. They imported slaves from the Black Sea region to supplement the local labor force. Sugar production by this system was established on Atlantic islands, using African labor, and then in the Americas by the Spanish and Portuguese. The French, English, and Dutch followed their lead and established sugar plantations on the Caribbean islands they held. Sugar production in the New World grew from about 20,000 tons in 1600 to about 200,000 tons by 1770. The Dutch became the official supplier of slaves to Spanish plantations in the New World and the chief supplier to most other regions. They made handsome profits until the end of the seventeenth century, when they were supplanted by the British.

Aware of the great Spanish territorial advantage in the New World and hoping for treasures such as the Spanish had found, the English, French, and Dutch were also ambitious to explore and settle North America. From the early sixteenth century, French, Dutch, English, and Portuguese seamen had fished and traded off Newfoundland. By 1630, small French and Scots settlements in Acadia (in modern Nova Scotia) and on the St. Lawrence River and English settlements in Newfoundland had been established to exploit the timber, fish, and fur of the north Atlantic coasts.

In England population growth and consequent unemployment, as well as religious discontent, created a large pool of potential colonists. The first English settlement to endure in what was to become the United States was established at Jamestown, named for James I, in Virginia in 1607. ("Virginia," named for Elizabeth I, the "virgin" queen, was an extremely vague designation for the Atlantic coast of North America and its hinterland.)

The Crown encouraged colonization, but a private company similar to the companies that financed long-distance trade was established to organize the enterprise. The directors of the Virginia Company were London businessmen. Investors and would-be colonists purchased shares. Shareholders among the colonists could participate in a colonial assembly, though the governor appointed by the company was the final authority.

The colonists arrived in Virginia with ambitious and optimistic instructions. They were to open mines, establish profitable cultivation, and search for sea routes to Asia. At first they struggled merely to survive. The indigenous peoples in Virginia, unlike those in Spanish-held territory, were not organized in urbanized, rigidly hierarchical societies that, after conquest, could provide the invaders with a labor force. Indeed, the native Americans in this region were quickly wiped out by European diseases. The introduction of tobacco as a cash crop a few years later saved the colonists economically—though the Virginia Company had already gone bankrupt and the Crown had assumed control of the colony. With the cultivation of tobacco, the Virginia colony became dependent on forced, eventually slave, labor.

Among the Virginia colonists were impoverished men and women who came as servants indentured to those who had paid their passage. Colonies established to the north, in what was called "New England," also drew people from the margins of English society: Early settlers there were religious dissidents. The first to arrive were the Pilgrims, who arrived at New Plymouth (modern Massachusetts) in 1620. They were religious separatists who had originally emigrated to the Netherlands from England. Following the Pilgrims came Puritans escaping escalating persecution under Charles I. The first, in 1629, settled under the auspices of another royally chartered company, the Massachusetts Bay Company. Among their number were many prosperous Puritan merchants and landholders. Independence

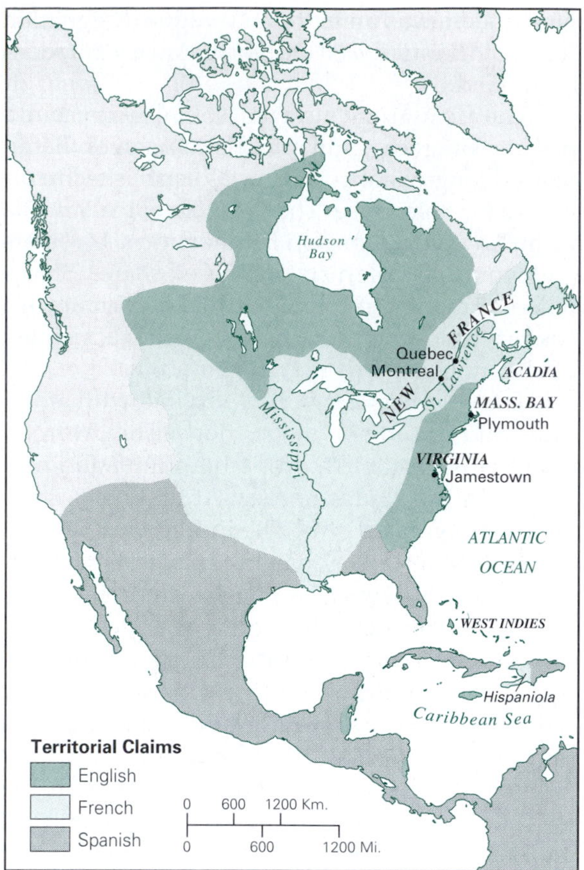

Map 14.2 British and French in North America, ca. 1700 By 1700 a veritable ring of French-claimed territory encircled the coastal colonies of England. English-claimed areas, however, were more densely settled and more economically viable.

from investors in London allowed them an unprecedented degree of self-government once the Massachusetts Bay colony was established.

Nevertheless, the colonies in North America were disappointments to England because they generated much less wealth than expected. Shipping timber back to Europe proved too expensive, fur traders found indigenous competition, and although certain colonists profited enormously from the tobacco economy, the mother country did so only moderately. The demand in Europe for tobacco never grew as quickly as the demand for sugar.

The colonies' greatest strength, from the English viewpoint, was that the settlements continued to attract migrants. By 1640, Massachusetts had some fourteen thousand European inhabitants. Through most of the next century, the growth of colonial populations in North America would result in an English advantage over the French in control of territory. In the long run, however, the size of the colonial communities would help lead them to seek independence.

The French began their settlement of North America at the same time as the English, in the same push to compensate for their mutual weakness vis-à-vis the Spanish (Map 14.2). The French efforts, however, had very different results, because of the scant number of colonists from France. There seems to have been less economic impetus for colonization from France than from England. And, after the French crown took over the colonies, there was no religious impetus, for only Catholics were allowed to settle in New France. Control by the Crown forced a traditional hierarchical political organization on the French colonies, and large tracts of land were set aside for privileged investors. There was little in North America to tempt people of modest means.

The first successful French colony was established in Acadia in 1605. A few years later, the intrepid explorer Samuel de Champlain (1567?–1635) navigated the St. Lawrence River and founded Quebec City. French explorers went on to establish Montreal, farther inland on the St. Lawrence (1642), and to explore the Great Lakes and the Mississippi River basin (see Map 14.2).

Such investment as the French crown was able to attract went into profitable trade, mainly in furs, not the difficult business of colonization. Although French men and women of Catholic religious orders sought new converts among the Indians, French trappers and traders ventured into wilderness areas without establishing European-style communities. Quebec remained more of a fur-trading outpost, dependent on supplies from France, than a thriving urban community. By the middle of the seventeenth century, all of New France had only about three thousand European inhabitants.

For both England and France the major profits and strategic interests in the New World lay to the south, in the Caribbean. The Dutch experience in North America reveals the degree to which North America was of secondary importance, for all colonial powers, to the plantation profits farther south. In 1624 the Dutch founded a trading center, New Amsterdam, at the site of modern New York City. In 1664 they relinquished it to the English in return for recognition of the Dutch claims to sugar-producing Guiana (modern Suriname) in South America. Consequently, by far the largest group of migrants to European-held territories in the Americas were forced migrants: African men and women sold into slavery and transported across the Atlantic. A conservative estimate is that approximately 1,350,000 Africans were transported as slave labor to the New World during the seventeenth century.

Marie de l'Incarnation, Colonial Settler Marie Guyart (1599–1672), as she was known in lay life, was an Ursuline nun who abandoned her own family in France to help found a convent and school for girls in Quebec, Canada. She welcomed both settlers' daughters and girls from native tribes to the school; she also learned several Amerindian languages during her life. *(Thomas Fisher Rare Book Library, University of Toronto)*

The Beginning of the End of Traditional Society

Within Europe, the economic impact of overseas trade was profound. Merchants and investors in a few of Europe's largest cities reaped great profits. Mediterranean trading centers such as Venice and Genoa, once the heart of European trade, fell into decline while Atlantic ports flourished. The population of Amsterdam increased from about 30,000 to 200,000 in the course of the seventeenth century.

All capital cities, however, not just seaports, grew substantially in the seventeenth century. Increasing numbers of government functionaries, courtiers and their hangers-on, and people involved in trade lived and worked in capital cities. These cities also grew from the demand such people generated for services and products. For the first time, cities employed vast numbers of country people. Perhaps as much as one-fifth of the population of England passed through London at one time or another, creating the mobile, volatile community so active in the English civil war and its aftermath.

The economy became more productive and flexible as it expanded, but social stratification increased. Patterns of consumption in cities reflected the economic gulfs between residents. Most people could not afford to buy imported pepper or sugar. Poverty increased in cities, even in vibrant Amsterdam, because they attracted people fleeing rural unemployment. As growing central governments increased their tax burdens on peasants, many rural people were caught in a cycle of debt; they abandoned farming and made their way to cities.

People on the margins of economic life were increasingly vulnerable to both economic forces and state power. Thousands of rural people, particularly those close to thriving urban centers, supplemented their farm income by means of the *putting-out system*, or cottage industry. An entrepreneur loaned, or "put out," raw materials to rural workers, who processed them at home and returned the finished products to the entrepreneur. In the long run, the putting-out system left workers open to exploitation of a new, more modern, sort. A local harvest failure might still endanger them, and so might a foreign war that affected the long-distance trade for their product.

Peasant rebellions recurred throughout the century. In western Europe, they were directed against escalating taxation. Countryfolk were accustomed to defending themselves as communities—against brigands and marauding soldiers, for example. Local gentry and even prosperous peasants sometimes led such revolts, convinced that they represented the legitimate interests of the community. The scale of peasant violence meant that at times thousands of troops had to be diverted from a state's foreign wars; as a matter of routine, soldiers accompanied tax officials to enforce collection all over Europe. Thus, as the ambitions of rulers grew, so did the resistance of ordinary people to the exactions of the state.

SUMMARY

The beginning of the seventeenth century was marked by religious turmoil and by social and political upheaval. By the end of the century, the former had faded as a source of collective anxiety, and the latter was largely resolved. Nascent political configurations in the Low Countries, in the Holy Roman Empire, and on the frontiers of eastern Europe had evolved into new centers of power: the Netherlands, Brandenburg-Prussia, and the Russia of Peter the Great. Most European states had moved from internal division—with independent provinces and aristocrats going their own way—to relative stability. This internal stability was both cause and consequence of rulers' desire to make war on an ever larger scale. By the end of the century, only those states able to field large armies were competitive on the European stage.

At the beginning of the century, overseas trade and colonization had been the near monopoly of Spain and Portugal; at the century's end, the English, French, and Dutch controlled much of the trade with Asia and were reaping many profits in the Americas. Beneath all these developments lay subtle but significant economic, social, and cultural shifts. One effect of the increased wealth generated by overseas trade and the increased power of governments to tax their subjects was a widening of the gulf between poor and rich. New styles of behavior and patterns of consumption highlighted differences between social classes. Overseas voyages had long-term effects on European attitudes. Along with the intellectual changes that culminated in the development of modern science, these shifts in attitude would have revolutionary consequences for European culture.

NOTES

1. Quoted in D. H. Pennington, *Europe in the Seventeenth Century*, 2d ed. (London: Longman, 1989), p. 508.

SUGGESTED READING

Alpers, Svetlana. *The Art of Describing: Dutch Art in the Seventeenth Century*. 1983. An innovative approach to Dutch art, considering it in its social and broader cultural context.

Aylmer, G. E. *Rebellion or Revolution? England from Civil War to Restoration*. 1987. A useful work that summarizes the important studies on each facet of the revolution; has an extensive bibliography.

Beik, William. *Absolutism and Society in Seventeenth-Century France*. 1984. A case study focusing on a province in southern France but nevertheless an important interpretation of the nature and functioning of the absolutist state; has an extensive bibliography.

Bercé, Yves-Marie. *Revolt and Revolution in Early Modern Europe*. 1987; and *History of Peasant Revolts*. 1990. The first work is a general, comparative survey of revolts and revolutionary movements of all sorts across Europe between 1500 and 1800; the second is a more intensive study of French peasant movements.

Bérenger, Jean. *A History of the Hapsburg Empire, 1273–1700*. 1990. A detailed and nuanced history of all the Habsburg domains and of the Habsburgs' relationship to Europe as a whole.

Boxer, C. R. *The Dutch Seaborne Empire*. 1965. The standard work detailing the development of the Dutch empire.

Collins, James B. *The State in Early Modern France*. 1995. An up-to-date synthesis by one of the leading scholars of French absolutism.

Curtin, Philip D. *The Rise and Fall of the Plantation Complex*. 1990. A good starting place for understanding the Europeans' establishment of plantation agriculture in the New World.

De Vries, Jan. *The Economy of Europe in an Age of Crisis, 1600–1750*. 1976. The single most important work on the development of the European economy in this period, integrating developments within and around Europe with the growth of overseas empires.

Gibson, Wendy. *Women in Seventeenth-Century France*. 1989. A comprehensive study of women's lives.

Goubert, Pierre. *The French Peasantry in the Seventeenth Century*. 1986; and *Louis XIV and Twenty Million Frenchmen*. 1970. Two works that consider political and social history from a broad analytic framework that includes long-term economic, demographic, and cultural data.

Hill, Christopher. *The World Turned Upside Down*. 1972. An exploration of Levellers and other groups of lower-class participants in the English revolution.

Howard, Michael. *War in European History*. 1976. A general study of warfare emphasizing the relationship between war making and state development.

Kirby, David. *Northern Europe in the Early Modern Period, 1492–1772*. 1990; and Oakley, Stewart P. *War and Peace in the Baltic, 1560–1790*. 1992. Two excellent surveys of the Baltic region in the early modern period.

Mack, Phyllis. *Visionary Women: Ecstatic Prophecy in Seventeenth-Century England*. 1992. An inquiry into the beliefs and practices of female prophets, including a discussion of the religious experience of ordinary people.

Pennington, D. H. *Europe in the Seventeenth Century*. 2d ed. 1989; and Bonney, Richard. *The European Dynastic States, 1494–1660*. 1991. Two general histories covering various portions of the century.

Riasanovsky, Nicolas V. *A History of Russia*. 2d ed. 1969. A reliable survey of Russian history from medieval times; has an extensive bibliography of major works available in English.

Ritchie, Robert C. *Captain Kidd and the War Against the Pirates*. 1986. An interesting work on the communities of castoffs and adventurers that grew up in the Caribbean during European expansion and their place in the Atlantic economic and political worlds.

Stone, Lawrence. *The Causes of the English Revolution, 1529–1642*. 1972. A brief and clear introduction.

Vierhaus, Rudolf. *Germany in the Age of Absolutism*. 1988. A concise survey of the development of German states from the end of the Thirty Years' War through the eighteenth century.

Wandycz, Piotr. *The Price of Freedom: A History of East Central Europe from the Middle Ages to the Present*. 1992. A lively survey of the histories of Poland, Hungary, and Bohemia.

Wolf, Eric R. *Europe and the People Without History*. 1982. A survey of European contact with and conquest of peoples after 1400; includes extensive treatments of non-European societies and detailed explanation of the economic and political interests of the Europeans.

CHAPTER 15

A Revolution in World-View

s famous as the confrontation between the religious rebel Martin Luther and Holy Roman Emperor Charles V in 1521 is the confrontation between the astronomer Galileo and the judges of the papal inquisition that ended on June 22, 1633. On that day, Galileo knelt before the seven cardinals who represented the inquisition to renounce his errors and receive his punishment. His "errors" included publishing scientific propositions that disagreed with views accepted by the church—particularly the view that the earth is stationary and does not spin on its axis and orbit the sun. As Galileo left the cardinals' presence, he is supposed to have muttered, "Eppur si muove" ("But it *does* move").

This seems a wonderful moment of historical drama, but we should be suspicious of it because it oversimplifies historical circumstances. The changes that we know as "the Reformation" and "the Scientific Revolution" were far more complex than the actions of a few individuals. And Galileo never made the defiant statement he is credited with.

Moreover, we cannot treat the new scientific views simply as truth overcoming ignorance and error. The history of scientific thought is not merely a history of discovery about the world; it is also a history of explanations of the world. From its beginnings the Scientific Revolution was a broad cultural movement. Copernicus, Galileo, and others contributed important new data to the pool of knowledge, but even more important was their collective contribution to a fundamentally new view of the universe and the place of the earth and human beings in it.

By the end of the seventeenth century, the idea of an infinite but orderly cosmos accessible to human reason had largely replaced the medieval vision of a closed universe centered on earth and suffused with Christian purpose. Religion became an increasingly subordinate ally of science as confidence in an open-ended, experimental approach to knowledge came to be as strongly held as religious conviction. It is because of this larger shift in world-view, not because of particular scientific discoveries, that the seventeenth century may be labeled the era of the scientific *revolution.*

Questions and Ideas to Consider

- What was the major contribution of Copernicus? Why was it so significant?
- How did most of the scientists support themselves? How did systems of patronage and appointment favor certain groups of people? Consider the experience of Copernicus or Tycho Brahe on the one hand, and that of Maria Sibylla Merian or Maria Winkelman on the other.
- Descartes fashioned a systematic explanation for the operations of nature that replaced the medieval view. What was it? Discuss some of the ways that his contemporaries responded to it. Consider, for example, Pascal, Cavendish, and Locke.
- How did the new science undermine traditional social and political hierarchies, and, in light of this, why did governments tend to support scientific research?
- Why did Hobbes and Locke disagree? How were their theories dependent on the rise of the new science, and how did they come to such different conclusions? Consider the political context of their work.

THE REVOLUTION IN ASTRONOMY

Because the Scientific Revolution was a revolution within science itself as well as a revolution in intellectual life more generally, we must seek its causes within the history of science as well as in the broader historical context. Many of the causes are familiar. They include the intellectual achievements of the Renaissance, the challenges that were posed by the discovery of the New World, the expansion of trade and production, the spread of literacy and access to books, and the increasing power of princes and monarchs.

The scientific origins of the seventeenth-century revolution in thought lie, for the most part, in developments in astronomy. Advances in astronomy spurred dramatic intellectual transformation because of astronomy's role in the explanations of the world and of human life that had been devised by ancient and medieval scientists and philosophers. In the early seventeenth century, fundamental astronomical tenets were successfully challenged. The consequence was the undermining of both the material explanation of the world (physics) and the philosophical explanation of the world (metaphysics) that had stood for centuries.

The Inherited World-View and the Sixteenth-Century Context

Ancient and medieval astronomy accepted the perspective on the universe that unaided human senses support—namely, that the earth is at the center of the universe and the celestial bodies rotate around the earth. The intellectual and psychological journey from the notion of a closed world centered on the earth to an infinitely large universe of undifferentiated matter was an immense process with complex causes.

The regular movements of heavenly bodies and the obvious importance of the sun for life on earth made astronomy a vital undertaking for both scientific and religious purposes in many ancient societies. Astronomers in ancient Greece carefully observed the heavens and learned to calculate and predict the seemingly circular motion of the stars and the sun about the earth. The orbits of a few of the lights in the sky were more difficult to explain, for they seemed to travel both east and west across the sky at various times and with no regularity that could be mathematically understood. These were called *planets*, from a Greek word meaning "wanderer."

We now know that all the planets orbit the sun at different speeds and at different distances from the sun. The relative positions of the planets thus constantly change; sometimes other planets

CHAPTER CHRONOLOGY

1543	Copernicus, *On the Revolution of Heavenly Bodies*
	Vesalius, *On the Fabric of the Human Body*
1576	Construction of Brahe's observatory begins
1591	Galileo's law of falling bodies
1609	Kepler's third law of motion
1610	Galileo, *The Starry Messenger*
1620	Bacon, *Novum Organum*
1628	Harvey, *On the Motion of the Heart*
1632	Galileo, *Dialogue on the Two Chief Systems of the World*
1637	Descartes, *Discourse on Method*
1660	Boyle, *New Experiments Physico-Mechanical*
1668	Cavendish, *Grounds of Natural Philosophy*
1687	Newton, *Principia*

are "ahead" of the earth and sometimes "behind." In the second century A.D. the Greek astronomer Ptolemy attempted to explain the planets' occasional "backward" motion by attributing it to "epicycles"—small circular orbits within the larger orbit. Although Ptolemy's mathematical explanations of the imagined epicycles were extremely complex, neither Ptolemy nor medieval mathematicians and astronomers were ever able fully to account for planetary motion.

Ancient physics, most notably the work of Aristotle (384–322 B.C.), explained the fact that some objects (such as cannonballs) fall to earth but others (stars and planets) seem weightless relative to the earth by presuming that objects are made up of different sorts of matter. Aristotle thought that different kinds of matter had different inherent tendencies and properties. In this view, all earthbound matter falls because it is naturally attracted to the earth.

The universe was thought to be literally a closed world with the stationary earth at the center. Revolving around the earth in circular orbits were the sun, the moon, the stars, and the planets. The motion of all lesser bodies was caused by the rotation of all the stars together in the crystal-like sphere in which they were embedded. In the Christian era, the Aristotelian explanation of the universe was infused with Christian meaning and purpose. The heavens were thought to be made of different, pure matter because they were the abode of the angels. Both earth and the humans who inhabited it were changeable and corruptible, but God had given it, and its human inhabitants, a unique and special place in the universe.

A few ancient astronomers theorized that the earth moved about the sun. Some medieval philosophers also adopted this heliocentric thesis (*helios* is the Greek word for "sun"), but it remained a minority view because it seemed to contradict both common sense and observed data. The sun and stars *appeared* to move around the earth with great regularity. Moreover, how could objects fall to earth if the earth was moving beneath them? Also, astronomers detected no difference in the angles from which observers on earth viewed the stars at different times. Such differences would exist, they thought, if the earth changed position by moving around the sun. It was inconceivable that the stars could be so distant that the earth's movement would produce no measurable change in its position with respect to the stars.

Several conditions of intellectual life in the sixteenth century encouraged new work in astronomy and led to a revision of the earth-centered world-view. The most important was the humanists' recovery of and commentary on ancient texts. Now able to work with new Greek versions of Ptolemy, mathematicians and astronomers discovered that his explanations for the motions of the planets were imperfect and not simply inadequately transmitted, as they had long believed. The discovery of the New World also undermined Ptolemy's authority by disproving many of his geographic assertions.

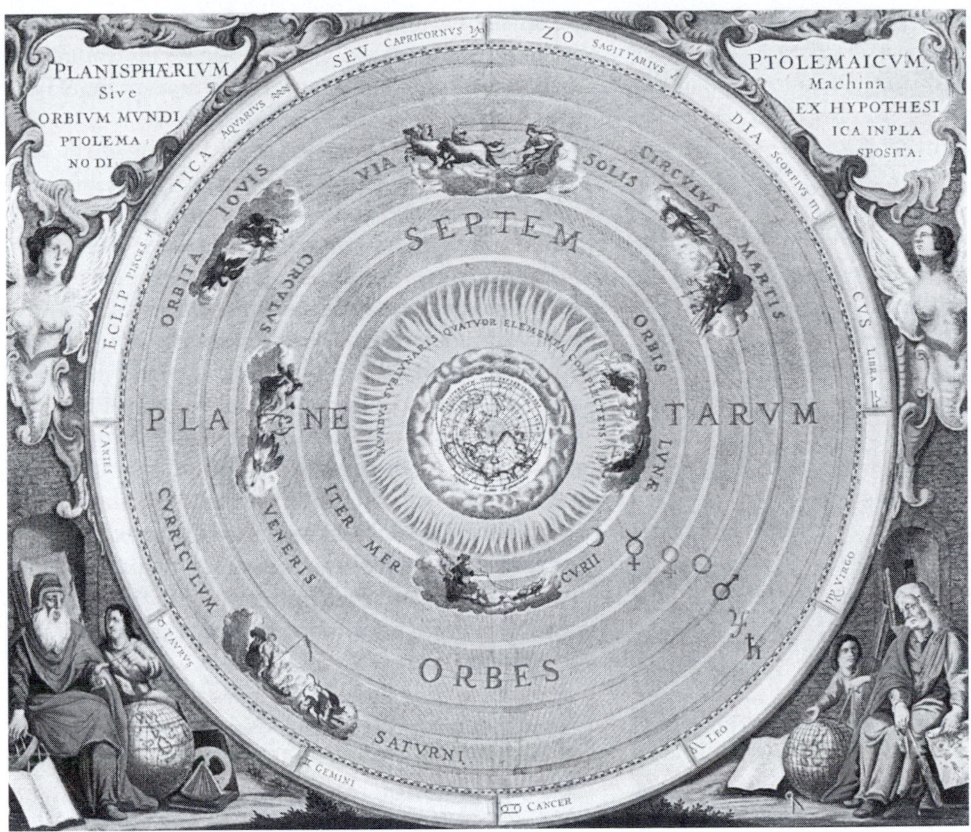

The Traditional Universe In this print from around 1600, heavenly bodies are depicted orbiting the earth in perfectly circular paths. In fact, the ancient astronomer Ptolemy believed that the planets followed complex orbits-within-orbits, known as *epicycles,* moving around the stationary earth. *(Hulton-Getty/Liaison)*

The desire to explain heavenly motions better was still loaded with religious significance in the sixteenth century and was heightened by the immediate need for reform of the Julian calendar (named for Julius Caesar). Ancient observations of the movement of the sun, though remarkably accurate, could not measure the precise length of the solar year. By the sixteenth century, the cumulative error of this calendar had resulted in a change of ten days: The spring equinox fell on March 11 instead of March 21. An accurate and uniform system of dating was necessary for all rulers and their tax collectors and recordkeepers but was the particular project of the church, because the calculation of the date of Easter was at stake.

Impetus for new and better astronomical observations and calculations arose from other features of the intellectual and political landscape as well. Increasingly as the century went on, princely courts became important sources of patronage for and sites of scientific activity. Rulers eager to buttress their own power by linking it symbolically to dominion over nature sponsored investigations of the world, as Ferdinand and Isabella had so successfully done, and displayed the marvels of nature at their courts. Sponsoring scientific inquiry also yielded practical benefits: better mapping of the ruler's domains and better technology for mining, gunnery, and navigation.

Finally, schools of thought fashionable at the time, encouraged by the humanists' critique of Scholastic tradition, hinted at the possibilities of alternative physical and metaphysical systems. One was Paracelsianism, named for the Swiss physician Philippus von Hohenheim (1493–1541), known as Paracelsus. Paracelsus offered an alternative to the theory, put forth by the ancient master, Galen (ca. 131–ca. 201), that the imbalance of bodily "humors" causes illness. He substituted a theory of chemical imbalance.

Neo-Platonism, another school of thought, had a more systematic and far-reaching impact. A revival primarily in Italian humanist circles of certain aspects of Plato's thought, Neo-Platonism emphasized the abstract nature of true knowledge: Things might not be as they seemed. Neo-Platonists prized mathematical investigation because they associated it with abstract truth. This provided a spur to astronomical studies, which, since ancient times, had been primarily concerned with mathematical analysis of heavenly movements (more than with physical explanations for them). Also, like Paracelsianism, Neo-Platonism had a mystical dimension. Neo-Platonists were particularly fascinated by the sun as a symbol of the one divine mind or soul at the heart of all creation.

The Copernican Challenge

Nicolaus Copernicus (1473–1543), the son of a prosperous Polish merchant, pursued wide-ranging university studies in philosophy, law, astronomy, and mathematics—first in Cracow in Poland and then in Bologna and Padua in Italy. In Italy he was exposed to Neo-Platonic ideas. He took a degree in canon law in 1503 and became a cathedral canon in the city of Frauenburg in East Prussia (modern Poland), where he pursued his interests in astronomy while carrying out administrative duties for the cathedral. When the pope asked Copernicus to assist with the reform of the Julian calendar, he replied that reform of the calendar required reform in astronomy. His major work, *On the Revolution of Heavenly Bodies* (1543), was dedicated to the pope in the hopes that it would help with the task of calendar reform—as indeed it did. The Gregorian calendar, issued in 1582, was based on Copernicus's calculations.

Copernicus did not assert that the earth and the other planets orbit the sun. Rather, he suggested that if we pretend this is the case we get a mathematical construct that is very useful for predicting the movements of planets, stars, and the sun. But though he did not claim that his heliocentric system corresponded to reality, we cannot be certain what he believed. He had searched in ancient sources for thinkers who believed the earth did move. Also, if he had not sensed that his work was a revolutionary description of the real world, why would he have waited until 1542, twelve years after finishing it, to send it to be published? For years, other astronomers familiar with his work had urged him to publish. Instead, he was on his deathbed when he first held the book in his hand.

Copernicus's work was immediately useful. The schema made possible a simpler prediction of planetary motion and accounted for most backward motion. But since Copernicus still assumed that the planets traveled in circular orbits, he retained some epicycles to account for the difference between his model and his observations. The Copernican account of planetary motion appealed to other astronomers of the age for both its usefulness and its beauty; as they worked with his calculations, they sought new evidence to support his theory.

But Copernican theory led to a conceptual revolution only gradually, because Copernicus had failed to resolve the physical problems his theory raised. If Copernicus were right, the earth would have to be made of the same stuff as other planets. But if the earth is not made of some special earth-stuff, why do objects "on" earth fall toward it? Also, Copernicus's system explained the motion of the stars as *apparent* movement due to the motion of the earth. This obviated the need for rotating crystalline spheres for the stars, but what about the planets? What made them move?

Copernicus was not as troubled by these questions as we might expect him to have been. Since ancient times, mathematical astronomy—the science of measuring and predicting the movement of heavenly bodies—had been far more important than and had proceeded independently of physical explanations for observed motion. Still, his theories directly contradicted many of the supposed laws of motion. The usefulness of his theories to other astronomers meant that the contradictions between mathematical and physical models for the universe would have to be resolved. Copernicus might be best understood as the last Ptolemaic astronomer, working within inherited questions and with known tools. His work did not constitute a revolution, but it certainly initiated one.

The First Copernican Astronomers

We can see the effects of Copernicus's work on the first generation of astronomers that followed him. His impressive computations rapidly won converts among fellow astronomers. Several particularly gifted astronomers continued to develop the Copernican system. By the second quarter of the seventeenth century, they and many others accepted the heliocentric theory as reality and not just as a useful mathematical fiction. The most important astronomers to build on Copernican assumptions were the Dane Tycho Brahe (1546–1601), the German Johannes Kepler (1571–1630), and the Italian Galileo Galilei (1564–1642).

Like generations of observers before him, Tycho Brahe had been stirred by the majesty of the regular movements of heavenly bodies. After witnessing a partial eclipse of the sun, he abandoned a career in government and became an astronomer. Brahe was the first truly post-Ptolemaic astronomer because he was the first to improve on the data that the ancients and all subsequent astronomers had used. Ironically, *no* theory of planetary motion could have reconciled the data that Copernicus had used: They were simply too inaccurate, based as they were on naked-eye observations and marred by errors of translation and copying, accumulated over centuries.

In 1576 the king of Denmark showered Brahe with properties and pensions enabling him to build an observatory, Uraniborg, on an island near Copenhagen. At Uraniborg, Brahe improved on ancient observations with large and very finely calibrated instruments that permitted precise measurements of celestial movements by the naked eye. His attention to precision and the frequency of his observations produced results that were twice as accurate as any previous data had been.

As a result of his observations, Brahe agreed with Copernicus that the planets rotate around the sun, not the earth. He still could not be persuaded that the earth itself moved, for none of his data supported such a notion. Brahe's lasting and crucial contribution was his astronomical data. They would become obsolete as soon as data from use of the telescope were accumulated about a century later. But in the meantime, they were used by Johannes Kepler to further develop Copernicus's model and arrive at a more accurate heliocentric theory.

Kepler was young enough to be exposed to Copernican ideas from the outset of his training, and he quickly recognized in Brahe's data the means of resolving the problems in Copernican analysis. Though trained in his native Germany, Kepler went to Prague, where Brahe spent the last years of his life after a quarrel with the Danish king, and became something of an apprentice to Brahe. After Brahe's death in 1601, Kepler kept his mentor's records of astronomical observation and continued to work at the imperial court as Rudolf II's court mathematician.

Kepler's contribution to the new astronomy, like that of Copernicus, was fundamentally mathematical. In it, we can see the stamp of the Neo-Platonic conviction about the purity of mathematical explanation. Kepler spent ten years working to apply Brahe's data to the most intricate of celestial motions—the movement of the planet Mars—as a key to explaining all planetary motion. Mars is close to the earth but is farther from the sun than the earth is. This combination produces very puzzling and dramatic variations in the movement of Mars apparent to an earthly observer.

The result of Kepler's work was laws of planetary motion that, in the main, are still in use. He eliminated the need for epicycles (see the caption on page 389) by correctly asserting that planets follow elliptical and not circular orbits and that the speed of a planet in its orbit slows proportionally as the planet's distance from the sun increases. He also showed that the distance of each planet from the sun and the time it takes each planet to orbit the sun are in a constant ratio.

Kepler's work was a breakthrough because it confirmed the Copernican heliocentric hypothesis mathematically. Kepler's laws invited speculation about the properties and motion of heavenly and terrestrial bodies alike; a new physics would be required to explain the novel motions Kepler had posited. Kepler himself, in Neo-Platonic fashion, attributed planetary motion to the sun:

> [The sun] is a fountain of light, rich in fruitful heat, most fair, limpid and pure . . . called king of the planets for his motion, heart of the world for his power. . . . Who would hesitate to confer the votes of the celestial motions on him who has been administering all other movements and changes by the benefit of the light which is entirely his possession?[1]

Galileo and the Triumph of Copernicanism

Galileo Galilei holds a pre-eminent position in the development of astronomy for several reasons. He provided compelling new evidence to support Copernican theory, and he contributed to the development of a new physics—or, more precisely, mechanics—that could account for the movement of bodies in new terms. Just as important, his efforts to publicize his findings and his condemnation by the church spurred debate about Copernican ideas in literate society.

Born to a minor Florentine noble family, Galileo studied medicine and mathematics at the University of Pisa and became professor of mathematics there in 1589 at the age of 25. He had already completed important work on mechanics and within three years was given a chair at the University of Padua, where Copernicus had once studied. He continued to work in mechanics during the 1590s but did not publish the results of his experiments until much later. Instead, he became famous for the results of his astronomical observations, which he published in 1610. *Sidereus Nuncius* (*The Starry Messenger*) described in lay language the results of his scrutiny of the heavens with a telescope that he had built.

Galileo was the first person that we know who used a telescope to look at the sky. In *The Starry Messenger,* he documented sighting new (previously invisible) stars, another blow to the ancient descriptions of the universe. He noted craters and other "imperfections" on the surface of the moon and the existence of moons orbiting the planet Jupiter. Three years later he published his observations of sunspots in *Letters on Sunspots.* Sunspots are regions of relatively cool gaseous material that appear as dark spots on the sun's surface. For Galileo the sunspots and the craters of the moon constituted proof that the heavens were not perfect and changeless but rather were like the supposedly "corrupt" and changeable earth.

Galileo's principal contribution to mechanics lay in his working out of an early theory of inertia. As a result of a number of experiments with falling bodies (balls rolling on carefully constructed inclines—not free-falling objects that, according to myth, he dropped from the Leaning Tower of Pisa), Galileo ventured a new view of what is "natural" to bodies. Galileo's view was that uniform motion is as natural as a state of rest. According to ancient and medieval theories, all motion needed a cause, and all motion could be explained in terms of purpose. "I hold," Galileo countered, "that there exists nothing in external bodies . . . but size, shape, quantity and motion."[2] In fact, Galileo retained the old assumption that motion was somehow naturally circular. Nevertheless, his theory was a crucial step in explaining motion according to new principles and in fashioning a world-view that accepted a mechanical universe devoid of metaphysical purpose. These theories were published only toward the end of his life, however. His astronomical theories were more influential at the time.

Galileo's books were widely read, and his work became common currency in the scientific societies already flourishing in his lifetime and in courtly circles where science was encouraged. In 1610, Galileo became court mathematician to Cosimo de' Medici, the grand duke of Tuscany (r. 1609–1620), as a result of the fame brought by *The Starry Messenger.* Soon after his arrival, however, rumors that "Galileists" were openly promulgating heliocentrism led to an investigation and, in 1616, the official condemnation of Copernicus's works by the inquisition in Rome. The condemnation allowed room for maneuver. After meeting personally with the pope, Galileo was assured that he could continue to use Copernican theory, but only as a theory.

In 1632, Galileo issued a bold response to that limitation. *Dialogue on the Two Chief Systems of the World* was perhaps the most important single source for the popularization of Copernican theory. The work consists of a debate among three characters on the merits of Copernican theory. Simplicio, the character representing the old world-view, was, as his name suggests, an example of ignorance, not wisdom. In this work, Galileo expressed his supreme confidence—bordering on arrogance—in his own powers and in human power generally to use reason to understand the physical world.

By publishing the *Dialogue,* Galileo defied the papal ban on advocating Copernicanism. In an earlier work, *Letter to the Grand Duchess Christina* (1615), Galileo had also been impolitic, trespassing on the church's authority to interpret the Scriptures. He was tried for heresy and forced to condemn his "errors" in 1633, though Pope Urban VIII (r. 1623–1644) intervened to give him the light sentence of house arrest at his villa in Tuscany. There, Galileo continued his investigations of mechanics until his death in 1642.

THE SCIENTIFIC REVOLUTION GENERALIZED

Galileo's work found such a willing audience because, like Kepler and Brahe, he was not working alone. Dozens of other scientists were attacking old problems from the fresh perspective offered by the breakthroughs in astronomy. Many of these thinkers addressed the metaphysical issues that their investigations inevitably raised.

The Promise of the New Science

Francis Bacon (1561–1626), lord chancellor of England during the reign of James I, wrote a utopian essay extolling the benefits of science for a peaceful society and for human happiness. In *New Atlantis,* published one year after his death, and in *Novum Organum* (1620), Bacon revealed his faith in science by advocating patient, systematic observation and experimentation to accumulate knowledge about the world. He argued that the proper method of investigation "derives axioms from . . . particulars, rising by gradual and unbroken ascent, so that it arrives at the most general axioms of all. This is the true way but untried."[3]

Bacon himself did not undertake experiments, though his widely read works were influential in encouraging both the *empirical method* (relying on observation and experimentation) and *inductive reasoning* (deriving general principles from particular facts). Bacon's writing reflected the fact that an interest in exploring nature's secrets and exercising "dominion over nature" had become an indispensable part of princely rule. Princely courts were the main source of financial support for science and a primary site of scientific work during Bacon's lifetime. Part of the impetus for this development came from the civic humanism of the Italian Renaissance, which had celebrated the state and service to it.

Rulers' newfound enthusiasm for science reflected the growing scope of their resources and ambitions: They wanted technical expertise in armaments, fortification, building projects in general, navigation, and mapmaking. The promise of the New World and the drive for overseas trade and exploration especially encouraged support of science. This took the form of geographical investigation, from mapmaking to navigation, as well as a variety of other empirical studies. For example, information was compiled about the new territory of Virginia, including the first dictionary of any Native American language.

Science could be an ideological as well as a practical tool. Most courts housed collections of marvels, specimens of exotic plants and animals, and mechanical contrivances. These demonstrated the ruler's interest in investigation of the world—his or her status, in other words, as an educated person. These collections and the work of court experts also enhanced the ruler's reputation as a patron and enlivened the image of the ruler's power. Galileo was playing off such expectations when he named some of his newly discovered bodies "Medician Stars."

Exploring the secrets of nature became an honorable activity for scholars and courtiers. By the beginning of the seventeenth century, private salons and academies were another major site of scientific investigation. These, too, had their roots in the humanist culture of Italy, where circles of scholars without university affiliations had formed.

The earliest scientific academy was the Accadèmia Segreta (Secret Academy), founded in Naples in the 1540s. The members pursued experiments together, in order, in the words of one member, "to make a true anatomy of the things and operations of nature itself."[4] For the rest of the sixteenth century and into the seventeenth, academies sprang up in many cities. The most celebrated was the Accadèmia dei Lincei, founded in Rome by an aristocrat in 1603. Its most famous member, Galileo, joined in 1611. The name "Lincei," *lynx*, was chosen because of the legendary keen sight of that animal, an appropriate mascot for "searchers of secrets."

Galileo's notoriety and the importance of his discoveries forced acceptance or rejection of Copernicanism on all communities. Throughout the seventeenth century, the investigation of natural phenomena continued in increasingly sophisticated institutional settings. The flowering of scientific thought in the seventeenth century occurred because of the specific innovations in astronomy and the general spread of scientific investigation that had been achieved by the end of Bacon's life.

New Cosmologies and New Procedures

Philosophers, mathematicians, and educated elites engaged in lively debate and practical investigation throughout Europe in the first half of the seventeenth century, but in France questions about cosmic order were posed at a time of political disorder. The years following the religious wars saw the murder of Henry IV, another regency, and further civil war in the 1620s (see page 344). In this environment, questions about order in the universe and the possibilities of human knowledge took on particular urgency. It is not surprising that it was a Frenchman, René Descartes (1596–1650), who created the first fully articulated alternative world-view.

Descartes's work emerged in dialogue with a circle of other French thinkers. His ideas became more influential among philosophers and lay people than those of some of his equally talented contemporaries because of his thoroughness and rigor, his mathematical expertise, and his graceful, readable French. His system was fully presented in his *Discourse on Method* (1637).

Descartes accepted Galileo's conclusion that the heavens and the earth are made of the same elements. In theorizing about the composition of matter, Descartes drew on ancient atomic models that previously had not been generally accepted. His theory that all matter is made up of identical bits, which he named "corpuscles," is a forerunner of modern atomic and quantum theories. Descartes believed that all the different appearances and behaviors of matter can be explained solely by the size, shape, and motion of these "corpuscles." Descartes's was an extremely mechanistic explanation of the universe. It permitted new, more specific observations and hypotheses and greater understanding of inertia. For example, because he reimagined the universe as being filled with "corpuscles" free to move in any direction, "natural" motion no longer seemed either circular (Galileo's idea) or toward the center of the earth (Aristotle's idea). The new understanding of motion would be crucial to Isaac Newton's formulations later in the century.

A Collection of Naturalia Displays of exotica, such as these specimens in Naples, symbolized the ruler's authority by suggesting his or her power over nature. *(From Ferrante Imperato,* Dell' Historia Naturale *[Naples, 1599]. By permission of the Houghton Library, Harvard University)*

The collapse of the old explanations about the world made Descartes and other investigators doubt not only what they knew but also their capacity to know anything at all. Their physical senses—which denied that the earth moved, for example—had been proved untrustworthy. Descartes's solution was to re-envision the human rational capacity, the mind, as completely distinct from the world—that is, as distinct from the human body—and the betraying sense data it offers. In a leap of faith, Descartes presumed that he could count on the fact that God would not have given humans a mind if that mind were to betray them. For Descartes, God became the guarantor of human reasoning capacity, and humans, in Descartes's view, were distinguished by that capacity. This is the significance of his famous claim "I think, therefore I am."

Descartes thus achieved a resolution of the terrifying doubt about the world by exalting the role of the human knower. The Cartesian universe was one of mechanical motion, not purpose or mystical meaning, and the Cartesian human being was pre-eminently a mind that could apprehend that universe. The term *Cartesian dualism* came to signify Descartes's notion that the material world of bodies and things is quite distinct from the mind of the human observer.

Descartes's ambitious view of human reason had important implications. One was the emphasis on *deductive reasoning* (a process of reasoning in which the conclusion follows necessarily from the stated premises), which naturally followed from his rejection of sense data. In actuality, Descartes did rely on sense data; he did experiments. But philosophically he emphasized logical sense above observed information. In the short run, Descartes's embrace of absolute certainty proved very useful to the advancement of knowledge because it gave natural philosophers the confidence to speculate despite their enormous uncertainty about specific problems.

Descartes's vision of the enhanced position of the individual knower, and of the power of the knower's reason, was also attractive to educated lay people. Elites used science to affirm their status in the world, which could now be expressed in terms of intellectual power and power over nature, rather than only as political power. Descartes was careful not to advocate the "madness" of applying reason to changing the state. The state alone had made humans civilized, he maintained; and although he and other thinkers had to rebuild knowledge of the universe from its foundations, he believed it was "unreasonable for an individual to conceive the plan of reforming a state by changing everything from the foundations."[5]

The notion of detached rationality appeared in other people's work around this time. Renaissance painters, for example, utilized the principles of linear perspective to present views of the world as detached still life. Michel de Montaigne (1533–1592) was also exploring a similar detachment (see page 352). Descartes's was the most radical detachment of all, for he claimed objectivity. Though much of Cartesian physics would be surpassed by Newton at the end of the century, Descartes's assumption about the objectivity of the observer would become an enduring part of scientific practice. The sense of detachment from the world also fostered a belief in humans' ability to control nature. In our own time, we have become aware of the limits of our ability to control nature, as well as the arbitrariness of Descartes's distinction between mind and body. In Descartes's day, the most radical aspect of his thought was the reduction of God from being an active presence in the world to serving as the guarantor of knowledge. Later generations of scientists would be fearful of Descartes's system because it seemed to encourage "atheism." In fact, a profound faith in God was necessary for Descartes's creativity in imagining his new world system—but the system did work without God. Although Descartes would have been surprised and offended by charges of atheism, he knew his work would antagonize the Catholic church. He moved to the Netherlands to study in 1628, and his *Discourse* was first published there.

A contemporary of Descartes, Blaise Pascal (1623–1662), challenged Descartes's confident rationalism by drawing attention to the limits of scientific knowledge. Son of a royal official, Pascal was one of the most brilliant minds of his generation. A mathematician like Descartes, he stressed the importance of mathematical representations of phenomena, built one of the first calculating machines, and invented probability theory. He also carried out experiments to investigate air pressure, the behavior of liquids, and the existence of vacuums.

Pascal's career alternated between periods of intense scientific work and religious retreat. Today he is best known for his writings on the human soul and psyche. His *Pensées* (*Thoughts,* 1669) consists of the published fragments of his defense of Christian faith, which remained unfinished at the time of his early death. Pascal's appeal for generations after him may lie in his assumption that matters of faith and feeling must also be open to investigation. His most famous statement, "The heart has its reasons which the reason knows not," can be read as a statement of the limits of the Cartesian world-view.

The new science had adherents and practitioners throughout Europe by 1650. Dutch scientists in the commercial milieu of the Netherlands, for example, had the freedom to pursue practical and experimental interests. The Dutch investigator Christiaan Huygens (1629–1695) worked on a great variety of problems, including air pressure and optics. He invented and patented the pendulum clock in 1657, the first device accurately to measure small units of time, essential for a variety of measurements.

In England, on the other hand, science was deeply informed by religion and politics because of the English civil war. In the 1640s natural philosophers with Puritan leanings were encouraged in their investigations by dreams that science, of the practical Baconian sort, could be used to bring about the perfection of life on earth and accelerate the end of history: the reign of the saints preceding the Second Coming of Christ. The best-known member of this group was Robert Boyle (1627–1691).

Boyle and his colleagues initially attacked the university system, still under the sway of Aristotelianism, and proposed widespread reform of education. But as the English revolution proceeded, they were forced to moderate many of their positions. Radical groups such as the Levellers believed that each person was capable of divine knowledge without the coercive hierarchy of officials of church and state. In response, Boyle and his colleagues worked to articulate a theoretical position that combined the orderliness of mechanism, a continued divine presence in the world, and a Baconian emphasis on scientific progress. This was attractive to the educated elite of the day because it offered the certainties of science without invalidating all of the authoritarian aspects of the old Christian world-view.

Boyle and his colleagues' most creative contribution was their refinement of experimental philosophy and practice. In 1660, Boyle published *New Experiments Physico-Mechanical*, describing the results of his experiments with an air pump he had designed and laying out general rules for experimental procedure. The work was significant for its nominal results (demonstrating that a vacuum could exist). The experiment is also interesting because Boyle's defense of the results did not meet modern standards of scientific rigor. When a Cambridge scholar criticized one of Boyle's interpretations of his experiments, Boyle replied that he could not understand his critic's objections, "the experiment having been tried both before our whole society [the Royal Society of London], and very critically, by its royal founder, his majesty himself."[6] Rather than debate differing interpretations, Boyle chose to fall back on the authority and prestige of the participants themselves. In English science in the mid-seventeenth century, the various aspects of the modern scientific profession—the agreement on principles, the acceptance of experimental procedures, and the authority of practitioners—were all being worked out simultaneously.

The Newtonian Synthesis: The Copernican Revolution Completed

It was the Englishman Isaac Newton (1642–1724) who completed the explanation of motion in the heavens and on earth that Copernicus's work had initiated and that Kepler, Galileo, and others had sought. In Newton's career, we can see how different the climate for science was by the second half of the seventeenth century. When Newton entered Cambridge University as a student in 1661, Copernicanism was studied, the benefits of scientific investigation were debated, and much attention was focused on the problems of Descartes's explanations of matter.

Like all the natural philosophers before him, Newton was as concerned by questions of metaphysics as by physics. In the 1680s, he devoted himself primarily to the study of church history, theology, and alchemy. As a student at Cambridge he was strongly influenced by the work of a group of Neo-Platonists who were critical of Cartesian dualism, which posited God as a cause of all matter and motion but removed God as an explanation for the behavior of matter. As Newton says in some of his early writing while a student, "However we cast about we find almost no other reason for atheism than this [Cartesian] notion of bodies having . . . a complete, absolute and independent reality."[7] Like all earlier natural philosophers, Newton had concerns that were both religious and scientific; he, too, sought to harmonize science with a securely Christian world-view following the "excesses" of the English revolution.

Newton combined his scientific skepticism and his religious certainty to posit the existence of gravity—a mysterious force that accounts for the movement of heavenly bodies. Others had speculated about the existence of gravity, but Newton's extraordinary contribution was the mathematical computation of the laws of gravity and planetary motion, which he combined with a fully developed concept of inertia. The concept of inertia, as it had been elaborated by Galileo, Descartes, and others were suggested the need for the concept of gravity. Otherwise, if a planet was "pushed" (say, in Kepler's view, by the "motive force" of the sun), it would continue along that course forever unless "pulled back" by something else.

In 1687, Newton published *Philosophiae Naturalis Principia Mathematica* (*Mathematical Principles of Natural Philosophy*). In this mathematical treatise—so intricate that it was inaccessible to lay people, even those able to read Latin—Newton laid out his laws of motion and expressed them as mathematical theorems that could be used to test future observations. Then he demonstrated that these laws also apply to the solar system, confirming the data already gathered about the planets. His supreme achievement was his law of gravitation, with which he predicted the discovery of an as-yet-unseen planet. This law states that every body, indeed every bit of matter in the universe, exerts over every other body an attractive force proportional to the product of their masses and inversely proportional to the square of the distance between them. Newton not only accounted for motion but united heaven and earth with a single explanatory scheme and created a convincing picture of an orderly nature.

Newton did not claim that his theorems resolved all the questions about motion and matter. He did not know what gravity actually is, and we still do not know today. Yet Newton's laws of motion still adequately account for most problems of motion. The fact that so fundamental a principle as gravity remains unexplained in no way diminishes Newton's achievement but is clear evidence about the nature of scientific understanding: Science provides explanatory schemas that account for many—but not all—observed phenomena. When a scientific explanation ceases to account satisfactorily for enough data, it collapses. No schema explains everything, and each schema contains open doorways that lead to further discovery and blind alleys that lead to mistaken impressions. Newton, for example, also studied alchemy during his most productive years. He assumed that the spiritual forces that somehow accounted for gravity could be harnessed to change metals into gold.

Other Branches of Science

Innovations in astronomy that led to the new mechanistic view of the behavior of matter did not automatically spill over to other branches of science. Developments in astronomy were very specific to that field. Other branches of science followed their own paths, though all were strongly influenced by the mechanistic world-view.

In chemistry, the mechanistic assumption that all matter was composed of small, equivalent parts was crucial to understanding the properties and behavior of compounds (combinations of elements). But knowledge of these small units of matter was not yet detailed enough to be of much use in advancing chemistry conceptually. Nevertheless, the flawed conceptual schema did not hold back all discovery and development. Lack of understanding of gases and the specific elements that compose them did not prevent the development and improvement of gunpowder, for example. Indeed, unlike the innovations in astronomy, conceptual innovation in chemistry and biology owed a great deal to the results of experiment and the slow accumulation of data.

A conceptual leap forward was made in biology in the sixteenth and seventeenth centuries, however. Because biological knowledge was mostly a byproduct of the practice of medicine, biological studies had been and remained very practical and experimental. But the discovery of *On Anatomical Procedures,* a treatise by the ancient master Galen, encouraged dissection and other practical research. Andreas Vesalius (1514–1564), in particular, made important advances by heed-ing Galen's exhortation to conduct anatomical research. Born in Brussels, Vesalius studied at the nearby University of Louvain in Belgium and then at Padua, where he was appointed professor of surgery. He ended his career as physician to Emperor Charles V and his son, Philip II of Spain. In his teaching at Padua he embodied newly discovered Galenic precepts by doing dissections himself rather than leaving the work to technicians. In 1543 he published versions of his lectures as an illustrated compendium of anatomy, *On the Fabric of the Human Body*. His dissections of human corpses, revealed in this work, demonstrated a number of errors in Galen's knowledge of human anatomy, much of which had been derived from dissection of animals. Neither Vesalius nor his immediate successors, however, questioned overall Galenic theory about the functioning of the human body, any more than Copernicus had utterly rejected Aristotelian physics.

The slow movement from new observation to changed explanation is clearly illustrated in the career of the Englishman William Harvey (1578–1657). Like Vesalius, Harvey was educated first in his own land and then at Padua, where he benefited from the tradition of anatomical research. Returning to England, Harvey became a practicing physician in London and at the courts of James I and Charles I.

Harvey postulated the circulation of the blood—postulated rather than discovered because, owing to the technology of the day, he could not observe the tiny capillaries where arterial blood flows into the veins. His vivisectional experiments on animals revealed the actual functioning of heart and lungs; from there he reasoned that circulation must occur. He carefully described his experiments and his conclusions in *On the Motion of the Heart* (1628).

Harvey's work challenged Galenic anatomy and, like Copernicus's discoveries, created new burdens of explanation. According to Galenic theory, the heart and the lungs helped each other to function. The heart sent nourishment to the lungs through the pulmonary artery, and the lungs provided raw material for the "vital spirit," which the heart gave to blood to produce and sustain life. One chamber of the heart was supposedly reserved for the cleansing of waste products from venous blood—thought to be entirely separate from the "nourishing" blood pumped out by the heart.

From his observations, Harvey came to think of the heart in terms consonant with the new mechanistic notions about nature: as a pump to circulate the blood. But Harvey did not leap to a new conceptualization of the body's function. Rather, he adjusted but did not abandon Galenic theories, for example, concerning how "vital spirit" was made. The lungs had been thought to "ventilate" the heart. In light of his discovery of the pulmonary transit (that all of the blood is pumped through the lungs and back through the heart), Harvey suggested that the lungs help the blood to concoct the "vital spirit." Only in this context could the heart be thought of as a machine, circulating this life-giving material.

Harvey's explanation of bodily functions thus did not constitute a rupture with Galenic tradition. But by the end of his life, Harvey's adjustments of Galenic theory were suggesting new conceptual possibilities. His work inspired additional research in physiology, chemistry, and physics. Robert Boyle's efforts to understand vacuums can be traced in part to questions Harvey raised about the function of the lungs and the properties of air.

SCIENCE AND SOCIETY

Scientists wrestled with questions about God, human ability, and the possibilities of understanding the world every bit as intensely as they attempted to find new explanations for the behavior of matter and the motion of the heavens. Eventually, the implications of the new scientific posture would affect thought and behavior throughout society. Once people no longer thought of the universe in hierarchical terms, it became easier to question the hierarchical organization of society. Once people questioned the authority of traditional knowledge about the universe, the way was clear for them to begin questioning traditional views of the state and social order.

Such profound changes of perspective happened gradually. In the short term, Louis XIV and other rulers welcomed the new science for its practical value, and the practice of science remained wedded to religion. The advances in science would eventually lead to revolutionary cultural change, but until the end of the seventeenth century traditional institutions and ideologies circumscribed this change.

The Rise of Scientific Professionalism

Institutions both old and new supported the new science developing in the sixteenth and seventeenth centuries. Universities were the setting for many scientific breakthroughs, but courts continued to serve as patrons of scientific activity. The development of the Accadèmia dei Lincei, to which Galileo belonged, and other academies was a step toward modern professional societies of scholars, although these new organizations also depended on patronage.

Royally sponsored scientific societies were founded in both England and France in the third quarter of the seventeenth century. The Royal Society of London, inaugurated in 1660, received royal recognition but no money and remained an informal institution sponsoring amateur scientific interests as well as specialized independent research. The Académie Royale des Sciences in France, established in 1666 by Jean-Baptiste Colbert, Louis XIV's minister of finance, sponsored research and supported chosen scientists with pensions. These associations were extensions to science of traditional kinds of royal recognition and patronage. Thus, the French Académie was well funded but tightly controlled by the government of Louis XIV, while the Royal Society of London received little of Charles II's precious resources or his scarce political capital.

An important role of academies and patrons was to support the publication of scientific work. The Accadèmia dei Lincei published two of Galileo's best-known works. The Royal Society of London published its fellows' work in *Philosophical Transactions of the Royal Society,* beginning in 1665.

The practice of seventeenth-century science took place in so many diverse institutions—academies, universities, royal courts—that neither *science* nor *scientist* was rigorously defined. Science as a discipline was not yet detached from broad metaphysical questions. Boyle, Newton, Pascal, and Descartes all concerned themselves with questions of religion, and all thought of themselves not as scientists but, like their medieval forebears, as natural philosophers. Natural philosophers belonged to the elite who met in aristocratic salons to discuss literature, politics, and science with equal ease and interest. Still, the narrowing of the practice of science to a tightly defined, truly professional community was becoming evident. Robert Boyle and his fellow advocates of experimentalism, for example, claimed that their procedures alone constituted true science.

The importance of court life and patronage to the new science had at first enabled women to be actively involved. Women ran important salons in France, aristocratic women everywhere were important sources of patronage for scientists, and women themselves were scientists, combining, as did men, science with other pursuits.

Noblewomen and daughters of gentry families had access to education in their homes, and a number of such women were active scientists—astronomers, mathematicians, and botanists. The astronomer Maria Cunitz (1610–1664), from Silesia (a Habsburg-controlled province, now in modern Poland), learned six languages with the support and encouragement of her father, a medical doctor. Later, she published a useful simplification of some of Kepler's mathematical calculations. Women from artisanal families might also receive useful training at home. Such was the case of the German entomologist Maria Sibylla Merian (1647–1717). Merian learned the techniques of illustration in the workshop of her father, an artist in Frankfurt. Later, she used her artistic training and her refined powers of observation to study and record the lives of insects and plants. Merian's career typifies many women's scientific careers in this period because it began within the artisanal tradition. She emerges as an extraordinary figure because her work was celebrated during her life and because of her ability to exit the tight confines of women's roles and follow an adventurous pursuit of science. In the 1670s she was an artist of some renown, but she was also working, raising children, and keeping house in a pattern usual to women of the artisan class. In 1692, however, she left her husband, taking refuge with a radical Protestant group that defended her right to divorce on the grounds that her husband was a nonbeliever. In 1699 she and her daughter, Dorothea, set off for the tropical Dutch colony of Suriname to collect and study the insects there. They traveled unaccompanied by a man and were not sponsored by any government or religious institution. After they returned, Merian's great work, *Metamorphosis of the Insects of Suriname*, established her as an important member of the scientific community of Amsterdam. Merian's life serves as an example of an extraordinary human being who managed to work despite tremendous cultural barriers; it also serves as a reminder of the many women who helped to advance the process of science by working at family-based, commercially motivated, artisanal crafts.

Margaret Cavendish (1623–1673) was a woman scientist from a very different tradition. Cavendish was the duchess of Newcastle. She worked at science in much the same way that many male English scientists did: from the comfort of an independent financial situation, and for the purpose of fulfilling her own intellectual desires. Cavendish wrote several major philosophical works, including *Grounds of Natural Philosophy* (1668). She was a Cartesian but was influenced by Neo-Platonism. She disagreed with Cartesian dualism in its strict separation of matter and mind, but she criticized English philosophers with whom she agreed on some matters because, like Descartes, she distrusted sense knowledge as a guide to philosophy. In many ways, she was disputing the contemporary belief that human knowledge of nature would lead to human control of nature—even control over natural causes and effects. Her arguments had considerable influence, but despite her accomplishments, she was barred from membership in the Royal Society of London.

Astronomers Elisabetha and Johannes Hevelius were one of many collaborating couples among the scientists of the seventeenth century. Women were usually denied pensions and support for their research when they worked alone, however. *(From Hevelius,* Machinae coelestis. *By permission of the Houghton Library, Harvard University)*

Women were regularly accepted in Italian academies but they were excluded from formal membership in the academies in London and Paris. They could use the academies' facilities, however, and received prizes from the societies for their work. One reason for the exclusion of women was the limited amount of patronage available: Coveted positions automatically went to men.

Moreover, the hierarchical distinction signified by gender made the exclusion of women a ready way to define the academies as special and privileged.

Cavendish was aware of the degree to which her participation in scientific life depended on informal networks and her personal wealth and status. (See the box "Margaret Cavendish Challenges Male Scientists.") Women scientists from more modest backgrounds, without Cavendish's resources, had to fight for the right to employment as public institutions gained importance as settings for the pursuit of science. The German astronomer Maria Winkelman (1670–1720), for example, tried to succeed her late husband in an official position at the Berlin Academy of Sciences in 1710. She had received advanced training and worked as an astronomer as a young woman. Her marriage to a leading astronomer was beneficial to them both, and she was her husband's unofficial partner during his tenure as astronomer to the academy. She attained a wide reputation for her abilities and discoveries (she found a new comet, for example, in 1702), and when he died she sought to continue her work to support her four children. The academy refused to extend an official position to Winkelman, despite her experience and accomplishments. The secretary of the academy stated:

> That she be kept on in an official capacity to work on the calendar or to continue with observations simply will not do. Already during her husband's lifetime the society was burdened with ridicule because its calendar was prepared by a woman. If she were now to be kept on in such a capacity, mouths would gape even wider.[8]

Winkelman worked in private observatories, and was able to return to the Berlin Academy only as the unofficial assistant to her son, whose training she herself had supervised.

The New Science and the Needs of the State

The new natural philosophy had implications for traditional notions about the state. The new world-view that all matter was alike and followed discernible natural laws gradually undermined political systems resting on a belief in the inherent inequality of persons and royal prerogative. By the middle of the eighteenth century, a fully formed alternative political philosophy would argue for more "rational" government in keeping with the rational, natural order of things. But change came slowly, and while it was coming, the state of Louis XIV and other rulers found much to admire and make use of in the new science.

Many new inventions were very attractive to governments and members of ruling elites. Experiments with vacuum pumps had important applications in the mining industry. The astronomy professor at Gresham College in London was required to teach navigation, and other professors at Gresham worked to improve the design of ships.

Governments also sponsored purely scientific research. Members of the elite, such as Colbert in France, recognized the opportunity not only for practical advances but also for prestige and, most important, confirmation of the orderliness of nature. It is hard to overestimate the psychological impact and intellectual power of this fundamental tenet of the new science—namely, that nature is an inanimate machine that reflects God's design not through its purposes but simply by its orderliness. Human beings could now hope to dominate nature in ways not possible before. Dominion, order, control—these were the goals of ambitious and powerful rulers in the seventeenth century.

Thus, in the short run, the new science supported a vision of order that was very pleasing to a monarch of absolutist pretensions. Louis XIV, among others, energetically sponsored scientific investigation by the Académie des Sciences and reaped the benefits in improved ships, increasingly skillful military engineers, and new industrial products.

Religion and the New Science

Because of Galileo's condemnation, the Catholic church is often seen as an opponent of scientific thought, and science and religion are often seen

Margaret Cavendish Challenges Male Scientists

In her preface to her earliest scientific work,* The Philosophical and Physical Opinions *(1655), Cavendish addresses scholars at Oxford and Cambridge Universities with deceptive humility. She implies that the seeming limitations of women's abilities are in fact the consequence of their exclusion from education and from participation in affairs.

Most Famously Learned,

I here present to you this philosophical work, not that I can hope wise school-men and industrious laborious students should value it for any worth, but to receive it without scorn, for the good encouragement of our sex, lest in time we should grow irrational as idiots, by the dejectedness of our spirits, through the careless neglects and despisements of the masculine sex to the female, thinking it impossible we should have either learning or understanding, wit or judgment, as if we had not rational souls as well as men, and we out of a custom of dejectedness think so too, which makes us quit all industry towards profitable knowledge, being imployed only in low and petty imployments which take away not only our abilities towards arts but higher capacities in speculations, so that we are become like worms, that only live in the dull earth of ignorance, winding ourselves sometimes out by the help of some refreshing rain of good education, which seldom is given us, for we are kept like birds in cages, to hop up and down in our houses . . . ; thus by an opinion, which I hope is but an erroneous one in men, we are shut out of all power and authority by reason we are never employed either in civil or martial affairs, our counsels are despised and laughed at and the best of our actions are trodden down with scorn, by the over-weening conceit men have of themselves and through a despisement of us.

Source: Moira Ferguson, ed., *First Feminists: British Women Writers, 1578–1799* (Bloomington and New York: Indiana University Press and The Feminist Press, 1985), pp. 85–86.

as antagonists. But this view is an oversimplification. Indeed, scientific thought remained closely tied to religion during the seventeenth century. Both religion and the Catholic church as an institution were involved in scientific advancement from the time of Copernicus. Copernicus himself was a cleric, as were many philosophers and scientists active in the early seventeenth century. This is not surprising, for most research in the sciences to this point had occurred within universities sponsored and staffed by members of religious orders.

Moreover, religious and metaphysical concerns were central to the work of virtually every scientist. The entire Cartesian edifice of reasoning about the world, for example, was founded on Descartes's certainty about God. God's gift of the capacity to reason was the only certainty that Descartes claimed. Copernicus, Kepler, and other investigators perceived God's purpose in the mathematical regularity of nature. In addition, traditional Christian views of the operations and purpose of the universe were evident in the work of all scientists from Copernicus to Newton—from Galileo's acceptance of perfect circular motion to Newton's theological writings.

Yet adjusting to a new view of nature in which God was less immanently and obviously represented was not particularly easy for the Catholic church. First of all, the church itself mirrored the hierarchy of the old view of the universe in its own hierarchy of believers, priests, bishops, popes, and saints. Moreover, in its sponsorship of institutions of higher learning, the church was the repository of the old view. In scientific disagreements spawned by the new theories, the church was both theoretically and literally invested in the old view.

Nevertheless, the church's condemnation of Galileo shocked many clerics, including a number of whom were scientists themselves, as well as three of Galileo's judges, who voted for leniency at his trial. Over the centuries, several apparent conflicts between scientific arguments and sacred teachings had been resolved with great intelligence and flexibility. Many scientists who were also clerics continued to study and teach the new science when they could; for example, Copernicanism was taught by Catholic missionaries abroad. (See the box "Encounters with the West: Jesuits and Astronomy in China.")

The rigid response of the church hierarchy to Galileo's challenge must be seen in the context of the Protestant Reformation, which, in the minds of the pope and others, had demonstrated the need for a firm response to any challenge. The condemnation of Galileo had a chilling effect on scientific investigators in most Catholic regions of Europe. They could and did continue their research, but many could publish results only by smuggling manuscripts to Protestant lands. Descartes, as we have seen, left France for the more tolerant Netherlands; he also sojourned at the Swedish court at the invitation of Queen Christina. After the middle of the seventeenth century, many of the most important empirical and theoretical innovations in science occurred in Protestant regions.

At first, Protestant leaders were not receptive to Copernican ideas because they defied scriptural authority. Protestant thinkers were also as troubled as Catholics by the metaphysical problems the new theories seemed to raise. In 1611, one year after the publication of Galileo's *Starry Messenger,* the English poet John Donne (1573–1631) reflected in "An Anatomie of the World" on the confusion about human capacities and social relationships that Copernican astronomy had caused:

> [The] new Philosophy calls all in doubt,
> The Element of fire is quite put out;
> The Sun is lost, and th'earth, and no man's wit
> Can well direct him where to look for it.[9]

The dilemma of accounting in religious terms for the ideas of Copernicus and Descartes became more urgent for Protestants as the ideas acquired an anti-Catholic status after the trial of Galileo in 1633. Religious, political, and scientific viewpoints became inextricably mixed. Religion did not merely remain in the scientists' panoply of explanations; it remained a fundamental building block of scientific thought, just as it remained central to most scientists' lives.

The Mechanistic World Order at the End of the Seventeenth Century

By the middle of the seventeenth century, political theory was beginning to show the impact of the mechanistic world-view. Political philosophers no longer viewed the world and human society as an organic whole in which each part was distinguished in nature and function from the rest. Thomas Hobbes, John Locke, and others reimagined the bonds that link citizens to each other and to their rulers.

Because of the political turmoil in England, Thomas Hobbes (1588–1679) spent much of his productive life on the Continent. After the beginnings of the parliamentary rebellion, he joined a group of royalist émigrés in France. He met Galileo and lived for extended periods in Paris, in contact with the circle of French thinkers that included Descartes.

Hobbes is best known today for *Leviathan* (1651), his treatise on political philosophy. Hobbes held a mostly Cartesian view of nature as composed of "self-motivated," atomlike structures. He understood people as no less mechanistic than the rest of nature. For him, people were made up of appetites of various sorts. The ideal state, concluded Hobbes, is one in which a strong sovereign controls the disorder that inevitably arises from the clash of desires. Unlike the medieval philosophers, Hobbes did not draw analogies between

~ ENCOUNTERS WITH THE WEST ~

Jesuits and Astronomy in China

The Italian Matteo Ricci (1552–1610) was one of the first of a series of Jesuit missionaries to establish himself at the imperial court in China. He was appreciative as well as critical of Chinese science, but his remarks are more interesting to us because they reveal that Ricci himself regarded expertise in mathematics and astronomy as worthy of esteem. Ricci's own scientific knowledge was crucial to his acceptance at court; Jesuit missionaries who followed Ricci in the seventeenth century found their scientific expertise equally valued, and several openly taught Copernican theory there.

The Chinese have not only made considerable progress in moral philosophy but in astronomy and in many branches of mathematics as well. At one time they were quite proficient in arithmetic and geometry, but in the study and teaching of these branches of learning they labored with more or less confusion. They divide the heavens into constellations in a manner somewhat different from that which we employ. Their count of the stars outnumbers the calculations of our astronomers by fully four hundred, because they include in it many of the fainter stars which are not always visible. And yet with all this, the Chinese astronomers take no pains whatever to reduce the phenomena of celestial bodies to the discipline of mathematics. Much of their time is spent in determining the moment of eclipses and the mass of the planets and the stars, but here, too, their deductions are spoiled by innumerable errors. Finally they center their whole attention on that phase of astronomy which our scientists term astrology, which may be accounted for the fact that they believe that everything happening on this terrestrial globe of ours depends upon the stars.

Some knowledge of the science of mathematics was given to the Chinese by the Saracens [Mongols], who penetrated into their country from the West, but very little of this knowledge was based upon definite mathematical proofs. What the Saracens left them, for the most part, consisted of certain tables of rules by which the Chinese regulated their calendar and to which they reduced their calculations of planets and the movements of the heavenly bodies in general. The founder of the family which at present regulates the study of astrology prohibited anyone from indulging in the study of this science unless he were chosen for it by hereditary right. The prohibition was founded upon fear, lest he who should acquire a knowledge of the stars might become capable of disrupting the order of the empire and seek an opportunity to do so.

Source: Louis J. Gallagher, trans., *China in the Sixteenth Century: The Journals of Matthew Ricci: 1583–1610* (New York: Random House, 1953), pp. 30–31.

the state and the human body (the king as head, judges and magistrates as arms, and so forth). Instead, Hobbes compared the state to a machine that "ran" by means of laws and was kept in good working order by a skilled technician—the ruler.

Hobbes's pessimism about human behavior and his insistence on the need for order imposed from above reflected his concern for order in the wake of political turmoil. This concern was one reason he was welcomed into the community of French philosophers, who were naturally comfortable with royalty as a guarantor of order. But Hobbes's work, like theirs, was a radical departure because it envisioned citizens as potentially

Science Gains an Audience The greatest scientific popularizer of the period was Bernard de Fontenelle. This illustration comes from his *Conversation on the Plurality of Worlds* (1686), and it reveals the audience for which the work was intended. A gentleman, sitting with a lady in a formal garden, gestures to a depiction of the solar system as it was then understood; the lady is presumed to understand and to be interested in the information. *(By permission of Houghton Library, Harvard University)*

equal and constrained neither by morality nor by natural obedience to authority.

Another Englishman, John Locke (1632–1704), offered an entirely different vision of social order. Locke's major works, *Essay on Human Understanding* (1690) and *Two Treatises on Government* (1690), combined the experimentalism of Robert Boyle, the systematizing rationality of Descartes, and other strands of the new scientific thought. Locke's treatises on government reflected his empiricism as well as his particular experiences as a member of elite circles in the aftermath of the English revolution. A trained physician, he served as personal physician and general political assistant to Anthony Ashley Cooper (1621–1683), Lord Shaftsbury, one of the members of Parliament most opposed to Charles II's pretensions to absolutist government. When James II acceded to the throne in 1685, Locke remained in the Netherlands, where he had fled to avoid prosecution for treason. He became an adviser to William of Orange and returned to England with William and Mary in 1688. Not surprisingly, Locke's view of the principles of good government reflected the pro-parliamentary stance of his political milieu.

Unlike Hobbes, Locke argued that people are capable of restraint and mutual respect in their pursuit of self-interest. The state arises from a contract that individuals freely enter into to protect themselves, their property, and their happiness from possible aggression by others. They can invest the executive and legislative authority to carry out this protection in monarchy or any other governing institution, though Locke believed the English Parliament was the best available model. Because sovereignty resides with the people who enter into the contract, rebellion against abuse of power is justified. Thus, Locke freed people from the arbitrary bonds of authority to the state.

Locke's status as a member of the elite of his society is apparent in his emphasis on private property, which he considered a fundamental human right. (See the box "Locke's View of the Purpose of Government.") Indeed, there was no place in his political vision for serious disagreement about the nature of property. Locke even found a justification for slavery. He also did not consider women to be political beings in the same way as men. The family, he felt, was a separate domain from the state, not bound by the same contractual obligations.

Locke's dismissal of women from the realm of politics and of questions of power and justice from the family was not an accident. The ability of Locke and many other seventeenth-century thinkers to imagine a new physical or political order was constrained by the prevailing view of gender as a "natural" principle of order and hierarchy. Gender distinctions are in the main socially ascribed roles that are easily misinterpreted as "natural" differences between women and men. Although Margaret Cavendish (see the box on page 403) and other women disputed the validity of such distinctions, men frequently used them. Locke's use of gender as an arbitrary organizing principle gave his political vision a claim to being "natural." The use of gender-specific vocabulary to describe nature itself had the effect of making the new objective attitude toward the world seem "natural." Works by seventeenth-century scientists are filled with references to nature as a woman who must be "conquered," "subdued," or "unveiled."

Traditional gender distinctions limited and buttressed most facets of political thought, but in other areas the fact of uncertainty and the need for tolerance were embraced. Another of Locke's influential works was the impassioned *Letter on Toleration* (1689). In it he argued that religious belief is fundamentally private and that only the most basic Christian principles need be accepted by everyone. Others went further than Locke by removing traditional religion as a fundamental guarantor of morality and order. Fostering such religious skepticism were religious pluralism in England and the irrationality of religious intolerance—demonstrated by Louis XIV's persecution of Protestants.

Pierre Bayle (1647–1706), a Frenchman of Protestant origins, argued that morality can be wholly detached from traditional religion. Bayle cited the philosopher Baruch Spinoza (1632–1677) as an example of morality. Spinoza believed the state to have a moral purpose and human happiness to have spiritual roots. Yet he was not a Christian at all but a Dutch Jew who had been ejected from his local synagogue for supposed atheism. One need hardly be a Christian to be a moral being, Bayle concluded.

Bayle's skepticism toward traditional knowledge was more wide-ranging than his views on religion. His best-known work, *Dictionnaire historique et critique* (*Historical and Critical Dictionary,* 1702), was a compendium of observations about virtually every thinker whose works were known at the time, including recent figures such as Descartes and Newton. Bayle was the first systematic skeptic, and he relentlessly exposed errors and shortcomings in all received knowledge. Informative, critical, and lively, his works were very popular with elite lay readers avid to take part in the revolutionary new worldview.

Locke's View of the Purpose of Government

In this passage from the second of his treatises on government, Locke describes men as naturally free and willing to enter into communities only for the protection of property. Notice how Locke justifies private property as "natural" by linking it to an individual's labor.

Men being . . . by nature all free, equal, and independent, no one can be put out of this estate and subjected to the political power of another without his own consent. The only way whereby any one divests himself of his natural liberty and puts on the bonds of civil society is by agreeing with other men to join and unite into a community for their comfortable, safe, and peaceable living amongst one another, in a secure enjoyment of their properties and a greater security against any that are not of it. This any number of men may do, because it injures not the freedom of the rest; they are left as they were in the liberty of the state of nature. When any number of men have so consented to make one community or government, they are thereby presently incorporated and make one body politic wherein the majority have a right to act and conclude the rest. . . . And thus that which begins and acutally constitutes any political society is nothing but the consent of any number of freemen capable of a majority to unite and incorporate into such a society. And this is that, and that only, which did or could give beginning to any lawful government in the world.

If man in the state of nature be so free . . . , and if he be absolute lord of his own person and possessions, equal to the greatest, and subject to nobody, why will he part with his freedom, why will he give up his empire and subject himself to the dominion and control of any other power?

The great and chief end, therefore, of men's uniting into commonwealths and putting themselves under government is the preservation of their property. . . . Though the earth and all inferior creatures be common to all men, yet every man has a property in his own person; this nobody has any right to but himself. The labor of his body and the work of his hands, we may say, are properly his. Whatsoever then he removes out of the state that nature has provided and left it in, he has mixed his labor with, and joined to it something that is his own, and thereby makes it his property. It being by him removed from the common state nature has placed it in, it has by this labor something annexed to it that excludes the common right of other men. For this labor being the unquestionable property of the laborer, no man but he can have a right to what that is once joined to, at least where there is enough and as good left in common for others. . . . As much land as a man tills, plants, improves, cultivates, and can use the product of, so much is his property. He by his labor does, as it were, enclose it from the common.

Source: Second Treatise, in John Locke, *Two Treatises of Civil Government* (London: G. Routledge & Sons, 1884).

SUMMARY

The Scientific Revolution began, as innovation in scientific thinking often does, with a specific problem whose answer led in unexpected directions. Copernicus's response to traditional astronomical problems led to scientific and philosophical innovation because of his solution and because of the context into which it was received.

Other scientists built on the theories of Copernicus, culminating in the work of Galileo, who supported Copernican theory with additional data and widely published his findings. The Frenchman Descartes was the first to fashion a systematic explanation for the operations of nature to replace the medieval view. The political climate in England, meanwhile, encouraged the development of experimental science and inductive reasoning. Isaac Newton provided new theories to explain the behavior of matter and expressed them in mathematical terms that applied to both the earth and the cosmos; with his work, traditional astronomy and physics were overturned.

Rulers made use of the new science for the practical results it offered despite the ideological challenge it presented to their power. By the end of the seventeenth century, the hierarchical Christian world-view grounded in the old science was being challenged on many fronts.

NOTES

1. Quoted in Thomas S. Kuhn, *The Copernican Revolution* (Cambridge, Mass.: Harvard University Press, 1985), p. 131.
2. Quoted in Margaret C. Jacob, *The Cultural Meaning of the Scientific Revolution* (Philadelphia: Temple, 1988), p. 18.
3. Quoted in Alan G. R. Smith, *Science and Society in the Sixteenth and Seventeenth Centuries* (New York: Science History Publications, 1972), p. 72.
4. Quoted in Bruce T. Moran, ed., *Patronage and Institutions: Science, Technology and Medicine at the European Court* (Rochester: The Boyden Press, 1991), p. 43.
5. Quoted in Jacob, *Cultural Meaning*, p. 59.
6. Quoted in Steven Shapin, *A Social History of Truth* (Chicago: University of Chicago Press, 1994), p. 298.
7. Quoted in Jacob, *Cultural Meaning*, p. 89.
8. Quoted in Londa Schiebinger, *The Mind Has No Sex?* (Cambridge, Mass.: Harvard University Press, 1989), p. 92.
9. *Complete Poetry and Selected Prose of John Donne*, ed. John Hayward (Bloomsbury, England: Nonesuch Press, 1929), p. 365; quoted in Kuhn, *The Copernican Revolution*, p. 194.

SUGGESTED READING

Biagioli, Mario. *Galileo Courtier.* 1993. A recent study that stresses the power of patronage relations to shape scientific process.

Bordo, Susan R. *The Flight to Objectivity: Essays on Cartesianism and Culture.* 1987. A collection that studies Descartes's work as a metaphysical and psychological crisis and discusses implications of Cartesian mind-body dualism.

Cohen, I. Bernard. *The Newtonian Revolution.* 1987. A brief introduction to Newton and the meaning of his discoveries; a good place to start on Newton.

Davis, Natalie Zemon. *Women on the Margins: Three Seventeenth-Century Lives.* 1995. The third section of this excellent study concentrates on Maria Sibylla Merian; rich in historical detail and cultural context.

Frank, Robert G., Jr. *Harvey and the Oxford Physiologists.* 1980. An explanation of Harvey's work in the context of traditional Galenic medicine and a discussion of the community of scholars who accepted and built on his innovations.

Geneva, Ann. *Astrology and the Seventeenth-Century Mind: William Lilly and the Language of the Stars.* 1995. Provides an excellent guide to the basics of seventeenth-century astrology.

Hall, A. Rupert. *The Revolution in Science, 1500–1800.* 1983. A thorough introduction to all scientific disciplines that de-emphasizes the larger context of scientific development but explains many of the innovations in detail.

Hunter, Michael. *Science and Society in Restoration England.* 1981. A study that sets English science in its political and cultural contexts; critical of Webster's classic study (see the next page).

Jacob, Margaret C. *The Cultural Meaning of the Scientific Revolution.* 1988. An account that moves from the Scientific Revolution through the industrial transformation of the nineteenth century.

———. *The Newtonians and the English Revolution.* 1976. A work that links the development of Newtonian science to its political and social context and examines the simultaneous evolution of religion that could accept the new science yet maintain traditional perspectives.

Kearney, Hugh. *Science and Change.* 1971. A readable general introduction to the Scientific Revolution.

Kuhn, Thomas. *The Copernican Revolution.* 1985. A readable treatment of the revolution in astronomy that also lucidly explains the Aristotelian world-view; the first thing to read to understand the Copernican revolution.

———.*The Structure of Scientific Revolutions.* 1970. A path-breaking work that argues that all scientific schemas are systems of explanation and that science progresses by shifting from one general paradigm to another, not from error to "truth."

Lindberg, D. C., and R. S. Westman. *Reappraisals of the Scientific Revolution.* 1990. Essays re-evaluating classic interpretations of the Scientific Revolution. Includes a rich bibliography.

Mandrou, Robert. *From Humanism to Science.* 1978. A general intellectual history of the period 1450–1650 that sets the Scientific Revolution in the context of broader intellectual, social, and economic currents.

Merchant, Carolyn. *The Death of Nature: Women, Ecology and the Scientific Revolution.* 1980. An important corrective interpretation that focuses on the changing definition of nature—particularly how nature became something to be dominated and consumed—and the way in which this definition reinforced negative cultural views of women.

Moran, Bruce T., ed. *Patronage and Institutions: Science, Technology and Medicine at the European Court.* 1991. A work that looks at royal courts as shaping and sustaining institutions for science from the early sixteenth century onward.

Redondi, Pietro. *Galileo Heretic.* 1987. A careful account of Galileo's confrontation with the church.

Schiebinger, Londa. *The Mind Has No Sex?* 1989. An examination of the participation of women in science and an explanation of how science began to reflect the exclusion of women in its values and objects of study.

Shapin, Steven, and Simon Schaffer. *Leviathan and the Air-Pump.* 1985. One of the most important studies of seventeenth-century science; it traces the conflict between Cartesian science, as represented by Hobbes, and experimental science, in the work of Boyle.

Thomas, Keith. *Religion and the Decline of Magic.* 1971. An exploration of the changing character of religious belief and "superstitious" practice; finds roots outside of science for changing, increasingly secular world-views.

Thoren, Victor E. *The Lord of Uraniborg: A Biography of Tycho Brahe.* 1990. An up-to-date study of the life and work of the Danish astronomer.

Webster, Charles. *The Great Instauration.* 1975. A classic study that links the development of the modern scientific attitude to the Puritan revolution in England.

Westfall, Richard S. *The Construction of Modern Science: Mechanisms and Mechanics.* 1977. A general treatment of the Scientific Revolution that emphasizes and explains the mechanistic world-view.

CHAPTER 16

Europe on the Threshold of Modernity, ca. 1715–1789

 customer in one of the growing number of cafés in Paris on February 10, 1778, might have wondered if the king himself was entering the city, such was the commotion as Parisians turned out to welcome a former resident. Now 84, this old man had journeyed to the city to preside at the opening of his latest play, but everyone realized that this most likely would be his last visit, and he was given a hero's welcome. Literary and political elites clamored to meet him; Benjamin Franklin brought his grandson to receive the old man's blessing. Though he was treated like royalty, the man was not a ruler, but a political thinker and writer: the philosopher Voltaire.

Voltaire was the best known of dozens of thinkers who made up the philosophical movement we know as the Enlightenment. The Enlightenment constituted a revolution in political philosophy, but it was much more. The era witnessed the emergence of an informed body of public opinion, critical of the prevailing political system, that existed outside the corridors of power. The relationship between governments and the governed had begun to change: Subjects of monarchs were becoming citizens of nations.

Frederick the Great of Prussia, Catherine the Great of Russia, and other rulers self-consciously tried to use Enlightenment precepts to guide their efforts at governing. They had mixed success. Powerful interests opposed their efforts at reform, and their own hereditary and autocratic power was incompatible with Enlightenment perspectives. Elites still sure of their power, as well as the traditional interests of states, dominated eighteenth-century politics.

Nevertheless, profound changes in economic, social, and political life began in this period. Economic growth spurred population growth, which in turn stimulated industry and trade. The increasing economic and strategic importance of overseas colonies made them focal points of international conflict. The dramatic political and social changes that began as the century closed had their roots in the intellectual, economic, and social ferment of eighteenth-century life.

Questions and Ideas to Consider

- What were the guiding principles of Enlightenment thought? What ideas did the various Enlightenment thinkers share? In what ways did they disagree? Consider, for example, the ideas of Voltaire, Smith, Rousseau, and Wollstonecraft.
- What were Enlightenment salons? Who generally ran them, and why were they so important?
- What was "enlightened monarchy"? To what degree did Catherine the Great of Russia succeed in implementing Enlightenment ideas?
- The eighteenth century was a period of warfare. What were the major issues of these conflicts?
- In the changing economy of the eighteenth century, states attempted to gain further control over their populations, and in many instances, people began to resist that control. Discuss the changing relationship between the state and those who made a living on the seas. Consider new attitudes toward piracy, privateering, navies, and traders.

THE ENLIGHTENMENT

One of Isaac Newton's countrymen wrote the following epitaph for the English scientist:

> Nature and Nature's Laws lay hid in Night.
> God said, "Let Newton be," and all was Light.

The most important works of Enlightenment philosophy reflected the intellectual confidence that Newton's work generated. The poet's assertion that "all was Light" evokes the confidence of an intellectual elite that felt it held a new key to truth. In this sense, the Enlightenment was nothing less than the transfer into general philosophy, particularly political and social thought, of the intellectual revolution that had already taken place in the physical sciences.

Enlightenment philosophy occurred in the context of increasingly widespread publications and new opportunities in literary societies, clubs, and salons for the exchange of views. This context shaped the outline of Enlightenment thought, which was for the most part an elite set of preoccupations. It also determined the radicalism of the Enlightenment, by helping to ensure that an entire level of society shared attitudes that were fundamentally critical of that society.

Voltaire and the Enlightenment

The Enlightenment was not so much a body of thought as an intellectual and social movement. Originating in France, it consisted, first, of the application to political and social thought of the confidence in the intelligibility of natural law that theoretical science had recently achieved. Enlightenment thinkers combined an optimistic belief in the intelligibility of the world and its laws with confidence in the human capacity to discern and work in concert with those laws. The most dramatic effect was the desacralizing of social and political bonds—a new belief that society could be grounded on rational foundations to be determined by humans, not arbitrary foundations determined by God.

A wide range of thinkers participated in the Enlightenment. In France they were known as *philosophes,* a term meaning not a formal philosopher but rather a thinker and critic. To most philosophes, the main agenda was clear. For too long, humans had been mired in ignorance, oppressed by arbitrary laws and institutions. Lack of proper education and the tyranny of the church had condemned them to ignorance. French thinkers singled out the Catholic church as the archenemy because of its opposition to their positive views of human nature and because it controlled much education and was still a force in political life.

The following passage from Voltaire's *Dictionnaire philosophique* (*Philosophical Dictionary,* 1764) is typical of his work in its casual format and biting wit and is also typical of the venomous Enlightenment view of the church:

> A hundred times [you clerics] have been spoken to of the insolent absurdity with which you condemned Galileo, and I shall speak to you for the hundred and first. . . . I desire that there be engraved on the door of your holy office: Here seven cardinals assisted by minor brethren had the master of thought of Italy thrown into prison at the age of seventy, made him fast on bread and water, because he instructed the human race.

The life of Voltaire (1694–1778) almost spanned the century. Born François-Marie Arouet to a middle-class family, he took the pen name Voltaire in 1718, after one of his early plays was a critical success. He produced a vast array of written work: plays, epic poems, novelettes—some of which have explicit philosophical or political content—as well as philosophical tracts. Voltaire moved in courtly circles. Mockery of the regent, the duke of Orléans, led to a year's imprisonment in 1717, and an exchange of insults with a leading courtier some years later led to enforced exile in Great Britain for two years.

After returning from Britain, Voltaire published his first major philosophical work. *Lettres philosophiques* (*Philosophical Letters,* 1734) revealed the influence of his British sojourn and helped to popularize Newton's achievement. Voltaire portrayed Great Britain as a more rational society than France. He was particularly impressed with the religious and intellectual toleration evident there. The British government had a more workable set of institutions, its economy was less crippled by the remnants of feudal privilege, and education was not strictly controlled by the church.

After the publication of his audacious *Lettres,* Voltaire was forced to leave Paris, and he resided for some years in the country home of a woman with whom he shared a remarkable intellectual and emotional relationship: Emilie, marquise du Châtelet (1706–1749). Châtelet was a mathematician and a scientist. She prepared a French translation of Newton's *Principia* while Voltaire worked at his accustomed variety of writing, which also included a commentary on Newton's work. Because of Châtelet's tutelage, Voltaire became more knowledgeable about the sciences and more serious in his efforts to apply scientific rationality to human affairs. He was devastated by her sudden death in 1749.

Shortly afterward, he accepted the invitation of the king of Prussia, Frederick II, to visit Berlin. His stay was stormy and brief because of disagreements with other court philosophers. He resided for a time in Geneva, until his criticisms of the city's moral codes forced yet another exile on him. He spent most of the last twenty years of his life at his estates on the Franco-Swiss border,

CHAPTER CHRONOLOGY

1721	Montesquieu, *Persian Letters*
1721–1742	Robert Walpole first British "prime minister"
1734	Voltaire, *Philosophical Letters*
1740–1748	War of the Austrian Succession
1748	Montesquieu, *The Spirit of the Laws;* Hume, *Essay Concerning Human Understanding*
1756–1763	Seven Years' War
1758	Voltaire, *Candide*
1751–1765	Diderot, The *Encyclopedia*
1762	Rousseau, *The Social Contract*
1764	Voltaire, *Philosophical Dictionary*
1772	First Partition of Poland
1776	Smith, *The Wealth of Nations*
1784	Kant, *What Is Enlightenment?*
1792	Wollstonecraft, *A Vindication of the Rights of Woman*
1795	Condorcet, *The Progress of the Human Mind*

Etablissement de la nouvelle Philosophie.
Notre Berceau fut un Caffé.

Café Society The caption under this contemporary illustration reads: "Establishment of the new philosophy; our cradle was the café." Cafés were one of the new settings where literate elites could discuss the new philosophy and explore its implications for social and political life. *(Musée Carnavalet, Paris/Edimedia)*

where he could be relatively free from interference by any government. There he produced his best-known satirical novella, *Candide,* in 1758. It criticized aristocratic privilege and the power of clerics as well as the naiveté of philosophers who took "natural law" to mean that the world was already operating as it should.

Voltaire's belief that one must struggle to overturn the accumulated habits of centuries was reflected in his political activity. He became involved in several celebrated legal cases in which individuals were pitted against the authority of the church, which was still backed by the authority of the state. In the most famous case, Jean Calas (1698–1762), a Protestant from southern France, was accused of murdering his son, allegedly to prevent him from converting to Catholicism. Calas maintained his innocence until his execution in 1762. Voltaire saw in this case the worst aspects of religious prejudice and injustice and worked tirelessly to establish Calas's innocence as a matter of principle and so that his family could inherit his property. In pursuit of justice in these cases, and in criticism of the church, Voltaire added a stream of political pamphlets to his literary output.

Voltaire died in Paris in May 1778, shortly after his triumphal return there. By then he was no longer the leader of the Enlightenment in strictly intellectual terms. Thinkers and writers more radical than he had come to prominence during his long life and had dismissed some of his beliefs, such as the notion that reform could be introduced by a monarch. But Voltaire had provided a crucial stimulus to French thought with his *Lettres philosophiques*. His importance lies also in his embodiment of the critical spirit of eighteenth-century rationalism: its confidence, its increasingly practical bent, its wit and sophistication.

The Variety of Enlightenment Thought

Differences among philosophes grew as the century progressed. In the matter of religion, for example, there was virtual unanimity of opposition to the Catholic church among French thinkers, but no unanimity about God. Voltaire was a *theist*—believing firmly in God as creator of the universe, but not a specifically Christian God. To some later thinkers, God was irrelevant—the creator of the world, but a world that ran continuously according to established laws. Some philosophes were atheists, arguing that a universe that ran according to discoverable laws needed no divine presence to explain, run, or justify it. In Protestant areas of Europe, in contrast to France, Enlightenment thought was often less hostile to Christianity.

Philosophes also pondered questions about the social and political order, as well as about human rationality itself. Charles de Secondat (1689–1755), baron of Montesquieu, a French judge and legal philosopher, combined the belief that human institutions must be rational with Locke's assumption of human educability. Montesquieu's treatise *De l'esprit des lois* (*The Spirit of the Laws*, 1748) went through twenty-two printings in just two years. In it Montesquieu maintained that laws were not meant to be arbitrary rules but derived naturally from human society: The more evolved a society was, the more liberal its laws. This notion provided a sense of the progress possible within society and government and deflated Europeans' pretensions in regard to other societies, for a variety of laws could be equally "rational" given differing conditions. Montesquieu is perhaps best known to Americans as the advocate of the separation of legislative, executive, and judicial powers that later became enshrined in the U.S. Constitution. To Montesquieu, this scheme paralleled the balance of forces observable in nature and seemed the best guarantee of liberty.

The "laws" of economic life were also investigated, most notably by the Scotsman Adam Smith in his treatise *An Inquiry into the Nature and Causes of the Wealth of Nations* (1776). A professor at the University of Glasgow, Smith (1723–1790) is best known today as the originator of "laissez-faire" economics: the assumption that an economy will regulate itself without government interference and, of more concern to Smith, without the monopolies and other restrictions on trade that were common in his day. Smith shared Locke's optimistic view of human nature and human rationality. Humans, Smith believed, can direct their drives and passions through their reason and inherent sympathy for one another. Thus, Smith said, in seeking their own achievement and well-being, they are often "led by an invisible hand" to benefit society as a whole.

Other philosophers disagreed about the nature and limits of human reason. David Hume (1711–1776) was radical in his critique of the human capacity for knowing, doubting even the reliability of sense data. These views, which he expounded in his *Essay Concerning Human Understanding* (1748), ran counter to the prevailing spirit of confidence in empirical knowledge.

Mainstream confidence in empirical knowledge and in the intelligibility of the world was quite evident in the *Encyclopédie* (*Encyclopedia*), a seventeen-volume compendium of knowledge, criticism, and philosophy assembled by leading philosophes in France and published between 1751 and 1765. The volumes were designed to contain state-of-the-art knowledge about arts, sciences, technology, and philosophy. The guiding philosophy of the project, set forth by its chief editor, Denis Diderot (1713–1784), was a belief that human happiness could be achieved through the advance of knowledge. The *Encyclopédie* intrigued and inspired intellectuals and was used by thousands of government officials and professionals. Catherine the Great, empress of Russia, remarked in a letter that she consulted its pages to find guidance concerning one of her reform schemes.

Reaction to the encyclopedia project illustrated the political context of Enlightenment thought as well as its philosophic premises. The Catholic church placed the work on the Index of prohibited books, and the French government might well have barred its publication but for the fact that the official who would have made the decision was drawn to Enlightenment thinking. Many other officials, however, worked to suppress it. By the late 1750s, losses in wars overseas had made French officials highly sensitive to political challenges of any kind. Thus, like Voltaire, the major contributors to the *Encyclopédie* were lionized by certain segments of the elite and persecuted by others.

The *Encyclopédie* reflected the complexities and limitations of Enlightenment thought on another score—the position of women. One might expect that the Enlightenment penchant for challenging received knowledge and traditional hierarchies would have led to revised views of women's abilities and rights. Indeed, some contributors did blame women's social and political inequality on the customs and laws that had kept women from education and valued public roles. However, others simply substituted scientific-sounding assertions of women's inferiority in place of traditional religious assertions of gender inequality.

Both positions were represented in Enlightenment thought as a whole. The assumption of the natural equality of all people provided a powerful reason for arguing the equality of women with men. Some thinkers, such as Mary Astell (1666–1731), challenged Locke's separation of family life from the public world of free, contractual relationships. (See the box "An English Feminist Criticizes Unenlightened Views of Women.") Most advocated increased education for women, if only to make them more fit to raise enlightened children. By the end of the century, the most radical thinkers were also advocating full citizenship rights for women and equal rights to property.

The best-known proponent of those views was an Englishwoman, Mary Wollstonecraft (1759–1797), the author of *A Vindication of the Rights of Woman* (1792). She argued that women had been weakened by excessive refinement. Like both sexes in the aristocracy, women of the middle class were taught to prize superficial, decorative attributes above more substantial virtues. Wollstonecraft wanted women to stop enjoying their frivolous privileges and the superficial praise that, she argued, masked insulting assumptions about their nature. She strenuously asserted that the responsibilities of citizenship, the leavening of education, and economic independence would make women happier, fuller human beings and that from this new position, women could help to work for the betterment of society. In any case, she noted, working women needed these rights simply to survive.

Wollstonecraft specifically criticized the misogynistic attitudes of Jean-Jacques Rousseau (1712–1778). Like Locke, Rousseau could conceive of the free individual only as male, and he grounded his critique of the old order and his novel political ideas in an arbitrary division of gender roles. Rousseau's view of women was part of a critique of the cosmopolitan elite society of his day, in which aristocratic women were fully involved. He believed that this society was corrupting and that the true citizen had to cultivate virtue and sensibility, not manners, taste, or refinement. Rousseau designated women as guarantors of the "natural" virtues of children and as nurturers of the emotional life and character of men—not as fully formed beings in their own right.

Rousseau's emphasis on the education and virtue of citizens was the underpinning of his larger political vision, set forth in *Du Contrat social* (*The Social Contract*, 1762). He imagined an egalitarian republic in which men would consent to be governed because the government would determine and act in accordance with the "general will" of the citizens. The "general will" was not majority opinion but rather what each citizen *would* want if he were fully informed and acting in accordance with his highest nature. The "general will" became apparent whenever the citizens met as a body and made collective decisions, and it could be imposed on all inhabitants. This was a breathtaking vision of direct democracy—but one with ominous possibilities, for Rousseau rejected the institutional brakes on state authority proposed by Locke and Montesquieu. Also Rousseau believed that the demands of citizenship in a direct democracy necessitated that half the population serve in an obedient, supportive role, that is, that women's lives be subordinated to those of male citizens.

Rousseau's emphasis on private emotional life anticipated the romanticism of the early nineteenth century (see page 467). It also reflected his own experience as the son of a humble family, always sensing himself an outcast in the brilliant world of Parisian salons. He had a love-hate relationship with this life, remaining attached to several aristocratic women patrons even as he decried their influence. His own personal life did not match his prescriptions for others. He completely neglected to give his four children the nurturing and education that he argued were vital; indeed,

An English Feminist Criticizes Unenlightened Views of Women

Both male and female writers criticized the failure of some Enlightenment thinkers to view ideas about women with the same rationalism that they brought to other subjects. One of the earliest was the Englishwoman Mary Astell (1666–1731). In this excerpt from **Some Reflections on Marriage** *(1700), Astell criticizes, in an ironic tone, negative assessments of women's capacities, Locke's separation of the public and private spheres, and the denial to women of the rights that men enjoy in public life.*

'Tis true, through want of learning, and that of superior genius which men, as men, lay claim to, she [the author] was ignorant of the natural inferiority of our sex, which our masters lay down as self-evident and fundamental truth. She saw nothing in the reason of things to make this either a principle or a conclusion, but much to the contrary.

If they mean that some men are superior to some women, this is no great discovery; had they turned the tables, they might have seen that some women are superior to some men. . . .

Again, if absolute sovereignty be not necessary in a state, how comes it to be so in a family? Or if in a family why not in a state, since no reason can be alleged for the one that will not hold more strongly for the other? If the authority of the husband, so far as it extends, is sacred and inalienable, why not that of the prince? The domestic sovereign is without dispute elected and the stipulations and contract are mutual; is it not then partial in men to the last degree to contend for and practice that arbitrary dominion in their families which they abhor and exclaim against in the state? For if arbitrary power is evil in itself, and an improper method of governing rational and free agents, it ought not to be practiced anywhere.

Source: Moira Ferguson, ed., *First Feminists* (Bloomington: Indiana University Press, 1985), pp. 191–193.

he abandoned them all to a foundling home. Rousseau's work reflected to an extreme degree a central tension in Enlightenment thought generally: It was part of elite culture as well as its principal critic.

The Growth of Public Opinion

It is impossible to understand the significance of the Enlightenment without an analysis of how it was a part of public life. Indeed, the clearest distinguishing feature of the Enlightenment may be the creation of an informed body of public opinion that stood apart from court society.

Increased literacy and access to books and other print media were an important part of the story. Perhaps more important, the kinds of reading that people favored began to change. We know from inventories made of people's belongings at the time of their death (required by inheritance laws) that ordinary people now read secular and contemporary philosophical works. As the availability of such works increased, reading itself evolved from a reverential encounter with traditional material to a critical encounter with new ideas. Solitary reading for reflection and pleasure became more widespread.

In the eighteenth century, forerunners of modern lending libraries made their debut. In Paris, for a fee, one could join a *salle de lecture* (literally, a "reading room"), where the latest works were available to members. Booksellers, whose num-

The Growth of the Book Trade Book ownership dramatically increased in the eighteenth century, and a wide range of secular works—from racy novelettes to philosophical tracts—was available in print. In this rendering of a bookshop, shipments of books have arrived from around Europe. Notice the artist's optimism in the great variety of persons, from the peasant with a scythe to a white-robed cleric, who are drawn to the shop by "Minerva" (the Roman goddess of wisdom). *(Musée des Beaux-Arts de Dijon)*

bers increased dramatically, found ways to meet readers' demands for inexpensive reading matter. One might, for example, pay for the right to read a book in the bookshop itself. In short, new venues encouraged people to see themselves not just as readers but as members of a reading public.

Among the most famous and most important of these venues were the Parisian salons, where Voltaire and others read aloud their works in progress and discussed them. The great majority of salons were run by women. Most were wealthy but of modest social status. They invited courtiers, bureaucrats, and intellectuals to meet in their homes at regular times each week. The *salonnières* (salon leaders) read widely in order to facilitate the exchange of ideas among their guests. This mediating function, along with the choice of guests, was crucial to the success of the salons. Manners and polite conversation had been a defining feature of aristocratic life since the seventeenth century, but they had largely been a means of displaying status and safeguarding honor. The leadership of the salonnières and the protected environment they provided away from court life enabled a further evolution of "polite society" to occur: Anyone with appropriate manners could participate as an equal.

The influence of salons was extended by the wide networks of correspondence that salonnières maintained. Perhaps the most famous salonnière in her day, Marie-Thérèse Geoffrin (1699–1777), corresponded with Catherine the Great, the reform-minded empress of Russia, as well as with philosophes outside of Paris and would-be participants in her salon. The ambassador of Naples regularly attended her salon before returning to his native city, from which he exchanged weekly letters with her. He reflected on the importance of salon leaders when he wrote from Naples, lamenting,

> [our gatherings here] are getting farther away from the character and tone of those of France, despite all [our] efforts. . . . There is no way to make Naples resemble Paris unless we find a woman to guide us, organize us, *Geoffrinise* us.[1]

Various clubs, local academies, and learned and secret societies copied some features of the salons of Paris. Hardly any municipality was without a private society that functioned both as a forum for political and philosophical discussion and as an elite social club. Ideas circulated beyond the membership of even the many far-flung clubs by means of print. Newsletters reporting the goings-on at salons in Paris were produced by some participants. Regularly published periodicals in Great Britain, France, and Italy also disseminated enlightened opinion in the form of reviews, essays, and published correspondence. Some of these journals had been established in the second half of the seventeenth century as a means to circulate the new scientific work. Subscribers now included Americans eager to keep up with intellectual life in Europe.

In all these arenas, Enlightenment ideas encouraged and legitimized a type of far-reaching political debate that had never before existed, except possibly in England during the seventeenth century. The first and greatest impact of the Enlightenment, particularly in France, was not the creation of a program for political change but the creation of a culture of politics that could generate change.

Art in the Age of Reason

Just as the market for books and the reading public expanded, so did the audience for works of art. The modern cultured public—a public of concertgoers and art-gallery enthusiasts—began to make its first appearance. Some performances of concerts and operas began to take place in theaters and halls outside the royal courts and were more accessible to the public.

Beginning in 1737, one section of the Louvre palace in Paris was devoted annually to public exhibitions of painting and sculpture (though by royally sponsored and approved artists). In both France and Britain, public discussion of art began to appear in published reviews: The role of art critic was born. Some works of art were now sold by public auctions, and as works became more available by such means, demand grew and production increased. Late baroque painters contributed to an exploration of private life and emotion sometimes called the "cult of sensibility." Frequently, they depicted private scenes of upper-class life, especially moments of intimate conversation or flirtation.

The cult of sensibility was fostered by literature as well. In England, the novels of Samuel Richardson (1689–1761)—*Pamela* (1740) and *Clarissa* (1747–1748)—explored personal psychology and passion. In the wake of these important works, the novel became an increasingly important genre for exploring human problems and relationships. Rousseau followed Richardson's lead in structuring his own novels, *La Nouvelle Héloïse* (1761) and *Emile* (1762). The cult of sensibility carried the message that honest emotion was a "natural" virtue and that courtly manners, by contrast, were irrational and degrading. The enormous popularity of Rousseau's novels came from the fact that their intense emotional appeal was considered to be uplifting.

There was a great revival of classical subjects and styles after the middle of the century. Classical revival architecture illustrated a belief in order, symmetry, and proportion. Americans are familiar with its evocations because it has been the architecture of their republic, but even churches were built in this style in eighteenth-century Europe. The classical movement in music reflected both the cult of sensibility and the classicizing styles in the visual arts. Embodied in the works of Austrians Franz Josef Haydn (1732–1809) and Wolfgang Amadeus Mozart (1756–1791), this movement saw the clarification of musical structures, such as the modern sonata and symphony, and enabled melody to take center stage.

Another trend in art was a fascination with nature and with the seemingly "natural" in human culture—less "developed" or more historically distant societies. Folk life, other cultures, and untamed nature itself began to be celebrated just when they were being more definitively conquered. Their disappearance made them exotic, and images of this exotic, natural world reinforced Europeans' sense of their own sophistication and dominance.

EUROPEAN RULERS AND EUROPEAN SOCIETY

Mindful of the lessons of the revolution in England and the achievements of Louis XIV, European rulers in the eighteenth century redoubled their efforts to govern with greater effectiveness. Some, like the rulers of Prussia and Russia, were encouraged in their efforts by Enlightenment ideas. In the main they, like Voltaire, believed that monarchs could be agents for change. In Austria, significant reforms were made, including the abolition of serfdom. The changes were uneven, however, and at times owed as much to traditional efforts at better government as to enlightened persuasion.

In all cases, rulers' efforts to govern more effectively meant continual readjustments in relationships with traditional elites. Whether or not elites played a formal role in the governing process, such as in the British Parliament, royal governments everywhere were still dependent on their participation. Enlightened monarchs were changing their view of themselves and their image from the diligent but self-glorifying image of Louis XIV to that of servant of the state. By redefining their role on a utilitarian basis, monarchs undermined the dynastic claim to rule. The state was increasingly seen as separate from the ruler.

France During the Enlightenment

It is one of the seeming paradoxes of the Enlightenment era that critical thought about politics flourished in France, an autocratic state. Yet in France there was a well-educated elite, a tradition of scientific inquiry, and a legacy of cultured court life that, since the early days of Louis XIV, had become the model for all Europe. French was the international intellectual language, and France was the most fertile center of elite cultural life. Both Adam Smith and David Hume spent portions of their careers in Paris and were welcomed into the salons. In fact, the French capital encouraged debate and dissent precisely because of the juxtaposition of the new intellectual climate with the institutional rigidities of the French political system—a system that excluded many talented and productive members of the elite from its privileged circles.

In the last decades of the reign of Louis XIV (d. 1715), many French people began to criticize the seemingly endless foreign wars. The intoxicating blend of stability, effective government, national interest, and the personal glory of the monarch was beginning to loose its hold on the French people.

Louis XIV was followed on the throne by his 5-year-old great-grandson, Louis XV (r. 1715–1774). During the regency, nobles clamored for the establishment of councils so that they could become more active partners in government. Likewise, the supreme law courts, the parlements, reclaimed the right of remonstrance—the right to object to royal edicts and thus to exercise some control over the enactment of laws. Throughout the years of Louis XV's reign, his administration locked horns with the parlements, particularly as royal ministers tried to cope with France's financial crises. Louis XIV had left the nation financially exhausted—in need of both money and new and more reliable ways to get money. During Louis XV's reign the pressures of further wars intensified the need for wholesale reform.

By the late 1760s, the weight of government debt finally forced the king into action. He threw his support behind the reforming schemes of his chancellor, Nicolas de Maupeou. Maupeou dissolved the parlements early in 1771 and created new law courts whose judges would not enjoy independent power.

Public opinion was split over this conflict between the monarch and the parlements. A number of Louis XV's ministers shared Enlightenment hopes of doing away with privileges such as the exemption of the nobility from taxation—and the Enlightenment views of the efficiency of creating economic change from the top. However, the role of consultative bodies and the separation of powers beloved of Montesquieu, himself a parlementaire, were much prized, and the parlements were the only institutions that could legitimately check monarchical powers.

From about the middle of the century, enlightened public opinion, nurtured in salons and other new settings, had begun proposing ways to enhance representation and consultation and implement reform. There were calls to revive the moribund Estates General, the cumbersome representative assembly last called in 1614, as well as for the establishment of new councils or local, decentralized representative assemblies. The workability of these proposals is less important than the fact that they were being made.

The Crown lost control of reform in 1774, when Louis XV died. His grandson, Louis XVI (r. 1774–1792), who was well-meaning but insecure, allowed the complete restoration of the parlements. Further reform efforts, sponsored by the king and several talented ministers, came to naught because of parlementary opposition. By the time an Estates General was finally called in the wake of further financial problems in 1788, the enlightened elites' habit of carrying on political analysis and criticism of government outside the corridors of power had given rise to a volatile situation.

Monarchy and Constitutional Government in Great Britain

After the deaths of William (d. 1702) and Mary (d. 1694), the British crown passed to Mary's sister, Anne (r. 1702–1714), and then to a collateral line descended from Elizabeth (d. 1662), sister of the beheaded Charles I. Elizabeth had married Frederick, elector of the Palatinate (and had reigned with him briefly in Bohemia at the outset of the Thirty Years' War), and her descendants were Germans, now electors of Hanover. The new British sovereign in 1714, who reigned as George I (r. 1714–1727), was both a foreigner and a man of mediocre abilities. Moreover, his claim to the throne was immediately contested by Catholic descendants of James II, who attempted to depose him in 1715 and his son, George II (r. 1727–1760), in 1745.

The second attempt was more nearly successful. In 1745, the son of the Stuart claimant to the throne, Charles (known in legend as Bonnie Prince Charlie), landed on the west coast of Scotland and marched south into England with surprising ease. Most of the British army (and George II himself) was on the Continent, fighting in the War of the Austrian Succession (see page 428). Scotland had been formally united with England in 1707 (hence the term "Great Britain" after that time), and Charles found some support among dissatisfied Scots.

But the vast majority of Britons did not want the civil war that Charles's challenge inevitably meant, especially on behalf of a Catholic pretender who relied on support from Britain's great rival, France. Landholders and merchants in lowland Scotland and northern England gathered militia to oppose Charles until regular army units returned from abroad. Charles's army, made up mostly of poor Highland clansmen, was destroyed at the Battle of Culloden in April 1746. Charles fled back to France, and the British government used the failed uprising as justification for the brutal and forceful integration of the still-remote Highlands into the British state.

Traditional Highland practices, from wearing tartans to playing bagpipes, were forbidden.

Land was redistributed to break the bonds of clan society. Thousands of Highlanders died at the battle itself, in prisons or deportation ships, or by deliberate extermination by British troops after the battle. Despite this serious challenge to the dynasty and the brutal response it occasioned, the British state enjoyed a period of relative stability as well as innovation in the eighteenth century. The events of the seventeenth century had reaffirmed both the need for a strong monarchy and the role of Parliament in defending elite interests. The power of Parliament was reinforced by the Act of Settlement, by which the Protestant heir to Queen Anne had been chosen in 1701.

It was in the eighteenth century that political parties—that is, distinct groups within the elite favoring certain foreign and domestic policies—came into existence. Two groups, the Whigs and the Tories, had begun to form during the reign of Charles II (d. 1685). The Whigs (named derisively by their opponents with a Scottish term for horse thieves) had opposed Charles's toleration of Catholicism and had wholly opposed his Catholic brother and successor, James II. Initially, the Whigs favored an aggressive foreign policy against continental opponents, particularly France. The Tories (also derisively named—for Irish cattle rustlers) tended to be staunch Anglicans uninterested in anti-Catholic agitation. They favored isolationism in foreign affairs and deference toward monarchical authority. Whigs generally represented the interests of the great aristocrats or wealthy merchants or gentry. Tories tended to represent the interests of provincial gentry and the traditional concerns of landholding and local administration. The Whigs were the dominant influence in government through most of the century to 1770. William and Mary as well as Queen Anne favored Whig religious and foreign policy interests.

The long Whig dominance of government was assisted by the talents of Robert Walpole (1676–1745). Walpole, from a minor gentry family, was brought into government in 1714 with other Whig ministers in George I's new regime. An extremely talented politician, he took advantage of the mistakes of other ministers and, in 1721, became both the first lord of the treasury and chancellor of the exchequer. There was not yet any official post or title of "prime minister," but the great contribution of Walpole's long tenure—1721–1742—was to create that office in fact, if not officially. He chose to maintain peace abroad where he could and thus presided over a period of recovery and relative prosperity that enhanced the stability of government.

Initially, Walpole was helped in his role as go-between for king and Parliament by George I's own limitations. The king rarely attended meetings of his council of ministers and, in any case, was hampered by his limited command of English. Gradually, the Privy Council of the king became something resembling a modern cabinet dominated by a prime minister. The notion of "loyal opposition" to the Crown within Parliament was also taking root. In some respects, the maturation of political life in Parliament resembled the lively political debates in the salons of Paris; political life was being legitimated on a new basis in both realms. In England, however, that legitimation was enshrined in a legislative institution, which made it especially effective and resilient.

Parliament was not yet representative of the British population. Because of strict property qualifications, only about 200,000 adult men could vote. In addition, representation was very uneven, heavily favoring traditional landed wealth. Agitation for reform began in the late 1760s as professionals, such as doctors and lawyers without landed property, and merchants in booming but underrepresented cities began to demand the vote. As the burden of taxation grew—the result of the recently concluded Seven Years' War—these groups felt increasingly deprived of representation. Indeed, many felt kinship and sympathy with the American colonists who opposed increased taxation by the British government on these same grounds and began a revolt in 1775.

The reform movement faltered over the issue of religion. In 1780, a tentative effort by Parliament to extend some civil rights to British Catholics provoked rioting in London (known as the Gordon Riots, after one of the leaders). The riots lasted for eight days and claimed three hundred lives. Pressure for parliamentary reform had been building as Britain met with reversals in its war against the American rebels, but this specter of a popular movement out of control temporarily ended the drive for reform.

"Enlightened" Monarchy

Arbitrary monarchical power might seem antithetical to Enlightenment thought, which stressed the reasonableness of human beings and their capacity to act in accord with natural law. Yet many contemporaries believed that the work of curtailing the influence of the church, reforming legal codes, and eliminating barriers to economic activity might be done most efficiently by a powerful monarch. Historians have labeled a number of rulers of this era "enlightened despots" because of the arbitrary nature of their power and the enlightened or reformist uses to which they put it.

"Enlightened despotism" aptly describes certain developments in the Scandinavian kingdoms in the late eighteenth century. In Denmark, the Crown had governed without significant challenge from the landholding nobility since the mid-seventeenth century. The nobility, however, had guaranteed its supremacy by means of ironclad domination of the peasantry. In 1784, a reform-minded group of nobles, led by the young Crown Prince Frederick (governing on behalf of his mentally ill father), began to apply Enlightenment remedies to the kingdom's economic problems. They encouraged freer trade and sought, above all, to boost agriculture by improving the status of the peasantry. With increased legal status and with land reform, which enabled some peasants to own the land they worked for the first time, agricultural productivity in Denmark rose dramatically. These reforms constitute some of the clearest achievements of any of the "enlightened" rulers.

In Sweden, in 1772, Gustav III (r. 1771–1796) staged a coup with army support that overturned the dominance of the Swedish parliament, the Riksdag. Bureaucrats more loyal to parliamentary patrons than to the Crown were replaced, restrictions on trade in grain and other economic controls were liberalized, the legal system was rationalized, the death penalty was strictly limited, and legal torture was abolished. Despite his abilities (and his charm), Gustav III was criticized for advancing reform by autocratic means in a kingdom with a strong tradition of representative government. In 1796 he was mortally wounded by an assassin hired by disgruntled nobles.

Another claimant to the title of "enlightened" monarch was Frederick II of Prussia (r. 1740–1786), "the Great." Although Frederick continued to reside in his imperial electorate of Brandenburg, the state he ruled was now referred to as "Prussia," the duchy his father had seized from Poland and ruled as king. In many ways, the Prussian state *was* its military victories, for Frederick's father and grandfather committed the resources of the state to a military machine of dramatic proportions. Prussia was a power on the European stage only because of the degree of that commitment.

The institutions that constituted the state and linked the various provinces under one administration were dominated by the needs of the military. There was no tradition of political participation—even by elites—and little chance of cultivating any. Nor was there any political or social room for maneuver at the lower part of the social scale. The rulers of Prussia had long ago acceded to the aristocracy's demand for tighter control over peasant labor. Thus, there was a stark limit to the kinds of social, judicial, or political reforms that Frederick could hope to carry out.

Frederick tried to introduce more efficient agricultural practices and improve the condition of peasants, but he met stiff resistance from noble landholders. He did succeed in abolishing serfdom in some regions. He tried to stimulate the economy by sponsoring state industries and trading monopolies but met opposition from the tightly controlled merchant communities. Simplifying and codifying the inherited jumble of local laws was a goal of every ruler. A law code published in 1794, after Frederick's death, was partly the product of his efforts.

Frederick's most distinctive "enlightened" characteristic was the seriousness with which he took his task as ruler. In his book *Anti-Machiavel* (1741) he argued that a ruler has a moral obligation to work for the betterment of the state. He styled himself as the "first servant" or steward of the state. However superficial this claim may appear, in his energy and diligence he compares favorably to Louis XV of France, who, having a much more wealthy and flexible society to work with, did much less.

Describing Frederick as "enlightened," however, masks the degree to which his activities reflected the traditional goals of security and prosperity as much as the impetus of "enlightened" thinking. Indeed, some of the most thoroughgoing administrative, legal, and economic reforms were accomplished in rival Austria entirely within such a traditional framework, during the reign of Maria Theresa (r. 1740–1780), the daughter of Emperor Charles VI (r. 1711–1740).

Maria Theresa was a remarkable ruler. Diligent and determined, she overcame the difficulties that surrounded her accession, survived the near dismemberment of Austrian territories in the war that opened her reign, and embarked on an energetic reform program to address the weaknesses in the state that the conflict had revealed (see page 428). The Austrian monarchy was still a highly decentralized state. Maria Theresa worked to streamline and centralize administration, finances, and defense. She created new centralized governing councils and, above all, reformed the tax system so that the Crown could better tap the wealth of its subjects. She established new courts of justice and limited the exploitation of serfs by landlords. In general, she presided over an effort to bypass many of the provincial and privatized controls on government still in the hands of the great nobility. She accomplished all of this without being in any way "enlightened" herself. For example, she had a traditional suspicion of freedom of the press and insisted on religious orthodoxy.

Her son, Joseph, was an interesting contrast. Self-consciously "enlightened," Joseph II (r. 1780–1790) carried out a variety of reforms that his mother had not attempted, including freedom of the press and limited freedom of religion. Some of his reforms were particularly dramatic, such as drastic curtailment of the death penalty and encouragement of widespread literacy. Many of Joseph's reforms, however, were simply extensions of his mother's. For example, he extended further legal protection to peasants and abolished hereditary serfdom in all Habsburg lands. And in some ways he was less successful than Maria Theresa had been. Though persuaded of the benefits of enlightened government, he was by temperament an inflexible autocrat, whose methods antagonized many of his most powerful subjects. Joseph's policies provoked simmering opposition and open revolt in a number of his lands, and some of his reforms were repealed even before his death.

Catherine the Great and the Empire of Russia

Another ruler who consciously staked a claim to the title "enlightened despot" was Catherine, empress of Russia (r. 1762–1796). Catherine was one of the ablest rulers in the eighteenth century and perhaps the single most able of all the rulers of imperial Russia. She combined intelligence with vision, diligence, and skill in handling people and choosing advisers. Her determination and political acumen were obvious early in her life in Russia simply from the fact that she survived at court. In 1745 she had been brought to Russia from her native Germany to marry the heir to the Russian throne. Treated badly by her husband, Tsar Peter III, Catherine engineered a coup against him in the summer of 1762. Peter was overthrown and killed, and Catherine ruled alone as empress for most of the rest of the century.

Catherine the Great, as she came to be called, was the true heir of Peter the Great in her abilities, policies, and ambitions. Under Catherine, Russia committed itself to general European affairs in addition to its traditional territorial ambitions. In situations involving the major European powers, Russia tended to ally with Britain (with which it had important trading connections, including the provision of timber for British shipbuilding) and with Austria (against their common foe, Turkey), and against France, Poland, and Prussia. In 1768, Catherine initiated a war against the Turks from which Russia gained much of the Crimean coast. She also continued Peter's efforts to dominate the weakened Poland. Here she was aided by Frederick the Great, who proposed the deliberate partitioning of Poland. In 1772, portions of Poland were gobbled up in the first of three successive "grabs" of territory (Map 16.1). Warsaw itself eventually landed in Prussian hands, but Catherine gained all of Belarus, Ukraine, and modern Lithuania—which had constituted the former duchy of Lithuania. Like any successful ruler of her age, Catherine counted territorial aggrandizement among her chief achievements.

Nevertheless, Catherine also counted herself a sincere follower of the Enlightenment. While young, she had received an education that bore the strong stamp of the Enlightenment. She took an active role in the intellectual community, corresponding with Voltaire over the course of many years and acting as patron to Diderot. One of Catherine's boldest political moves was the secularization of church lands. Although Peter the Great had extended government control of the church, he had never touched church lands. Catherine licensed private publishing houses and permitted a burgeoning periodical press. The number of books published in Russia tripled during her reign. This enriched cultural life helped bring forth a great flowering of Russian literature in the early nineteenth century.

Catherine the Great Catherine was a German princess who had been brought to Russia to marry another German, Peter of Holstein-Gottorp, who was being groomed as heir to the Russian throne. There had been several Russian monarchs of mixed Russian and German parentage since the time of Peter the Great's deliberate interest in and ties with other European states. *(Wernher Collection, Somerset House, London)*

The stamp of the Enlightenment on Catherine's policies was also visible in her attempts at legal reform. In 1767 she convened a legislative commission and provided it with a guiding document, the *Instruction,* which she had written. The commission was remarkable because it comprised representatives of all classes, including peasants, and provided a place for the airing of grievances. Catherine hoped for a general codification of law as well as reforms such as the abolition of torture and capital punishment—reforms that made the *Instruction* radical enough to be banned in other countries. She did not propose changing the legal status of serfs, however, and class differences made the commission unworkable in the end. Most legal reforms were accomplished piecemeal and favored the interests of landed gentry. Property rights were clarified and strengthened; judicial procedures were streamlined but constructed to include legal privileges for the gentry.

Like the Austrian rulers, Catherine undertook far-reaching administrative reform to create more

Map 16.1 The Partitions of Poland and the Expansion of Russia, 1772–1795 Catherine the Great acquired modern Lithuania, Belarus, and Ukraine, which had once constituted the duchy of Lithuania, part of the multi-ethnic Polish kingdom.

effective local units of government. Here again, political imperatives were fundamental, and reforms in local government strengthened the hand of the gentry. The legal subjection of peasants in serfdom was also extended as a matter of state policy to help win the allegiance of landholders in newly acquired areas. Gentry, on whom the stability of her government depended, were rewarded with estates and serfs to work them.

Catherine's reign was marked by one of the most massive and best-organized peasant rebellions of the century. Occurring in 1773, the rebellion expressed the grievances of the thousands of peasants who joined its ranks and called for the abolition of serfdom. The revolt took its name from its Cossack leader, Emelian Pugachev (d. 1775), and also reflected the dissatisfaction with the Russian government of this semiautonomous people.

The dramatic dilemmas Catherine faced illustrated both the promise and the costs of state formation throughout Europe. State consolidation permitted the imposition of internal peace, a coordinated economic policy, and the reform of justice, but at the price of coercion of the population. Thus, we can see from the alternative perspective of Russia the importance of the political sphere that was opening up in France and being consolidated in England.

STATES IN CONFLICT

In the eighteenth century a new constellation of states emerged to dominate politics on the Continent. Along with the traditional powers of England, France, and Austria were Prussia in central Europe and Russia to the east (see Map 16.1). Certain characteristics common to all these states account for their dominance, and none was more crucial than their ability to field effective armies. Traditional territorial ambitions accounted for many wars in the eighteenth century, but the increasing importance of overseas trade and colonization was the most significant source of conflict between England and France.

A Century of Warfare: Circumstances and Rationales

The large and small states of Europe continued to make war on each other for both strategic and dynastic reasons. The expense of war, the number of powerful states involved, and the complexities of their interests meant that wars were preceded by the careful construction of complex systems of alliances and followed by the changing control of many bits of territory.

States fought over territory that had obvious economic and strategic value. Although rational and defensible "national" borders were important, collecting isolated bits of territory was still the norm. The wars between European powers became extremely complex strategically; for example, France might strike a blow against Austria by invading an Italian territory in order to use it as a bargaining chip in the eventual peace negotiations.

The state of military technology, tactics, and organization shaped the outcome of most conflicts. In the eighteenth century, weapons and tactics became increasingly refined. More reliable muskets were used. A bayonet that could slip over a musket barrel without blocking the muzzle was invented. Coordinated use of bayonets required even more rigorous drilling of troops. Artillery and cavalry forces were also subjected to greater standardization of training. One sure result of the new equipment and tactics was that war became more expensive than ever before. It became increasingly difficult for small states such as Sweden to compete. Prussia, a small and relatively poor state, supported large forces by means of an extraordinary bending of civil society to the needs of the army. In Prussia, twice as many people were in the armed forces, proportionally, as in other states, and a staggering 80 percent of meager state revenue went to support the army.

Most states introduced some form of conscription in the eighteenth century. The very poor often volunteered for army service to improve their lives, but the conscription of peasants imposed a significant burden on peasant communities and a sacrifice of productive members to the state. Governments everywhere supplemented volunteers and conscripts with mercenaries and even criminals, as necessary, to fill the ranks without tapping the wealthier elements of the community. Common soldiers were increasingly seen not as members of society but as its rejects. A French war minister commented that armies had to consist of the "scum of people and of all those for whom society has no use."[2] Brutality became an accepted tool for governments to use to manage such groups of men. From the eighteenth century, the army increasingly became an instrument of social control used to manage and make use of individuals who otherwise would have had no role in society.

The Power of Austria and Prussia

Major continental wars had a marked impact on the balance of power among states in western and central Europe. The first of these, now known as the War of the Austrian Succession, began in 1740. Emperor Charles VI died that year without a male heir, and his daughter, Maria Theresa, succeeded him. Charles VI had negotiated tirelessly to persuade the various provinces of the Habsburg monarchy and the states of Europe to accept the Pragmatic Sanction, an act recognizing his daughter as his heir. In 1740, however, Frederick II of Prussia took advantage of Habsburg vulnerability by invading the wealthy Habsburg province of Silesia (see Map 16.1), to which he had a hereditary claim of sorts.

Maria Theresa proved a much more tenacious opponent than Frederick had anticipated. In the end, he was lucky to be able to hold onto Silesia, which was on the northern edge of Maria Theresa's territories. Although Austrian forces were never able to dislodge Frederick, they did best most of the forces ranged against them by their perpetual opponent, France, and other German states allied with Frederick.

The War of the Austrian Succession dragged on until 1748, when a final treaty was signed. Austria's succession was not disrupted and its lands were not dismembered. Prussia, because of the annexation of Silesia and the psychological impact of victory, emerged as a power of virtually equal rank to the Habsburgs in Germany.

The unprecedented threat that Austria now felt from Prussia caused a veritable revolution in alliances across Europe. So great in Austrian minds was the change in the balance of power that Austria was willing to ally with France, its traditional enemy, in order to isolate Prussia. In the years before what would later be known as the Seven Years' War (1756–1763), Austrian officials approached France to propose a mutual defensive alliance—a move that became known as the "Diplomatic Revolution." Sweden and Russia, with territory to gain at Prussia's expense, joined the alliance system.

Frederick initiated hostilities in 1756, hoping, among other outcomes, to prevent consolidation of the new alliances. Instead, he found that he had started a war against overwhelming odds. Limited English aid kept him in the field. The English, engaged with France in the overseas conflict known as the French and Indian War, wanted France to be heavily committed on the Continent. What saved Frederick was Russia's withdrawal from the alliance against him when a new ruler took the throne there in 1762. Prussia managed to emerge intact—though strained economically and demographically.

The results of the war confirmed Prussia and Austria as the two states of European rank in German-speaking Europe. Their rivalry would dominate German history until the late nineteenth century.

The Atlantic World: Trade, Colonization, Competition

The importance of international trade and colonial possessions to the states of western Europe grew dramatically in the eighteenth century. Between 1715 and 1785, Britain's trade with North America rose from 19 to 34 percent of its total trade, and its trade with Asia and Africa rose from 7 to 19 percent of the total. By the end of the century, more than half of all British trade was carried on outside of Europe; for France, the figure was more than a third.

European commercial and colonial energies were concentrated in the Atlantic world, where the profits were the greatest. The population of British North America grew from about 250,000 in 1700 to about 1.7 million by 1760. The densely settled New England colonies provided a market for manufactured goods from the mother country, though they produced little by way of raw materials or bulk goods on which traders could make a profit. Maryland and Virginia produced tobacco, the Carolinas rice and indigo. England re-exported all three throughout Europe, at considerable profit.

The French in New France, numbering only 56,000 in 1740, were vastly outnumbered by the British colonists. Nevertheless, the French successfully expanded their control of territory in Canada. Despite native resistance, the French extended the fur trade—the source of most of the profits that New France generated—west and north along the Great Lakes, consolidating their hold as they went by building forts. They cut into the British trade run out of Hudson Bay to the north and contested the mouth of the St. Lawrence River and the Gulf of St. Lawrence. The British held Nova Scotia and Newfoundland, the French held Cape Breton Island, and both states fished the surrounding waters.

The commercial importance of all of these holdings, as well as those in Asia, paled beside the profits generated by the Caribbean colonies. The British held Jamaica and Barbados; the French, Guadeloupe and Martinique; the Spanish, Cuba and San Domingo; and the Dutch, a few small islands. Sugar produced by slave labor was the major source of profits, along with other cash crops such as coffee, indigo, and cochineal (another dyestuff). The tiny Dutch possession of Guiana on the South American coast required twice as many visits by Dutch ships as the Dutch East India Company sent into Asia.

The economic dependence of the colonies on slave labor meant that the colonies were tied to their home countries not with a two-way commercial exchange but with a three-way "triangle" trade (Map 16.2). European manufactures were shipped to western ports in Africa, where they were traded for slaves. The enslaved Africans were then transported to South America, the Caribbean, or North America, where planters bought and paid for them with profits from their sugar and tobacco plantations. (See the box "Encounters with the West: An African Recalls the Horrors of the Slave Ship.") Sugar and tobacco were then shipped back to the mother country to be re-exported at great profit throughout Europe. Merchants in cities such as Bordeaux in France and Liverpool in England invested heavily in the slave trade and the re-export business.

The proximity and growth of French and British settlements in North America ensured conflict (see Map 16.3). The Caribbean and the coasts of Central and South America were strategic flashpoints as well. The British were making incursions along the coastline claimed by Spain and were trying to break into the monopoly of trade between Spain and its vast possessions in the region. Public opinion in both Britain and France became increasingly sensitive to colonial issues. For the first time, tensions abroad would fuel a major conflict between two European states.

Great Britain and France: Wars Overseas

In the eighteenth century, England became the dominant naval power in Europe. Its navy protected its far-flung trading networks, its merchant fleet, and the coast of England itself. England had strategic interests on the Continent as well and consistently promoted a variety of powers there, so that no one of them could pose too great a threat to England, its coastline, or its widespread trading system. The French, who had dispatched a fleet to aid the Stuart claimant to the British throne (see page 421), seemed a particular threat.

A second, dynastic consideration in continental affairs was the electorate of Hanover, the large principality in western Germany that was the native territory of the Hanoverian kings of England. Early in the century especially, the interests of this German territory were a significant factor in British foreign policy. Unable to field a large army, given their maritime interests, the British sought protection for Hanover in alliances and subsidies for allies' armies on the Continent. The money for these ventures came from the profits on overseas trade.

After the death of Louis XIV in 1715, England's energies centered on colonial rivalries with France, its greatest competitor overseas. There were three major wars between England and France in colonial regions. The first two were concurrent with the major land wars in Europe: the War of the Austrian Succession (1740–1748) and the Seven Years' War (1756–1763). The third war

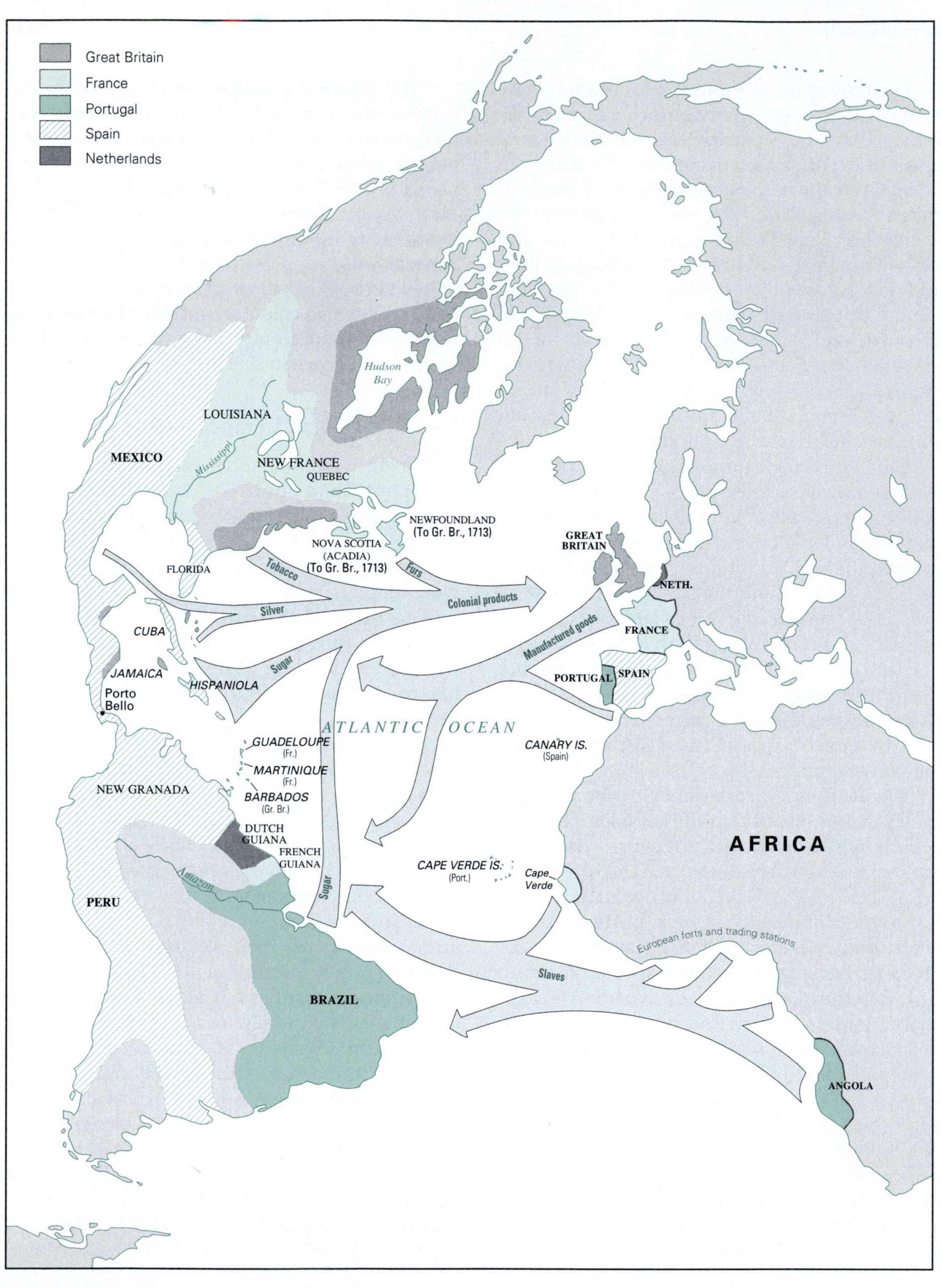

Great Britain
France
Portugal
Spain
Netherlands
Hudson Bay
LOUISIANA
MEXICO
Mississippi
NEW FRANCE
QUEBEC
NEWFOUNDLAND
(To Gr. Br., 1713)
NOVA SCOTIA
(ACADIA)
(To Gr. Br., 1713)
FLORIDA
Tobacco
Furs
Colonial products
Silver
CUBA
Sugar
JAMAICA
HISPANIOLA
Porto Bello
Manufactured goods
GREAT BRITAIN
NETH.
FRANCE
PORTUGAL
SPAIN
ATLANTIC OCEAN
GUADELOUPE
(Fr.)
MARTINIQUE
(Fr.)
BARBADOS
(Gr. Br.)
CANARY IS.
(Spain)
NEW GRANADA
DUTCH GUIANA
FRENCH GUIANA
AFRICA
CAPE VERDE IS.
(Port.)
Cape Verde
Amazon
Sugar
PERU
European forts and trading stations
Slaves
BRAZIL
ANGOLA

ENCOUNTERS WITH THE WEST

An African Recalls the Horrors of the Slave Ship

Olaudah Equiano (ca. 1750–1797) was one of the few Africans sold into slavery in the Americas to leave a written record of his experiences. An Ibo from the Niger region, he first experienced slavery as a boy when kidnapped from his village by other Africans. But nothing prepared him for the brutality of the Europeans who bought and shipped him to Barbados, in the British West Indies. He eventually regained his freedom and received an education.

The first object which saluted my eyes when I arrived on the [African] coast was the sea and a slaveship . . . waiting for its cargo. . . . When I was carried on board I was immediately handled, and tossed up, to see if I were sound, by some of the crew. . . . I was soon put down under the decks, and there I received such a salutation in the nostrils as I had never experienced in my life; so that, with the loathsomeness of the stench . . . I became so sick and low that I was not able to eat. . . . I now wished for the last friend, death, to relieve me; but soon, to my grief, two of the white men offered me eatables; and, on my refusing to eat, one of them held me fast by the hands and laid me across, I think, the windlass, and tied my feet while the other flogged me severely.

One day, when we had a smooth sea and a moderate wind, two of my wearied countrymen, who were chained together, preferring death to such a life of misery, somehow made through the nettings and jumped into the sea; immediately another dejected fellow who [was ill and so not in irons] followed their example. . . . Two of the wretches were drowned, but they got the other and afterwards flogged him unmercifully for thus attempting to prefer death to slavery. In this manner we continued to undergo more hardships than I can now relate. Many a time we were near suffocation for want of fresh air. . . . This, and the stench of the necessary tubs, carried off many.

Source: Philip D. Curtin, *Africa Remembered* (Madison: University of Wisconsin Press, 1967), pp. 92–96.

coincided with the rebellion of British colonies in North America—the American Revolution—beginning in the 1770s. Inevitably more committed to affairs on the Continent than were the British, the French were able to hold their own successfully in both arenas during the 1740s, but by 1763, though pre-eminent on the Continent, they had lost many of their colonial possessions to the English.

Map 16.2 The Atlantic Economy, ca. 1750 The "triangle trade" linked Europe, Africa, and European colonies in the Americas. The most important component of this trade for Europe was the profitable plantation agriculture that depended on enslaved Africans for labor.

In the 1740s, France and England tested each other's strength in scattered colonial fighting, which began in 1744 and produced a few well-balanced gains and losses. Peace was made in 1748 but tension was renewed almost immediately at many of the strategic points in North America. The French reinforced their encirclement of British colonies with more forts along the Great Lakes and the Ohio River. The French and Indian War was sparked when British troops (at one point led by the colonial commander George Washington) attempted to strike at these forts in 1754.

In India, meanwhile, the French and the British attempted to strengthen their commercial footholds by making military and political alliances with local Indian rulers. A British attack on a French convoy provoked a declaration of war by France in May 1756, three months before fighting in the Seven Years' War broke out in Europe. For the first time, a major war between European nations had started and would be fought in their overseas possessions, signifying a profound change in the relation between Europe and the rest of the world.

The French had already committed themselves to an alliance with Austria and were increasingly involved on the Continent after Frederick II initiated war there in August 1756. Slowly, the drain of sustaining war both on the Continent and abroad began to tell, and Britain scored major victories against French forces after an initial period of balanced successes and failures. The French lost a number of fortresses on the Mississippi and Ohio Rivers and on the Great Lakes and, finally, also lost the interior of Canada with the fall of Quebec and Montreal in 1759 and 1760, respectively (Map 16.3).

In the Caribbean, the British seized Guadeloupe, the main French sugar-producing island. Superior resources in India enabled the British to take several French outposts there. The cost of involvement on so many fronts meant that French troops were short of money and supplies. They were particularly vulnerable in North America because the territory they had occupied remained sparsely settled and dependent on the mother country for food.

By the terms of the Peace of Paris in 1763, France regained Guadeloupe. In India, France retained many of its trading stations but lost its political and military clout. British power in India was also enhanced by victories over the Indian rulers who had sided with the French. British political rule in India, as opposed to merely a mercantile presence, began at this time. The British now also held Canada. They emerged as the preeminent world power among European states.

ECONOMIC EXPANSION AND SOCIAL CHANGE

The intellectual and cultural ferment of the Enlightenment laid the groundwork for domestic political changes to come, just as British victories in the Seven Years' War shifted the balance of power abroad. More subtle and more profound changes were occurring in the European countryside, however: Population, production, and consumption were beginning to grow beyond the bounds that all preceding generations had known.

More Food and More People

Throughout European history, there had been a delicate balance between available food and numbers of people to feed. Population growth had accompanied increases in the amount of land under cultivation. From time to time, population growth surpassed the ability of the land to produce food, and people became malnourished and prey to disease.

There were few ways to increase the productivity of land. Peasants safeguarded its fertility by alternately cultivating some portions while letting others lie fallow or using them as pasture. Manure provided fertilizer, but during the winter months livestock could not be kept alive in large numbers. Limited food for livestock meant limited fertilizer, which in turn meant limited production of food for both humans and animals.

After the devastating decline in the fourteenth century due to the Black Death, the European population experienced a prolonged recovery, and in the eighteenth century the balance that had previously been reached began to be exceeded for the first time. Population growth occurred because of a decline in the death rate for adults and a simultaneous increase in the birthrate in some areas owing to earlier marriages.

The primary reason adults were living longer, despite the presence of various epidemic diseases, was that they were better nourished and thus better able to resist disease. Food production increased because of the introduction of new crops

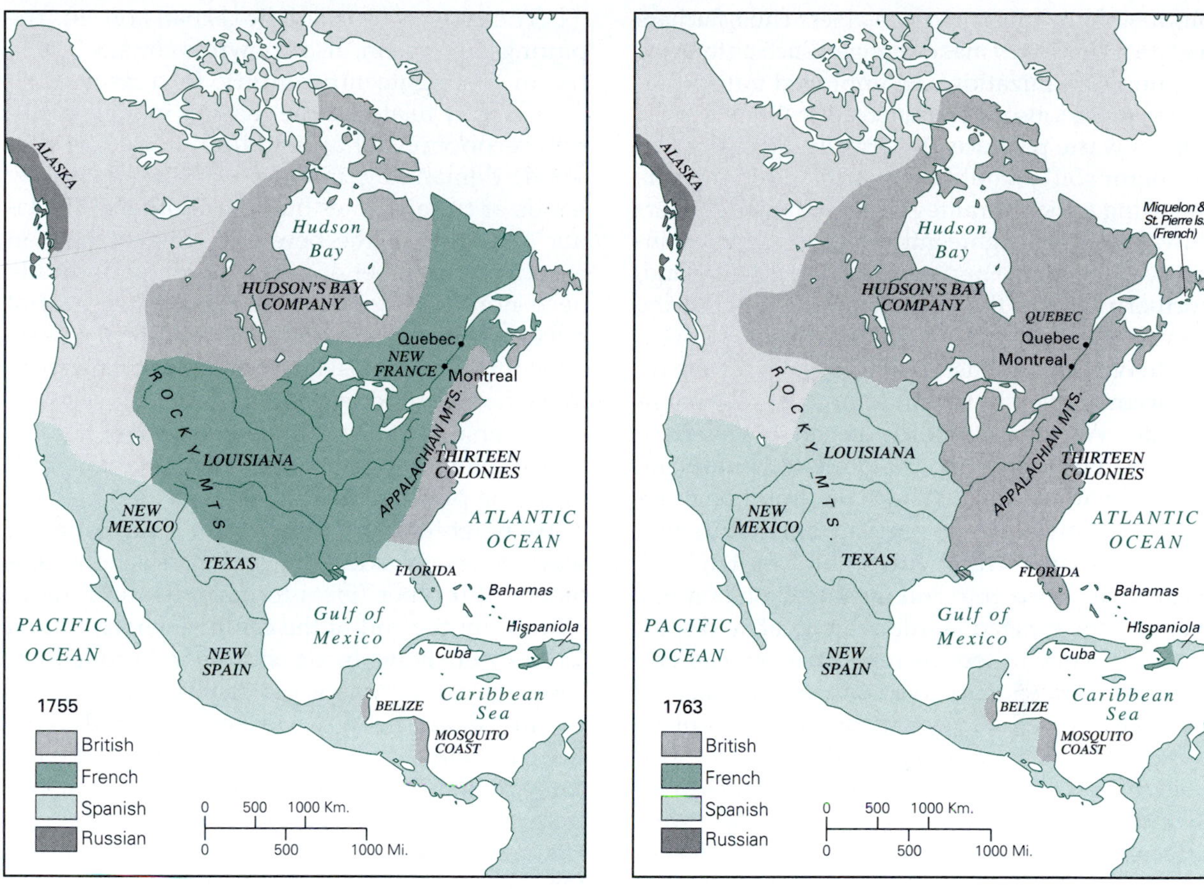

Map 16.3 British Gains in North America The British colonies on the Atlantic coast were effective staging posts for the armies that ousted the French from North America by 1763. However, taxes imposed on the colonies to pay the costs of the Seven Years' War helped spark revolt—the American Revolution—a decade later.

and other changes in agricultural practices. The cumulative effect of these changes was so dramatic that historians have called them an "agricultural revolution." The new crops included fodder, such as clover, legumes, and turnips, which did not deplete the soil and could be fed to livestock over the winter. The greater availability of animal manure, in turn, boosted grain production. The potato, introduced from the Americas in the sixteenth century, is nutrient-dense and can feed more people per acre than can grain.

More food being produced meant more food available for purchase. A family that could purchase food might decide to convert its farm into a dairy farm. In such a case, many families could be supported from a piece of land that had formerly supported a single family engaged in traditional agriculture. Over a generation or two, several children might share the inheritance of what had previously been a single farm, yet each could make a living from his or her share, and population could grow as it had not done before.

Capitals like London and Amsterdam and trading centers such as Glasgow and Bordeaux were booming. Such cities demanded not only grain but also specialized produce such as dairy products and fruits and vegetables. Thus, farmers had an incentive to make changes, such as to dairy farming. Urbanization and improved transportation networks also encouraged agriculture because human waste produced by city dwellers—known as "night soil"—could be distributed in the surrounding agricultural regions to increase soil fertility. By the late eighteenth century, pockets of intensive, diversified agriculture existed in England, northern France, the Rhineland in Germany, the Po Valley in Italy, and Catalonia in Spain.

In other areas, changes in agriculture were often accompanied by a shift in power in the countryside. Wealthy landlords began to invest in change in order to reap the profits of producing for the new markets. Where the traditional authority of the village to regulate agriculture was weak, peasants were vulnerable. In England, weak village structure and the attraction of urban markets encouraged landlords to treat land speculatively. They raised the rents farmers paid and changed cultivation patterns on the land that they controlled directly. They appropriated the village common lands, a process known as *enclosure*, and used them for cash crops such as sheep (raised for their wool) or beef cattle. Many rural people were driven off the land or made destitute by the loss of the resources of common lands.

Thus, the agricultural revolution that allowed the population to grow because of an increased production of food per individual inhabitant did not mean increased prosperity for most people.

The Growth of Industry

Agricultural changes fostered change in other areas of economic and social life. As more food was grown with less labor, peasants were freed to do other work. Since there was work to be had making other products that people needed, the nonagricultural population continued to grow. More people meant more consumers, and the demand for goods helped continue the cycle of population growth, changes in production, and economic expansion. A combination of forces increased the number of people who worked at producing a few essential materials and products.

There was a dramatic expansion in the putting-out system, also known as cottage industry, in the eighteenth century, for reasons that were closely related to the changes in the agricultural economy. All agricultural work was seasonal, demanding intensive effort and many hands at certain times but few at others. The labor demands of the new crops meant that an even larger number of people might periodically need nonfarm work to make ends meet. Rural poverty, whether as a result of traditional or new agricultural methods, made manufacturing work in the home attractive to more people.

Overseas trade spurred the demand in Europe's colonies for cloth and other finished products. The production of cloth expanded also because heightened demand led to changes in the way cloth was made. Wool was increasingly combined with other fibers to make less expensive fabrics. By the end of the century wholly cotton fabrics were being made cheaply in Europe from cotton grown in America by slave labor.

In the Middle Ages, weavers had produced a luxury-quality cloth, and their profits came not from demand, which was relatively low, but from the high prices consumers paid. In the eighteenth century, cheaper kinds of cloth were made for mass consumption. Producing more became important.

The invention of machines to spin thread in the late eighteenth century brought a marked increase in the rate of production and profound changes to the lives of rural workers who had been juggling agricultural and textile work according to season and need. The areas of England, France, and the Low Countries where the new technologies were introduced stood, by the end of the century, on the verge of a massive industrial transformation that would have dramatic political and social consequences.

Control and Resistance

The economic changes of the century produced both resistance and adaptation by ordinary people and, at times, direct action by state authorities. Sometimes ordinary people coped in ways that revealed their desperation. In many cities, the number of abandoned children rose greatly because urban families, particularly recent immigrants from the countryside, could not support their offspring. The major cities of Europe put increasing resources into police forces and city lighting schemes. Charitable institutions run by cities, churches, and central governments expanded. By 1789, for example, there were more than two thousand *hôpitaux*—poorhouses for the destitute and ill—in France. The poor received food and shelter but were forced to work for the city or to live in poorhouses against their will. Men were sometimes taken out of poorhouses and forced to become soldiers.

Resistance and adaptation were particularly visible wherever the needs of common people conflicted with the states' desire for order and for revenue. Consider, for example, the suppression of piracy. Piracy had been a way of life for hundreds of Europeans and colonial settlers since the sixteenth century. From the earliest days of exploration, European rulers had authorized men known as privateers to commit acts of war against specific targets; the Crown took little risk and was spared the cost of arming the ships but shared in the plunder. True piracy—outright robbery on the high seas—was illegal, but the difference between piracy and privateering was often small. As governments' and merchants' desire for regular trade began to outweigh that for the irregular profits of plunder, and as national navies developed in the late seventeenth century, a concerted effort to eliminate piracy began.

Life on the seas became an increasingly vital part of western European economic life in the eighteenth century, and it began to resemble life

An Idle Apprentice Is Sent to Sea, 1747 In one of a series of moralizing engravings by William Hogarth, the lazy apprentice, Tom, is sent away to a life at sea. The experienced seamen in the boat introduce him to some of its terrors: On the left dangles a cat-o'-nine-tails, and on the distant promontory is a gallows, where pirates and rebels meet their fate. *(Reproduced with permission)*

on land in the amount of compulsion it included. English-speaking seamen alone numbered about thirty thousand around the middle of the eighteenth century. Sailors in port were always vulnerable to forcible enlistment in the navy by impressment gangs, particularly during wartime. A drowsy merchant sailor sleeping off a night of celebrating with newgotten wages could wake up to find himself aboard a navy ship. Press gangs operated throughout England and not just in major ports, for authorities were as interested in controlling "vagrancy" as in staffing the navy. Merchant captains occasionally filled their crews by such means, particularly when sailing unpopular routes.

Like soldiers in the growing eighteenth-century armies, sailors in the merchant marine as well as the navy could be subjected to brutal discipline and appalling conditions. Merchant seamen attempted to improve their lot by trying to regulate their relationship with ships' captains. Contracts for pay on merchant ships became more regularized, and seamen often negotiated their terms very carefully, including, for example, details about how rations were to be allotted. Sailors might even take bold collective action aboard ship. The English-language term for a collective job action, *strike,* comes from the sailing expression "to strike sail," meaning to lower the sails so that they cannot fill with wind. Its use dates from the eighteenth century, from "strikes" of sailors protesting unfair conditions.

Seafaring men were an unusual group because they were a large and somewhat self-conscious community of workers for wages. Not until industrialization came into full swing a century later would a similar group of workers exist within Europe itself.

SUMMARY

It is important not to exaggerate the degree to which circumstances of life changed in the eighteenth century. The economy was expanding and the population growing beyond previous limits, and the system of production was being restructured. But these changes happened incrementally over many decades and were not recognized for the fundamental changes they were.

Most of the long-familiar material constraints were still in place. Roads, on which much commerce depended, were generally impassable in bad weather. Shipping was relatively dependable and economical—but only relatively. Military life likewise reflected traditional constraints. Despite technological changes and developments of the state to equip, train, and enforce discipline, the conduct of war was still hampered by problems of transport and supply that would have been familiar to warriors two centuries before.

Similarly, though some rulers were inspired by precepts of the Enlightenment, all were guided by traditional concerns of dynastic aggrandizement and strategic advantage. Among the reading public, the women who held Enlightenment salons, and even the leading Enlightenment authors, there was no consensus as to the level of equality desirable in a society. There was certainly a great deal of fear associated with democracy—and there would be for a long time to come.

The most visible and dramatic change would happen first in politics, where goals and expectations nurtured by Enlightenment philosophy clashed with the rigid structure of the French state. Whether they were referring to the rights of women, or religious toleration, or the ideal form of government, Enlightenment philosophes argued that thinking based on empirically established facts or demonstrable logic could discover truths more conducive to human happiness than the pronouncements of tradition, church, and monarch. Even if only a limited number of people understood the specifics of the ideas being advanced, the Enlightenment generally fostered reading and education as routes to freedom and power, advocated change, and suggested that traditional social hierarchies might be questioned. Yet the Enlightenment was not simply an intellectual movement. It also encompassed the public and private settings where "enlightened" opinion flourished. The revolutionary potential of Enlightenment thought came from belief in its rationality and from the fact that it was both critical of its society and fashionable to practice.

NOTES

1. Quoted in M. S. Anderson, *Europe in the Eighteenth Century,* 3d ed. (London: Longman, 1987), pp. 218–219.
2. Dena Goodman, *The Republic of Letters: A Cultural History of the French Enlightenment* (Ithaca: Cornell University Press, 1994), p. 89.

SUGGESTED READING

Carsten, F. L. *The Origins of Prussia.* 1982. An introduction to the growth of the Prussian state in the seventeenth and eighteenth centuries.

Chartier, Roger. *The Cultural Uses of Print in Early Modern France.* 1987. A discussion of changes in reading habits and in the uses of printed materials throughout the eighteenth century in France.

Cipolla, Carlo. *Before the Industrial Revolution.* 1976. A comprehensive treatment of the development of the European economy and technology through this period.

Colley, Linda. *Britons: Forging the Nation, 1707–1837.* 1992. A history of the British that emphasizes the interrelationships of political, social, and cultural history.

Darnton, Robert. *The Literary Underground of the Old Regime.* 1982. One of several important works by Darnton on the social history of print culture.

Devine, T. M. *Clanship to Crofters' War: The Social Transformation of the Scottish Highlands.* 1994. A brief and readable study that follows the destruction and transformation of Highland culture from the Late Middle Ages to the nineteenth century.

De Vries, Jan. *The Economy of Europe in an Age of Crisis, 1600–1750.* 1976. Essential reading for understanding the changes in Europe's economy and in its trade and colonial relationships throughout the world.

Doyle, William. *The Old European Order, 1660–1800.* 1978. A general history.

Gagliardo, John. *Enlightened Despotism.* 1968. A general introduction to the concept and to the rulers of the era.

Gay, Peter. *The Enlightenment: An Interpretation.* 2 vols. 1966–1969. A detailed study of Enlightenment thought by one of its foremost modern interpreters.

———. *Voltaire's Politics.* 1959. A lively introduction to Voltaire's career as a political and social reformer.

Goldgar, Anne. *Impolite Learning: Conduct and Community in the Republic of Letters, 1680–1750.* 1995. Erudite study of international literary and scientific communities.

Goodman, Dena. *The Republic of Letters: A Cultural History of the French Enlightenment.* 1994. Indispensable for understanding the social context of the Enlightenment and the role of women.

Gullickson, Gay. *Spinners and Weavers of Auffay.* 1986. Focuses on a specific community in western Europe, providing a detailed analysis of the changes in the European economy in the seventeenth and eighteenth centuries.

Hubatsch, Walter. *Frederick the Great.* 1981. A biography that illuminates Frederick's system of government.

Hufton, Olwen. *The Poor of Eighteenth-Century Paris.* 1974. An analysis of the lives of the poor and the responses of the state.

Kennedy, Paul. *The Rise and Fall of British Naval Mastery.* 1976. The authoritative work on the rise of British seapower from the sixteenth century to modern times.

Laslett, Peter. *The World We Have Lost.* 1965. An innovative study of premodern society and culture, emphasizing the differences in habits and values that separate our society from preindustrial times.

Madariaga, Isobel de. *Russia in the Age of Catherine the Great.* 1981. The best recent biography of Catherine.

Parry, J. H. *Trade and Dominion: The European Overseas Empires in the Eighteenth Century.* 1971. A reliable survey of developments.

Treasure, Geoffrey. *The Making of Modern Europe, 1648–1780.* 1985. A broad study covering political, social, economic, and cultural developments.

CHAPTER 17

Revolutionary Europe, 1789–1815

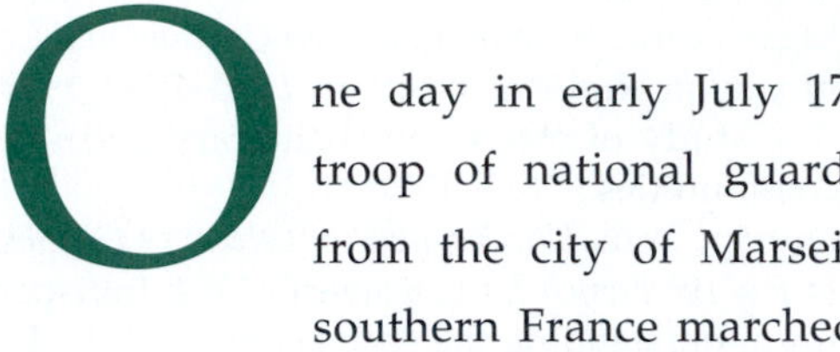

One day in early July 1792, a troop of national guardsmen from the city of Marseille in southern France marched into Paris, singing as they came:

Allons enfants de la patrie,	(Come, children of the nation)
Le jour de gloire est arrivé	(The day of glory is at hand)
Contre nous de la tyrannie	(Against us is raised)
L'étendard sanglant est levé!	(The bloody standard of tyranny!)

Their song, soon known as the "Marseillaise," became famous as the rally cry of the French Revolution and three years later was officially declared the French national anthem. This choice is appropriate, for the Revolution, which was unfolding that July, profoundly shaped the growth and character of modern France.

Part of the Revolution's significance lay in the power of symbols, such as the "Marseillaise," to challenge an old political order and legitimate a new one. Challenges to the power of the king were not new, but the Revolution overthrew his right to rule at all. Indeed, in the course of this Revolution, Louis XVI was transformed from the divinely appointed father of his people to an enemy of the people, worthy of execution. A new political world was emerging.

The Revolution began because of a governmental financial crisis, and at several important junctures it was further ignited by bread shortages, but these material causes led only to remarkable innovation (both horrible and hopeful) because of the intellectual and political climate in which they occurred. Enlightenment philosophy influenced the decisions of French public figures and inspired the imaginations of the people. The example of the American Revolution moved the French reformers to believe that change was both desirable and possible. Expectations ran high.

In its initial phase, the French Revolution established the principle of constitutional government and ended many traditional political privileges. These moderate gains were swept aside as the Revolution became increasingly radical. The reasons for this were various, including the king's intransigence, foreign war, counterrevolution, and food riots. Most dangerous, perhaps, was inexperience with the compromises and delays necessary in the normal processes of democratic institutions. The Revolution's most radical phase, the Terror, produced its most effective legislation but also its worst violence.

Today the Revolution is considered the initiation of modern European as well as modern French history. Events in France reverberated throughout Europe because the overthrow of Louis XVI threatened other monarchs. By the late 1790s the armies of France would be led in outright conquest of other European states by one of the most talented generals in European history, Napoleon Bonaparte. What he brought to the continental European nations was an amalgam of imperial aggression and revolutionary fervor.

Questions and Ideas to Consider

- In what ways did the American Revolution influence the French? Consider the ideological influences as well as the economic demands of the American Revolution and the experiences of Lafayette and other French officers.
- Over the course of the French Revolution, many people took an active role in politics for the first time. Consider the experience of Parisian women. In what ways, old and new, were they able to express their views and effect political change?
- What were the goals of the Terror? Did it achieve these goals? Scholars have long debated the moral significance of the Terror. What do you think? If great and arbitrary violence is necessary to create a regime of greater democracy and freedom, is such violence acceptable?
- Did Napoleon preserve the democratic and social accomplishments of the Revolution or dismantle them? Give evidence for both possible conclusions. Which do you think is more persuasive?
- Discuss the notion of political legitimacy. How do symbolic images and gestures help to give permanence and authority to a regime? Name several important symbols and symbolic acts of the revolutionary period.

BACKGROUND TO REVOLUTION

When the American colonists declared their independence from Britain in 1776, there were many consequences: British trading interests were challenged, French appetites for gains at British expense were whetted, and notions of "liberty" seemed more plausible and desirable. The victory of the American colonies in 1783, followed by the writing of the United States Constitution in 1787, heightened the appeal of liberal ideas elsewhere. There were attempts at liberal reform in several states, including Ireland, the Netherlands, and Poland. However, the American Revolution had the most direct impact on later events in France because the French had been directly involved in the American struggle.

Revolutionary Movements Around Europe

The war against the American colonies was not firmly supported by the British people. Many Britons had divided loyalties, and many others were convinced that the war was being mismanaged and called for reform of the ministerial government. In addition, a reform movement in Ireland began to spring up in 1779. The reformers demanded greater autonomy from Britain. Like the Americans, Irish elites felt like disadvantaged junior partners in the British Empire. Following the example of the American rebels, middle- and upper-class Anglo-Irish set up a system of locally sponsored voluntary militia to

CHAPTER CHRONOLOGY

May 5, 1789	Meeting of Estates General
June 17, 1789	Third Estate declares itself the National Assembly
June 20, 1789	Tennis Court Oath
July–August 1789	Storming of the Bastille (July 14); abolition of feudalism (August 4); Declaration of the Rights of Man and of the Citizen (August 27)
October 5–6, 1789	Women's march on Versailles; Louis XVI's return to Paris
July 1790	Civil Constitution of the Clergy
June 1791	Louis XVI attempts to flee Paris; is captured and returned
September 1791	New constitution is implemented; Girondins dominate newly formed Legislative Assembly
April 1792	France declares war on Austria
August 10, 1792	Storming of the Tuileries; Louis XVI arrested
September 21, 1792	National Convention declares France a republic
January 21, 1793	Louis XVI is guillotined
February 1793	France declares war on Britain, Spain, and the Netherlands
June 1793	Radical Jacobins purge Girondins
July 1793	Robespierre assumes leadership of Committee of Public Safety
July 1793–July 1794	Reign of Terror
July 1794	Robespierre is guillotined
August 1794	Thermidorian reaction begins
October 1795	Directory is established
November 1799	Napoleon seizes power
1804	Napoleon proclaimed emperor; Napoleonic Code
1805	Battle of Trafalgar; Battle of Austerlitz
1812	Invasion of Russia
1814	Napoleon abdicates
1815	Battle of Waterloo

resist British troops if necessary. The Volunteer Movement was undercut when greater parliamentary autonomy for Ireland was granted in 1782, following the repeal of many restrictions on Irish commerce. Unlike the Americans, the Irish elites faced an internal challenge to their own authority—the Catholic population whom they had dominated for centuries—so they were willing to reach an accommodation with the British government.

Meanwhile, a political crisis with constitutional overtones was also brewing in the Netherlands. Tensions between the stadholder of the House of Orange and the merchant oligarchies of the major cities deepened during the American Revolution, because the Dutch were engaged in a commercial war against the British, to whom the stadholder was believed to be sympathetic. The conflict ceased to be wholly traditional because the representatives of the various cities, calling themselves the Dutch "Patriot" party, made wide claims to "liberty," like those of the American revolutionaries. Also, middling urban dwellers, long disenfranchised by these oligarchies, demanded "liberty," too—that is, political enfranchisement within the cities—and briefly took over the Patriot movement. An invasion in 1787 restored the power of the stadholder, the prince of Orange.

Both the Irish "volunteers" and the Dutch "Patriots," though members of very limited movements, echoed the American rebels in practical and ideological ways. Both were influenced by the economic and political consequences of Britain's relationship with its colonies. Both were inspired by the success of the American rebels and their claims for political self-determination.

Desire for political reform flared in Poland as well during this period. Reform along lines suggested by Enlightenment precepts was accepted as a necessity by Polish leaders after the first partition of Poland in 1772 had stripped the state of some of its wealthiest territories (see Map 16.1 on page 426). In 1788, however, reforming gentry in the *sejm* (representative assembly) went further, establishing a commission to write a constitution following the American example. The resulting document, known as the May 3 (1791) Constitution, was the first codified constitution in Europe; it was read and admired by George Washington.

The Constitution established a constitutional monarchy. However, Catherine the Great, empress of Russia, would not tolerate a constitutional government so close to her own autocratic regime; she ordered an invasion of Poland in 1792. The second, more extensive partition of Poland ensued, to be followed in turn in 1794 by a widespread insurrection against Russian rule. The uprising was mercilessly suppressed by Russian and Prussian troops. Unlike the Americans from whom they drew inspiration, the Poles' constitutional experiment was doomed by the power of its neighbor. A third partition in 1795 wiped Poland off the map—a situation that persisted for over 120 years.

The American Revolution and the Kingdom of France

As one of Britain's greatest commercial and political rivals, France naturally was drawn into Britain's struggle with its North American colonies. The consequences for France were momentous. First, the huge expense of aid for the American rebels helped accelerate a financial crisis in the French monarchy. Second, French involvement exposed many French aristocrats and common soldiers to the "enlightened" international community.

Rivalry with Great Britain gave France a special relationship with the American colonies and their fight for independence. In the Seven Years' War (1756–1763), France had lost many of its colonies, and some of the king's ministers pressed for an aggressive colonial policy to make up for these losses. The American Revolution seemed to offer the perfect opportunity. The French extended covert aid to the Americans from the very beginning of the conflict in 1775. After the first major American victory—at the Battle of Saratoga in 1777—France recognized the United States, established an alliance with them, and committed French troops. This support was decisive. In 1781 the French fleet kept reinforcements from reaching the British force besieged at Yorktown by George Washington. The American victory at Yorktown effectively ended the war; the colonies' independence was formally recognized by the Treaty of Paris in 1783.

The effect on France was complicated. Aid for the Americans saddled France with a debt equal to one-quarter of the government's total debt. A less tangible effect was also important. About nine thousand French soldiers, sailors, and aristocrats participated in the war. The best known was the Marquis de Lafayette, who became an aide to George Washington and helped command American troops. For many humble men, the war was simply employment. For others, it was a quest of sorts. For them, the Enlightenment belief in the rationality of men, natural rights, and natural laws by which society should be organized was brought to life in America.

Exposure to the American conflict occurred at the French court, too. Beginning in 1775, a permanent American mission to Versailles lobbied hard for aid and later managed the flow of that assistance. The chief American emissary was Benjamin Franklin (1706–1790), whose writings and scientific experiments were already known to French elites. His talents—among them a skillful exploitation of a simple, Quakerlike demeanor—succeeded in promoting the idealization of America at the French court.

The United States Constitution and the various state constitutions and debates surrounding them were all published in Paris and much discussed in salons and at court. America became the prototype of what Enlightenment philosophy said was possible. It was hailed as the place where the irrationalities of inherited privilege did not prevail. A British observer, Arthur Young (1741–1820), believed that "the American revolution has laid the foundation of another in France, if [the French] government does not take care of itself."[1]

By the mid-1780s there was no longer a question of whether the French regime would experience reform but rather what form the reform would take. The royal government was almost bankrupt. A significant minority of the politically active elite was convinced of the fundamental irrationality of France's system of government.

The Crisis of the Old Regime

The *Old Regime*—a term for the political structure that existed before the Revolution—was brought to the point of crisis in the late 1780s. Three main factors can be discerned: (1) an antiquated system for collecting revenue; (2) institutional constraints on the monarchy that defended privileged interests; and (3) an elite public opinion that envisioned thoroughgoing reform and pushed the monarchy in that direction. Another factor was the ineptitude of the king, Louis XVI (r. 1774–1793).

Louis was a kind, well-meaning man better suited to carry out the responsibilities of a petty bureaucrat than to be king. The queen, the Austrian Marie Antoinette (1755–1793), was unpopular. She was regarded with suspicion by those for whom the alliance with Austria had never felt natural. She, too, was politically inept and widely rumored to be selfishly wasteful of royal resources.

The fiscal crisis of the monarchy was an outgrowth of the system in which the greatest wealth was protected by traditional privileges. At the top of the social and political pyramid were the nobles, a legal grouping that included warriors and royal officials. Since nobility conferred exemption from much taxation, the royal government could not directly tax its wealthiest subjects.

This situation existed throughout much of Europe, a legacy of the individual contractual relationships that had formed the political and economic framework of medieval Europe. Unique to France was the strength of the institutions that defended this system. Of particular importance were the royal law courts, the parlements, which claimed a right of judicial review over royal edicts. All the Parlementaires were noble. Louis XV (d. 1774) had successfully undermined the power of the parlements, but Louis XVI buckled under pressure and restored them to full power.

Deficit financing had been a way of life for centuries. After early efforts at reform, Louis XIV (d. 1715) had reverted to such old expedients as selling offices, which only added to the weight of privileged investment in the old order. England had established a national bank to free its government from the problem, but the comparable French effort early in the century had been undercapitalized and had failed.

Short-term economic crises added to the problem. During Louis XVI's reign there were several years of disastrously poor harvests, and there was a persistent downturn in the economy. The weakness of the economy proved to be a crucial reason for the failure of overall reform.

The king employed able finance ministers, who tried to replace the tangle of taxes with a simpler system in which all would pay and to eliminate local tariffs, which were stifling commerce. The parlements and many courtiers and aristocrats, as well as ordinary people, resisted.

Ordinary people did not trust the "free market" (free from traditional trade controls) for grain; most feared that speculators would buy up the grain supply and people would starve. Trying to implement such reforms in a time of grain shortage almost guaranteed their failure. Moreover, many supported the parlements out of self-interest and because they were the only institution capable of standing up to the monarchy. Yet not all members of the elite opposed reform. The imprint of "enlightened" public opinion shaped in salons and literary societies was apparent in the thinking of some aristocrats.

In 1787 the king called an "Assembly of Notables"—an ad hoc group of elites—to support him in facing down the parlements and implementing reform. He found little support even among men known to be sympathetic to reform. Some did not support particular reforms. Others, reflecting the influence of the American Revolution, maintained that a "constitutional" body such as the Estates General, which had not been called since 1614, needed to make these decisions.

Ironically, nobles and clergy who opposed reform supported the call for the Estates General, for they assumed that they could control its deliberations. Since the three Estates met and voted separately by "order"—clergy (First Estate), nobles (Second Estate), and commoners (Third Estate)—the clergy and nobles could nullify whatever the Third Estate might propose.

In 1788 deputies to the Estates General were elected by intermediate assemblies chosen by wide male suffrage. Louis assumed there was widespread loyalty to the monarchy in the provinces, and he wished to tap into it by means of this voting. Louis also agreed that the Third Estate should have twice as many deputies as the other two Estates, but he did not authorize voting by head rather than by order.

Louis faced a critical situation when the Estates General convened in May 1789. Political pamphlets abounded arguing that the Third Estate deserved enhanced power because it had the mandate of the people. The most important pamphlet was *What Is the Third Estate?* (1789) by Joseph Emmanuel Sieyès (1748–1836), a church official from the diocese of Chartres. The sympathies of Abbé Sieyès, as he was known, were with the Third Estate: His career had suffered because he was not noble. Sieyès argued that the Third Estate represented the nation because it did not reflect special privilege.

Among the deputies of the first two Estates were some men, like the Marquis de Lafayette (1757–1834), who were sympathetic to reform. More important, the elections had returned to the Third Estate a large majority of deputies who reflected the most radical political thought possible for men of their standing. Most were lawyers or government functionaries but, like Sieyès, of low social rank. They frequented provincial academies, salons, and political societies. They were determined on reform and had little stake in the system as it was.

1789: The Revolution Begins

The three Estates met at Versailles, and the ineptness of the Crown quickly became clear. On the first day of the meetings, Louis and his ministers failed to introduce a program of reforms for the deputies to consider. This failure raised doubt about the monarchy's commitment to reform. More important, it allowed the political initiative to pass to the Third Estate. The deputies challenged the Crown's insistence that the three Estates meet and vote separately. Deputies of the Third Estate refused to be certified (that is, to have their credentials officially recognized) as members of only the Third Estate rather than as members of the Estates General as a whole.

For six weeks the Estates General was unable to meet officially, and the king did nothing to break the impasse. During this interlude, more and more deputies were won over to the notion that the three Estates should meet together and that the reform process must begin in the most systematic way: France must have a written constitution.

By the middle of June, more than thirty reformist members of the clergy were sitting jointly with the Third Estate, which had invited the deputies of all three Estates to meet and be certified together. On June 17 the Third Estate declared itself the National Assembly of France. At first the king did nothing, but when the deputies arrived on the morning of June 20, they discovered they had been locked out of the hall. Undaunted, they assembled instead in a nearby indoor tennis court and produced the document that has come to be known as the "Tennis Court Oath." It was a collective pledge to meet until a written constitution had been achieved.

The king continued to handle the situation with both ill-timed self-assertion and attempts at compromise. As more and more deputies from the First and Second Estates joined the National Assembly, Louis "ordered" the remaining deputies to join it, too. Simultaneously, however, he ordered troops to come to Paris, which stirred unrest in the capital. Paris, with a population of about 600,000 in 1789, was one of the largest cities in Europe. Some assumed the king intended to starve Paris and destroy the National Assembly. Already they considered the Assembly to be a guarantor of acceptable government.

It took little—the announcement of the dismissal of a reformist finance minister—for Paris to erupt in demonstrations and looting. Crowds besieged City Hall and the royal armory, where they seized thousands of weapons. A popular militia formed as citizens armed themselves. Armed crowds assailed other sites of royal authority, including the huge fortified prison, the Bastille, on the morning of July 14. The Bastille now held only

The Tennis Court Oath It was raining on June 20 when the deputies found themselves barred from their meeting hall and sought shelter in the royal tennis court. Their defiance created one of the turning points of the Revolution; the significance was recognized several years later by this painting's artist. *(Photographie Bulloz)*

a handful of petty criminals, but it was a symbol of royal power and, it was assumed, held large supplies of arms. The siege was successful because the garrison had not been given firm orders to fire on the crowds if necessary.

The citizens' victory was a great embarrassment to royal authority. The king had to embrace the popular movement. He came to Paris and in front of a crowd at City Hall donned the red and blue cockade worn by the militia and ordinary folk as a badge of resolve and defiance. This symbolic action signaled the legitimation of politics based on new principles.

Encouraged by events in Paris, inhabitants of cities and towns around France staged similar uprisings. In many, the machinery of royal government broke down completely. City councils, officials, and even Parlementaires were thrown out of office. Popular militias took control of the streets. There was a simultaneous wave of uprisings in rural areas. Most of them were the result of food shortages, but their timing added momentum to the political protests in urban areas. These events forced the members of the National Assembly to pass legislation to satisfy popular protests against economic and political privileges.

On August 4 the Assembly issued a set of decrees abolishing the remnants of powers that landlords had enjoyed since the Middle Ages, including the right to compel peasants to labor for them and the bondage of serfdom itself. Although largely symbolic, because serfdom and forced labor had been eliminated in much of France, these changes were hailed as the "end of feudalism." A blow was also struck at established religion by abolishing the *tithe*, an important church tax. At the end of August, the Assembly issued a Declaration of the Rights of Man and the Citizen, a bold assertion of principles condemning the old order.

In September, the deputies debated the king's role in a new constitutional government. Deputies known as "monarchists" fought with more radical deputies over the role of elites in government and whether the king should hold legislative veto power. After deliberation, the Assembly reached a compromise. The king was

Women's March on Versailles On October 5, 1789, Parisian marketwomen marched the 12 miles to Versailles, some provisioning themselves with tools, stolen firearms, and horses as they left the capital. *(Jean-Loup Charmet)*

given a three-year suspensive veto—the power to suspend legislation. This was still a formidable amount of power but a drastic limitation of his formerly absolute sovereignty.

Again, Louis resorted to troops. This time, he called them directly to Versailles, where the Assembly sat. News of the troops' arrival provoked outrage, which increased with the threat of another grain shortage. Early on the morning of October 5, women in street markets in Paris responded to the food shortages with immediate collective action, shouting for bread at the steps of City Hall. Women often led protests over bread shortages, because they procured food for their families. But this bread riot became political. A crowd of thousands gathered and decided to go all the way to Versailles, accompanied by the popular militia (now called the "National Guard"), to petition the king directly. At Versailles, they presented a delegation to the National Assembly, and a joint delegation of the women and deputies was dispatched to see the king. Louis ordered stored grain supplies distributed in Paris, and he agreed to accept the constitutional role that the Assembly had voted for him. The entire royal family was escorted back to Paris by militia and city women. The king was now in the hands of his people. He was still king, but his powers were limited, and his authority was badly shaken. The Assembly had begun to govern in the name of the "nation."

THE FRENCH REVOLUTION

The French Revolution was a complicated affair; consensus and stability were extremely elusive. Even among elites convinced of the need for reform there was a wide range of opinion. The people of Paris continued to be an important force for change. Country people also became active, primarily in resisting changes forced on them by the central government. The continuing problems that had precipitated the Revolution in the first place—the indebtedness of the government, economic difficulties, and recurrent shortages of grain—remained unresolved. All of the wrangling within France was further complicated by foreign reaction. Managing foreign war soon became a routine burden for the fragile revolutionary governments.

The First Phase Completed, 1789–1791

At the end of 1789, Paris was in ferment, but there was no disastrous division between king and Assembly. The capital continued to be the center of lively political debate. Salons continued to meet; academies and private societies proliferated. Deputies to the Assembly swelled the ranks of these societies or helped to found new ones. Several would be important throughout the Revolution—particularly the Jacobin Club, named for the monastic order whose buildings the members used as a meeting hall.

The clubs represented a wide range of revolutionary opinion. Some, in which ordinary Parisians were well represented, focused on economic policies that would directly benefit common people. Women were active in a few of the more radical groups. Monarchists dominated other clubs. At first similar to the salons and debating societies of the Enlightenment era, the clubs increasingly became both sites of political action and sources of political pressure on the government. A bevy of popular newspapers also contributed to the vigorous political life in the capital.

The broad front of revolutionary consensus began to break apart as the Assembly forged ahead with decisions about the constitution and with policies necessary to remedy France's still-desperate financial situation. The largest portion of the untapped wealth of the nation lay with the Catholic church, an obvious target for anticlerical reformers. The Assembly seized most of the vast properties of the church and declared them national property to be sold for revenue. The clergy became salaried officials of the state. Monasteries were abolished; monks and nuns were granted pensions to permit them to continue working as nurses and teachers where possible.

Since revenue was needed faster than church property could be inventoried and sold, government bonds (*assignats*) were issued against the eventual sale of the properties. Unfortunately, in the cash-strapped economy, the bonds were treated like money, their value became inflated, and the government never realized the hoped-for profits. The Civil Constitution of the Clergy, which required clergy to swear an oath of loyalty to the state, was passed by the Assembly in July 1790 because the clerical deputies opposing it were outvoted. More than half of the clergy did take the oath of loyalty. Those who refused, concentrated among the higher clergy, were in theory thrown out of their offices. Antirevolutionary sentiment grew among people to whom the church was still important.

Meanwhile, the Assembly proceeded with administrative and judicial reform. The deputies abolished the medieval provinces as administrative districts and replaced them with uniform *départements* (departments). They declared that local officials would be elected—a revolutionary dispersal of power that had previously belonged to the king.

As work on the constitution drew to a close in the spring of 1791, the king decided that he had had enough. Louis was now a virtual prisoner in the Tuileries Palace in the heart of Paris. Afraid for himself and his family, he and a few loyal aides worked out a plan to flee France. The king and the members of his immediate family set out incognito on June 20, 1791. However, the royal party missed a rendezvous with a troop escort and was stopped along the way—and recognized.

Louis and his family were returned to Paris and now lived under lightly disguised house arrest. The circumstances of his flight were quickly discovered. He had intended to invade France with Austrian troops if necessary. Thus, in July 1791, just as the Assembly was completing its proposal for a constitutional monarchy, the constitution it had created began to seem unworkable because the king was not trustworthy.

Editorials and popular demonstrations against the monarchy echoed these sentiments. On September 14 the king swore to uphold the constitution. He had no choice. The event became an occasion for celebration, but tensions remained. Though a liberal document for its day, the constitution reflected the views of the elite deputies who had created it. The right to vote, based on a minimal property qualification, was given to about half of all adult men. But these men only chose electors, for whom the property qualifications were higher. The electors in turn chose the deputies to national bodies and also local officials.

Further, no political rights were accorded to women. Educated women had joined Parisian clubs such as the *Cercle sociale* (Social Circle), where opinion favored extending rights to women. Through such clubs, these women had tried to influence the National Assembly. But the Assembly granted neither political rights nor legal equality to women, nor did it pass other laws beneficial to women such as legalizing divorce or mandating female education. The prevailing view of women among deputies seemed to reflect those of the Enlightenment philosophe Rousseau, who imagined women's competence to be entirely circumscribed within the family. *A Declaration of the Rights of Woman* was drafted by a woman named Olympe de Gouges to draw attention to the treatment of women in the constitution.

The fragility of the new system became clear soon after the constitution was implemented. Since the National Assembly had declared that its members could not serve in the first assembly elected under the constitution, the members of the newly elected Legislative Assembly, which began to meet in October 1791, lacked any of the cohesiveness that would have come from collective experience. Also, unlike the previous National Assembly, they did not represent a broad range of opinion but were mostly republicans.

In fact, the Legislative Assembly was dominated by republican members of the Jacobin Club known as Girondins, after the region in France from which many of the club's leaders came. The policies of these new deputies and continued pressure from the ordinary citizens of Paris would cause the constitutional monarchy to collapse in less than a year.

The Second Revolution and Foreign War, 1791–1793

An additional pressure on the new regime soon arose from outside France. Antirevolutionary aristocratic émigrés had taken refuge in German states and were planning to invade France. Although the German rulers did little to aid the émigrés, Austria and Prussia declared in the Declaration of Pilnitz of August 1791 that they would intervene if necessary to support the monarchy in France.

The threat of invasion seemed more real to the revolutionaries in Paris than it actually was. Many deputies wanted war. They assumed that the outcome would be a French defeat, which would lead to a popular uprising that would rid them, at last, of the monarchy. In April 1792, under pressure from the Assembly, Louis XVI declared war against Austria. From this point, foreign war would be an ongoing factor in the revolution.

At first, the war was a disaster for France. The army had not been reorganized into an effective fighting force after the loss of many aristocratic officers and the addition of newly self-aware citizens. On one occasion, troops insisted on putting an officer's command to a vote. The defeats heightened criticism of the monarchy.

By July 1792, tensions had become acute. There was a severe grain shortage due to a poor harvest and the needs of the armies; Austrian and Prussian troops were threatening to invade; and the populace was better organized and more determined than ever before. In each of the forty-eight "sections"—administrative wards—of Paris a miniature popular assembly thrashed out the issues of the day just as deputies in the nationwide Legislative Assembly did. Derisively called *sans-culottes,* "without knee pants" (worn by the elite), the Parisians in the section assemblies included shopkeepers, artisans, and laborers. Their political organization enhanced their influence with the Assembly, the clubs, and the newspapers in the capital. By late July most sections of the city had approved a petition calling for the exile of the king, the election of new city officials, the exemption of the poor from taxation, and other radical measures.

In August they took matters into their own hands. On the night of August 9, after careful preparations, the section assemblies sent representatives who constituted themselves as a new city government with the aim of "saving the state." They then proceeded with an organized assault on the Tuileries Palace, where the royal family was living. In the bloody confrontation, hundreds of royal guards and citizens died. The king and his family were imprisoned in one of the fortified towers in the city, under guard of the popularly controlled city government.

The storming of the Tuileries inaugurated the second major phase of the Revolution: the establishment of republican government in place of the monarchy. Since some deputies had fled, the people of Paris now physically dominated the Legislative Assembly. The Assembly was dissolved to make way for another body to be elected by universal manhood suffrage. On September 20, that assembly—known as the National Convention—began to meet. The next day, the Convention declared the end of the monarchy and began to work on a constitution for the new republic.

Coincidentally, on the same day, French forces won their first real victory over the allied Austrian and Prussian forces. It was a profound psychological victory. A citizen army had defeated professional, royal forces. The new republican regime let it be known that its armies were not merely for self-defense but for the liberation of all peoples in the "name of the French Nation."

The Convention faced the divisive issue of what to do with the king. Louis had not done anything truly treasonous, but some of the king's correspondence, discovered after the storming of the Tuileries, provided a pretext for charges of treason. The Convention held a trial for him, lasting from December 11, 1792, to January 15, 1793. He was found guilty by an overwhelming vote (683 to 39). Less certain was the sentence: Louis was condemned to death by a narrow majority, 387 to 334. On January 21, 1793, Louis mounted the scaffold in a public square near the Tuileries and was beheaded.

The Faltering Republic and the Terror, 1793–1794

In February 1793, the French republic was at war with virtually every state in Europe, except the Scandinavian kingdoms and Russia. Moreover, the regime faced massive and widespread counterrevolutionary uprisings within France. Nevertheless, for a time, the republican government functioned adequately. In May 1793, it passed the first Law of the Maximum, which tried to fix the price of grain so that urban people could afford their staple food.

The Convention established an executive body, the Committee of Public Safety. As the months passed, it acted with greater and greater autonomy to institute various policies and eradicate internal and external enemies. The broadly based republican government represented by the Convention began to disintegrate. In June 1793, a group of extreme Jacobins, pushed by the Parisian sections, purged the Girondin deputies from the Convention and arrested many of them. The Girondins were republicans who favored an activist government in the people's behalf, but they were less radical than the Jacobins and less willing to share power with the citizens of Paris. After the purge, the Convention still met, but most authority was held by the Committee of Public Safety.

New uprisings against the regime began. Added to counterrevolutionary revolts by peasants and aristocrats were new revolts by Girondin sympathizers. As resistance to the government mounted and the foreign threat continued, a dramatic event in Paris led the Committee of Public Safety officially to adopt a policy of political repression. A well-known figure of the Revolution, Jean Paul Marat (1743–1793), publisher of a radical republican newspaper very popular with ordinary Parisians, was murdered on July 13 by Charlotte Corday (1768–1793), a fervent supporter of the Girondins and their moderate republicanism. Shortly afterward, a long-time member of the Jacobin Club, Maximilien Robespierre (1758–1794), joined the Committee and called for "Terror"—the systematic repression of internal enemies.

Robespierre embodied all the contradictions of the policy of Terror. He was an austere, almost prim, man who lived very modestly—a model, of sorts, of the virtuous, disinterested citizen. The policies followed by the government during the year of his greatest influence, from July 1793 to July 1794, included generous, rational, and humane actions to benefit ordinary citizens as well as the policy of official Terror. (See the box "Robespierre Justifies the Terror.")

The guillotine had been at work against identified enemies of the regime since the previous autumn, but now a more energetic apparatus of terror was instituted. The Law of Suspects allowed citizens to be arrested simply on vague suspicion of counterrevolutionary sympathies. Revolutionary tribunals made arbitrary arrests and rendered summary judgments. In October a steady stream of executions began, beginning with the queen, imprisoned since the storming of the Tuileries the year before. The imprisoned Girondin deputies followed, and then the process continued relentlessly. In Paris there were about 2600 executions from 1793 to 1794.

Around France, verdicts from revolutionary tribunals resulted in approximately 14,000 executions. Another 10,000 to 12,000 people died in prison. Ten thousand or more were killed, usually by summary execution, after the defeat of counterrevolutionary uprisings. For example, 2000 people were summarily executed in Lyon when a Girondin revolt collapsed there in October. The repression in Paris, however, was unique because of the city's role in the nation's political life. The aim of the repression was not merely to quash resistance; it was also to stifle dissent. The victims in Paris included sans-culottes as well as aristocrats and former deputies.

The Terror notwithstanding, the government of the Committee of Public Safety was effective in providing direction for the nation at a critical time. It instituted the first mass conscription of citizens into the army (*levée en masse*), which created an effective popular army for the first time in the modern world. In the autumn of 1793, this army won impressive victories. Accomplishments in domestic policy included an extended

Robespierre Justifies the Terror

In this excerpt from a speech before the Convention in December 1793, Robespierre justifies the revolutionary government's need to act in an extraconstitutional manner. He echoes Rousseau's notion of a highly abstract sense of the public good.

The defenders of the Republic must adopt Caesar's maxim, for they believe that "nothing has been done so long as anything remains to be done." Enough dangers still face us to engage all our efforts. It has not fully extended the valor of our Republican soldiers to conquer a few Englishmen and a few traitors. A task no less important, and one more difficult, now awaits us: to sustain an energy sufficient to defeat the constant intrigues of all the enemies of our freedom and to bring to a triumphant realization the principles that must be the cornerstone of public welfare. . . . Revolution is the war waged by liberty against its enemies; a constitution . . . crowns the edifice of freedom once victory has been won and the nation is at peace. . . . The principal concern of a constitutional government is civil liberty; that of a revolutionary government, public liberty. [A] revolutionary government is obliged to defend the state itself against the factions that assail it from every quarter. To good citizens revolutionary government owes the full protection of the state; to the enemies of the people it owes only death.

Is a revolutionary government the less just and the less legitimate because it must be more vigorous in its actions and freer in its movement than ordinary government? . . . It also has its rules, all based on justice and public order. . . . It has nothing in common with arbitrary rule; it is public interest which governs it and not the whims of private individuals.

Thanks to five years of treason and tyranny, thanks to our credulity and lack of foresight . . . Austria and England, Russia, Prussia, and Italy had time to set up in our country a secret government to challenge the authority of our own. . . . We shall strike terror, not in the hearts of patriots, but in the haunts of foreign brigands.

Source: George Rudé, ed., *Robespierre* (Englewood Cliffs, N.J.: Prentice-Hall, 1967), pp. 58–63.

Law of the Maximum (September 1793) that applied to necessary commodities other than bread. Extensive plans were made for a system of free and universal primary education. Slavery in the French colonies was abolished in February 1794. Divorce, first legalized in 1792, was made easier for women to obtain.

In the name of "reason" and progress, traditional rituals and rhythms of life were changed. One reform of long-term significance was the introduction of the metric system of weights and measures. Equally "rational" but not ultimately successful was the elimination of the traditional calendar. The traditional days, weeks, and months were replaced by forty-day months and *decadi* (ten-day weeks with one day of rest). All saints' days and Christian holidays were eliminated. The years had already been changed—Year I had been declared with the founding of the republic in 1792.

Churches were rededicated as "temples of reason." Believing that atheism left people with no basis for personal or national morality, Robespierre sought to promote a cult of the Supreme Being. Public festivals organized around this principle were solemn civic ceremonies intended

Robespierre the Incorruptible A lawyer who had often championed the poor, Robespierre was elected to the Estates General in 1789 and was a consistent advocate of republican government from the beginning of the Revolution. His unswerving loyalty to his political principles earned him the nickname "the Incorruptible." *(Musée des Beaux-Arts, Lille)*

to ritualize and legitimize the new political order. The various innovations were not necessarily welcomed. The French people generally resented the elimination of the traditional calendar. In the countryside, there were massive peasant uprisings over the loss of poor relief, community life, and familiar ritual.

Divorce law and economic regulation were a boon, especially to urban women, but women's participation in sectional assemblies and in all organized political activity—which had been energetic and widespread—was banned in October 1793. The particular target of the regime was the Society of Revolutionary Republican Women, a powerful club representing the interests of female sans-culottes. By banning women from political life, the regime hoped to ground its legitimacy, since the seemingly "natural" exclusion of women might make the new system of government appear part of the "natural" order. Elimination of women's clubs and women's participation in section assemblies also excluded a source of popular power from which the regime was now trying to distance itself.

Several critics of Robespierre and his allies were guillotined because they differed with them on policy and on the continuing need for the Terror itself. Their deaths helped precipitate the end of the Terror by further shrinking Robespierre's power. Deputies to the Convention finally dared to move against Robespierre in July 1794. French armies had scored a major victory over Austrian troops on June 26, so there no longer seemed to be any need for the Terror. In late July (the month of Thermidor, according to the revolutionary calendar), the Convention voted to arrest Robespierre. On July 28 and 29, Robespierre and his associates—about a hundred in all—were guillotined, and the Terror ended.

Thermidorian Reaction and the Directory, 1794–1799

After the death of Robespierre, the Convention reclaimed many of the executive powers that the Committee of Public Safety had seized. The Convention dismantled the apparatus of the Terror and forced the revolutionary tribunals to adopt ordinary legal procedures. The Convention also passed into law some initiatives, such as expanded public education, that had been proposed in the preceding year but not enacted. This phase of the Revolution that followed the Terror is called the "Thermidorian Reaction" because it began in the month of Thermidor (July 19–August 17).

The stability of the government, however, was threatened from the outset. There were counterrevolutionary uprisings in western France and popular uprisings against the Terror throughout France. Officials of the previous regime were lynched, and prorevolutionary groups were massacred by their fellow citizens.

With the apparatus of Terror dismantled, the Convention was unable to enforce controls on the supply and price of bread. Thus, economic difficulties and a hard winter produced famine by the spring of 1795. In May crowds marched on the Convention, chanting "Bread and the Constitution of '93," referring to the republican constitution drafted by the Convention but never implemented. The demonstrations were forcefully dispersed.

Fearful of a renewed, popularly supported Terror, or even of desperate popular support for a royalist uprising, the Convention drafted a new constitution. The new plan allowed fairly widespread (but not universal) male suffrage, but only for electors, who would choose the deputies. Property qualifications for being an elector were very high, so all but elite citizens were effectively disenfranchised.

In the fall of 1795, as the Convention was preparing for new elections, a final popular uprising shook Paris. When a crowd of twenty thousand or more converged on the Tuileries Palace, the officer in charge ordered his troops to fire. Parisian crowds never again seriously threatened the government, even though living conditions worsened as food prices soared. The army officer who issued the command to fire was Napoleon Bonaparte.

A new government took office under the provisions of the new constitution. It was called the Directory for the executive council of five men chosen by the upper house of the new legislature. To avoid the concentration of authority that had produced the Terror, the members of the Convention had tried to enshrine separation of powers in the new system. However, because of unsettled conditions throughout France, the governments under the Directory were never stable and never free from attempted coups. The most spectacular challenge, the Conspiracy of Equals, was led by extreme Jacobins who wanted to restore popular government and promote greater equality of property. The conspiracy ended with arrests and executions in 1797.

In 1799, conditions reached a critical juncture. France was again at war with a coalition of states and was faring badly. The demands of the war effort, together with other economic woes, brought the government again to the brink of bankruptcy. The government seemed to be losing control of the countryside; there were continued royalist uprisings and local political vendettas.

Two members of the Directory now invited General Napoleon Bonaparte to help them form a government that they could more strictly control. They plotted with Napoleon and his brother Louis Bonaparte to seize power on November 9, 1799.

THE NAPOLEONIC ERA

Talented, daring, and ruthless, Napoleon Bonaparte (1769–1821) was able to assess the situation in France and profit from the general state of political confusion. His audacity and personal magnetism were matched by his determination: He was a charismatic man of action who seemed capable of delivering both high ideals and social order. Once in power, he stabilized the political scene by enshrining in law the more conservative gains of the Revolution. He also used his abilities as a general to continue France's wars of conquest.

Napoleon's troops, in effect, exported the Revolution when they conquered most of Europe. Law codes were reformed, governing elites were opened to talent, and public works were undertaken in most states under French control. Yet French conquest also meant domination, pure and simple, and involvement in France's rivalry with Britain.

Napoleon: From Soldier to Emperor, 1799–1804

Napoleon was from Corsica, a Mediterranean island that had passed from Genoese to French control in the eighteenth century. The second son of a large gentry family, he was educated at military academies in France, and he married the politically well-connected widow Joséphine de Beauharnais (1763–1814), whose aristocratic husband had been a victim of the Terror.

By 1799, Napoleon was well known and popular because of his military victories. He had demonstrated his reliability and ruthlessness in 1795 when he ordered troops guarding the Convention to fire on the Parisian crowd. In 1796 and 1797 he conquered all of northern Italy, forcing Austria to relinquish that territory as well as the Austrian Netherlands, which revolutionary armies had seized in 1795. He then commanded an invasion of Egypt in an attempt to strike at British influence and trade connections in the eastern Mediterranean. The Egyptian campaign failed in its goals, but individual spectacular victories during the campaign ensured Napoleon's military reputation.

Napoleon's partners in the new government after the November coup in 1799 soon learned of his great political ambition and skill. In theory, the new system was to be a streamlined version of the Directory: Napoleon was to be first among equals in a three-man executive—First Consul, according to borrowed Roman terminology. But Napoleon soon asserted his primacy among them and began not only to dominate executive functions but also to bypass the various legislative bodies in the new regime.

Napoleon was careful to avoid heavy-handed displays of power. He cleverly sought ratification of each stage of his assumption of power through national plebiscites—a national referendum in which all eligible voters could vote for or against Napoleon's proposal. One plebiscite was for a new constitution in 1800; another, in 1802, confirmed support for his claim to consulship for life. Critical to the success of his increasingly authoritarian regime was his effort to include, among his ministers, advisers, and bureaucrats, men of many political stripes—Jacobins, reforming liberals, even former Old Regime bureaucrats. He welcomed many exiles back to France, including all but the most ardent royalists.

Napoleon combined toleration with ruthlessness. Between 1800 and 1804 he imprisoned, executed, or exiled dozens of individuals for alleged Jacobin agitation or royalist sympathies. His final gesture to intimidate royalist opposition came in 1804 when he kidnapped and coldly murdered a Bourbon prince who had been in exile in Germany.

By the terms of the Treaty of Amiens in 1802, Napoleon made peace with Britain, France's one remaining enemy. The short-lived peace only papered over the two countries' commercial and strategic rivalries, but it gave Napoleon room to establish his rule more securely in France. One of the most important steps had already been accomplished by the Concordat of 1801. The aim of this treaty with the pope was to solve the problem of church-state relations that for years had caused antirevolutionary rebellions. The agreement allowed for the resumption of Catholic worship and the continued support of the clergy by the state but also accepted the more dramatic changes accomplished by the Revolution. Church lands that had been sold were guaranteed to their new owners. Protestant churches were allowed and their clergy was paid, although Catholicism was recognized as the "religion of the majority of Frenchmen." Later, Napoleon granted new rights to Jews.

Napoleon Crossing the Great St. Bernard This stirring portrait by the great neoclassical painter Jacques-Louis David memorializes Napoleon's 1796 crossing of the Alps before his victorious Italian campaign, as a general under the Directory. The painting depicts the moment heroically rather than realistically (Napoleon wisely crossed the Alps on a sure-footed mule, not a stallion), in part because it was executed in 1801–1802. Napoleon, as First Consul, wanted images of himself that would justify his increasingly ambitious claims to power. *(Louvre © R.M.N.)*

The law code that Napoleon established in 1804 was much like his accommodation with the church in its limited acceptance of revolutionary gains. His Civil Code reflected the revolutionary legacy in its guarantee of equality before the law and its requirement for the taxation of all social classes; it also enshrined modern forms of property ownership and civil contracts. But neither the code nor Napoleon's political regime fostered individual rights, especially for women. Women lost all the rights they had gained during the Revolution. Fathers' control over their families was enhanced. Divorce was no longer permitted except in rare instances. Women lost all property rights when they married, and they generally faced legal domination by fathers and husbands.

More in keeping with the goals of the Revolution, Napoleon put France on a better financial footing by establishing a national bank. He also streamlined and centralized the administrative system, set up in 1789, by establishing the office of prefect to govern the départements. All prefects were appointed by Napoleon.

Some of these legal and administrative changes occurred after Napoleon's final coup—declaring himself emperor. This was a bold move, but Napoleon approached it dexterously. Years before, Napoleon had begun to sponsor an active court life appropriate to imperial pretensions.

The empire was proclaimed in May 1804 with the approval of the Senate; it was approved by another plebiscite. Members of Napoleon's family were given princely status, and a number of his favorites received titles. These brought no legal privileges but signaled social and political distinctions of great importance. Old nobles were allowed to use their titles again on this basis.

Conquering Europe, 1805–1810

Napoleon maintained relatively peaceful relations with other nations while he consolidated power at home, but the truces did not last. Tensions with the British quickly re-escalated when Britain resumed aggression against French shipping in 1803, and Napoleon countered by seizing Hanover, the ancestral German home of the English king. Then Napoleon seized several Italian territories and extended his influence in other German states. By 1805, all the states of Europe were threatened. Napoleon began to gather a large French force on the northern coast of France, with which he could invade England.

The British fleet, commanded by Horatio Nelson (1758–1805), intercepted the combined French and Spanish fleets that were to have been the invasion flotilla and inflicted a devastating defeat off Cape Trafalgar in southern Spain (see Map 17.1) on October 21, 1805. The victory ensured British mastery of the seas and contributed to Napoleon's eventual defeat.

In December 1805, after some preliminary small-scale victories, Napoleon's army confronted a Russian force near Austerlitz, north of Vienna (see Map 17.1). Tsar Alexander I (r. 1801–1825) led his own troops into a battle that he ought to have avoided. Austrian reinforcements could not reach him in time, and French armies shattered the Russian forces. The Battle of Austerlitz was Napoleon's most spectacular victory. Austria sued for peace. In further battles in 1806, French forces defeated Prussia as well as Russian armies once again. Prussia was virtually dismembered by the subsequent Treaty of Tilsit (1807), but Napoleon tried to work out terms to make Russia into a contented ally. His hold on central Europe would not be secure with a hostile Russia.

Napoleon defeated Austria in the Battle of Wagram in July 1809 and, like Russia, Austria accepted French political and economic hegemony in a sort of alliance. By 1810, Napoleon had transformed most of Europe into allied or dependent states (Map 17.1). The only exceptions were Britain and the parts of Spain and Portugal that continued to resist France with British help.

The states least affected by French hegemony were its reluctant allies: Austria, Russia, and the Scandinavian countries. Most affected were the territories incorporated into France. These included the Austrian Netherlands, territory along the Rhine, and territories in Italy that bordered France. These regions were occupied by French troops and were treated as though they were départements of France itself.

In most other regions, some form of French-controlled government was in place, usually headed by a member of Napoleon's family. In northern Italy and, initially, in the Netherlands, where "sister" republics had been established after French conquests under the Directory, Napoleon imposed monarchies. Napoleon's brother Joseph was made king of Spain. Western German states of the Holy Roman Empire that had allied with Napoleon against Austria were organized into the Confederation of the Rhine, with Napoleon as its "Protector." In 1806, after a thousand years, the Holy Roman Empire ceased to exist.

Napoleon's domination of these various regions had complex, at times contradictory, consequences. French rule brought political and economic reform akin to that of the early phases of the Revolution, now enshrined in the Napoleonic Civil Code. Equality before the law was decreed, ending noble exemption from taxation where it still existed. In general, the complex snarl of medieval taxes and tolls was replaced with straightforward property taxes from which no one was exempt. As a consequence, tax revenues rose dramatically—by 50 percent in the kingdom of Italy, for example. Serfdom and forced labor were also abolished, as they had been in France in August 1789.

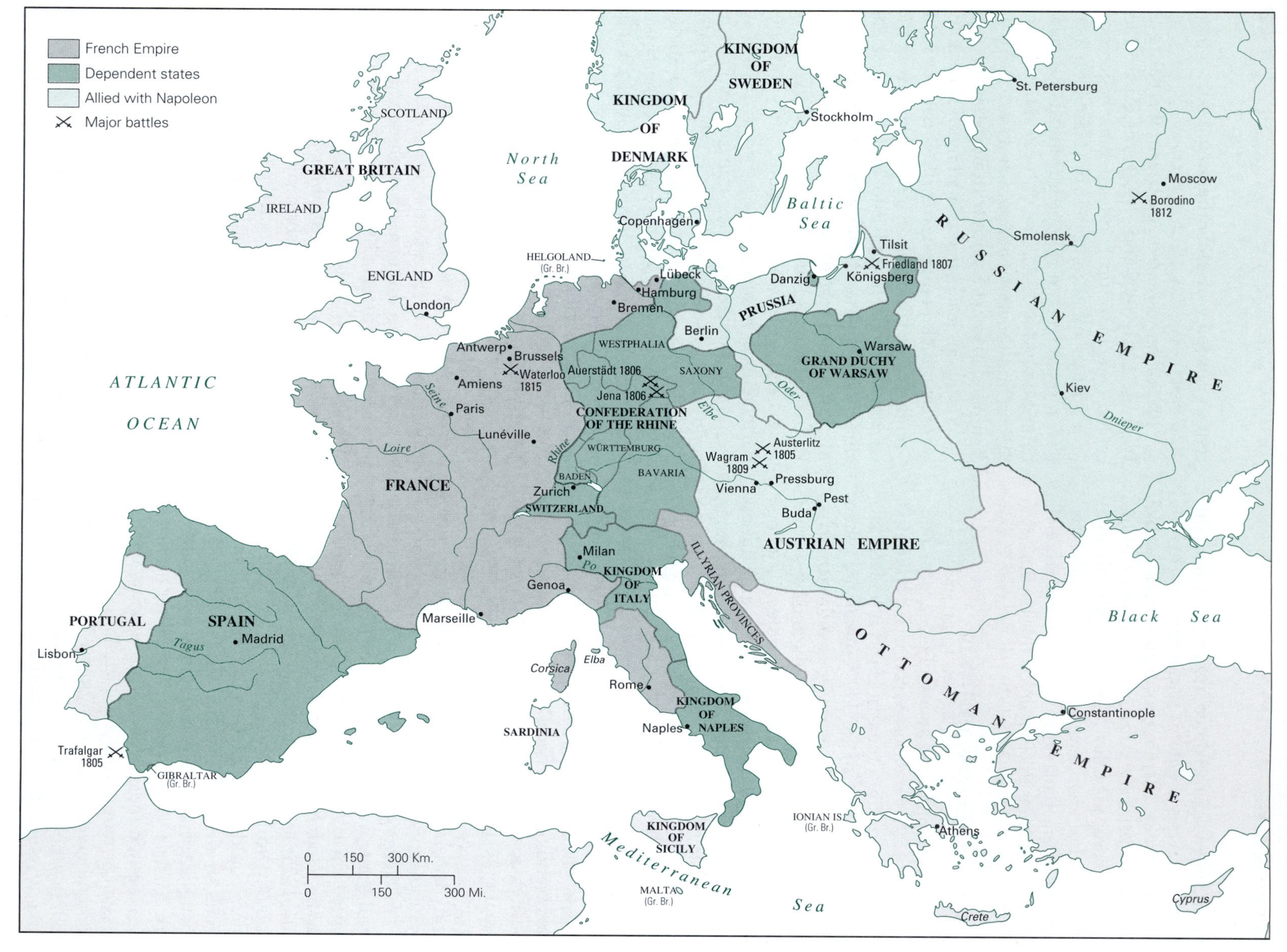
French Empire
Dependent states
Allied with Napoleon
Major battles
SCOTLAND
GREAT BRITAIN
IRELAND
ENGLAND
London
North Sea
ATLANTIC OCEAN
KINGDOM OF DENMARK
KINGDOM OF SWEDEN
Copenhagen
Stockholm
St. Petersburg
Baltic Sea
Moscow
Borodino 1812
Smolensk
RUSSIAN EMPIRE
Kiev
Dnieper
Tilsit
Friedland 1807
Königsberg
Danzig
PRUSSIA
HELGOLAND (Gr. Br.)
Lübeck
Hamburg
Bremen
Berlin
GRAND DUCHY OF WARSAW
Warsaw
Oder
Antwerp
Brussels
Waterloo 1815
Amiens
Seine
Paris
Lunéville
WESTPHALIA
SAXONY
Auerstädt 1806
Jena 1806
CONFEDERATION OF THE RHINE
Elbe
Loire
Rhine
WÜRTTEMBURG
BAVARIA
BADEN
FRANCE
Zurich
SWITZERLAND
Austerlitz 1805
Wagram 1809
Pressburg
Vienna
Pest
Buda
AUSTRIAN EMPIRE
Milan
Po
KINGDOM OF ITALY
ILLYRIAN PROVINCES
Genoa
Marseille
PORTUGAL
SPAIN
Madrid
Tagus
Lisbon
Corsica
Elba
Rome
KINGDOM OF NAPLES
Naples
SARDINIA
Trafalgar 1805
GIBRALTAR (Gr. Br.)
Black Sea
OTTOMAN EMPIRE
Constantinople
IONIAN IS. (Gr. Br.)
Athens
KINGDOM OF SICILY
Mediterranean Sea
MALTA (Gr. Br.)
Crete
Cyprus
0 150 300 Km.
0 150 300 Mi.

In most Catholic regions, the church was subjected to the terms of the Concordat of 1801. The tithe was abolished, church property seized and sold, and religious orders dissolved. Though Catholicism remained the state-supported religion in these areas, Protestantism was tolerated and Jews were granted rights of citizenship. Secular education, at least for boys, was encouraged.

And yet Napoleon would countenance only those aspects of France's revolutionary legacy that he tolerated in France itself. Meaningful participatory government was everywhere suppressed. This came as a blow to the Netherlands, which had experienced its own democratizing "Patriot" movement and had enjoyed republican self-government after invasion by French armies during the Revolution. Throughout the Napoleonic Empire, many of the benefits of streamlined administration and taxation were offset by the drain of continual warfare; deficits rose three- and fourfold, despite increased revenues.

Although true self-government was not allowed, a broad segment of the elites in all regions was won over to cooperation with Napoleon by being welcomed into his bureaucracy or into the large multinational army, the Grande Armée. Their loyalty was cemented when they bought confiscated church lands.

The impact of Napoleon's Continental System was equally mixed. Under this system, the Continent was closed to all British shipping and British goods. The effects were widespread but uneven, and smuggling became a major enterprise. Regions heavily involved in trade with Britain or its colonies or dependent on British shipping suffered in the new system, as did overseas trade in general when Britain gained dominance of the seas after Trafalgar. However, the closing of the Continent to British trade, combined with increases in demand resulting from the need to supply Napoleon's armies, spurred the development of continental industries, at least in the short run. This industrial growth, enhanced by the improvement of roads, canals, and the like, formed the basis for further industrial development.

Map 17.1 Napoleonic Europe, ca. 1810 France dominated continental Europe after Napoleon's victories. Though French control would collapse quickly after defeats in Russia and Spain in 1812, the effects of French domination were more long-lasting.

Defeat and Abdication, 1812–1815

Whatever its achievements, Napoleon's empire was ultimately precarious because of the hostility of Austria and Russia and the belligerence of Britain. Austria resented losing the Austrian Netherlands and lands in northern Italy. Russian landowners and merchants were angered when their vital trade in timber for the British navy was interrupted and when supplies of luxury goods, brought in British ships, began to dwindle. A century of close alliances with German ruling houses made alliance with a French ruler extremely difficult politically for Tsar Alexander I.

It was Napoleon, however, who ended the alliance by provoking a breach with Russia. He had reluctantly divorced Joséphine in 1809 because their marriage had not produced an heir, and he agreed to marry one of Alexander's younger sisters. Then he backed out and accepted the Austrian princess Marie Louise instead. In addition, he seized lands along the German Baltic seacoast belonging to a member of Alexander's family. When Alexander threatened a rupture of the alliance if the lands were not returned, Napoleon mounted an invasion. Advisers warned him about the magnitude of the task—particularly about the preparations needed for winter fighting in Russia, but their warnings went unheard.

Napoleon's previous military successes had stemmed from a combination of strategic innovations and audacity. Napoleon divided his forces into independent corps. Each corps included infantry, cavalry, and artillery. Organized in these workable units, his armies could travel quickly by several separate routes and converge in massive force to face the enemy. Leadership on the battlefield came from a loyal and talented officer corps that Napoleon had fashioned by welcoming returning aristocrats and favoring rising new talent. The final ingredient in the successful formula was the high morale of French troops under Napoleon. Napoleon's English nemesis, Arthur Wellesley (1769–1852), duke of Wellington, once remarked that Napoleon's presence on a battlefield was worth forty thousand men.

The campaign against Russia began in June 1812. It was a spectacular failure. Napoleon had gathered a force of about 700,000 men—about half from France and half from allied states—a force twice as large as Russia's. The strategy of quickly moving independent corps and assembling massive forces could not be implemented because of these large numbers. The supply system—always Napoleon's weakness—was simply not up to the task. Bold victories had often enabled Napoleon's troops to live off the countryside while they waited for supplies to catch up with them. But when the enemy attacked supply lines, when the distances traveled were very great, when the countryside was impoverished, or when battles were not decisive, Napoleon's strategies proved unworkable. In varying degrees, these conditions prevailed in Russia.

By the time the French faced the Russians at Borodino, the principal battle of the Russian campaign, the Grande Armée had been on the march for two and a half months and stood at less than half its original strength. After the indecisive but bloody battle, the French occupied and pillaged Moscow but found scarcely enough food and supplies to sustain them. When Napoleon finally led his troops out of Moscow late in October, the fate of the French forces was all but sealed. The army marched south to reach the warmer and better-provisioned Ukraine but was turned back by Russian troops. The French then retreated out of Russia. French soldiers who had not died in battle died of exposure or starvation or were killed by Russian peasants when they wandered away from their units. Of the original 700,000 French and allied troops, fewer than 100,000 made it out of Russia.

In the meantime, Napoleon had left his army. A coup attempt in Paris prompted him to return home before the French people realized the extent of the disaster in Russia. The collapse of his reign had begun, spurred by a coincidental defeat in Spain. By the time Napoleon got back to Paris, his brother Joseph had been expelled from Spain, and an Anglo-Spanish force led by the duke of Wellington was poised to invade France.

Napoleon's most able generals rallied what remained of his troops and held off Prussian and Russian forces in the east until he arrived in April 1813 with a new army of raw recruits. With Britain willing to subsidize the allied armies, Tsar Alexander determined to destroy Napoleon, and the Austrians now anxious to share the spoils, Napoleon's empire began to crumble. Napoleon's forces were crushed in a massive "Battle of Nations" near Leipzig in October, during which some of his troops from German satellite states deserted him on the battlefield. The allies invaded France and forced Napoleon to abdicate on April 6, 1814. Napoleon was exiled to the island of Elba, off France's Mediterranean coast, but was installed as the island's ruler and treated somewhat royally.

The restored French king faced significant challenges. Louis XVIII (r. 1814–1824) was the brother of the executed Louis XVI; he took the number eighteen out of respect for Louis XVI's son, who had died in prison. In addition to the task of establishing his own legitimacy, he faced enormous practical problems, including pensioning off thousands of unemployed soldiers still loyal to Napoleon.

Napoleon saw his chance and returned surreptitiously to France on February 26, 1815. He had only a small band of attendants with him, but when the king sent soldiers to prevent Napoleon from advancing to Paris, they joined him instead. Louis XVIII abandoned Paris to the returned emperor.

Napoleon's triumphant return lasted one hundred days. Though many soldiers welcomed his return, ordinary French citizens had become disenchanted with him since the defeat in Russia, and with the high costs, in conscription and taxation, of raising new armies. Napoleon's reappearance galvanized the divided allies, who had been haggling over a peace settlement, into unity. Napoleon tried to strike first, but he was defeated by British and Prussian troops at Waterloo (in modern Belgium) on June 18, 1815. This time he was exiled to the tiny, remote island of St. Helena in the South Atlantic, from which escape would be impossible. He died there in 1821.

THE IMPACT OF REVOLUTION ON FRANCE AND THE WORLD

There had been extraordinary upheaval in France between 1789 and 1815, and yet this period began with Louis XVI on the throne and ended with Louis XVIII on the throne. That continuity had significance, but it could not mask the profound changes that had occurred in matters of political legitimacy, national sovereignty, and popular consciousness. The Revolution had changed the fundamental premises of political life in Europe.

The Significance of Revolution in France

Although the French monarchy was restored in 1815, the new king governed with a small group of representatives of the elite, whose participation slowly widened. The Revolution had established new principles on which to base a government: the right of "the people," however narrowly defined, to participate in government and enjoy due process of law.

Another legacy of the revolutionary era was a centralized political system. The nation was divided into *départements* rather than provinces. For the first time, a single code of law applied to all French people. Most officials—from département administrators to city mayors—continued to be appointed by the central government until the late twentieth century. The government sponsored national scientific societies, a national library and archives, and a system of teachers' colleges and universities. Particularly under Napoleon, there was a spate of canal- and road-building.

Napoleon's legacy, like that of the Revolution itself, was mixed. His self-serving reconciliation of aristocratic pretensions with the opening of careers to men of talent helped to ensure the long-term success of revolutionary principles from which the elite as a whole profited. His reconciliation of the state with the Catholic church helped stabilize his regime and preserve some revolutionary gains, since the restored monarchy could not renege on these arrangements. But Napoleon could hardly eliminate the antirevolutionary bent of the church, and it continued to be a reactionary force in France. The Napoleonic Code was a uniform system of law for the nation. But although it guaranteed equality under the law for men, it enshrined political and legal inferiority for women.

Napoleon's return to power in 1815 reflected the degree to which his power was always rooted in military adventurism and the loyalty of soldiers and officers. His bravado suggests the importance of personal qualities to the success of an authoritarian regime. But the swiftness of his collapse suggests that the legitimacy and security of his empire were as uncertain as the legitimacy and security of the revolutionary governments.

Although Louis XVIII acknowledged the principle of constitutionalism, it rested on fragile footing. Indeed, the fragility of new political systems was one of the most profound lessons of the Revolution. Politics, the Revolution revealed, takes place in part on a symbolic level. Symbols are effective because they link a specific political system to a broader, fundamental system of values. The religious symbolism used by the monarchy linked royal government to divine order. Similarly, the cults of reason and the Supreme Being promoted by Robespierre were attempts to link patriotism and support of the government to universal principles. Other, more limited, symbols were constantly in use: the red and blue cockades that supporters of the National Assembly put in their caps; the "liberty cap" that Louis XVI donned on one occasion; various representations of the abstract notion of "Liberty" in popular newspapers and journals.

Before the Revolution started, there was a significant shift in notions about political legitimacy. The deputies who declared themselves to be the National Assembly in June 1789 already believed that they had a right to do so. In their view, they represented "the nation," and their voice had legitimacy for that reason. The deputies brought to Versailles not only their individual convictions but also their experience in social settings where those ideas were well received. In their salons, clubs, and literary societies, they had experienced the familiarity, trust, and sense of community that are essential to effective political action.

The deputies' attempt to transplant their sense of community into national politics was not wholly successful. The National Assembly had scarcely inaugurated a secure system when its deputies undermined its workability by making themselves ineligible to hold office under the new constitution. Factions, competing interests, and clashes of personality were fatal to the government because it was so new—it did not have the authority and legitimacy that accrue over time, and its members were inexperienced. The British parliamentary system, by comparison, though every bit as elitist as the narrowest of the representative systems during the French Revolution, had a long history as a workable institution for lords, commoners, and rulers. This shared experience was an important counterweight to differences over issues, so that Parliament as an institution both survived political crises and helped solve them.

The Impact of the Revolution Overseas

Although French conquests in Europe were quickly overturned, the brief French domination had lasting effects. Elites were exposed to modern bureaucratic management, and equality under the law transformed social and political relationships. Although national self-determination had an enemy in Napoleon, the breaking down of ancient political divisions provided important practical grounding for later cooperation among elites in nationalist movements across Europe.

Europe's overseas colonies felt the impact of the Revolution in several ways. The British tried to take advantage of Napoleon's preoccupation with continental affairs by seizing French colonies and the colonies of the French-dominated Dutch. In 1806 they seized the Dutch colony of Capetown—crucial for support of trade around Africa—as well as French bases along the African coast. In 1811 they grabbed the island of Java. In the Americas, French sugar colonies in the Caribbean were particularly vulnerable to English seapower. The sugar island of Haiti was an exception because British aggression there occurred in the context of a local revolution.

In Haiti the French Revolution had a direct impact. The National Assembly in Paris delayed abolishing slavery in French colonies, despite the moral appeal of such a move, because of pressure from the white planters on Haiti and out of fear that the French government would lose some of its profitable sugar trade. But the example of revolutionary daring in Paris and confusion about ruling authority invited challenges to authority in the colonies.

Many white planters hoped to seize the opportunity the Revolution provided to gain political and economic independence from France. White planter rule in Haiti was challenged, in turn, by wealthy people of mixed European and African descent and then by a full-fledged slave rebellion, beginning in 1791. (See the box "Encounters with the West: A Planter's Wife on the Haitian Slave Revolt.") Britain sent aid to the rebels when it went to war against the French revolutionary government in 1793. Only when the republic was declared in Paris and the Convention abolished slavery did the Haitian rebels abandon alliances with France's enemies and attempt to govern in concert with the mother country.

France never regained control of Haiti. Led by a former slave, François Dominique Toussaint-Louverture (1743–1803), the new government of Haiti tried to run its own affairs, though without formally declaring independence from France. Napoleon, early in his rule, decided to tighten control of the profitable colonies by reinstituting slavery and ousting the independent government of Haiti. In 1802, French forces fought their way onto the island. They captured Toussaint-Louverture, who died shortly thereafter in prison. But in 1803 they were forced to leave by another rebellion prompted by the threat of renewed slavery.

ENCOUNTERS WITH THE WEST

A Planter's Wife on the Haitian Slave Revolt

The following are excerpts from two letters of Madame de Rouvray, a wealthy planter's wife living in the French colony of Saint-Domingue (the western half of the island of Hispaniola), to her married daughter in France. The decree of May 15, 1791, that Madame de Rouvray mentions in her first letter granted civil rights to free persons of mixed race. Tensions between white planters, on the one hand, and mulattos and modest white settlers who favored revolutionary changes, on the other, enabled the well-organized slave rebellion to be dramatically successful. It began in late August 1791 and is the backdrop to Madame de Rouvray's second letter. Madame de Rouvray and her husband fled the island—renamed Haiti, the Native American term for Hispaniola, after the revolt—for the United States in 1793.

July 30, 1791 I am writing to you from Cap [a city on the island] where I came to find out what the general mood is here. . . . All the deputies who make up the general assembly [of the colony] left here the day before yesterday to gather at Léogane [another city]. If they conduct themselves wisely their first action should be to send emissaries to all the powers who have colonies with slaves in order to tell them of the decree [of May 15] and of the consequences that will follow from it, and ask for help from them in case it happens that the National Assembly actually abolishes slavery too, which they will surely do. After their decree of May 15, one cannot doubt that that is their plan. And you understand that all the powers who have slave colonies have a common interest in opposing such a crazy plan because the contagion of liberty will soon infect their colonies too, especially in nearby Jamaica. It is said that [the English] will send a ship and troops [which] would be wonderful for us. Your father thinks it won't be long before the English take control here.

September 4, 1791 If news of the horrors that have happened here since the 23rd of last month have reached you, you must have been very worried. Luckily, we are all safe. We can't say whether our fortunes are also safe because we are still at war with the slaves who revolted [and] who have slaughtered and torched much of the countryside hereabouts. . . . All of this will gravely damage our revenues for this year and for the future, because how can we stay in a country where slaves have raised their hands against their masters? . . . You have no idea, my dear, of the state of this colony; it would make you tremble. Don't breathe a word of this to anyone but your father is determined, once the rebels have been defeated, to take refuge in Havanna.

Source: M. E. McIntosh and B. C. Weber, *Une Correspondance familiale au temps des troubles de Saint-Domingue* (Paris: Société de l'Histoire des Colonies Françaises et Librairie Larose, 1959), pp. 22–23, 26–28. Trans. by Kristen B. Neuschel.

The View from Britain

Today the city of Paris is dotted with public monuments that celebrate Napoleon's victories. One of the main train stations is the Gare (Station) d'Austerlitz. A column in a city square, crowned with a statue of Napoleon, was made from the metal of enemy cannon captured at Austerlitz.

In London, another set of events and another hero is celebrated. In Trafalgar Square stands a statue of Lord Nelson, the British naval commander whose fleet destroyed a combined French and

Spanish fleet in 1805. Horatio Nelson was a brilliant tactician, whose innovations in maneuvering ships in the battle line resulted in stunning victories at Trafalgar and, in 1798, at the Nile Delta, which limited French ambitions in Egypt and the eastern Mediterranean. Trafalgar looms large in British history because it ensured British mastery of the seas, which enabled the British to seize colonies formerly ruled by France and its allies.

Since the late eighteenth century, the British had steadily made other gains abroad. In 1783, Britain had lost control of thirteen of its North American colonies; however, it had more successfully resolved the Irish rebellions. Similarly, in the Caribbean, British planter families, like Irish elites, were willing to accept tighter rule from the mother country in return for greater security against their subject population. In India, the East India Company was increasing its political domination and economic stranglehold on Indian manufacture and trade.

The British economy would expand dramatically in the nineteenth century as industrial production grew. The roots for that expansion can be found in this period in the countryside of Britain, where changes in agriculture and in production were occurring. These roots also lay in Britain's overseas possessions by the profits made there and also, increasingly, by the control of sources of raw materials, notably raw cotton raised in India. The export of Indian cotton grew significantly during the revolutionary period as part of an expanding trading system that included China, the source of tea.

Not every conquest had direct economic payoffs, but British elites were sure that strategic domination was a desirable step, wherever it could be managed. One Scottish landholder, writing in the opening years of the nineteenth century, spoke for many when he said that Britain needed an empire to ensure its greatness and that an empire of the sea was an effective counterweight to Napoleon's empire on land. Much as the French were at that moment exporting features of their own political system, the British, he said, could export their constitution wherever they conquered territory.

Thus, England and France were engaged in similar phases of expansion in this period. In both, the desire for power and profit drove policy. In each, myths about heroes and about the supposed benefits of domination masked the state's self-interest. In both, the effects of conquest would become a fundamental shaping force in the nineteenth century.

SUMMARY

The French Revolution was a watershed in European history because it successfully challenged the principles of hereditary rule and political privilege on which European states had hitherto been governed. The Revolution began when a financial crisis forced the monarchy to confront the desire for political reform by a segment of the French elite. Political philosophy emerging from the Enlightenment and the example of the American Revolution moved the French reformers to action. In its initial phase, the French Revolution established the principle of constitutional government and ended many of the traditional political privileges of the Old Regime.

The Revolution moved in more radical directions because of the intransigence of the king, the threat of foreign invasion, and the actions of republican legislators and Parisian citizens. Its most radical phase, the Terror, produced the most effective legislation for ordinary citizens but also the worst violence of the Revolution. A period of unstable conservative rule that followed the Terror ended when Napoleon seized power.

Though Napoleonic rule enshrined some of the gains of the Revolution, it also subjected France and most of Europe to the great costs of wars of conquest. After Napoleon, the French monarchy was restored but forced to accept many limitations on its power as a result of the Revolution. Indeed, hereditary rule and traditional social hierarchies remained in place in much of Europe, but they would not be secure in the future. The legacy of revolutionary change would prove impossible to contain in France or anywhere else.

NOTES

1. Quoted in Owen Connelly, *The French Revolution and Napoleonic Era* (New York: Holt, Rinehart and Winston, 1979), p. 32.

SUGGESTED READING

Baker, Keith Michael, ed. *The French Revolution and the Creation of Modern Political Culture.* 1987. A collection of essays by diverse scholars emphasizing the Revolution as a period of change in political culture.

Chartier, Roger. *The Cultural Origins of the French Revolution.* 1991. An interpretation of intellectual and cultural life in the eighteenth century with a view to explaining its revolutionary results; has a good bibliography.

Connelly, Owen. *Blundering to Glory: The Campaigns of Napoleon.* 1992. A new assessment of Napoleon's military achievements by an expert on Napoleonic warfare.

Furet, François. *Interpreting the French Revolution.* 1981. The major work by the outstanding French scholar of the Revolution of the current generation, written in reaction to liberal and Marxist interpretations.

Hufton, Olwen. *Women and the Limits of Citizenship in the French Revolution.* 1992. A series of essays by the leading scholar on the history of women in the Revolution.

Hunt, Lynn. *The Family Romance of the French Revolution.* 1992. A study of political ideology and symbolic politics emphasizing the vast cultural consequences of killing the king and queen.

———. *Politics, Culture and Class in the French Revolution.* 1984. A survey and assessment of other interpretations of the Revolution, emphasizing the role of symbols and symbolic politics.

James, C. L. R. *The Black Jacobins.* 1938. The classic study of the Haitian revolution in the context of events in Europe.

Jordan, D. P. *The King's Trial.* 1979. A readable study of Louis XVI's trial and its importance.

Landes, Joan. *Women and the Public Sphere in the Age of the French Revolution.* 1988. An analysis of the uses of gender ideology to fashion the new political world of the revolutionaries.

Lefebvre, Georges. *The Coming of the French Revolution.* Translated by R. R. Palmer. 1947. A beautifully written Marxist interpretation. The greatest work of this important French historian.

Lyons, Martyn. *Napoleon Bonaparte and the Legacy of the French Revolution.* 1994. A clear, readable, and up-to-date synthesis of scholarship on Napoleon.

Markham, Felix. *Napoleon.* 1963. The best biography in English of Napoleon.

Palmer, R. R. *The Age of Democratic Revolution.* 2 vols. 1959. A study of the American and European revolutions and their reciprocal influences; erudite and immensely readable.

Rudé, George. *The Crowd in the French Revolution.* 1959. A classic Marxist assessment of the importance of common people to the progress of the Revolution.

———. *Twelve Who Ruled.* 1941. A study of the principal figures of the Terror by one of the greatest American historians of the French Revolution.

Soboul, Albert. *The Sans-Culottes.* 1972. A study of the workers of Paris who were active in the Revolution, by Lefebvre's successor as the foremost Marxist historian of the Revolution.

Sutherland, D. M. G. *France, 1789–1815.* 1986. A dense and detailed treatment, with extensive bibliography, that emphasizes the revolutionary over the Napoleonic period.

Sydenham, M. *The First French Republic, 1792–1804.* 1974. A useful survey of the relatively neglected phases of the Revolution.

Tackett, Timothy. *Priest and Parish in Eighteenth-Century France.* 1977. A study of rural Catholic life before the Revolution and after the impact of the Civil Constitution of the Clergy.

CHAPTER 18

Restoration, Reform, and Revolution, 1814–1848

In 1791, in the midst of revolution, the comte de Provence had fled his homeland, disguised as a foreign merchant. Shunted from country to country he lived in exile, depending on subsidies from foreign courts. Since the revolutionaries had beheaded his brother, Louis XVI, and a nephew had died in captivity, when he returned to France after twenty-three years abroad, he did so as king of France, Louis XVIII (r. 1814–1824).

With Louis's return to French soil in April 1814, the Bourbons were restored. In many other states, too, with the fall of Napoleon, monarchy and aristocracy attempted to reassert, to "restore," their authority. Historians often call the period from 1814 to 1832 in Europe the "restoration." Yet the old world could not be re-created—from the beginning, efforts to restore it were challenged by forces that had appeared during the revolutionary years.

The Great Powers tried to re-establish as much of the old European state system as possible, but the international arrangements of the victorious powers—Austria, Great Britain, Prussia, and Russia—were soon shaken by outbreaks of nationalist fervor. Nationalists aimed either to create larger political units, as in Italy and Germany, or to win independence from foreign rule, as in Greece.

Domestically, the attempt to set the clock back also had limited success. The conservatism of European rulers and their opposition to change were at odds with the new dynamism of European society. Between 1800 and 1850, Europe's population increased by nearly 50 percent, from around 190 million to 280 million. Population growth and the development of industry created large cities where there had been small towns or rural areas. Manufacturing in factories was on the rise, reshaping class structures and the lives of workers. Romanticism, liberalism, and other systems of thought were redefining the relationship of the individual to society.

In 1814, European statesmen had consciously tried to forestall revolution, but in less than a generation they were challenged by waves of protest and violence, most notably in the revolutions of 1848. Revolutionaries did not win all their goals, and in many cases the forces of order crushed them. Yet major intellectual, social, and political changes had occurred by midcentury.

Questions and Ideas to Consider

- Was the "restoration" worked out at the Congress of Vienna a true restoration of prerevolutionary Europe?
- What were the major ideas of romanticism? Why did romantic artists and intellectuals reject the classicism of the Enlightenment?
- Women found that both romanticism and socialism could be used to support gender equality. How? Consider the ideas of George Sand, Harriet Taylor Mill, Zoé Gatti de Gamond, and Flora Tristan.
- In western Europe, the political systems established in 1815 underwent important transformations by the 1830s. Reforms were instituted in many aspects of government. Discuss the mixture of conservatism and liberalism that shaped these transformations.
- What were the common factors of the revolutions of 1848? What were the results of these revolts? How is it that England avoided these upheavals?

THE SEARCH FOR STABILITY: THE CONGRESS OF VIENNA

The defeat of Napoleon put an end to French dominance in Europe. In September 1814 the victorious powers of the Quadruple Alliance—Austria, Great Britain, Prussia, and Russia—convened a conference in Vienna to negotiate the terms of peace. The victors sought to draw territorial boundaries advantageous to themselves and to provide long-term stability on the European continent.

Although many small powers attended the Congress of Vienna, their role was limited to ratifying the large states' decisions. Having faced a powerful France that had mobilized popular forces with revolutionary principles, the victors decided to erect an international system to remove such threats. They restored the European order that had existed before the French Revolution. Thus, following principles of "legitimacy and compensation," they redrew the map of Europe (Map 18.1). Rulers who had been overthrown were restored to their thrones. As we have seen, the eldest surviving brother of Louis XVI of France became King Louis XVIII. In Spain, Ferdinand VII was restored to the throne from which Napoleon had toppled him and his father. The restoration, however, was not complete. Certain new realities had to be recognized. For example, Napoleon had consolidated the German states; the process was acknowledged with the creation of a loose German Confederation.

Negotiators at the Congress of Vienna strengthened the territories bordering France, enlarged Prussia, created the kingdom of Piedmont-Sardinia, joined Belgium to Holland, and provided the victors with spoils and compensation for territories bartered away. Russia's reward for its contribution to the war effort was most of Poland and all of Finland, which had belonged to Sweden. Sweden's king was compensated for the loss of Finland by being permitted to rule in a joint union over Norway, formerly under the Danish crown. Denmark was punished for adhering to the Napoleonic alliance longer than the victorious allies thought was appropriate. Britain acquired a number of colonies and naval outposts. Thus, even as they proclaimed their loyalty to the prerevolutionary past, conservative statesmen changed the map of Europe.

The leading personality at the Congress of Vienna was the Austrian foreign minister, Prince

CHAPTER CHRONOLOGY

EUROPEAN REVOLUTIONS, 1820–1831

January 1820	Spain
July 1820	Naples
August 1820	Portugal
March 1821	Piedmont; Greece
December 1825	Russia
July 1830	France
August 1830	Belgium
September 1830	Brunswick; Saxony; Hesse-Cassel
November 1830	Poland
February 1831	Revolt in Piedmont, Modena, and Parma; revolt in Papal States

EUROPEAN REVOLUTIONS, 1848

January	Sicily
February	France
March	Austria, Hungary, Croatia, Lombardy, Prussia
April	Bohemia
May	German National Assembly convenes in Frankfurt
January 1849	Roman Republic declared

Clemens von Metternich (1773–1859), who presided over the meetings. An aristocrat in exile from the Rhineland, which had been annexed by revolutionary France, he had gone into the service of the Habsburg empire and risen to become its highest official. Personal charm, tact, and representation of a state that for the time being was satisfied with its territories made Metternich seem a disinterested statesman. His influence at the Congress was great.

Made wary by their long war against France, the four powers of the Quadruple Alliance had pledged before the Congress of Vienna to cooperate to prevent any future French aggression. They planned to meet periodically to resolve all European issues, creating what was known as the "Concert of Europe." At Vienna the wily French foreign minister, Count Charles Talleyrand (1754–1838), was able to insinuate himself into the councils of the four Great Powers. The desire of Russia and Prussia for sizable territorial gains alarmed Austria and Great Britain, and France joined them in limiting Russian and Prussian ambitions. At Talleyrand's insistence, France was counted as one of five Great Powers.

The Concert of Europe, including France, met several times to try to resolve subsequent crises. Underlying the states' cooperation was the principle of a common European destiny.

IDEOLOGICAL CONFRONTATIONS

The international and domestic political systems established in 1815 were modified by a series of challenges and even revolts, culminating in revolutions throughout Europe in 1848. The order established in 1815 was inspired by conservatism. Its challengers advocated competing ideologies: romanticism, nationalism, liberalism, and socialism.

Conservatism

The architects of the restoration justified their policies with doctrines based on the ideology of conservatism, emphasizing the need to preserve the existing order. Conservatism emerged as a coherent movement during and after the French Revolution in reaction to the forces of change.

Edmund Burke (1729–1797), a British statesman and political theorist, launched one of the first intellectual assaults on the French Revolution. The revolutionary National Assembly had asserted that ancient prerogatives were superseded by the rights of man and principles of human equality based on natural law. In *Reflections on the Revolution in France* (1790), Burke said that such claims were abstract and dangerous and that the belief in human equality undermined the social order. Government should be anchored in tradition, he argued. No matter how poorly the French monarchy and its institutions had served the nation, they should be preserved; their very longevity proved their usefulness. Burke's writings were widely read and influential on the Continent.

In the English-speaking world, one of the most popular writers, Hannah More (1745–1833), who with her four sisters ran a prosperous school, saw piety as a rampart against rebellion. In a series of moral tracts, *Cheap Repository Tracts,* she advocated the acceptance of the existing order and the solace of religious faith. Costing but a penny, the tracts were often handed out by the rich together with alms or food to the poor. More was the first writer in history to sell over a million copies; within three years the sales doubled. Conservative values thus spread to a very large audience in both Britain and the United States, where one of her works appeared in thirty editions.

A more extreme form of conservatism was ultraroyalist or counterrevolutionary ideology. Its proponents wanted to restore society to its prerevolutionary condition. They had often had personal experience of the upheavals of the Revolution. Count Joseph de Maistre (1753–1821), a Savoyard (from the Franco-Italian border region) nobleman whose estates were occupied by the invading French, described monarchy as a God-given form of government in his *Considerations on France* in 1796. De Maistre advocated stern government control, including the generous use of the death penalty, to keep people loyal to throne and altar.

In Germany the influential thought of Georg Wilhelm Friedrich Hegel (1770–1831), philosophy professor at the University of Berlin, was interpreted by many of his disciples as a defense of the conservative order re-established by the restoration. In Hegel's view, history was propelled from one stage to another by the "world spirit" incarnate in the dominant power. Just as Rome had fulfilled divine plans by dominating the ancient world, so Napoleon was hailed by Hegel as a "world soul." The emperor's fall convinced Hegel that the true world soul was incarnate in the victorious allies, particularly Prussia. The state, Hegel said, showed "the march of God in the world"; the existing power, reactionary and authoritarian, was divinely ordained.

Conservatism was also influenced by romanticism, with its glorification of the past, taste for pageantry, and belief in the organic unity of society. But not all conservatives were romantics. Metternich, for instance, saw his work as the attempt of an enlightened mind to restore the world put in turmoil by the French Revolution. (See the box "Metternich's Cure for Europe.")

Romanticism

The romantic movement emerged in the 1760s as a rebellion against rationalism and persisted until the 1840s. It was primarily a movement in the arts. Writers, painters, and composers consciously rebelled against the Enlightenment and its values. In contrast to the philosophes with their emphasis on reason, romantics praised emotion and feeling. Jean-Jacques Rousseau's strong appeal to sentiment was taken up by the German writer Johann Wolfgang von Goethe (1749–1832), who declared that "Feeling is everything." Goethe's *Sorrows of Young Werther* (1774), the most widely read book of the era—Napoleon had a copy by his bedside—depicted the passions of the hero, who, depressed by unrequited love, kills himself. Many readers dressed in "Werther clothes" (tight black pants, blue vest, and an open yellow shirt) and in some cases emulated the tragic hero by committing suicide.

The Enlightenment studied nature for the principles that it could impart; romantics worshiped nature for its inherent beauty. The German composer Ludwig van Beethoven (1770–

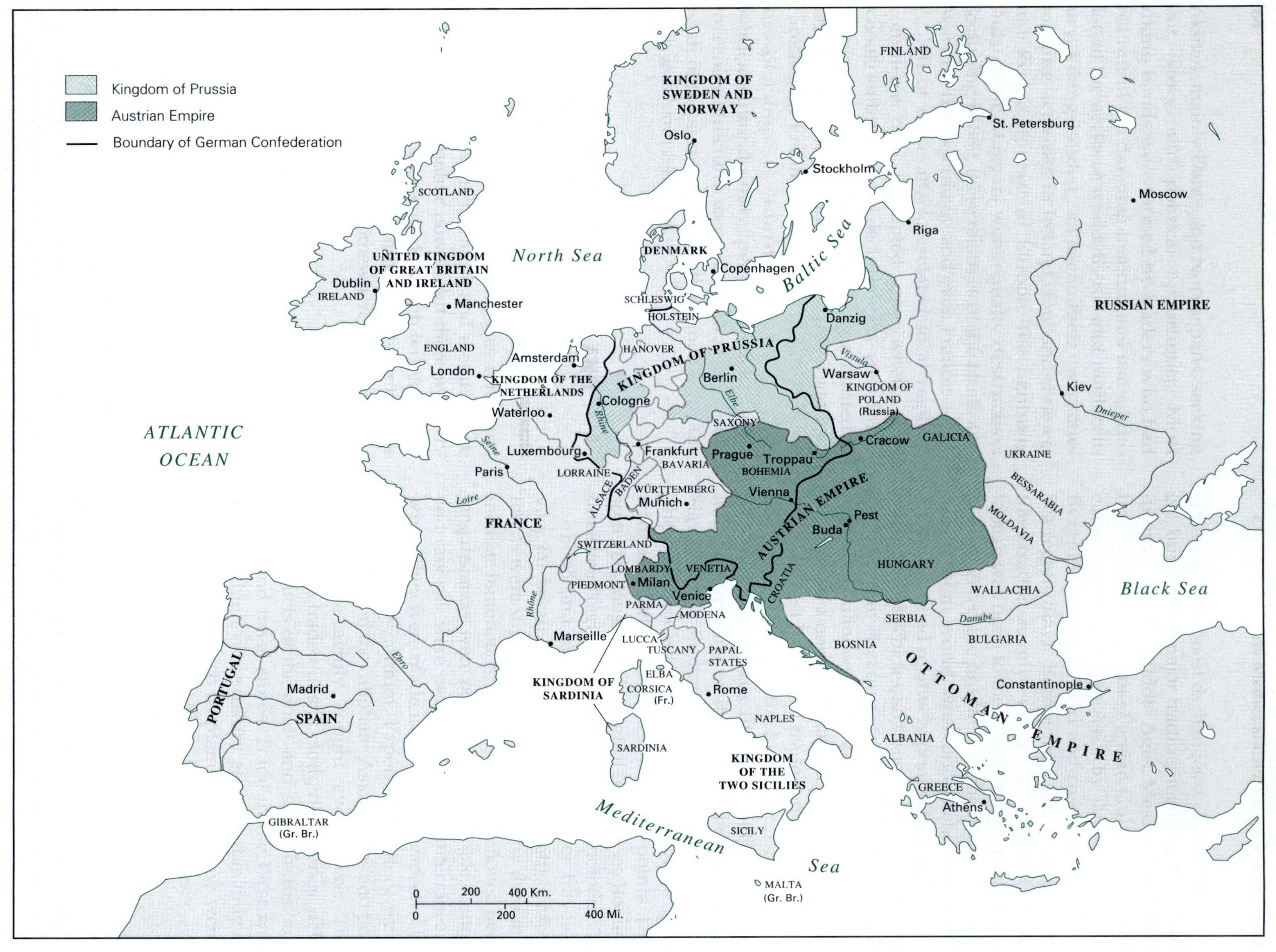

Kingdom of Prussia
Austrian Empire
Boundary of German Confederation
ATLANTIC OCEAN
North Sea
Baltic Sea
Black Sea
Mediterranean Sea
KINGDOM OF SWEDEN AND NORWAY
FINLAND
St. Petersburg
Oslo
Stockholm
Moscow
Riga
RUSSIAN EMPIRE
SCOTLAND
UNITED KINGDOM OF GREAT BRITAIN AND IRELAND
Dublin
IRELAND
Manchester
ENGLAND
London
DENMARK
Copenhagen
SCHLESWIG
HOLSTEIN
HANOVER
KINGDOM OF PRUSSIA
Danzig
Vistula
Warsaw
KINGDOM OF POLAND (Russia)
Kiev
Dnieper
Amsterdam
KINGDOM OF THE NETHERLANDS
Berlin
Elbe
Cologne
Rhine
Waterloo
SAXONY
Cracow
GALICIA
UKRAINE
Luxembourg
Frankfurt
BAVARIA
Prague
Troppau
BOHEMIA
Seine
Paris
LORRAINE
ALSACE
BADEN
WÜRTTEMBERG
Munich
Vienna
AUSTRIAN EMPIRE
BESSARABIA
MOLDAVIA
Pest
Buda
Loire
FRANCE
SWITZERLAND
HUNGARY
LOMBARDY
VENETIA
CROATIA
PIEDMONT
Milan
Venice
WALLACHIA
PARMA
MODENA
SERBIA
Danube
Rhône
Marseille
LUCCA
TUSCANY
PAPAL STATES
BOSNIA
BULGARIA
Ebro
PORTUGAL
Madrid
SPAIN
KINGDOM OF SARDINIA
ELBA
CORSICA (Fr.)
Rome
OTTOMAN EMPIRE
Constantinople
NAPLES
ALBANIA
SARDINIA
KINGDOM OF THE TWO SICILIES
GREECE
Athens
GIBRALTAR (Gr. Br.)
SICILY
MALTA (Gr. Br.)
0 200 400 Km.
0 200 400 Mi.

Metternich's Cure for Europe

Metternich, Austria's foreign minister from 1809 to 1848, had an impact beyond his empire's borders, providing much of the leadership of the reactionary regimes of Europe between 1815 and 1848. In this secret letter to Russia's Tsar Alexander I, Metternich analyzed the current ailments of Europe and saw their cure in firm support for king and church.

Kings have to calculate the chances of their very existence in the immediate future; passions are let loose, and league together to overthrow everything which society respects as the basis of its existence; religion, public morality, laws, customs, rights, and duties all are attacked, confounded, overthrown, or called in question. . . .

Having now thrown a rapid glance over the first causes of the present state of society, it is necessary to point out in a more particular manner the evil which threatens to deprive it, at one blow, of the real blessings, the fruits of genuine civilisation, and to disturb it in the midst of its enjoyments. This evil may be described in one word—presumption; the natural effect of the rapid progression of the human mind towards the perfecting of so many things. This it is which at the present day leads so many individuals astray, for it has become an almost universal sentiment. . . .

The Governments, having lost their balance, are frightened, intimidated, and thrown into confusion, by the cries of the intermediary class of society, which, placed between the Kings and their subjects, breaks the sceptre of the monarch, and usurps the cry of the people. . . .

We are convinced that society can no longer be saved without strong and vigorous resolutions on the part of the Governments. . . . By this course the monarchs will fulfill the duties imposed upon them by Him who, by entrusting them with power, has charged them to watch over the maintenance of justice, and the rights of all, to avoid the paths of error and tread firmly in the way of truth. . . .

. . . [L]et the Governments govern. . . . Let them not encourage by their attitude or actions the suspicion of being favourable or indifferent to error: let them not allow it to be believed that experience has lost its rights to make way for experiments which at the least are dangerous.

Source: Metternich to Emperor Alexander, Troppau, December 15, 1820, in Prince Richard Metternich, ed., *Memoirs of Prince Metternich, 1815–1829,* vol. 3, trans. Mrs. Alexander Napier (New York: Scribner & Sons, 1881), pp. 455, 458–459, 468–470, 474.

1827) wrote his *Pastoral* Symphony in praise of nature. The English poets William Wordsworth (1770–1850) and Samuel Taylor Coleridge (1772–1834) treated untamed wilderness as a particular subject of wonder. Fellow Englishman Joseph Turner (1775–1851) displayed the raw passions of the sea in his paintings *Fire at Sea* (1834) and *Snowstorm, Steamboat Off a Harbour's Mouth* (1842). To paint the latter, Turner is said to have tied himself to a ship's mast and braved a snowstorm for four hours. The Frenchman Théodore Géricault (1791–1824) also portrayed the impotence of human beings in the face of the natural world. His *Raft of the "Medusa,"* widely considered the most important painting of French romanticism, depicted an actual shipwreck off the coast of Africa. Passionate and dark, the painting includes all of romanticism's key themes: an exotic setting, powerful natural forces, and grand displays of human emotion.

Map 18.1 Europe in 1815 The map of Europe was redrawn at the Congress of Vienna.

Géricault: Raft of the "Medusa" This painting depicts a scandalous tragedy that occurred in 1816. A French government ship had been wrecked due to the incompetence of the captain, who had been appointed on the basis of his nobility and not his seamanship. Lacking sufficient lifeboats, 150 passengers were left on a makeshift raft. Before their chance rescue thirteen days later, most had died, and some of those who survived had engaged in cannibalism and murder. Partially because the government tried to hide these facts, Géricault's painting became an important symbol of antigovernment sentiment. *(Erich Lessing/Art Resource, NY)*

In their pursuit of feeling, many romantics rediscovered religion. In some areas of Europe, popular religion had anticipated the artists' romantic sensibilities. France experienced a revival of Catholicism. In the German states, pietism, which emerged in the seventeenth and eighteenth centuries, stressed the personal relationship of the individual to God. The influence of pietism, with its emphasis on feeling and emotion, spread throughout central Europe in schools and churches.

In England piety and emotionalism in religion expressed itself in the popularity of Methodism. Founded in the 1730s by the English preacher John Wesley (1703–1791), this movement emphasized salvation by faith. Appealing especially to the poor and desperate, Methodism had gained 70,000 members when it split off from the Church of England in the 1790s; within a generation it quadrupled its flock.

The philosophes had derided the Middle Ages, but romantics celebrated them. Sir Walter

Scott (1771–1832) in Scotland and Victor Hugo (1802–1885) in France celebrated chivalry and the age of faith in such popular works as *Ivanhoe* (1819) and *The Hunchback of Notre Dame* (1831). Painters frequently took as their theme Gothic buildings or ruins. Architects imitated the Gothic style in both private and public buildings.

After the French Revolution, monarchs and nobles ceased sponsoring art on a grand scale and were expected to conduct their lives soberly. Cut off from royal patronage, artists had to depend on members of the new middle class to buy paintings and books and attend plays and musical performances. Earning a livelihood had been difficult for artists in the past, but now it became even more so. Forced to live marginally, they cultivated the image of the artist as a bohemian, deliberately rejecting the conventions of society. The romantic period gave rise to the notion of the starving genius, alienated from society, loyal only to art.

Romantics often celebrated individualism. For this reason, they accepted unusual behavior—even when it challenged existing power relations and proprieties. The French writer Amandine-Aurore Dupin (1804–1876), better known by her pen name, George Sand, spoke for the emancipation of women from the close supervision of their husbands, fathers, and brothers. Sand practiced the freedom she preached, dressing like a man, smoking cigars, and openly pursuing affairs with the writer Prosper Mérimée (1803–1870), the poet Alfred de Musset (1810–1857), and the composer Frédéric Chopin (1810–1849). The English writer Mary Ann Evans (1819–1892), like George Sand, adopted a male pseudonym, George Eliot. She conducted her life in a nonconformist manner, living with a married man. The adoption of male pen names by both writers attests to the hostility that intellectual women still faced.

Determined to overthrow the smug present and create a new world, romantics consciously turned their backs on the classical tradition. Victor Hugo called for "no more rules, no more models" to constrain the human imagination. Such figures as the English romantic poet Percy Bysshe Shelley (1792–1822), the writer Mary Wollstonecraft (1759–1797), the painter Eugène Delacroix (1798–1863), and the poet George Gordon, Lord Byron (1788–1824), each expressed some aspect of romantic individualism, dedication to grand, passionate causes, and respect for the power of nature.

Nationalism

The ideology of nationalism emerged in this era. *Nationalism* is the belief that people derive their identity from their nation and owe their nation their primary loyalty. The idea of a "nation" grew out of the idea of a "country." While a country can be defined by its land and its government, a nation *is* its people. Nations tend to define themselves as a group of people with a common language and religion, as well as common traditions, daily habits, and shared historical experiences. No nation can claim all of these, and many areas that actually can claim many of these are not in fact nations. Nineteenth-century nationalists argued fiercely over what qualifications constituted a nation.

In an era that saw the undermining of traditional religious values, nationalism offered a new locus of faith. To people distressed by the erosion of the old order, nationalism held out the promise of a new community. Nationalism became an ideal espoused as strongly as religion. The Italian nationalist Giuseppe Mazzini (1805–1872) declared that nationalism was "a faith and mission" ordained by God. The religious intensity of nationalism helps explain its widespread appeal.

Many forces shaped nationalism. Its earliest manifestation, cultural nationalism, had its origins in Rousseau's ideas of the organic nature of a people. Johann Gottfried Herder (1744–1833), Rousseau's German disciple, declared that every people has a "national spirit." To explore the unique nature of this spirit, intellectuals all over Europe began collecting folk poems, songs, and tales. In an effort to document the spirit of the German people, the Grimm brothers, Jacob (1785–1863) and Wilhelm (1786–1859), collected fairy tales by traveling around German territories and asking women to recite the stories handed down from their own mothers. Fairy tales such as "Little Red Riding Hood" and "Snow White" had long been created and recounted by women, as many of their themes indicate. In making them public, the nationalist movement legitimated these stories but masked their true authors.

Political nationalism was born in the era of the French Revolution. When revolutionary France was attacked by neighboring countries ruled by kings and dukes, the Legislative Assembly called on the French people to rise and save the nation. The realm of the king of France had become the French nation.

Intellectuals in Germany and Italy embraced the spirit of nationalism, challenging France's claim to the right to lead the peoples of Europe. They argued variously that Germans were endowed with a special genius that had to be safeguarded for the well-being of all humankind or that Italians ought to be pre-eminent in Europe because they were the descendants and heirs of ancient Rome. Culture could also be invoked for the purpose of throwing off a foreign yoke. In the 1810s, as part of a campaign to free Greece from the Turks, Greek intellectuals re-issued the classics of ancient Greek literature in "purified" language, closer to classical Greek. Their purpose was to remind the population that they were the sons and daughters of Hellas.

For the most part, early nineteenth-century nationalism was generous and cosmopolitan in its outlook—excepting the French Revolution and the Napoleonic era. Herder and Mazzini believed that each of Europe's peoples was destined to achieve nationhood and that the nations of Europe would then live peacefully side by side. The members of dedicated nationalist groups like Young Germany and Young Italy were also members of Young Europe.

It is important to remember, though, that in the first half of the nineteenth century most people were likely to feel local and regional affinities more than national loyalties. Only after decades of propaganda would the ideology win wide support, and only then did it become natural for Europeans to think of dying for their nation.

Liberalism

Liberalism was a direct descendant of the Enlightenment's critique of eighteenth-century absolutism. Nineteenth-century liberals believed that individual freedom was best safeguarded by the reduction of government powers. They wanted to impose constitutional limits on government, to establish the rule of law, to sweep away all state regulation of the economy, and to ensure a voice in government for men of property and education. Liberalism was influenced by romanticism, with its emphasis on individual freedom and the imperative of the human personality to develop to its full potential.

Liberalism was both an economic and a political theory. In 1776, Adam Smith (1723–1790), the influential Scottish economist, published *An Inquiry into the Nature and Causes of the Wealth of Nations,* a systematic study of the economic knowledge of his era. Smith advocated freeing national economies from the fetters of the state. Under the mercantilist system, prevalent throughout Europe until about 1800, the state had regulated the prices and conditions of manufacture (see page 362). Smith argued for letting the forces of the marketplace shape economic decisions. He was the founder of the classical school of economics; this school rested on the belief that economics is subject to basic unalterable laws, which can be discerned and applied in the same fashion as natural laws. The economy is driven as if by an "invisible hand." In France, advocates of nonintervention by government in the economy were called supporters of *laissez faire* (to leave alone).

Wages and employment were also seen as subject to the law of supply and demand. Thomas Malthus (1766–1834), an Anglican minister, published *An Essay on the Principle of Population* in 1798. Malthus posited that if employers paid their workers higher salaries, workers would be able to afford to marry earlier and have more children, thus glutting the labor market and driving wages down. He wanted wages to be kept at subsistence level. Workers, Malthus suggested, are "themselves the cause of their own poverty."

The third giant among classical economists was the retired English stockbroker David Ricardo (1772–1823), who set forth his ideas in *Principles of Political Economy* (1817). Ricardo saw the capitalist system as typified by what he called the "iron law of wages." Since capitalists' major expenses were wages, to be competitive they had to keep depressing wages. According to the school of classical economics, the economy is driven by laws, and intervention of any sort will only make things worse.

In the political realm, liberals argued that power must be limited to prevent despotism. The French Revolution had proclaimed that the purpose of government is to ensure the happiness of humankind. As Thomas Jefferson (1743–1826), another child of the Enlightenment, asserted in the Declaration of Independence (1776), among the "unalienable rights" of individuals are "life, liberty, and the pursuit of happiness." The purpose of government is to safeguard and promote those rights.

The Enlightenment had posited natural law as the basis of government. French liberals in the nineteenth century continued to see human liberty as founded on natural law, but their English counterparts were less theoretical in outlook. The Englishman Jeremy Bentham (1748–1832) argued that the purpose of government is to provide "the greatest happiness of the greatest number." Bentham and his disciples believed that the test of government is its usefulness; they were known as "utilitarians."

John Stuart Mill (1803–1873), a disciple of Bentham, was the foremost proponent of liberalism, seeing it as ensuring the development of a free society. Individuals could best develop their talents if they were not hampered by the interference of the state. In his essay *On Liberty*, one of the fundamental documents of nineteenth-century liberalism, Mill argued for the free circulation of ideas—even false ones. In the free marketplace of ideas, false ideas will be defeated and truth will be vindicated. Mill also asserted that a free society should be free for all its members. In 1830, Mill met Harriet Taylor (1807–1856), an English feminist who became his wife years later (after her first husband's death). Harriet Taylor Mill's influential essay, "Enfranchisement of Women" (1851), had a tremendous impact on John Stuart Mill. After her death, he wrote his famous *On the Subjection of Women* (1861), crediting her with "all that is striking and most profound" in this work. Both Taylor and Mill asserted that women should vote and have access to equal educational opportunities as well as to the professions. Such equality would not only be just but would also have the advantage of "doubling the mass of mental faculties available for the higher service of humanity." Some people advocated women's right to vote on the principle that women would bring a special morality to the ballot box. Harriet Taylor and John Stuart Mill, however, were among those who argued that women deserved equal rights on the same liberal principles that gave men their rights.

Clearly, liberalism came in many forms. In the second half of the century, many people came to believe that the laws of the marketplace could not be allowed to operate without intervention. Even Mill grew to believe that some controls on market forces were needed to protect workers and consumers. Also, many liberals came to fear the masses and therefore vigorously opposed democracy. When less fortunate Frenchmen denounced the property requirements that prevented them from voting, the liberal statesman François Guizot (1787–1874) smugly replied, "Get rich."

In politics, however, the basic tenets of the liberal credo—the sanctity of human rights, freedom of speech and freedom to organize, the rule of law and equality before the law, and the abolition of torture—eventually became so widely accepted that even conservative and socialist opponents of liberalism accepted them as fundamental rights.

Socialism

The notion that human happiness can best be assured by the common ownership of property had been suggested by individuals as different as the Greek philosopher Plato (427?–347 B.C.) and Sir Thomas More (1478–1535), the English author of

Utopia. Troubled by the condition of the working classes, thinkers in Britain and France developed theories that, beginning in the 1820s, were called "socialist." Socialists believed that the "social" ownership of property, unlike private ownership, would benefit society as a whole.

In 1796, during the French Revolution, Gracchus Babeuf (1760–1797), a minor civil servant, participated in the Conspiracy of Equals (see page 452). The Revolution, however haltingly, had proclaimed political equality for its citizens, but it had failed to bring economic equality. Babeuf decided to resort to revolution to bring about a "communist" society—a society in which private property would be abolished and all property would be owned in common. Work would be provided for everyone; medical services and education would be free to all. Babeuf's plan was discovered and he was guillotined, but his theories and his example of conspiratorial revolutionary action would influence later socialists.

Several other important French thinkers made contributions to European socialism. Curiously, a French aristocrat, Henri de Saint-Simon (1760–1825), emphasized the need "to ameliorate as promptly and as quickly as possible the moral and physical existence of the most numerous class." The proper role for the state, Saint-Simon declared, was to ensure the welfare of the masses. Europe should be governed by a council of artists and scientists who would oversee the economy and ensure that everyone enjoyed a minimum level of well-being. Young intellectuals who gravitated to Saint-Simonism took on the master's faith in the capacity of technology to transform society. They became the dynamic entrepreneurs and engineers who in the 1850s would build up the French banking, investment, and rail systems.

Another vital contribution to socialist thought came from thinkers who tried to imagine an ideal world on an even wider scale. They were later derisively dismissed as dreamers, as builders of utopias, fantasy worlds (the Greek word *utopia* means "no place"). One of the earliest and most notable utopians was the Welsh mill-owner Robert Owen (1771–1858). In New Lanark, Scotland, beginning in 1800 he ran a successful cotton mill. He provided generously for his workers, guaranteeing them a job and a decent education for their children. In his writings Owen suggested the establishment of self-governing communes that would own the means of production. Essentials would be distributed to all members according to their needs. Owen's ideas for the new society included equal rights for women.

Owen received little support from fellow manufacturers and political leaders. In 1824 he established in New Harmony, Indiana, an ideal new society that was to be a model for others. Within four years of its founding, New Harmony ran into economic difficulty and was torn by internal dissension. Disheartened, Owen abandoned the community and returned to Britain.

Another influential contributor to early socialist theory was the Frenchman Charles Fourier (1772–1837). A clerk and salesman, Fourier wrote out his vision of the ideal future society in great detail. It would consist of cooperative organizations called "phalanxes," each with 1600 inhabitants who would live in harmony with nature and one another. Everyone would be assured of gainful employment. Work would be made enjoyable by rotating jobs and by sharing pleasurable and unpleasurable tasks. Cooperative communes often faced the issue of who would carry out the unpleasant tasks. Fourier thought that because children enjoy playing with dirt, they should be put in charge of picking up garbage.

Fourier's belief in equality of the sexes gave him an important female following. In Belgium, the activist Zoé Gatti de Gamond (1806–1854) cofounded a phalanx for women. She believed that if women could be assured of economic well-being, other rights would follow. Also inspired by Fourier, Flora Tristan (1801–1844) was an effective advocate for workers' rights. In her book *Union Ouvrière (Workers' Union),* she suggested that workers should contribute to establish a "Worker's Palace" in every town, where the sick and disabled would have shelter and the workers' children could be given a free education. Like Fourier, she saw a profound link between the concerns of socialism and feminism and championed women's rights as prerequisite for a just society. Arguing that worker solidarity was damaged when underpaid women were employed in place of men, Tristan concluded that women's rights and worker's rights were profoundly interdependent. Crossing France on foot, she spread the word of workers' solidarity and self-help.

There were other approaches. The French socialist journalist Louis Blanc (1811–1882) saw in democracy the means of bringing into existence a socialist state. By securing the vote, the common people could win control of the state and direct it to serve their needs. The state could be induced to buy up banks, insurance companies, and railway systems and set up a commercial and retail chain that would provide jobs for workers and set reasonable prices. Once the workers controlled the state by the ballot, the state would establish worker-run workshops. The idea was to "Let each produce according to his aptitudes and strength; let each consume according to his need."

Blanc's contemporary, Louis Blanqui (1805–1882), suggested a more violent mode of action. He advocated seizure of the state by a small, dedicated band of men devoted to the welfare of the working class who would install communism for the equality of all. Blanqui was a perpetual conspirator, confined to state prisons for much of his long life. The thought of Blanqui and the other socialists would play a major role in shaping the thinking of the most important socialist of the nineteenth century, Karl Marx.

RESTORATION AND REFORM

Despite the new ideologies that emerged to challenge the existing order, efforts at restoration appeared successful until at least 1830. Indeed in central and eastern Europe, from the German states to Russia and the Ottoman Empire, the political systems established in 1815 would persist virtually unchanged until midcentury. In western Europe, however, important transformations would occur by the 1830s as reaction gave way to reform. Then in 1848, widespread revolution would break out on much of the Continent. The language of liberalism and nationalism and even the newer idiom of socialism would be heard on the barricades, in popular assemblies, and in parliamentary halls.

France

The restoration of the Bourbons in France turned the clock back not to 1789 but closer to 1791, when the country had briefly enjoyed a constitutional monarchy, and it went beyond that in maintaining the Napoleonic Code with its provisions of legal equality.

Louis XVIII granted France a charter confirming political and religious liberties and legal equality. The new constitution provided for a parliament with an elected lower house, the Chamber of Deputies, and an appointed upper house, the Chamber of Peers. Although suffrage to the Chamber of Deputies was limited to a small elite of men with landed property—100,000 voters, about 0.2 percent—it was a concession to representative government that had not existed in the Old Regime. Louis XVIII was unusual among European rulers because he accepted some aspects of the principle of popular sovereignty proclaimed by the French Revolution.

Louis was succeeded by his ultrareactionary brother, Charles X (r. 1824–1830). The new king encouraged passage of an indemnity bill to pay the aristocratic émigrés for property lost during the Revolution and Napoleon's regime. Bourgeois and lower-class taxpayers were outraged. Many resented the increased power granted the clergy and were shocked by the introduction of the death penalty for acts deemed sacrilegious. Charles X's dissolution of the National Guard, one of the bastions of the middle class, further alienated the bourgeoisie. Frustration mounted with an economic downturn in 1827, marked by poor harvests and increased unemployment in the cities. On July 26, 1830, after the humiliating defeat of his party at the polls, the king issued a set of decrees suspending freedom of the press, dissolving the Chamber of Deputies, and stiffening property qualifications for voters in subsequent elections. The king appeared to be engineering a coup against the existing political system.

The first to protest were the Parisian journalists and typesetters, directly threatened by the censorship laws. On July 28, others joined the protest and began erecting barricades across many streets and calling for a republic. After killing several hundred protesters, the king's forces lost control of the city. The uprising, known as "the three glorious days," drove the king into exile. However, the idea of a republic frightened the middle classes. A liberal constitutional monarchy seemed safer. Better organized than the republicans, they prevailed on the Chamber of Deputies to offer the throne to the king's cousin, the liberal-minded duke of Orléans, Louis Philippe (1773–1850).

Louis Philippe proclaimed himself "King of the French," acknowledging that he reigned at the behest of the people. Freedom of the press was reinstated; suffrage was extended to twice as many voters as before. The July Monarchy, named after the month in which it had been established by revolution, legitimated itself by celebrating the revolution of 1789. Louis Philippe commissioned huge canvasses celebrating great moments of the Revolution. On the site where the Bastille had been razed in 1789, the government erected a large column with the names of the victims of the July 1830 revolution, suggesting a continuity between those who had fought tyranny in 1789 and 1830.

But the regime allowed celebration only of the period until 1791, when France had a constitutional monarchy. Now that the revolution of 1830 had established a constitutional monarchy, the regime was suggesting, any further uprisings were illegitimate.

The July Monarchy was challenged from many quarters. Many people were nostalgic for the republic that had existed under the Revolution. Others longed for the glories of the Napoleonic era. Shortly after the revolution of 1830, another downturn in the economy led to further unemployment, followed by an epidemic of cholera that affected most of Europe. Also contributing to the unsettled atmosphere was labor agitation—including some bloody uprisings in Lyon in 1831 and 1834. In the countryside there were rumors of mass arson. In the face of unrest, the monarchy often resorted to censorship and other forms of repression. Foreign visitors from more authoritarian societies were impressed by France's apparently liberal institutions (see the box "Encounters with the West: A Moroccan Description of the French Freedom of the Press"), but many French liberals saw the regime as a travesty of the promises it had represented in 1830. Inaugurated by revolution, in a few years it would face revolution.

Great Britain

In comparison to the rest of Europe, Great Britain enjoyed considerable constitutional guarantees and a parliamentary regime. Yet liberals and radicals found their government retrograde and repressive. Traumatized by the French Revolution, the ruling class clung to the past, certain that advocates for change were Jacobins in disguise.

Social unrest beset Britain as it faced serious economic dislocation. The arrival of peace in 1815 led to a sudden drop in government expenditures and the return to the workplace of several hundred thousand men who had been away at war. The poor and the middle classes were incensed by the economic advantages that the landed classes, dominating Parliament, had secured for themselves in 1815 in passing the Corn Law. This legislation imposed high tariffs on imported "corn"—that is, various forms of grain. It thus shielded the domestic market from international competition and allowed landowners to reap huge profits at the expense of consumers. In response, there were demonstrations, petitions, protest marches, and other challenges to the authorities.

In August 1819, sixty thousand people gathered in St. Peter's Fields in Manchester to demand universal suffrage for men *and* women, an annual Parliament, and other democratic reforms. The crowd was peaceful and unarmed, but when a speaker whom the government con-

ENCOUNTERS WITH THE WEST

A Moroccan Description of the French Freedom of the Press

In 1845–1846 a Moroccan diplomatic mission visited Paris; the ambassador's secretary, Muhammad as-Saffar (d. 1881), wrote an account of this visit. He was struck by many aspects of French society, and in the following passage he described France's press.

The people of Paris, like all the French—indeed, like all of [Europe]—are eager to know the latest news and events that are taking place in other parts [of the world]. For this purpose they have the gazette. [In] these papers . . . they write all the news that has reached them that day about events in their own country and in other lands both near and far.

This is the way it is done. The owner of a newspaper dispatches his people to collect everything they see or hear in the way of important events or unusual happenings. Among the places where they collect the news are the two Chambers, the Great and the Small, where they come together to make their laws. When the members of the Chamber meet to deliberate, the men of the gazette sit nearby and write down everything that is said, for all debating and ratifying of laws is matter for the gazette and is known to everyone. No one can prevent them from doing this. . . .

. . . [I]f someone has an idea about a subject but he is not a member of the press, he may write about it in the gazette and make it known to others, so that the leaders of opinion learn about it. If the idea is worthy they may follow it, and if its author was out of favor it may bring him recognition.

No person in France is prohibited from expressing his opinion or from writing it and printing it, on condition that he does not violate the law. . . .

In the newspapers they write rejoinders to the men of the two Chambers about the laws they are making. If their Sultan demands gifts from the notables or goes against the law in any way, they write about that too, saying that he is a tyrant and in the wrong. He cannot confront them or cause them harm. Also, if someone behaves out of the ordinary, they write about that too, making it common knowledge among people of every rank. If his deeds were admirable, they praise and delight in him, lauding his example; but if he behaved badly, they revile him to discourage the like.

Moreover, if someone is being oppressed by another, they write about that too, so that everyone will know the story from both sides just as it happened, until it is decided in court. One can also read in it what their courts have decided.

Source: Susan Gilson Miller, ed. and trans., *Disorienting Encounters—Travels of a Moroccan Scholar in France in 1845–1846. The Voyage of Muhammad as-Saffar* (Berkeley: University of California Press, 1992), pp. 150–153. Reprinted by permission of the Regents of California and the University of California Press.

sidered a rabble-rouser took to the podium, mounted soldiers charged, attempting to arrest him. In the ensuing melee, eleven people were killed and four hundred wounded. The British public was shocked by this use of violence against peaceful demonstrators. Parliament responded in autumn 1819 by passing the Six Acts, which outlawed freedom of assembly and effectively imposed censorship.

The government began to embrace change in the 1820s. The provisions that prevented Catholics from holding any government position

"Peterloo" Massacre In August 1819 at St. Peter's Fields in Manchester, a crowd demanding parliamentary reform was charged by government troops, leading to bloodshed. Many English people derided the event and called it "Peterloo." *(Public Record Office)*

were removed in 1829. The number of crimes punishable by death was reduced to just one, homicide. Prison reforms were made. Sir Robert Peel (1788–1850), heir to a manufacturing fortune and an enthusiastic reader of Bentham's works, was the driving force behind many of these reforms. He became home secretary in 1828, and the following year he organized an efficient London police force, known ever after as "bobbies" in his honor, to control crime and contain popular protests.

The major political issue facing Britain in the early nineteenth century was the composition of Parliament. It did not reflect the dramatic population shifts that had occurred since the seventeenth century. Industrialization had transformed mere villages into major cities, but those cities had no representation in Parliament, while localities that had lost population were still represented.

News of the July 1830 revolution in Paris encouraged liberals to push for reform and frightened some conservatives into softening their opposition. In 1831 the liberal Whig government of Earl Grey (1764–1845), a hereditary peer who was well attuned to the demands of the middle class, introduced a reform bill abolishing or reducing representation for sparsely populated areas and granting representation for the populous and unrepresented cities. The bill, which came to be known as the "Great Reform Bill of 1832," also widened the franchise by lowering property qualifications.

The reform was not particularly radical. Only the upper layers of the middle class were enfranchised, or one of seven adult males. The old franchise had not excluded women from the vote, but the new law did so. Still, Parliament better reflected the shift of economic power from agricultural landowners to the industrial and commercial classes. The bill's passage revealed the ability of the political system to bring about reform peacefully.

More reforms followed. The Poor Law of 1834 had a mixed impact. It denied aid to the able-bodied, no matter how destitute, offering them only the option of entering workhouses, where prisonlike conditions deterred all but the most desperate. But the law also abolished the long-standing policy of providing government supplements to very low salaries, which had made it unnecessary for employers to pay workers a living wage. The law of 1834 may thus have played some role in raising wages. Though harsh toward the poor, the Poor Law was an acknowledgment of a national responsibility for the underprivileged.

There were colonial reforms as well. In Britain opposition to slavery had been voiced since the 1780s. Slavery was an affront to liberal principles, and its persistence threatened the empire—in 1831, sixty thousand slaves rebelled in Jamaica. Parliament took heed of the call for change and in

1833 abolished slavery in the British Empire. The antislavery campaign led to the extension of British power into Africa. Having abolished the slave trade in 1807, the British worked to compel other nations to end it. The British navy patrolled the coast of West Africa, trying to suppress the traffic in humans. The minor settlements it established as bases for these patrols made Britain the predominant European power along the coast, foreshadowing the increasing European intrusion into African affairs.

Parliament's reforming zeal stimulated support for *Chartism*, a movement intended to transform Britain into a democracy. In 1838 political radicals with working-class support drew up a "people's charter" calling for universal male suffrage, equal electoral districts, salaries and the abolition of property qualifications for members of Parliament, the secret ballot, and annual general elections. Chartists hoped to end the dominance of narrow upper classes in Parliament. Chartism won wide support among men and women in the working class, sparking demonstrations and petition drives of unprecedented size. Women participated to a larger extent than in any other political movement of the day, founding over a hundred female Chartist organizations. Some Chartists, especially female members, asked for women's suffrage, but this demand was not supported by the overall membership.

Chartism lost some of its followers during a temporary economic upswing. The movement then fell under the sway of advocates of violence, who scared off many artisans and potential middle-class supporters. Lacking popular support, Chartism failed as a political movement. Still, it drew public attention to an integrated democratic program whose main provisions (except for yearly elections) would be adopted piecemeal over the next half-century.

In 1839 urban businessmen founded the Anti–Corn Law League for the purpose of abolishing the Corn Law of 1815, which was increasing the price of grain. Manufacturers knew that low food prices would allow them to pay low wages. The Corn Law was also unpopular with workers, who wanted bread at a price they could afford. The anti–Corn Law movement proved more effective than Chartism because it had the support of the middle classes. Parliament, alarmed by the threat of famine after the poor harvest of 1845, repealed the Corn Law in 1846.

Although repeal did not affect the price of grain, it was a milestone in British history because it showed how organized groups could bring about economic and social reform by putting pressure on Parliament. It also underscored what the Great Reform Act of 1832 had already revealed: Political and economic power was shifting away from the landed gentry to the urban industrial classes. The British political system responded more flexibly to this change than did the political systems of the Continent. When revolution broke out on the Continent, it did not cross the English Channel.

Spain

The term *liberal* was first coined in Spain, where the fate of liberals prefigured what would happen elsewhere in continental Europe. In 1812 the national parliament, the Cortes, elected during the Napoleonic occupation, issued a democratic constitution that provided for universal manhood suffrage and a unicameral legislature with control over government policy. Supporters and admirers of the constitution in Spain became known as "liberals," or friends of liberty.

The Bourbon king Ferdinand VII (r. 1808, 1814–1833) had been overthrown by Napoleon and replaced by his brother, Joseph Bonaparte (r. 1808–1813). In 1814, Ferdinand returned to power, promising to respect the 1812 constitution. But Ferdinand was a believer in the divine right of kings. He had no real intention of abiding by a document drawn up by the educated middle classes that reflected their anticlericalism and desire for power. Ferdinand drew his support from the aristocracy and from segments of the general population still loyal to the call of throne and altar. Liberals were arrested or driven into exile.

Ferdinand's plan to restore Spain to its earlier prominence included a reassertion of control over its American colonies. The Spanish dominions had grown restless in the eighteenth century, for they had witnessed the advent of an independent United States and French occupation of Spain itself. The dominions refused to recognize the Napoleonic regime in Madrid and became increasingly self-reliant. Their attitude did not change when French control of Spain ended. Ferdinand refused to compromise with the overseas territories. Instead, he gathered an army to subdue them. Some liberal junior officers, declaring the army's loyalty to the constitution of 1812, won support from the rank and file, who balked at going overseas. The military mutiny coincided with a sympathetic provincial uprising to produce the "revolution of 1820," the first major assault on the European order established in 1815 at the Congress of Vienna. Ferdinand appealed to the European powers for help. France intervened and crushed the uprising.

Ferdinand's reactionary regime was restored in Spain but could not regain its American colonies. The British, sympathetic to the cause of Latin American independence and eager for commercial access to the region, opposed reconquest. Naval dominance of the seas rendered Britain's opposition effective. The United States, meanwhile, had recognized the independence of the Latin American republics and wished to see their independence maintained. In 1823, President James Monroe issued the statement known as the Monroe Doctrine, proclaiming U.S. opposition to any European colonization or intervention in the affairs of independent republics in the Americas. The United States lacked the military power to back this proclamation, but the British navy effectively enforced it. By 1825 all Spain's colonies on the mainland in Central and South America had won their freedom.

The newly independent states patterned their regimes on the model of Spanish liberalism; all of them had constitutions, separation of powers, and guaranteed human rights. Brazil, the Portuguese empire in the Americas, was a monarchy for most of the rest of the nineteenth century, as was Mexico for a short time, but the other states all became republics, opting for what was then an unusual form of government. Although most of the Latin regimes eventually became despotic, lip service continued to be paid to liberal values.

When Ferdinand died in 1833, Spain was torn by competing claims to the succession. A civil war between liberal and conservative factions led to extreme cruelty on both sides. The moderates and liberals won, but the military gained the upper hand in governing. A constitutional government was established, but the real power lay in the hands of the army. Several officers served as dictators of the country, replacing each other in a series of coups. One of them, General Ramón Narváez (1799–1868), brutally ran the country from 1844 to 1851. When he was on his deathbed, he was asked whether he forgave his enemies. He answered, "I have no enemies. I have shot them all."

Austria and the German States

The Austrian Empire's far-flung territories seemed to its Habsburg rulers to require a firm hand (see Map 18.1). Liberalism, which challenged imperial power, could not be countenanced. Nor, in this multinational empire, could nationalism be tolerated. The emperor, Francis I (r. 1792–1835), was opposed to any change; his motto was "Rule and change nothing." Prince Metternich, Francis's chief minister, viewed the French Revolution of 1789 and its aftermath as a disaster. Metternich established a network of secret police and informers to spy on the imperial subjects and keep them in check.

In most of the German states, the political order was authoritarian and inflexible. The states of Baden and Württemberg in the west and Bavaria in the south had been granted constitutions by their rulers, although effective power remained in the hands of the ruling houses. The king of Prussia had repeatedly promised a constitution, but none had materialized. A central, representative Diet would not meet until 1847. Prussia was ruled by an alliance of the king and the *Junkers,* the landowning aristocrats who staffed the officer corps and the bureaucracy. Both the officer corps and the bureaucracy were efficient enough to serve as models for the rest of Europe. Where Prussia lagged by liberal standards was in its political institutions.

Throughout the German states, the urban middle classes, intellectuals, journalists, university professors, and students were frustrated with the existing system. They were disappointed by the lack of free institutions and the failure of the patriotic wars against Napoleon to create a united Germany. University students formed *Burschenschaften,* or brotherhoods, whose slogan was "Honor, Liberty, Fatherland." Metternich imposed a policy of reaction on the Germanic Confederation and had it adopt the Carlsbad Decrees in July 1819, establishing close supervision over the universities, censorship of the press, and dissolution of the youth groups. Wholesale persecution of liberals and nationalists followed.

The outbreak of revolution in Paris in 1830 inspired further political agitation. Mounting demands for national unity led to the prosecution of outspoken liberals. Many associated with the nationalist Young Germany movement fled abroad. Nationalist fervor swept the German states again in the 1840s. The patriotic song "Deutschland, Deutschland über alles" ("Germany, Germany above all"), which became Germany's national anthem half a century later, was written at this time. Some German rulers who had been reluctant to support the national idea in the past now attempted to coopt it. In Bavaria, King Ludwig II built the Walhalla, named after the hall where fallen heroes gather in Germanic lore; Ludwig's Walhalla was to be a "sacred monument" to German unity, adorned with statues of famous Germans. The Cologne Cathedral, unfinished in its construction, became a symbol of German enthusiasm; from all over Germany donations came in to complete it. Prussia's King William Frederick IV (r. 1840–1861) declared it "the spirit of German unity and strength." These events suggested a broadening base for nationhood.

Italy

Austria continued to wield considerable power over the Italian states. In addition to Lombardy and Venetia, which it acquired in 1815 (see Map 18.1), Austria had dynastic ties to several ruling houses in the central part of the peninsula and political alliances with others, including the papacy. The only ruling house free of Austrian ties—and hence looked to by nationalists as a possible rallying point for the independence of the peninsula—was the Savoy dynasty of Piedmont-Sardinia.

Italy consisted of eight political states, and it was in Austria's interest to maintain disunity. Many Italian rulers imposed repressive policies, knowing that they could count on Austrian assistance in case of a popular uprising. Metternich's interventions to crush liberal rebellions generated hatred of Austria among Italian nationalists. Political reaction in the Italian states cannot be wholly blamed on Austria, however. Piedmont, which was free of Austrian influence, nevertheless embraced restoration. When the royal house of Savoy returned to power in 1815, it nullified all the laws passed during Napoleon's reign and banned from government service all officials who had served the French.

Throughout Italy, there was resistance to the restoration. The Carbonari (literally, "charcoal burners," suggesting men of simple occupations), a nationalist conspiratorial group that had been formed to fight the French occupation, after 1815 targeted the restoration regimes. In March 1821, liberal-minded young army officers in Piedmont, inspired by recent events in Spain, proclaimed their support of a constitution and their desire to evict Austria from Italy. The movement, essentially military, did not win much popular support. With the help of Austria, Piedmontese loyal to the monarch crushed the uprising.

A decade later, catalyzed by the July revolution in Paris, the same forces came to the fore. An uprising broke out in Piedmont, then spread to the Papal States and Modena. The revolt was aimed at the authoritarian rulers of the various Italian states, but it was also in support of a united Italy. Led by intellectuals and some members of the middle classes, the uprisings were fragmented by the participants' primary loyalties to their individual states and cities. The Austrians promptly crushed hopes for the liberty and unity of Italy.

Russia

By far the most autocratic of the European states was tsarist Russia. Since 1801 it had been ruled by Alexander I (r. 1801–1825), an enigmatic character whose domestic policy wavered between liberalism and reaction and whose foreign policy vacillated between brutal power politics and apparently selfless idealism. When the Congress of Vienna awarded additional Polish lands to Russia, he demonstrated his liberalism to the world by granting Poland a liberal constitution. But he offered no such constitution to his own people. He and his council discussed terms for the abolition of serfdom in 1803 and again in 1812, but like so many of his plans this one was not implemented. Although he earnestly desired freedom for the serfs, he was unwilling to impose any policy detrimental to the interests and privileges of the landed gentry.

Toward the end of his rule, Alexander became increasingly authoritarian and repressive, probably in response to growing opposition. Western liberal ideas, including constitutionalism, were adopted by Russian military officers who had served in western Europe, by Russian Freemasons who corresponded with Masonic lodges in western Europe, and by Russian intellectuals who read Western liberal political tracts. These groups formed secret societies with varying programs. Some envisioned Russia as a republic, others as a constitutional monarchy, but all shared a commitment to the abolition of serfdom and the establishment of a freer society.

Alexander died in December 1825, leaving it unclear which of his brothers was to succeed him. The younger brother, Nicholas, claimed to be the legal heir. Military conspirators declared in favor of the older brother, Constantine, in the belief that he favored a constitutional government. The "Decembrist uprising," as the ensuing struggle is known, quickly failed. The revolt in the Russian capital was badly coordinated with uprisings planned in the countryside, and Nicholas moved quickly to crush the rebellion. He had the leaders executed, sent to Siberia, or sent into exile. Despite its tragic end, the Decembrist uprising served as an inspiration to Russians resisting tsarist oppression throughout the nineteenth century.

Coming to the throne after crushing a revolt, Nicholas I (r. 1825–1855) was obsessed with the danger of revolution and determined to suppress all challenges to his authority. The declared goal of his rule was to uphold "orthodoxy, autocracy, and nationality." Nicholas created a stern, centralized bureaucracy to control all facets of Russian life. He established the modern Russian secret police, called the "Third Section"; it was above the law—a state within the state. The tsar supported the primacy of the Russian Orthodox church within Russian society; the church in turn upheld the powers of the state. Nicholas also used nationalism to strengthen the state, glorifying the country's past and trying to Russify non-Russian peoples, especially the Poles, by imposing the Russian language on them.

Russia's single most overwhelming problem was serfdom. Economically, serfdom had little to recommend it; free labor was far more efficient. Moreover, public safety was threatened by the serfs' dissatisfaction with their lot. During Nicholas's thirty-year reign there were over six hundred peasant uprisings. Nicholas understood that serfdom had to be abolished for Russia's own good, but he could envision no alternative. Emancipation, he believed, would only sow further disorder. Except for a few minor reforms, he did nothing. Nicholas's death, followed by Russia's defeat in the Crimean War, eventually ended the institution that had held nearly half of the Russian people in bondage.

The Ottoman Empire

In its sheer mass, the Ottoman Empire continued to be a world empire. It extended over three continents. In Africa it ran across the whole North African coast. In Europe it stretched from Dalmatia (on the Adriatic coast) to Constantinople. In Asia it extended from Mesopotamia (present-day Iraq) to Anatolia (present-day Turkey). But it was an empire in decline, seriously challenged from within by nationalist movements and from outside by foreign threats.

The Ottoman bureaucracy, once the mainstay of the government, had fallen into decay. In the past, officials had been recruited and advanced by merit; now lacking funds, Constantinople sold government offices. Tax collectors ruthlessly squeezed the peasantry. By the eighteenth century the Janissaries, formerly an elite military force, had become an undisciplined band that menaced the peoples of the Ottoman Empire—especially those located at great distances from the capital. The reform-minded Sultan Selim III (r. 1789–1807) sought to curb the army, but he was killed by rebellious Janissaries, who forced the new ruler, Mahmud II (r. 1808–1839), to retract most of the previous improvements. The worst features of the declining empire were restored.

The Serbs and the Greeks successfully revolted against Ottoman rule at about the same time. The Serbs did so under the leadership of Milosh Obrenovich (r. 1815–1839). He was a formidable figure but success was determined from outside: Russia took an interest in fellow Slavs and members of the Orthodox faith, and in 1830 they pressured Constantinople to recognize Milosh as hereditary ruler over an autonomous Serbia. The Greek struggle was also determined by larger powers. Greeks encountered the ideas of the French Revolution and dedicated themselves to restoring Greek independence. The rest of Europe, excited by the idea of an independent Greece restored to its past greatness, widely supported the Greek movement for freedom. The Great Powers intervened in 1827, sending their navies and sinking Turkish ships. In 1830 an international agreement spelled out Greek independence.

When Egypt challenged the Ottoman Empire the Great Powers again intervened, this time on the empire's behalf. Mehemet Ali, the Egyptian ruler, modernized his army and used it to wrest Syria away in 1831. Britain and Russia helped Constantinople win it back because they were concerned that the Ottoman Empire might collapse and thus threaten the region's balance of power. The survival of the Ottoman Empire was beginning to depend on the goodwill of the Great Powers.

THE REVOLUTIONS OF 1848

From France in the west to Poland in the east, at least fifty separate revolts and uprisings shook the Continent in 1848, the most extensive outbreak of violence in nineteenth-century Europe. The revolts had an impact far beyond Europe's borders. Brazilians, inspired by the example of the European revolutions, rose up against their government. In Bogotá, Colombia, church bells rang to celebrate the announcement of a republic in France. And as a result of the Parisian revolution, slaves in French colonies were emancipated.

Roots of Rebellion

There were many reasons for the outbreak of discontent. In the countryside, changes in access to land (such as land enclosure) frustrated peasants. Although in the past many had enjoyed free access to village commons, increasingly these were coming under private control. Also, the poor were once allowed to forage in the forests for firewood, but the limitation of this right now led to frequent conflicts.

Points of friction were made worse by growing populations that put pressure on available resources. In the cities, artisans were being undercut by the putting-out system, or cottage industry, in which capitalists had goods produced in the countryside by cottagers—part-time artisans who supported themselves partly through agriculture and were thus willing to work for lower wages. Crises in the crafts hurt the journeymen; they had to serve far longer apprenticeships and in many cases could never expect to be masters. Where the guild system still existed, it was in decline.

These developing concerns came to a crisis as a result of the economic depression of 1845–1846. In 1845 a crop disaster, including the spread of the potato blight, destroyed the basic food of the poor in northern Europe. Food prices doubled from what they had been in the early 1840s. An industrial downturn accompanied these agricultural disasters, creating massive unemployment. Municipal and national governments seemed unable to deal with the crowding, disease, and unsanitary conditions. Tensions ran high in the cities, the sites of national governments. Revolts were triggered by discontent, but also by the hope for change.

France

Once again the spark for revolution was ignited in Paris. Economic crisis had a severe impact in the French capital. In some occupations as many as half the people were out of work. The price of bread had shot up to over one franc a pound, which meant that the entire salary of the average male worker—a franc a day—would not buy enough bread to sustain him. Thousands of workers were ready to pour into the streets to protest the government's seeming indifference to their desperation.

Meanwhile, liberals were agitating for the expansion of suffrage. When political meetings were forbidden in 1847, they resorted to banquets featuring long-winded toasts indistinguishable from political speeches. Such a banquet was scheduled for Paris on February 22, 1848, to celebrate the birthday of George Washington—an icon to French liberals. When the government banned the meeting, mass demonstrations broke out. Unlike the British with their professional urban police, the French had no forces trained in crowd control. The government called in the military, whose tactics were more appropriate to engaging an enemy army than to containing civilians. On February 23, soldiers guarding the Ministry of Foreign Affairs panicked and shot into a crowd; fifty-two people died.

Word spread that the government was shooting at the people. To protect themselves, residents of the traditionally revolutionary neighborhoods near the Bastille square erected barricades. On February 24, protesters attacked police and army posts and surrounded the royal palace. The National Guard, a civilian force recruited from the artisan and middle class and charged with restoring order, had become sympathetic to the protesters. Louis Philippe resigned as king and fled for London under the pseudonym "Mr. Smith."

The abruptness of the king's departure left the opposition in disarray. The protesters shared one goal, the extension of suffrage, but otherwise diverged sharply. The new regime, hastily organized under the pressure of a mob invasion of the Chamber of Deputies, lacked consensus. The provisional government consisted of well-known liberal opponents of the July Monarchy such as the poet Alphonse de Lamartine (1790–1869) and the journalist Alexandre Ledru-Rollin (1807–1874). Under pressure from the radicals, socialist journalist Louis Blanc and a worker known only as Albert also joined the government. At first, there was cooperation between liberal supporters of constitutional democracy and radical republicans committed to economic justice. Under the strain of events, however, the coalition fell apart by late spring.

Bowing to pressure from the poor and unemployed of Paris, the government established national workshops and a commission headed by Louis Blanc to study the problems of the poor. The national workshops were not a substitute for the capitalist order, as Louis Blanc had intended, but a stopgap measure to enable the unemployed to earn a livelihood. They nevertheless represented the most ambitious plan that any French government had yet undertaken to combat the misery of the poor.

The new republic was quick to institute other reforms. It abolished slavery in the colonies and the death penalty for political crimes. Imprisonment for debt ceased, and the workday was limited to ten hours in Paris, eleven hours in the départements. The most radical move was the adoption of universal male suffrage. In 1789 men had identified citizenship as a distinctly male prerogative, and they continued to do so.

In the general euphoria over human liberties, women asserted their rights. A new woman's newspaper, *La Voix des Femmes* (*The Voice of*

Women), argued for equal pay, political rights, and educational opportunities. Many of the militants took their cue from the women who had fought for their rights in 1789. Women's political clubs flourished in the capital as well as in Lyon and lesser provincial towns. (See the box "A Revolutionary of 1848 Calls for Women's Political Rights.") When women's political clubs petitioned for the vote, the revolutionary government abolished them. In light of women's active role at the barricades that had toppled the monarchy, this was a bitter disappointment.

The first universal-manhood elections took place in April. The results were surprising. Nearly everyone expected enfranchisement of the poor and uneducated to bring about the election of radicals. Most of France's population, however, consisted of rural peasants, and most peasants distrusted the radicalism of the capital and resented the tax increases needed to support social programs. Peasants tended to vote for their social superiors: the local landowner, notary, or lawyer. Even Paris elected mostly moderate deputies. The new National Assembly elected by popular vote did not look much different from that of the July Monarchy. Among the new deputies, there were only seventeen workers and no peasants.

The government was soon at loggerheads with the radical workers in Paris. Under conservative pressure, in May the Assembly disbanded the national workshops, which were extremely expensive. At the news of the closings, people who depended on the workshops rose up in despair. After days of fighting in which 1500 were killed and 12,000 arrested, government forces regained control of the city. Passionate feelings on both sides led to savagery: Corpses were mutilated, and severed heads were paraded through

Revolutionary Women In this cartoon, entitled "The Divorced Women," Daumier ridicules women who fought for their rights in the revolution of 1848. They are seen as divorced, deprived of male companionship, and probably therefore crazed. This kind of depiction was one of many ways in which women were discouraged from participating in politics. *(Jean-Loup Charmet)*

A Revolutionary of 1848 Calls for Women's Political Rights

Jeanne Deroin was a French advocate of women's suffrage who served as editor of the newspaper representing women, **L'opinion des femmes,** *during the revolution of 1848. Frustrated that women were denied a role in the political process, she tried to run for parliament in 1849. In an election poster and in correspondence with a socialist paper, which although socially radical was opposed to female suffrage, Deroin proclaimed the rights of women.*

I present myself for your votes, out of devotion to the consecration of a great principle: the civil and political equality of the sexes.

It is in the name of justice that I appeal to the sovereign people against negating the great principles that are the foundation for the future of our society.

If using your right, you call upon women to take part in the work of the Legislative Assembly, you will consecrate our republican dogmas in all their integrity: Liberty, Equality, Fraternity for all women as well as for all men.

A Legislative Assembly composed entirely of men is incompetent to make the laws that rule a society of men and women, as an assembly composed entirely of privileged people to debate the interests of workers, or an assembly of capitalists to sustain the honor of the country. . . .

It is precisely because woman is equal to man, and yet not identical to him, that she should take part in the work of social reform and incorporate in it those necessary elements that are lacking in man, so that the work can be complete.

Liberty for woman, as well as for man, is the right to utilize and to develop one's faculties freely.

Life's unity can be considered to be in three parts: individual life, family life, and social life; this is a complete life. To refuse woman the right to live the social life is to commit a crime against humanity.

. . . this is a holy and legitimate protest against the errors of the old society and against a clear violation of our sacred principles of liberty, equality, and fraternity.

Source: Election poster to the Electors of the Department of Seine, *L'opinion des femmes,* April 10, 1849; *La Démocratie pacifique,* April 13, 1849. Trans. K. Offen. Reprinted in Susan Groag Bell and Karen M. Offen, eds., *Women, the Family, and Freedom: The Debate in Documents,* vol. I (Stanford: Stanford University Press, 1983), pp. 280–281.

the streets. Both the liberal Alexis de Tocqueville and the socialist Karl Marx called the June uprisings class warfare between the poor and the rich.

After the June uprisings, the propertied classes looked to the authorities for security. Of the several candidates for president in 1848, Louis Napoleon (1808–1873), a nephew of Napoleon Bonaparte, appealed to the largest cross section of the population. The bourgeoisie was attracted by the promise of authority and order, while peasants remained loyal to the memory of Napoleonic glory. Workers were impressed by Louis Napoleon's vaguely socialistic program.

Louis Napoleon received nearly three times as many votes as all his opponents combined. His government was conservative, composed of men of the old order. Three years later, Louis Napoleon dissolved the National Assembly by force and established a personal dictatorship. In 1852 he declared himself Emperor Napoleon III.

Austria

In Austria, news of the overthrow of Louis Philippe and agitation in the German states prompted demonstrations and petitions calling for a constitution and the dismissal of Metternich, the symbol of the reactionary order. In the face of growing opposition, Metternich resigned, and the army withdrew from Vienna, which appeared to have fallen under the control of students and workers. On March 15, 1848, the imperial court, surrounded by crowds of students and workers, announced its willingness to issue a constitution. Even more important was the decision to abolish serfdom. There had been fear of a serf uprising, but the relatively generous terms of the emancipation mollified the peasantry.

The promised constitution was issued, but it was drafted by the emperor rather than by representatives of the people. It was probably acceptable to the male middle classes because it enfranchised them, but students and workers who favored popular sovereignty opposed it. Mass demonstrations and an invasion of the prime minister's office prompted the court to leave Vienna for Innsbruck on May 17.

The government also faced revolts in the non-German parts of the empire: in Italy, Hungary, the

Celebrating the Revolution of 1848 in Vienna What social issues are idealized in this painting of a barricade on May 26, in the early stage of the Austrian Revolution? Consider some of the individual groups of people and their interactions. Compare the women here with the portrayal of political women in Daumier's "The Divorced Women" on page 485. *(Historische Museen der Stadt Wien)*

Czech lands, and Croatia. In March, Vienna acquiesced to Hungary's demands; thereafter, Hungary was joined to the Austrian Empire by personal union to the emperor. Constitutional government was established in Hungary, but participation in the political process was limited to Magyars, who were the largest ethnic group but who made up only 40 percent of the population. The other peoples of Hungary—Romanians, Slovaks, Croats, and Slovenes—preferred the more distant rule of German Vienna to Magyar authority.

Many nationalities rallied to the Austrian Empire in 1848 for their own reasons—fear of falling under German rule in Bohemia, fear of Magyar rule in Hungary, fear of Polish rule in Galicia (the Austrian part of Poland)—and the empire survived. There was no solidarity among the various nationalities that rose up against Vienna's rule, yet the danger nationalism posed to its survival was clearly revealed.

The revolutions in Austria and its possessions were suppressed as soon as the court was able to gather an army and send it against the rebels. Prague was bombarded into submission in June and Vienna in November 1848. Absolutist rule was re-established by Prince Felix von Schwarzenberg (1800–1852), chief minister to the new emperor, Francis Joseph (r. 1848–1916).

Italy

In the years before 1848, the Italian peninsula was in the grip of economic hardship and social unrest; nationalists and liberals hoped somehow to see their program of a united and free Italy implemented. The election in 1846 of Pius IX (r. 1846–1878) was seen as a harbinger of change. The pope was not only a religious leader but also the secular ruler of the Papal States. Pius appeared to be a liberal and a supporter of Italian unification. In January 1848, a revolution forced the king of Sicily to grant a constitution to his subjects. The Sicilian revolution was the first to erupt in Europe, but it was news of the Paris uprising in February that stimulated revolutions elsewhere in Italy.

Italians under Austrian rule revolted, forcing the Austrians to evacuate their Italian possessions. The middle classes, though eager to be free of Austrian rule, saw working-class radicals as a threat. They believed that annexation to nearby Piedmont would provide security from both Austria and the lower classes. The king of Piedmont, Charles Albert (r. 1831–1849), reluctantly decided to unite Italy under his throne if doing so would prevent the spread of radicalism to his kingdom. On March 24, 1848, he declared war on Austria but was defeated in July and had to sue for an armistice.

The pope had expressed sympathy for Italian unification but provided no support for the cause. Republicans, disappointed by the pope's abandonment of the national cause, forced him to flee. In January 1849 they declared the Roman Republic. Hope ran high that it would become the capital of a united republican Italy. Giuseppe Mazzini was to be a member of the governing triumvirate. In Piedmont, Charles Albert declared war on Austria once again, in March 1849. Within six days his army was defeated, and he resigned his throne to his son, Victor Emmanuel II (r. 1849–1878).

The Austrians quickly reconquered their lost provinces and helped restore their puppets to power. Louis Napoleon, the newly elected president of France, eager to curry favor with Catholic voters, sent French troops to Rome, restoring the pope to power in July 1849. Nevertheless, profound liberal ideas—constitutional government, universal suffrage, abolition of the remnants of the Old Regime—had been expressed and in some cases implemented, though briefly. Most reforms were rescinded, but Piedmont's liberal constitution, the *Statuto,* implemented in 1848, was retained and later became the constitution of a united Italy.

The German States

News of the February uprising in Paris also acted as a catalyst for change in the German states. In response to large public demonstrations in the grand duchy of Baden in southwestern Germany, the duke—reluctant to suffer the same fate as Louis Philippe—dismissed his conservative prime minister and installed in March 1848 a government sympathetic to the aspirations of middle-class liberals. As the king of Württemberg observed, "I cannot mount on horseback against ideas." The wisest course appeared to be compromise. He and many of his fellow dukes and princes changed their governments, dismissing their cabinets and instituting constitutions.

Up to this point Prussia was untouched by the revolutionary wave. But when news of Metternich's fall reached Berlin on March 16, middle-class liberals and artisans demonstrated for reforms. To appease his subjects, King Frederick William IV appointed a liberal businessman to head a new government. Representative government was introduced, and suffrage was extended, though it was still restricted to men of property.

The revolutionary outbreaks in the German states in 1848 were triggered by dissatisfaction with local economic and political conditions, not by agitation for German unification. But once the revolutions had taken hold, preoccupying the two largest states, Prussia and Austria—which both opposed unification lest it undermine their power—the question of a single Germany quickly came to the fore. In March 1848, a self-appointed national committee invited five hundred prominent German liberals to convene in Frankfurt to begin the process of national unification.

The vast majority of those elected to the first all-German National Assembly came from the liberal professions; only four were artisans, and one a peasant. The liberals rejoiced that they controlled the new parliament, but it was unrepresentative and lacked broad popular support.

The first all-German elected legislature met in May 1848 to create a unified Germany. The most ambitious plan envisioned a *Grossdeutschland,* or large Germany, consisting of all the members of the Germanic Confederation. Such a country would have included many non-Germans, including Poles, Czechs, and Danes. The proponents of *Kleindeutschland,* or small Germany, which would exclude Austria and its possessions, saw their solution as a more likely scenario for national unity, although it would exclude many Germans. They succeeded in the end, largely because the reassertion of Austrian imperial power in the fall of 1848 made the areas under Vienna's control ineligible for inclusion.

The Frankfurt assembly formed a provisional government in June 1848. But since the individual states, including Prussia and Austria, did not recognize the assembly's authority, it was utterly powerless. The minister of war could not raise any soldiers, and the minister of finance could not impose taxes. The United States, enthusiastic about a new republic consciously modeled on its own, was one of the few nations to accept an ambassador from the all-German government.

The parliament might have succeeded if it had called for a national uprising against the princes, but the liberals in Frankfurt were loath to do so. They distrusted the populace. Force remained in the hands of the traditional authorities. In the fall of 1848, the king of Prussia brought soldiers into Berlin and dissolved the Prussian assembly. The Prussian reassertion of royal power, though partial, was a signal for other German rulers in late 1848 to dismiss their liberal ministers.

The moment for liberalism and national unification had passed by the time the Frankfurt assembly drew up a constitution in the spring of 1849. The parliament offered the throne to Frederick William IV, king of Prussia, because he ruled the largest state within the designated state boundaries and had the power of the Prussian army. But Frederick William feared that accepting the throne would lead to war with Austria. Also, he also did not want an office offered by representatives of the people. Disappointed, most members of the Frankfurt assembly went home. A series of uprisings in favor of German unity were crushed by the Prussian army.

So German unification failed. Liberalism was unable to bring about German unity; other means would be required to do so.

SUMMARY

The revolutions of 1848 released many of the forces for change that had been gathering strength since 1815. In spite of the Congress of Vienna's effort to restore the old order after Napoleon's fall, the generation after 1815 established a new order. The ideas of change that had powered the French Revolution of 1789 continued to shape an era that claimed to be rolling history back to prerevolutionary times. Liberalism contested authoritarianism.

Reform-minded regimes in Europe improved the lives of people in colonies overseas, abolishing slavery in British and then French colonies. Some states even turned away from monarchy and experimented with republicanism, a form of government that until then many had thought fit only for small states. All of the Latin American colonies except Mexico became republics on gaining independence from Spain. In Europe during 1848–1849 the French, German, Hungarian, and Roman republics were proclaimed. These experiments suggested new modes of political organization that were to become common in the following century.

The generation after 1815 experienced revolutions frequently and broadly. These uprisings usually failed, and the forces of order were able to recapture power. Yet the status quo was altered. In many cases absolutist rulers had to grant constitutions and accept ministers who were not their choice. Even though most of these arrangements were temporary, they established an important precedent. Unusual in the first half of the century, constitutions now became the norm. Nationalism arose in these years. The desire for national independence and unity was voiced in Italy, Germany, Hungary, Poland, and the land of the Czechs.

The middle classes found their position strengthened after 1848. They did not dominate the political system, but their influence was increasing with the growth of entrepreneurship. Middle-class professionals were recruited into the civil services of states determined to streamline their operation in order to withstand revolution more effectively. Revolutionary fervor waned after 1848, but the current of economic and social change continued to transform Europe. It is to these economic and social changes that we turn next.

SUGGESTED READING

Agulhon, Maurice. *The Republican Experiment*. 1983. A work that stresses how the splits between different French political groups made it difficult for revolutionaries to achieve their goals.

Anderson, Benedict. *Imagined Communities*. 1983. A noted anthropologist underscores the extent to which a nation is an "imagined community."

Brock, Michael. *The Great Reform Act*. 1973. An account that emphasizes the sense of crisis on the eve of the Great Reform Act.

Bushnell, David, and Neill Macaulay. *The Emergence of Latin America in the Nineteenth Century*. 1988. A brief but suggestive synthesis.

Carlisle, Robert B. *The Proffered Crown: Saint-Simonianism and the Doctrine of Hope*. 1987. A work that shows the originality of Saint-Simonian thought and its continuity after the founder's death.

Harrison, J. F. C. *Quest for the New Moral World: Robert Owen and the Owenites in Britain and America*. 1969. A good biography that views the movement as affected by contemporary religious notions of a coming millennium.

Hobsbawm, E. J. *The Age of Revolution, 1789–1848*. 1962. A compellingly argued book that describes the era as being dominated by two simultaneous revolutions, the French Revolution and the industrial transformation.

Jardin, André, and André-Jean Tudesq. *Restoration and Reaction, 1815–1848*. 1988. A general survey of France.

Johnson, Paul. *The Birth of the Modern World Society, 1815–1830*. 1991. A weighty but readable book providing a panoramic view of the era. Particularly strong in providing biographical sketches of some of the major figures.

Jones, Gareth Stedman. *The Languages of Class: Studies in English Working-Class History, 1832–1982*. 1983. A work that considers Chartism as a movement of the politically disenfranchised seeking a voice within the political system.

Kedourie, Elie. *Nationalism*. 1960. An account that describes the German romantics as developers of modern nationalism and creators of an essentially pernicious force.

Kissinger, Henry. *A World Restored*. 1957. A study by a future U.S. secretary of state that emphasizes the efforts of diplomats to build an international order resistant to revolution.

Lincoln, W. Bruce. *Nicholas I: Emperor and Autocrat of All the Russias*. 1978. A biography of the tsar, revealing the ruler's dedication to preserve the autocratic regime and its values.

Pinkney, David H. *The French Revolution of 1830*. 1972. The standard work on the subject.

Porter, Roy, and Mikulas Teich, eds. *Romanticism in National Context*. 1988. An up-to-date series of essays on romanticism in different national settings.

Price, Roger. *The Revolutions of 1848*. 1989. A general history of the European revolutions describing them as the result of discontent with an economic and political system.

Sheehan, James J. *German History, 1770–1866*. 1989. A survey of the variety and contrast of the German experience.

———. *German Liberalism in the Nineteenth Century*. 1978. The standard work revealing the difficulties that German liberals faced as early as the first half of the nineteenth century.

Sked, Alan. *The Decline and Fall of the Habsburg Empire, 1815–1918*. 1989. A brief, clear study stressing the threat the revolutions of 1848 posed to imperial survival.

Sperber, Jonathan. *The European Revolutions, 1848–1851*. 1994. The best up-to-date synthesis.

Taylor, Barbara. *Eve and the New Jerusalem*. 1983. A study of socialism and feminism in the nineteenth century that pays particular attention to the Owenite movement.

Woolf, Stuart Joseph. *A History of Italy, 1700–1860*. 1979. A consideration of the problems of political divisions in Italian life.

CHAPTER 19

The Industrial Transformation of Europe, 1750–1850

In the 1830s, the French socialist Louis Blanqui suggested that just as France had experienced a political revolution, so Britain was undergoing an "industrial revolution." Eventually, that expression entered the general vocabulary to describe the advances in production that occurred first in England and then in most of western Europe. Many economic historians now emphasize how gradual the changes were and question the appropriateness of the term. In the expanse of history, however, these vast transformations—in production, transportation, information, and construction—all occurred at an extraordinary pace.

Industrial development left its mark on just about every sphere of human activity. Economic activity became increasingly specialized. The unit of production changed from the family to a larger and less personal group. Significant numbers of workers left farming to enter mining and manufacturing, and major portions of the population moved from the countryside to the city. Machines replaced or supplemented manual labor.

The economic changes physically transformed Europe. Greater levels of production were achieved, and more wealth was created than ever before. Factory chimneys belched soot into the air. Miners in search of coal, iron ore, and other minerals cut deep gashes into the earth. Cities grew quickly, and Europe became increasingly urban.

Industrialization created unprecedented advancement and opportunity as well as unprecedented hardships and social problems. Different groups tried various strategies to strike a balance between the positive and negative effects. Many entrepreneurs and their sympathizers supported liberal principles based on classical economics. Workers, with a growing sense of solidarity, struggled for their common interests. Out of the socialist ideologies of the early nineteenth century, Karl Marx forged a militant ideology to address the needs of the industrial working class.

Questions and Ideas to Consider

- Why did industrialization begin where and when it did? Consider social, cultural, and economic factors.
- Describe the circumstances of the working class in industrialized, urban Europe. How did the situation differ for women, men, and children? How did the family function as an economic unit?
- Industrialization had harsh consequences on the environment. Describe both the immediate and the long-term effects.
- What were "friendly societies"? How were they different from unions?
- How does Marxism differ from the ideas of the utopian socialists? Compare the ideas of Flora Tristan, Charles Fourier, and Robert Owen (see pages 474–475) to those of Karl Marx.

SETTING THE STAGE FOR INDUSTRIALIZATION

No one can say with certainty which conditions were necessary for the industrialization of Europe. Nevertheless, we do know why industrialization did not spread widely to the rest of the world in the nineteenth century. A certain combination of conditions—geographic, cultural, economic, demographic—helped make industrialization possible in Europe.

Why Europe?

A fortunate set of circumstances seems to explain why Europe was the stage for industrial development. Since the Middle Ages, political transformations in western Europe had reduced risk and uncertainty while encouraging productive investment. With the development of legal due process, rich merchants did not run the risk of having their wealth confiscated—as they did, for instance, in the Ottoman Empire. The unfolding of state power in Europe reduced the frequency of brigandage—still common in many parts of the world—and thus encouraged trade. Discrepancies in risk are apparent in the differences in interest rates on borrowing money in the eighteenth century: 3 percent in England, 36 percent in China.

In Europe, disparities of wealth, though serious, were less extreme than in other parts of the world; thus, there was a better market for goods. At the time western Europe industrialized, the average yearly income per person was equivalent to $500—more than in many non-Western societies even today. And nearly half of the population was literate, again a very high proportion compared to non-Western societies.

Although population grew in Europe during the eighteenth century, late marriages and limited family sizes kept its rise in check; hence European society was rarely overwhelmed by the pressures of population. In India and China, by contrast, population growth was so dramatic that society had to be fully engaged in feeding the people and could not be readily mobilized for other production.

Europe enjoyed a measure of cultural, political, and social diversity unknown elsewhere. Challenges to the dominant religious and political powers had brought some religious diversity—a rarity outside the West. Diversity encouraged a culture that tolerated and eventually promoted innovation. Competitiveness drove states to try to catch up with each other. Governments actively encouraged industries and commerce to enrich a country and make it more powerful than its neighbors. None of these factors alone explains why industrialization occurred, but their combination seems to have facilitated the process when it did occur.

The industrialization of Europe radically transformed power relationships between the industrial West and nonindustrial Africa, Asia, and

CHAPTER CHRONOLOGY

1712	Steam-operated water pump invented by Thomas Newcomen
1733	Flying shuttle introduced by John Kay
1764	Spinning jenny invented by James Hargreaves
1769	Water frame invented by Richard Arkwright
	Steam engine improved by James Watt
1779	The "mule" invented by Samuel Crompton
1784	Chlorine gas as a textile bleach discovered by C. L. Berthollet
1793	Cotton gin invented by Eli Whitney
1811–1812	Luddites smash textile machinery in Britain
1848	General Workers' Brotherhood founded in Germany
	Communist Manifesto published by Karl Marx and Friedrich Engels
1859	Samuel Smiles publishes *Self-Help*
1868	Trades Union Congress founded in Britain

South America. By 1900 the latter were overwhelmed by the economic and military power of the former. Within Europe, power shifted to the nations that were most industrialized. Britain was the first to industrialize, and as France had been the dominant power in the eighteenth century, so Britain dominated the nineteenth. Britain was widely admired and seen not only as an economic model but also as a political and cultural one.

Transformations Accompanying Industrialization

A number of transformations preceded or accompanied and helped define the industrializing era. Changes in commerce, agriculture, population behavior, and transportation were the major stimuli of industrial development.

Changes in agriculture during the eighteenth century had dramatically increased the productivity of the land. In addition, new, more efficient plows enabled farmers to cultivate more land than ever before. The wealth created by agriculture allowed for investment in industry and for expenditures on infrastructure, such as roads and canal systems, useful to industry. The new crops and the more efficient cultivation meant fewer farmworkers were necessary to feed the growing population, and surplus labor expanded the new urban industries.

In the seventeenth and eighteenth centuries, European trade had increased significantly, enriching businessmen and making them aware of the fortunes to be made in local and distant markets. A new dynamic ethos took hold of businessmen eager to venture into untried fields of economic endeavor.

The population continued to grow during the years of industrial transformation. It was significant enough to promote industrialization, yet not so large as to put a brake on economic expansion. From 1750 to 1850 the population of Europe doubled. This growing group of people supplied the labor force for the new industries and provided a large surge in consumers of industrial goods.

In the countryside industrialization was foreshadowed by a form of production that had developed in the seventeenth century—the putting-out system, or cottage industry (see page 434). During the winter and at other slack times, peasants took in handwork such as spinning, weaving, or dyeing. Entrepreneurs discovered that some individuals were better than others at specific tasks. Rather than have one household process the wool through all the steps of production until it was a finished piece, the entrepreneur would buy wool from one family, then take it to another to spin, a third to dye, a fourth to weave, and so on.

Some historians believe that this form of production, called *protoindustrialization*, laid the basis for industrial manufacture. Like the latter, it depended on specialization and supplied goods to a market beyond the producers' needs. In some areas, for instance, Flanders and northern Italy, protoindustry was followed by industrial manufacture; in other regions, such as western France, it became a substitute for industry. In still other areas, like Catalonia and the Ruhr region of western Germany, industry flourished without the previous development of cottage industries. Although cottage industry was an important contributor to industrialization in some regions, it did not play a role in every case.

A less ambiguous prerequisite for industry was a good transportation network. Transportation had improved significantly in the eighteenth century. Better roads were built; coaches and carriages were constructed to travel faster and carry larger loads. Government and private companies built canals linking rivers to each other or to lakes. All this made possible the movement of raw materials to manufacture and from there to market without too great an increase in the price of the finished good. In Great Britain these transformations occurred simultaneously with industrialization; on the Continent they preceded economic change.

In Britain, industrialization had begun before rail-building; yet once railroad expansion occurred, beginning in the 1830s, orders for iron rails, steam engines, and wagons sustained and advanced industrial growth. (See the box "Encounters with the West: A Persian Discovers the British Rail System.") On the Continent rail-building promoted industrialization, notably in Germany and later in Italy.

INDUSTRIALIZATION AND EUROPEAN PRODUCTION

Several important technological advances powered European industry, and breakthroughs in one field often led to breakthroughs in others. The first two industries to be affected were textiles and iron. New forms of energy drove the machinery, and novel forms of directing labor enhanced production. At first limited to the British Isles, industry spread to the Continent, a development that occurred unevenly in various regions.

Advances in the Cotton Industry

A series of inventions in the eighteenth century led the way to the mass manufacture of textiles. The flying shuttle, introduced in Britain in 1733 by John Kay (1704–1764), accelerated the weaving process to such an extent that it increased the demand for thread. This need was met in the 1760s by James Hargreaves (d. 1778), who invented the spinning jenny, a device that spun thread from wool or cotton. Improved spinning machines, such as the "mule" of Samuel Crompton (1753–1827), increased the efficiency of the spinning jenny so that by 1812 one spinner could produce as much yarn as two hundred had made before. In 1769, Richard Arkwright (1732–1792), a barber and wigmaker, invented the water frame. This huge spinning machine drove two pairs of rollers, moving at different speeds. It was installed in a single establishment with three hundred employees, forming the first modern factory. The frame was originally powered by horses or by a waterfall, but in 1777 Arkwright had James Watt construct a steam engine to operate it. With these innovations, cotton manufacturing increased 130-fold between 1770 and 1841.

In the past, finished cloth had been soaked in buttermilk and spread out in the meadows to be bleached by the sun. That method was hardly practical for the unprecedented quantities of cloth rolling out of the factories. The introduction

ENCOUNTERS WITH THE WEST

A Persian Discovers the British Rail System

In 1836 a delegation of three Persian princes visited England. Traveling widely, they had the opportunity to meet important Englishmen and to inspect and experience some of the new technological advances, including the railroad. One of the princes, Najaf-Kuli Mirza, wrote down his observations. In this entry on the new British rail system, he attempts to describe its workings to fellow Persians.

All the wonderful arts which require strong power are carried on by means of steam, which has rendered immense profits and advantages. The English then began to think of steam coaches, which are especially applicable to their country, because it is small, but contains an enormous population. Therefore, in order to do away with the necessity for horses, and that the land which is sown with horse-corn [rye] should be cultivated with wheat, so as to cause it to become much more plentiful (as it is the most important article of food), and that England might thereby support a much greater population, they have with their ingenious skill invented this miraculous wonder, so as to have railroads from the capital to all parts of the kingdom.

Thus, by geometrical wisdom, they have made roads of iron, and where it was necessary these roads are elevated on arches. The roads on which the coaches are placed and fixed are made of iron bars. The coach is so fixed that no air or wind can do it any harm and twenty or thirty coaches may be fixed to the first in the train, and these one after the other.

All that seems to draw these coaches is a box of iron, in which they put water to boil, as in a fire-place; underneath this iron box is like an urn, and from it rises the steam which gives the wonderful force: when the steam rises up, the wheels take their motion, the coach spreads its wings, and the travellers become like birds. In this way these coaches go the incredible distance of forty miles an hour.

We actually travelled in this coach, and we found it very agreeable, and it does not give more but even less motion than horses; whenever we came to the sight of a distant place, in a second we passed it. The little steam engine possesses the power of eighteen horses.

Source: Najaf-Kuli Mirza, *Journal of a Residence in England and of a Journey to and from Syria* II (London, 1839, Reprinted, Farnborough, England: Gregg International Publishers, 1971), pp. 11–12.

of sulfuric acid solved the problem. It was a far more economical bleach than buttermilk and sunlight and could be produced in commercial quantities. It in turn was replaced in the 1790s when the Frenchman C. L. Berthollet (1748–1822) discovered the bleaching powers of chlorine gas. Entrepreneurs or artisans made many of the other industrial inventions, but the breakthroughs in bleaching demonstrated that more and more, industry would be fueled by advances in scientific knowledge.

The cotton-manufacturing industry in Great Britain was based on cotton grown mainly in the U.S. South. Manufactured cotton was comfortable to wear, easy to wash, and cheap enough to compete with all handmade textiles. The popularity of cotton may have improved public health as well, for people could now own several changes of clothing and keep them clean. The higher demand for raw material put pressure on cotton growers in the United States, who opened up new land.

British Cotton Manufacture Machines simultaneously performed various functions. The carding machine (front left) separated cotton fibers, readying them for spinning. The roving machine (front right) wound the cotton onto spools. The drawing machine (rear left) wove patterns into the cloth. Rich in machines, this factory needed relatively few employees; most were women and children. *(The Granger Collection, New York)*

In 1793, the American Eli Whitney (1765–1825) invented the cotton gin, a device that mechanically removed the seeds from cotton. The cotton gin meant that more cotton could be processed and thus more could be grown. It increased the profitability of the U.S. southern plantation economy and the attractiveness of slave labor.

The cotton industry in Britain showed how local manufacturing could produce a ripple effect across the oceans. Among those benefiting overseas were American farmers, cotton traders, and merchants, as well as consumers of English cotton cloth around the world. Elsewhere, people were adversely affected—in Africa, where slaving raids increased, and in India, where local spinners were driven out of business.

No longer, as in preindustrial trade, were all goods locally made; nor did the consumer meet producers and buy from them. Increasingly, specialization became the norm. The results were high production and a low price for the finished product. For human beings, this often meant a sense of separation from the finished product and a loss of the pride and individuality of craftwork.

Iron, Steam, and Factories

Charcoal had traditionally fueled the smelting of iron. Britain, however, ran out of wood before other European countries did and needed an alternative source of fuel. There was plenty of coal, but it contained contaminating impurities, particularly sulfur. The discovery that coal in a blast furnace could smelt iron without contamination triggered the iron industry's use of coal. In 1777, the introduction of a steam engine to operate the blast furnace considerably increased efficiency. The output of the English iron industry doubled between 1788 and 1796 and again in the following eight years. Relatively cheap and durable iron machines replaced wooden machines, which had worn out rapidly. The new machines fueled further advances. The industrial change that had started with cotton was continued by breakthroughs in the use of iron and coal.

Before the age of industry, the basic sources of power were humans, animals, wind, and water. Humans and animals were limited in their capacity to drive the large mills needed to grind corn or operate a sawmill. Wind power was unreliable, and water-driven mills depended on the seasons—streams dried up in the summer and froze in the winter. And water mills could be placed only where there was a waterfall. The steam engine changed everything because it was a constant power source that could be located just about anywhere. The steam engine was first used to pump out coal mines. As mining shafts were dug ever deeper, water in the mines became an increasing hindrance. In 1712, Thomas Newcomen (1663–1729) invented a steam-operated water pump. James Watt (1736–1819) improved on the Newcomen engine considerably, making it twice as efficient in energy output. Eventually he made it capable of converting the reciprocating motion of the piston to rotary motion. This breakthrough enabled the steam engine to power a variety of machines. Its use spread rapidly. Cotton production in Britain grew more than 400-fold between 1840 and 1860. Assisted by machines, workers were enormously more productive than when they depended on hand-operated tools. In 1700 spinning 100 pounds of cotton took 50,000 worker-hours; by 1825, it took only 135.

The steam engine centralized the workplace. With the machine as a central power source, it became practical to organize work in factories. Large, austere edifices sometimes inspired by military architecture, factories imposed rigorous work discipline. The tall factory chimney became a common sight on the industrial landscape.

Factories ranged in size from small food-manufacturing operations to large textile mills. In the first half of the nineteenth century, the average number of employees in English and French textile mills was between two and three hundred. Some plants were big, but in 1850 the small workshop, worked by the owner and his relatives or a handful of employees, was still the most common site of manufacturing in Britain.

British production became truly industrial only after 1850. For decades industry coexisted with the artisan trades and other nonindustrial occupations, and indeed in a number of cases it aided their growth. Cheap industrially manufactured thread allowed handweaving to survive. Skilled craftsmen made by hand many of the machines and boilers used in factories. Income from the new industries created a wealthy middle class, which consumed more handmade goods and employed a great number of domestic servants; except for agriculture, domestic service was the single largest field of employment for women. In 1850 factory labor did not dominate the economy of western Europe, but it had become clear that it would be increasingly difficult for handmade products to compete.

Inventions and Entrepreneurs

The industrial age was triggered by inventions, and it was sustained by the steady flow of new ones. In the decade 1700–1709, 22 patents had been issued in Britain; between 1840 and 1849, 4581 were granted. Something revolutionary was occurring. People were seeing in their lifetime sizable growth in productivity, both in the factory and on the farm. Rather than cling to traditional methods, many entrepreneurs challenged tradition. In this age of invention, innovation was prized as never before.

Most of the early British industrialists belonged to merchant families; very few were landed noblemen, industrial workers, or artisans. However, in the iron industry, it was not uncommon for metalworkers to build a modest iron mill and then enlarge it. That was also the case with potters. Josiah Wedgwood (1730–1795), who pioneered the industrial manufacturing of china, came from a long line of artisan potters and is a good example of a self-made man. The thirteenth child of a potter who died when Josiah was 9 years old, he went to work for his brother as an apprentice and gradually established himself on his own. Richard Arkwright was a barber before his invention of the water frame brought him a knighthood and a fortune of half a million pounds. Many entrepreneurs began as farmers, became involved in the putting-out system, and graduated to industrial manufacture. Yet a disproportionate number of the early manufacturers were university educated. In fact, the self-made man was more the exception than the rule. Most entrepreneurs came from relatively privileged backgrounds.

Entrepreneurs took considerable financial risk when they invested in new enterprises. Most entrepreneurs ran a single plant by themselves or with a partner, but even in the early stages, some ran several plants. In 1788, Richard Arkwright and his partners had eight mills. Some enterprises were vertically integrated, controlling all stages of production. The entrepreneurs' dynamism and boldness fostered the growth of the British industrial system, making the small nation the "workshop of the world."

Britain's Lead in Industrial Innovation

Britain led the way industrially for many reasons. It was the first European country to have a standard currency, tax, and tariff system. It enjoyed the most emancipated labor. Although Britain was by no means an egalitarian society, it accommodated some movement between the classes. Ideas and experiments were readily communicated among entrepreneurs, workers, and scientists. Although other countries had scientific societies, several societies in Britain brought together theoreticians and businessmen—for example, the Lunar Society in Birmingham and the Literary and Philosophical Society in Manchester.

Britain was far more open to dissent than were other European countries at the time. The lack of conformity was reflected in religious diversity, as well as a willingness to try new methods of production. In fact, the two often went together. A large proportion of British entrepreneurs were Quakers or belonged to one of the dissenting (non-Anglican) churches. Perhaps they were accustomed to questioning authority and treading new paths. They were also well educated and, as a result of common religious bonds, inclined to provide mutual aid, including financial support.

England had gained an increasing share of international trade since the seventeenth century. This trade provided capital for investment in industrial plants. The world trade network also ensured that Britain had a market beyond its borders, as well as access to the raw materials it needed for its industry, the most important of which was cotton.

Earlier than its competitors, Britain had a national banking system to provide capital for expanding industries. In addition to numerous London banks, there were six hundred provincial banks by 1810. Banking could flourish because Britons had wide experience in trade, had accumulated considerable wealth, and had found a constant demand for credit.

Geographically, Britain was also fortunate. Coal and iron were located close to each other (Map 19.1). A relatively narrow island, Britain has easy access to the sea. This was a strategic advantage, for water was by far the cheapest means of transportation. Compared to the Continent, Britain had few tolls, and goods could move around easily.

On the whole, British workers were better off than their continental counterparts. They were more skilled, earned higher wages, and had discretionary income to spend on the manufactured

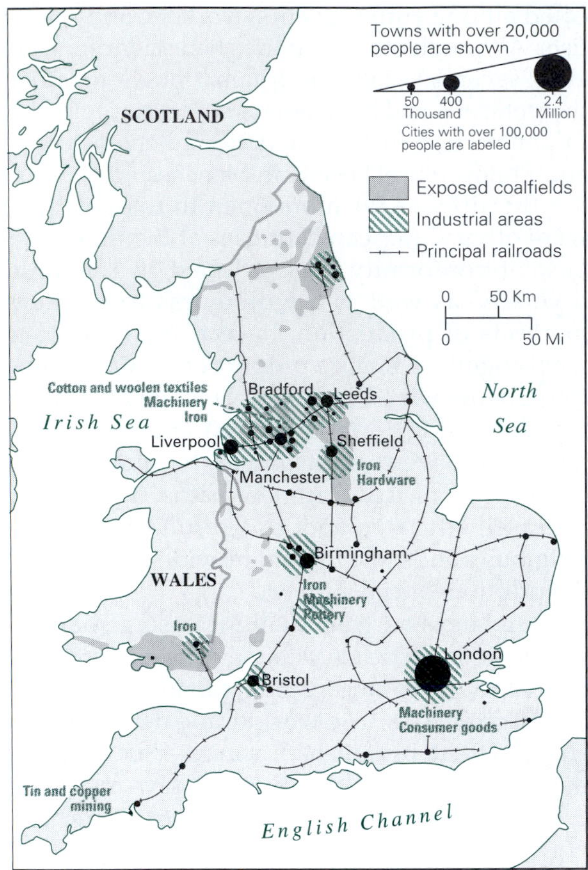

Map 19.1 The Industrial Transformation in England, ca. 1850 Industry developed in the areas rich in coal and iron fields. Important cities sprang up nearby and were linked to each other by a growing rail network.

goods now for sale. But because their wages were higher than wages on the Continent, there was an incentive for British business owners to find labor-saving devices and reduce the number of workers needed for production.

Population in Great Britain increased by 8 percent in each decade from 1750 to 1800. This swelling population expanded the market for goods. The most rapid growth occurred in the countryside, causing a steady movement of people from rural to urban areas. The presence of this work force was another contributing factor in Britain's readiness for change.

The timing of the industrial transformation in Britain was influenced by plentiful harvests in the years 1715–1750, creating low food prices and thus making possible low industrial wages. The demand for industrial goods was reasonably high. Farmers with good earnings could afford the new iron manufactured plows. It is likely that the income from farming helped bring about population growth, improvements to the transportation system, and the growing availability of capital for investment. Each change triggered more change, and the cumulative effect was staggering (see Map 19.1).

The Spread of Industry to the Continent

The ideas and methods that were changing industry in Britain spread to the Continent by direct contact and emulation. Visitors came to Britain, studied local methods of production, and returned home to set up blast furnaces and spinning works inspired by British design. Some visitors even resorted to industrial espionage, smuggling blueprints of machines out of Britain. Although a British law forbade local artisans from emigrating, some did leave, including entrepreneurs who helped set up industrial plants in France and Belgium. By the 1820s, British technicians were all over Europe.

The first country on the Continent to industrialize was Belgium, which had won its independence from the Netherlands in 1830. Like Britain, Belgium had iron and coal in proximity (Map 19.2). Belgium also had a long tradition of working cloth and iron and could readily adapt new methods to increase production of both. Belgium's location between Britain and Germany fostered the development of railroads. And railbuilding facilitated industrialization by providing fast and cheap transportation and stimulating the iron industry. The Belgian government encouraged industrial modernization by building railroads and investing in the shipping industry. In the early years it kept tariffs high to protect nascent industries; later it negotiated free-trade agreements to provide expanded markets for its manufacturers.

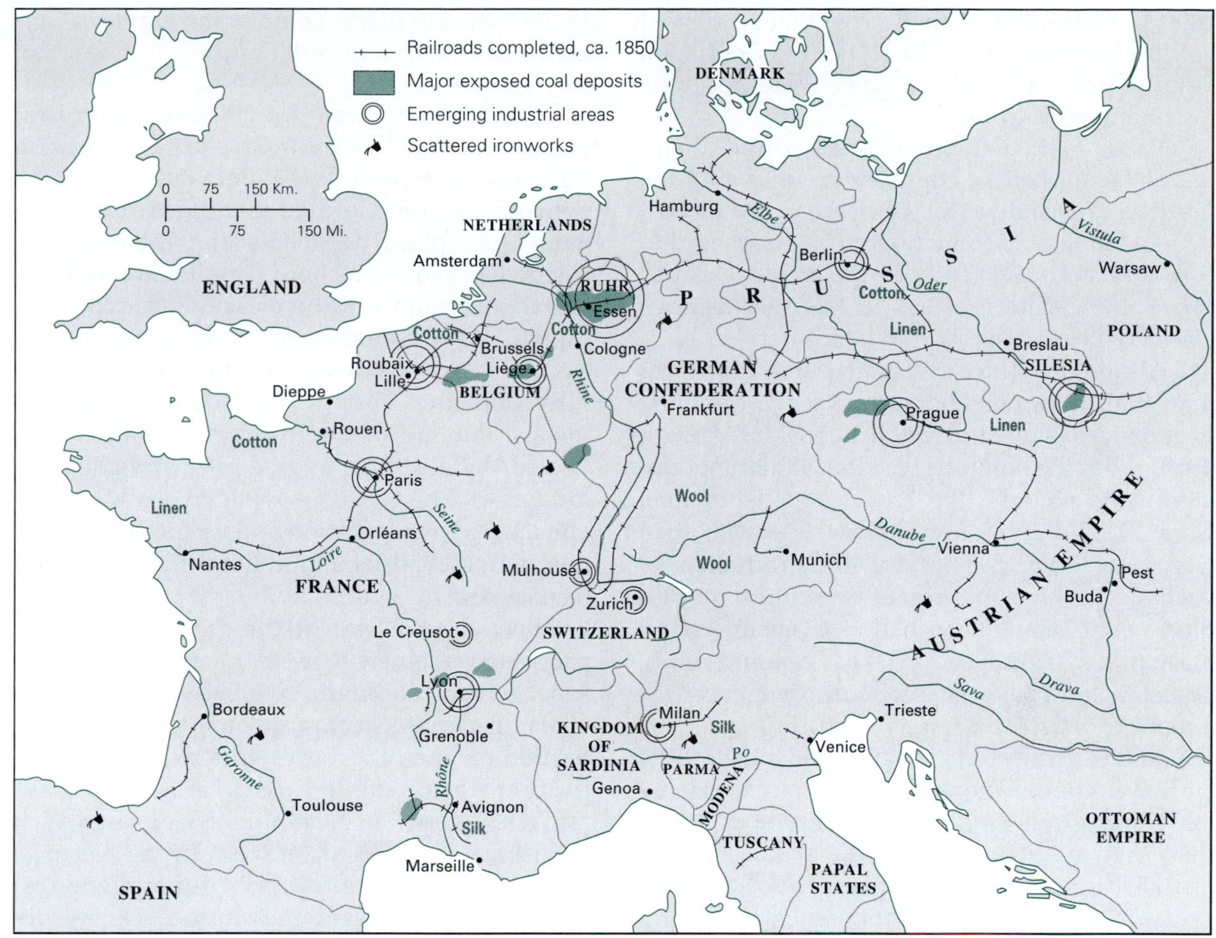

Map 19.2 Continental Industrialization, ca. 1850 Despite the fact that industry had begun on the Continent by the mid-nineteenth century, it was still sparse there, as was the rail network.

In the eighteenth century France seemed a more likely candidate for economic growth than Britain. France's overseas trade was growing faster than Britain's. In 1780, France's industrial output was greater than Britain's, though production per person was less. In the nineteenth century, however, while Britain's industry boomed, France's lagged behind. Why?

Historians have suggested several reasons. The war and revolution of the late eighteenth century were certainly contributing factors. They slowed economic growth and cut France off from the flow of information and new techniques from Britain. Moreover, in the 1790s, when the French peasants pressured for legislation to ease their situation, the revolutionaries responded positively. Thus, the misery of the peasantry was somewhat relieved, and peasants felt no urgency to leave the land and provide a cheap and ready labor supply, as in Britain. Further, since the Napoleonic Code of 1804 abolished primogeniture, younger sons were not forced off the land when their father died. Population figures provide another reason. Between

1800 and 1914, the population of France grew at half the average rate of the rest of the Continent. Finally, iron and coal in France were not close together (see Map 19.2).

Thus, French manufacturers found themselves facing British competition. By being the first to industrialize, the British had the advantage of being able to manufacture goods and to corner markets efficiently and relatively cheaply. The French were the first to feel the negative effects of being an industrial latecomer.

Although France's growth rate was lower than that of its neighbors, the French economy experienced slow but nearly constant growth throughout the nineteenth century. Taking population into account, the French did better than Great Britain and only slightly less well than Germany. From 1810 to 1850, the production of coal and the consumption of raw cotton quintupled. In 1830, France had 130 steam-driven machines; by 1852, it had 16,000. In ceramics, glass, porcelain, and paper manufacturing, France was a pioneer. Most French manufacturing, however, remained small; the typical firm had a handful of employees. Production by artisans, rather than by mass industrial production, continued longer there than in Britain or Germany.

The invasions of Germany by Napoleon caused considerable destruction but also brought some positive economic benefits. The example of the French Revolution led to important socioeconomic changes. Restrictive guilds declined. The French occupiers suppressed the small German states with their many tariffs and taxes, established a single unified legal system—which survived even after 1815—and introduced a single standard of measurement based on the metric system.

Governments in the German Confederation played an important role in the adoption of improved methods of manufacturing. The Prussian government invested in a transportation network to carry raw materials for processing and finished goods to their markets. To spur both trade and industrial growth, Prussia took the lead in creating a customs union, the *Zollverein*, which abolished tariffs among its members. By 1834 a German market embracing eighteen German states with a population of 23 million had been created.

German industrial growth accelerated dramatically in the 1850s. Massive expenditures on railways created a large demand for metal, which pressured German manufacturers to enlarge their plant capacities and increase efficiency. Germany was not yet politically unified, but the German middle classes saw economic growth as the route to prominence in Europe. Germany's growth was phenomenal. It successfully emulated Britain, overtook France, and toward the end of the nineteenth century pioneered the electrical engineering and chemical industries. The Germans avoided costly and inefficient experimentation and adapted the latest methods; they also entered fields the British had neglected.

Even by the end of the century, however, progress remained slow in many areas of Europe. As long as Russia retained serfdom (until 1861), it would lack the mobile labor force needed for industrial growth. And until late in the century, the ruling Russian aristocracy hesitated to adopt an economic system in which wealth was not based on land. In the Austrian Empire, Bohemia was the only important industrial center; otherwise, the empire was heavily agrarian (see Map 19.2).

The impoverished southern Mediterranean countries experienced little economic growth. With mostly poor soil, their agriculture yielded only a meager surplus. Spain, lacking coal or access to other energy sources, could not easily diversify its economic base. There was some industry in Catalonia, especially around Barcelona, but it did not have much impact on the rest of the country. The Italian peninsula was still industrially underdeveloped in the middle of the nineteenth century.

Although by midcentury only a few European nations had experienced industrialization to any great extent, many more would do so by the end of the century, pressured by severe competition from their more advanced neighbors. The potential threat was political and military as well as economic, for the industrialized nations represented military might and superiority. As compared to the rest of the world, Europe in the nineteenth century had a distinct material culture increasingly based on machine manufacture. Although only some regions of Europe were industrialized, many Europeans came to view their continent as obviously "superior" and the other continents as "inferior."

THE TRANSFORMATION OF EUROPE AND ITS ENVIRONMENT

Industry changed the traditional methods of agriculture, commerce, trade, and manufacture. It also transformed people's lives, individually and collectively. It altered how they made a livelihood, where and how they lived, and how they thought of themselves. Because industry required specialization, the range of occupations expanded dramatically.

The advent of industry transformed the way society functioned. Until the eighteenth century, the basis of influence and power was hereditary privilege, which meant aristocratic birth and land. The aristocracy did not disappear, but in the late eighteenth century it was challenged by a class of people whose wealth was self-made and whose influence was based on economic contributions to society. Cities grew dramatically as a result of industrialization, and Europeans faced urban problems and the pollution of their air and water.

Urbanization and Its Discontents

A sociologist at the end of the nineteenth century observed, "The most remarkable social phenomenon of the present century is the concentration of population in cities."[1] The number and size of cities had grown as never before. The major impetus for urban growth was the concentration of industry in cities and the resulting need of large numbers of urban workers for goods and services.

Industrialization was not the only stimulus. France provides many examples of urban growth with little industry. Increased commercial, trading, and administrative functions also led to the growth of cities. Neither Holland, Italy, nor Switzerland experienced much industrial development in the first half of the nineteenth century, yet their cities grew. In general, however, industry transformed people from rural to urban inhabitants.

Urban growth in some places was dramatic. In the entire eighteenth century, London grew by only 200,000; in the first half of the nineteenth century, it grew by 1.4 million, more than doubling its size. Liverpool and Manchester experienced similar growth. Census figures show that by 1851 Britain was a predominantly urban society, the first country to have as many people living in cities as in the countryside. For Germany that date was 1891, for France 1931. Although the proportion of people who were urban varied from place to place, the trend was clear.

In some cases factories were built in the countryside far from any town; as they prospered, cities grew up around them. In other cases industry gave rise to dramatic growth in once-modest towns. As industry stimulated urban growth, it was fueled in turn by urbanization. Large cities provided a labor pool and convenient markets for goods. The concentration of people encouraged the exchange of ideas. A large city was likely to have scientific societies and laboratories where engineers and scientists could discuss new ideas. After midcentury, industrialization was driven more and more by scientific and technical breakthroughs made in urban environments.

Cities pulled in people from near and far. Usually, the larger the city, the stronger its ability to attract migrants from great distances. While the medium-sized French town of Saint-Etienne drew migrants from the nearby mountains, Paris drew from the entire country. Industrial centers attracted people from beyond the nation's borders. The Irish arrived in large numbers to work in the factories in Lancashire, Belgians came for mining work in northern France, and Poles sought employment in the Ruhr in western Germany. Industrial activity stimulated world trade and shipping, taking merchant sailors far from home. Africans and Asians settled in port cities such as Amsterdam, Marseille, and Liverpool. Many large cities had heterogeneous populations, which included people of different languages, religions, and national origins, as well as, in some cases, of different races.

With the growth of cities came a multitude of urban ills. In the first half of the nineteenth century, mortality rates were higher in the cities than the countryside. There was a dramatic social inequality in the face of death. Factoring in the high child mortality rate, the average age at death for members of gentry families in Liverpool in 1842 was 35; for members of laborers' families it was 15. In 1800 boys living in urban slums were 8 inches shorter than their more fortunate contemporaries.

The rapid growth of the cities caught local authorities unprepared, and in the early stages of industrialization city life was particularly severe for the poor. Urban slums developed. The most notorious London slum was St. Giles, which became a tourist attraction because of its squalor. In many cities, large numbers of people were crammed into small areas. The houses were built back to back on small lots and had insufficient lighting and ventilation. Overcrowding was the norm. One study of a working-class parish in central London in midcentury showed three-quarters of the families living in single rooms. On one particular street, between twelve and twenty people were sleeping in each room. In Preston in 1842, 2400 persons slept three to a bed.

Sanitation was rudimentary or nonexistent. A single privy in a courtyard was likely to serve dozens of tenants—in some notorious cases in Britain and France, a few hundred. Waste from the privy might drain through open sewers to a nearby river, which was likely to be the local source of drinking water. Or the privy might be connected to a cesspool from which wastewater would seep and contaminate nearby wells. Some tenants lacked toilets and relieved themselves in the street. In the 1830s people living in the poorest sections of Glasgow stored human waste in heaps alongside their houses and sold it as manure.

In manufacturing towns factory chimneys spewed soot, and everything was covered with dirt and grime. Smoke created the famous London fog, which not only reduced visibility but posed serious health risks. City streets were littered with refuse; rotting corpses of dogs and horses were common. In 1858 the stench was so severe that the British House of Commons had to suspend its sessions.

It is not surprising that cholera, a highly infectious disease transmitted through contaminated water, swept the European urban centers. In the 1830s one of the first epidemics of modern times struck Europe, killing 100,000 in France, 50,000 in Britain, and 238,000 in Russia. Typhoid fever, also an acute infectious disease, hit mostly the poor but did not spare the privileged. Queen Victoria of Great Britain nearly died of it, and her husband, Prince Albert, did.

The Working Classes and Their Lot

In 1842 a middle-class observer traveling in industrial Lancashire noted that around the mills and factories there had developed a "population [that] like the system to which it belongs is NEW . . . hourly increasing in breadth and strength."[2] A French countess, using the pen name Daniel Stern, wrote in her memoirs of France in the 1830s and 1840s of the emergence of "a class apart, as if it were a nation within the nation," working in factories and mines, called "by a new name: the industrial proletariat."[3]

As industry advanced, more and more people depended on it for a livelihood. In the putting-out system, when there was an agricultural downturn, a cottager could spend more time on hand labor, and when there was a slack in demand for hand labor, the cottager could devote more time to the land. But people living in industrial cities were totally dependent on manufacturing. Neither skilled nor unskilled workers were assured of regular employment: Any downturn in the economy led to layoffs or loss of

St. Giles The most notorious London slum was St. Giles, whose human squalor made it a tourist attraction. *(Harvard College Library)*

jobs. In addition, the introduction of new industries often devastated laborers in older forms of production.

Most factory work was dirty and laborious, in grim plants with heavy machinery. Sixteen-hour days were common, and child labor was widespread. Because there were no safety provisions, the workers were prone to accidents—especially new workers unaccustomed to work routines or experienced workers untrained on new machines. Few factory owners protected their workers against dangerous substances or circumstances. Mercury used in hat manufacturing gradually poisoned the hatmakers and often led to dementia—the origin of the term *mad hatter*. Lead used in paints and pottery also had a devastating impact on workers' health. Metal grinding caused serious health problems. In Sheffield in 1842, three-quarters of the cutlery workers had lung disease by the age of 40. In the 1840s the British military rejected four of ten rural volunteers because of some health deficiency; in the industrializing cities the rate of rejection was 90 percent.

Usually physically lighter than boys and often underfed, girls were faced with heavy labor that undermined their health. In 1842, 18-year-old Ann Eggley, a mineworker since the age of 7, hauled carriages loaded with ore weighing 800 pounds for twelve hours a day. She testified to a parliamentary commission that she was so tired from her work that when she came home she often fell asleep before even going to bed. Isabel Wilson, another mineworker, testified that she had given birth to ten children and had suffered five miscarriages. These women—overworked, exhausted, vulnerable to disease, and especially endangered by complications from giving birth—faced premature death. The mortality rate for adult women during the era of industrial transformation was slightly higher than that for men. The situation changed only toward the end of the nineteenth century.

Wages were so low that workers normally spent between two-thirds and three-fourths of their income on food. Family survival depended as much on intelligent purchasing and economizing as it did on money earned. Skill in negotiating the consumer economy could mean the difference between life and death. Women made the family's clothes, raised chickens or pigs, tended a potato patch, took in other families' laundry, collected rags to sell, and stretched food in whatever ways possible. Bread was the largest single item consumed; in Britain and Germany people also ate a lot of potatoes. A little bacon or other meat gave flavor to the meal, but meat was rarely consumed as a main course. Men generally took the choice piece of meat and the largest amount of food. Women and children ate what was left.

Despite such hardship, industrialization did increase wealth from the beginning. "Optimist" historians argue that some of the new wealth trickled down to the lower levels of society. "Pessimist" historians say that a downward flow did not necessarily occur. Statistics suggest that by the 1840s workers' lives in Britain did improve. Their real incomes rose by 40 percent between 1800 and 1850. In part this advance was due to an increase in the numbers of skilled workers, who were paid more than their unskilled counterparts. Although factory workers' wages took time to improve, they were usually higher than wages in the handicrafts. In Lille, in northern France, in the 1830s women in spinning mills were paid one-quarter to one-half more than lacemakers, whose work was done by hand.

Factory workers benefited not only from increased earnings but from the relatively low prices of many basic goods. In London, the price of 4 pounds of household bread fell from 15 pennies at the beginning of the nineteenth century to 8½ pennies in the 1830s. As the cost of cloth declined, there was a marked improvement in the dress of working-class people. In Germany workers' wages did not increase appreciably between 1800 and 1829, but by 1850 they had increased by 25 percent and by 1870 by another 50 percent.

Industrialization and the Family

Industrialization dramatically changed the character of the working-class family and household. Table 19.1 reveals the existence of a variegated, hierarchical work force with clear, separate functions and specified salaries. Job segregation reserved the best-paying jobs, such as carpenter and the running of certain machinery, for men. Especially in the textile industries, factory owners employed children and women in the lowest positions and paid them considerably less. Women generally received from 30 to 50 percent of men's wages, children from 5 to 25 percent. In 1839, Thomas Heath, a weaver in Spitalfields, a London neighborhood, earned 15 shillings a week, his wife but 3 shillings.

Factory work often undermined the ability of families to take care of their children. As farmers or cottagers, parents had been able to work and supervise their children at the same time. The factory, however, often separated the parents from their children. Many children were given heavy burdens at an early age, and it was not uncommon for an older child, sometimes only 5 or 6 years old, to be entrusted with the care of his or her sibling. Suzanne Monnier, the daughter of a French worker, described in her memoirs how her mother on giving birth had the 9-year-old Suzanne kiss her new sister and told her, "This is not a sister I am giving you, but a daughter."

Other workers resorted to more dangerous methods of child care. They might send a newborn to a "babyfarm," to individuals in the countryside who were paid to take care of the child. Very often these babies were neglected, and their mortality rate was extremely high. In many cases, babyfarming was no more than a camouflaged form of infanticide. Mothers who kept their children at home but were obliged to leave them unwatched during factory hours sometimes

Table 19.1 Wage Differentials in Verviers, Belgium, 1836–1869

		Wages (francs per day)				
		1836	1846	1856	1863	1869
Male Occupations	Carpenter*	1.90	2.25	2.65	2.87	3.50
	Dyer	1.40	1.46	1.60	2.60	3.37
	Spinner	1.80	1.90	2.90	3.12	3.40
	Tanner*	1.83	2.00	2.25	3.00	3.25
	Hand weaver*	1.97	1.70	2.85	3.00	3.00
	Joiner*	1.98	2.00	2.25	2.75	3.00
	Presser	1.47	1.78	1.78	2.15	3.00
	Comber	0.84	1.27	1.50	1.75	2.65
	Laborer	—	1.25	1.50	1.87	2.50
Female Occupations	Mender	0.73	0.80	1.10	1.40	2.25
	Wool sorter	0.98	1.08	1.70	1.85	2.00
	Seamstress*	0.73	0.80	1.10	1.40	—
	Scourer	0.70	0.75	0.85	1.35	1.62
Children's Occupation	Piecener	—	0.70	0.90	1.10	1.60

*Artisans. (Those not starred were industrial workers.)

Source: Adapted from Chamber of Commerce of Verviers, *Rapport général sur la situation du commerce et de l'industrie en 1868* (Verviers, 1869), p. 69; repr. in George Alter, *Family and the Female Life Course—The Women of Verviers, Belgium, 1849–1880* (Madison: University of Wisconsin Press, 1988), p. 103. Used by permission of the University of Wisconsin Press.

pacified them with opium, readily available from the local druggist.

Working-class women carried a heavy burden in the family. In addition to sometimes working outside the home, they were responsible for running the household, managing the family income, and taking care of the children—providing most of the nurture and supervision they required. Because of the many demands on married women, their employment pattern followed the life cycle. Young women might work before marriage or before giving birth, then stay home until the children were older, and then return to work. Factory work had a harsh impact on women's lives, but most women did not work in factories; far more were in agriculture, crafts industries (which still flourished despite poor working conditions), and domestic service.

Some sectors of industry had a large proportion of women in them. In France, for example, where textiles were still the predominant product after the turn of the nineteenth century, women made up two-thirds of the textile work force as late as 1906. In iron and, later, steel plants, men were dominant. But in Belgium, women represented a full 15 percent of miners.

The textile industry found employment for children once they were over the age of 5 or 6. Their size made them useful for certain jobs, such as reaching under machines to pick up loose cotton. Because of their small hands they were also hired as "doffers," taking bobbins off frames and replacing them. Elizabeth Bentley began work as a doffer in 1815 at the age of 6. At the age of 23, when she testified before a parliamentary commission, she was "considerably deformed . . . in consequence of this labor." (See the box "The Young Girl in the Factory.")

Families changed their behaviors, but continued to function as cooperative economic units. Grandparents often moved from the country to live with the family and take care of children.

The Young Girl in the Factory

Reformers in Parliament, among them Michael Sadler, denounced the appalling conditions in the factories. Sadler was appointed to head a commission to hold hearings; workers appeared before it giving vivid descriptions of their lot. Public and parliamentary outrage at the conditions revealed by these hearings led to the Factory Act of 1833. Among the witnesses was Elizabeth Bentley, a 23-year-old weaving machine operator, who gave the following testimony.

What age are you?—23 . . .

What time did you begin to work in a factory?—When I was 6 years old. . . .

What were your hours of labor? . . . —From 5 in the morning till 9 at night, when they were thronged.

For how long have you worked that excessive length of time?—For about half a year.

What were your usual hours of labor when they were not so thronged?—From 6 in the morning till 7 at night.

What time was allowed for your meals?—40 minutes at noon. . . .

Your labor is very excessive?—Yes, you have not time for anything.

Suppose you flagged a little, or were too late, what would they do?—Strap us. . . .

Girls as well as boys?—Yes.

Severely?—Yes.

Could you eat your food well in that factory?—No, indeed, I had not much to eat, and the little I had I could not eat it, my appetite was so poor, and being covered with dust; and it was no use taking it home, I could not eat it . . . .

Did you live far from the mill?—Yes, two miles.

Had you a clock?—No, we had not. . . .

Were you generally there in time?—Yes; my mother has been up at four o'clock in the morning and at two o'clock; the colliers used to go to their work at about three or four o'clock, and when she heard them stirring she has got up out of her warm bed, and gone out and asked them the time; and I have sometimes been at Hunslet Car at 2 o'clock when it was steaming down with rain, and we have had to stay till the mill was opened [at 5 A.M.].

Source: Great Britain, *Sessional Papers, House of Commons,* Hearing of June 4, 1832, vol. XV (1831–1832), pp. 195–197.

A study of Verviers, an industrial city in eastern Belgium, showed that at mid-nineteenth century a sizable number of children over the age of 20 continued to live with their parents and contribute to the financial well-being of the family unit. When industrial workers married, they often settled with their spouses on the same street or in the same neighborhood where their parents lived. Although industry had the potential to undermine traditional family structures—sometimes giving women unprecedented opportunities to survive outside the family—the historical evidence shows that the family economic unit was the most effective way for men and women to survive in the industrial world.

The Land, the Water, and the Air

Industrialization seriously challenged the environment, transforming the surface of the earth, the water, and the air. To run the new machinery, coal was mined in increasing amounts. Iron and

Manchester, England, 1851 A small, unimportant town of 20,000 in the 1750s, Manchester—as a result of industrialization—had 400,000 inhabitants in 1850. In this 1851 painting, the polluted industrial city is contrasted with its idealized rural suburb. *(The Royal Collection © 1993 Her Majesty Queen Elizabeth II)*

other minerals were also in great demand. The exploitation of coal ushered in the modern age of energy use, in which massive amounts of nonrenewable resources are consumed.

To extract coal and other minerals, miners dug deep tunnels. Millions of tons of earth, rock, and other debris were removed from underground. This material, plus slag and other waste from the factories, was heaped up in mounds that at times covered acres of land, creating new geological formations. In one district in England in 1870, a million cubic yards of soda waste occupied 50 acres.

People cut down millions of trees to supply the wood to build shafts for coal, iron, and tin mines, or to make charcoal for glassmaking. Between 1750 and 1900, industrial and agricultural needs led to the clearing of 50 percent of all the forests ever cleared. Many of Europe's major forests disappeared or were seriously diminished. Deforestation in turn sped up soil erosion.

Factories dumped waste ash into rivers, changing their channels and making them considerably shallower. Because of pollution from industrial and human waste, by 1850 no fish could survive in the lower Thames River in England. Smoke and soot darkened the skies. Foul odors from factories could be detected at several miles' distance. Not merely unpleasant, various air pollutants caused cancer and lung disease.

RESPONSES TO INDUSTRIALIZATION

The misery of people in the new industrial classes was disquieting evidence of the impact of industrialization. What should be done about the working classes—or for them? These new classes developed their own sense of a common interest and fate. The result was a resounding cry for political and social democracy that began in the first half of the nineteenth century and became increasingly insistent. Many solutions were proffered. The proposals became powerful ideologies shaping the nineteenth and twentieth centuries, not only in Europe but also in most of the world.

Middle-Class Ideology

The classical economists of the late eighteenth and early nineteenth centuries (see page 472) had argued in favor of laissez faire, the policy of nonintervention by the government in the economy. The laws of supply and demand, they contended, if allowed to operate unhindered, would provide for the well-being of both the individual and society. Their arguments formed the basis of middle-class ideology in the nineteenth century.

The classical economists' argument that government should do nothing to regulate industry and trade was now extended to mean that government should do nothing to regulate the distribution of wealth. The gospel of free enterprise spawned elaborate justifications of the tremendous differences in living conditions between rich and poor. *Self-Help* by Samuel Smiles (1812–1904), published in 1859, was such a justification—and one of the most influential books of the nineteenth century. *Self-Help* argued that the rich were rich because they deserved it—if the poor lived thrifty, industrious lives, the good life would come to them too. Although some people made extraordinary fortunes during the industrial transformation, others were barely surviving, unable to resort to the old sources of aid, for industrialization had broken down the charity and mutual-aid systems of the church and village. Yet Smiles argued that nothing need be done to help, for improvement depended on the character of the individual, not on society. Considering the ability of Smiles's books to assuage feelings of guilt in the middle class, their extraordinary popularity is not surprising.

Building on earlier liberals' advocacy of laissez-faire policies, others also argued against any government action to improve the condition of the working classes. The British social theorist Herbert Spencer (1820–1903) took the lessons of classical economics to extremes. Although he lived on inherited money, he asserted that wealth reflected innate virtue and poverty indicated innate vice. According to Spencer, the state should guarantee the right of everyone to pursue freedom as long as the pursuit did not infringe on others. In *Social Statics* (1851), Spencer opposed relief for the poor on the grounds that it unfairly deprived some—the rich—of their property. He also argued that schooling was outside the authority of the state.

Applying to human society Charles Darwin's principle of "survival of the fittest" (see page 559), Spencer was a Social Darwinist. Society, he believed, should be established in such a way that the strongest and most resourceful would survive. The weak, poor, and improvident were not worthy of survival. If the state helped them survive—such as by providing education—it would only perpetuate the unfit. Spencer's harsh doctrines were widely acclaimed.

Many of those who favored laissez-faire policies criticized some aspects of the market economy, however. In France in the first half of the nineteenth century, commentators on the factory system, including industrialists, expressed fear that factory work would undermine the stability of family life and hence of society itself. At midcentury, in the face of unsanitary urban conditions, child labor, and other alarming results of industrialization, some governments began to intervene in areas of concern that would have been unthinkable a half-century earlier.

The Growth of Working-Class Solidarity

At some point workers stopped thinking of themselves as members of a given craft and began to think of themselves as members of the working class. The decline of the guilds, which had included apprentices and masters, rich and poor, was one factor in this shift. Unlike the skilled handicrafts that required years of apprenticeship, much of industrial production did not require lengthy periods of training. The system of dependence between apprentice and master became irrelevant. Although guilds faded in importance, the solidarity and language born of the guild system continued to shape workers' attitudes throughout much of the nineteenth century. New experiences also reinforced the sense of belonging to a group and sharing common aspirations.

Cultural forces fostered workers' sense of solidarity. The common language of religion and shared religious practice united workers, and many religious groups were born as a result. Emphasis on equality before God fueled the sense of injustice in a world where some lived in luxury while others worked for a pittance. Joanna, a self-proclaimed prophet active in the 1810s in England, announced both salvation and the coming of a new world of material well-being. In France, workers believed the new society would come about by their martyrdom; like Jesus, the workers would suffer, and from their suffering would emerge a new, better society. Ideas of social justice were linked in the country-side with religious broadsides speaking of "Jesus the worker."

Social institutions also encouraged class unity. In the eighteenth century both husband and wife were usually in the same craft. By 1900 it became more common for workers to marry across their crafts, thereby strengthening the sense of solidarity that encompassed the working class as a whole.

Other cultural and social factors created bonds among workers. Housing was increasingly segregated. Workers lived in low-rent areas—in slums in the center of cities or in outlying areas near the factories. Thus, urban workers lived close together, in similar conditions of squalor and hardship. Entrepreneurs who built factories or established mineworks in the countryside had to provide housing in order to attract and retain workers. Although this housing was sometimes better than the quarters of urban workers, it nevertheless reinforced the workers' solidarity and sense of commonality.

Workers increasingly spent their leisure time together, drinking in pubs and taverns, attending theaters and new forms of popular entertainment such as the circus, or watching traditional blood sports like boxing or cockfights. Popular sports emerged in the 1880s. In sports such as soccer, which developed in England at this time, both players and fans were drawn overwhelmingly from the working class.

Faced with the uncertainties of unemployment and job-related accidents, in addition to disease and other natural catastrophes, workers formed so-called friendly societies in which they pooled their resources to provide mutual aid. These societies, descendants of the benefit organizations of the Middle Ages and Renaissance, combined business activity with feasts, drinking bouts, and other social functions.

Friendly societies had existed as early as the seventeenth century, but they became increasingly popular after industrialization. Their strength in a region often reflected the degree to which the area was industrialized. First started to provide aid for workers in a particular trade, they soon included members in several crafts. They federated into national organizations, so that a worker who moved to a new town could continue membership in the new locale. Connected by common membership in friendly societies, workers expressed group solidarity beyond their individual occupations. Though far from accomplished, a working class was in the making.

Collective Action

Militant and in some cases violent action also strengthened workers' solidarity. In 1811–1812, British hand weavers, faced with competition from mechanized looms, organized in groups claiming to be led by a mythical General Ned Ludd. In the name of economic justice and to protect their livelihood, the "Luddites," as the general's followers were called, smashed machines or threatened to do so. To bring the Luddite riots under control, twelve thousand troops were dispatched, and in January 1813, British authorities executed ten people for Luddism. Similarly, in Saxony in eastern Germany in the 1830s and 1840s, weavers went on machine-crushing campaigns.

In Lyon, France, in 1831 and 1834, workers led uprisings demanding fair wages for piecework. Angered when silk merchants lowered the amount they would pay, the workers marched in the streets bearing banners proclaiming "Live Working or Die Fighting." Troops were brought in to restore order to the riot-torn city. Although conditions of the silk trade had been the immediate impetus for the uprising, the workers appealed for help to workers in other trades.

Labor agitation increased in the 1840s in much of Europe; a wave of strikes involving twenty thousand workers broke out in Paris in 1840. In the summer of 1842, an industrial downturn in England led to massive unemployment and rioting. During the summer of 1844 in Silesia, in eastern Prussia, linen handloom weavers desperate because of worsening conditions brought on by competition from machine-made cotton fabrics attacked the homes of the wealthy.

Labor unions were illegal in Britain until 1825, in Prussia until 1859, and in France until the 1860s. The advantages offered by unions were well understood. As a French workers' paper declared in 1847, "If workers came together and organized . . . nothing would be able to stop them." An organized group could threaten to withhold labor if the employer did not grant decent wages and acceptable conditions. Unions made workers a countervailing force to the factory owners.

Discipline in the factory was often severe. Workers had to conform to rigid rules not only in the workplace but also away from it. Workers in some factories were forbidden to read certain newspapers, had to attend religious services, and could marry only with the owners' permission. Workers resisted these attempts at control. They wanted freedom from outside regulation, and unions were a way to ensure that freedom.

The process of unionization was difficult. By 1850 many countries had passed laws supporting employers against the workers. Censorship and the use of force against organized strikes were not uncommon. Population growth made it difficult for workers to withhold labor lest they be replaced by others only too willing to take their place. Foreign workers—for example, the Irish who streamed into England and the Belgians and Italians who streamed into France—were often desperate for work and not well informed about local conditions.

In many countries, workers formed unions before they were legalized. Most were centered around a single craft or a single industry. In Britain, however, there were early attempts to organize unions on a national basis. In 1834, Welsh socialist Robert Owen (1771–1858) helped launch the Grand National Consolidated Trades Union. The organization's goal was to use the principles of cooperation to unite all of labor against the capitalist system. Internal strife and government repression kept this organization from succeeding. Not until 1868 was a federal structure created for the British unions—the Trades Union Congress.

In Germany the General Workers' Brotherhood was founded in 1848. Its first members came from many walks of life, but eventually its membership included workers only. Most were craftsmen and artisans: skilled workers such as cigar makers, book printers, typesetters. The year after its founding, the General Workers' Brotherhood had 15,000 members and 170 locals. After 1859, when labor unions were legalized, they grew significantly.

The composition of union membership evolved over time. Because labor unions originated in the crafts tradition, the earliest members were skilled craftsmen who organized to protect their livelihood from the challenges of industrialization. Literate and long-time residents of their communities, they provided the labor movement with much of its leadership and organization. Skilled craft workers played a strong role in developing a sense of class consciousness. The language and institutions they had developed over decades and sometimes over centuries became the common heritage of workers in general.

Workers looked to political action as the means to improve their situation. In the 1830s and 1840s, English workers agitated for the right to vote; they saw voting as a way to put themselves on equal footing with the privileged and win better conditions. When the Great Reform Bill of 1832 failed to grant them the vote, many workers backed the Chartist movement of the 1840s (see page 479).

In France urban laborers had played an important part in the various stages of the Revolution of 1789, and they continued to shape political events. In July 1830 workers helped topple the Bourbon monarchy and bring Louis Philippe (r. 1830–1848) to the throne. They insisted that their labor had created the wealth of the nation and that their self-sacrifice had brought in a freer government. Workers were disappointed by their failure to win political representation under the July Monarchy, and their sense of betrayal strengthened their class solidarity.

However vague their ideas, European workers showed that their organizations were legitimate representatives of the people and that the lot of the worker should be the concern of government. In general, workers upheld the ideal of a moral economy—one in which all who labored got a just wage and a minimum level of well-being was assured to all.

The working class was never a monolithic group. It consisted of people with varying skills, responsibilities, and incomes. Many skilled workers looked with contempt on the unskilled. If both sexes worked side by side, there was little solidarity between them. Men worried that the presence of women devalued their work because women were regularly paid. Men often excluded women from their unions and even went on strike to force employers to discharge women. An exception to this practice was Belgium, where labor organizations were remarkably receptive to female members. Nor was there solidarity across nationalities. Foreign workers were heartily despised. British workers were hostile to their Irish colleagues, the French to the Belgians and Italians in their midst. Thus, many forces fostered dissension in the working class in the nineteenth century. Nevertheless, various experiences broadened and deepened workers' sense of a common fate and goal.

The middle classes came to believe that all workers formed a single class. By the mid-nineteenth century, they had developed a clear fear of workers, not only as individuals but as a group, as a class. It was not unusual for members of the elite to refer to workers as "the swinish multitude" or, as the title of a popular English book put it, *The Great Unwashed* (1868). In France reference was alternately made to "the dangerous classes" and "the laboring classes." Not just workers but even the privileged seemed to see relations between the groups as a form of class war.

Marx and Marxism

Socialism provided a powerful language for the expression of working-class interests. Many of the workers enfranchised in the latter part of the century joined political parties espousing this doctrine. As we have seen, socialism existed before Karl Marx came on the scene. Henri de Saint-Simon and Charles Fourier in France and Robert Owen in Great Britain were its foremost prophets (see page 474). Marx drew on their theories and gave them a very special twist; in the end his became the dominant form of socialist thought.

Karl Marx (1818–1883), the son of a lawyer, grew up in the Rhineland, in western Germany, an industrializing area that was particularly open to political ideas and agitation. The Rhineland had been influenced by the ideas of the French Revolution and was primed for political radicalism. As a young man Marx studied philosophy at the University of Berlin and joined a group known as the "Young Hegelians," self-declared disciples of the idealist philosopher G. W. F. Hegel (1770–1831). Marx showed an early interest in political liberty and socialism. In 1842–1843 he edited a newspaper that spoke out for freedom and democracy in Germany. The following year in Paris, he met several of the French socialist writers. Even as a young man, he was perceived by his contemporaries as brilliant and extraordinarily determined.

Because of his radical journalism, he was exiled from the Rhineland and lived briefly in Paris, then Brussels. In 1849 he settled in London, where he lived for the rest of his life, dedicated to establishing his ideas on what he viewed as scientific bases. Deriving a modest income from writing for the *New York Daily Tribune* and from funds provided by his friend and collaborator Friedrich Engels (1820–1895), Marx was never able to provide well for his family, which constantly lived on the edge of poverty. Of the six children born to the Marx household, three died in infancy.

In 1848, Marx and Engels published the *Communist Manifesto.* A pamphlet written for the Communist League, a group of Germans living in exile, the manifesto was an appeal to the workers of the world. The league deliberately called itself "Communist" rather than "Socialist." Communism was a radical program, bent on changing property relations by violence; socialism was associated with peaceful transformation. The pamphlet was too late and too obscure to influence the revolutions of 1848. However, it laid out Marx's basic ideas, calling on the working class to rise—"You have nothing to lose but your chains"—and create a society that would end the exploitation of man by man. The exploitation of women was not especially interesting to Marx. Marxists noted that even in the poorest household, husbands were tremendously privileged over their wives, but most merely insisted that after "the revolution" such injustices would end.

Karl Marx Through his writings and agitation, Marx transformed the socialism of his day and created an ideology that helped shape the nineteenth and twentieth centuries. *(Corbis-Bettmann)*

A number of political and polemical works flowed from Marx's pen, but most of them remained unpublished during his lifetime. The first volume of his major work, *Capital,* was published in 1867; subsequent volumes appeared posthumously. Marx agreed with Hegel that human history has a goal. Hegel believed that the goal was the realization of the world spirit (see page 467); Marx believed it was the abolition of capitalism, the victory of the proletariat, the disappearance of the state, and the liberation of all humankind.

Whereas Hegel thought that ideas govern the world, Marx insisted that material conditions determine it. Hegel said that truth evolves by a "dialectic method": A person states a proposition and then states its opposite; from the clash of the two emerges a synthesis that leads to a higher truth. Marx called his philosophy "dialectic materialism." Following Hegel, he posited a world of change but said that it was embedded in material conditions, not in a clash of ideas. Ideas, to Marx, were but a reflection of the material world.

Marx grouped human beings into classes based on their relationship to factories and machines—the means of production. Capitalists were one class, because they owned the means of production. Workers were a separate class—the proletariat—because they did not own any of the means of production and their income came from their own hands. Because these two classes had different relationships to the means of production, they had different—in fact, antagonistic—interests and were destined to engage in a class struggle.

Marx saw the conflict as necessary to advance human history, and he sought to validate his thesis by the study of the past. In the Middle Ages, he pointed out, the feudal class dominated society but eventually lost the struggle to the commercial classes. Now, in turn, the capitalists were destined to be overwhelmed by the rising proletariat.

Marx found not only justification for but irrefutable proof of the "scientific" basis of his ideas in history and economics. Capitalism was creating the forces that would supplant it. The large industrial plants necessitated an ever greater work force with a growing sense of class interest. The inherently competitive nature of capitalism would inevitably drive an increasing number of enterprises out of business, and there would emerge a form of monopoly capitalism, abusive of both consumers and workers. As a result of ever more savage competition, more businesses would fail, and more workers would become unemployed. Angry and frustrated, workers would overthrow the system that had abused them for so long: "The knell of private property has sounded. The expropriators will be expropriated." The proletariat would take power and to solidify its rule would temporarily exercise the "dictatorship of the proletariat." Once that had taken place, the state would wither away, class war would end, and the ideal society would prevail. History would be over.

Marx's study of economics and history proved to him that socialism was not only desirable—as the utopians had thought—but inevitable. The laws of history dictated that capitalism would collapse, having created within itself the means of its own destruction—namely, the rising proletariat. For millions of people, Marxism was a doctrine of hope founded on scientific principles.

SUMMARY

Industrial transformation altered the face of Europe. The process, which started around 1750 in parts of England, spread by 1850 to other states of Europe. The proximity of coal and iron, the relative ease of domestic transportation, a culture open to innovation and entrepreneurship, and the existence of an already relatively dynamic economy help explain why Britain was the first nation to industrialize.

Economies based on industry changed power relations within Europe and altered the relationship of Europe to the rest of the world. As a result of the transformation in its economy Britain became in the nineteenth century the most powerful nation in Europe and achieved worldwide influence. Although Europe was industrialized only in certain areas, many Europeans came to think of their continent as economically and technologically superior to the rest of the world.

Industry changed the nature of work for large numbers of Europeans. Machines replaced human energy in the workplace. By the application of science and technology, manufacturing productivity increased significantly. A decreasing number of people worked in agriculture, and more entered manufacturing. Population patterns changed; cities grew dramatically, and for the first time European cities had over a million inhabitants.

The massing of workers in factories and urban areas called attention to their misery and also to their potential power. Eager to improve their lives and working conditions, workers began to express their solidarity. They organized into groups that were more broadly based and therefore more powerful than workers' groups of the past. As workers began to think of themselves as a group, the dominant groups within society began to perceive them as such.

Confronted by the realities of industrialization, many people changed their intellectual convictions. It was obvious that the laissez-faire system could not meet many workers' needs. Classical liberal economists revised their orthodoxy; the state became more interventionist, trying to remove some of the worst abuses.

Drawing on earlier strands of socialism, Karl Marx articulated this ideology in a new and compelling way. Marxism gave a powerful voice to the new proletarian class that industrialization had created, and it was to cast a shadow far into the next century.

NOTES

1. Adna Ferrin Weber, *The Growth of Cities in the Nineteenth Century: A Study in Statistics* (New York: Macmillan, 1899; Ithaca, N.Y.: Cornell University Press, 1963), p. 1.
2. W. Cooke Taylor, *Notes of a Tour in the Manufacturing Districts of Lancashire, in a Series of Letters to His Grace the Archbishop of Dublin* (London, 1842), pp. 4–6. Quoted in E. P. Thompson, *The Making of the English Working Class* (New York: Vintage, 1963), p. 191.
3. Marie de Flavigny d'Agoult [Daniel Stern], *Histoire de la Révolution de 1848,* 2d ed., vol. 1 (Paris, 1862), p. 7, quoted in Theodore S. Hamerow, *The Birth of a New Europe: State and Society in the Nineteenth Century* (Chapel Hill: University of North Carolina Press, 1983), pp. 206–207.

SUGGESTED READING

Alter, George. *Family and the Female Life Course: The Women of Verviers, Belgium, 1849–80.* 1988. A reminder that women were usually not continuously in the industrial work force but entered and exited according to family needs.

Brimblecombe, Peter. *The Big Smoke: A History of Air Pollution in London Since Medieval Times.* 1987. An account of the causes of pollution and the attempts to control it.

Chinn, Carl. *Poverty Amidst Prosperity: The Urban Poor in England, 1834–1914.* 1995. Concentrates on the harsher aspects of industrialization.

Deane, Phyllis. *The First Industrial Revolution.* 1965. An excellent discussion of the importance of changes in production techniques.

Hilden, Patricia P. *Women, Work, and Politics: Belgium, 1830–1914.* 1993. Reveals the unique experience of women in the industrial work force in the first continental country to industrialize.

Himmelfarb, Gertrude. *The Idea of Poverty: England in the Early Industrial Age.* 1983. A work that describes the image of the poor among Victorian middle-class observers.

Hohenberg, Paul M., and Lynn Hollen Lees. *The Making of Urban Europe, 1000–1950.* 1985. A good general introduction to the impact of industry on urbanization, emphasizing less the pathology of cities and more their resilience.

Kelly, Alfred, ed. *The German Worker: Working-Class Autobiographies from the Age of Industrialization.* 1987. A collection of workers' accounts of their lives.

Landes, David S. *Prometheus Unbound.* 1969. A standard work emphasizing technological and cultural factors as explanations for industry.

Lynch, Katherine A. *Family, Class, and Ideology in Early Industrial France: Social Policy and the Working-Class Family, 1825–1848.* 1988. A study of social concerns in France over the corrosive impact of industry on working-class families.

Maynes, Mary Jo. *Taking the Hard Road.* 1995. An analysis of French and German workers' experiences during industrialization.

Mazlish, Bruce. *The Meaning of Karl Marx.* 1984. An easy-to-read introduction to the man and his thought, emphasizing the shaping of both by the era in which Marx lived.

Mokyr, Joel. *The Lever of Riches: Technological Creativity and Economic Progress.* 1990. A work that provides a comparative study of Western and Chinese technology, emphasizing cultural elements as explanations for the industrialization of the West.

Nardinelli, Clark. *Child Labor and the Industrial Revolution.* 1990. A work that represents child labor as less harsh than some contemporaries claimed and as a rational adjustment to existing economic conditions.

O'Brien, Patrick K., and Roland Quinault, eds. *The Industrial Revolution and British Society.* 1993. A broad set of essays on the origins and impact of industry on British society.

Pollard, Sidney. *Peaceful Conquest.* 1981. A reminder that although industrialization started in England, it occurred not throughout the whole country but only in specific regions; likewise when industry spread to the Continent, it spread only to specific regions.

Sylla, Richard, and Gianni Toniolo, eds. *Patterns of European Industrialization.* 1991. A volume describing the patterns of industrialization in a comparative perspective.

Thompson, E. P. *The Making of the English Working Class.* 1963. A work that emphasizes cultural factors that encouraged the development of working-class consciousness in England.

Tilly, Louise, and Joan Scott. *Women, Work and Family.* 1978. A description of the family wage economy in which all members contributed to the economy of the family, especially in the early stages of industrialization.

CHAPTER 20

New Powers and New Tensions, 1850–1880

In 1866 when Prince Charles, a member of the Prussian royal family, was offered the throne of Romania, he reportedly had to look at a map to locate his future kingdom. His puzzlement was partly understandable, for a united Romania had existed for only five years. The prince and his contemporaries in the generation after 1848 witnessed the emergence of several new nation-states. And as the map of Europe changed, a much enlarged and more powerful United States also emerged.

The changing political scenery was accompanied by the development of new political institutions. To meet the demand for popular participation in government so dramatically expressed in 1848, every European state, except the Ottoman and Russian Empires, found it necessary to have a parliament. Rare before midcentury, such institutions became common thereafter. No longer was the demand for popular participation seen as a threat to the existing political and social order. In fact, popular participation, or the appearance of it, gave the existing order a legitimacy it had not enjoyed since the French Revolution. Nationalism flourished during this period, emerging as a decisive force in European affairs and in the United States, where it promoted territorial expansion and a determination to preserve the Union.

These political transformations occurred in an era of unprecedented economic growth and prosperity, touched off by the discovery of gold in California in 1848. The increased supply of gold allowed for the expansion of credit, which led to the founding of new banks and mass investments in growing industries. The iron output of Britain, France, and Germany tripled in the years between 1850 and 1878. During this same period the standard of living of every class rose significantly in industrializing nations. The middle class expanded dramatically, while the elites sought to re-establish their power in new ways.

In the first half of the century, international relations had been dominated by the congress system, in which representatives of the major European states met periodically to preserve the balance of power. This order disappeared in the second half of the century, as political leaders pursued the narrow interests of their state. Instead of negotiation, brute military force, or the threat of it, was employed to resolve international conflict. This was *Realpolitik,* a policy in which war became a regular instrument of statecraft, and its chief practitioner was the Prussian chancellor Otto von Bismarck.

Questions and Ideas to Consider

- What was the "congress system"? How did the Crimean War and the subsequent peace treaty change the system of international order? Were the decisions of the Congress of Paris honored?
- Why did Cavour want Napoleon III to help him win Italian unification? Why was Napoleon III willing to help? What does Napoleon III's decision to sign a treaty with Austria suggest about his attitude toward an Italian nation?
- Like Italian unification, German unification was won through military force, not liberal idealism. Yet the new Italian state was dominated by liberal Piedmont, while Germany was dominated by authoritarian Prussia. Discuss some of the other formative characteristics of the new German nation.
- In the United States, expansion—and tensions over the new territories—helped lead to the Civil War. Afterward, the democratic structure strained to adjust to new citizens and new calls for political participation. Discuss the political status of African Americans and women in this period.
- What was the Paris Commune? What kind of government was set up in France in its aftermath?

THE CHANGING SCOPE OF INTERNATIONAL RELATIONS

The Crimean War and its aftermath shaped European international relations for several decades. A new level of mutual suspicion arose, leading nations to act in their own self-interest and ignore the concerns of the other major players in the international system.

The Crimean War as a Turning Point, 1854–1856

The Crimean War had many causes. Principally, however, it was ignited by the decision of French and British statesmen to contain Russian power in the Balkans and keep it from encroaching on the weakening Ottoman Empire. Russian claims to have the right to intervene on behalf of Ottoman Christians had led to war between the two states in October 1853. The defeat of the Ottoman navy at Sinope in November left the Ottoman Empire defenseless.

British and French statesmen had considerable interest in the conflict. Britain had long feared that the collapse of the Ottoman Empire would lead Russia to seek territorial gains in the Mediterranean. Such a move would challenge Britain's supremacy. An explosion of public sentiment against Russia also obliged the British government to take an aggressive stance. Meanwhile, the French emperor, Napoleon III, viewed defeat of Russia as a way to eclipse one of the states most dedicated to preserving the existing European borders. He wanted to undermine existing power relations, hoping that a new order would lead to increased French power and influence. Napoleon also imagined that fighting side by side with Britain could lay the foundation for Anglo-French friendship. And so England and France rushed to defend the Ottoman Empire and declared war on Russia in March 1854.

The war was poorly fought on all sides. Leadership was woefully inadequate. The Russians had a standing army of a million men but never managed to use more than a fraction of

Crimean War This photograph shows the interior of the Sevastopol fortress after it had been battered into surrender. The Crimean War was the first conflict to be documented by photographers. *(Courtesy of the Board of Trustees of the Victoria & Albert Museum)*

CHAPTER CHRONOLOGY

1851	Louis Napoleon's coup d'état in France
1854–1855	Crimean War
1860	Italy united under Piedmontese rule
1861	The abolition of serfdom in Russia
1861–1865	Civil War in the United States
1862	Bismarck appointed prime minister of Prussia
January 1864	Austria and Prussia attack Denmark and occupy Schleswig and Holstein
June 1866	Austro-Prussian War
1867	The North German Confederation
	The "Second Reform Bill" in England
1870	Rome joined to Italy and becomes its capital
March–July 1870	Crisis over Hohenzollern candidacy for Spanish throne
July 19, 1870	France declares war on Prussia
1871	The Paris Commune and formation of the Third Republic
January 18, 1871	The German Empire declared in the Hall of Mirrors in Versailles
1878	Congress of Berlin

that number due largely to poor communications and supply systems. In Britain, failures in military supplies and leadership were denounced in the press and in Parliament. For the first time the press played an active role in reporting war, and photography brought to readers at home the gruesome realities of battle.

One of the few heroic figures to emerge from this conflict was Florence Nightingale (1820–1910), who organized a nursing service to care for the British sick and wounded. Before she arrived, there were five times more casualties from disease than from enemy fire. Her efforts produced a remarkable reduction of such casualties. Through the tremendous force of her intelligence and personality, she established new levels of cleanliness and order in hospitals. In the wake of her successes Nightingale was often described as an angelic maternal figure. However, her early writing demonstrates that she was not seeking to extend the female role of nurturer to the larger

Florence Nightingale in the Crimean War

Florence Nightingale used her influential family connections to win an appointment to the Crimean battlefield. Once there, she organized nursing for the wounded and was able to secure additional personnel and medical supplies for her hospital. In this letter, Nightingale describes the plight of the wounded in an army lacking sufficient supplies.

We have no room for corpses in the wards. The Surgeons pass on to the next, an excision of the shoulder-joint—beautifully performed and going on well—ball lodged just in the head of the joint, and fracture starred all round. The next poor fellow has two stumps for arms—and the next has lost an arm and leg. As for the balls, they go in where they like, and do as much harm as they can in passing. That is the only rule they have. The next case has one eye put out, and paralysis of the iris of the other. He can neither see nor understand. But all who can walk come into us for Tobacco, but I tell them that we have not a bit to put into our own mouths. Not a sponge, nor a rag of linen, not anything have I left. Everything is gone to make slings and stump pillows and shirts. These poor fellows have not had a clean shirt nor been washed for two months before they came here, and the state in which they arrive from the transport is literally *crawling*. I hope in a few days we shall establish a little cleanliness. But we have not a basin nor a towel nor a bit of soap nor a broom—I have ordered 300 scrubbing brushes. But one half the Barrack is so sadly out of repair that it is impossible to use a drop of water on the stone floors, which are all laid upon rotten wood, and would give our men fever in no time. . . .

I am getting a screen now for the Amputations, for when one poor fellow, who is to be amputated tomorrow, sees his comrade today die under the knife it makes impression—and diminishes his chance. But, anyway, among these exhausted frames the mortality of the operations is frightful.

Source: Letter to Dr. William Bowman, November 14, 1854, in Sue M. Goldie, ed., *"I Have Done My Duty": Florence Nightingale in the Crimean War, 1854–56* (Iowa City: University of Iowa Press, 1987), pp. 37–38.

society but searching for a way to avoid the cloistered, domestic role that women of the time were expected to fill. By almost single-handedly creating the idea and practice of nursing as a professional calling, Nightingale broadened the range of respectable middle-class female behavior and opened up another avenue of employment for working-class women. (See the box "Florence Nightingale in the Crimean War.")

The war ended in December 1855 when Russia surrendered the fortified port of Sevastopol after a long, bitter siege. Nightingale's efforts notwithstanding, the Crimean War killed three-quarters of a million people—more than any European war between the end of the Napoleonic Wars and World War I. The slowness with which each side mobilized, the lack of planning and foresight in staging battles, the large number of fatalities from causes other than enemy fire—all were reminiscent of hostilities from earlier eras. It was a futile, senseless war whose most important consequence was political, for it unleashed dramatic new changes in the international order.

The Congress of Paris and Its Aftermath

The former combatants met in Paris in February 1856 to work out a peace treaty. Their decisions—which pleased no one—shaped relations among European states for the next half-century. Russian statesmen were especially discontented. The Congress of Paris forbade Russia from having a fleet in the Black Sea and forced it to withdraw from the provinces of Moldavia and Wallachia, where it had enjoyed the right of intervention since the 1830s. Tsar Nicholas I had expected Austrian assistance in the war in return for his help in crushing the Hungarian rebellion in 1849. Instead, Austria's leaders had not only withheld aid but threatened to join the Western alliance. Nor did French leaders feel their nation had benefited. Although holding the congress in Paris flattered the emperor's pride, no other clear advantages emerged for France. The north Italian state of Piedmont, which had joined the allies, gained from the congress only a vague statement on the unsatisfactory nature of the existing situation in Italy. Prussia was invited to attend the congress only as an afterthought and hence also felt slighted.

Although the war seemed to have sustained the integrity of the Ottoman Empire, the peace settlement weakened it indirectly by dictating reforms in the treatment of its Christian populations. These reforms impaired the empire's ability to repress growing national movements. British political leaders, galled by the heavy sacrifices of the war, moved toward isolationism in foreign policy.

In the past the congress system had tried to ensure that no major power was dissatisfied enough to subvert the existing distribution of power, but the Crimean War and the peace treaty changed the situation. In the first half of the century the international order had been upheld in part by the cooperation of the conservative Eastern powers: Russia, Austria, and Prussia. Now these powers were rivals, and their competition contributed to growing instability in the international system. By and large, the decisions reached in Paris were either disregarded or unilaterally revised.

ITALIAN UNIFICATION

In the words of Prince von Metternich of Austria, Italy at midcentury was nothing but a "geographic expression." The revolution of 1848 had revealed an interest in national unification, but the attempt had failed. Yet within a dozen years what many believed to be impossible would come to pass. Idealists like Giuseppe Mazzini (1805–1872) had preached that Italy would be unified by its people, who would rise and establish a free republic. Instead, it was unified by royalty, by war, and with the help of a foreign state.

After the failed 1848 revolution, various Italian rulers resorted to repression. In Modena, the Habsburg duke Francis V jailed liberals, closed the universities, and personally caned passersby who did not tip their hat to him. In the Papal States, men were imprisoned for "appearing inclined to novelty." Pope Pius IX, who first had appeared sympathetic to Italian unification, opposed it as soon as he realized it was attainable only by war against Catholic Austria. In Parma, the duke was assassinated in 1854—to the relief of his people—and the uprising that accompanied this desperate act was suppressed by three thousand Austrian troops sent in by the duke's ally, the Habsburgs.

Compared to this dismal record, the kingdom of Piedmont in northern Italy appeared stable and successful. It was the only Italian state that kept the liberal constitution it had adopted in 1848, and it welcomed political refugees from other Italian states. Economically, it was a beacon to the rest of Italy, establishing modern banks and laying half the rail lines on the peninsula.

Since the late eighteenth century, some Italians had called for a *risorgimento*, a political and cultural renewal of Italy. By the mid-nineteenth century the idea was actively supported by a small, elite group of the educated middle class. For merchants, industrialists, and professionals, a unified state would provide a larger stage on which to pursue their ambitions. Members of these groups founded the National Society, a grassroots unification movement. This organization now looked to Piedmont to lead the peninsula to national unity.

Cavour Plots Unification

The statesman who was to catapult Piedmont to leadership in the dramatic events leading to

Italian unification was Count Camillo di Cavour (1810–1861). The son of a Piedmontese nobleman and high government official, he grew up speaking French, the language of the court in Piedmont, and mastered Italian only as an adult. Cavour was sympathetic to the aspirations of the middle class and saw in Britain and France models of what Italy ought to become, a liberal and economically advanced society.

Short, fat, and nearsighted, Cavour hardly cut a heroic figure. Yet he was ambitious, hardworking, and driven to succeed. In 1850 he joined the government of Piedmont. Two years later he was appointed prime minister. He shared the general enthusiasm of the middle classes for an Italian nation, but his vision probably did not include the entire Italian peninsula, only its north and center, which would dominate the rest of the peninsula in a loose federation. One fateful lesson he had learned from the failures of 1848 was that foreign help would be necessary to expel the Austrians from the peninsula.

When the Crimean War broke out in 1854, Cavour steered Piedmont to the allied side, hoping to advance his cause. He sent twenty thousand troops to the Crimea, one-tenth of whom died. This act gained him a seat at the Congress of Paris, where his presence boosted the kingdom's prestige—and where he and Napoleon III had an opportunity to meet and size each other up.

Napoleon III favored Italian liberation from Austrian rule and some form of unification of the peninsula. Austria had been France's traditional opponent; destroying its power in Italy might strengthen France. The French emperor and the Piedmontese prime minister met secretly in July 1858 at Plombières, a French spa, to discuss how Italian unity could be achieved. They agreed that Piedmont would stir up trouble in one of Austria's Italian territories in an effort to goad the Austrians into war. France would help the Piedmontese expel Austria from the peninsula, and the new Piedmont, doubled in size, would become part of a confederation under the papacy. In exchange, the French emperor demanded the cession of Nice and Savoy. Although Savoy was the heartland of the Piedmont kingdom, Cavour reluctantly agreed.

War between Austria and Piedmont broke out in April 1859. By June the combined Piedmontese and French forces had defeated the Austrians at Magenta and Solferino (Map 20.1). The bloodiness of these battles impressed contemporaries: The color magenta was named after the color of the blood flowing on the battlefield, and when a Swiss humanitarian, Henri Dunant (1828–1901), organized emergency services for both French and Austrians wounded at Solferino, he proposed the founding of voluntary relief societies in every nation, called the Red Cross.

Instead of following up these victories, Napoleon III decided to end the fighting. He was truly shocked by the bloodshed he had witnessed—and alarmed by Prussian mobilization on the Rhine on behalf of Austria. Also, there were popular uprisings in some other Italian states in June (Ravenna, Ferrara, Bologna), which Napoleon III feared might lead to requests for union. Such union would result in a much larger independent state than he had anticipated. Without consulting his ally, Napoleon signed an armistice with the Austrians, allowing Austria to keep part of Lombardy and all of Venetia and to participate in an Italian Confederation. Cavour was outraged by Napoleon's betrayal and resigned as prime minister; he returned to office, however, in January 1860.

Unification Achieved, 1860

The overthrow of the Austrian-backed rulers in Parma, Modena, and Tuscany led these areas in 1860 to vote in plebiscites to join Piedmont. Farther south, in central Italy, agitation against papal misrule also inclined the people of the Papal States toward Piedmont.

Cavour had envisioned no more than a united northern Italy. Unexpected events in the south, however, dramatically changed that vision. The centuries-old misgovernment of Naples led to an uprising, abetted by the revolu-

Map 20.1 The Unification of Italy, 1859–1870 Piedmontese leadership and nationalist fervor united Italy.

tionary firebrand Giuseppe Garibaldi (1807–1882), a rival of Cavour who favored unification and won a large popular following. In May 1860, with but a thousand poorly armed, red-shirted followers, he set sail for Sicily to help the island rise up against its Bourbon ruler. Winning that struggle, Garibaldi's forces crossed to the mainland. Victory followed victory, and enthusiasm for Garibaldi grew. His army swelled to 57,000 men, and he won the entire Kingdom of the Two Sicilies.

Threatened by the advance of Garibaldi's power, Cavour sent his army into the Papal States in September 1860. This action, a brutal attack on a weak state that had not harmed Piedmont, was viewed by many Catholics as aggression against the spiritual head of their church. However, as Cavour explained to his parliament, political necessity required it. The interests of Piedmont and the about-to-be-born Italy superseded traditional morality.

Although Garibaldi was a republican, he was convinced that Italy could best achieve unity under the king of Piedmont, and he willingly submitted the southern part of Italy, which he controlled, to the king, Victor Emmanuel II (r. 1849–1878). Thus by November 1860, Italy was united under Piedmontese rule (see Map 20.1). The territories that came under Piedmontese control all affirmed their desire to be part of the new Italy in plebiscites based on universal male suffrage. By huge majorities, the populations voted affirmatively. Undoubtedly there was pressure from the occupying army and the upper classes. Voting was not secret, and fraud was widespread. But the plebiscite gave legitimacy to the new state and won sympathy from liberally inclined states abroad.

Austria still held Venetia in the northeast; Rome and its environs were still held by the pope with the support of a French garrison. But within a decade, a propitious international situation enabled the fledgling country to acquire both key areas. After Austria was defeated in the Austro-Prussian War in 1866, Venetia was ceded to Italy. Then the Franco-Prussian War forced the French to evacuate Rome, which they had occupied since 1849. Rome was joined to Italy and became its capital in 1870. Unification was complete (see Map 20.1).

The Problems of Unified Italy

National unity had been achieved, but it was frail. The nation was divided between the modernizing north and the traditional south. From the beginning, the north behaved like a conquering state—sending its officials to the south, raising taxes, and imposing its laws. In 1861 an uprising of disbanded Neapolitan soldiers and brigands broke out. To crush the revolt, half the Italian army was sent south; the civil war lasted five years and produced more casualties than the entire effort of unification.

Other divisions remained. In 1861 only 2.5 percent of the population spoke the national language, Florentine Italian. The north was far more industrialized than the rural south. In the south, child mortality was higher, life expectancy was lower, and illiteracy approached 90 percent. The two regions seemed to belong to two different nations.

Piedmont imposed strong central control, resolutely refusing a federal system of government, which many Italians had hoped for. Piedmont was determined to project its power onto the rest of the peninsula and feared that any other form of government might lead to disintegration of the new state. The Civil War in the United States suggested the dangers of a federal system of government.

Piedmont imposed its constitution on unified Italy. This constitution limited suffrage to men of property and education, less than 2 percent of the population. Further, although parliamentarism was enshrined in the constitution, Cavour's maneuvering as prime minister had kept governments from being answerable to the parliament. Still, although Italian parliamentarism was far from complete, a liberal state recognizing legal equality and freedom of association had been established, providing more freedom for its citizens than the peninsula had seen for centuries.

The new Italian state was weakened by the hostility of the Catholic church. When Piedmont annexed Rome in 1870, the pope retained control of only a few square blocks around the papal palace, the Vatican. The popes considered themselves prisoners of the new Italian state and denounced it and all those who supported it, including those participating in elections. Thus the new state was contested by many Catholics, who refused to recognize it for decades.

In 1870, Italy, with its 27 million people, was the sixth most populous European nation. It was too small to be a great power and too large to accept being a small state. Italian statesmen found it difficult to define their country's role in international politics, and they lacked a firm consensus on Italy's future.

GERMAN UNIFICATION

Like Italy, Germany began as a collection of polities, first loosely united in the Holy Roman Empire and then, after 1815, equally loosely organized in the German Confederation. As Piedmont had done in Italy, Prussia, the most powerful German state, led the unification movement. And just as Italy had in Cavour a strong leader who imposed his will, German unification had a ruthless and cunning leader: Otto von Bismarck, prime minister of Prussia.

In 1848, German unification under Prussian leadership had appeared likely until the king of Prussia refused to accept a throne offered by an elected assembly. When national unity was ultimately achieved, it was due not to popular decision but to military force and the imposition of Prussian absolutism over the whole country.

The Rise of Bismarck

Austria under Metternich had always treated Prussia as a privileged junior partner. After Metternich's fall in 1848, rivalry erupted between the two German states. Each tried to use for its own aggrandizement the desire for national unity that had appeared during the revolution of 1848.

In March 1850, Prussia invited various German rulers to a meeting in Erfurt to consider possible unification under its sponsorship. Austria, which had been excluded, insisted that the "Erfurt Union" be dissolved. Austrian leaders backed their demands with the threat of war; Prussia had to scuttle the Erfurt Union and accept Austrian leadership in Germany. At that time the Prussian military was not strong enough to challenge Austria. The new Prussian king, William I (r. 1861–1888), was committed to expanding the size and effectiveness of the army. When liberals in parliament opposed the increased costs that this would require, the king dissolved Parliament and appointed Otto von Bismarck as prime minister in 1862.

Bismarck was a Junker, a Prussian aristocrat known for his reactionary views, who had opposed the liberal movement in 1848. Bismarck sought to heighten Prussian power in Germany and throughout Europe. He faced down the newly elected parliament, telling the Budget Commission in 1862, "The position of Prussia in Germany will be decided not by its liberalism but by its power . . . not through speeches and majority decisions are the great questions of the day decided—that was the mistake of 1848–49—but by 'iron and blood.'"[1]

Bismarck tried to win over the liberals by suggesting that with military force at its disposal, Prussia could lead German unification. But the liberals resisted, and the Parliament voted against the military reforms. Bismarck decided to carry out the military measures anyway and to collect the taxes that would make them possible. The liberals who opposed Bismarck represented the business and professional classes who had received the vote as a result of the 1848 revolution. They had not implemented effective political or social programs, and they did not enjoy mass support. Bismarck met with no organized resistance.

German liberals were faced with a dilemma: Did they value nationhood or the principles of liberty more? In other countries statehood had preceded the development of liberalism, thus avoiding the conflict. Even in Italy, the liberals had faced a less harsh dilemma, for unification was led by the liberal state of Piedmont. That was not the case in Germany, where the natural leader, Prussia, had a long tradition of militarism and authoritarianism.

Bismarck's genius was to exploit the growing desire for German unification. Professional and cultural organizations now often extended beyond a single state, for instance, the German Commercial Association, the Congress of German Jurists, and the German Sharpshooters League. Many individual German states, each calculating possible political gains, launched proposals for unification in the 1860s. Although it had yet to find much resonance among the lower classes, the idea of a united Germany was gaining a wider audience.

Prussian Wars and German Unity

Neither the Prussian king nor Bismarck's fellow aristocrats were nationalists. Believing in a strong Prussia, they feared that a united Germany might dilute Prussian power and influence. German unification had been part of the liberals' program, not the conservatives'. Bismarck had to be clever. His first move was to enlarge Prussia's role in Germany at the expense of Austria. The provocation was a crisis over Schleswig-Holstein (Map 20.2). These two provinces, ethnically and linguistically German (except for northern Schleswig), were ruled by Denmark. When the Danish king, contrary to earlier treaty obligations, attempted to connect Schleswig more closely to the Crown in 1863, Holstein felt threatened. Although it was under Danish rule, Holstein was also a member of the German Confederation and called on the Confederation for protection. Acting on behalf of the Confederation, Prussia and Austria intervened, sending troops who won a quick, cheap victory in 1864. Prussia occupied Schleswig, and Austria took Holstein.

Joint military action in no way united Prussia and Austria, who continued to be bitter rivals for domination of Germany. Bismarck believed that war was the only means to win this contest, and conflicts over the administration of Schleswig and Holstein served as a pretext to start one. With no declaration of war, Prussia attacked Austrian-administered Holstein in June 1866 and defeated the Austrian army at Sadowa (Königgrätz) on July 3. Austria sued for peace.

Prussia annexed its smaller neighbors who had supported Austria, thus creating a contiguous state linking Prussia with the Rhineland. This enlarged Prussia intended to dominate the newly formed North German Confederation, comprising all the states north of the Main River. Henceforth Austria was excluded from German affairs.

These events transformed Bismarck into a popular hero. Elections held on the day of the battle returned a conservative pro-Bismarck majority to the Prussian parliament. The legislature, including a large number of liberals mesmerized by the military victory, voted retroactively to legalize the illegal taxes that had been levied since 1862 to upgrade the military. The liberals rationalized that national unity ought to be gained first, with liberal constitutional institutions secured later. It did not turn out that way.

Bismarck hoped that the southern German states would eventually merge with the North German Confederation. Economically they continued to be dependent as a result of the Zollverein (the customs union). Many southern Germans favored unity, especially business people who saw in it the hope of an improved economy.

The Franco-Prussian War and Unification, 1870–1871

French leaders were determined to prevent German unity. They feared the loss of influence in the southern German states that had tradition-

Map 20.2 The Unification of Germany A series of military victories made it possible for Prussia to unite Germany under its domain.

ally been France's allies. More important, since the mid-seventeenth century, French security had been linked to a weak and divided Germany.

Both Berlin and Paris anticipated war. And war came soon enough, precipitated by a crisis over the Spanish succession. In 1868, a Catholic member of the Hohenzollerns, the reigning Prussian monarch's family, was offered the Spanish throne. The French viewed this candidacy as an unacceptable expansion of Prussian power. As passions heated, Bismarck was elated at the prospect of war. But the Prussian king was not. On July 12, 1870, he withdrew the young prince's candidacy, removing the cause for war. Bismarck was bitterly disappointed. Not satisfied, the French pushed their luck. On July 13 the French ambassador met the king of Prussia at Ems and demanded guarantees that no Hohenzollern would ever again be a candidate to the Spanish throne. The Prussian king refused.

William telegraphed an account of his meeting to Bismarck. The chancellor edited what became known as the Ems dispatch, making the exchange seem like a deliberate snub to the French ambassador. Faced by a flood of emotional demands for redress of the imagined slight to French national honor, Napoleon III declared war on July 19.

The Prussians led a well-planned campaign. An army of 384,000 Prussians was rushed by rail to confront 270,000 Frenchmen. Within a few weeks, Prussia won a decisive victory at Sedan, taking the French emperor prisoner on September 2. But the French continued the struggle, despite the odds. Infuriated, the Prussians resorted to extreme measures, taking hostages and burning down whole villages. They laid siege to Paris, starving and bombarding its beleaguered population.

Throughout Germany the outbreak of the war was met with general enthusiasm for the Prussian cause. Exploiting this popular feeling, Bismarck called on the other German states to accept the unification of Germany under the Prussian king. Reluctant princes, such as the king of Bavaria, were bought off with bribes. On January 18, 1871, the German princes met in the Hall of Mirrors of the Versailles palace, symbol of past French greatness, and acclaimed William I as *Kaiser*—German for emperor (see Map 20.2).

In May 1871 the Treaty of Frankfurt established the peace terms. France was forced to give up the provinces of Alsace and Lorraine and to pay a heavy indemnity of five billion francs. These harsh terms embittered the French, leading many to desire revenge and establishing a formidable barrier to future relations between France and Germany.

The Character of the New Germany

German unity had been forged by a series of wars—against Denmark in 1864, Austria in 1866, and France in 1870—and lacked the popular democratic base that had been present in Italy. Because the military had been instrumental in the formation of the new German *Reich* (German for empire), it remained dominant in the new state. Italian unity had been sanctioned by plebiscites. The founding act of the new Reich was the meeting of the German rulers on the soil of a defeated neighbor. Thus the rulers placed themselves above popular sanction.

The constitution of the new Germany was remarkably democratic on the surface. It provided for an appointed upper house, the *Bundesrat*, representing the individual German states, and a lower house, the *Reichstag*, which was elected by universal manhood suffrage. The latter seemed a surprising concession from Bismarck, the authoritarian aristocrat. But he knew the liberals lacked mass support and gambled that he would be able to create majorities that could be manipulated for his purposes.

The dominant state in the new Germany was, of course, Prussia, which also had two-thirds of its population. Within the Bundesrat, Prussia had 17 of the 43 seats and could block any legislation it opposed with the aid of only a few other states. The king of Prussia occupied the post of emperor, and the prime minister—now called the chancellor—was responsible not to parliament but to the emperor, as were the other cabinet members. The emperor alone could make foreign policy and war, command the army, and interpret the constitution. The authoritarianism of Prussia had been projected onto all of Germany.

The emergence of a strong, united Germany disrupted the European balance of power. In February 1871 the British political leader Benjamin Disraeli observed that the unification of Germany was "a greater political event than the French revolution of last century. . . . There is not a diplomatic tradition which has not been swept away. You have a new world. . . . The balance of power has been entirely destroyed."[2] Germany had become the dominant power on the Continent.

PRECARIOUS SUPRANATIONAL EMPIRES

In an age of nationalism that saw the creation of two new nation-states—Italy and Germany—the two multinational empires found themselves in a precarious position. The Habsburg and Ottoman Empires consisted of peoples speaking different languages, holding different religious beliefs, and having different historical traditions. In the past such multinational states had been quite normal in Europe, but in the nineteenth century they became increasingly anomalous. The peoples living under the authority of Vienna and Constantinople became more and more restive. Facing this severe challenge, the Austrian and Ottoman Empires attempted to strengthen themselves by restructuring their institutions.

The Dual Monarchy in Austria-Hungary

Austrian statesmen sensed the vulnerability of their empire. By 1860 they had lost much of their Italian possessions; in Hungary they met with resistance from the Magyars, a powerful group still resentful they had not won independence in 1848; and they faced the bitter struggle for German supremacy in Prussia. To give his government credibility, in February 1861, Emperor Francis Joseph (r. 1848–1916) issued what became known as the February Patents, which liberalized the government, guaranteed civil liberties, and provided local self-government and an elected parliament.

The need to safeguard the remaining territories was clear. By 1866 the Austrian Habsburgs were no longer a German or Italian power (Venetia had been handed over to a united Italy). The strongest challenge to Habsburg rule came from Hungary, where the Magyars insisted on self-rule, a claim based on age-old historic rights and Vienna's initial acceptance of autonomy in 1848. Since Magyar cooperation was crucial, the government entered into lengthy negotiations with Magyar leaders in 1865. The outcome was the Compromise of 1867, which created a new structure for the empire that lasted until 1918. The agreement divided the Habsburg holdings into Austria in the west and Hungary in the east, linked by the person of the emperor of Austria, Francis Joseph, who was also king of Hungary. Hungary had full internal autonomy and participated jointly in imperial affairs—state finance, defense, and foreign relations. The new state created by the compromise was known as the dual monarchy of Austria-Hungary.

The emperor of the new state of Austria-Hungary had come to the throne as an 18-year-old in that year of crisis, 1848. Francis Joseph was a well-meaning monarch who took his duties seriously. He spoke several of his subjects' languages. In both halves of the empire, he was a much-loved, regal figure who provided a visible symbol of the state.

The compromise confirmed Magyar dominance in Hungary. Although numerically a minority, Magyars controlled the Hungarian parliament, the army, the bureaucracy, and other state institutions. They opposed self-rule by the Croats, Serbs, Slovaks, Romanians, and others in the kingdom and attempted a policy of Magyarization—teaching only Hungarian in the schools, conducting all government business in Hungarian, and giving access to government positions only to those fully assimilated in Magyar culture. This arrangement created frustrations and resistance among the various nationalities under their rule.

The terms of the compromise also gave the Hungarians a voice in imperial foreign policy. Magyars feared that the Slavic groups outside the empire who planned to form independent states or had already done so would inspire fellow Slavs in Austria-Hungary to revolt. To prevent that, the Hungarians favored an expansionist foreign policy in the Balkans, which the monarchy gladly embraced. Having lost its influence in Germany, Austria-Hungary found in the Balkans an area in which to assert itself. The policy was fraught with risks and, by bringing more discontented Slavs into the empire, led to hostility with other states.

The Ailing Ottoman Empire

At midcentury the Ottoman Empire was still one of the largest European powers, but it faced unrest within its borders and threats by the expansionist designs of its neighbors. The ailing empire was commonly referred to as "the sick man of Europe." Over the next twenty-five years, the empire shed some of its territory and modernized its government, but nothing could save it from decline in the face of nationalist uprisings in its Balkan possessions.

As early as the 1840s, the Ottoman Empire had begun various reform movements to bring more security to its subjects. Known as the *Tanzimat,* these changes were initiated by Sultan Abdul Mejid (r. 1839–1861), with the help of his able prime minister, Reshid Mustafa Pasha (1800–1858). Reshid had served as the Ottoman ambassador in London and Paris and was familiar with Western institutions, which he admired and wished to emulate. The reforms introduced security of property, equality of taxation, and equality before the law regardless of religion. Tax collection was regularized.

These reforms were strengthened by further edicts after the Crimean War. Contacts with the West encouraged Turks to think of transforming their empire into a more modern, Westernized state. Many young intellectuals were impatient with the rate of change, however, and, unable freely to express their opinions at home, some went into exile in the late 1860s to Paris and London. Their hosts called them the "Young Turks," an expression that became synonymous with the desire for change and improvement.

Alarmed by challenges to its rule, the central government began to turn away from reform, and in 1871 the sultan decided to assert his personal rule. His inability successfully to wage war and hold onto the empire led to dissatisfaction, and in the spring of 1876 rioters demanded and won the establishment of constitutional government. Within less than a year, however, the new sultan, Abdul Hamid II (r. 1876–1909), dismissed the constitutional government and reverted to personal rule.

Opposition to the government increased, fueled by nationalist fervor. The empire tolerated religious diversity and did not persecute people because of their religion. But the central administration had lost control over its provincial officials, who were often corrupt and tyrannical. Much of the Balkan region was isolated from any benign control Constantinople might have wished to exercise. Christians, the majority population in the Balkans, blamed their suffering on Islamic rule, and many were inspired by the 1821 Greek war of independence and the revolutions of 1848 to seek their own independence.

The Romanians, who lived mainly in the adjoining provinces of Moldavia in the north and Wallachia in the south, began to express nationalist sentiments in the late eighteenth century. These sentiments were nurtured by Western-educated students, who claimed for their countrymen illustrious descent from Roman settlers of antiquity. News of revolution in Paris in 1848 helped trigger a revolt in both provinces demanding unification and independence. This uprising was quickly crushed by the Turks.

In 1856 the Congress of Paris had removed Russia's right of protection over Moldavia and Wallachia and provided for a referendum to determine their future. In 1859 the two provinces chose a local military officer, Alexander Cuza (r. 1859–1866), as ruler of each territory; and in

1862, the Ottoman Empire recognized the union of the two principalities in the single, autonomous state of Romania. At the Congress of Berlin in 1878, the full independence of Romania was recognized. Thus, in less than a quarter-century, two provinces of the Ottoman Empire merged and gained full sovereignty.

The path to independence was much more violent for the Bulgars. When a nationalist uprising in Bulgaria broke out in May 1876, the Christian rebels attacked not only symbols of Ottoman authority but also peaceable Turks living in their midst. The imperial army, aided by local Turk volunteers, quickly re-established Ottoman authority. Incensed by the massacre of fellow Muslims, the volunteers resorted to mass killing, looting, and burning of Christian villages. The "Bulgarian horrors" shocked Europe and made the continuation of Turkish rule unacceptable.

The Bulgar crisis was resolved by the Balkan wars of 1876–1878, which were provoked by the uprising of the westernmost Ottoman provinces of Bosnia and Herzegovina. Since many of the inhabitants of these two provinces were Serbs, they had the sympathy of Serbia, which believed it could unify the southern Slavs. Together with the neighboring mountain state of Montenegro, Serbia declared war on the Ottoman Empire. They were savagely defeated by the Turks.

Russia, which saw itself as the protector of the Slavic peoples, also declared war on the empire and forced the sultan to sue for peace. The resulting Treaty of San Stefano, signed in March 1878, excluded the Ottoman Empire from Europe and created a huge, independent Bulgaria as essentially a Russian satellite. The British, Austrians, and French were shocked at the extent to which the San Stefano treaty favored Russia. Under their pressure, the European powers met in Berlin in 1878 to reconsider the treaty. The Congress of Berlin reduced the size of the Bulgarian territory, allowing the rest to revert to Constantinople. Bosnia and Herzegovina were removed from Ottoman rule and put under that of Austria-Hungary (see Map 22.3 on page 595). Constantinople was forced to acknowledge the independence of Serbia, Montenegro, and Romania and the autonomy of Bulgaria. The British insisted on being given the island of Cyprus to administer, an outpost from which they might prevent further challenges to the balance of power.

Nationalistic Uprising in Bulgaria In this 1879 lithograph, Bulgaria is depicted in the form of a maiden—protected by the Russian eagle, breaking her chains, and winning liberty from the Ottoman Empire. *(St. Cyril and Methodius National Library, Sofia)*

Thus Turkey was plundered, not only by its enemies but also by the powers that had intervened on its behalf. When France complained that it received no compensation, it was given the chance to grab Tunisia, another Ottoman province. The work of the congress reflected the power politics that now characterized international affairs. Neither morality nor international law restrained ambition.

THE EMERGENCE OF A POWERFUL UNITED STATES, 1840–1880

Across the seas a new power emerged in these years, the United States. It enlarged its territories, strengthened its national government, and broadened its democracy by including a large category of people previously excluded from the political process—African Americans. But these achievements came at the expense of the bloodiest conflict in American history, the Civil War. And through it all, this great democracy refused to enfranchise its female members, despite tremendous efforts by those lobbying for woman suffrage.

Territorial Expansion and Slavery

In the nineteenth century the United States gained huge territories through westward expansion. In 1803, President Thomas Jefferson, negotiating with the French, secured the Louisiana Purchase, which nearly doubled the size of the United States. In 1810, 1813, and 1819, Florida was acquired from Spain. Some Americans looked even farther, moving into Mexican-held territories in the Southwest and British-held territories in the Pacific Northwest. The United States, some began to insist, was destined to occupy the whole North American continent; expansion would fulfill what was often called America's Manifest Destiny. In 1845, Congress annexed Texas; in 1846 the United States gained the southern part of the Oregon territory after threatening war against Britain. Declaring war on Mexico in the same year, the United States won California and the Southwest in 1848. The United States now spanned the continent from the Atlantic to the Pacific.

The nature of the U.S. government was transformed in these years: From being a weak institution exercising authority only in a limited number of domains, the federal government became a powerful authority. This change represented the only practical resolution of regional disagreements that threatened to tear the country apart in the mid-nineteenth century.

Beginning in the 1820s the United States saw serious sectional clashes between east and west as well as north and south. The latter were more important. Many issues divided the two regions, notably a conflict between the industrial interests of the North and the agrarian interests of the South. What particularly sharpened this divide was the issue of slavery. As the United States annexed new territories, the question of whether they would be slave or free divided the North and South; the North opposed the spread of the "peculiar institution," while much of the South, fearing isolation, favored its spread.

The issue of slavery was passionately debated for decades. Some Americans wanted slavery abolished throughout the United States; if that could not be done, some of the most committed abolitionists advocated the secession of free states from the Union. On the other side, southerners threatened that if their way of life—meaning a society based on slavery—were not assured, then the South would secede. The threat of secession was lightly and frequently made by partisans of various causes for many decades. Commitment to national unity was weak.

The election of the Illinois Republican Abraham Lincoln (1809–1865) as president in November 1860 appeared to the South as a final blow. Lincoln opposed the spread of slavery beyond its existing borders and hence appeared to threaten its future. Within a few weeks, the South reacted to Lincoln's election.

Beginning in December 1860 a number of southern states voted to secede from the Union, forming in February 1861 the Confederate States of America. The South saw its cause as being one of states' rights, claiming that the people of each state had the right to determine their destiny. Southern states seized federal funds and property, and in April 1861 the Confederates bombarded federally held Fort Sumter, an island fort in the harbor of Charleston, South Carolina. Lincoln, inaugurated in March 1861, was determined to put down the insurrection and preserve the Union. A calamitous civil war (1861–1865) had begun.

Civil War and National Unity

The North had many advantages over the South. It was nearly three times as populous as the South, it had a strong industrial base that could supply an endless stream of manufactured weapons, and it had a more extensive rail system allowing for better transport of men and materiel to the front. Although there were a number of important military engagements between the two parties, the North essentially strangled the South, which toward the end of the war was short of men, money, and supplies.

During the war and its aftermath, the government took measures that centralized power in the United States, changing the nation from a loose federation of states to a more centrally governed entity. As one historian has noted, the United States changed from "they" to "it." The federal government intruded into areas of life from which it had before been absent. Slaves, previously considered property, were declared by Lincoln to be free with the Emancipation Proclamation in 1863. The Union imposed conscription, instituted a federal income tax, and replaced state banks with a uniform national banking system. The federal government provided massive subsidies for a national railroad system, and with the Morrill Land Grant College Act of 1862, it created a national system of state universities. As Senator John Sherman of Ohio declared during the war, "the policy of this country ought to be to make everything national as far as possible."

The principle of state sovereignty, which the Southern states had espoused and which the North had tried to accommodate before the war, now lay defeated. The North occupied the South in an attempt to "reconstruct" it. Reconstruction included efforts to root out the Confederate leadership and ensure full civil and political rights for the newly emancipated African Americans. The government also embarked on a short-lived campaign to provide freed slaves with enough land to assure them of a livelihood—another example of federal authority at work.

The Frontiers of Democracy

One of the major transformations in the United States that began in the 1820s was the inclusion of an ever greater number of people in the political process. By the late 1820s, under the impact of popular pressure, states abandoned restrictions on voting, and most adult white men received the vote. Symbolic of this new "age of the common man" was the election of Andrew Jackson as U.S. president in 1828. All his predecessors had been men of education and property—some were even described as "Virginia aristocrats"—but Jackson represented himself as a self-made man, a rugged frontiersman. State legislatures had in the past elected members to the presidential Electoral College, but in response to public calls for change, state legislatures altered the system so that Electoral College members were selected by direct popular vote.

National presidential campaigns became rough-and-tumble affairs, with emotional appeals to the public. Scurrilous attacks, many untrue, were mounted against opponents. Campaigns began to revolve around easily grasped symbols. When William Henry Harrison ran for president in 1840 he was depicted as a simple frontiersman; his supporters wore log-cabin badges, sang log-cabin songs, and carried log-cabin replicas on floats in parades. Such paraphernalia became a common sight in American elections. If some contemporary observers, such as the Frenchman Alexis de Tocqueville (1805–1859), were disappointed at the lack of a thoughtful and deliberate process in choosing political leaders, they thought democracy was nowhere in the world as fully developed as in the United States, where it foreshadowed the future of other societies.

When Abraham Lincoln was elected in 1860, nobody of his social standing occupied an equivalent position in Europe. At the news of his assassination in 1865, workmen and artisans, seeing in the dead president a kindred spirit, stood for hours in line outside the U.S. legation in London and the consul general's office in Lyon (France) to sign a book of condolence to express their sorrow. It was also a form of tribute to a nation that had elected a backwoodsman born in a log cabin to its highest office.

The frontiers of democracy appeared to have widened after the Civil War when amendments to the U.S. Constitution granted African American men full equality with white men. Slavery was forbidden throughout the United States, and citizenship was granted to all, regardless of "race, color, or previous condition of servitude." All American men were guaranteed the right to vote. During the first few years of Reconstruction, white men who had supported the Confederacy were deprived of the right to vote, and African American men represented a large voting bloc in the South. As a result, for the first time the United States saw the election of a black governor as well as several lieutenant-governors, senators, congressmen, postmasters, and innumerable county and town officials who were black. After the end of military occupation of the South, however, local white power reasserted itself and the rights of African Americans were sharply curtailed. Yet, compared to the situation before the Civil War, African Americans had advanced significantly.

Legislation allowing African American men to vote contrasted dramatically with the political situation of women in America. This was particularly true because women in the North had helped lead the movement to abolish slavery. In so doing, they had learned the processes of democratic action—writing petitions and gathering signatures, collecting funds, making speeches, and holding demonstrations. They had also learned, and personalized, the language of Enlightenment emancipatory ideals and liberal self-determinism. The first women's rights movement had been organized by Elizabeth Cady Stanton (1815–1902) and Lucretia Mott (1793–1880) in 1848. These women and others, most notably Susan B. Anthony (1820–1906) and Lucy Stone (1818–1893), were important abolitionists as well. For many women, struggling for the rights of slaves caused them to recognize the injustice of their own political situation. When emancipation of the slaves finally arrived, they expected that black men and all women would be given the vote simultaneously. Instead, only black men got the vote.

Some of the white women were enraged to see those for whom they had labored suddenly transported to a political status that surpassed their own. They asked their white countrymen why an uneducated ex-slave should be able to influence public policy and a highly educated white woman should not. However, most black women felt that it was more important to secure black male suffrage than to hold out for universal suffrage. Some white women agreed and the women's movement split along these lines.

Still, by 1880 the United States had been transformed by unprecedented territorial expansion as well as the ordeal of the Civil War, which brought about the extension of federal authority and—however hesitatingly—the rights of citizenship to new groups. A large, powerful democracy had arisen on the North American continent.

STABILITY IN VICTORIAN BRITAIN

The mid-nineteenth century was a period of exceptional wealth and security for Britain as the population as a whole began to share in the benefits of industrialization. Britain enjoyed both social and political peace. The political system was not challenged, as it had been after the Napoleonic Wars. A self-assured, even smug, elite—merchants, industrialists, and landowners—developed a political system reflecting liberal values.

Parliamentary Government

Although suffrage was still very restricted, the parliamentary system became firmly established, with a government clearly responsible to the electorate. The importance of Parliament was symbolized by the splendor and size of the new building in which it met, finished in 1850. The form of government developed in its halls after midcentury represented a model that aroused the curiosity and envy of much of the world. (See the box, "Encounters with the West: A Japanese View of the British Parliament.") As we have

ENCOUNTERS WITH THE WEST

A Japanese View of the British Parliament

In 1862 the Japanese government sent its first diplomatic mission to Europe. Accompanying the delegation was its young translator, Fukuzawa Yukichi (1835–1901). Intrigued by what he saw and eager to interest his fellow Japanese in the West, Fukuzawa published several books. In fact, all books about the West in Japan came to be known as "Fukuzawa-bon." Toward the end of his life in his* Autobiography *he described how, while in London, he had tried to understand the workings of the British Parliament.

Of political situations at that time, I tried to learn as much as I could from various persons that I met in London . . . though it was often difficult to understand things clearly as I was as yet unfamiliar with the history of Europe. . . . A perplexing institution was representative government. When I asked a gentleman what the "election law" was and what kind of an institution the Parliament really was, he simply replied with a smile, meaning I suppose that no intelligent person was expected to ask such questions. But these were the things most difficult of all for me to understand. In this connection, I learned that there were different political parties—the Liberal and the Conservative—who were always "fighting" against each other in the government.

For some time it was beyond my comprehension to understand what they were "fighting" for, and what was meant, anyway, by "fighting" in peace time. "This man and that man are 'enemies' in the House," they would tell me. But these "enemies" were to be seen at the same table, eating and drinking with each other. I felt as if I could not make much out of this. It took me a long time, with some tedious thinking, before I could gather a general notion of these separate mysterious facts. In some of the more complicated matters, I might achieve an understanding five or ten days after they were explained to me. But all in all, I learned much from this initial tour of Europe.

Source: The Autobiography of Fukuzawa Yukichi, trans. Eiichi Kiyooka (Tokyo: Hokuseida Press, 1948), pp. 138, 143–144.

seen, Parliament consisted of an upper, hereditary House of Lords and a lower, elected House of Commons. Increasingly, the royal cabinet became answerable to Parliament.

In the twenty years after 1846, five different parties vied for power. Depending on the issue, parties and factions coalesced to support particular policies. After 1867, however, a clear two-party system emerged: Liberal and Conservative (Tory), both with strong leadership. This development gave the electorate a distinct choice. The Conservatives sought to preserve traditional institutions and practices, while the Liberals tended to be open to change.

Gladstone, Disraeli, and the Two-Party System

Heading these parties were two strong-minded individuals who dominated British political life for over a generation: William E. Gladstone (1809–1898), a Liberal, and Benjamin Disraeli (1804–1881), a Conservative. Gladstone came from an industrial family and married into the aristocracy; Disraeli was the son of a Jewish man of letters who had converted to Christianity. His father's conversion made his career possible —before the 1850s, Jews were barred from Parliament. Gladstone and Disraeli were master debaters;

Parliament and the press hung on their every word. Each was capable of making speeches lasting five hours or more and conducting debates that kept the house in session until 4 A.M. The rivalry between the two men thrilled the nation and made politics a popular pastime.

The competition between the Liberals and Conservatives led to a further extension of suffrage in 1867. The Second Reform Bill lowered property qualifications, extending the vote from 1.4 to 2.5 million electors out of a population of 22 million, and gave new urban areas better representation. Although some in Parliament feared that these changes would lead to the masses capturing political power—"a leap into the dark," one member called it—no radical change ensued. Extending the vote to clerks, artisans, and other skilled workers made them feel more a part of society and thus bolstered the existing system. John Stuart Mill, then a member of Parliament, championed the cause of women's suffrage (see page 585), but he had few allies and his effort failed.

As the extension of voting rights increased the size of the electorate, the parties became larger and stronger. Strong party systems meant a clear alternation of power between the Liberals and the Conservatives. With an obvious majority and minority party, the monarch could no longer play favorites in choosing a prime minister. The leader of the majority party had to be asked to form a government. Thus, even though Queen Victoria (r. 1837–1901) detested Gladstone, she had to ask him to form governments when the Liberals won parliamentary elections.

The creation of a broad-based electorate meant that politicians had to make clear appeals

Illustration of the Royal Family from *A Book of English Song* By carefully depicting herself as a devoted wife and mother, Queen Victoria appealed to her middle-class subjects and reflected their social ideals. In reality, she resented much about motherhood, privately complaining of the inconvenience and burden of childbirth and child rearing.

to the public and its interests. Public election campaigns became part of the political scene. The democratic "American" style of campaigning appealed to the common man. Also borrowed from across the seas was the "Australian ballot"—the secret ballot—adopted in 1872. This protected lower-class voters from intimidation by their employers, landowners, or other social superiors. In 1874 the first two working-class members of Parliament were elected, sitting as Liberals. Although their victory represented a very modest gain for workers' representation, it presaged the increasingly democratic turn Britain would take.

FRANCE: FROM EMPIRE TO REPUBLIC

Unlike Britain, which gradually transformed into a parliamentary democracy, France took a more tumultuous path. Revolutions and war overthrew existing political systems and inaugurated new ones. Each time the French seemed to have democracy within reach, the opportunity slipped away.

The People's Emperor, Napoleon III

The constitution of the Second French Republic provided for a single four-year presidential term. Frustrated by this limitation, Louis Napoleon by a coup d'état extended his presidency to a ten-year term in 1851. The following year, he called for a plebiscite to confirm him as Napoleon III (r. 1852–1870), emperor of the French. Although both of these moves were resisted in the countryside, the resistance was put down by massive repression.

In the rest of the country, huge majorities of voters endorsed first the prolonged presidency and then the imperial title. The new emperor seemed different from his predecessors. He believed in popular sovereignty (he maintained universal male suffrage, introduced in 1848), he did not pretend to reign by divine grace, and he repeatedly tested his right to rule by appealing to the popular vote. He seemed to combine order and authority with the promises of the Revolution—equality before the law, careers open to talent, and the abolition of hereditary rights.

The mid-nineteenth century was a period of prosperity for most Frenchmen, including urban workers and peasants. Louis Napoleon, in his youth the author of a book on pauperism, introduced policies congenial to labor, but repressive measures were also initiated. On the one hand, workers were required to keep a booklet in which their conduct was to be recorded by their employers; on the other hand, workers were granted limited rights to organize strikes, and labor unions were virtually legalized. The emperor expressed his desire to improve the workers' lot, and the government took a few concrete steps, such as providing some public housing. Slum clearance during the rebuilding of Paris drove many from their homes to the outskirts of the city, but it did provide healthier conditions for those who stayed behind, and the ambitious urban projects provided work for many (see page 553). Other public works projects, such as ports, roads, railroads, and monumental public buildings, also created jobs. For many, Louis Napoleon—the heir to the great Napoleon—was an incarnation of national glory.

Not all the French supported the emperor; many republicans could not forget that he had usurped the constitution of 1848. In protest, some went into exile, including the poet Victor Hugo. When Napoleon began to liberalize the government beginning in 1860 by easing censorship and making his government more accountable to the parliament, it facilitated the expression of opposition views. A coordinated republican opposition rebuked the economic policies of the empire.

Widespread hostility to the influence of the Catholic church—and the desire for more extensive freedoms of expression and assembly—helped forge a republican alliance of the middle classes and workers. This alliance was particularly powerful in the large cities and in some southern regions notorious for their opposition to central government control. Republicanism was better organized than in earlier years and had a more explicit program. Its proponents were prepared to take over the government, if the opportunity arose.

By 1869 the regime, which declared itself a "liberal empire," had fully evolved into a constitutional monarchy, responsible to the Legislative Corps, the lower house of the parliament. It might have endured, but in July 1870, Napoleon III rashly declared war against Prussia over the Ems dispatch and its fabricated slight to French national honor (see page 528). Defeat destroyed the empire. In September, at news of the emperor's capture, the republican opposition in the Legislative Corps declared a republic. It continued the war but had to sign an armistice in January 1871.

The leader of the new government was an old prime minister of Louis Philippe, Adolphe Thiers (1797–1877). To sign a definite peace, the provisional government held elections. The liberals, known as republicans since they favored a republic, were identified with continuing the war; the conservatives, mostly royalists, favored peace. Mainly because of their position on this issue, the royalists won a majority from a country discouraged by defeat.

The Paris Commune, 1871

The new regime had no time to establish itself before an extraordinary uprising shook France in the spring of 1871. The uprising was called the Paris Commune, a name that harked back to 1792–1794, when the Paris crowds had dictated to the government. The Commune insisted on its right to home rule. It was seen by both radicals and conservatives as a workers' revolt that was seeking to establish a workers' government. Karl Marx described it as the "bold champion of the emancipation of labor."

Although labor discontent played a role in the Paris Commune, other forces also contributed, most notably the Prussian siege of Paris during the Franco-Prussian War. Paris had become radicalized during the siege: The rich had evacuated the city. The remaining Parisians, largely working class, suffered much because of the siege. Angered at the lack of recognition for their economic needs and their courage in withstanding the Prussians, they rose up against the new French government. Under their pressure, the Commune, composed largely of artisans, began governing the city.

In March 1871 the Commune declared itself free to carry out policies without hindrance from the central government in Versailles. During the two months that it lasted, Parisians developed a wide range of political clubs, public rituals, and cooperative workshops. They experimented with many socialist initiatives and, in general, the experience was described as exhilarating and celebratory. Political debates took place in every bar and meeting place; women formed separate clubs and also took an active part in many of the general clubs and events. Overall, the Commune's goals were quite moderate: It sought free universal education, a fairer taxation system, a minimum wage, and disestablishment of the official Catholic church. When the government sent forces to crush the Commune, soldiers set buildings on fire to force the Parisians out, and Parisians set official buildings on fire both to slow the soldiers and to burn the records of debt. Later, it was said that political women had set the fires. Such rumors and images of wild women proliferated as conservatives later tried to impose order by forcing women back into the domestic sphere. The end of the Commune was bloody: 25,000 people were massacred, 40,000 arrested, and several thousand deported.

The crushing of the Paris Commune signified the increasing power of the centralized state. The modern state had the strength to squelch popular revolts that in the past had seriously threatened regimes. Western Europe would not again witness a popular uprising of this magnitude.

Creation of the Third Republic, 1871–1875

Despite its brutality, the crushing of the Commune by Thiers's new government reassured many Frenchmen. "The Republic will be conservative, or it will not be," declared Thiers. The question now at hand was what form the new government would take. The monarchist majority offered the throne to the grandson of Charles X.

Manet: The Barricade In a detail from this 1871 painting, Edouard Manet catches a scene from the Paris Commune of 1871. With barricades, the communards are trying to protect themselves from the onslaught of government troops. Although fewer than a thousand government soldiers died, over 25,000 communards were killed. *(Reproduced by courtesy of the Board of Directors of the Budapest Museum of Fine Arts)*

However, he insisted he would become king only if the *tricouleur*—the flag of the Revolution, which long since had become a cherished national symbol—were replaced by the white flag of the House of Bourbon. The monarchists realized their project was unfeasible. France remained a republic. The republic, as Thiers put it, "is the regime which divides us the least."

By 1875 the parliament had approved a set of basic laws that became the constitution of the Third Republic. The parliament was to consist of two chambers: the Chamber of Deputies, elected by universal male suffrage, and the Senate, chosen indirectly by local officials. The two houses sitting jointly elected the president, who was to occupy essentially a ceremonial role as chief of state. The head of government—the premier—and his cabinet were responsible to the parliament. A century after the French Revolution, a lasting republican system of government in France was finally launched.

RUSSIA AND THE GREAT REFORMS

By the 1840s concern about the archaic nature and structure of Russian government was mounting. Many officials lamented the tendency of a timid bureaucracy to lie and mislead the public. Defeat in the Crimean War widened the critique of Russian institutions. Calls for *glasnost*—greater openness—became the leading motif in the great reforms of the 1860s.

The Abolition of Serfdom, 1861

The chief problem that needed resolution was serfdom. Educated opinion had long denounced serfdom as immoral, but this was not the principal reason for its abolition. Serfdom was abolished because it presented clear political disadvantages in both the domestic and international domains. The new tsar, Alexander II (r. 1855–1881), feared that if the abolition of serfdom did not come from above, it would occur from below—by a violent serf rebellion that would sweep away everything in its path, including the autocracy itself.

Serfdom was also linked to Russia's place in the world. Defeat in the Crimean War suggested that Russia could not depend on a soldiery of serfs for its defense. The Russian army would be more powerful if it consisted of free men with a stake in their society. In addition, the victorious Western states had won in part because their industrial might had furnished better weaponry and transportation networks. Industrial progress required a mobile labor force, not one tied to the soil. For many educated Russians, the defeat in the Crimea revealed general Russian backwardness; it was time to abolish serfdom.

In April 1861, the tsar issued a decree freeing the serfs. It was a radical measure to emancipate 22 million people from a system that allowed them to be bought and sold, separated from their families, and treated in the cruelest ways imaginable. Emancipation represented a compromise with the gentry, which had reluctantly agreed to liberate its serfs but insisted on compensation. As a result, the newly liberated peasants had to reimburse the government with mortgage payments for fifty years. The peasants received some land, but its value was vastly overrated and its quantity insufficient for peasant families. To make ends meet, the freed peasants continued working for their former masters.

The mortgage payments and taxes imposed on the peasants by the central government were handled by the local commune, the *mir.* The mir determined how the land was to be used, and it paid collectively for the mortgage and taxes on the land. As a consequence, the commune was reluctant for the peasants to leave the land, and they could do so only with its permission. Freed from serfdom, the peasants still suffered many constraints.

The tsar and his advisers feared the large mass of uneducated peasants as a potential source of anarchy and rebellion. Thus they depended on the mir to preserve control even though the commune system had some inherent economic disadvantages. Increased productivity benefited the commune as much as the individual peasant; hence there was little incentive for land improvement, and yields remained low.

Reforms in Russian Institutions

Alexander was called the "tsar emancipator" by his contemporaries, but he was wedded to the principles of autocracy. His aim in abolishing serfdom and introducing other reforms was to modernize and strengthen Russia and stabilize his divinely mandated rule. Like most Russians, Alexander believed that only the firm hand of autocracy could hold together a large, ethnically diverse country.

Clearly, however, the sudden freedom of 22 million illiterate peasants threatened to overwhelm existing institutions, and some changes had to be made. Although he surrendered no powers, Alexander did reform the government and the judicial and military systems so they could deal more effectively with all the changes in Russian society.

Government reform had paramount importance. Between about 1800 and 1850, the Russian population had increased from 36 to 59 million, and it had become more and more difficult to administer this vast country. Overcentralized, with a poorly trained civil service, the government was unable to cope with the problems of its people. Emancipation of the serfs greatly exacerbated this situation; an enormous number of people, freed from their owners' control, were abruptly in need of services. Thus in 1864 a law was passed providing for local governments, or *zemstvos*, at the village and regional level, giving Russians the authority and the opportunity to use initiative in local matters.

The zemstvos were largely controlled by the gentry and not particularly democratic. They were forbidden to debate political issues, and their decisions could be overridden or ignored by local officials appointed by the tsar. Some hoped that the zemstvos could become the basis for self-government at the national level and looked for the creation of an all-Russian zemstvo. But such hopes were firmly squelched by the tsar, who jealously insisted on undiminished power.

The tsar also created an independent judiciary that ensured equality before the law, public jury trials, and uniform sentences. Russian political leaders recognized that public confidence in the judiciary was a prerequisite for the development of commerce and industry. Businessmen would no longer fear arbitrary intervention by capricious officials and could develop enterprises in greater security.

In addition, censorship of the press was abolished. Under the previous tsar, Nicholas, all ideas that did not conform to government policy were censored. Censorship prevented the central government from being well informed about public opinion or the effects of its policies on the country. Under Alexander, openness in the press was viewed as a remedy for corruption and the misuse of power.

Reform also extended to the Russian army. Its structure and methods became more Western. Military service, previously limited to peasants, became the obligation of all Russians. Access to the officer corps was to be by merit rather than by social connection.

Although the tsarist regime remained autocratic and repressive, the reforms undertaken by Alexander II meant that a new page had been turned in Russian history.

SUMMARY

Novel configurations of power appeared in the period from about 1850 to 1880 as new or enlarged states were created through warfare or the threat of force. Liberal nationalists in the early nineteenth century had believed that Europe would be freer and more peaceful if each people had a separate nation, but they were now proved wrong. The Crimean War and its aftermath replaced the congress system, which had sought a balance of power among partners, with a system of rival states pursuing their own self-interest. The international order was severely shaken as Italy and Germany emerged from the center of Europe and Romania and Bulgaria were carved out of the Ottoman Empire in the east.

Both new and existing states faced a choice between federalism and centralized rule. In the process of unification, Italy and Germany could have opted for a loose federal union, but both Piedmont and Prussia chose central control. And the crushing of the Paris Commune spelled the doom of those who wanted a France of decentralized self-governing units. Strong, centralized governments increasingly became the norm. That was also the case across the ocean in the United States, where North and South fought a bloody civil war over the issues of slavery and state sovereignty, and the victorious federal government imposed its will on the rebellious states.

To achieve legitimacy, however, governments had to appear to have the consent of their peoples. Hence all European rulers except those of the Ottoman and Russian Empires found it necessary to have a parliament. France and Britain became increasingly democratic in these years, answerable to a growing electorate. In the United States white males already enjoyed freer and more open institutions than existed anywhere else, and the post–Civil War era marked a further enlargement of political participation when African American men were granted the rights of citizenship. Women did not have the right to vote in any of these states, but the women's suffrage movement had begun.

Two major changes for which liberals in 1848 had agitated had become reality: freer political institutions and the organization of nation-states. Although neither of these was fully implemented everywhere, both appeared to have been successfully established. Many Europeans could easily believe they were living in an age of optimism.

NOTES

1. Quoted in Otto Pflanze, *Bismarck and the Development of Germany*, vol. 1 (Princeton: Princeton University Press, 1990), p. 184.
2. Quoted in William Flavelle Monypenny and George Earle Buckle, *The Life of Benjamin Disraeli: Earl of Beaconsfield*, vol. 2 (London: John Murray, 1929), pp. 473–474.

SUGGESTED READING

Bensel, Richard Franklin. *Yankee Leviathan: The Origins of Central State Authority in America, 1859–1877.* 1990. Emphasizes the extent to which the Civil War led to centralization of government in the United States.

Blake, Robert. *Disraeli.* 1966. The authoritative biography of the Victorian statesman who helped shape the British parliamentary system.

Carr, William. *The Wars of German Unification.* 1991. A careful examination of the three wars that led to unification.

Coppa, Frank J. *The Wars of Italian Independence.* 1992. Views Italian unification within an international context.

Engle, Barbara Alpern. *Between the Fields and the City: Women, Work, and Family in Russia, 1861–1914.* 1994. An interesting and careful study of the complex experience of emancipation.

Evans, Eric J. *The Forging of the Modern State: Early Industrial Britain, 1783–1870.* 1983. Considers the development of political parties for the period covered in this chapter.

Goldfrank, David M. *The Origins of the Crimean War.* 1994. Blames the Russian Tsar Nicholas I for irresponsibly launching the war.

Grew, Raymond. *A Sterner Plan for Italian Unity.* 1963. Studies the role of the National Society in advancing the cause of unification.

Jelavich, Charles and Barbara. *The Establishment of the Balkan National States, 1804–1920.* 1977. Traces the emergence of independent states from the Ottoman Empire.

Kolchin, Peter. *Unfree Labor: American Slavery and Russian Serfdom.* 1987. The most recent study of Russian serfdom, of particular interest to American readers.

Lincoln, W. Bruce. "The Problem of Glasnost in Mid-Nineteenth Century Russian Politics." *European Historical Quarterly*, 11 (April 1981): 171–188. Considers the origins of the concept in the Russian bureaucracy.

Pearton, Maurice. *The Knowledgeable State: Diplomacy, War and Technology Since 1830.* 1982. Emphasizes the contribution of breakthroughs in science, technology, and social organization to military matters.

Pflanze, Otto. *Bismarck and the Development of Germany. I: The Period of Unification, 1815–1871.* 1990. Emphasizes Bismarck's flexibility and ability to improvise to accomplish long-range goals.

Rich, Norman. *Why the Crimean War? A Cautionary Tale.* 1985. Argues that the war was caused by the Western powers' decision to eliminate the Russian threat to the Ottoman Empire.

Shapiro, Ann-Louise. *Housing the Poor of Paris, 1850–1902.* 1985. A good discussion of the effect housing reform had on the working class.

Shaw, Stanford J. *History of the Ottoman Empire and Modern Turkey. II: Reform, Revolution and Republic: The Rise of Modern Turkey, 1808–1975.* 1977. Emphasizes the success of reform in the Ottoman Empire and sees its decline as essentially due to foreign aggression.

Sheehan, James. *German Liberalism in the Nineteenth Century.* 1978. Emphasizes the environment that conditioned the shaping of liberalism in a country that unified late and had to deal with a fast-emerging working class.

Sked, Alan. *The Decline and Fall of the Habsburg Empire, 1815–1918.* 1989. Provides a revisionist interpretation, concentrating on the strengths of the empire.

Smith, Dennis Mack. *Cavour and Garibaldi, 1860.* 1954. Contrasts the heroic, but sometimes naive, Garibaldi with the master manipulator, Cavour.

Smith, Page. *A People's History*, vols. 4 and 5. 1981 and 1982. Vol. 4 describes the development of the United States from 1828 to 1860. Vol. 5 covers the Civil War and Reconstruction. Both are marked by vivid prose and strong narrative.

Smith, William H. C. *Napoleon III.* 1972. Provides a sympathetic view of Napoleon III as a staunch believer in popular sovereignty who was devoted to the welfare of his people.

Williams, Roger L. *The French Revolution of 1870–1871.* 1969. Describes the Commune as the continuation of the French revolutionary tradition.

CHAPTER 21

The Age of Optimism, 1850–1880

The first department store, "Bon Marché" (the good buy), opened its doors in Paris in the 1850s. The store sold a large range of products that previously had been available only in separate specialty shops, and it bought them in quantities that made it possible to lower prices considerably. Constructed of glass and iron, Bon Marché represented the new, modern age: technologically impressive, convenient, and opulent. The shoppers themselves exemplified the ideals of the age, for they were largely women: As men became increasingly associated with managing production in this age of "separate spheres," women became associated with managing consumption. The department store was where the "idle" middle-class woman negotiated the market for the benefit of her family, shopping for what her preindustrial counterpart would have made by hand.

In many ways, the department store serves as a summary of the various changes experienced by prosperous regions of the West after midcentury. Industrial innovation had lowered the price of glass and steel, so that these huge emporiums could be built at reasonable cost. Railroads brought customers from outside the city. The penny press provided advertising for the department store, while the expansion of the postal system facilitated catalog sales. And the higher incomes available to many people allowed them to purchase more than just the necessities. The consumer society had begun.

The new levels of European wealth also contributed to a change in attitudes. This was an era shaped to a large extent by a growing, optimistic middle class, convinced it was living in an age of progress. The application of science and technology to social problems created confidence that the world could be improved. The fertility of the soil was increased; the burgeoning cities were sanitized and regulated. Scientists used new methods to study and combat disease. Public authorities founded schools and trained teachers. Transportation and communication rapidly improved.

However, as many artists and intellectuals pointed out, not all of society benefited from the fruits of progress. Democracy and legal equality seemed on the rise, yet women were everywhere disenfranchised and often held the legal status of children. Eastern and southern Europe changed little, and even in the western part a large group of the population still lived in great misery. Some cities carried out ambitious programs of urban renewal, but others continued to neglect slums. Still, the tone of the age was set by the ascendant middle class in western Europe, which embraced change and believed that the era was heading toward even more remarkable improvements.

Questions and Ideas to Consider

- Why is late-nineteenth-century culture associated with the middle class? Describe middle-class values. What was the ideology of "separate spheres"?
- How did the lives of the working class change during this period? Did a separate spheres ideology exist for this class? Why or why not?
- Why did this period experience so much urban renewal? What were the plans and goals of Baron Haussmann's rebuilding of Paris?
- Although the 1850s to 1880s saw a growing women's suffrage movement, women's rights activists worked for a variety of goals aside from the vote. What were they? What tactics were used to achieve them?
- The successes of science in this period promoted a general sense of optimism, but the new theories often gave rise to new fears. Discuss the impact of Darwin's evolutionary theory as well as the new ideas in physics and chemistry.

INDUSTRIAL GROWTH AND ACCELERATION

Beginning in the 1850s, western Europe experienced an unprecedented level of economic expansion. Manufacturers created new products and employed new sources of energy. An enlarged banking system provided more abundant credit to fund the expansion. Scientific research was systematically employed to improve methods of manufacture. A revolution in transportation speedily delivered goods and services to distant places. For many Europeans, daily life was profoundly changed.

The "Second Industrial Revolution," 1850–1914

The interrelated cluster of economic changes that began after 1850 is often called the "second industrial revolution." It was characterized by a significant speedup in production and the introduction of new materials such as mass-produced steel, synthetic dyes, and aluminum. Manufacturers replaced the traditional steam engine with stronger steam-powered turbines or with machines powered by new forms of energy—petroleum and electricity.

The invention of new products and methods of manufacture spurred industrial expansion. The second half of the nineteenth century has often been called the "age of steel." Up to then, steel production had been limited by the expense involved in its manufacture, but in 1856, Sir Henry Bessemer (1813–1898) discovered a much cheaper method, which produced in twenty minutes the same amount of steel previously produced in twenty-four hours. Over the next three decades, further advancements came from the French and English, halving the price of steel in Great Britain. Increased steel production made possible the expansion of the rail system, the creation of a steamship fleet, and an explosive growth in the building industry. No longer was steel a rare alloy used only for the finest swords and knives; it became the material that defined the age.

Significant changes in the supply of credit further stimulated economic expansion. Discovery of gold in California and Australia led to the inflow of huge amounts of the precious metal to Europe, expanding the supply of money and credit. This led to the establishment of the modern banking system.

CHAPTER CHRONOLOGY

1820s	The omnibus is introduced in France
1829	Robert Stephenson runs the *Rocket*
1833	Invention of the telegraph
1840	Introduction of the penny stamp
1848	The Public Health Bill in England
	Seneca Falls Women's Rights Convention
1850s	Clipper ships
	Invention of the tramway
1851	Crystal Palace Exhibition
1859	Darwin publishes his doctrine of evolution
1863	Building of underground railroad in London
1864	Pope Pius IX issues the *Syllabus of Errors*
1865	Transoceanic telegraph cable installed
1869	Opening of Suez Canal
1875	Alexander Graham Bell invents the telephone
	Electric lights in Paris
1885	Pasteur's rabies vaccine

Each advance made possible additional changes. Increased wealth and credit accelerated further expansion of industrial plants and the financing of an ambitious infrastructure of roads, railroads, and steamships, which in turn boosted trade. Between 1800 and 1840, the value of world trade had doubled. From 1850 to 1870 it increased 260 percent.

By the 1880s scientific discoveries increasingly fueled industrial improvements. Electricity began to be more widely used, replacing coal as a source of energy. Synthetic dyes revolutionized the textile industry, as did alkali in the manufacture of soap and glass. Dynamite, invented by the Swedish chemist Alfred Nobel (1833–1896) in the 1860s, made it possible to level hills and blast tunnels through mountains, facilitating construction. Five years after Nobel's death, his will established a prestigious prize named after its donor to honor significant contributions to science and peace.

Transportation and Communications

The rail system grew dramatically in the middle decades of the nineteenth century. When the English engineer Robert Stephenson (1803–1859) demonstrated his steam locomotive, the *Rocket*, in 1829, it ran on a track that was one-and-a-half miles long. By 1880 the total European railroad mileage was 102,000 (Map 21.1). In 1888 the Orient Express line opened, linking Constantinople to Vienna and thus to the rest of Europe. Meanwhile, the cost of rail transport steadily decreased, allowing for its greater use. Ocean transportation also changed dramatically. In 1869, the Suez Canal opened, reducing the distance between London and Bombay by 40 percent. More efficient ships were developed; by midcentury the clipper ship could cross the Atlantic in fourteen days. Steamships were also built, though they did not dominate ocean traffic until the 1890s. By 1880, European shipping carried nearly three times the cargo it had thirty years earlier.

The optimism born of conquering vast distance was reflected in a popular novel, *Around the World in Eighty Days* (1873), by the French writer Jules Verne (1828–1905). The hero, Phineas Fogg, traveled by balloon, llama, ostrich, steam locomotive, and steamship to accomplish in eighty days a feat that, only thirty years earlier, would have taken at least eleven months. Such was the impact of the new technology—and the Suez Canal.

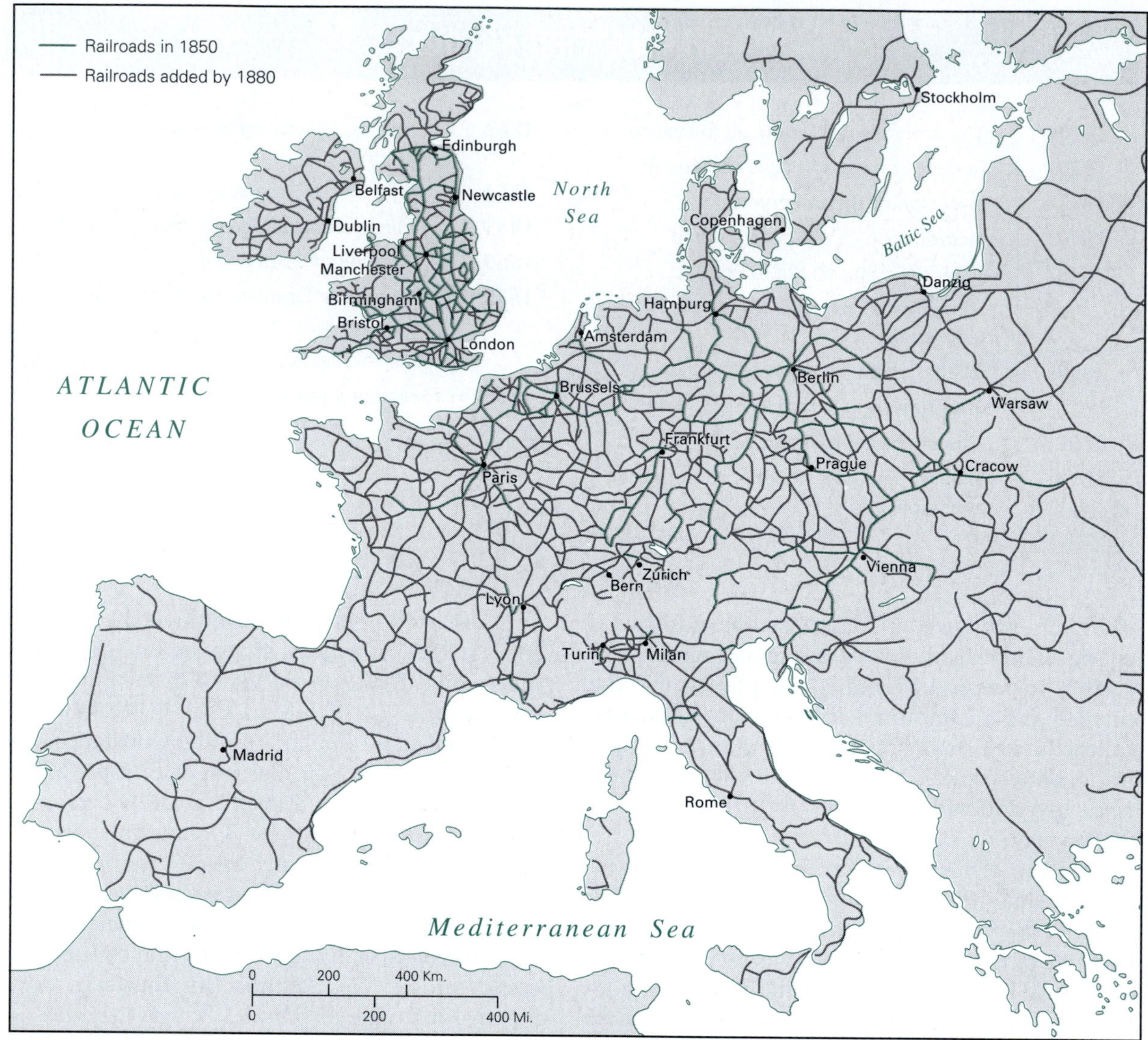

Map 21.1 Railroads of Western Europe, 1850 and 1880 During the mid-nineteenth century, European states built railroads at an increasing rate, creating a dense network by the 1880s. (*Adapted from Norman J. G. Pounds,* An Historical Geography of Europe, 1800–1914 *[New York: Cambridge University Press, 1985].*)

Along with the new speed, advances in refrigeration changed food transport. Formerly, refrigeration could be achieved only with ice cut out of frozen lakes, but this changed in the 1870s with the introduction of mechanical ice-making machines. By the 1880s dairy products and meat were being transported vast distances by rail and even across the seas by ship. Thanks to these advances, the surplus food of the Americas and Australia, rich in grasslands, could offer Europe a cheaper and far more varied diet.

The Suez Canal Opened in 1869, the canal significantly shortened the voyage by ship from Europe to East Asia. The Suez Canal exemplified the speeding up of transportation and communication in the second half of the nineteenth century. *(AKG London)*

Regular postal service was another a child of the new era, because railroads and increased efficiency lowered the cost. In Great Britain the number of letters mailed in a year increased from 7 per person in 1840 to 32 by 1880. Combined with the transoceanic telegraphy system (1865) and the invention of the telephone (1875), regular postal service transformed the world of information. Now travelers could easily communicate with those at home, business could be transacted at a distance, and news from distant parts of the globe—of earthquakes, revolutions, or the outbreak of war—could reach Europe within minutes. In 1875 the American inventor Alexander Graham Bell (1847–1922) invented a machine capable of transmitting the human voice by electrical impulses; in 1879 the first telephones were installed in Germany; two years later they appeared in France.

The speedy linking of distant places called attention to the need to standardize time. Until then, countries typically had innumerable time zones; each town established its time according to the location of the sun. Railroad traffic made these quaint differences a source of annoyance to travelers and railroad officials, and it became imperative to have a standard time for each European nation. The electric telegraph made it possible to set that time to the second.

CHANGING CONDITIONS AMONG SOCIAL GROUPS

Industrial advances transformed the traditional structure of European society. Fewer people worked the land; more worked in industry. The social and political influence of the landed aristocracy waned as wealth became far less dependent on the ownership of land. To varying degrees, this influence now had to be shared with the growing middle class. Although life for both industrial and farm workers generally improved in this period, there were great disparities, as many people continued to suffer from profound deprivation.

The Declining Aristocracy

Always a small, exclusive group, the European aristocracy represented less than 1 percent of the population in the nineteenth century. Many people of noble birth were quite poor and economically indistinguishable from their non-noble neighbors. Others owned vast estates and were fabulously wealthy.

Some ennoblements were of recent origin. In England, most titles were less than a hundred years old, having originally been conferred on individuals for service to the state, the arts, or the economy. In France both Napoleons had ennobled persons they wished to honor. In Germany, Bismarck arranged for the Kaiser to ennoble the Jewish banker Gerson Bleichröder (1822–1893) for helping finance the wars of the Prussian state.

As distinctions blurred between the aristocracy and the upper middle class, marriages were often arranged between the children of noble families in financial straits and children of wealthy merchants desiring status. Many nobles who previously had shunned manufacture became industrialists and bankers. Idle members of the nobility were now somewhat rare. Although many aristocrats still enjoyed a lavish lifestyle, others were far more restrained and might be mistaken for successful business people. Nobles played varied roles across Europe, generally dominating the ranks of officers, diplomats, and high-ranking civil servants. Many successful industrialists were also of noble birth. Their continued importance was obvious, but in most European states, nobles could no longer assert privileges based exclusively on birth.

The Expanding Middle Class

Up to the eighteenth century, society had been divided into legally separate orders based on birth. In the nineteenth century, it became more customary to classify people by their economic function. The large new group of industrialists, professionals, and merchants came to be known as the "middle class." These people were also frequently described as *bourgeois*, a term that had originated in the twelfth century to describe the new wealthy class based on urban occupations. The nineteenth century is often described as "the bourgeois century," especially in western Europe, where the middle class helped fashion much of society.

The middle class expanded dramatically in the wake of industrialization. More trade and manufacture meant more entrepreneurs and managers, while the increasingly complex society called for more engineers, lawyers, accountants, bankers, merchants, architects, and doctors. As industries matured, the increasing use of machinery and better industrial organization meant that fewer additional workers and more clerks and bureaucrats were needed. In the 1870s about 10 percent of urban working-class people reached lower-middle-class status by becoming storekeepers, lower civil servants, clerks, or salespeople.

Import-export businesses, insurance companies, and department stores provided opportunities of this kind, as did the expansion of government services. In the second half of the nineteenth century, France increased its teacher corps by 80,000 and the British postal service increased its staff sixfold. The significance for individuals was great. When the son or daughter of peasants became the village postmaster, a schoolteacher, or a clerk in a major firm, his or her whole family rose to the lower stratum of the middle class. Even more than income or material comfort, the promise of social respectability enticed the lower classes to strive for membership in the middle class. In midcentury Britain, the middle class represented 15 percent of the population; by 1881, 25 percent. Elsewhere, the proportion was lower, but it was growing in number and strength as the economy expanded.

A widening subgroup of the middle class consisted of members of the professions, those whose prestige rested on the claim of exclusive expertise in a particular field. In the early nineteenth century, requirements for exercising a profession varied, depending on the country. In France and Prussia, government regulation stipulated the qualifications necessary to practice medicine; in England anyone might practice it. As the professions attempted to create a monopoly for themselves and eliminate rivals, they established more standards. Medical doctors, for instance, began requiring specialized education to distinguish themselves from herbalists, midwives, and other rivals. By midcentury either professional associations or the state itself accredited members of the professions. Women had limited access to professions; typically their opportunities were confined to lower teaching positions and, as a result of Florence Nightingale's efforts (see page 519), nursing.

Middle-Class Lifestyles

The standard of living of the middle class varied considerably, from the wealthy entrepreneur who bought a château, or built one, to the bourgeois who dwelled in a modest apartment. But all members of the middle class lived in new standards of comfort. Their homes had running water, upholstered furniture, and enough space to provide separate sleeping and living quarters. They had several changes of clothing and consumed a varied diet. They read books and subscribed to newspapers and journals.

In some areas suburban living became fashionable. For further relief from the crowded cities, visits to resorts became popular. Throughout Europe, resort towns sprang up, devoted principally to the amusement of the well-off. It became fashionable to "take the waters"—bathing in hot springs and drinking the mineral waters thought to have special attributes. For the first time, tourism became big business. Thomas Cook (1808–1892), an Englishman, organized tours to the Crystal Palace exhibition of 1851 (see page 558). Discovering the large market for travel tours, he began running tours in England and on the Continent. Beginning in 1835, a German publisher, Karl Baedeker (1801–1859), issued a tourist guide to the Rhine, followed by guidebooks to various European countries and the Middle East. The Baedeker guides provided the pattern for the multitude of guidebooks that followed.

New wealth and leisure time also led to more hotels, restaurants, and cafés. In 1869 there was a hotel in Paris with seven hundred well-appointed rooms. Vienna's National Hotel, with three hundred rooms, had steam heat, spring water on every floor, and an icehouse providing cool drinks. At home or away, the bourgeois valued comfort.

Members of the middle class shared certain attitudes about the conduct of their lives. They believed their successes were due not to birth but to talent and effort. They wanted to be judged on their merits, and they were expected to abide by strict moral principles. Their lives were supposed to be disciplined, especially with regard to sex and drink. The age was called "Victorian" because the middle class in Britain saw in the queen who reigned for two-thirds of the century a reflection of its own values. "Victorian morality," preached but not always practiced, was often seen as hypocritical. Male sexuality was expected and condoned while female sexuality was repressed and negated. As a result, sexual behavior was veiled in social anxiety, and women were seen as either respectable virgins and mothers or disruptive mistresses and prostitutes. As the middle class increasingly dominated society, its values became the social norms. Public drunkenness was discouraged, and anti-alcohol movements

Ladies' Bicycling Fashion This new mode of transportation suggested possibilities for female emancipation. *(From Karin Helm (ed.),* Rosinen aus der Gartenlaube *[Gutersloh: Signum Verlag, n.d.]. Reproduced with permission.)*

vigorously campaigned against drinking. Public festivals were regulated, making them more respectable and less rowdy. In several countries, societies for the protection of animals agitated against blood sports such as cockfights.

In spite of their differences in education, wealth, and social standing, most of the bourgeoisie resembled one another in dress, habits of speech, and deportment. Bourgeois men dressed somberly, in dark colors, and avoided decoration, reflecting their activity in the hard world of machines, money, and scientific attitudes. Such dress also reflected a conscious attempt to emphasize the achievement-oriented attitudes of the bourgeoisie in contrast to what was seen as the frivolous nobility.

The values that applied to bourgeois women were quite different. Confined to the running of the family home, bourgeois women expressed themselves through their clothes and their homes. They created extravagant, huge, beribboned dresses that literally took up space and defined their environments. Women's decorative ornamentation also defined the middle-class home. With the world of business and machines seen as ruthless and unforgiving, the home was reconceived from a place of production and reproduction to a haven of purity and love. Whereas the husband was limited to work for profit and was expected to be strong and rational, the wife was limited to work for affection and religious devotion and was expected to be gentle and emotional. Women did a great deal of work: They decorated and redecorated their homes with the seasons and the styles, supervised their servants, kept the accounts, watched over the children's homework and religious education, and involved themselves in charitable works. (See the box "Advice on Running the Middle-Class Household.") Yet all this activity was explicitly undervalued in a world concerned with material and intellectual progress. In the decades around midcentury, the idea of two separate spheres—one male and public, the other female and private—reached its height.

It is also true that many bourgeois women helped their husbands or fathers in the office, the business, or the writing of scientific treatises. Others achieved success on their own terms, running their own businesses, writing, painting, teaching. When Rosa Bonheur (1822–1899) was excluded from nude sketching sessions at her art school because she was a woman, she began painting animals and became the best-known painter of domestic animals in the nineteenth century.

The expectation that middle-class women would marry and be taken care of by their husbands led to the provision of inferior education for girls and young women. The husband's responsibility to support his wife—and any un-

Advice on Running the Middle-Class Household

In 1861 Isabella Mary Mayson Beeton, a London housewife, published **Mrs. Beeton's Book of Household Management**, *which in Britain was outsold only by the Bible. Her popular book provided British middle-class women with advice on running their households and reflected their values concerning discipline, frugality, and cleanliness.*

As with the commander of an army, or the leader of an enterprise, so is it with the mistress of a house. Her spirit will be seen through the whole establishment; and just in proportion as she performs her duties intelligently and thoroughly, so will her domestics follow in her path. Of all those acquirements, which more particularly belong to the feminine character, there are none which take a higher rank, in our estimation, than such as enter into a knowledge of household duties; for on these are perpetually dependent the happiness, comfort, and well-being of a family. . . .

Early rising is one of the most essential qualities which enter into good Household Management, as it is not only the parent of health, but of innumerable other advantages. Indeed, when a mistress is an early riser, it is almost certain that her house will be orderly and well-managed. . . .

Cleanliness is indispensable to health, and must be studied both in regard to the person and the house, and all that it contains. . . .

Frugality and economy are home virtues, without which no household can prosper. . . .

Charity and benevolence are duties which a mistress owes to herself as well as to her fellow-creatures; and there is scarcely any income so small, but something may be spared from it. . . . Great advantages may result from visits paid the poor, for there being, unfortunately, much ignorance, generally amongst them with respect to all household knowledge, there will be opportunities for advising and instructing them in a pleasant and unobtrusive manner, in cleanliness, industry, cookery, and good management. . . .

A housekeeping account-book should invariably be kept, and kept punctually and precisely. . . .

. . . The treatment of servants is of the highest possible moment as well to the mistress as to the domestics themselves. On the head of the house the latter will naturally fix their attention; and if they perceive that the mistress's conduct is regulated by high and correct principles, they will not fail to respect her. If, also a benevolent desire is shown to promote their comfort, at the same time that a steady performance of their duty is exacted, then their respect will not be unmingled with affection, and they will be more solicitous to continue to deserve her favour.

Source: Isabella Mary Mayson Beeton, *Mrs. Beeton's Book of Household Management* (London: S. O. Beeton, 1861), pp. 1–6.

married female members of their family—was often a source of great anxiety for men. For women, the problem was deeply frustrating. Even if they were brighter and more intellectually curious than their brothers, young girls did not receive an equal education. Proponents of women's rights argued strenuously for equal access to education and the professions. Slowly, secondary and university education was made available to young women, and very slowly they began to enter the professions.

Women more easily penetrated the lower levels of middle-class occupations. By the 1890s, two-thirds of primary schoolteachers in England

and half the post office staff in France were women; by 1914 nearly half a million women were working as shop assistants in England. Some new technologies created jobs that became heavily feminized, such as the positions of typist and telephone operator.

The Workers' Lot

Working-class women had always worked. They were generally paid much less than their male counterparts, but the jobs were there, families needed everyone to work, and there was no status to defend through enforced idleness. The increased prosperity and productivity of the period gradually improved the conditions of both male and female workers after 1850. Their wages and standard of living rose, and they enjoyed more job security. The workers' increased income enabled them to enjoy a better diet. In France the average number of calories consumed per adult male increased by one-third between 1840 and 1890. The quality of food also improved; people consumed more meat, fish, eggs, and dairy products.

In some ways, factory work became harder. There was an increased emphasis on efficiency, fewer informal breaks, and new machines that increased the tempo of work, frequently leading to accidents and exhaustion. Legislation gradually reduced the length of the workweek. The British workweek, typically 73 hours in the 1840s, was reduced to 56 hours in 1874. In France it was reduced to 10 hours a day, in Germany to 11.

As workers had more time and more money, their leisure patterns changed. Some leisure activities that had previously been limited to the upper classes became available to workers. Dance halls, popular theaters, and other enterprises sprang up to entertain them and make a profit. The railroad took them to resort towns for holidays.

Although most workers believed their lot had improved, they were aware that a vast gulf separated them from the middle and upper classes. In the 1880s in the northern French industrial city of Lille, the combined estates of 20,000 workers equaled that of one average industrialist. In Paris the gluttonous rich ate multicourse meals and the leftover scraps were collected by special vendors and sold to the poor.

Although a few members of the working class were able to enter the lower levels of the middle class, most remained mired in the same jobs as their parents and grandparents. Poverty was still pervasive, and urban diseases, such as tuberculosis, were common. Compared to the middle class, the workers continued to live in shabby and limited circumstances.

The Transformation of the Countryside

Before the nineteenth century, the countryside had hardly changed at all, but beginning at midcentury it was radically transformed. Agriculture became increasingly efficient, and the food supply grew significantly. More land was cultivated, and the yield per acre increased. In 1760 an agricultural worker in England could feed himself and one other person; by 1841 he could feed himself and 2.7 others. The population of Europe nearly doubled between 1800 and 1880, and yet it was nourished better than ever before.

The higher yields were due to an increased use of manure, augmented in the 1870s and 1880s by saltpeter imported from Chile and chemical fertilizers manufactured in Europe. In the 1850s steam-driven threshing machinery was introduced in some parts of western Europe. Organizational techniques borrowed from industry, including specialization and the insistence on regularity in the workplace, also contributed to greater productivity.

Life in the countryside became less isolated. Improved roads and dramatically expanded rail lines enabled farmers to extend their markets beyond the local area. In Brittany, in western France, a rail line to Paris led to a boom in dairy farming. Not only did rail lines connect farms to cities, but national school systems brought teachers into the villages. The local dialects and in some cases distinct languages that peasants had spoken for generations were replaced by a standardized national language. Local costumes became less common as styles adopted in the cities spread to the countryside via consumer catalogs. The farm girls who went to the cities to work as maids in middle-class homes returned to their villages with urban and middle-class ideals. Likewise, the military draft brought village youth into contact with urban folk and further spread city values to the countryside.

Even so, the rural world remained distinct from urban society. Many of the forces that contributed to modernity exacerbated rural problems. The expansion of manufacturing in cities contributed to the decline of cottage industry in rural areas, where agricultural workers had relied on the putting-out system to provide supplementary income. Thus, farmworkers were idle during slack seasons, and rural unemployment grew. In many cases railroads bringing goods made elsewhere wiped out some of the local markets on which cottage industry had depended. The steamship lowered the cost of transporting grain from distant Canada and Argentina, which often undersold wheat grown in Europe. The resultant crisis, worsened by a rural population explosion, led to the emigration of millions, who left the land for towns and cities or even migrated across the seas to the Americas and Australia. Although this process was painful for large segments of the rural population, the result was that for those who were able to remain on the land the situation eventually improved.

These developments had a striking effect on western Europe, but eastern Europe was hardly touched by them. In Russia, the average agricultural yield per acre in 1880 was one-quarter that of Great Britain. The land sheltered a large surplus population that was underemployed and contributed little to the economy. In the Balkans, most peasants were landless and heavily indebted.

URBAN PROBLEMS AND SOLUTIONS

By 1851 the majority of English people lived in cities; by 1891 the majority of Germans did as well. To cope with urban growth and its attendant problems—epidemics, crowding, traffic jams—cities developed public health measures and introduced planning and rebuilding programs. They adapted the new technologies to provide such urban amenities as streetlights, public transportation, water and sewer systems, and police forces. Cities became safer and more pleasant places to live, although city dwellers continued to suffer high mortality rates.

City Planning and Urban Renovation

Most of Europe's cities had begun as medieval walled cities and had grown haphazardly into major industrial centers. Their narrow, crooked streets could not accommodate the increased trade and daily movement of goods and people, and traffic snarls were common. City officials began to recognize that broad, straight avenues would resolve the traffic problem and bring sunlight and fresh air into the narrow and perpetually dank lanes and alleys. In the 1820s, London saw the first ambitious street-widening initiative. On Regency Street, old hovels were torn down and replaced with fancy new houses, and the poor were usually displaced. Later projects followed this pattern.

The most extensive program of urban rebuilding took place in midcentury Paris. Over a period of eighteen years, Napoleon III and his aide, Baron Georges Haussmann (1809–1891), transformed Paris from a dirty medieval city to a beautiful modern one. Broad, straight avenues were carved through what had been dingy slums. The avenues were lined with trees and graced with elegant houses. Enhancing the city were public monuments and buildings, such as the new opera house. The tremendous costs of this ambitious scheme kept the city of Paris in debt for decades. In addition, the slum-removal program drove tens of thousands of the poorest Parisians to the outskirts of the city, leading to greater social segregation than had previously existed.

Haussmann's extensive work in Paris served as a model for other cities, and although none was rebuilt as extensively, many underwent significant improvements. The cities of Europe

Pissarro: L' avenue de l' Opéra, Sunlight, Winter Morning Camille Pissarro, one of the leading impressionists, portrayed the broad new avenue designed by Baron Haussmann. The avenue leads to the new opera, in background, also planned during the Second Empire. (*Musée Saint-Denis, Reims/Giraudon/Art Resource, NY*)

began to display an expansive grace and sense of order, supporting the middle-class belief that theirs was an age of progress.

The Introduction of Public Services

Beginning at midcentury, government at the central and local levels helped make cities more livable by legislating sanitary reforms and providing public transportation and lighting. In the 1820s medical practitioners had observed that disease and higher mortality were related to dirt and the lack of clean air, clean water, and sunshine. Since diseases spreading from the poorer quarters of town threatened the rich and powerful, there was a general interest in improving public health by clearing slums, broadening streets, and supplying clean water.

Reform began in England, where the lawyer and civil servant Edwin Chadwick (1800–1895) drafted important plans for reform that became the basis for legislation. The Public Health Bill of 1848 established national standards for urban sanitation and required cities to regulate the installation of sewers and the disposal of refuse. The 1875 Health Act required cities to maintain certain basic health standards such as clean water and drainage.

As running water in the home became standard rather than a luxury, bathing became more common. The English upper classes had learned the habit of daily baths from their colonial experience in India; on the Continent it was not the custom until about the third quarter of the nineteenth century. French artist Edgar Degas (1834–1917) frequently painted bath scenes portraying the new European habit.

All these changes had a direct impact on the lives of city dwellers. Life became healthier, more comfortable, and more orderly. Between the 1840s and 1880, London's death rate fell from 26 per thousand to 20 per thousand. There was a decline in the incidence of diseases associated with filthy living conditions. Improved water supplies provided a cleaner environment and reduced the prevalence of water-borne diseases such as cholera and typhoid. In addition, a number of states became involved in the fight against disease: Norway and Sweden introduced mandatory vaccination for smallpox in 1810 and 1816, respectively. England followed in 1867 and Germany in the 1870s.

Other improvements also contributed to a better quality of life. With the introduction of urban transportation, city dwellers no longer had to live within walking distance of their work. Early public transportation was seen in the French omnibus service of the 1820s—a system of horse-drawn carriages following fixed routes. The bicycle also became an important means of transportation for some city dwellers. New gaslights made cities easier and safer to move around at night. The first electric lights appeared in Paris in 1875, although they were not common until the end of the century.

Cities significantly expanded their police forces to impose order, control criminal activity, and discourage behavior deemed undesirable, such as dumping garbage on the street, relieving oneself in public, or singing loud, raucous songs late at night. In 1850 London was the best-policed city in Europe with a five-thousand-man force, and Paris had around three thousand policemen. The numbers continued to increase.

SOCIAL AND POLITICAL INITIATIVES

New groups emerged to tackle the social and political inequalities of the period, as well as the critical urban problems that had followed in the wake of economic growth. The women's movement emerged. The state intervened in the economy in new ways. Private charitable groups sprang up. And socialist parties, exclusively dedicated to improving the lot of workers, gained in numbers and strength.

Feminism

A significant women's movement developed in the second half of the nineteenth century. In 1840, women working for the abolition of slavery found themselves barred from attending the World Anti-Slavery Convention in London. The outrage of the excluded U.S. delegates helped to inspire the organization of the first Women's Rights Convention, held in Seneca Falls, New York, in 1848. In Europe, similar conventions and associations appeared throughout the 1850s and 1860s.

In France, many of these associations formed during the political movements of 1848 and 1871. In both of these upheavals, women worked and fought alongside men and expected to reap some political and economic benefits. For instance, the Commune Commission for Education ruled to raise the salaries of women teachers to match those of men, "seeing that the necessities of life are as imperative for women as for men."[1] In general, these goals were not achieved. The government's re-establishment of order was, in both cases, partially structured around returning women to the private sphere. For instance, after the "June Days" of 1848, the government forbade women to form political clubs.

The strongest women's rights movement of the period developed in England. Largely made up of middle-class women from reform-minded families, the movement was led by Barbara Bodichon (1827–1891). Bodichon had written a pamphlet investigating the lack of legal rights for women, especially after they married. Incensed by what she found, she put together a petition asserting that married women ought to have control of their property and earnings. The petition was signed by a number of distinguished women of the day, including the poet Elizabeth Barrett Browning, the novelist Elizabeth Gaskell, and the political theorist Harriet Martineau. When Parliament rejected the proposal in 1856, the women around Bodichon redoubled their efforts.

These women and those who later joined them launched a number of important initiatives in the 1860s—a club where women could read and discuss issues, the feminist *Englishwoman's Journal*, and the Society for the Promotion of the Employment of Women to give women the skills they would need to be clerks and bookkeepers, instead of just governesses. They continued to lobby Parliament for married women's right to control their earnings and won this battle in 1878; in 1882 they secured married women's control of their own property.

Another major women's rights initiative, the repeal of the Contagious Disease Acts, was led by Josephine Grey Butler (1828–1906). In 1864, in response to the spread of venereal disease, the English government had given police in a number of ports and towns the right to arrest and examine any woman suspected of being a prostitute. Suspicion could be based on little more than a woman walking alone after dark. The acts clearly held women to blame for disease, put the burden of controlling prostitution on the prostitutes rather than their customers (or the wider economic system), and put all women, of whatever class, in danger of harassment by the state.

Butler, who came from a family of reformers, had fought to abolish slavery and had worked for the spread of education to impoverished women. The humiliating ideas behind the Contagious Disease Acts radicalized her—to the distress of some of her more conservative supporters. Through Butler's tireless efforts, and using political techniques she had learned in her abolitionist work, the acts were overturned in England in the 1880s. Butler also called attention to the plight of prostitutes on the Continent. Butler believed that women needed to obtain extensive political power, writing that "we have passed through an education—a noble education. God has prepared in us, in the women of the world, a force for all future causes which are great and just."[2]

The women's movement led by Barbara Bodichon put its numbers and prestige behind Butler's campaign and, in these same years, also campaigned for women's education. Although British universities admitted women, the University of London did not grant them degrees until after 1878, and the most prestigious British institutions, Oxford and Cambridge, did not grant degrees to women until after World War I. The situation was similar in the rest of Europe. In spite of discriminatory laws, harassment by male students, and initial obstruction by professional and accrediting groups, a few female doctors and lawyers practiced in England by the 1870s and on the Continent in the following decades.

The women's movement also continued to press for the right to vote, supporting John Stuart Mill in his run for Parliament and forming the Women's Suffrage Committee to organize further initiatives (see page 473). Nightingale, Martineau, and others, such as the mathematician Mary Somerville, joined 1499 prominent women in petitioning for the vote in 1866 but made little progress. In the coming century, women would use more aggressive tactics and achieve a great deal.

State Intervention in Welfare

The difficult conditions industry imposed on workers led to debates in several countries about the need for the state to protect the workers. The growing militancy of organized labor also forced the authorities to consider ways to meet the workers' needs. Although some rejected government intervention in the free market, others argued that the laws of supply and demand had caused wrongful exploitation—especially in the cases of very young children and pregnant women. Also, some advocates for worker protections were motivated by fear rather than compassion, as organized labor grew increasingly militant and socialist parties gained strength.

To correct some of the worst abuses, the Scottish philanthropist Robert Owen (1771–1858) agitated in Parliament for the first effective British factory act, which passed in 1819. The act forbade labor for children under the age of 9 and limited the workday of older children to twelve hours. Then, beginning in 1833, a series of factory acts further limited the work hours of children and women in factories and mines and funded inspections to enforce these laws. French laws protecting children were passed as early as 1841, but it was not until 1874 that funding was approved to enforce them. When France's defeat in the Franco-Prussian War was blamed on inadequate troops due to a falling birthrate—especially in comparison to its rival Germany—the government began to limit the work hours of children and women. French bourgeois liberals advocated "Solidarism," an ideology of mutual social responsibility intended to appease moderate socialists and defuse class war.

In Germany, the Kaiser's government wanted to show workers the benefits they could gain from the state so they would abandon the growing Socialist party. In the 1880s the government provided a comprehensive welfare plan that included health insurance and old-age pensions. By offering these benefits to the people on its own initiative, the German government enacted reform without seeming to have been forced. The German government was the first to express a national responsibility for the welfare of its citizens, and German social programs became models for the rest of Europe.

In much of Europe, however, the state did little on behalf of workers' welfare. In eastern Europe, where industry was still in its infancy, there was no protection of workers. More surprising was Belgium's inaction: It was the earliest country on the Continent to industrialize and one of the last to provide protection from the harsh industrial conditions.

The middle and upper classes supplemented government programs by developing private initiatives to better the workers' lot. Concern among these groups and individuals arose from a mixture of pity for workers' condition, religious teachings about their responsibilities for the less fortunate, and fear of the consequences of unrelieved misery. In Paris, three thousand private charitable organizations were founded between 1840 and 1900; their combined outlay in aid equaled the public charity available. In London the sum of £6 million—more than the total budget of many European states—was spent to aid the poor in 1890.

Middle- and upper-class women were largely responsible for volunteer charity work. Socially prohibited from working for profit and responsible for the spiritual well-being of the family, women embraced charity work as a focus for their talents and energies. By the end of the nineteenth century, as many as half a million Englishwomen were contributing their time to provide charity to the less fortunate. In Sweden women founded refuges for the destitute, old-age homes, a children's hospital, an asylum for the mentally handicapped, and various societies to promote female industry.

In Catholic and Protestant countries, the churches had traditionally identified with the rights of employers and seemed to ignore the lot of the workers. However, a number of Christians, lay and clerical, began to emphasize the need to address social issues. In Germany, Bishop Wilhelm von Ketteler (1811–1877) preached the need for the well-off to take responsibility for the less privileged. His message was taken up in France, Italy, and Spain among what became known as "social Catholics." In England, Protestants' concern for the poor was evidenced by the founding of the Salvation Army in 1878. Religious groups also hoped they could win converts among the poor by demonstrating concern for their plight.

Increasingly, states, municipalities, volunteer groups, and churches accepted responsibility for the well-being of others. This trend marked the beginning of an evolution that would eventually lead to the welfare state in much of twentieth-century Europe.

Educational and Cultural Opportunities

At the beginning of the nineteenth century, governments took little responsibility for providing education. The upper classes educated their children with private tutors, parents from more modest economic groups taught their children what they knew, and the poor attended the few small schools run by charitable and religious groups. With the rise of national democracies, however, leaders grew concerned that only an educated electorate could vote responsibly. Governments also wanted a chance to indoctrinate children in beliefs that would lend stability to the country: enthusiasm for the present form of government; nationalism, especially in opposition to any common enemy; and secular rationalism—especially for boys. England and France initiated mandatory primary school education in the 1880s. In Britain, one million children attended school in 1865; by 1880 more than three million attended.

Public education included not only reading, writing, and arithmetic but other skills as well. By insisting on punctuality and obliging students to carry out repetitive skills such as copying letters, words, or sentences, schools encouraged people to fit into the emerging industrial society. Obedience and respect for authority and the government were also taught, shaping the nation's future soldiers, factory workers, mothers, and voters. Secondary education was, on the whole, available only to the wealthy and the upper-middle class. University was available only to the sons of the elite, with the exception of a very small number from the lower-middle class.

In the spirit of public education, grand exhibitions were set up, and libraries, museums and art galleries gradually became accessible to the general public. The greatest public symbol of progress was the Great Exhibition of 1851, held in London and housed in the Crystal Palace. This was the first World's Fair, and with 100,000 objects on display—half from Great Britain and its empire and the other half from foreign nations—it was intended to celebrate the accomplishments of the century, of industry, of each nation, and of an imagined bountiful future. The Crystal Palace itself was an immense glass and steel marvel of technology that became a model for the Bon Marché (see page 543) and many other architectural wonders of the nineteenth-century world. During peak attendance, 110,000 people were in the building at the same time, having come from all over the world and from all classes. Indeed, the entrance fee was lowered on certain days to ensure that the working class could view the stunning opulence and abundance and its promise for the future.

Despite the exuberant mood at the Great Exhibition, there were signs of the darker side of progress. A display of new cannons by the German arms manufacturer Alfred Krupp hinted of the coming mechanization of war. Colonial displays were enjoyed as collections of exotic delights, but they were also reminders that the European empires rested on the domination of other peoples. For some visitors, the most troubling aspect of the Great Exhibition was the crass materialism of it all. Charles Dickens complained, "There's too much," and many agreed. Nevertheless, world's fairs took place frequently for several decades as each nation sought to demonstrate its grandeur to the world.

Less ornate, but considerably more permanent, new libraries and museums also brought a wide range of cultural experiences to the general public. Between 1840 and 1880, the number of large libraries in Europe increased from forty to five hundred. The French national public library, the Bibliothèque Nationale, was established in Paris in the 1860s. Constructed of iron and glass, it was an impressive monument to the idea of an expanded reading public. Many provincial cities, as well as the glittering capitals of Europe, were endowed with new libraries.

Less grandiose, but probably more important for mostly rural populations, were the traveling libraries. Museums and art galleries, which in the previous century had been open to only a select few, gradually became accessible to the general public. The first museum to open to the public was the Louvre in Paris after the French Revolution. The rest of Europe lagged behind in making their cultural heritage available to the masses. The British Museum was open only to the wealthy, for there was widespread fear of the possible destruction that the "vulgar classes" might cause if they were allowed to visit. But the sedate behavior of the crowds during the Crystal Palace exposition reassured British authorities, and finally, in 1879, the museum was opened daily—without restrictions.

CULTURE IN AN AGE OF OPTIMISM

The improving economic and material conditions of the second half of the nineteenth century buoyed European thinkers. Many believed that women and men were becoming more enlightened, and they expressed faith in humankind's ability to transform the world with new scientific and technical breakthroughs. The world seemed knowable and perfectible. This faith advanced secularism while it undermined the certainties of traditional religion. The arts reflected these new values, emphasizing realism and science—as well as an underlying foreboding of the dark side of this "age of optimism."

Darwin and the Theory of Evolution

By midcentury most thinkers accepted the notion of change and transformation of society—and by analogy of the natural environment. The intellectual culture of the era was dominated by positivism, a philosophy of French thinker Auguste Comte (1798–1857). Viewing human progress as inevitable and ever increasing, positivists upheld the significance of empirical investigation and scientific thought, confident that their methods would assure the continued progress of humanity.

In the field of geology, the Englishman Charles Lyell (1797–1875) maintained that the earth was far older than the Bible suggested. He argued that its geological formations—the mountains, valleys, and seas—had been subjected to natural forces that, over hundreds of thousands, even millions, of years, had transformed them. Most educated people accepted his theory (there were, after all, seashells on mountaintops), which led many to wonder if the animal kingdom had also evolved.

Although evolution in the biological realm had been suggested as early as the end of the eighteenth century, Charles Darwin (1809–1882) was the first to offer a plausible explanation of the process. As the naturalist on an official British scientific expedition in the 1830s, he had visited the Galápagos Islands off the coast of South America. There he found species similar to but different from those on the mainland—and different from one another. Darwin hypothesized that they were not the result of separate creation but that they had adapted differently to their varying environments. Darwin had read Malthus's *Essay on the Principle of Population* (see page 472), and it influenced his reasoning. Darwin observed that there are almost always more creatures born than can be supported by the environment. This gives rise to what Darwin called a "struggle for existence," in which some creatures die off. Those that survive do so because they have some attribute that proved helpful in their specific environment. The survivors reproduce and pass on the helpful attributes to the next generation. Darwin called this imperceptible but continuous evolutionary mech-anism "natural selection." Though Darwin understood that the "fittest" creature for a given environment might not be the smartest, most complex, or most noble, many thought that his theory confirmed the era's faith in progress. Darwin did not suggest that human beings also evolved until *Descent of Man* (1871), where he clearly stated that humans had developed like other species of the animal kingdom. (See the box "Darwin's Basic Laws of Evolution.")

Many Christians were shocked by Darwin's assertions, and some denounced his findings.

Darwin's Basic Laws of Evolution

Darwin's* On the Origin of Species *(1859) uses several kinds of arguments. In the passage below, Darwin suggests an objection to his theory and then refutes it. He also uses metaphors from geology and animal domestication to help his theory seem familiar. Lastly, he distances evolution from charges of atheism and vulgarity.

Nothing at first can appear more difficult to believe than that the more complex organs and instincts have been perfected, not by means superior to, though analogous with, human reason, but by the accumulation of innumerable slight variations, each good for the individual possessor. Nevertheless, this difficulty, though appearing to our imagination insuperably great, cannot be considered real if we admit the following propositions, namely, that all parts of the organisation and instincts offer, at least, individual differences—that there is a struggle for existence leading to the preservation of profitable deviations of structure or instinct—and, lastly, that gradations in the state of perfection of each organ may have existed, each good of its kind. The truth of these propositions cannot, I think, be disputed. . . .

As geology plainly proclaims that each land has undergone great physical changes, we might have expected to find that organic beings have varied under nature, in the same way as they have varied under domestication. And if there has been any variability under nature, it would be an unaccountable fact if natural selection had not come into play. . . .

There is grandeur in this view of life, with its several powers, having been originally breathed by the Creator into a few forms or into one; and that, whilst this planet has gone cycling on according to the fixed law of gravity, from so simple a beginning endless forms most beautiful and most wonderful have been, and are being evolved.

Source: Charles Darwin, *On the Origin of Species by Means of Natural Selection*, 6th ed., vol. 2 (1872; reprint, New York: Appleton, 1923), pp. 267–268, 279, 305–306.

Some atheists and anticlerics celebrated evolutionary ideas as proofs against religion. Most moderate Christians, however, saw no reason why God could not have created the world through natural forces. Still, in the long run, Darwinism did much to undermine the authority of religion and literal interpretations of the Bible because, for the first time, there was a reasonable secular answer to the question of human existence.

Physics, Chemistry, and Medicine

Dramatic scientific breakthroughs in the nineteenth century reinforced the belief that human beings could understand and control nature. In physics, laws regarding electricity, magnetism, and thermodynamics were articulated by Michael Faraday (1791–1867), James Clerk Maxwell (1831–1879), and James Joule (1818–1889). In 1869, Russian chemist Dmitri Mendeleev (1834–1907) developed the periodic table, leaving blank spaces for several unknown elements whose discovery he predicted. When several were later discovered, it further added to the prestige of science.

Prolific research yielded discoveries in one field of knowledge that could be transferred to another. For example, chemists produced new dyes, enabling biologists to color slides of microorganisms and better study their evolution. Scientific breakthroughs also led to technical advancements that had industrial uses; for instance, inventions in chemistry led to the development of the first artificial fertilizers in 1842 and synthetic dyes in the 1850s.

Science became increasingly specialized. In the eighteenth century, the scientist had been a learned amateur practicing a hobby. In the nineteenth century, as the state and industry became increasingly involved in promoting scientific research, the scientist became a professional, employed by a university, a hospital, or other institution. New theories and discoveries were disseminated by scientific journals and at meetings of scientific associations.

Internationally, scientific cooperation became common, but there was also much nationalist rivalry. When cholera broke out in Egypt in 1883, a French and a German team of scientists rushed to the area to discover its cause. The German team, led by Robert Koch (1843–1910), uncovered the cholera bacillus as the source; on returning to his homeland Koch was feted as a national hero who had vindicated German superiority in science.

Around the midcentury mark, a number of important breakthroughs occurred in medicine. Before the development of anesthesia, surgery had been nearly impossible. With only alcohol to dull the patient's pain, even the swiftest surgeons could manage only modest surgical procedures. In the 1840s, the introduction of ether and then chloroform allowed for more extensive surgery. Painkillers were also increasingly used in childbirth, a procedure made popular when Queen Victoria herself used chloroform to ease her pain.

The greatest change in medicine was the shift from seeing disease as an imbalance in the patient's physical and moral system to understanding that it was caused by microscopic organisms. Among the many figures involved in making this conceptual leap, Louis Pasteur (1822–1895) was the most significant. Pasteur also pioneered certain methods of disease prevention. He demonstrated that the body could build up immunities to a disease when vaccinated by a weaker form of the bacilli that caused it. His were not the first vaccines: People had long noticed that milkmaids' exposure to cowpox made them immune to smallpox, and in the eighteenth century, the English physician Edward Jenner (1749–1823) had developed a successful vaccine based on this principle. However, until Pasteur, no one knew why it worked or how to apply the procedure to other diseases.

The development of measures to prevent contamination also followed the pattern of observation preceding understanding. The Hungarian doctor Ignaz Semmelweiss (1818–1865) noticed that if he delivered a baby just after performing an autopsy, the new mother often contracted puerperal fever and died. He found that he could radically reduce infection rates by washing his hands with a chlorine solution before touching patients. Effective but inexplicable, Semmelweiss's method was lambasted and his career was ruined. Later, in England, the surgeon John Lister (1827–1912) developed an effective disinfectant, carbolic acid, to kill the germs that caused gangrene and other infections in surgical patients. Incidents of puerperal fever were reduced when midwives and especially doctors—who so often carried germs from sickbeds into healthy homes—began washing their hands and sterilizing equipment. Surgery was transformed as the diminished risk of infection allowed for more operations. The first surgical kidney removal took place in 1876; the first successful brain surgery in modern times occurred three years later.

The increasingly scientific base of medicine and its visible success in combating disease improved its reputation. The medical profession began to control access to its ranks by establishing powerful professional associations: The British Medical Association was founded in 1832, the American association in 1847, and the German association in 1872. Medical journals also emerged to spread scientific knowledge.

Science was fashionable. In 1869, Empress Eugénie in France had Louis Pasteur come to tea, draw blood from her finger, and examine it under a microscope, all to the astonishment of her guests. Some frogs, brought in for experimentation, escaped down palace corridors. The spectacle of science as the chic entertainment of an empress was a reminder of the increasing attention it commanded in the later nineteenth century.

Birth of the Social Sciences

The scientific method, so effective in uncovering the mysteries of nature, was now applied to history, society, and psychology. History flourished in the nineteenth century. In an era of vast transformations, many people were eager to employ scientific methods to explore their past. The father of modern historical writing is the German Leopold von Ranke (1795–1886). Departing from the tradition of earlier historians, who explained the past as the fulfillment of some overall purpose such as God's will or the liberation of humanity, Ranke insisted that the role of the historian was to "show how things actually were." Like a scientist, the historian must be objective and dispassionate. History became a discipline with common standards of evidence. Historians studied and interpreted original (or "primary") sources; they collected and published their findings; and they founded professional organizations and published major journals.

New social sciences emerged in this period. Anthropology had been the subject of speculative literature for hundreds of years, but it now combined interest in non-European societies with a search for biological sources of the intelligence and character of Europeans. The Anthropological Society, founded in Paris in 1859, searched for differences in the brains of factory workers and professionals, women and men, criminals and the law-abiding, and various nationalities and races. Led by the medical doctor Paul Broca (1824–1880), French anthropologists measured thousands of heads and reading their own prejudices into the measurements, they pronounced women, members of the working class, and nonwhite races to be naturally inferior. Even at the time some anthropologists, such as the Frenchman Léonce Manouvrier (1850–1927), argued against these methods and conclusions, and today they are considered quite meaningless. Anthropology is now understood as the comparative study of people in differing societies, but in its origins it gave apparent "scientific" backing to the era's racism, sexism, and classism.

In Britain, the main anthropological theorist was Edward Tylor (1832–1917). The son of a brass manufacturer, Tylor traveled because of ill health and came into contact with non-European peoples, who aroused his curiosity. He believed that societies were subject to discoverable scientific laws that followed evolutionary patterns. Theorizing that evolution had to do with geography as well as time, he believed that as one became distanced from Europe, humankind became increasingly primitive. The contemporary African was at a level of development similar to that of Europeans in an earlier era. Tylor believed that the conditions of non-Europeans were due not to biology but to a function of their institutions. Although they disagreed on the causes, both physical and social anthropologists generally believed in the superiority of the European race. Tylor was appointed to the first university chair in anthropology in 1884. Anthropology was slower to gain legitimacy as a profession in France because the science of human difference and inequality clashed with the stated ideals of the new democratic government. Sociology gained professional status considerably earlier.

The term *sociology*, originally coined by Comte, meant the study of society. This study began in earnest in the latter part of the century, for three reasons. First, the rise of statistics in the 1840s demonstrated that cases of human distress like suicide, disease, and infant mortality could be predicted. Even though these predictions related to the whole society and not to individuals, prediction implied the possibility of control. Second, Darwinism had sparked theorists like Herbert Spencer in England to investigate the natural evolution of human behaviors (see page 510). Third, the secular French government was concerned that society could not remain ethical in the absence of religion, and it seemed that sociology might help solve this problem. Emile Durkheim (1858–1917) led the new discipline of sociology by insisting that it was a verifiable science and that it could provide a nonreligious, factual morality. He occupied the first chair of sociology at a French university in 1887 and later founded a journal of sociology.

In the past, history, anthropology, and sociology had been the purview of amateurs; now professional historians, anthropologists, and sociologists were engaged full time in research and teaching. This led to significant advances in several disciplines, but it also led to the fragmentation and compartmentalization of knowledge. People of broad learning and expertise became far less common.

The Challenge to Religion

The scientific claims of the era seemed to clash with the traditions of religion. A number of scientists, including Darwin himself, found their Christian faith undermined by theories on evolution. Although most Europeans continued to be strongly influenced by traditional religious beliefs, they appeared less confident than in earlier eras.

After the revolutions of 1848, religion was regarded as a bulwark of order. In France, Napoleon III gave the Catholic church new powers in education, and the bourgeoisie flocked to worship. In Spain, moderates who had been anticlerical began to support the church, and in 1851 they signed a concordat declaring Roman Catholicism "the only religion of the Spanish nation." In Austria in 1855, the state surrendered to the bishops full control over the clergy, the seminaries, and the administration of marriage laws.

The papacy had been nearly overthrown in 1848, and in 1860 it lost most of its domains to Italy. Thus Pope Pius IX became a sworn enemy of liberalism, and in the *Syllabus of Errors* (1864) he condemned a long list of what he perceived to be modern errors, among them "progress," "liberalism," and "modern civilization." To establish full control over the clergy and believers, the Lateran Council in 1870 issued the controversial doctrine of papal infallibility, declaring that the pope, when speaking officially on faith and morals, was infallible. This doctrine became a target of anticlerical opinion.

The political alliance the Catholic church struck with reactionary forces meant that when new political groups came to power they moved against the church. Since the church had discouraged the unification of Italy, conflict raged between the church and the new state. When Protestant Prussia unified Germany, Chancellor Bismarck eyed Catholics with suspicion and launched a campaign against them, the *Kulturkampf* ("cultural struggle").

In France, the revolutionaries of 1789 had vilified the church along with the monarchy, for both were seen as authoritarian, hierarchical, and conservative. The antagonism between scientific republicans and religious monarchists had only grown since then. Democrats of the early Third Republic bitterly resented the church's support of the monarchist party. Anticlerics were also strongly influenced by Comte's ideas of positivism, believing that France would not be a free country until the power of the church was diminished and its antiscientific disposition was overcome. The Third Republic reduced the role of the church in education as well as some other clerical privileges.

Movements toward state secularism were sometimes accompanied by an acceptance of religious diversity. In 1854 and 1871, England opened university admission and teaching posts at all universities to non-Anglicans. Anti-Catholicism, at times a popular and virulent movement, declined in the 1870s. In France, the position of religious minorities improved. Some of the highest officials of the Second Empire were Protestants, as were some early leaders of the Third Republic.

Legal emancipation of Jews, started in France in 1791, eventually spread to the rest of the Continent. England removed restrictions on Jews when the House of Commons, in 1858, and the House of Lords, in the following decade, allowed Jews to serve in Parliament. Germany and Austria-Hungary granted Jews the rights of citizenship in the 1860s. Social discrimination continued, however, and Jews were not accepted as equals in most of European society. Although some Jews occupied high office in France and

Italy, in Germany and Austria-Hungary they had to convert before they were eligible.

In the expanding economy of western Europe, where the condition of most people was improving, the enhanced opportunities for Jews aroused relatively little attention. In other parts of Europe, they were not so fortunate. When they moved into commerce, industry, and the professions in eastern Europe, they were resented. Rashes of violence against them, called *pogroms,* broke out in Bucharest, capital of Romania, in 1866 and in the Russian seaport of Odessa in 1871. Although economic rivalries may have fueled this anti-Semitism, they do not completely explain it. In most cases anti-Jewish sentiment occurred in the areas of Europe least exposed to liberal ideas of human equality and human rights.

As the continued anti-Semitism showed, religion was still a passionate issue in the nineteenth century. In fact, despite the rise of secularism, religiosity grew in some ways. In France there were frequent reported sightings of the Virgin Mary. A shepherdess in 1858 claimed to have seen and spoken with her at Lourdes, which became an important shrine whose waters were reputed to heal the lame and the sick. In 1872 construction of a rail line allowed 100,000 people a year to visit the town.

Church attendance continued to be high, especially in rural areas. In England villagers usually attended church, many twice or more each Sunday, and children attended Sunday schools. Advances in printing made it possible to distribute large quantities of cheap religious tracts to a sizable and avid readership. The faithful eagerly engaged in proselytizing, sending missionaries to all corners of the globe.

Art in the Age of Material Change

The new era of technology, science, and faith in progress was reflected in the arts. Photography, for instance, had a direct impact on painting. Experiments in the late eighteenth century and the inventions of the Frenchman Louis Daguerre (1789–1851) made the camera relatively usable in the 1830s. By the 1860s, photographic services were in high demand; in Paris alone, thirty thousand people made a living from photography and allied fields. After the invention of the miniature camera in the 1870s and celluloid film in the 1890s, the camera came into wide use. Unlike paintings, photography was accessible to the public. Many Europeans became amateur photographers—Queen Victoria and Prince Albert had a darkroom at Windsor Castle.

The ability of photography to depict a scene with exactitude had a significant impact on art. On the one hand, it encouraged artists to reproduce on the canvas a visual image akin to that of a photograph. On the other hand, in England, the pre-Raphaelites reacted against materialism, copying the symbolic imagery and innocent style of painters prior to Raphael.

In a scientific spirit, many artists discarded myths and symbols, describing the world as it actually appeared to them—everyday life in all its grimness. The realist painter Gustave Courbet (1819–1877) proclaimed himself "without ideals and without religion." Similarly, his fellow Frenchman, Jean-François Millet (1814–1875), refused to romanticize peasants as earlier artists had, depicting the harsh conditions in which they labored. In painting historical scenes, artists undertook meticulous research of the landscape, architecture, fauna, and costumes of their subjects. To paint the Dead Sea in *The Scapegoat,* English artist Holman Hunt (1827–1910) traveled all the way to Palestine to guarantee an accurate portrayal of the site.

In the past, artists had been concerned about perfectly balanced composition. Under the influence of photography, they began to paint incomplete, off-center pictures. *Orchestra of the Paris Opera* by French artist Edgar Degas looks as if it has been cropped, with only half of a musician showing on each edge and the top half of the ballet dancers missing.

In 1874, Degas (1834–1917), Claude Monet (1840–1926), Camille Pissarro (1830–1903), Auguste Renoir (1840–1919), Alfred Sisley (1839–1899), and Berthe Morisot (1841–1895) opened an exhibition in Paris that a critic disparagingly called "impressionist." The impressionist artists

Courbet: The Stone Breakers This realistic 1849 painting depicts the rough existence of manual laborers. The bleakness of the subject matter and the style in which it was carried out characterized much of the realistic school of art. (The Stone Breakers, *1849 [destroyed 1945], by Gustave Courbet [1819–1877], Gemaldegalerie, Dresden, Germany/Bridgeman Art Library, London/New York)*

increasingly painted outdoors, in the natural light. Monet was particularly interested in painting several views of the same scene, showing how the image of a street or cathedral varied with small changes in viewpoint, weather, and time of day.

The school of realism also influenced literature, especially the novel. In realist novels, life was not glorified or infused with mythical elements; the stark existence of daily life was seen as a suitable subject. Charles Dickens (1812–1870), who came from a poor background and had experienced the inhumanity of the London underworld, wrote novels depicting the lot of the poor with humor and sympathy. The appalling social conditions he described helped educate his large middle-class audience on the state of the poor. And yet, reflecting his own rise to the middle class, he provided numerous examples of individuals who improved their circumstances through cleverness and hard work.

Another realist, the French novelist Gustave Flaubert (1821–1880), consciously debunked the romanticism of his elders. His famous novel, *Madame Bovary*, describes middle-class life as bleak, boring, and meaningless. The heroine seeks to escape the narrow confines of provincial life through adulterous and disastrous affairs.

Emile Zola (1840–1902), another Frenchman, belonged to the naturalist school of literature—distinguished from realism by its interest in precise, objective analysis offered without philosophical or moral commentary. The writer, Zola claimed, should be like a surgeon or chemist, providing a scientific cause and record of human behavior. In his Rougon-Macquart series,

ENCOUNTERS WITH THE WEST

A Chinese Official's Views of European Material Progress

Educated in European universities, Ku Hung-Ming rose to become a high official in the Chinese court. His essays were penned under the impact of the European military intervention in China during the Boxer Rebellion in 1900. Ku denounced European notions of superiority over Asia, arguing that material progress was an inappropriate measure of a civilization.

In order to estimate the value of a civilisation, it seems to me, the question we must finally ask is not what great cities, what magnificent houses, what fine roads it has built and is able to build; what beautiful and comfortable furniture, what clever and useful implements, tools and instruments it has made and is able to make; no, not even what institutions, what arts and sciences it has invested: the question we must ask, in order to estimate the value of a civilisation,—is, *what type of humanity, what kind of men and women it has been able to produce.* In fact, the man and woman,—the type of human beings—which a civilisation produces, it is this which shows the essence, the personality, so to speak, the soul of that civilisation. Now if the men and women of a civilisation show the essence, the personality and soul of that civilisation, the language which the men and women in that civilisation speak, shows the essence, the personality, the soul of the men and women of that civilisation. . . .

To Europeans, and especially to unthinking practical Englishmen, who are accustomed to take what modern political economists call "the standard of living" as the test of the moral culture of or civilisation of a people, the actual life of the Chinese and of the people of the East at the present day, will no doubt appear very sordid and undesirable. But the standard of living by itself is not a proper test of the civilisation of a people. The standard of living in America at the present day, is, I believe, much higher than it is in Germany. But although the son of an American millionaire, who regards the simple and comparatively low standard of living among the professors of a German University, may doubt the value of the education in such a University, yet no educated man, I believe, who has travelled in both countries, will admit that the Germans are a less civilised people than the Americans.

Source: Ku Hung-Ming, *The Spirit of the Chinese People,* 2d ed. (Beijing: Commercial Press, 1922), pp. 1, 144–145.

which describes the lives of several generations of a family, Zola incorporated the anthropological ideas of the era. His characters are deeply defined by their heredity, such that a moral or a criminal ancestor determines a character's biological destiny either to succeed or to fall into degradation.

The Russian novelist Leo Tolstoy (1828–1910) brought a new perspective to the historical novel in *War and Peace.* Instead of a heroic approach to battle, he showed individuals caught in forces beyond their control. Small and insignificant events, rather than major ones, seem to govern human destiny. Another Russian novelist often associated with the realist school, Feodor Dostoyevsky (1821–1881), aimed to portray realistically the psychological dimensions of his characters in *Crime and Punishment* (1866), *The Idiot* (1868), and *The Brothers Karamazov* (1879–1880). Though realism was often associated with science, Dostoyevsky used it to emphasize the spiritualism of his characters. When his books were translated into French and English, they had a striking effect on readers in western Europe.

Although material progress was generally celebrated in this era, a number of intellectuals reacted against it. Many feared the uniformity and valuelessness of a world based on mass production and consumption. They denounced the smug and the self-satisfied. In Britain, the historian Thomas Carlyle (1795–1881) wrote that his was not the age of progress but of selfishness and spiritual decline.

Another Englishman, John Ruskin (1819–1900), looked back to the Middle Ages as an ideal era in human history. People then did not produce with machines, but exercised craftsmanship; they had a stronger sense of community and labored for the common good. Ruskin was one of the founders of the Arts and Crafts movement, which emphasized the need to produce goods for daily use with an eye for beauty and originality. "Industry without art is brutality," Ruskin warned. As is clear in the works of Zola and Flaubert, French intellectuals also tended to reject the modern vision of progress. And some abroad were also unimpressed. (See the box "Encounters with the West: A Chinese Official's Views of European Material Progress.")

Thus, all was not optimistic in the age of optimism. If many people celebrated what they viewed as an age of progress, others claimed that under the outer trappings of material comfort lay a frightening ignorance of aesthetic, moral, and spiritual values.

SUMMARY

During the second half of the nineteenth century, advances in industry created for many westerners an era of material plenty, providing more comforts to a larger population than ever before. It was a self-confident age that believed in progress and anticipated further improvements in its material and intellectual environment.

Economic changes transformed the class structure of many European countries, and middle-class values and tastes defined the second half of the century. Perhaps the most striking of these middle-class values was the ideology of separate spheres based on gender. Men and women both struggled with the constraints of this ideal, but it was most confining for women, and women's movements arose all over Europe. The new wealth and technologies of this period led to improvements in both the countryside and the cities. Governments provided new services such as public education, cultural facilities, and expanded welfare.

The material changes in society were reflected in intellectual currents. Change and evolution were embraced as an explanation for the origin of species. A new confidence in scientific research led to many scientific and technical breakthroughs. Novelists and painters aimed to dissect the world around them, creating realism in the arts. Some intellectuals, however, criticized the worship of industry, science, and materialism.

Progress, as Europeans were to learn in a later era, was two-edged: The very forces that improved life for many also threatened it. The same breakthroughs in chemistry that led to the development of artificial fertilizers also provided more powerful military explosives. The expansion of education and reduction of illiteracy meant an end to ignorance but also the creation of a public that could more easily absorb messages of hate against a rival nation or against minorities at home. Material progress and well-being continued, but there were new forces in the shadows that would ultimately undermine the comforts, self-assurance, and peace of this age.

NOTES

1. Quoted in Edith Thomas, *The Women Incendiaries* (London: Secker and Warburg, 1976), p. 100, as cited in Bonnie S. Anderson and Judith P. Zinsner, *A History of Their Own*, vol. 2 (New York: Harper and Row, 1988), p. 282.
2. Quoted in F. K. Prochaska, *Women and Philanthropy in Nineteenth-Century England* (Oxford: Clarendon Press, 1980), p. 220, as cited in Anderson and Zinsner, p. 184. The discussion of Butler is indebted to Anderson and Zinsner, pp. 181–184.

SUGGESTED READING

Adams, Carole Elizabeth. *Women Clerks in Wilhelmine Germany*. 1988. Provides a history of female store employees.

Bowler, Peter J. *Evolution—The History of an Idea*. Rev. ed. 1989. Written by a scientist who examines the history and development of the concept while evaluating the scientific merit of the debates.

Briggs, Asa. *Victorian Things*. 1989. Provides an amusing and instructive history of the various new objects that became part of consumer culture.

Chadwick, Owen. *The Secularization of the European Mind in the Nineteenth Century*. 1973. Considers the rise and spread of secular attitudes at the cost of religion.

Clark, T. J. *Image of the People: Gustave Courbet and the 1848 Revolution*. 1973. Explores the impact of the sociopolitical environment on Courbet's paintings and the audience's reactions to them.

Cocks, Geoffrey, and Konrad H. Jarausch, eds. *German Professions, 1800–1950*. 1990. Describes the relationship between the professions and the state.

Geison, Gerald L., ed. *Professions and the French State, 1700–1900*. 1984. Considers the development of the various professions in France.

Goldstein, Jan. *Console and Classify: The French Psychiatric Profession in the Nineteenth Century*. 1987. Excellent examination of the rise of psychiatry within the broader cultural, intellectual, religious, and political history of France.

Hobsbawm, Eric J. *The Age of Capital, 1848–1875*. 1979. Particularly strong on social and economic developments.

Lees, Andrew. *Cities Perceived: Urban Society in European and American Thought, 1820–1940*. 1985. Depicts how various writers in Europe and the United States perceived their cities.

Mayer, Arno. *The Persistence of the Old Regime—Europe to the Great War*. 1981. Argues for the persistence of the aristocracy throughout the nineteenth century.

Miller, Michael B. *The Bon Marché—Bourgeois Culture and the Department Store, 1869–1920*. 1981. Views the first and largest department store in Paris as both manifestation and promoter of bourgeois culture.

Peterson, M. Jeanne. *Family, Love, and Work in the Lives of Victorian Gentlewomen*. 1989. Offers a revisionist examination of the view that women were passive in the Victorian era.

Pilbeam, Pamela. *The Middle Classes in Europe, 1789–1914: France, Germany, Italy, and Russia*. 1990. Reviews the formation and values of the bourgeoisie in four continental European nations.

Pinkney, David. *Napoleon III and the Rebuilding of Paris*. 1958. The standard work on the urban renewal of Paris.

Pool, Phoebe. *Impressionism*. 1985. Studies the origins, accomplishments, and legacies of impressionism.

Prochaska, F. K. *Women and Philanthropy in Nineteenth Century England*. 1980. Reveals the important role women played in charity work throughout the century.

Robertson, Priscilla. *An Experience of Women and Change in Nineteenth Century Europe*. 1982. Describes the private lives of bourgeois women in the nineteenth century, emphasizing the differing national cultural traditions.

Smith, Bonnie G. *Ladies of the Leisure Class—The Bourgeoises of Northern France in the Nineteenth Century*. 1981. Emphasizes the separate world of domesticity bourgeois women created and maintained.

Thompson, F. M. L. *The Rise of Respectable Society—A Social History of Victorian Britain, 1830–1910*. 1988. Depicts considerable social mobility and well-being in Britain in the second half of the nineteenth century.

Walkowitz, Judith. *City of Dreadful Delight*. 1993. Fascinating study of the nineteenth-century urban world.

Weber, Eugen. *Peasants into Frenchmen: The Modernization of Rural France, 1870–1914*. 1976. A lively description of the process by which the French peasantry was modernized.

Weisberg, Gabriel P., ed. *The European Realist Tradition*. 1982. A multinational study revealing the pervasiveness of realism in European art.

Youngson, A. J. *The Scientific Revolution in Victorian Medicine*. 1979. A record of innovation in British medicine.

CHAPTER 22

Escalating Tensions, 1880–1914

In the spring of 1914, U.S. President Woodrow Wilson, concerned over the growing international crisis, sent his aide, Colonel Edward House, to Europe. The colonel toured several capitals—Berlin, Paris, and London—and on May 29, 1914, he reported, "The situation is extraordinary. It is militarism run stark mad. Unless some one . . . can bring about a different understanding there is one day to be an awful cataclysm."[1] This prediction was far more accurate than House could have imagined; nine weeks later Europe was at war.

Yet the preceding years in Europe had on the whole been peaceful and prosperous. Contemporaries often characterized the generation before the war as *"la belle époque"*—the beautiful era. A growing economy provided expanding opportunities for many. The arts flourished and were celebrated. Parliamentary government continued to spread; in several nations, suffrage was extended. Yet hand in hand with these trends of apparent progress came troubling new tendencies. Several developments in the generation before 1914 undermined and threatened all the accomplishments of these years.

In many societies, governing became more complex as populations increased. The population of Europe jumped from 330 million in 1880 to 460 million in 1914. A larger population coupled with extended suffrage meant that more people participated in the political system, but it became harder to find consensus. The example of democracy in some countries led to frustration in the autocratic ones. In the same way, prosperity and economic growth aroused resentment in those who did not share in the benefits.

Intellectuals revolted against what they viewed as the smug self-assuredness of earlier years. They no longer felt certain that the world was knowable, stable, subject to comprehension and mastery by rational human beings. Some jettisoned rationality, glorifying emotion, irrationality, and, in some cases, violence.

The anxieties and tensions that beset many Europeans took a variety of forms. Ethnic minorities became the target of hatreds. Overseas, non-Europeans were forcibly put under white domination as European states embarked on a race for empire throughout the world. On the European continent, states increasingly felt insecure, worried that they would be subject to attack. They established standing armies, shifted alliances, drafted war plans, and, ultimately, went to war.

Questions and Ideas to Consider

- Socialism had a variety of champions between 1880 and 1914. Describe some of the contrasting strategies and goals. Consider the Fabians, Ferdinand Lassalle, Karl Kautsky, and Clara Zetkin.
- Colonial conquest was not very lucrative and often quite costly. Why did the Europeans pursue new overseas empires in the late nineteenth century?
- By the end of the nineteenth century, Britain, France, and Italy were all having difficulty winning broad consensus for their policies. Why? Discuss the violent tactics associated with the Irish "home-rule" issue, the women's suffrage movement, the 1907 strikes in the Midi, and the Sicilian labor movement.
- Why were the states of Europe unafraid of war in 1914?
- How did World War I begin? How did France, Britain, and Germany get involved in a struggle over the Balkans?

FROM OPTIMISM TO ANXIETY: POLITICS AND CULTURE

Many of the beliefs and institutions that had seemed so secure in the "age of optimism" came under attack in the next generation. Forces hostile to liberalism became increasingly vocal. In the arts and philosophy, confidence was replaced by doubt, relativism, and a desire to flee the routines of everyday life.

The Erosion of the Liberal Consensus

In 1850 liberalism appeared to be the ascendant ideology, and liberals assumed that with the passage of time more and more people would be won over to their world-view. But by 1900, liberalism was facing serious challenges. Principles eroded within the liberal camp, while various ideas and movements—some new, some rooted in the past—eroded the liberal consensus. Prominent among these were socialism, anarchism, a new political right, racism, and anti-Semitism.

The undermining of the liberal consensus began among liberals themselves, who, in the face of changing circumstances, retreated from some of their basic tenets. One of the principal emphases of liberalism had always been free trade. But under the pressure of economic competition, liberals supported tariffs at home and created closed markets for the mother country overseas in the empire.

Historically, liberals had stood for the expansion of civil liberties, yet several groups were denied their rights. Power remained an exclusively male domain, and liberal men saw nothing wrong or inconsistent in denying women the vote and equal access to education and professional advancement. In the face of labor agitation, many liberals no longer unconditionally supported civil liberties and favored instead the violent crushing of strikes.

Similarly, liberals had always upheld the sanctity of private property, but under the pressure of events, they abandoned this principle as an absolute goal. To ensure workers' safety, they placed limits on employers by passing legislation on working conditions. In some countries, they supported progressive income taxes, which many perceived as a serious invasion of private property. When it became clear that a free market was unable to meet many human needs, liberals

CHAPTER CHRONOLOGY

1864	Founding of the International Workers' Association
1873	Three Emperors' League (Germany, Austria-Hungary, and Russia)
1879	Alliance between Germany and Austria
	Bismarck bans the Socialist party
1882	Triple Alliance (Germany, Austria, and Italy)
1884	Renewal of Three Emperors' League
	Fabian Society founded in Britain
1886	Gladstone proposes home rule for Ireland
1887	Reinsurance Treaty (Germany and Russia)
1889	Second International
1893	Independent Labour party established in Britain
1894	Franco-Russian Alliance
1897	Dreyfus affair rages in France
1898	Battle of Omdurman
1899	Kipling's poem "White Man's Burden"
1903	Pankhurst founds the Women's Social and Political Union
1904	Anglo-French Entente
1905	Einstein proposes the theory of relativity
	Law separating church and state in France
1907	Anglo-Russian Entente
1911	Italy occupies Libya
1914	Archduke Francis Ferdinand and his wife assassinated

supported the introduction of welfare programs in several countries. These reforms were intended to strengthen the state by winning support from the masses, but they constituted a breach of liberal principles. The meaning of liberalism was changing and amid such inconsistency and uncertainty, many began to feel that liberal ideology could not deal with the problems of the day.

The Growth of Socialism and Anarchism

Among the groups challenging the power and liberal ideology of the middle classes were the socialist parties, both Marxist and non-Marxist, whose goal was to alleviate the plight of the workers. Socialists varied in their notions of how their goals should be achieved. Some thought they could be achieved gradually and peacefully; others were dedicated to a violent overthrow of capitalist society. Some felt that "the woman question" could be solved after the triumph of socialism; others asserted that oppression based on sex and oppression based on class were fundamentally linked, and both required immediate attention.

In Britain, where the Liberal party was more responsive to the needs of workers than in other European states, a separate socialist party, the Independent Labour party, was established relatively late, in 1893. More influential in the late nineteenth century was the Fabian Society, founded in 1884 and championed by such figures as the social investigators Beatrice Webb (1858–1943) and Sidney Webb (1859–1947) and the playwright George Bernard Shaw (1856–1950). The Fabians believed that by gradual, democratic means, factories and land could be transferred from the private sector to the state, which would employ them for the benefit of society as a whole. Socialism would come into being not through class war but through enlightened ideas. This gradualist approach became the hallmark of British socialism.

In Germany there were two competing socialist parties. The first, founded in 1863 by Ferdinand Lassalle (1825–1864), viewed universal suffrage as the means of assuring workers' well-being. A second socialist party, formed in 1868 and influenced by Marx, called for a workers' revolution. In 1875 the two parties united around a common program.

Unification did not prevent the German Social Democratic party from a bitter debate soon to be echoed in all European socialist parties. A German socialist leader, Eduard Bernstein (1850–1932), who had visited England and soaked up the influence of the Fabians, argued in his book, *Evolutionary Socialism* (1898), that Marx was wrong in his assumption that capitalism necessarily led to increasing wretchedness for the working class. Working conditions had actually improved. By piecemeal democratic action workers could gradually win power and legislate on behalf of their interests. Since he argued for a revision of Marxist theory, Bernstein was labeled a "revisionist."

Opposing Bernstein in this debate was the party theoretician Karl Kautsky (1854–1938). Although Kautsky agreed that in material terms the workers' lot had not worsened, he insisted that workers were worse off in political terms. In Germany, he argued, workers could come to power only if they first overthrew autocracy. A violent revolution would be necessary to institute socialism. Although the German Social Democratic party officially rejected revisionism and seemed to embrace the doctrine of a violent proletarian revolution, it in fact practiced the former. It had become a part of established society and was not ready to overthrow it.

Similarly ambiguous developments occurred in neighboring France. One of Marx's French disciples, Jules Guesde (1845–1922), founded a socialist party with a strong working-class membership devoted to carrying on a workers' revolution. Opposing his brand of socialism was Jean Jaurès (1859–1914), an idealistic schoolteacher who saw socialism as an ethical system. Jaurès believed that socialism could be achieved peacefully, in cooperation with the more enlightened members of the middle class. In 1905 the socialist parties led by Guesde and Jaurès merged, and Jaurès became virtual party leader. Although Jaurès' brand of gradual democratic socialism influenced the daily functioning of the party, the French Socialist party formally continued to adhere to Guesde's doctrine of revolution. In 1914, on the eve of war, Jaurès called on his government to avoid war, and a furious nationalist assassinated him for it.

Another movement that sought to liberate the downtrodden was anarchism, which proclaimed that humans could be free only when the state had been abolished. According to anarchist theory, in a stateless society people would naturally join together in communes and share the fruits of their labor. Some anarchists believed their goal could be reached by attacking authority. The Russian nobleman Michael Bakunin (1814–1876), frustrated at the authoritarianism of his homeland, became a lifelong anarchist. He challenged tsarism at home and participated in the 1848 revolutions throughout Europe. He viewed all governments as repressive and declared war on them: "The passion for destruction is also a creative passion." His ideas were particularly influential in Italy, Spain, and parts of France, especially among the artisan classes.

Many anarchists of this period wanted to bring about the new society by "propaganda of the deed." An attack on the bastions of power, these anarchists believed, could bring about the dissolution of the state. They formed secret terrorist organizations that assassinated heads of state or those close to them. Between 1894 and 1901, the president of France, the prime minister of Spain, the empress of Austria, the king of Italy, and the president of the United States were killed by anarchists. These murders fixed the popular image of anarchism as a violence-prone ideology and produced no particular improvement in the lives of the working-class people.

Without accepting the anarchists' methods, some in the labor movement shared their hostility toward parliamentary institutions. A working-class program, labor activists argued, could be implemented only by a pure workers' movement, such as unionization. According to this line of thought, known as *syndicalism* (after the French word for unions), workers should amass their power in unions and, at the right moment, carry out a general strike, crippling capitalist society and bringing it down.

European socialism also attempted to have an international presence. In 1864, Marx had participated in the founding of the International Workers' Association, which fell prey to internal dissension and dissolved after a few years. It was followed by a more robust organization, the Second International, in 1889. The movement's staunchly patriarchal outlook was challenged by the socialist-feminist theoretician Clara Zetkin (1857–1933). In her important work of 1889, *The Question of Women Workers*, Zetkin argued that feminism and socialism were fundamentally linked: Men were oppressed by bosses, women were oppressed by bosses and men, and freedom for all could come only from economic emancipation. Later feminists would argue that cultural stereotypes of inferiority and social double standards needed to be addressed along with economics, but Zetkin was successful for her time. Impressed by her logic and pressured by her followers, the German Socialist party began supporting women's suffrage in 1895.

Male or female, socialists were concerned over the worsening relations among European states. As early as 1893 the International called on European states to resolve their conflicts by mandatory arbitration. In 1907, sensing impending war, the International called on the workers to strike and refuse military service. However, once war broke out most socialists were swept up in nationalist fervor and went willingly to war. Zetkin and others who hoped the workers of the world would refuse to fight each other were bitterly disappointed.

The New Right, Racism, and Anti-Semitism

The traditional opponents of liberalism on the political right were the conservatives, wedded to preserving the existing order. Beginning in the 1880s, however, a populist "new right" emerged. Although conservatives had been wary of nationalism, the new right embraced it. Many in the new right rejected doctrines of human equality and embraced racist ideologies.

Racist thinking was common in the nineteenth century. Many Europeans believed that they were the epitome of humankind while members of other races belonged to lesser groups. In midcentury the Frenchman Arthur de Gobineau (1816–1882) published his *Essay on the Inequality of Human Races,* declaring that racial inequality "dominates all other problems and is the key to it." Biologists and early anthropologists made similar statements, giving racism a scientific aura. Some races were relegated to near subhuman levels.

These ideas helped fuel anti-Semitism. For centuries Jews had been the object of suspicion and bigotry. Originally, the basis of the prejudice was religious. As early as the Middle Ages, however, the argument emerged that "Jewish blood" was different. With the popularization of scientific racist thinking in the nineteenth century, Jews were commonly viewed as a separate race, unworthy of the same rights as Christians.

Historically, Christians had relegated the Jews in their midst to marginal positions. In the Middle Ages, when land was the basis of wealth and prestige, Jews had been confined to such urban trades as cattle trading and moneylending. They incurred high risks by lending money: They often were not paid back and faced unsympathetic courts when they tried to collect on debts. To counteract these risks, Jewish moneylenders charged high interest rates that gave them the reputation as usurers.

The emancipation of the Jews, which began in France with the Revolution and spread to Germany and Austria by the 1860s, provided them opportunities they had not had before, and some members of society found it hard to adjust to the prominence a few Jews gained. Because their increased prominence and success occurred concurrently with the wrenching social transformations of industrialization and urbanization, anti-Semites pointed to the Jews as the perpetrators of these unsettling changes. Many people perceived Jews as prototypical of the new capitalist class. Although most Jews were of modest means, resentment of the rich often was aimed at Jews.

Political movements based on anti-Semitism were founded in the 1880s. They depicted Jews as dangerous and wicked and called for their exclusion from the political arena and certain professions. In some cases they suggested that Jews be expelled from the state. The mayor of Vienna, Karl Lueger (1844–1928), was elected on an anti-Semitic platform. In Berlin, the emperor's chaplain, Adolf Stöcker (1835–1909), founded an anti-Semitic party. In France, Edouard Drumont (1844–1917) published one of the best-sellers of the second half of the nineteenth century, *Jewish France,* which attributed all the nation's misfortunes to the Jews.

In Russia organized *pogroms*, or mass attacks, on Jews killed two thousand people in the 1880s and one thousand in 1905, frightening 2 million Jews into exile, mostly to the United States. Russian Jews lived under social as well as legal disabilities, winning full emancipation only with the Bolshevik Revolution of 1917.

In the face of growing hostility, some Jews speculated that they would be safe only in their own nation. The Austrian Jewish journalist Theodore Herzl (1860–1904), outraged by the Dreyfus affair in France, in which a Jewish officer was imprisoned on trumped-up charges of treason (see page 587), founded the Zionist movement. He advocated establishing a Jewish state in the Jews' ancient homeland of Israel. In the beginning, the Zionist movement won a following only in eastern Europe, where the Jews were particularly ill-treated, but in 1948, it would lead to the founding of the state of Israel.

Various manifestations of anti-Semitism revealed the vulnerability of the principle of toleration, one of the basic tenets of liberalism. It became eminently clear that racism, with its penchant for irrationality and violence, could easily be aroused.

Irrationality and Uncertainty

In contrast to the confidence in reason and science that prevailed at midcentury, the era starting in the 1880s wrestled with the issues of irrationality and uncertainty—in philosophy, in science, in the arts, even in religion. The positivism of the earlier era had neglected the emotive and intuitive aspects of life. By the 1890s a neoromantic mood, emphasizing emotion and feeling, stirred major intellectual movements.

The intellectuals who matured in the 1890s, and thus are known as "the generation of 1890," stressed the extent to which irrational forces guide human beings and their relation to one another. Nonetheless, they remained strongly affected by the positivists, adopting their scientific methods to study irrationality and hoping to find ways to make human beings more rational. Following this group came those intellectuals who matured around 1905, known as the "generation of 1905." Like their seniors, they believed human beings were irrational and the world was unknowable, but they did not express any regret at this condition. Rather, they glorified it.

The intellectual trends of the 1890s were exemplified in the work of the Austrian Sigmund Freud (1856–1939), who founded *psychoanalysis*, a method of treating psychic disorders by exploring the unconscious. Freud believed that people were motivated not only by observed reality but also by their unconscious feelings and emotions. Whereas earlier physicians had described hysteria as a physical ailment, Freud saw its roots as psychological, the result of unresolved inner conflicts. Although Freud's work was influenced by rational methods, he stressed that irrational forces played a significant role in human behavior.

In philosophy, the tension between reason and emotion was expressed in the work of the German philosopher Friedrich Nietzsche (1844–1900), who proclaimed that rationality had led humankind into a meaningless abyss. Reason would not resolve human problems, but neither would religion now that modernity had broken it down. Nietzsche famously announced that "God is dead." He celebrated this because he saw Judeo-Christian ideas of good and evil as part of a "slave morality" that cherished obedience and docility over independence and heroism. With no God, humankind was free of outside constraints. Nietzsche admonished his readers to challenge existing institutions and accepted truths and to create new ones. Realizing that these ideas could be terribly dangerous if misunderstood, he warned his readers against such misconceptions, but to little avail. Across Europe, interpretations of Nietzsche's ideas were often used to support violent, racist doctrines.

In contrast to Nietzsche, the French philosopher Henri Bergson (1859–1940) reflected the values of the generation of 1905. He argued that science—and indeed life—must be interpreted not rationally but intuitively. "Science," Bergson declared, "can teach us nothing of the truth; it can only serve as a rule of action." Meaningful truths could best be understood emotively, such as the truth of religion, literature, and art.

The scientists of this period seemed to underscore the philosophers' conclusions. In 1905, the German physicist Albert Einstein (1879–1955) proposed the theory of relativity, which undermined the certainties of Newtonian physics. Einstein demonstrated that time and space are not absolute but exist relative to the observer. Much of the research in atomic theory also revealed variations and unexplained phenomena. The work of German physicist Max Planck (1858–1947) in quantum theory showed that energy was absorbed or emitted not continuously, as previously assumed, but rather discontinuously. Some scientists were finding it increasingly difficult to believe in ultimate certainties.

In the arts, the idea of being *avant-garde*—French for "at the forefront"—took hold among creative people. Artistic movements proclaimed idiosyncratic manifestos and constantly called for the rejection of existing forms of expression and the creation of new ones. The symbolists in France and Italy, the expressionists in Germany, the futurists in Italy, and the secessionists in Austria all reflected the sense that they were living through a fractured period.

Uncomfortable with the mass culture of their day, many artists no longer wanted to portray public ideals; rather, they tended to be interested in portraying their inner conflicts and emotions. The public at large found it difficult to decipher the meaning of the new art, but a number of patrons confirmed the avant-garde artists' talent and insight.

Unlike the realists who preceded them, artists in the 1890s surrendered to neoromanticism, trying to investigate and express inner forces. As the French painter Paul Gauguin (1848–1903) noted, the purpose of painting was to communicate not how things looked but the emotions they conveyed. The Russian Wassily Kandinsky (1866–1944) asked viewers of his art to "look at the picture as a graphic representation of a mood and not as a representation of objects." Artists appeared to be examining the hidden anxieties of society. The Austrian artist Egon Schiele (1890–1918) and the Norwegian painter Edvard Munch (1863–1944) emphasized scenes of violence, fear, and sheer horror.

Religion, too, felt the effects of these intellectual trends. Although large numbers of people still held traditional religious beliefs and followed traditional practices, indifference to organized religion spread. In urban areas of western Europe, church attendance declined. But with the decline of traditional Christian practices, various forms of mysticism became more widespread. Some people were attracted to Eastern religions like Buddhism and Hinduism and other mystical beliefs. These attitudes may have reflected a loss of faith in Western culture itself. As the century came to an end, a number of intellectuals argued that their culture was destined for decline.

THE NEW IMPERIALISM

The age of empire building that started in Europe in the sixteenth century seemed to have ended by 1750. Then, in the 1880s, the European states launched a new era of expansionism and conquered an unprecedented amount of territory. In only twenty-five years, Europeans seized 10 million square miles and subjugated 500 million people—half of the world's non-European

Munch: The Scream Painted in 1893, this work reflects the fear and alienation of modern life. *(Edvard Munch,* The Scream, *1893. Tempera and oil pastel on cardboard. 91 × 73.5 cm. Photo: J. Lathion, Nasjonalgalleriet, Oslo)*

population. European expansion was also manifest in a massive movement of people; between 1870 and 1914, 55 million Europeans migrated overseas, mainly to Australia, the United States, Canada, and Argentina.

This era of ambitious conquest is often called the "new imperialism" to differentiate it from the earlier stage of empire building. Whereas the earlier imperialism focused on the Americas, nineteenth-century imperialism centered on Africa and Asia. And unlike that in the earlier period, the new imperialism occurred in an age of mass participation in politics and was accompanied by expressions of popular enthusiasm.

Economic and Social Motives

The hope of profit overseas was crucial in the dynamic of the new imperialism. When the British explorer Henry Stanley (1841–1904) returned from Africa in the late 1870s, he told the Manchester Chamber of Commerce, "There are forty million people beyond the gateway of Congo, and the cotton spinners of Manchester are waiting to clothe them." An economic downturn in 1873 had led to a decade-long European depression, and many hoped that colonization would help solve this economic crisis. Colonies, it was believed, would provide markets for European goods that would stimulate production at home. "Colonial policy is the daughter of industrial policy," declared French Prime Minister Jules Ferry (1832–1893). Rising tariff walls between European nations made colonial markets especially attractive.

However, there is considerable evidence that colonies did not represent large markets for the mother countries. In 1914, France's colonies represented only 12 percent of its foreign trade. Great Britain's trade with its colonies represented one-third of its foreign trade, but most of that was with the settlement colonies and not those acquired through direct conquest. As for Germany, colonial trade represented less than 1 percent of its exports. France, Germany, and Great Britain continued to be one another's main customers. Still, many Europeans contended that the colonies would turn out to be profitable in the long run.

Some proponents of empire, known as social imperialists, argued that possession of an empire could resolve social issues by giving employment to the working classes and thus keeping them satisfied with their lot. British colonial secretary Joseph Chamberlain (1836–1914) was a vigorous proponent of empire and claimed that if it were lost, "half at least of our population would be starved." His fellow imperialist Cecil Rhodes (1853–1902) claimed that Britain's empire was saving the country "from a murderous civil war." In Belgium, King Leopold II (r. 1865–1909) believed that the political strife between Catholics and liberals in his state could be overcome by territorial acquisition overseas.

An empire could be an outlet for a variety of domestic frustrations, especially for nations concerned about overpopulation. German and Italian imperialists often argued that their nations needed colonies to settle their multiplying poor. Once the overseas territories were acquired, however, few found them attractive for settlement.

Nationalistic Motives

To a large extent, empire building was triggered by the desire to assert national power. At the end of the nineteenth century, two major powers emerged: Russia and the United States. Compared to them, western European nations seemed small and insignificant, and many of their leaders believed they needed to acquire large territories to compete effectively on the world stage.

The British Empire, with India as its crown jewel, was the largest, most powerful, and apparently wealthiest of all the European domains. It was the envy of Europe. Although the real source of Britain's wealth and power was the country's industrial economy, many people believed possession of a vast empire explained Britain's success. And so the British example stimulated other nations to carve out empires.

Once the European states entered the fray, they excited mutual suspicion and fear. When the French appeared to be expanding in West Africa in the 1890s, the British, afraid they would be cut off from the trade of the Niger Valley, aggressively conquered huge tracts of land that previously had been ignored. The French had begun their conquests believing that they needed to reach the Niger before the British did (Map 22.1). Thus the scramble for Africa was triggered by European rivalries, by fear of missing an opportunity that would never return. Similarly in Asia, Britain annexed Burma in 1885 under the impression that France was about to do so, while France expanded in Indochina in the 1880s and 1890s for fear the British would beat them to the punch.

France, defeated by Prussia in 1870, found in its colonies proof that it was still a Great Power. Germany and Italy, which formed their national identities relatively late, cast a jealous eye on the British and French Empires and decided that if they were to be counted as Great Powers, they too would need overseas colonies. King Leopold II of Belgium spun out plans to acquire colonies to compensate for his nation's small size. And Britain, anxious at the emergence of rival economic and political powers in the late nineteenth century, viewed its colonies as a guarantee for the future.

Worldwide strategic concerns also stimulated expansion. Because the Suez Canal assured the route to India, the British established a protectorate

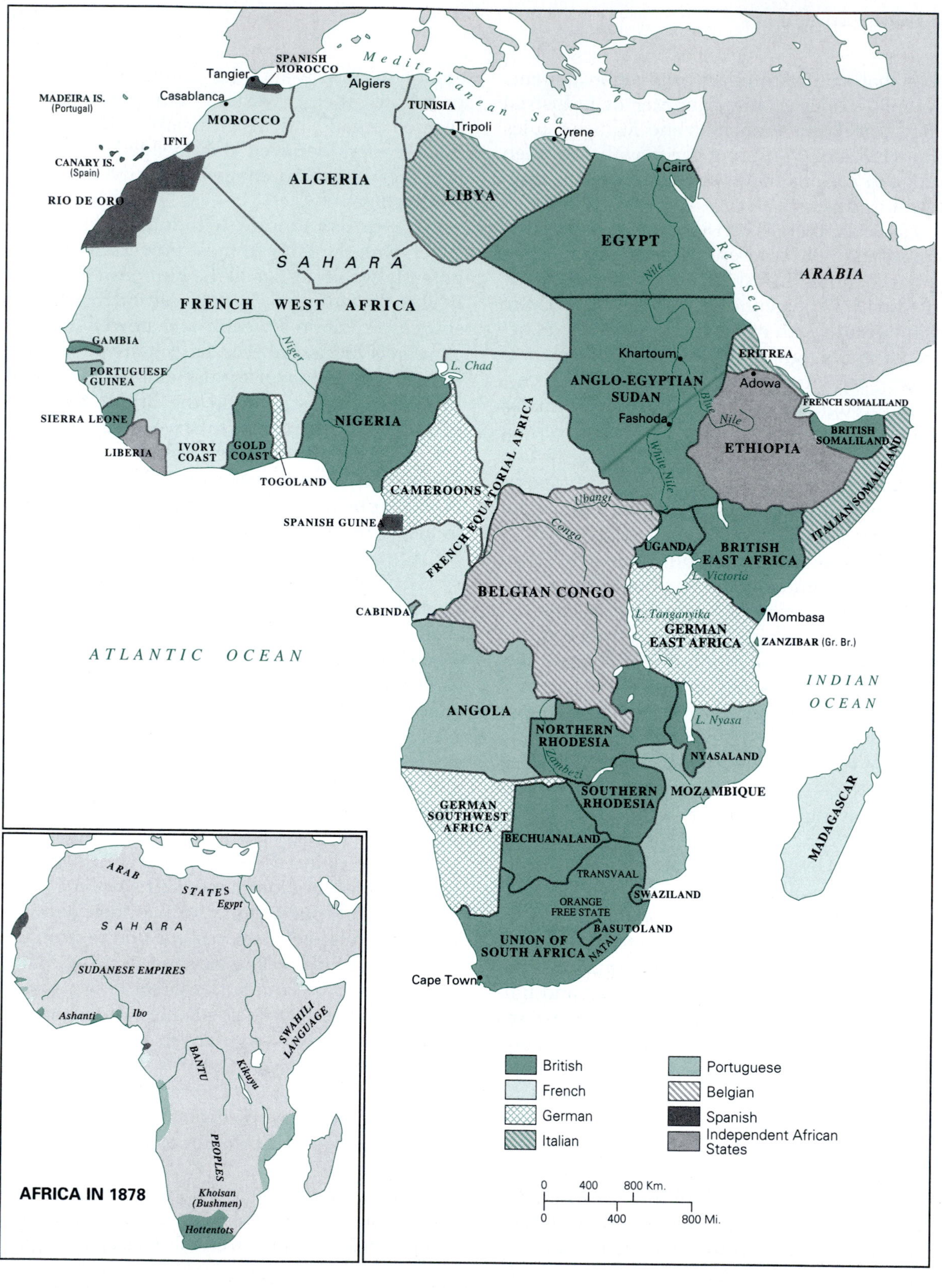

Mediterranean Sea
Tangier
SPANISH MOROCCO
Algiers
MADEIRA IS. (Portugal)
Casablanca
TUNISIA
MOROCCO
Tripoli
Cyrene
IFNI
CANARY IS. (Spain)
Cairo
ALGERIA
LIBYA
RIO DE ORO
EGYPT
Red Sea
Nile
ARABIA
SAHARA
FRENCH WEST AFRICA
GAMBIA
Niger
Khartoum
ERITREA
L. Chad
PORTUGUESE GUINEA
ANGLO-EGYPTIAN SUDAN
Adowa
FRENCH SOMALILAND
Fashoda
Blue Nile
SIERRA LEONE
NIGERIA
BRITISH SOMALILAND
ETHIOPIA
LIBERIA
IVORY COAST
GOLD COAST
White Nile
TOGOLAND
CAMEROONS
Ubangi
ITALIAN SOMALILAND
SPANISH GUINEA
FRENCH EQUATORIAL AFRICA
Congo
UGANDA
BRITISH EAST AFRICA
L. Victoria
BELGIAN CONGO
CABINDA
L. Tanganyika
Mombasa
GERMAN EAST AFRICA
ZANZIBAR (Gr. Br.)
ATLANTIC OCEAN
INDIAN OCEAN
ANGOLA
L. Nyasa
NORTHERN RHODESIA
Zambezi
NYASALAND
SOUTHERN RHODESIA
MOZAMBIQUE
GERMAN SOUTHWEST AFRICA
MADAGASCAR
BECHUANALAND
TRANSVAAL
SWAZILAND
ORANGE FREE STATE
BASUTOLAND
UNION OF SOUTH AFRICA
NATAL
Cape Town
British
French
German
Italian
Portuguese
Belgian
Spanish
Independent African States
0 400 800 Km.
0 400 800 Mi.
AFRICA IN 1878
ARAB STATES
Egypt
SAHARA
SUDANESE EMPIRES
Ashanti
Ibo
SWAHILI LANGUAGE
BANTU
Kikuyu
PEOPLES
Khoisan (Bushmen)
Hottentots

over Egypt in 1882. Then, in 1900, fearing that a rival power might threaten their position by encroaching on the Nile, they established control over the Nile Valley all the way south to Uganda. Russian expansion southward into central Asia toward Afghanistan was intended to avert a British takeover of this area, while the British movement northwestward to Afghanistan was designed to prevent Russia from encroaching on India. The "great game" played by Russia and Britain in central Asia lasted the entire nineteenth century, ending only in 1907.

Much of the expansion was due to the desire to control the often turbulent frontiers of newly acquired areas. Once these frontiers had been brought under control, there were, of course, new frontiers that had to be subdued. As the Russian foreign minister remarked, "The chief difficulty is to know where to stop." The imperial powers rarely did.

Much of the pace and direction of empire building was directed not by European governments but by "the man on the spot," the European official dispatched overseas. In 1883, British Prime Minister Gladstone sent General Charles Gordon (1833–1885) to the Sudan to supervise the withdrawal of British troops who had temporarily entered the country. Gordon disregarded his orders and tried to overthrow the local political and religious leader, the Mahdi, who counterattacked and killed Gordon. In the face of public outrage over the killing, the British annexed the Sudan.

Similarly, in 1883 France dispatched Commander Henri Rivière (1827–1883) to the southern part of Vietnam, already under French authority. Exceeding his orders, Rivière marched northward, and he and his troops were massacred. When news reached Paris, the National Assembly unanimously voted an expedition of twenty thousand men, who more than avenged the hapless commander. They brought northern Vietnam under French control.

Map 22.1 Africa in 1914 European powers conquered most of Africa in the late nineteenth century. Only Liberia and Ethiopia were left unoccupied by 1914.

Other Ideological Motives

In addition to the search for profit and nationalistic pride, a strong sense of mission was used to rationalize imperialism. Because Europeans were endowed with technical and scientific know-how, many imperialists believed it was Europe's duty to develop Africa and Asia. Railroads, telegraphs, hospitals, and schools would transform colonial peoples by opening them to what were seen as the beneficent influences of Europe. If necessary, these changes would be realized by force.

Influenced by Darwinian evolutionary theory, many argued that just as competition among species existed in nature, so did groups of humans struggle for survival. Dubbed "Social Darwinists," these thinkers envisioned a world of fierce competition. They believed that the most serious struggle was among the races.

At the same time that Europeans were making substantial material progress as a result of industrialization, their widescale expansion overseas brought them into contact with Africans and Asians who had not created an industrial economy. Europeans assumed that the dramatic disparity between their own material culture and that of colonial peoples was proof of their innate superiority.

Social Darwinists claimed that the laws of nature dictated the eclipse of weaker races and the victory of the stronger and presumably better race. Others believed that the "white man" had an obligation to dominate and lead the "lesser breeds" to a "higher stage." The British author Rudyard Kipling (1865–1936) celebrated this view in his poem "White Man's Burden" (1899):

Take up the White Man's burden—
Send forth the best ye breed—
Go bind your sons to exile
To serve your captives' need. . . .

Pointing to historic antecedents, imperialists colored their activities with a hue of heroism. Many Europeans took satisfaction in the idea that their countries were performing feats akin to those of ancient Rome or the Crusaders, spreading "civilization" to far-flung empires. Colonial writers, including Kipling, celebrated the heroism of white "men of action," while portraying "natives" as cowardly and weak.

Missionary groups were motivated by strong ideals favoring expansion. David Livingstone (1813–1873), a missionary doctor who had explored central and East Africa in the 1850s, had come across slave caravans and other practices that he found shocking. If the area were opened to commerce, he proclaimed, then Christianity and civilization would follow. His *Travels* and posthumous *Last Journals* were widely read by the British public, and they seemed to suggest that Africa would be vastly improved if it were "opened" to European contact. Missionaries were gripped by the notion of millions of "heathens" in Africa and Asia, and they welcomed European expansion to ensure the spread of Christianity.

Missionaries sometimes unwittingly started incidents that ended in conquest because they explicitly threatened indigenous social and political structures as well as religions. The execution of French missionaries in Vietnam in 1851 and 1852 led to reprisals by the French navy. The killing of missionaries in China also brought intervention by Europe. In Madagascar, competition between British Protestant and French Catholic missionaries for influence over the Malagasy queen precipitated French military intervention and conquest in 1896.

Much of the literature celebrating empire building described it in gendered terms. European men were seen as proving their virility by going overseas, conquering, and running empires. This image did not change when women heroically explored distant lands. For instance, Englishwoman Mary Kingsley (1862–1900) went on two exploration trips into Africa. Her popular books focused British interest on overseas territories, but they did not shake the established view that empire was a manly enterprise.

Conquest, Administration, and Westernization

Industrialization gave Europeans the means to conquer overseas territories. They manufactured rapid-fire weapons and had steam-driven gunboats and oceangoing vessels. Telegraphic communications allowed Europeans to gather information and coordinate military and political decision making. Such advantages made them virtually invincible in colonial conflicts. One remarkable exception was the defeat of the Italians in Adowa in 1896, when they faced an Ethiopian force that was superior in numbers and better armed.

Conquest was often brutal. In September 1898, British-led forces, armed with the recently developed machine gun, slaughtered twenty thousand Sudanese at the Battle of Omdurman. From 1904 to 1908, an uprising in southwest Africa against German rule led to the killing of an estimated sixty thousand of the Herero people; the German general, who had expressly given an order to exterminate the whole population, was awarded a medal by William II. In many colonies resistance continued long after conquest had officially been declared. Continuous skirmishes, in some cases full-scale wars, were fought. In Indochina, it took the French twenty years to defeat the "Scholars' Revolt," led by mandarins who resisted the protectorate.

Colonial governments could be brutally insensitive to the needs of the indigenous peoples. (See the box "Encounters with the West: Chief Montshiwa Petitions Queen Victoria.") To save money, France in the 1890s put large tracts of land in the French Congo under the administration of private rubber companies, which systematically and violently coerced the local people to collect rubber. When the scandal broke in Paris, the concessionary companies were abolished and the French state re-established its control.

The most notorious example of exploitation, terror, and mass killings was the Belgian Congo. Leopold II of Belgium had acquired it as a personal empire, and he mercilessly exploited it and its people. An international chorus of condemnation finally forced the king to surrender his empire and put it under the administration of the Belgian government, which abolished some of the worst features of Leopold's rule.

Though brutal and exploitive, imperialism's spread of Western technologies and values had

ENCOUNTERS WITH THE WEST

Chief Montshiwa Petitions Queen Victoria

In 1885 Bechuanaland in southern Africa became a British protectorate. The Bechuana leaders saw British protection as a means to prevent takeover by the Boers, Dutch-speaking white settlers who were aggressively expanding in South Africa. The British were cavalier about their responsibilities, however, and a few years later allowed the British South Africa Company, a particularly exploitive enterprise, to take control of Bechuanaland. In protest, Chief Montshiwa (1815–1896), a major chief of the Baralong people, petitioned Queen Victoria for redress. His petition was supported by missionary lobbying, and most of Bechuana was saved from the clutches of the company.

Mafeking, 16 August, 1895

To the Queen of England and Her Ministers:

We send greetings and pray that you are all living nicely. You will know us; we are not strangers. We have been your children since 1885.

Your Government has been good, and under it we have received much blessing, prosperity, and peace. . . .

We Baralong are very astonished because we hear that the Queen's Government wants to give away our country in the Protectorate to the Chartered Company; we mean the B[ritish] S[outh] A[frica] Company.

Our land there is a good land, our fathers lived in it and buried in it, and we keep all our cattle in it. What will we do if you give our land away? My people are increasing very fast and are filling the land.

We keep all the laws of the great Queen; we have fought for her; we have always been the friends of her people; we are not idle; we build houses; we plough many gardens; we sow. . . .

Why are you tired of ruling us? Why do you want to throw us away? We do not fight against your laws. We keep them and are living nicely.

Our words are No: No. The Queen's Government must not give my people's land in the Protectorate to the Chartered Company. . . .

Peace to you all, we greet you;
Please send a good word back.

I am etc,

Montshiwa

Source: S. M. Molema, *Montshiwa, 1815–1896* (Cape Town: G. Struik, 1966), pp. 181–182.

some positive results. By 1914, Great Britain had built 40,000 miles of rail in India—nearly twice as much as in Britain. In India and Egypt, the British erected hydraulic systems to irrigate previously arid lands. Colonials built cities often modeled on the European grid system, and some neighborhoods were equipped with running water and modern sanitation. Schools, patterned after those in Europe, taught the imperial language and spread Western ideas and scientific knowledge—though to only a small percentage of the population.

Colonial rulers imposed laws and practices modeled after those of the home country. In India the colonial administration prided itself on

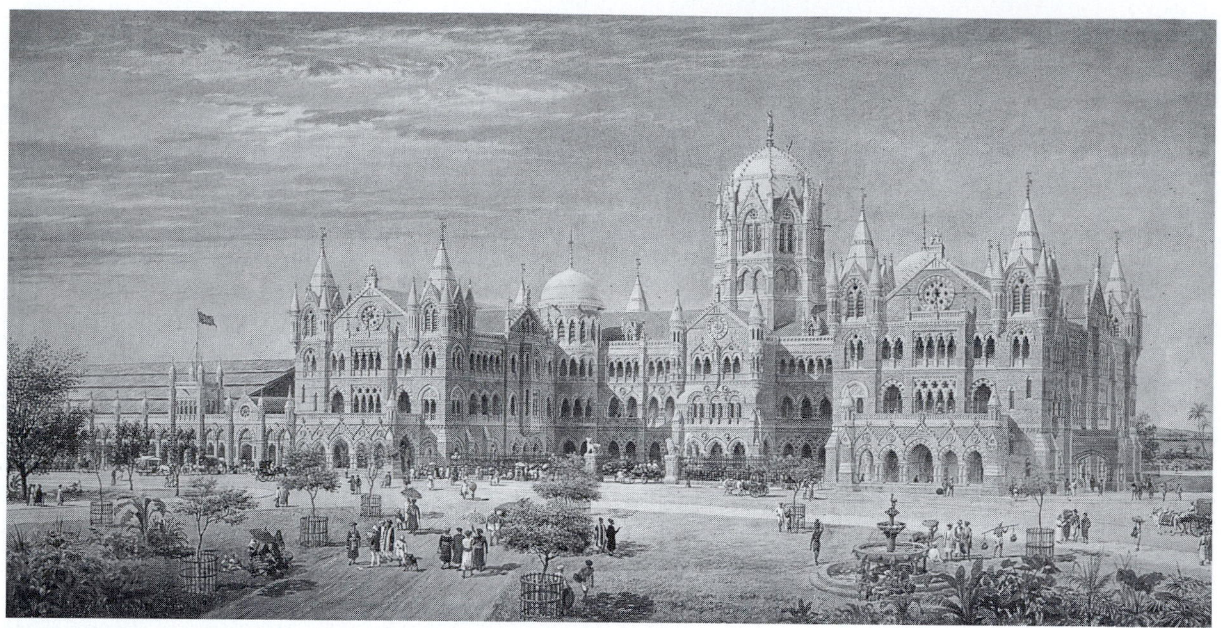

Victoria Terminus, Bombay Europeans' tendency to transfer values and institutions to their colonies included the export of architectural style. Various traditional European architectural styles, mainly the neo-Gothic that was so popular in nineteenth-century England, shaped this edifice, completed in 1888. *(The British Library, Oriental and India Office Collections)*

safeguarding the condition of Indian women by, for instance, abolishing in 1829 the tradition of "suttee," whereby widows were burned on their husband's funeral pyre. However, European models sometimes reduced the rights of indigenous women. In Hindu law a wife could leave her husband, but British law introduced into India the right of a husband to force his wife to return to him. In Kerala, in the southern part of the subcontinent, inheritance and descent were matrilineal (meaning they followed the mother's family line); the British tried to legislate this tradition out of existence since it disturbed their notion of the proper relationship between the sexes.

The European empire builders created political units that had never existed before. The British joined the whole Indian subcontinent under a single authority for the first time. Through a common administration, rail network, and trade, Britain gave Indians the sense of a common condition, leading in 1885 to the founding of the India Congress party. Initially the party demanded reforms within the British colonial system; eventually it became the major nationalist group and called for constitutional government, representative assemblies, and the rule of law.

The ties of empire affected metropolitan cultures as well. The Hindi word for bandit became the English word *thug;* the Hindi number five, denoting the five ingredients necessary for a particular drink, became *punch.* Scenes from the colonial world often were the themes of European art, such as Paul Gauguin's paintings of Tahiti. After the turn of the century, Pablo Picasso's cubism reflected his familiarity with African art. In running the largest empire in the world, the British cultivated competitive sports and stern schooling, which, they believed, would develop "character." A growing number of people from the colonies also came to live in European cities. By 1900 some former colonists, despite various forms of discrimination, had become full participants in the life of their host country; two East Indians won election to the British parliament in the 1890s.

Overseas Migrations and the Spread of European Values

European migration overseas had begun with the expansion of European power abroad in the sixteenth century. Around 6 million people left Europe between the sixteenth and eighteenth centuries. These numbers pale in comparison to the 55 million Europeans who left the Continent for the New World, Australia, and New Zealand between 1870 and 1914 (Map 22.2).

Economic crises and overpopulation in rural Europe led many men and women to look overseas for new opportunities. They either settled permanently or labored as migrant workers to save enough money to bring back home to pay the mortgage or buy more land for their families. As many as three-quarters of all immigrants to the United States were young men. This shifted with changing economic situations: During some decades women who were domestic servants dominated Irish immigration to the United States.

The introduction of the steamship provided cheap and rapid communications with other continents. A transatlantic ticket did not cost much, and in many cases employers in the Americas advanced the price of a ticket in efforts to recruit labor. The trip was relatively short—a crossing from Liverpool to New York took no more than two weeks. In the past people had trekked for weeks from their village to the city in search of work; in the same amount of time they could now reach New York or Buenos Aires. Many envisioned the move as temporary. Of the 34 million migrants to the Americas, about a third returned to Europe. Many were truly seasonal workers, known as swallows in Italian, who went back and forth between Europe and the Americas every year.

Increased literacy, cheaper printing, and the ease of correspondence with the outside world spread what was called "America fever." Between 1900 and 1906, 3 million letters were sent to eastern Europe from the United States, and correspondence to relatives and friends boasted of the material advantages of life in the New World. A Swede who had settled in the United States wrote home, "And I can tell you that here we do not live frugally but here one has egg pancake and canned fish and fresh fish and fruits of all kinds, so it is different from you who have to sit and hold herring bones." Such letters, often reprinted in local newspapers or gathered in pamphlets, unleashed mass waves of migration.

Certain European groups migrated to specific areas. Scandinavians settled in the upper Midwest of the United States, Italians in Argentina, Germans in Paraguay, Britons in South Africa, Portuguese in Brazil, each group deeply influencing its adopted land. The upper Midwest was known as "the great desert," but Scandinavians used farm techniques from their homelands to cultivate these dry lands. German Mennonites who settled in Kansas brought with them a strain of wheat that became the basis of the state's prosperity. Durban in South Africa looks like an English city, and the Germans who came to Milwaukee, Wisconsin, made it a city of beer and strong socialist convictions.

Emigration scattered peoples and extended cultures overseas. By 1914 nearly half of all the Irish and Portuguese lived outside Europe. The settlers consumed many European goods and produced for the European market, increasing the centrality of Europe in the world market. The migrations across the globe were an added force to that of imperial conquest, further putting Europe's imprint on peoples and societies abroad.

THE DEMOCRATIC POWERS

By the end of the nineteenth century, most of Europe's political systems were in crisis. The major powers with democratic institutions—Great Britain, France, and Italy—confronted volatile public opinion and had difficulty winning broad consensus for their policies. They struggled with

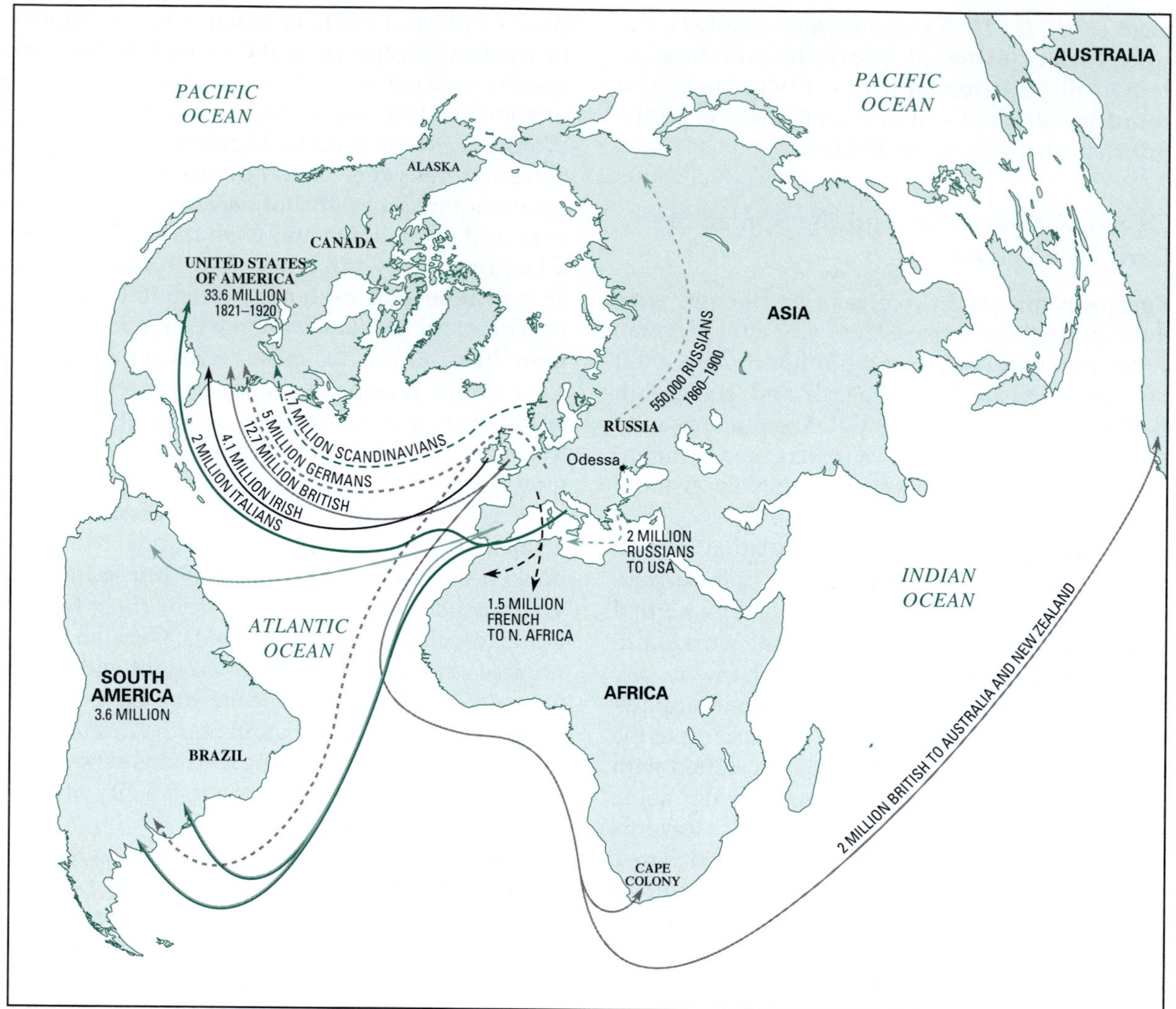

Map 22.2 European Migrations, 1820–1910 Throughout the nineteenth century, millions of Europeans left home for overseas; most headed for the United States. (*Source:* Reproduced from *The Times Atlas of World History*, 3d ed., by kind permission of Times Books. Some data from Eric Hobsbawm, *The Age of Empire, 1875–1914* [New York: Pantheon, 1987].)

new challenges emerging from an expanded electorate. Turning away from the democratic precept of resolving differences through the ballot and legislation, many people—both in government and out—were willing to resort to extraparliamentary means, including violence, to see their interests prevail.

Great Britain

In Great Britain the Reform Bill of 1884 had transformed the political landscape by doubling suffrage—giving the vote to two of every three adult men. To appeal to this enlarged electorate politicians were tempted to make promises that were often broken, to the frustration of their constituents. It was also more difficult to reach a compromise in a Parliament that no longer consisted of a fairly limited class of people with common interests and values. The British political system was faced with issues it was unable to resolve peacefully, and it was obliged—uncharacteristically—to resort to force or the threat of force.

As in earlier periods, Ireland proved to be a persistent problem. The political consciousness of the Irish had risen considerably, and they seethed under alien rule. In an attempt to quell Irish opposition in 1886, Prime Minister Gladstone proposed autonomy, or "home rule," for Ireland. The most serious objection to this plan was that if Ireland, a predominantly Catholic country, ruled itself, the Protestant majority in Ulster would be overwhelmed. "Home rule is Rome rule," chanted the supporters of Ulster Protestantism. Among Gladstone's own Liberals, many opposed changing the existing relationship between England and its possession. They seceded from the Liberals and formed the Unionist party, which, in coalition with the Conservatives, ruled the country from 1886 to 1905. When the Liberals returned to power in 1906, they proposed home rule again, but it was obstructed in the House of Lords and delayed until September 1914.

In the process of debating the Irish issue, many segments of British society resorted to extralegal tactics and even violence. Protestants in northern Ireland armed themselves, determined to resist home rule. Catholic groups, also armed, insisted on the unity of the island under home rule. The Conservative party in Britain, which opposed home rule, called on Ulster to revolt. British officers threatened to resign their commissions rather than fight Ulster. Only the outbreak of world war in 1914 delayed a showdown over Ireland, and then for only a few years.

Returned to power in 1906, the Liberals committed themselves to a vast array of social reforms but were frustrated by the difficulty of getting their program through the House of Lords. The feisty Liberal chancellor of the Exchequer, David Lloyd George (1863–1945), expressed his outrage that the will of the people was being thwarted by a handful of magnates in the House of Lords, sitting there not by election but by hereditary right.

The Liberals' social reform program included old-age pensions. To finance them, Lloyd George proposed raising income taxes and death duties and levying a tax on landed wealth. A bill with these measures easily passed the House of Commons in 1909 but was stymied in the upper chamber, where many members were prominent landowners. The House of Lords technically had the power to amend or reject a bill passed by the Commons, but for nearly 250 years it had been understood that it did not have the right to reject a money bill. Nonetheless, motivated by economic self-interest and personal spite against the Liberals, a majority in the House of Lords voted against the bill.

In reaction, in 1911, the Liberal government sponsored a bill to limit the House of Lords to a suspensive veto. This would mean that a bill defeated in the House of Lords could be prevented from going into effect for only a predetermined period—in this case, two years. The bill was quickly passed by the House of Commons, but the House of Lords had to be compelled to pass it: At the request of the government, the king threatened to appoint four hundred new lords. Under this threat, the House of Lords passed the bill.

During the debate over the bill, Conservatives, supposedly the upholders of decorum, resorted to brawling and refused to let the prime minister speak—for the first time in British parliamentary history. The British Parliament, considered the best model of free institutions, had shown itself unable to resolve issues in a reasoned manner.

Violence also appeared in another unexpected place: the women's suffrage movement. Most liberal men, when speaking of the need to extend human liberty, had excluded the female gender. Women had begun to organize groups devoted to winning the vote in the middle of the nineteenth century (see page 555). Their methods were peaceful—and they had little success. In the early twentieth century, both these factors changed.

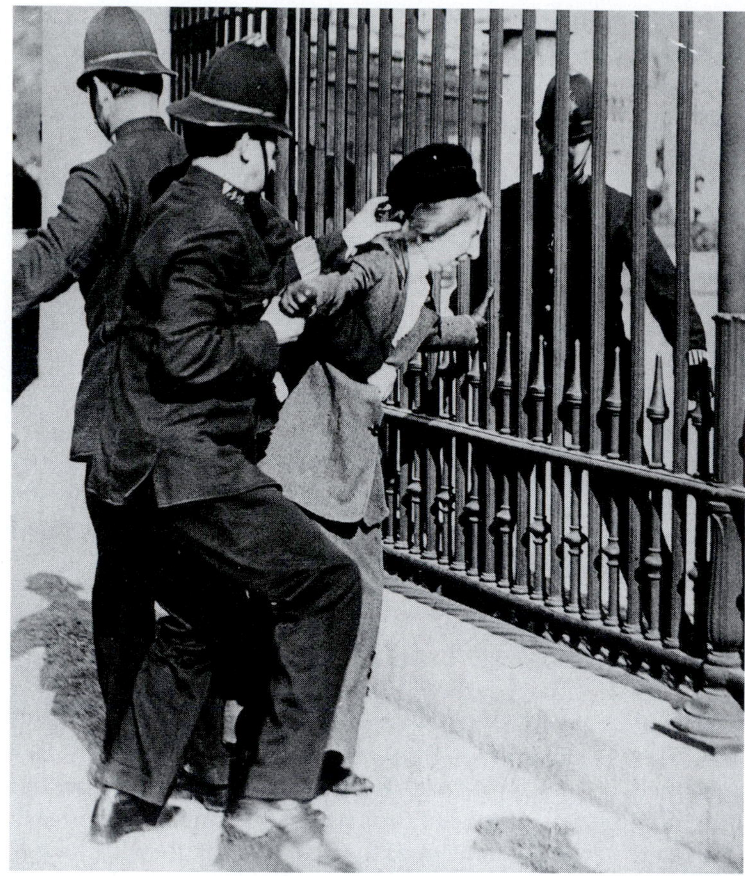

A Suffragist Attempts to Chain Herself to the Gates of Buckingham Palace, 1914 In their effort to win the vote, women resorted to public protests, and the police often violently intervened. *(Popperfoto/Archive Photos)*

In 1903, Emmeline Pankhurst (1858–1928) and her two daughters founded the Women's Social and Political Union, whose goal was immediate suffrage. Angered by their lack of progress, the suffragists (referred to by contemporaries as "suffragettes") led by the Pankhursts began in 1906 a more militant program of protest—disturbing proceedings in Parliament, breaking windows at the prime minister's residence, burning down empty houses, dropping acid into mailboxes, and throwing bombs. There were even threats on the lives of the prime minister and king. Suffragists who were arrested often engaged in hunger strikes. In a painful and humiliating process, the authorities force-fed the women. Female protesters were also physically attacked by male thugs. (See the box "Pankhurst on Women's Rights.") At the dawn of World War I, protesters for women's suffrage had drawn considerable attention to their cause. Women's contributions to the war effort would make it difficult for governments to continue to ignore their demands.

France

The Third Republic, founded in 1870 after France's humiliating defeat at the hands of the Prussians, also continued to face an ongoing series of crises. Challenged by enemies on the political left and right, the regime found itself buffeted from all sides.

The French government contributed to an unstable political situation by its lack of strong leadership. The need to build coalitions among the several parties in the parliament rewarded politicians who had moderate programs and

Pankhurst on Women's Rights

In 1908 the suffragists, led by Emmeline Pankhurst, issued a handbill calling on the people of London to "rush" Parliament and win the vote for women. The legal authorities interpreted their action as a violation of the peace, and several suffragists, including Pankhurst, were put on trial. They put up a spirited defense, in which Pankhurst movingly explained her motives for leading the suffragist cause.

I want you to realise how we women feel; because we are women, because we are not men, we need some legitimate influence to bear upon our law-makers.

Now, we have tried every way. We have presented larger petitions than were ever presented for any other reform, we have succeeded in holding greater public meetings than men have ever had for any reform, in spite of the difficulty which women have in throwing off their natural diffidence, that desire to escape publicity which we have inherited from generations of our foremothers; we have broken through that. We have faced hostile mobs at street corners, because we were told that we could not have that representation for our taxes which men have won unless we converted the whole of the country to our side. Because we have done this, we have been misrepresented, we have been ridiculed, we have had contempt poured upon us. The ignorant mob at the street corner has been incited to offer us violence, which we have faced unarmed and unprotected by the safeguards which Cabinet Ministers have. We know that we need the protection of the vote even more than men have needed it. . . .

We believe that if we get the vote it will mean better conditions for our unfortunate sisters. We know what the condition of the woman worker is . . . and we have been driven to the conclusion that only through legislation can any improvement be effected, and that that legislation can never be effected until we have the same power as men have to bring pressure to bear upon our representatives and upon Governments to give us the necessary legislation. . . .

I should never be here if I had the same kind of power that the very meanest and commonest of men have—the same power that the wife-beater has, the same power that the drunkard has. I should never be here if I had that power, and I speak for all the women who have come before you and other magistrates. . . .

If you had power to send us to prison, not for six months, but for six years, for sixteen years, or for the whole of our lives, the Government must not think that they can stop this agitation. It will go on. . . .

We are here not because we are law-breakers; we are here in our efforts to become lawmakers.

Source: F. W. Pethick Lawrence, ed. *The Trial of the Suffragette Leaders* (London: The Women's Press, 1909), pp. 21–24.

were flexible. Thus there was little premium on firm ideas and commitments. Further, lackluster leadership appealed to republicans, who continued to fear that a popular leader might—as Louis Napoleon had in 1851—exploit his support to make himself dictator.

The regime lurched from scandal to scandal. The most notorious was the Dreyfus affair. In October 1894, Captain Alfred Dreyfus (1859–1935) of the French army was arrested and charged with passing military secrets to the German embassy. Dreyfus seems to have attracted suspicion because he was the only Jewish officer on the general staff. The evidence was flimsy—a letter written in a handwriting that some thought resembled that of Dreyfus.

Using this letter and materials that later turned out to be forged, the army court-martialed Dreyfus and sentenced him to life imprisonment on Devil's Island off the coast of South America. By March 1896, the general staff had evidence that it was another officer, Major Esterhazy, who was actually the spy. But to reopen the case would be to admit the army had made an error, and the general staff refused to do so.

By late 1897, when the apparent miscarriage of justice became widely known, French society split over "the affair." The political left, including many intellectuals, argued for reopening the case. For them it was crucial that justice be carried out. The army and its supporters, right-wing politicians, royalists, and Catholics, argued that the decision should not be changed. As the bulwark against internal and foreign threats, the army should be above challenge, and the fate of a single man—guilty or innocent—was immaterial.

The affair unleashed a swirl of controversy and rioting, which led the government to order a retrial in 1899. But the court again found Dreyfus guilty—this time with "extenuating circumstances" and the recommendation that he be pardoned. Finally, in 1906, Dreyfus was fully exonerated. He ended his days as a general in the army that had subjected him to so much suffering.

The strong encouragement Catholics had given to those who supported the original verdict confirmed the republicans' belief that the church was a menace to the regime. The Radical party, the staunchest backers of Dreyfus, won the elections in 1898. Despite its title, the Radical party favored moderate social reforms. It was uncompromising, however, in its anticlericalism. In 1905 the parliament passed a law separating church and state, ending the privileged position the Catholic church had enjoyed. Violent language and physical confrontations on both sides accompanied this separation. Catholics trying to prevent state officials from entering churches to take required inventories sometimes resorted to force, using weapons or, in one case, a bear chained to the church. Armed soldiers broke down church doors and dragged monks away.

Labor problems also triggered confrontations with the government. Increased labor militancy produced long, drawn-out strikes, which in 1904 alone led to the loss of 4 million labor-days. There was agitation in the countryside, too, particularly in 1907 in the Midi, the south of France. This region had witnessed increased rural proletarianization as population grew and larger landholdings were concentrated under smaller numbers of owners. Rural militancy led to a revolt in 1907. Troops were sent in, killing dozens and winning for the Radical government the title "government of assassins."

Italy

Although unification had taken place in 1860, Italy found genuine unity elusive. The country was plagued by regionalism, social strife, and an unrepresentative political system. As in the past, the south especially challenged the central government. Assertive regionalism, brigandage, and poverty hardened the areas resistant to most government programs.

The parliamentary system established in 1860 was far from democratic. Property qualifications limited suffrage to less than 3 percent of the population. And government corrupted and co-opted the opposition so that electoral choice was short-circuited.

Between 1870 and 1890 the Italian government introduced some important reforms, but it was difficult to improve the standard of living for a people undergoing rapid population growth. In the fifty years after unification, the population increased from 25 to 35 million. In the south, a few wealthy landowners held large *latifundia*, or private estates, while the majority of the peasants were landless and forced to work for minimum wages. In the north, industrialization had started, but the region was not rich in coal or iron. To be competitive, industry paid very low wages, and the workers lived in abject misery.

Conditions on the land and in the factory led to widespread protests, followed by stern government repression. In 1893 a Sicilian labor movement won the adherence of 300,000 members, who seized land and attacked government offices. The government responded with massive force. In 1896, with unrest spreading throughout the peninsula, the government placed half the provinces under military rule. A cycle of violence and counterviolence gripped the nation. In this general atmosphere of violence, an anarchist killed King Umberto I on July 29, 1900.

After the turn of the century, a new prime minister, Giovanni Giolitti (1842–1928), tried to bring an end to the upheaval. He showed a spirit of cooperation toward the workers. Seeking to broaden his popularity by appealing to nationalist fervor, Giolitti launched an attack on Libya in 1911, wresting it from the ailing Ottoman Empire. The territory was arid and bereft of economic promise, but its conquest was championed as a proof of national virility and the foundation of national greatness.

Domestically, the nation also returned to force. A wave of workers' discontent seized the nation again, and in June 1914 a national strike led to rioting and the seizure of power in many municipalities, including Bologna. In the Romagna, an independent workers' republic was proclaimed. It took 100,000 government troops ten days to restore order. The workers' actions led some nationalist right-wing extremists to form "volunteers for the defense of order," anticipating the vigilante thugs who were to make up the early bands of Italian fascism.

THE AUTOCRACIES

Four major autocracies dominated central and eastern Europe: Germany, Austria-Hungary, the Ottoman Empire, and Russia. If the democracies were faced with difficulties in these years, the autocracies faced even more severe problems. Resistance to the autocracies included broad popular challenges to the German imperial system, the reduction of Austria-Hungary into a nearly ungovernable empire, and revolution in the Russian and Ottoman Empires.

Germany

Although Germany had a parliament, the government was answerable to the Kaiser, not the people's electoral representatives. And in the late nineteenth century, Prussia, the most reactionary part of the country, continued to dominate.

To rule effectively, Chancellor Otto von Bismarck maneuvered and intrigued to quell opposition. In the face of socialist growth, he used an attempt to assassinate the emperor as the excuse to ban the Socialist party in 1879. He succeeded in winning over both conservative agrarian and liberal industrial interests by supporting tariffs on imported foodstuffs and industrial goods. He also turned against the Catholics, who were lukewarm toward Protestant Prussia, persecuting them and their institutions. These measures, however, did not prevent the growth of the Socialist and Catholic Center parties.

Unfortunately for Bismarck, whose tenure in office depended on the goodwill of the emperor, William I died in 1888, to be succeeded first by his son, Frederick, who ruled only a few months, and then by his grandson, William II (r. 1888–1918). The young Kaiser William intended to rule as well as reign, but he was ill fit to govern. Convinced of his own infallibility, he bothered to learn very little. He hated any hints of limitation to his powers, announcing, "There is only one ruler in the Reich and I am he. I tolerate no other." He dismissed Bismarck. The schism between the two men was ideological as well as personal. William believed that Bismarck's suppression of the socialists had been ineffective and divisive. He ended the ban against the Social Democrats and sought to undermine their popularity through more subtle means, such as propaganda in the state schools.

The emperor was determined to make Germany a world power. He wanted it to have colonies, a navy, and major influence among the Great Powers. This policy, *Weltpolitik*, or "world politics," alarmed Germany's neighbors, but within Germany, it won support. Steel manufacturers and shipbuilders received lucrative contracts; workers seemed assured of employment.

Although the nationalist appeals impressed many Germans, the nation could not be easily managed. The emperor's autocratic style was challenged, and his behavior was increasingly viewed as irresponsible. In the elections of 1912, one-third of all Germans voted for the Socialist party. Thus the largest single party in the Reichstag was at least rhetorically committed to the downfall of the capitalist system and autocracy. Labor militancy reached new heights. In 1912, 1 million workers—a record number—went on strike. More and more Germans pressed for a parliamentary system with a government accountable to the people's elected representatives.

The emperor could not tolerate criticism. He frequently talked about using the military to crush socialists and the parliament. To some observers it seemed likely that the days of German autocracy were numbered—or that there would be a violent confrontation between the army and the people.

Austria-Hungary

The Austro-Hungarian Empire also faced a series of crises. In an age of intense nationalism, a multinational empire was an anomaly, as Emperor Francis Joseph (r. 1848–1916) himself acknowledged. Although the relationship between the two parts of the empire was regulated by the compromise of 1867 (see page 529), the agreement did not prevent conflict between Austria and Hungary, particularly over control of their joint army.

In the Hungarian half of the empire, the Magyars found it increasingly difficult to maintain control of the other nationalities. The Hungarian government resorted to censorship and jailings to silence nationalist leaders. In the Austrian half of the empire, the treatment of nationalities was less harsh, but the government was equally strife-ridden.

There were no easy solutions to the conflicts that the empire faced. Since much of the national agitation was led by middle-class intellectuals, the Habsburg government introduced universal male suffrage in 1907 in an effort to undercut their influence. However, the result was an empire even more difficult to govern. It became nearly impossible to find a workable majority within a parliament that included thirty ethnically based political parties.

The virulence of debate based on nationality and class divisions grew to unprecedented extremes. Within the parliament, deputies threw inkwells at each other, rang sleigh bells, and sounded bugles. Parliament ceased to be relevant. By 1914 it had been dissolved and Austria was being ruled by decree. Emperor Francis Joseph feared the empire would not survive him.

The Ottoman Empire

In the years before 1914, no political system in Europe suffered from so advanced a case of dissolution as the Ottoman Empire, undermined by both secessionist movements within its borders and aggression from other European powers. Sultan Abdul Hamid II (r. 1876–1909) ruled the country as a despot and authorized mass carnage against those who contested his rule, earning him the title of the "Great Assassin."

Young, Western-educated Turks—the "Young Turks"—dismayed at one-man rule and the continuing loss of territory and influence, overthrew Abdul Hamid in a coup in July 1908. They set up a government responsible to an elected parliament. The Young Turks hoped to stem the loss of territory, but their efforts had the opposite effect. The various nationalities of the empire resented the attempts at "Turkification," the imposition of Turkish education and administration. Renewed agitation broke out in Macedonia, Albania, and among the Armenians. The government carried out severely repressive measures to end the unrest, killing thousands of Armenians.

For foreign powers, the moment seemed propitious to plunder the weakened empire. In 1911, Italy occupied Libya. Greece, Bulgaria, and Serbia formed an alliance, the Balkan League, which prosecuted a successful war against the empire in 1912. Albania became independent, and Macedonia was partitioned among members of the league. The empire thus lost its European possessions except for the capital, Constantinople, and a narrow strip of surrounding land.

Russia

Through the great reforms of the 1860s (see pages 539–541), the Russian autocracy had attempted to resolve many of the problems facing its empire and people. But the reforms and the major social changes of the period unleashed new forces, making it even more difficult for the tsars to rule.

The needs of a modernizing country led to an increase in the number of universities. The newly educated Russian youths began almost instantly an ardent, sustained critique of autocracy. In the absence of a large group upholding liberal, advanced ideas, university students and graduates, who came to be known as the intelligentsia, saw it as their mission to transform Russia. In the 1870s, university youths by the thousands organized a populist movement, hoping to bring change to the countryside. These youths included young women, known at the time as "Russian Amazons," who coupled their fight for peasants' rights with dedication to women's emancipation.

These youthful idealists intended to educate the peasants and make them more politically aware. But they met with suspicion from the peasantry and repression by the government. Large numbers of populists were arrested and put on trial. Frustrated, some disaffected young radicals formed the People's Will, which turned to murdering public officials to hasten the day of revolution.

Although the regime intensified repression, it also sought to broaden its public support. But in 1881, just as Tsar Alexander II was about to take a small step toward a parliamentary form of government, he was assassinated by members of the People's Will. The new ruler, Tsar Alexander III (r. 1881–1894), who had witnessed the assassination, blamed his father's leniency for his death and sought to weaken his reforms. When Alexander's son, Nicholas II (r. 1894–1917), succeeded his father on the throne in 1894, he declared he would be as autocratic as his father. But he was a pleasant man who wanted to be liked. He lacked the forcefulness to establish a coherent policy for his troubled country.

Since the great reforms, serious problems had accumulated that threatened the stability of the regime. In the countryside the situation worsened steadily as the population exploded. The provisions that had accompanied the freeing of the serfs left considerable discontent. The peasants were not free to come and go as they pleased; they had to have the permission of the village council. Agriculture remained inefficient, far inferior to that of western Europe; hence the allotted land was insufficient to feed the peasants.

The modernization of Russia had changed it more dramatically and rapidly than any other central or eastern European state. In the 1890s an ambitious railroad-expansion program had triggered industrial development. Some factories and mining concerns were unusually large, with as many as six thousand employees. When workers grew incensed at their condition, they engaged in massive strikes that crippled industry.

Revolutionary socialist groups continued to flourish. The heirs to the populists were the Social Revolutionaries, who believed that the peasants would bring socialism to Russia. In 1898 the Russian Social Democratic party was founded. In 1903 this Marxist party split between the Mensheviks and the Bolsheviks. The Mensheviks insisted that Russia had to go through the stages of history Marx had predicted—to witness the full development of capitalism and its subsequent collapse—before socialism could come to power. The Bolsheviks, a minority group, were led by Vladimir Lenin (1870–1924), who insisted that a revolutionary cadre could seize power on behalf of the working class. Lenin favored a small, disciplined party, like the People's Will, while the Mensheviks favored a more open, democratic party.

At the turn of the century these groups were small and played a limited role in the mounting opposition to tsarism. But popular opposition

Workers' Demonstration in Moscow, 1905 In 1905 workers as well as peasants protested against the Russian autocracy. To bring the revolution under control, Nicholas II was obliged to grant several concessions. *(Novosti)*

soon grew in the face of Russian military ineptness in the war against Japan, which had broken out in February 1904 in a dispute over northern Korea. Antagonism to the tsarist regime escalated as a result of social tensions, heightened by an economic slowdown.

In January 1905, a series of demonstrations, strikes, and other acts of collective violence began. Together, they were dubbed "the revolution of 1905." One Sunday in January 1905, 400,000 workers seeking redress of their grievances gathered in front of the tsar's palace. Rather than hear their protests, officials ordered soldiers to fire on them, resulting in 150 deaths and hundreds more wounded. "Bloody Sunday" angered the populace. The tsar, instead of being viewed as an understanding, paternal authority, had become the murderer of his people. As reports reached Russia of more defeats in the war with Japan, the regime's prestige was further undermined. By September 1905, Russia had to sue for peace. Challenged in the capital, where independent workers' councils called *soviets* had sprung up, the government also lost control over the countryside, the site of widespread peasant uprisings.

Nicholas hoped to split the forces challenging him by meeting the demands for parliamentary government and granting major constitutional and civil liberties. At the end of October, the tsar established an elective assembly, the Duma, with restricted male suffrage and limited political power. When it quickly became the arena for criticism of autocracy, he suspended it and changed its electoral base and rules of operations.

The government tried to win support by reducing the peasants' financial obligations and extending local self-rule to the peasants, but it was not enough. Between emancipation and 1914 the peasant population had grown by 50 percent, but it acquired only 10 percent more land. In 1891 famine had broken out in 20 provinces, killing a quarter of a million people. Rural poverty and discontent were widespread.

Labor unrest also mounted among industrial workers. In 1912 there were 725,000 strikers, but by the first half of 1914 there were twice that number. When the French president visited St. Petersburg on the eve of the outbreak of the war, barricades were rising in workers' neighborhoods.

THE COMING WAR

Instability and upheaval characterized international relations in the years between 1880 and 1914. However, there was nothing inevitable about the outbreak of war. Good common sense dictated against it, and some intelligent people predicted that in the new modern era, war had become so destructive that it was unthinkable. Nevertheless, the Great Powers pursued diplomatic and military policies that brought them to its brink.

Power Alignments

Germany enjoyed an unchallenged position in the international order of the 1870s and 1880s. It was allied with Russia and Austria-Hungary in the Three Emperors' League, formed in 1873 and renewed by treaty in 1884. And it was part of the Triple Alliance with Austria and Italy. France was isolated, without allies. Britain, with little interest in continental affairs, appeared to be enjoying its "splendid isolation."

Germany's alliance system was not free from problems. Austria-Hungary and Russia were at loggerheads over control of the Balkans. How could Germany be the friend of both? To reassure the Russian government, Bismarck signed the Reinsurance Treaty in 1887, promising that Germany would not honor its alliance with Austria if the latter attacked Russia. After Bismarck's resignation in 1890, William II allowed the Reinsurance Treaty to lapse. Alarmed, the Russians signed the Franco-Russian Alliance in January 1894, by which each side pledged to help the other in case either was attacked by Germany.

The Great Powers on the Continent were now divided into two camps, the Triple Alliance (Germany, Austria-Hungary, and Italy) and the Franco-Russian Alliance. Britain formally belonged to neither. For a time it leaned toward the German-led alliance because France and Russia both rivaled Britain for influence in Asia, and France challenged Britain for control of Africa. However, distrust of Germany led Britain and France to resolve their difficulties overseas. In 1904, Britain and France signed an understanding, or *entente*, resolving their rivalries in Egypt, and in 1907, Great Britain and Russia regulated their competition for influence in Persia (present-day Iran) with the Anglo-Russian Entente. Now the Triple Alliance faced the Triple Entente of Great Britain, France, and Russia.

The Momentum for War

A series of crises solidified these alignments to the point where their members were willing to go to war to save them. France's attempts to take over Morocco twice led to conflict with Germany. In 1905, Germany insisted that an international conference discuss the issue and deny France this kingdom adjacent to its colony of Algeria. In 1911, when France grabbed Morocco anyway, Germany accepted the situation only after extorting compensation from the French, who deeply resented what they viewed as German bullying.

Britain also began to view Germany as a serious international menace. Over the years, Britain had developed a navy equal to none. An island nation, dependent on international trade for its economic survival, Britain saw its navy as a necessity. Germany began building its own navy in the 1890s, expressly for the purpose of challenging Britain's supremacy on the seas.

The heightened international rivalry forced the European states to increase their arms expenditures. In 1906 the British introduced a new class of ships with the launching of the *Dreadnought.* Powered by steam turbines and heavily armored, it was faster than any other ship and could not be easily sunk. Its ten 12-inch guns made it a menace on the seas. When Germany built equivalent ships, British naval supremacy was gone. Britain was feeling less secure than at any time since the Napoleonic Wars, and it continued an expensive and feverish naval race with Germany.

In Germany the changing military capacity of Russia created great anxieties. When Japan defeated the tsarist empire in 1905, the Russian military was revealed to be inferior. As a result Germany was not particularly afraid of its eastern neighbor. But stung by that humiliation, Russia had quickly rebuilt its army and planned to establish an extensive rail network in the west. To many Germans, their country appeared encircled by Russia and France. Beginning in 1912 many in the military and within the government started thinking about a preventive war. If war was inevitable, many Germans argued, it should occur before Russia became even stronger.

Many political leaders viewed the escalating arms race as a form of madness. Between 1904 and 1913 French and Russian arms expenditures increased by 80 percent; that of Germany by 120 percent; Austria-Hungary by 50 percent; and Italy by 100 percent. British Foreign Secretary Sir Edward Grey (1862–1933) warned that if the arms race continued, "it will submerge civilization."

On the whole warfare was not feared. Except for short, victorious colonial wars, the Western powers had not experienced a major conflict since the Crimean War. Russia's war against Japan in 1905 had been a calamity, but Russia could imagine that this was a nonreplicable disaster. Most policymakers believed that the next war would be short. The wars of the past half-century, notably the Austro-Prussian War of 1866 and the Franco-Prussian War of 1870, had been decided in a few weeks. Many of Europe's leaders did not dread war enough to make a major effort to prevent it.

It was the territorial rivalry between Austria and Russia that triggered international disaster. For decades the two empires had vied for control of the Balkans (Map 22.3). In 1903, following a bloody military coup that killed the king and queen of Serbia, a pro-Russian party took control of the Serbian government. It spread anti-Austrian propaganda and sought to unify under its banner the Slavs living in the Balkans, including those under Austrian rule. Many Austrian officials became convinced that the survival of the Austro-Hungarian Empire required that Serbia be destroyed.

On June 28, 1914, the heir to the Habsburg throne, Archduke Francis Ferdinand, visited Sarajevo in Austrian-ruled Bosnia. A young Bosnian Serb nationalist, hostile to Austrian rule, who had been trained and armed by a Serb terrorist group called the Black Hand, assassinated the archduke and his wife.

The assassination of the heir to the throne provided Austria with a pretext for military action. Kaiser William II, fearing that failure to support Vienna would lead to Austrian collapse and a Germany bereft of any allies, urged Austria to attack Serbia. On July 23, Austria issued an ultimatum to Serbia, deliberately worded in such a way as to be unacceptable. When Serbia refused the ultimatum, Austria declared war on July 28.

Perceived self-interest motivated each state's behavior in the ensuing crisis. Russia's status as a Great Power demanded that it not allow its client state to be humiliated, much less obliterated. In the past the French government had acted as a brake on Russian ambitions in the Balkans. France now counseled restraint, but it did not withhold its aid. France feared isolation in the face of what it perceived as growing German aggressiveness and believed that to remain a Great Power, it needed to help its ally.

German leaders may have seen the crisis as a propitious moment to begin a war that was going to occur sooner or later anyway. Germany declared war on Russia and, assuming that France would come to Russia's aid, invaded France through Belgium. The British, concerned by the threat to their ally France, and outraged by the violation of Belgian neutrality to which all the Great Powers had been signatories since 1839, declared war on Germany. Events had hurtled forward between the Austrian declaration of war on Serbia on July 28 and the British decision on August 4. Europe was at war.

Map 22.3 The Balkans in 1914 By 1914 the Ottoman Empire was much diminished, containing virtually none of Europe. Political boundaries did not follow nationality lines. Serbia was committed to unite all Serbs at the expense of the Austro-Hungarian Empire.

SUMMARY

On the surface, the years from 1880 to 1914 seemed comfortable. More people than ever before enjoyed material advantages and an improved standard of living. Literacy spread. Death rates went down; life expectancy rose. But a revolution of rising expectations had been created, and people grew more demanding, insisting in sometimes violent ways on their political and economic rights. Although mass movements such as socialism and the women's suffrage movement generally made use of peaceful means in their campaigns to change society, some of their members advocated and employed force. Anarchism appeared to stalk Europe. And in turn, states did not hesitate to use force in efforts to quell various protest movements, even resorting to martial law.

Reflecting these trends, intellectuals like Freud and Bergson and artists like Schiele and Munch suggested that there was a hidden, irrational dimension of life beneath surface appearances. Behind the façade of security lay many disturbing impulses such as racism, anti-Semitism, and the desire to replace the emerging democracies with dictatorships.

In their relations with Africa and Asia, Europeans resorted to force to an unprecedented degree, conquering most of Africa and much of Asia. The new empires were intended to provide Europe with new sources of wealth, trade, and the trappings of power. Europeans found it natural to regard themselves as belonging to a master race, destined to dominate the world.

Although most Europeans were optimistic about their future, some had serious doubts. Intellectuals spoke of decadence and decline. Statesmen, anxious to avoid the threat of national decline, resorted to extreme measures such as empire building overseas and armed competition in Europe. Among European thinkers and statesmen, force became widely accepted as the means to an end, and some leaders—notably those of Austria-Hungary and Germany—favored war over negotiation in July 1914.

The major powers—except Britain, confident in its naval dominance—built up large standing armies with millions of men and much modern equipment. Europe's network of alliances created more tension. If there were some leaders who feared war, more dreaded the consequences of not fighting, believing that war would save their regimes from the internal and external challenges they faced. Few could foresee the dire consequences of such a choice.

NOTES

1. Charles Seymour, ed. *The Intimate Papers of Colonel House,* vol. 1 (Boston: Houghton Mifflin, 1926), p. 249.

SUGGESTED READING

Baumgart, Winfried. *Imperialism—The Idea and Reality of British and French Colonial Expansion, 1880–1914.* 1989. A comparative study, emphasizing the political aspects of imperialism.

Brédin, Jean-Denis. *The Affair: The Case of Alfred Dreyfus.* 1986. The most authoritative account, written by a French lawyer; covers both the details of the affair and its context.

Bridge, F. R. *The Habsburg Monarchy Among the Great Powers, 1815–1918.* 1990. Contrary to most works on the Habsburg empire, praises Austrian leaders for preserving the empire as long as they did.

Clark, Linda L. *Schooling the Daughters of Marianne.* 1984. A study of the schooling and socialization of girls in France at the turn of the century.

Gay, Peter. *Freud—A Life for Our Time.* 1988. An admiring study by a prominent historian and trained psychoanalyst.

Hobsbawm, Eric. *The Age of Empire, 1875–1914.* 1987. A fine survey, emphasizing social change, by a leading British historian.

Hoerder, Dirk, and Leslie Page Moch, eds. *European Migrants—Global and Local Perspectives.* 1996. A collection of up-to-date articles on migrations of Europeans.

Hughes, H. Stuart. *Consciousness and Society: The Reorientation of European Social Thought, 1890–1930.* 1979. A classic on changes in European social thought.

Joll, James. *The Origins of the First World War.* 1984. A clear, concise, readable history emphasizing strategic interests and nationalist passions leading to the outbreak of the war.

Katz, Jacob. *From Prejudice to Destruction, 1700–1933.* 1980. A survey of two centuries of European anti-Semitism.

Kennedy, Paul. *The Rise and Fall of the Great Powers, 1500 to 2000.* 1987. Masterfully summarizes the factors that led to the shifting fates of the Great Powers.

Kohut, Thomas A. *Wilhelm II and the Germans—A Study in Leadership.* 1991. A psychohistorical study, analyzing the German emperor's youth and unsatisfactory relations with his parents.

Levine, Philippa. *Victorian Feminism.* 1987. Shows that Victorian women were involved in several campaigns for their rights, including the suffragist movement.

Mayeur, Jean-Marie, and Madeleine Réberioux. *The Third Republic—From Its Origins to the Great War, 1871–1914.* 1987. The most up-to-date survey of France in these years, emphasizing the emergence of republican government and the challenges it faced.

Silverman, Debora L. *Art Nouveau in Fin-de-Siècle France: Politics, Psychology, and Style.* 1989. An examination of the relationship among psychology, politics, and art.

Strobel, Margaret. *European Women and the Second British Empire.* 1991. Considers the role of women in the formation of the British Empire.

Teich, Mikulas, and Roy Porter, eds. *Fin de Siècle and Its Legacy.* 1990. A collection of critical essays summarizing the cultural trends at the end of the century.

Tickner, Lisa. *The Spectacle of Women: Imagery of the Suffrage Campaign, 1907–1914.* 1988. An extensively illustrated study of radical suffragism in Britain.

Townshend, Charles. *Political Violence in Ireland.* 1983. Studies the social and economic origins of violence in Ireland since 1848.

Wilson, Keith, ed. *Decisions for War, 1914.* 1995. A collection of articles, based on the most recent scholarship, highlighting the actions of the major and some minor powers in the crises of July 1914.

CHAPTER 23

War and Revolution, 1914–1919

s the European powers prepared for a military showdown, an Egyptian-Sudanese intellectual, Mohammed Ali Duse (1867–1944), contemplated the long-term consequences the war might have: "We can only watch and pray. Unarmed, undisciplined, disunited, we cannot strike a blow; we can only await the event. But whatever that may be, all the combatants, the conquerors and the conquered alike, will be exhausted by the struggle, and will require years for their recovery, and during that time much may be done. Watch and wait! It may be that the non-European races will profit by the European disaster. God's ways are mysterious."[1] Duse was right. The fighting that began in August 1914 would become the first "world war"—a dramatic turning point in world history and the beginning of the end of European hegemony.

In Europe the overwhelming majority initially welcomed the war, but the eventual consequences for Europeans were often cataclysmic, most dramatically in the countries that met defeat. Long-standing empires and dynasties fell apart, so the map of Europe had to be redrawn after the war. World War I, known to contemporaries as "the Great War," shattered the old European order, with its assumptions of superiority, rationality, and progress.

The war proved such a turning point because the fighting, which had been expected to produce a quick result, instead bogged down in a stalemate during the fall of 1914. By the time it finally ended, in November 1918, the war had strained the whole fabric of life, affecting everything from economic organization to literary vocabulary, from journalistic techniques to the roles of women and men. The war also led to a communist revolution in Russia that had an incalculable impact on the subsequent history of the twentieth century.

Questions and Ideas to Consider

- How did the new technologies in warfare favor those in the defensive position? What were the consequences of this?
- "Total war" required new social arrangements and innovative techniques to control public opinion. What changes occurred at the home front? What were their long-term results?
- Why did the Russian Revolution end Russia's participation in the war? Why was Lenin so concerned that the revolution spread to other European countries?
- In 1918, Germany was in a relatively favorable military situation. Many Germans wanted to work out a compromise peace while they had the chance, but military leaders persuaded Emperor William II to keep fighting. Why?
- What were the major concerns of each nation at the end of the war? In light of these concerns, was the Paris peace settlement a success?

THE UNFORESEEN STALEMATE, 1914–1917

When the war began in August 1914, enthusiasm and high morale, based on expectations of quick victory, marked both sides. But fighting on the crucial western front led to a stalemate by the end of 1914, and the particularly brutal encounters of 1916 made it clear that this was not the sort of war most had expected at its start. By early 1917 the difficulties of the war experience brought to the surface underlying questions about what it was all for—and whether it was worth the price.

August 1914: The Domestic and Military Setting

The outbreak of fighting early in August produced a wave of euphoria and a remarkable degree of domestic unity. To many, war came almost as a relief; at last, the issues that had produced tension and intermittent crisis for the past decade would find definitive solution.

An unexpected display of patriotism by the socialist left fed the sense of domestic unity and high morale. Despite their long-standing call for international proletarian solidarity, members of the socialist parties of the Second International rallied to their respective national war efforts almost everywhere in Europe. To socialists and workers, national defense against a more backward aggressor seemed essential to the eventual creation of socialism. French socialists had to defend France's democratic republic against autocratic and militaristic Germany; German socialists had to defend German institutions, and the strong socialist organizations that had proven possible within them, against repressive tsarist Russia. The German Socialists' vote for war credits in the Reichstag on August 4 dramatically symbolized working-class support for the war.

In France the government had planned, as a precaution, to arrest roughly one thousand trade union and socialist leaders in the event of war, but no such arrests seemed necessary when the war began. Instead, the order of the day was "Sacred Union," which even entailed Socialist participation in the new government of national defense. Germany enjoyed a comparable "Fortress Truce," including an agreement to suspend labor conflict during the war, although no Socialist was invited to join the war cabinet.

The high spirits of August were possible because so few Europeans could foresee what they were getting into. It would be "business as usual," as the British government put it—no shortages, no rationing, no massive government intervention. Each side had reason for optimism: The forces of the Triple Entente outnumbered those of Germany and Austria-Hungary, but the Central Powers had potential advantages in equipment, coordination, and speed over their more dispersed adversaries.

After the fighting began, a second tier of belligerents intervened one by one, expanding the war's scope and complicating its strategy. In November 1914 the Ottoman Empire, fearful of Russia, joined the Central Powers, thereby extending

CHAPTER CHRONOLOGY

August 1914	Fighting begins
September 1914	French forces hold off the German assault at the Marne
May 1915	Italy declares war on Austria-Hungary
February–December 1916	Battle of Verdun
July–November 1916	Battle of the Somme
January 1917	Germans resume unrestricted submarine warfare
March 1917	First Russian revolution: fall of the tsar
April 1917	U.S. declaration of war
July 1917	German Reichstag war-aims resolution
November 1917	Second Russian revolution: the Bolsheviks take power
March 1918	Treaty of Brest-Litovsk between Germany and Russia
March–July 1918	Germany's last western offensive
July 1918	Second Battle of the Marne
July–November 1918	French-led counter-offensive
November 1918	Armistice: fighting ends
January 1919	Peace congress convenes at Paris
June 1919	Victors impose Treaty of Versailles on Germany

the war along the Russo-Turkish border and on to Mesopotamia and the approaches to the Suez Canal in the Middle East. For Arabs disaffected with Ottoman rule, the war presented an opportunity to take up arms—with the active support of Britain and France. Italy, after dickering with both sides, committed itself to join the Entente with the Treaty of London of April 1915. This secret agreement specified the territories Italy was to receive in the event of Entente victory—primarily the Italian-speaking areas still within Austria-Hungary. In September 1915, Bulgaria entered the war on the side of the Central Powers, seeking territorial advantages at the expense of Serbia. Romania intervened on the side of the Entente in August 1916, hoping to seize Transylvania from Hungary.

Thus the war was fought on a variety of fronts (Map 23.1). This fact, combined with uncertainties about the role of sea power, led to ongoing debate among military decision makers about strategic priorities. Because of the antagonism that the prewar German naval buildup had caused, some expected that Britain and Germany would quickly be drawn into a decisive naval battle. Britain promptly instituted an effective naval blockade of Germany, but the great showdown on the seas never materialized. World War I proved fundamentally a land war.

Germany faced not only the long-anticipated two-front war against Russia in the east and France and Britain in the west; it also had to look to the southeast, given the precarious situation of Austria-Hungary. On the eastern front, Germany managed decisive victories during 1917 and 1918, forcing first Russia, then Romania, to seek a separate peace. But it was the western front that proved decisive.

Into the Nightmare, 1914

With the lessons of the wars of German unification in mind, both sides had planned for a short war based on rapid offensives. According to the

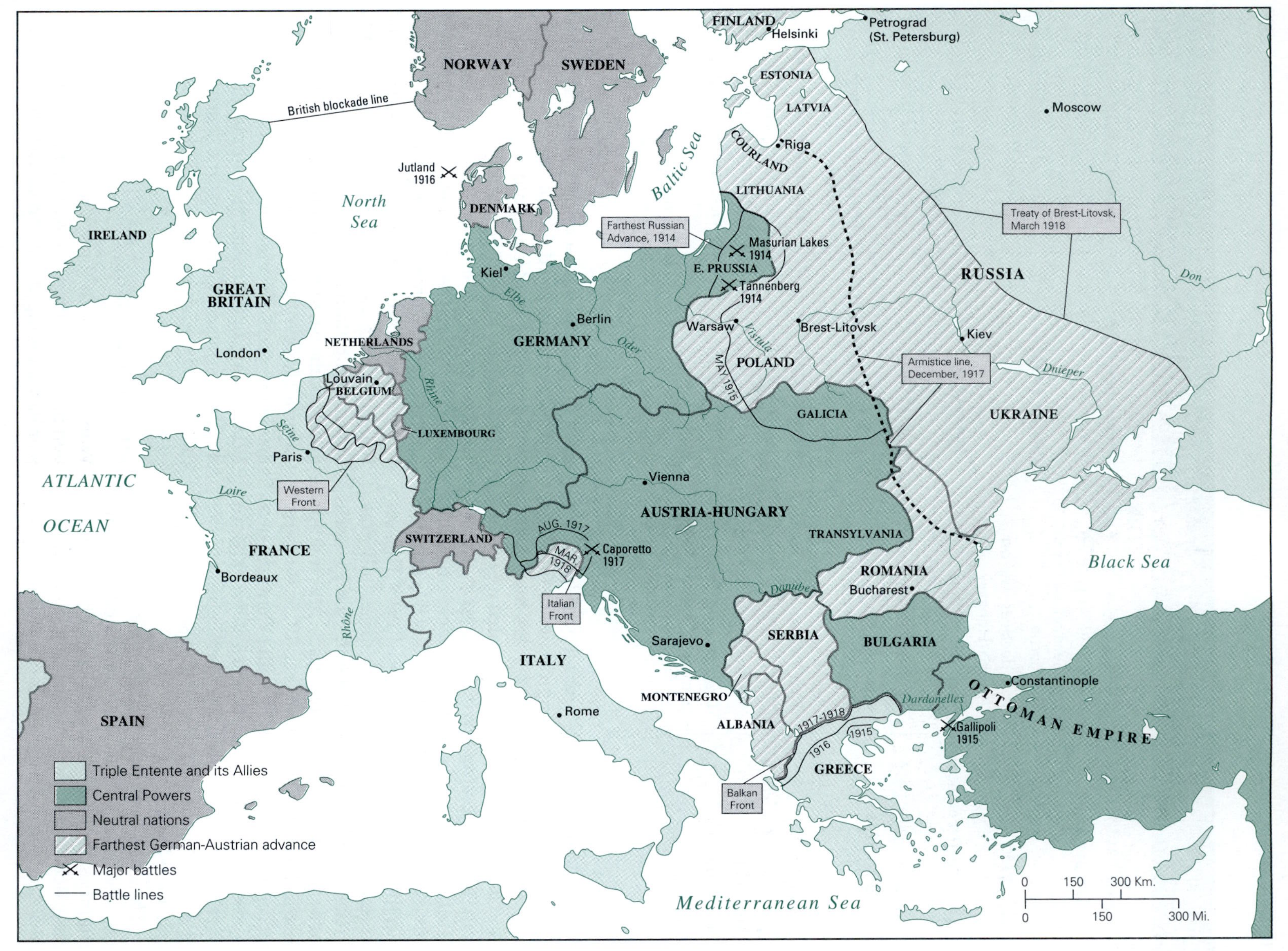

FINLAND
Helsinki
Petrograd
(St. Petersburg)
NORWAY
SWEDEN
British blockade line
ESTONIA
LATVIA
Moscow
COURLAND
Riga
Jutland
1916
North
Sea
Baltic Sea
LITHUANIA
DENMARK
IRELAND
Treaty of Brest-Litovsk,
March 1918
Farthest Russian
Advance, 1914
Masurian Lakes
1914
E. PRUSSIA
Kiel
GREAT
BRITAIN
Tannenberg
1914
RUSSIA
Don
Elbe
Berlin
Warsaw
Vistula
Brest-Litovsk
Kiev
NETHERLANDS
GERMANY
Oder
MAY 1915
POLAND
Armistice line,
December, 1917
Dnieper
London
Louvain
BELGIUM
Rhine
GALICIA
UKRAINE
LUXEMBOURG
Seine
Paris
Vienna
ATLANTIC
OCEAN
Loire
Western
Front
AUSTRIA-HUNGARY
AUG. 1917
TRANSYLVANIA
SWITZERLAND
Caporetto
1917
MAR. 1918
FRANCE
ROMANIA
Black Sea
Bordeaux
Danube
Bucharest
Italian
Front
Rhône
Sarajevo
SERBIA
BULGARIA
ITALY
Constantinople
MONTENEGRO
Dardanelles
OTTOMAN EMPIRE
Rome
SPAIN
ALBANIA
1917-1918
1915
Gallipoli
1915
1916
GREECE
Balkan
Front
Triple Entente and its Allies
Central Powers
Neutral nations
Farthest German-Austrian advance
Major battles
Battle lines
Mediterranean Sea
0
150
300 Km.
0
150
300 Mi.

No Trenches in Sight Spirits were high early in August 1914, as soldiers like these in Paris marched off to war. None foresaw what fighting this war would be like. None grasped the long-term impact the war would have. *(Archives Larousse-Giraudon)*

Schlieffen Plan, drafted in 1905, Germany would concentrate first on France, devoting but one-eighth of its forces to containing the Russians, who were bound to need longer to mobilize. After taking just six weeks to knock France out of the war, Germany would then concentrate on Russia. French strategy, crafted by General Joseph Joffre (1852–1931), similarly relied on rapid offensives. The boys would be home by Christmas—or so it was thought.

Map 23.1 Major Fronts of World War I Although World War I included engagements in East Asia and the Middle East, it was essentially a European conflict, encompassing fighting on a number of fronts. A vast territory was contested in the east, but on the western front, which proved decisive, fighting was concentrated in a relatively small area.

Although German troops encountered more opposition than expected from the formerly neutral Belgians, they moved through Belgium into northern France during August. By the first week of September they had reached the Marne River, threatening Paris and forcing the French government to retreat south to Bordeaux. But French and British troops under Joffre counterattacked September 6–10, forcing the Germans to fall back. By holding off the German offensive at this first Battle of the Marne, the Entente had undercut the Schlieffen Plan—and with it, it turned out, any chance of a rapid victory by either side.

During the rest of the fall of 1914, each side tried—unsuccessfully—to outflank the other. When active fighting ceased for the winter in November, a military front of about 300 miles had been established all the way from Switzerland

Trench Warfare British soldier guards a trench at Ovillers, on the Somme, in July 1916.
(Trustees of the Imperial War Museum)

to the North Sea. This line failed to shift more than 10 miles in either direction over the next three years. The result of the first six weeks of fighting on the western front was not gallant victory by either side but a grim and unforeseen stalemate.

The two sides settled into a war of attrition, constructing an elaborate network of defensive trenches. Enemy trenches were sometimes within shouting distance, so there was occasionally banter back and forth, even attempts to entertain the other side. But the trenches quickly became almost unimaginably grim—filthy, ridden with rats and lice, noisy and smoky from artillery fire, and foul-smelling, partly from the odor of decaying bodies.

As defensive instruments the trenches proved quite effective, especially because each side quickly learned to take advantage of barbed wire, mines, and machine guns to defend its positions. The machine gun had been developed before the war as an offensive weapon; few anticipated the decided advantage it would give the defense. It proved possible to defend trenches even against massive assaults—and to impose heavy casualties on the attackers. In 1916 the tank was introduced to counter the machine gun, but, as skeptics had warned, tanks proved too unreliable to be widely effective. Although the French used them to advantage in the decisive Allied offensive in 1918, tanks were not crucial to the outcome of the war.

Though the defensive trenches had formidable advantages, neither side could give up the vision of a decisive offensive to break through on the western front. The troops were periodically called on to go "over the top" and then across "no man's land" to assault the enemy trenches. Again and again, such offensives proved futile, producing incredibly heavy casualties: "Whole regiments gambled away eternity for ten yards of wasteland."[2]

For the soldiers on the western front the war became a nightmarish experience in a hellish

Into the Trenches

As the initial offensives on the western front turned into stalemate, ordinary soldiers on both sides began to experience unprecedented forms of warfare in an eerie new landscape. Writing home to his family from France in November 1914, a young German soldier, Fritz Franke (1892–1915), sought to convey what this new war was like. He was killed six months later.

Yesterday we didn't feel sure that a single one of us would come through alive. You can't possibly picture to yourselves what such a battlefield looks like. It is impossible to describe it, and even now, when it is a day behind us, I myself can hardly believe that such bestial barbarity and unspeakable suffering are possible. Every foot of ground contested; every hundred yards another trench; and everywhere bodies—rows of them! All the trees shot to pieces; the whole ground churned up a yard deep by the heaviest shells; dead animals; houses and churches so utterly destroyed by shellfire that they can never be of the least use again. And every troop that advances in support must pass through a mile of this chaos, through this gigantic burial ground and the reek of corpses.

In this way we advanced on Tuesday, marching for three hours, a silent column, in the moonlight, toward the Front and into a trench as Reserve, two to three hundred yards from the English, close behind our own infantry.

There we lay the whole day, a yard and a half to two yards below the level of the ground, crouching in the narrow trench on a thin layer of straw, in an overpowering din which never ceased all day or the greater part of the night—the whole ground trembling and shaking! There is every variety of sound—whistling, whining, ringing, crashing, rolling . . . [ellipses in the original] the beastly things pitch right above one and burst and the fragments buzz in all directions, and the only question one asks is: "Why doesn't one get me?" Often the things land within a hand's breadth and one just looks on. One gets so hardened to it that at the most one ducks one's head a little if a great, big naval-gun shell comes a bit too near and its grey-green stink is a bit too thick. Otherwise one soon just lies there and thinks of other things. . . .

One just lives from one hour to the next. For instance, if one starts to prepare some food, one never knows if one may'nt have to leave it behind within an hour. . . .

. . . Above all one acquires a knowledge of human nature! We all live so naturally and unconventionally here, every one according to his own instincts. That brings much that is good and much that is ugly to the surface.

Source: A. F. Wedd, ed., *German Students' War Letters,* translated and arranged from the original edition of Dr. Philipp Witkop (London: Methuen, 1929), pp. 123–125.

landscape. Bombardment by new, heavier forms of artillery scarred the terrain with huge craters, which then became muddy, turning the landscape into a near swamp. (See the box "Into the Trenches.") Beginning early in 1915, tear gas, chlorine gas, and finally mustard gas were used by both sides. Although the development of gas masks significantly reduced its impact, the threat of poison gas added another horrible element to the experience of those who fought the war. The notions of patriotism, comradeship, duty, and glory began to seem absurd.

Although the Germans had been denied their quick victory in the west, by the end of 1914 they occupied much of Belgium and almost one-tenth of France, including major industrial areas and mines producing most of France's coal and iron. On the eastern front, the Germans had won some substantial advantages in 1914—but not a decisive victory.

The first season of fighting in the east suggested that the pattern there would not be trench warfare but rapid movement across a vast but thinly held front. When the fighting began in August, the Russians came more quickly than anticipated, confronting an outnumbered German force in a reckless invasion of East Prussia. By mid-September German forces under General Paul von Hindenburg (1847–1934) and his chief of staff, General Erich Ludendorff (1865–1937), repelled the Russian advance, taking a huge number of prisoners and seriously demoralizing the Russians.

As a result of their victory in East Prussia, Hindenburg and Ludendorff emerged as heroes, and they would play major roles in German public life thereafter. Hindenburg became chief of staff of the entire German army in August 1916, but the able and energetic Ludendorff remained at his side, and Ludendorff gradually assumed control of the whole German war effort, both military and domestic.

Seeking a Breakthrough, 1915–1917

In 1916, German leaders decided to launch a massive offensive against the great French fortress at Verdun, hoping to inflict a definitive defeat on France. The Germans gathered 1220 pieces of artillery for attack along an 8-mile front. Included were thirteen "Big Bertha" siege guns, weapons so large that nine tractors were required to position each of them; a crane was necessary to insert the shell, which weighed over a ton. The level of heavy artillery firepower that the Germans applied at Verdun was unprecedented in the history of warfare.

German forces attacked on February 21, taking the outer defenses of the fortress, and appeared poised for victory. The tide turned, however, when General Philippe Pétain (1856–1951) assumed control of the French defense at Verdun. Pétain had the patience and skill necessary to organize supplies for a long and difficult siege. Moreover, he proved able to inspire affection and confidence among his men. By July the French had repelled the German offensive, although only in December did they retake the outer defenses of the fortress. The French had held in what would prove the war's longest, most trying battle—one that killed 600,000 men on both sides. For the French the Battle of Verdun would remain the epitome of the horrors of World War I.

Meanwhile, early in July 1916, the British had led a major attack at the Somme River that was similarly bloody—and that affected Britain much as Verdun affected France. On the first day the British suffered 60,000 casualties, including 21,000 killed. Fighting continued into the fall, though the offensive proved futile. One-third of those involved, or over 1 million soldiers, ended up dead, missing, or wounded.

Dominated by the devastating battles at Verdun and the Somme, the campaigns of 1916 marked the decisive end to the high spirits of the summer of 1914. Both sides suffered huge losses apparently for nothing. By the end of 1916, the front had shifted only a few miles from its location at the beginning of the year.

The French turned to new military leadership, replacing Joffre with Robert Nivelle (1856–1924), who sought to prove himself with a new offensive during the spring of 1917. Persisting even as it became clear that this effort had no chance of success, Nivelle provoked increasing resistance among French soldiers, some of whom were refusing to follow orders by the end of May.

With the French war effort in danger of collapse, the French government replaced Nivelle with General Pétain, the hero of the defense of Verdun. Pétain re-established discipline by adopting a conciliatory approach—improving food and rest, visiting the troops in the field, listening, even dealing relatively mercifully with most of the resisters. To be sure, many of the soldiers who had participated in this near-mutiny were court-martialed, and over 3400 were convicted. But of the 554 sentenced to death, only 49 were actually executed.

1917 as a Turning Point

Meanwhile, the Germans decided to concentrate on the eastern front in 1917 in an effort to knock Russia out of the war. The German offensive helped spark revolution in Russia, and in December 1917, Russia's new regime asked for a separate peace. This freed the Germans to concentrate on the west, but by this time France and Britain had a new ally.

On April 6, 1917, the United States entered the war on the side of the Entente in response to Germany's controversial use of submarines. Germany lacked sufficient strength in surface ships to break Britain's naval blockade, so the Germans deployed submarines to interfere with shipping to Britain. Submarines, however, were too vulnerable to be able to surface and confiscate goods, so the Germans had to settle for sinking suspect ships with torpedoes. In February 1915, Germany served notice that it would torpedo not only enemy ships but also neutral ships carrying goods to Britain. This German response was harsh, but so was the British blockade, which violated a number of earlier international agreements about the rights of neutral shipping and the scope of wartime blockades.

In May 1915 a German sub torpedoed the *Lusitania*, a British passenger liner, killing almost 1200 people. Partly because 128 of those killed were Americans, U.S. President Woodrow Wilson issued a severe warning, which contributed to the German decision in September 1915 to pull back from unrestricted submarine warfare. But as German suffering under the British blockade increased, pressure steadily mounted to put the subs back into action.

The issue provoked bitter debate among German leaders. Chancellor Theobald von Bethmann-Hollweg and the civilian authorities opposed resumption out of fear it would provoke the United States to enter the war. But Ludendorff and the military prevailed, arguing that even if the United States did intervene, U.S. troops could not get to Europe in time to have a major impact. Germany announced the resumption of unrestricted submarine warfare on January 31, 1917, and the United States responded with a declaration of war on April 6. Although it would take at least a year for the American troops to arrive in force, the entry of the United States gave the Entente at least the promise of more fighting power.

THE EXPERIENCE OF TOTAL WAR

As the war dragged on, the distinction between the military and civilian spheres blurred. Suffering increased on the home front, and unprecedented governmental mobilization of society proved necessary to wage war on the scale that had come to be required. Because it became "total" in this way, the war affected not simply international relations and the power balance but also culture, society, and the patterns of everyday life.

Hardship on the Home Front

The war meant food shortages, and thus malnutrition, for ordinary people in the belligerent countries, although Britain and France, with their more favorable geographical positions, suffered considerably less than others. Germany was especially vulnerable and promptly began suffering under the British naval blockade. With military needs taking priority, the Germans encountered shortages of the chemical fertilizers, farm machinery, and draft animals necessary for agricultural production. The government began rationing bread, meat, and fats in 1915. The scarcity of foodstuffs produced sharp increases in diseases like rickets and tuberculosis and in infant and childhood mortality rates in Germany.

The need to pay for the war produced economic dislocations as well. Government borrowing covered some of the cost, but to cover the rest governments all over Europe found it more palatable to inflate the currency, by printing more money, than to raise taxes. The idea was that the enemy would be made to pay once victory had been achieved. But financing the war this way meant rising prices and severe erosion of purchasing power for ordinary people all over Europe. In both France and Germany, the labor truce of 1914 gave way to increasing strike activity during 1916.

With an especially severe winter in 1916–1917 adding to the misery, there were serious instances of domestic disorder, including strikes and food riots, in many parts of Europe during 1917. In Italy, there were major strikes in Turin and other cities over wages and access to foodstuffs. The strains of war even fanned the flames in Ireland, where an uneasy truce over the home-rule controversy had accompanied the British decision for war in 1914. Unrest built up again in Ireland, culminating in the Easter Rebellion in Dublin in 1916. The brutality with which British forces crushed the uprising intensified demands for full independence.

Domestic Mobilization

Once it became clear that the war would not be over quickly, leaders realized that the outcome would not be determined on the battlefield alone. Victory required mobilizing all of the nation's resources and energies. So World War I became a total war, involving the whole society.

The British naval blockade on Germany, which made no distinction between military and nonmilitary goods, was a stratagem characteristic of total war. The goal was to damage Germany's long-term war-making capacity. And the blockade did prove significant, partly because Germany had not made effective preparations—including stockpiling—for a long war.

By the end of 1916, Germany had developed a militarized economy, with all aspects of economic life coordinated for the war effort. Under the supervision of the military, state agencies, big business, and the trade unions were brought into close collaboration. The new system included rationing, price controls, and compulsory labor arbitration, as well as a national service law enabling the military to channel workers into jobs deemed vital to the war effort. Also, the Germans did not hesitate to exploit the economy of occupied Belgium, requisitioning foodstuffs even to the point of causing starvation among the Belgians themselves. They forced 62,000 Belgian workers to work in German factories under conditions of virtual slave labor. Although this practice was stopped in February 1917, by then nearly a thousand Belgian workers had died in German labor camps.

Although Germany presented the most dramatic example of domestic coordination, the same pattern was evident everywhere, even in France, with its economic individualism and distrust of an interventionist state. In Britain, the central figure was David Lloyd George (1863–1945), appointed to the newly created post of minister of munitions in 1915. During his year in that office, ninety-five new factories opened, soon overcoming the shortage of guns and ammunition that had impeded the British war effort until then. In fact, types of ammunition that had formerly taken a year to manufacture were now being produced in weeks, even days. His performance as munitions minister made Lloyd George seem the one person who could organize Britain for victory. He became prime minister in December 1916.

Shifting Gender Roles

The war effort quickened the long-term socioeconomic changes associated with industrialization. Government orders for war materiel fueled industrial expansion. The needs of war spawned new technologies—advances in food processing and medical treatment, for example—that would carry over into peacetime. And with so many men needed for military service, women were called on to assume new economic roles—running farms in France, for example, or working in the new munitions factories in Britain.

During the course of the war, the number of women employed in Britain rose from 3.25 million to 5 million. (See the box "Domestic Mobilization and the Role of Women.") In Italy, 200,000

Domestic Mobilization and the Role of Women

Early in 1917, the British writer Gilbert Stone published a remarkable collection of statements intended to illuminate the new experiences that British women were encountering in the workplace. The following passage by Naomi Loughnan, a well-to-do woman who worked in a munitions factory, makes it clear that the new work experience during the war opened the way to new questions about both gender and class.

Engineering mankind is possessed of the unshakable opinion that no woman can have the mechanical sense. If one of us asks humbly why such and such an alteration is not made to prevent this or that drawback to a machine, she is told, with a superior smile, that a man has worked her machine before her for years, and that therefore if there were any improvement possible it would have been made. As long as we do exactly as we are told and do not attempt to use our brains, we give entire satisfaction, and are treated as nice, good children. Any swerving from the easy path prepared for us by our males arouses the most scathing contempt in their manly bosoms. . . . Women have, however, proved that their entry into the munitions world has increased the output. Employers who forget things personal in their patriotic desire for large results are enthusiastic over the success of women in the shops. But their workmen have to be handled with the utmost tenderness and caution lest they should actually imagine it was being suggested that women could do their work equally well, given equal conditions of training—at least where muscle is not the driving force. This undercurrent of jealousy rises to the surface rather often, but as a general rule the men behave with much kindness, and are ready to help with muscle and advice whenever called upon. If eyes are very bright and hair inclined to curl, the muscle and advice do not even wait for a call.

The coming of the mixed classes of women into the factory is slowly but surely having an educative effect upon the men. "Language" is almost unconsciously becoming subdued. There are fiery exceptions who make our hair stand up on end under our close-fitting caps, but a sharp rebuke or a look of horror will often bring to book the most truculent. . . . It is grievous to hear the girls also swearing and using disgusting language. Shoulder to shoulder with the children of the slums, the upper classes are having their eyes pried open at last to the awful conditions among which their sisters have dwelt. Foul language, immorality, and many other evils are but the natural outcome of overcrowding and bitter poverty. If some of us, still blind and ignorant of our responsibilities, shrink horrified and repelled from the rougher set, the compliment is returned with open derision and ribald laughter. . . . On the other hand, attempts at friendliness from the more understanding are treated with the utmost suspicion, though once that suspicion is overcome and friendship is established, it is unshakable.

Source: Naomi Loughnan, "Munition Work," in Gilbert Stone, ed., *Women War Workers: Accounts Contributed by Representative Workers of the Work Done by Women in the More Important Branches of War Employment* (New York: Thomas Y. Crowell, [1917]), pp. 35–38.

women had war-related jobs by 1917. Women also played indispensable roles at the front, especially in nursing units. The expanded opportunities of wartime intensified the debate over the sociopolitical role of women that the movement for women's suffrage had stimulated. Some antiwar

Mobilizing Women Responding to appeals like this, women quickly become prominent in the munitions industry in Britain as elsewhere. The chance to perform valued public roles during the wartime emergency proved a watershed for many women. *(Trustees of the Imperial War Museum)*

feminists argued that women would be better able than men to prevent wars. Women should have full access to public life, not because they could be expected to respond as men did but because they had a distinctive—and valuable—role to play. At the same time, by giving women jobs and the opportunity to do many of the same things men had done, the war undermined the stereotypes that had long justified restrictions on women's political roles and life choices.

For many women, serving their country in this emergency situation afforded a new sense of accomplishment, as well as a new taste of independence. Women were now much more likely to have their own residences and go out in public on their own, eating in restaurants, even smoking and drinking. Yet while many seized new opportunities and learned new skills, women frequently had to combine paid employment with housework and child rearing, and those who left home—to serve in nursing units, for example—often felt guilty about avoiding traditional family roles.

Propaganda and the "Mobilization of Enthusiasm"

Because the domestic front was crucial to sustaining a long war of attrition, it became ever more important to shore up civilian morale as the war dragged on. The result was the "mobilization of enthusiasm"—the manipulation of collective passions by national governments on an unprecedented scale. Everywhere there was extensive censorship, even of soldiers' letters from the front. Because of concerns about civilian morale, the French press carried no news of the Battle of Verdun and its horrifying casualties. In addition, systematic propaganda included attempts to discredit the enemy, even through outright falsification.

At the outset of the war, the brutal behavior of the German armies in Belgium made it easy for the French and the British to discredit the Germans. At Louvain late in August 1914 the Germans responded to alleged Belgian sniping by shooting a number of hostages and setting the town on fire, destroying the famous old library at the university. This notorious episode led the London *Times* to characterize the Germans as "Huns," a reference to the Mongol tribe that invaded Europe in the fourth century. Stories about German soldiers eating Belgian babies began to circulate.

The unprecedented propaganda combined with the unexpected destruction to give the war an increasingly catastrophic aura. Some came to believe that real peace with an adversary so evil, so different, was simply not possible. Thus, there must be no compromise, but rather total victory, no matter what the cost. At the same time, however, war-weariness produced a tendency to seek a "white peace," a peace without victory for either side. Both sets of impulses were at work in 1917, when dramatic events in Russia changed the meaning of the war for everyone involved.

TWO REVOLUTIONS IN RUSSIA: MARCH AND NOVEMBER 1917

Strained by war, the old European order finally cracked in Russia in 1917. Revolution against the tsarist autocracy seemed at first to lay the foundations for parliamentary democracy. But by the end of the year, the Bolsheviks, the smallest and most extreme of Russia's major socialist parties, had taken power, an outcome that was hardly conceivable when the revolution began.

The Wartime Crisis of the Russian Autocracy

The Russian army performed better than many had expected during the first year of the war, and as late as June 1916, it was strong enough for a successful offensive against Austria-Hungary. Russia had industrialized sufficiently by 1914 to sustain a modern war, at least for a while, and the country's war production increased significantly by 1916. But Russia suffered from problems of leadership and organization that made it less prepared for a long war than the other belligerents. Even early in 1915, perhaps a fourth of Russia's newly conscripted troops were sent to the front without weapons, instructed to pick up rifles and supplies from the dead.

Tsar Nicholas II (1868–1918) assumed personal command of the army in August 1915, but his absence from the capital only accelerated the deterioration in government. An illiterate but charismatic Siberian monk, Grigori Rasputin (ca. 1872–1916), had won favor at court for his alleged ability to control the hemophilia of the tsar's son, Alexis, the heir to the throne. With the tsar away, Rasputin emerged as the key political power and made a shambles of the state administration. Many educated Russians wondered if pro-German elements at court were responsible for the government chaos. Asked one Duma deputy of the government's performance, "Is this stupidity, or is it treason?" Finally, late in December 1916, Rasputin was assassinated by aristocrats seeking to save the autocracy, an act that indicated how desperate the situation was becoming.

By the end of 1916, the immediate difficulties of war had combined with the strains of rapid wartime industrialization to produce a revolutionary situation in Russia. The country's urban population had increased rapidly, and now the cities faced severe food shortages. Strikes and demonstrations spread from Petrograd (the former St. Petersburg) to other cities during the first two months of 1917. In March renewed demonstrations in Petrograd, spearheaded by women protesting the lack of bread and coal, led to revolution.

The March Revolution and the Provisional Government

At first, the agitation that began in Petrograd on March 8, 1917, appeared to be just another bread riot. Even when it turned into a wave of strikes, the revolutionary parties expected it to be crushed by the Petrograd garrison. But when called out to help the police break up the demonstrations, the soldiers generally avoided firing at the strikers. Within days, they were sharing weapons and ammunition with the workers; the garrison was going over to what was now becoming a revolution.

Late in the afternoon of March 12, leaders of the strike committees, delegates elected by factory workers, and representatives of the socialist parties formed a *soviet*, or council, following the example of the revolution of 1905, when such soviets had first appeared (see page 592). Regiments of the Petrograd garrison also began electing representatives, soon to be admitted to the Petrograd Soviet, which officially became the Council of Workers' and Soldiers' Deputies. This soviet was now the ruling power in the Russian capital. It had been elected and was genuinely representative—though of a limited constituency of workers and soldiers. Following the lead of Petrograd, Russians elsewhere began forming soviets, so that over 350 local units were represented when the first All-Russian Council of Soviets met in Petrograd in April. The overwhelming majority of representatives were Mensheviks and Socialist Revolutionaries; only about one-sixth were Bolsheviks.

On March 14 a committee of the Duma, recognizing that the tsar's authority had been lost for good, persuaded Nicholas to abdicate, then formed a new provisional government. Because it derived from the Duma elected in 1907, under extremely limited suffrage, this government was supposed to be temporary and pave the way for an elected constituent assembly, which would establish fully legitimate institutions.

Russia had apparently experienced the bourgeois revolution necessary to develop a Western-style parliamentary democracy. Even from an orthodox Marxist perspective, this was the revolution to expect, and Marxists could only help consolidate bourgeois democracy. The pursuit of socialism could take place within that new political framework. But the March revolution proved only the beginning.

The provisional government had to operate with the potentially more radical Petrograd Soviet, the keystone of the network of soviets across the country, looking over its shoulder. At first the Petrograd Soviet was perfectly willing to give the provisional government a chance to govern. In this bourgeois revolution, it was not up to socialists and workers to take responsibility by participating directly in government. Even among the Bolsheviks, there was widespread support for acceptance of the new government. Although the Bolshevik leader, Vladimir Lenin, disagreed, he was in exile in Switzerland.

The provisional government took important steps toward Western-style liberal democracy, establishing universal suffrage, civil liberties, autonomy for ethnic minorities, and labor legislation, including provision for an eight-hour workday. In response to pressure from feminists, women obtained the right to vote in all elections—along with a host of civil rights including the right to equal pay. But the government failed in two key areas, fostering discontents that the Bolsheviks soon exploited. First, it persisted in fighting the war. Second, it dragged its feet on agrarian reform.

The provisional government's determination to renew the war effort stemmed from genuine concern about Russia's obligations to its allies, about the country's national honor and position among the great powers. The educated, well-to-do Russians who led the new government expected that ordinary citizens, now free, would fight with renewed enthusiasm, like the armies that had grown from the French Revolution over a century before. These leaders failed to grasp how desperate the situation of ordinary people had become.

The March revolution had begun in the cities, but in the aftermath the peasantry had moved into action as well, seizing land and sometimes burning the houses of their landlords. By midsummer, a full-scale peasant war seemed to be in the offing in the countryside, and calls for radical agrarian reform became increasingly insistent. Partly from expediency, partly from genuine concern for social justice, the provisional government promised a major redistribution of land, but it insisted that the reform be carried out legally—not by the present provisional government, but by a duly elected constituent assembly.

Calling for elections would thus seem to have been the first priority, but the new political leaders kept putting it off. As unrest grew in the countryside, the authority of the provisional government diminished and the soviets gained in stature.

The Bolsheviks Come to Power

In the immediate aftermath of the March revolution, the Bolsheviks had not seemed to differ substantially from their rivals in the socialist movement. But the situation began to change in April, when Lenin returned from exile in Switzerland, thanks partly to the help with transportation that the German military provided. The Germans assumed—correctly, it turned out—that the Bolsheviks would undermine the Russian war effort. Largely through the force of Lenin's leadership, the Bolsheviks soon assumed the initiative.

Lenin (1870–1924), born Vladimir Ilich Ulianov, came from a comfortable upper-middle-class family. He was university-educated and trained as a lawyer. After an older brother was executed in 1887 for participating in a plot against the tsar's life, Lenin followed him into revolutionary activity. He was arrested for the first time in 1895, then exiled to Siberia. After his release in 1900, he made his way to western Europe, where he remained, except for a brief return to Russia during the revolution of 1905, until the renewal of revolution in 1917.

The Bolshevik party was identified with Lenin from its beginning in 1903, when it emerged from the schism in Russian Marxist socialism. Because of his emphases, Bolshevism came to mean discipline, organization, and a special leadership role for a revolutionary vanguard. Lenin proved effective because he was a stern and somewhat forbidding figure, disciplined, fiercely intelligent, sometimes ruthless. As a Bolshevik colleague put it, Lenin was "the one indisputable leader . . . a man of iron will, inexhaustible energy, combining a fanatical faith in the movement, in the cause, with an equal faith in himself."[3]

When Lenin began taking the initiative in 1917, his reading of the situation astonished even many Bolsheviks. He held that the revolution was about to pass from the bourgeois-democratic to a socialist phase involving dictatorship of the proletariat in the form of government by the soviets. It was time, then, for active opposition to

Lenin as Leader Although he was in exile during much of 1917, Lenin's leadership was crucial to the Bolshevik success in Russia. He is shown here addressing a May Day rally in Red Square, Moscow, on May 1, 1919. *(ITAR-TASS/Sovfoto)*

the provisional government, and this meant both criticism of the war, as fundamentally imperialist, and calls for the distribution of land from the large estates to the peasants. This latter measure had long been identified with the Socialist Revolutionaries; most Bolsheviks had envisioned collectivization and nationalization instead.

Lenin believed that a Bolshevik-led revolution in Russia would provide the spark to ignite the proletarian revolution elsewhere in Europe, especially in Germany. Although some remained skeptical, Lenin's strategic vision won acceptance among most of his fellow Bolsheviks.

In April 1917 moderate socialists still had majority support in the soviets, so the Bolsheviks sought to build gradually, postponing any decisive test of strength. Events escaped the control of the Bolshevik leadership in mid-July when impatient workers, largely Bolshevik in sympathy, took to the streets of Petrograd on their own. The provisional government had no difficulty getting military units to quell the uprising, killing two hundred in the process. Though this disturbance had developed spontaneously, Bolshevik leaders felt compelled to offer public support, and this gave the government an excuse to crack down on the Bolshevik leadership. Lenin managed to escape to Finland.

With the Bolsheviks on the defensive, counterrevolutionary elements in the Russian military attempted a coup. The provisional government, now led by the young Socialist Revolutionary Alexander Kerensky (1881–1970), had to rely on whomever could offer help—including the Bolsheviks. Bolshevik propaganda led the soldiers to refuse orders from their counterrevolutionary commanders. Within days, the Bolsheviks won their first clear-cut majority in the Petrograd Soviet, then shortly gained majorities in most of the other soviets as well.

During the fall of 1917, the situation became increasingly volatile, eluding control by anyone. People looted food from shops; peasants seized land, sometimes murdering their landlords. Desertions and the murder of officers increased within the Russian military.

With the Bolsheviks at last the dominant power in the soviets, Lenin, from his hideout in Finland, began urging the Bolsheviks to prepare for armed insurrection. The task of organizing the seizure of power fell to Leon Trotsky (1870–1940), who skillfully modified Lenin's aggressive strategy by playing up its defensive character. He argued that the provisional government would continue dragging its feet, inadvertently giving right-wing officer leagues time for another counterrevolutionary coup. This notion led people who wanted simply to defend the Petrograd Soviet to support the Bolsheviks' initiative.

During the night of November 9, armed Bolsheviks and regular army regiments occupied key points in Petrograd, including railroad stations, post offices, telephone exchanges, power stations, and the national bank. Able to muster only token resistance, the provisional government collapsed. In contrast to the March revolution, which had taken about a week, the Bolsheviks took over the capital and overthrew the government literally overnight, and almost without bloodshed. A wave of popular euphoria followed. But though the Bolsheviks had taken Petrograd, they would need three more years and a civil war to extend their control across the whole Russian Empire. No one yet knew if the Bolshevik Revolution in Russia would ignite revolution elsewhere in war-weary Europe, or if the Bolshevik regime could survive in Russia on its own.

The Russian Revolution and the War

Having stood for peace throughout the revolution, the Bolsheviks promptly moved to get Russia out of the war, agreeing to an armistice with Germany in December 1917. They hoped that Russia's withdrawal would speed the collapse of the war effort on all sides and that this, in turn, would intensify the movement toward revolution elsewhere in Europe. The Russian Revolution, they believed, was but a chapter in a larger story. As Lenin noted to Trotsky, "If it were necessary for us to go under to assure the success of the German revolution, we should have to do it.

The German revolution is vastly more important than ours."[4]

The Bolsheviks hoped to spark wider revolution by demonstrating the imperialist basis of the war. They published the tsarist government's secret documents concerning the war—the treaties and understandings specifying how the spoils were to be divided in the event of victory. In doing so, the Bolsheviks hoped to show ordinary people elsewhere that this had been, all along, a war on behalf of capitalist interests. The Bolshevik initiative added fuel to the controversy already developing in all the belligerent countries over the war's purpose and significance.

THE NEW WAR AND THE ENTENTE VICTORY, 1917–1918

Because the stakes of the war changed during 1917, the outcome, once the war finally ended in November 1918, included consequences that Europeans could not have foreseen in 1914. German defeat brought revolution against the monarchy and the beginning of a new democracy. Grand new visions competed to shape the postwar world.

The Debate over War Aims

The French and British governments publicly welcomed the March revolution in Russia, partly because they expected Russia's military performance to improve under new leadership, but also because the change of regime seemed to have highly favorable psychological implications. With Russia no longer an autocracy, the war could be portrayed—and experienced—as a crusade for democracy. At the same time, the March revolution could only sow confusion among the many Germans who had understood the war as a matter of self-defense against reactionary Russia. But the November revolution required a deeper reconsideration for all the belligerents.

Entente war aims agreements, like the Treaty of London that had brought Italy into the war in 1915, had remained secret until the Bolsheviks published the tsarist documents. Products of old-style diplomacy, those agreements had been made by a small foreign policy elite within the governing circles of each country; even the elected parliaments were generally not aware of them. The debate over war aims that developed in 1917 thus became a debate over decision making as well. In addition, there were exhortations for all the parties in the war to renounce annexations and settle for a white peace. It was time to call the whole thing off and bring the soldiers home.

To counter such sentiments, the idealistic U.S. president, Woodrow Wilson (1856–1924), insisted on the potential significance of an Allied victory. First in his State of the Union speech of January 1918, and in several declarations thereafter, Wilson developed "Fourteen Points" to guide the new international order. Notable among them were open diplomacy, free trade, reduced armaments, self-determination, a league of nations, and a recasting of the colonial system, recognizing the rights of the indigenous populations.

Lenin and Wilson, then, offered radically different interpretations of the war, with radically different implications. Yet they had something in common compared to the old diplomacy. They seemed to represent a whole new approach to international relations—and the possibility of a more peaceful world. Thus they found an eager audience among the war-weary peoples of Europe.

In Germany, antiwar sentiment grew within the Social Democratic party (SPD), finally leading the antiwar faction to split off and form the Independent Socialist party (USPD) in April 1917. A large-scale debate on war aims, linked to considerations of domestic political reform, developed in the Reichstag by the summer of 1917 and culminated in the Reichstag war-aims resolution of July 19. Affirming that Germany's purposes were solely defensive, the measure passed by a solid 60 percent majority. Germany, too, seemed open to a white peace.

But just as the dramatic events of 1917 interjected important new pressures for moderation and peace, pressures also mounted in the opposite direction. War aims grew more grandiose as it began to seem that the war offered an opportunity to secure advantages for the more contentious world that would follow. The shape of the present war convinced top German officials that Germany's geography and dependence on imports made it especially vulnerable in a long war. The purpose of the war for Germany increasingly seemed the conquest of the means to fight the next war on a more favorable footing.

When Germany established the terms of peace with Russia, it became clear how radically annexationist Germany's war aims had become. The outcome of negotiations at Brest-Litovsk early in 1918 was a dictated peace that Russia finally had no choice but to accept. Germany was to annex 27 percent of Russia's European territory, including the agriculturally valuable Ukraine, 40 percent of its population, and 75 percent of its iron and coal. All the German Reichstag parties except the Socialists accepted the terms of the treaty, which produced a new wave of enthusiasm for a victorious peace.

France, less vulnerable geographically than Germany, tended to be more modest. But news of the terms the Germans had imposed at Brest-Litovsk inflamed the French, supporting the notion that France must push on to definitive victory in order to secure substantial advantages against the German menace.

The Renewal of the French War Effort

The domestic division in France that followed the failure of Nivelle's offensive reached its peak in the fall of 1917. In November, with pressure for a white peace intensifying and France's ability to continue fighting in doubt, President Raymond Poincaré called on Georges Clemenceau (1841–1929) to lead a new government. The 76-year-old Clemenceau was known as a "hawk"; his appointment portended a stepped-up prosecution of the war.

Clemenceau moved decisively on both the domestic and military levels. By cracking down on the antiwar movement—imprisoning antiwar leaders, suppressing defeatist newspapers—he stiffened morale. Choosing a new commander of all Allied forces in the west, Clemenceau bypassed Pétain and picked General Ferdinand Foch (1851–1929). From Clemenceau's perspective, Pétain was too passive, even defeatist. After some initial friction, Clemenceau let Foch have his way on the military level, and the two proved an effective leadership combination.

The German Gamble, 1918

As the campaign of 1918 began, Germany seemed in a relatively favorable military position: Russia had been knocked out at last, and American troops were yet to arrive. Moderates in Germany wanted to take advantage of the situation to work out a compromise peace. But the military leadership persuaded Emperor William II that Germany could still win a definitive victory on the western front if it struck quickly. Germany would be out of reserves by summer, so the alternative to decisive victory in the west would be total German defeat.

The German gamble almost succeeded. From March to June 1918, German forces seized the initiative in four months of sustained attacks. By May 30 they had again reached the Marne, where they had been held in 1914, and again Paris, only 37 miles away, had to be evacuated (see Map 23.1). As late as mid-July, Ludendorff remained confident of victory, but by mid-August it was becoming clear that Germany lacked the manpower to exploit its successes.

By mid-1918, American involvement was becoming a factor. On June 4, over a year after the U.S. declaration of war, American troops went into action for the first time, bolstering French forces along the Marne. It was a small operation, in which the Americans' performance was amateurish compared to that of their battle-seasoned allies. But as the Allied counterattack proceeded, 250,000 U.S. troops were arriving every month, boosting Allied morale and battlefield strength. By early August the whole western front began to roll back. With astonishing suddenness, the outcome was no longer in doubt, although most expected the war to drag on into 1919. Few realized how desperate Germany's situation had become.

Military Defeat and Political Change in Germany

In late September, Ludendorff realized that his armies could not stop the Allied advance, so he informed the government that to avoid invasion, Germany had to seek an immediate armistice. Hoping to secure favorable peace terms and to make politicians take responsibility for the defeat, Hindenburg and Ludendorff asked that a government based on greater popular support be formed. A leading moderate, Prince Max von Baden (1867–1929), became chancellor, and the Reichstag again became significant after its eclipse during the virtual dictatorship of the military. Prince Max replaced Ludendorff with General Wilhelm Groener (1867–1939), who seemed more democratic in orientation. It was clear that ending the war could not be separated from the push for political change in Germany.

After securing a written request for an armistice from Hindenburg, Prince Max sent a peace note to President Wilson early in October, asking for an armistice based on Wilson's Fourteen Points. During the month that followed, Prince Max undertook a series of measures, passed by the Reichstag and approved by the emperor, that reformed the constitution, expanding voting rights in Prussia and making the chancellor responsible to the Reichstag. At last Germany had a constitutional monarchy. President Wilson encouraged speculation that Germany could expect better peace terms if William II were to abdicate and Germany became a republic. But if it seemed likely that Germany was to become a parliamentary democracy, it was also possible to imagine a more radical change, perhaps inspired by the Russian example.

A radical outcome seemed a real possibility. As negotiations for an armistice proceeded in October 1918, the continuing war effort produced instances of mutiny in the navy and breaches of discipline in the army. By early November workers' and soldiers' councils were being formed all over the country, just as in Russia the year before. In Munich, on November 7, antiwar socialists led an uprising of workers and soldiers that expelled the king of Bavaria and proclaimed a new Bavarian republic, which sought its own peace negotiations with the Allies. In Berlin on November 9, thousands of workers took to the streets to demand an immediate peace, and the authorities could not muster enough reliable military force to move against them.

The senior army leadership grew concerned that the collapse of governmental authority would undermine the ability of army officers even to march their troops home. So Hindenburg and Groener persuaded the emperor to abdicate. Having lost the support of the army, William II accepted the inevitable and left for exile in the Netherlands.

With the German right, including the military, in disarray, and the centrist parties discredited by their support for what had become an annexationist war, the initiative passed to the socialists. But the socialists had divided in 1917, mostly over the question of response to the war. To many leftist socialists, the fact that the reformist mainstream of the SPD had supported the war for so long had discredited the party irrevocably. The most militant of these leftist socialists, led by Rosa Luxemburg (1870–1919) and Karl Liebknecht (1871–1919), envisioned using the workers' and soldiers' councils as the basis for a full-scale revolution.

Partly to head off the extreme left, SPD moderates proclaimed a parliamentary republic on November 9, just hours before the revolutionaries proclaimed a soviet-style republic. The next day the soldiers' and workers' councils in Berlin elected a provisional executive committee, to be led by the moderate socialist Friedrich Ebert (1871–1925). As the new republic sought to consolidate itself, the radical leftists continued to promote further revolution. So for Germany the end of the war meant a leap into an unfamiliar democratic republic, which had to establish itself in conditions not only of military defeat and economic hardship but also of incipient revolution on the extreme left.

Birth from military defeat was especially disabling for the new republic because the German people were so little prepared for the defeat when it came. Censorship had kept the public from any grasp of Germany's real situation, so the request for an armistice came as a shock. At no time during the war had Germany been invaded from the west, and in mid-1918 the German army had seemed on the brink of victory. It appeared inconceivable that Germany had lost on the battlefield. Thus the "stab in the back" myth, the notion that political intrigue had undermined the German military effort, developed to explain what seemed an inexplicable defeat.

THE OUTCOME AND THE IMPACT

After the armistice officially ended the fighting on November 11, 1918, those responsible for a formal peace settlement faced unprecedented challenges. The war's casualties included the Habsburg and Ottoman Empires, so the peacemakers had to deal not just with defeated adversaries but with a changed political and territorial order. And the volatile sociopolitical situation in the wake of war and revolution inevitably colored their deliberations. After all that had happened since August 1914, it was not clear what a restoration of peace and order would require.

The Costs of War

Raw casualty figures do not begin to convey the war's human toll, but they afford some sense of the magnitude of the catastrophe. Estimates differ, but it is generally agreed that from 10 to 13 million military men lost their lives, with another 20 million wounded. In addition, between 7 and 10 million civilians died as a result of the war and its hardships. In the defeated countries, food shortages and malnutrition continued well after the end of the fighting. Adding to the devastation in 1918 was a pandemic of influenza that killed 20 million people worldwide.

Germany suffered the highest number of military casualties, but France suffered the most in proportional terms. Two million Germans were killed, with another 4 million wounded. Military deaths per capita for France were roughly 15 percent higher than for Germany—and twice as severe as for Britain. Of 8 million Frenchmen mobilized, over 5 million were killed or wounded. Roughly 1.5 million French soldiers, or 10 percent of the active male population, were killed—and this in a country already concerned about demographic decline. The other belligerents also suffered in great numbers. Among the military personnel killed were 2 million Russians, 500,000 Italians, and 114,000 Americans. Especially in light of the assumptions about European superiority and progress, this unprecedented bloodletting deeply affected the European self-image. It was the worst loss of life Europe had suffered since the Black Death of the fourteenth century.

Economic costs were heavy as well. Europeans found themselves reeling from inflation and saddled with debt, especially to the United States, once the war was over. Although the immediate transition to a peacetime economy did not prove as difficult as many had feared, the war and its aftermath produced an economic disequilibrium that lingered, helping to produce a worldwide depression in 1929.

The Search for Peace

The war had begun because of an unmanageable nationality problem in Austria-Hungary, and it led not simply to military defeat for Austria-Hungary but to the abdication of the emperor and the breakup of the Habsburg monarchy. The end of the war brought bright hopes for self-determination to the Czechs, Slovaks, Poles, Serbs, and Croats. Even before the peacemakers began deliberating in January 1919, some of these groups had begun creating a new order on their own. A popular movement of Czechs and Slovaks established a Czechoslovak republic on October 29, 1918, and a new Yugoslavia and an independent Hungary also emerged from indigenous movements. Some of these new amalgams of ethnic groups would unravel in the future, for many of these countries lacked traditions of self-government that might have helped them to survive.

The triumph of a revolutionary regime in Russia immeasurably complicated the situation, because in the unsettled conditions of the former Habsburg territories, as in Germany, the revolution seemed poised to spread in the wake of defeat—precisely according to the script the Russian revolutionaries were reading to the world. Still a precarious minority within Russia in 1918, the Bolsheviks continued to bank on revolution elsewhere in Europe until 1920. Shortly after taking power, they had rechristened themselves "Communists," partly to jettison the provincial Russian term *bolshevik*, but especially to underline their departure from the old reformist socialists of the Second International. Communism meant revolution along Russian lines. Before they were suppressed, enthusiastic Communist regimes governed for brief periods in parts of Hungary and Czechoslovakia and in the German state of Bavaria.

Fears that the Russian Revolution might spread fueled foreign intervention in Russia in June 1918, when 24,000 French and British troops entered the country. As long as the war with Germany lasted, military concerns helped justify this course, but after the armistice of November 1918, the intervention became overtly anticommunist. A series of thrusts, involving troops from fourteen countries at one time or another, struck at Russia from diverse points on its huge border. That effort aided the counterrevolutionary Whites, especially members of the old elites dispossessed by the Bolsheviks, who waged a civil war against the communists from 1918 to 1920. Although there was never a coordinated strategy between the Whites and the foreign troops, foreign intervention was intended to help topple the new regime.

The fourth prewar regime to disappear was the Ottoman Empire, which had controlled much of the Middle East in 1914. The Arab revolt against the Turks that developed in the Arabian peninsula in 1916 did not achieve its major military aims, though it endured, causing some disruption to the Turkish war effort. Its success was due partly to the collaboration of a young British officer, T. E. Lawrence (1888–1935), who proved an effective military leader and an impassioned advocate of the Arab cause. The support that Britain had offered the Arabs suggested that independence, perhaps even a single Arab kingdom, might follow from a defeat of the Ottoman Empire.

But British policy toward the Arabs was uncertain and contradictory. Concerned about the Suez Canal, the British government sought to tighten its control in Egypt by declaring it a protectorate in 1914. British and French diplomats agreed on a division of the Ottoman territories in the Middle East into colonial spheres of influence. France would control Syria and Lebanon, while Britain would rule Palestine and Mesopotamia, or present-day Iraq.

Potentially complicating the situation in the region was Zionism, the movement to establish a Jewish state in Palestine. Led by Chaim Weizmann (1874–1952), a remarkable Russian-born British chemist, Zionists reached an important milestone when British foreign secretary Arthur Balfour (1848–1930) cautiously announced, in the Balfour Declaration of November 1917, that the British government "looked with favor" on the prospect of a "Jewish home" in Palestine. At this point, British leaders sympathetic to Zionism saw no conflict in embracing the cause of the Arabs against the Ottoman Turks at the same time; indeed, Arabs and Jews, each seeking self-determination, could be expected to collaborate.

In the heat of war, the British established their policy for the former Ottoman territories of the Middle East without careful study. Thus, they made promises and agreements that were not entirely compatible.

The Peace Settlement

The peace conference opened in Paris in January 1919. Its labors led to five separate treaties, with each of the five defeated states, known collectively as the Paris peace settlement. The first and most significant was the Treaty of Versailles with Germany, signed in the Hall of Mirrors of the Versailles Palace on June 28, 1919. Treaties were also worked out, in turn, with Austria, Bulgaria, Hungary, and finally Turkey, in August 1920.

This was to be a dictated, not a negotiated, peace. Germany and its allies were excluded, as was renegade Russia. Having won the war, France, Britain, the United States, and Italy were to call the shots on their own, with the future of Europe and much of the world in the balance. However, spokesmen for many groups—from Slovaks and Croats to Arabs, Jews, and pan-Africanists—were in Paris as well, seeking a hearing for their causes. Both the Arab Prince Faisal (1885–1933), who would later become king of Iraq, and Colonel T. E. Lawrence were there to plead for an independent Arab kingdom. (See the box "Encounters with the West: Prince Faisal at the Peace Conference.") The African American leader W. E. B. Du Bois (1868–1963), who took his Ph.D. at Harvard in 1895, led a major pan-African congress in Paris concurrently with the peace conference.

The fundamental challenge for the peacemakers was to reconcile the conflicting visions of the postwar world that had emerged by the end of the war. U.S. President Wilson represented the promise of a new order of peace and cooperation. Clemenceau, now the French prime minister, stressed that only a permanent preponderance of French military power over Germany, and not some utopian league of nations, could guarantee a lasting peace. The negotiations at Paris centered on this fundamental difference between Wilson and Clemenceau. Although Britain's Lloyd George took a hard line on certain issues, he also sought to mediate, helping engineer the somewhat awkward compromise that resulted. When, after the peace conference, he encountered criticism for the outcome, Lloyd George replied, "I think I did as well as might be expected, seated as I was between Jesus Christ and Napoleon Bonaparte."[5]

In Article 231 of the final treaty, the peacemakers assigned responsibility for the war to Germany and its allies. The treaty forced Germany to pay reparations to reimburse the victors for the costs of the war; Article 231, the so-called "War Guilt Clause," seemed to establish a moral basis for these exactions. The determination to make Germany pay for what had become an enormously expensive war was one of the factors militating against a compromise peace in 1917. Thus the peacemakers decided to fix a reparations responsibility, although the amount to be paid was not established until 1921.

In addition, Germany was forced to dismantle much of its military apparatus. The treaty severely restricted the size of the German army and navy, and Germany was forbidden to manufacture or possess military aircraft, submarines, tanks, heavy artillery, or poison gas. France took back Alsace and Lorraine, the provinces it had lost to Germany in 1871 (Map 23.2). But for France, the crucial security provision was the treatment of the adjacent Rhineland section of Germany itself. For fifteen years Allied troops were to occupy the west bank of the Rhine River in Germany—the usual military occupation of a defeated adversary. But this would be only temporary. The long-term advantage for France was the permanent demilitarization of all German territory west of the Rhine and a strip of 50 kilometers along its east bank.

French interests also helped shape the settlement in east-central Europe. Wilsonian principles called for self-determination, but in this area of great ethnic complexity, ethnic differences were not readily sorted out geographically. So that Germany would again face potential enemies from both east and west, the French envisioned building a network of allies starting with the new Poland, created from Polish territories formerly in the German, Russian, and Austro-Hungarian Empires. That network might come to include Czechoslovakia, Yugoslavia, and Romania as well. These states would be weak enough to remain under French influence but, taken together, strong enough to replace Russia as a force against Germany.

The new Czechoslovakia not only was an amalgam of Czechs and Slovaks but also included Germans and Magyars. Indeed, Germans, mostly from the old Bohemia, made up 22 percent of the population of Czechoslovakia. Yugoslavia had an even more diverse population. French policymakers were so determined to foster a strong Czechoslovakia and Yugoslavia that they ordered the

ENCOUNTERS WITH THE WEST

Prince Faisal at the Peace Conference

With the war nearing its end in October 1918, British authorities permitted Faisal ibn-Husayn (1885–1933) to set up a provisional Arab state, with its capital at Damascus. In the memorandum of January 1919 that follows, Faisal outlined the Arab position, mixing pride and assertiveness with a recognition that the Arabs would continue to need the support and help of Western powers.

We believe that our ideal of Arab unity in Asia is justified beyond need of argument. If argument is required, we would point to the general principles accepted by the Allies when the United States joined them, to our splendid past, to the tenacity with which our race has for 600 years resisted Turkish attempts to absorb us, and, in a lesser degree, to what we tried our best to do in this war as one of the Allies. . . .

We believe that Syria, an agricultural and industrial area thickly peopled with sedentary classes, is sufficiently advanced politically to manage her own internal affairs. We feel also that foreign technical advice and help will be a most valuable factor in our national growth. We are willing to pay for this help in cash; we cannot sacrifice for it any part of the freedom we have just won for ourselves by force of arms.

. . . The world wishes to exploit Mesopotamia rapidly, and we therefore believe that the system of government there will have to be buttressed by the men and material resources of a great foreign Power. We ask, however, that the Government be Arab, in principle and spirit, the selective rather than the elective principle being necessarily followed in the neglected districts, until time makes the broader basis possible. . . .

In Palestine the enormous majority of the people are Arabs. The Jews are very close to the Arabs in blood, and there is no conflict of character between the two races. In principles we are absolutely at one. Nevertheless, the Arabs cannot risk assuming the responsibility of holding level the scales in the clash of races and religions that have, in this one province, so often involved the world in difficulties. They would wish for the effective super-position of a great trustee. . . .

In our opinion, if our independence be conceded and our local competence established, the natural influences of race, language, and interest will soon draw us together into one people; but for this the Great Powers will have to ensure us open internal frontiers, common railways and telegraphs, and uniform systems of education. To achieve this they must lay aside the thought of individual profits, and of their old jealousies. In a word, we ask you not to force your whole civilisation upon us, but to help us to pick out what serves us from your experience. In return we can offer you little but gratitude.

Source: J. C. Hurewitz, *Diplomacy in the Near and Middle East: A Documentary Record: 1914–1956* (Princeton, N.J.: D. Van Nostrand, 1956), vol. 2, pp. 38–39.

French police to force the spokesmen for Slovak and Croat separatism to leave Paris. Thus, Poland, Czechoslovakia, Yugoslavia, and Romania ended up as large as possible. Austria, Hungary, and Bulgaria, on the other hand, were diminished. What remained of Austria, the German part of the old Habsburg empire, was prohibited from choosing to join Germany.

Concern to contain and weaken Communist Russia was also at work in the settlement

Boundaries of German, Russian, and Austro-Hungarian empires in 1914
Areas lost by Austro-Hungarian Empire
Areas lost by Russian Empire
Areas lost by German Empire
Areas lost by Bulgaria
Areas lost by Ottoman Empire
Demilitarized Zones
Boundaries of 1926
Areas controlled under mandates from the League of Nations, 1920
NORWAY
SWEDEN
FINLAND
Oslo
Helsinki
Stockholm
Leningrad (St. Petersburg)
Tallinn
ESTONIA
North Sea
GREAT BRITAIN
DENMARK
Copenhagen
Baltic Sea
Riga
LATVIA
Memel
LITHUANIA
Vilnius
NETHERLANDS
Amsterdam
Danzig
POLISH CORRIDOR
EAST PRUSSIA
GERMANY
RUSSIAN EMPIRE
(Became Union of Soviet Socialist Republics, 1922)
Volga
Brussels
BELGIUM
RUHR
Cologne
Berlin
POLAND
Warsaw
Paris
Seine
LUX.
Weimar
Frankfurt
Rhine
Elbe
Oder
Vistula
FRANCE
LORRAINE
ALSACE
Strasbourg
Prague
CZECHOSLOVAKIA
GALICIA
Kiev
Don
Dnieper
Ural
Loire
Bern
SWITZ.
Geneva
Vienna
AUSTRIA
S. TYROL
Locarno
Milan
Po
Venice
Rhône
Budapest
HUNGARY
BESSARABIA
Trieste
Zagreb
CROATIA
ROMANIA
Genoa
Rapallo
Belgrade
ITALY
YUGOSLAVIA
Bucharest
Danube
Corsica
Rome
SERBIA
BULGARIA
Sofia
MONTENEGRO
(To Yugoslavia 1921)
Black Sea
Caspian Sea
Batum
Baku
Sardinia
Naples
ALBANIA
Kars
Istanbul
(Constantinople)
Ankara
TURKEY
Tabriz
GREECE
Sicily
Izmir
(Smyrna)
Athens
PERSIA
(IRAN)
Annexed by Turkey 1939
Aleppo
TUNISIA
(French)
Mediterranean Sea
SYRIA
(French Mandate)
Tigris
Euphrates
Crete
Cyprus
(Gr. Br.)
Baghdad
IRAQ
(MESOPOTAMIA)
(British Mandate)
Kut el Amara
Beirut
Damascus
PALESTINE
(British Mandate)
Amman
Jerusalem
TRANSJORDAN
(British Mandate)
Basra
KUWAIT
(Gr. Br.)
Suez Canal
Cairo
NEUTRAL ZONES
NEJD
(SAUDI ARABIA)
LIBYA
(Italian)
EGYPT
(Independent 1922)
Red Sea
Nile
Riyadh
Medina
0 200 400 Km.
0 200 400 Mi.

in east-central Europe. A band of states in east-central Europe, led by France, could serve not only as a check to Germany but also as a shield against the Russian threat. Romania's aggrandizement came partly at the expense of the Russian Empire, as did the creation of the new Poland. Finland, Latvia, Estonia, and Lithuania, all part of the Russian empire for over a century, now became independent states (see Map 23.2).

The overall settlement cost Germany almost 15 percent of its prewar territory, including major iron- and coal-producing regions, as well as about 10 percent of its prewar population. But the great bitterness that developed in Germany over the terms of the peace stemmed above all from a sense of betrayal. In requesting an armistice, German authorities had appealed to Wilson, who seemed to be saying that the whole prewar international system, not one side or the other, had been to blame for the current conflict. In 1919, however, the peacemakers treated Germany as the guilty party, greatly intensifying the sting of defeat.

Although Wilson had been forced to compromise with French interests in dealing with east-central Europe, he achieved a potentially significant success in exchange—the establishment of the League of Nations. According to the League covenant worked out by April, disputes among member states were to be settled no longer by war but by mechanisms established by the League. Other members were to participate in sanctions, from economic blockade to military action, against a member that violated League provisions.

Map 23.2 The Impact of the War: The Territorial Settlement in Europe and the Middle East The defeat of Russia, Austria-Hungary, Germany, and Ottoman Turkey opened the way to major changes in the map of east-central Europe and the Middle East. A number of new nations emerged in east-central Europe, while in the Arab world the end of Ottoman rule meant not independence but new roles for European powers.

Wider Consequences

How could Wilsonian hopes for a new international order be squared with the imperialist system, which seemed utterly at odds with the ideal of self-determination? As Mohammed Ali Duse had anticipated in 1914 (see page 597), the war had sown the seeds of dramatic change. Elites among the colonial peoples tended to support the war effort in the hopes of achieving greater autonomy. The Indian leader Mohandas Gandhi (1869–1948), for example, who had been educated in the West and admitted to the English bar in 1889, actively supported the British war effort, even helping recruit Indians to fight on the British side. But his aim was to speed Indian independence, and he led demonstrations that embarrassed the British during the war. After over a century of British rule, the war unleashed expectations and demands that led the British, in 1917, to promise home rule for India.

Colonial peoples participated directly in the war on both sides. In sub-Saharan Africa, for example, German-led Africans fought against Africans under British or French command. France brought colonial subjects from West and North Africa into front-line service during the war. The experience expanded political consciousness among the peoples subject to European imperialism.

Duse's *African Times and Orient Review* found reason for optimism in March 1917: "[A] Franco-British success will mean a greater freedom of the peoples we represent than they have previously experienced. The once despised black man is coming to the front in the battle for freedom, and the freedom which he helps to win for the white man, must also be meted out to him when the day of reckoning arrives."[6] The same line of thinking led China and Siam (now Thailand) to associate with the Allied side in 1917, in an effort to win international stature and thereby eventually to regain their lost sovereignty. China sent 200,000 people to work in France to help ease France's wartime labor shortage.

German colonies and Ottoman territories were not simply taken over by the victors, in the old-fashioned way, but came under the authority of the League, which assigned them as mandates to one of the victorious powers, which was to report back to the League annually. There were various classes of mandates, based on how prepared for sovereignty the area was taken to be. In devising this system, the Western powers formally recognized for the first time that non-Western peoples under Western influence had rights and that, in principle, they were progressing toward independence.

Still, the mandate approach to the colonial question was a halting departure at best. Although Britain granted considerable sovereignty to Iraq in 1932, the victorious powers generally operated as before, assimilating the new territories into their existing empires. Given the hopes raised in the Arab world during the war, this outcome produced a sense of betrayal among Arab leaders, who had expected complete independence.

The Chinese also felt betrayed. The victors acquiesced in special rights for Japan in China, causing a renewed sense of humiliation among Chinese elites and provoking a wave of popular demonstrations. In this instance, Western leaders were allowing a non-Western power, Japan, access to the imperial club, but they were hardly departing from imperialism. Those whose political consciousness had been raised by the war came to believe not only that colonialism should end, but that the colonial peoples would themselves have to take the lead in ending it.

In the United States, debate arose over the American role as President Wilson sought Senate ratification of the peace treaty. Wilson's opponents worried about U.S. commitments to France and Britain and that League membership would compromise U.S. sovereignty. An isolationist backlash had developed as Americans increasingly questioned whether the United States had been wise to become involved, for the first time, in a war in Europe. Late in 1919, at the height of the debate, Wilson suffered a disabling stroke. The Senate then refused to ratify the peace treaty, thereby keeping the United States out of the League of Nations. By 1920 the United States seemed to be pulling back from the leadership role it had been poised to play in 1918.

During the peace conference, a member of the British delegation, the economist John Maynard Keynes (1883–1946), resigned to write *The Economic Consequences of the Peace* (1920), which helped undermine confidence in the whole settlement. Keynes charged that the vindictive policy of the French, by crippling Germany with a punishing reparations burden, threatened the European economy and thus the peace of Europe over the long term. The lack of consensus about the legitimacy of the peace profoundly increased the postwar sense of disillusionment.

After the war was over, many of those who had fought it felt a sense of ironic betrayal; their prewar upbringing, the values and assumptions they had inherited, had not equipped them to make sense of what they had lived through. Beginning in the late 1920s a wave of writings about the war appeared. Many were memoirs, such as *Goodbye to All That* by the English writer Robert Graves (1895–1985) and *Testament of Youth* by Vera Brittain (1893–1970), who had served as a British army nurse at the front. The most famous exploration of the war was the antiwar novel *All Quiet on the Western Front* (1929) by German writer Erich Maria Remarque (1898–1970), which sold 2.5 million copies in twenty-five languages in its first eighteen months in print.

Although Remarque had seen front-line action, his novel said more about the cynical mood after the war than it did about the actual experience of those in the trenches. By the end of the 1920s an element of mythmaking was creeping into these efforts to make sense of the war experience. Still, there was something undeniably genuine in the laments of loss of innocence, in the sense of belonging to a "lost generation," that marked much of this writing. Not only were many friends dead or maimed for life, but all the sacrifices seemed to have been in vain.

What followed from the war, most fundamentally, was a sense that Western civilization was neither as secure nor as superior as it had seemed. The celebrated French poet Paul Valéry (1871–1945), speaking at Oxford shortly after the war, observed that "we modern civilizations have learned to recognize that we are mortal like the others. We had heard . . . of whole worlds vanished, of empires foundered. . . . Elam, Nineveh, Babylon were vague and splendid names; the total ruin of these worlds, for us, meant as little as did their existence. But France, England, Russia . . . these names, too, are splendid. . . . And now we see that the abyss of history is deep enough to bury all the world."[7] Valéry went on to warn that the transition to peace would be even more difficult and disorienting than the war itself. So traumatic might be the convulsion that Europe might be shown up for what it was in fact—a pathetically small corner of the world, a mere cape on the Asiatic landmass. Astounding words for a European, yet even Valéry, for all his foresight, could not anticipate what Europe would go through in the decades to follow.

SUMMARY

Europe was optimistic on the eve of war. After a century of relative peace and apparent progress, people everywhere believed that the war would be brief, purifying, and jubilantly successful. The nations of the Triple Entente and the Central Powers all believed that the war would confirm their own cultural, technological, and even racial superiority. Instead, in the west, trench warfare gave the defense the advantage, creating a tedious and traumatic stalemate that stretched over four years. In the east, the war produced an even more shocking outcome: the Russian Revolution.

For all the belligerent countries, this long war of attrition was made possible by industrial technology, but it was ultimately dependent on the will of the people. As such, controlling popular opinion became crucial to the war effort. Soldiers had to be kept obedient, dedicated, and optimistic. Women had to be recruited for munitions work and other previously masculinized labors. Colonial subjects of the European nations were also drawn into the war with promises of recognition and emancipation.

People wanted to believe that the world would be better after the war and that their nation would somehow be reimbursed for the emotional, physical, and financial tolls that the war had taken. When U.S. troops finally broke the stalemate, its allies could believe that such recompense was on the way. Before long, however, it became clear that most wartime wishes would not soon be fulfilled. The serious discrepancies between expectation or perception and reality would have profound consequences.

As the Treaty of Versailles demonstrated, after World War I the chief struggle in the West would be between those who would attempt to recreate the prewar world and the values that it now seemed to represent and those who wanted to create a new world with new values. In either case, the disintegration of the old order produced a sense of vulnerability hard to overcome. The vast casualties, the terrifying new weapons, the destruction of monuments—all gave the war an apocalyptic aura that heightened its psychological impact.

By destroying the Habsburg empire and the imperial regime in Germany, World War I seemed to have solved the immediate problems that caused it. Yet the war also produced a new set of tumultuous circumstances. The Russians had produced a communist revolution and were angling for other countries to join them. In many nations, women's demand for the vote could no longer be ignored after their great service and sacrifice. New nations were born out of the peace settlement, while others were pressing for recognition. And still, for most, the magnitude of violence itself created the greatest of the changes: A deep sense of disillusionment and doubt replaced Europe's optimism and expectation of eternal progress.

NOTES

1. From *African Times and Orient Review*, August 4, 1914; quoted in Imanuel Geiss, *The Pan-African Movement*, translated by Ann Keep (London: Methuen & Co., 1974), pp. 229–230.
2. Thus wrote the German poet Ivan Goll in 1917; quoted in Modris Eksteins, *Rites of Spring: The Great War and the Birth of the Modern Age* (Boston: Houghton Mifflin, 1989), p. 144.
3. By A. N. Potresov, as quoted in Richard Pipes, *The Russian Revolution* (New York: Random House, Vintage, 1991), p. 348.

4. Quoted in Koppel S. Pinson, *Modern Germany: Its History and Civilization*, 2d ed. (New York: Macmillan, 1966), p. 337.
5. Quoted in Walter Arnstein, *Britain Yesterday and Today: 1830 to the Present*, 6th ed. (Lexington, Mass.: D. C. Heath, 1992), p. 266.
6. Unsigned editorial, *African Times and Orient Review*, March 1917; quoted in Geiss, *The Pan-African Movement*, p. 479, n. 2.
7. Paul Valéry, *Variety*, 1st series (New York: Harcourt, Brace, 1938), pp. 3–4.

SUGGESTED READING

Becker, Jean-Jacques. *The Great War and the French People*. 1985. A landmark study of the relationship between battlefield fortunes and wider public responses as France bore the brunt of the fighting during World War I.

Brayborn, Gail, and Penny Summerfield. *Out of the Cage: Women's Experiences in Two World Wars*. 1987. A comparative study of the impact of the two world wars on women, relying especially on direct testimony.

Eksteins, Modris. *Rites of Spring: The Great War and the Birth of the Modern Age*. 1989. An original and provocative exploration of the relationship between culture and the war experience.

Ellis, John. *Eye-Deep in Hell: Trench Warfare in World War I*. 1989. A compelling account of life and death in the trenches, covering topics from trench construction to eating, drinking, and sex. Includes striking photographs.

Fitzpatrick, Sheila. *The Russian Revolution, 1917–1932*. 2d ed. 1994. An ideal introductory work that places the events of 1917 in the sweep of Russian history.

Fromkin, David. *A Peace to End All Peace: The Fall of the Ottoman Empire and the Creation of the Modern Middle East*. 1989. A detailed but gripping account of the role of the war and the peace process in transforming the lands of the Ottoman Empire.

Fussell, Paul. *The Great War and Modern Memory*. 1975. A widely admired study of the attempts to forge the new language, through literature, necessary to make sense of the British war experience.

Hanna, Martha. *The Mobilization of Intellect: French Scholars and Writers During the Great War*. 1996. Challenges the widespread notion that World War I galvanized a unified assault of French intellectuals against German culture.

Higonnet, Margaret Randolph, et al., eds. *Behind the Lines: Gender and the Two World Wars*. 1987. Sophisticated essays on the role of women during the two world wars, concerned especially with the impact of war on gender definition.

Hough, Richard. *The Great War at Sea, 1914–1918*. 1983. A survey of naval operations, featuring the British navy. Includes photographs.

King, Jere Clemens, ed. *The First World War*. 1972. A superior documentary history, with selections on an array of topics, from military operations to diplomacy to the role of women in the war.

Kocka, Jürgen. *Facing Total War: German Society, 1914–1918*. 1984. Using concepts of class and monopoly capitalism in a flexible way, a leading German historian analyzes the impact of the war on German society.

Leed, Eric J. *No Man's Land: Combat and Identity in World War I*. 1979. A pioneering study of the experience of World War I, which explores its challenge to masculine identity.

Mayer, Arno J. *The Politics and Diplomacy of Peacemaking: Containment and Counterrevolution at Versailles, 1918–1919*. 1967. Emphasizes the impact of domestic political concerns and fears of spreading revolution.

Mosse, George L. *Fallen Soldiers: Reshaping the Memory of the World Wars*. 1990. Shows how the encounter with mass death in World War I led to new ways of sanctifying and justifying war.

Service, Robert. *Lenin: A Political Life*. 3 vols. 1985, 1991, 1995. A landmark, readable biography that does justice both to Lenin's ruthlessness and to the visionary purpose that made him one of the decisive actors of the twentieth century.

Sharp, Alan. *The Versailles Settlement: Peacemaking in Paris, 1919*. 1991. A brief, clear, and balanced overview that seeks to do justice to the magnitude of the task the peacemakers faced.

Von Laue, Theodore H. *Why Lenin? Why Stalin? Why Gorbachev? The Rise and Fall of the Soviet System*. 3d ed. 1993. A widely used survey. Accents the larger context of international preoccupations that helped shape the revolution and the system that developed from it.

Winter, J. M. *The Experience of World War I*. 1989. An ideal introductory work that proceeds via concentric circles from politicians to generals to soldiers to civilians, then to the war's long-term effects.

———. *Sites of Memory, Sites of Mourning*. 1995. Using an effective comparative approach, a leading authority argues that Europeans relied on relatively traditional means of making sense of the bloodletting of World War I.

CHAPTER 24

From Stability to Crisis, 1919–1939

In 1925, Josephine Baker (1906–1975), a black entertainer from St. Louis, moved to Paris and quickly became a singing and dancing sensation. Also a favorite in Germany, she was the most famous of the African American entertainers who took the cultural capitals of Europe by storm during the 1920s. After the disillusioning experience of war, many Europeans found a valuable infusion of vitality in Baker's jazz music, exotic costumes, and "savage," uninhibited dancing.

The attraction to African Americans as primitive, vital, and sensual reflected a good deal of racial stereotyping, and black performers like Baker sometimes played to them. But there really was something fresh and uninhibited about American culture, especially its African American variant. Baker herself was a woman of great sophistication who became a French citizen in 1937, participated in progressive causes, and was decorated for her secret intelligence work in the anti-Nazi resistance during World War II.

The prominence of African Americans in European popular culture during the 1920s was part of a wider infatuation with all things American. As expatriates gathered in the Paris salon of the American writer Gertrude Stein (1874–1946), a new set of cultural values began to take shape. Old conventions had been shattered, and Stein represented the artistic innovation and social freedom that had appeared in the wake of the war.

But when the Great Depression began at the end of the decade, serious sociopolitical strains became evident throughout most of the Western world, and the open culture of the 1920s grew tense and constricted. The mechanisms used to realign the international economy after World War I seemed effective for most of the 1920s, but by 1929, they were beginning to backfire. The promise of democracy, so bright in the 1920s, was beginning to darken.

The Sensational Josephine Baker A native of St. Louis, the African American Josephine Baker moved to Paris in 1925 and quickly created a sensation in both France and Germany as a cabaret dancer and singer. Playing on the European association of Africa with the wild and uninhibited, she featured unusual poses and exotic costumes. *(Hulton-Getty/Liaison)*

New forms of government were emerging in Stalinist Russia and fascist Italy—both of which relied heavily on violence and intimidation. In Germany, the rise to power of the Nazi leader Adolf Hitler intensified the ideological polarization in Europe, and his policies produced a series of diplomatic crises that eventually led to a new European war.

Questions and Ideas to Consider

- To many, the rise of mass society meant cultural innovation and a democracy more responsive to the will of the people. Others saw only a debasement of cultural standards. Discuss some of the specific positions on both sides of this debate.
- Who was the "new woman," and what did she symbolize during the prosperous 1920s? How were women represented in the anxious years after 1929?
- Because its failure led to Nazism, the Weimar Republic has been much scrutinized. What might its leaders have done differently to produce a more viable democracy? Are the republic's immediate problems enough to explain its failure, or was Germany's history of authoritarianism crucial as well?
- What were the central positions of Nazism? Did Nazism succeed electorally because most people agreed with these positions?
- Compare the regimes of fascist Italy, Nazi Germany, and Stalinist Russia. Were they all totalitarian? In what ways can it be said that Nazi Germany had more in common with Stalinist Russia than it did with fascist Italy?

ECONOMY AND SOCIETY IN THE INTERWAR YEARS

Readjustment to peace caused wild economic swings just after the war, yet by the later 1920s, Europe was enjoying renewed prosperity. Culture also seemed vibrant and optimistic in the 1920s. By the close of the decade, however, Europe was in crisis. In the wake of the Wall Street crash of 1929, a cataclysmic depression struck the world economy. With the Great Depression came extraordinary suffering for many and great anxiety for many others. The creation of a "mass society"—through literacy, democracy, and technology—had seemed progressive and emancipatory in the 1920s. In the 1930s, many began to worry that the masses were too easily led and deceived, and too eager to lower cultural standards.

New Trends in Labor and Lifestyle

The wartime spur to industrialization produced a large increase in the industrial labor force all over Europe, and a good deal of labor unrest accompanied the transition to peacetime. Some of that agitation challenged factory discipline and authority relationships. Business leaders and publicists fostered a new cult of efficiency and productivity, partly by adapting Taylorism and Fordism, influential American ideas about mass production. On the basis of his "time-and-motion" studies of factory labor, Frederick W. Taylor (1856–1915) argued that breaking down assembly line production into small, repetitive tasks was the key to maximizing efficiency. In contrast, Henry Ford (1863–1947) linked the gospel of mass production to mass consumption. In exchange for accepting the discipline of the assembly line, the workers should be paid well enough to be able to buy the products they produced—even automobiles. Not all Europeans welcomed the new ideas from America. In the new cult of efficiency some saw an unwelcome sameness and a debasement of cultural ideals.

In light of the major role women had played in the wartime labor force, the demand for women's suffrage proved irresistible in Britain, Germany, and much of Europe, though not yet in France or Italy. Although female employment remained higher than before the war, many women were pushed out of the work force to make jobs available to the returning soldiers. Working-class women continued to work, of necessity, but often lost their higher-paying war jobs. Still, many women felt freer as fashion and culture in the 1920s and 1930s deliberately broke away from the stultifying bourgeois respectability that had so constrained the actions of women. The "new woman," with short hair, a job, and her own apartment, was a central symbol of modernity. Dance crazes and jazz concerts defined a new culture of freedom in which women could function with considerable autonomy.

The desire to be "modern" also produced a more open, unsentimental, even scientific discussion of sexuality and reproduction. The new "rationalization of sexuality" fed demands that governments provide access to sex counseling, birth control, and even abortion as they assumed ever greater responsibilities for promoting public health. This direction was especially prominent in Germany, although German innovators learned from experiments in the new Soviet Union and from the birth control movement that Margaret Sanger (1883–1966) was spearheading in the United States. The more open and tolerant attitude toward sexuality fostered the development of a gay subculture, prominent

CHAPTER CHRONOLOGY

March 1919	Founding of the Italian fascist movement
November 1920	End of fighting in the Russian civil war
October 1922	Mussolini becomes Italian prime minister
January 1924	First Labour government in Britain
	Death of Lenin
August 1924	Acceptance of the Dawes Plan on German reparations
October 1925	Locarno Agreement
May 1926	Beginning of general strike in Britain
August 1929	Acceptance of the Young Plan on German reparations
October 1929	U.S. stock market crash leads to Great Depression
January 1933	Hitler becomes German chancellor
March 1935	Hitler announces rearmament in defiance of the Versailles treaty
October 1935	Italy invades Ethiopia
July 1936	Beginning of the Spanish civil war

in the vibrant cabaret scene that emerged in Berlin during the 1920s.

Arts and Leisure in the "Roaring Twenties"

As the new prosperity spread the fruits of industrialization more widely, ordinary people increasingly set the cultural tone, partly through new mass media like film and radio. To some, the advent of mass society portended a welcome revitalization of culture and a more authentic kind of democracy, while others saw only a decline in standards and a susceptibility to populist demagoguery.

With the eight-hour day increasingly the norm, growing attention was devoted to leisure. More and more people began to have the time and means to take vacations. European beach resorts grew crowded. An explosion of interest in soccer among Europeans paralleled the growth of baseball and college football in the United States. Huge stadiums were built across Europe.

During the early 1920s radio became a commercial venture, reaching a mass audience in Europe, as in the United States. Although movies had begun to emerge as vehicles of popular entertainment before the war, they came into their own during the 1920s, when the names of film stars became household words for the first time. The rapid development of film showed that new, more accessible media could nurture extraordinary innovation. Germany led the way with such films as *Metropolis* (1927) and *The Blue Angel* (1930), but the Russian Sergei Eisenstein (1898–1948) became perhaps the most admired filmmaker of the era with *Potemkin* (1925), his brilliant portrayal of the Russian revolution of 1905. And American film was on the rise: Marlene Dietrich (1901–1992) was among a number of German film celebrities who went to Hollywood.

Perhaps the quintessential positive symbol of the postwar period was air travel. The new technology symbolized freedom and possibility, and the American pilots Charles Lindbergh (1902–1974) and Amelia Earhart (1897–1937) captured the European imagination with their bravery. Earhart's feminism won her many fans as well. It seemed that there still were heroes, despite the ironies of the war and the ambiguities of the peace.

Cultural Anxiety and Alienation

World War I had accelerated the long-term "modernization" process toward large industries, cities, and bureaucracies, and toward mass politics, society, and culture. That process was positive, even liberating, in certain respects, but it was also disruptive and disturbing. Thus a wide variety of concerns were expressed by intellectuals and artists in the years between the two world wars.

Many artists and writers attempted to capture the agonies of the war. The German artist Käthe Kollwitz (1867–1945) portrayed in sculpture and woodcuts the intense emotions of bereaved parents and orphaned children. Her own son had died in the war, and her images came to represent the grief and exhaustion of the era.

While Kollwitz depicted the ordeals of the masses, others began to worry over their character—and the fate of the culture they now controlled. In *Revolt of the Masses* (1930), the influential Spanish thinker José Ortega y Gasset (1883–1955) concluded that ordinary people were intolerant and illiberal, incapable of creating standards, and content with the least common denominator. Communism and fascism indicated the violence and intolerance of the new mass age. But Ortega found the same tendencies in American-style democracy.

Concern with cultural decline was widespread. To Sigmund Freud, the eruption of violence and hatred during the war and after indicated a deep, instinctual problem in the human makeup. In his gloomy essay *Civilization and Its Discontents* (1930), he suggested that the progress of civilization entails the bottling up of aggressive instincts, which are directed inward as guilt or left to erupt in violent outbursts.

The sense that there is something incomprehensible, even nightmarish, about modern civilization, with its ever more complex bureaucracies, technologies, and cities, found vivid expression in the works of the Czech Jewish writer Franz Kafka (1883–1924), most notably in the novels *The Trial* and *The Castle*, published posthumously in the mid-1920s. In a world that claimed to be increasingly rational, Kafka's individual is the lonely, fragile plaything of forces utterly beyond reason, comprehension, and control. In such a world, the quest for law, or meaning, or God is futile and ridiculous.

While some sought renewal from within the tradition, others insisted that a more radical break was needed—but also that the elements for a viable new cultural tradition were available. Reflecting on the situation of women writers in 1928, the British novelist Virginia Woolf (1882–1941) showed how women in the past had suffered from the absence of a tradition of writing by women. By the 1920s, women had made important strides, but Woolf suggested that they had to study their historical role in order to go further. Culture advances by drawing on the accomplishments of the past, but, explained Woolf, women's work and accomplishments were not written about and were thus lost to history. Most basically, women needed greater financial independence so that they could have the time for scholarship, the leisure of cultivated conversation, and the privacy of "a room of one's own." Woolf wrote about a hypothetical "Shakespeare's sister," suggesting that women geniuses had been born but had never been given the most rudimentary requirements of time, space, and respect. Woolf asserted that although the work of her own generation of women might not be noticed, it would eventually change the world for a future Shakespeare's sister, so that "when she is born again she shall find it possible to live and write her poetry."[1]

A very different effort to establish a new tradition developed in Paris in the early 1920s as the poet André Breton (1896–1966) spearheaded the surrealist movement. Surrealism grew directly from Dada, an artistic movement that had emerged during the war. Protesting the war, Dada artists developed shocking, sometimes nihilistic, forms to deal with a reality that seemed senseless and out of control. Some made collages from trash; others indulged in nonsense or relied on chance. The results were sometimes amusing and often disturbing. By the early 1920s, the surrealists were adapting Dada's use of chance to gain access to the subconscious, which they believed contains a deeper truth.

Readjustment and the New Prosperity

In their effort to return to normal, governments were quick to dismantle wartime planning and control mechanisms. The needs of war had stimulated innovations that helped fuel the economic growth of the 1920s. New industries such as chemicals, electricity, and advanced machinery led the way to a new prosperity in the 1920s. The automobile, a plaything for the wealthy before the war, began to be mass-produced in western Europe. In France, which had pioneered automotive manufacture, the production of automobiles shot up dramatically, from 40,000 in 1920 to 254,000 in 1929.

But the heady pace masked problems that lay beneath the relative prosperity of the 1920s, even in victorious Britain and France. While new industries prospered, old ones declined in the face of new technologies and stronger foreign competition. In Britain, the industries responsible for the country's earlier industrial preeminence—textiles, coal, shipbuilding, and iron and steel—were now having trouble competing. Rather than investing in new technologies, companies in older industries sought government protection and imposed lower wages and longer hours on their workers. At the same time, British labor unions resisted the mechanization necessary to make older industries more competitive.

Rather than realistically assessing Britain's prospects in the more competitive international economy, British leaders sought to return to the prewar situation, based on the gold standard, and with London the world's financial center. For many Britons, the government's announcement in 1925 that the British pound was again freely convertible to gold at 1914 exchange rates was an indication that normality had returned at last. Yet the return to 1914 exchange rates overvalued the pound relative to the U.S. dollar, making British goods more expensive in export markets and making it still more difficult for aging British industries to compete. Further, Britain no longer had the capital to act as the world's banker. By trying to do so, Britain became all the more vulnerable when the international economy reached a crisis in 1929.

In Britain the Labour party supplanted the Liberals to become the dominant alternative to the Conservatives by the early 1920s. The Labour party got a brief taste of power when Ramsay MacDonald (1866–1937) formed Britain's first Labour government in January 1924. As a result, the governmental elite was significantly expanded to include those with working-class backgrounds.

Although the rise of Labour was significant, it was the Conservative leader Stanley Baldwin (1867–1947) who set the tone for British politics between the wars in three stints as prime minister between 1923 and 1937. Baldwin deliberately departed from the old aristocratic style of Conservative politics. He was the first British prime minister to use radio effectively, and he made an effort to foster good relations with workers. Yet Baldwin's era was one of growing social tension.

With exports declining, unemployment remained high in Britain throughout the interwar period, never falling below 10 percent. The coal industry, the country's largest employer, had become a particular trouble spot in the British economy. In 1926, a coal miners' strike turned into a general strike, involving almost all of organized labor—about 4 million workers—in the most notable display of trade-union solidarity Britain had ever seen. For nine days the British economy stood at a virtual standstill.

If the structural decline of older industries was clearest in Britain, inflation and its psychological impact was most prominent in Germany and France. In response to German foot-dragging in paying reparations, the French sent troops to occupy the Ruhr industrial area in January 1923. By the summer it was clear that the move had backfired, transforming an already serious inflationary problem, stemming from wartime deficit spending, into one of the great hyperinflations in history. At its height, when it took 4.2 trillion marks to equal a dollar, Germans were forced to take wheelbarrows of paper money to buy groceries. Simply printing the necessary currency was a severe strain for the government. By the end of 1923, the government managed to stabilize prices through currency reform and drastically reduced government spending. But the rampant inflation had wiped out the life savings of ordinary people while profiting speculators and those in debt, including some large industrialists. This inequity left scars that remained even as Germany enjoyed a measure of prosperity in the years that followed. Inflation was less dramatic in France, but it was severe there, too—and particularly upsetting because before the war the value of the French franc had been stable for over a century.

Although some in prewar France had worried about falling behind rapidly industrializing Germany, the victory seemed to have vindicated France's more cautious, balanced economy, with its blend of industry and agriculture. Thus, the prewar mistrust of rapid industrial development continued, and the French pulled back even from the measure of state responsibility for the economy that had developed during the war. Government grants helped reconstruct almost eight thousand factories, but most were simply rebuilt as they were before the war. Moreover, the working class benefited little from the relative prosperity of the 1920s. Housing remained poor, wages failed to keep up with inflation, and France continued to lag behind other countries in social legislation.

The Great Depression

Although the stock market crash of October 1929 in the United States helped usher in the world economic crisis of the early 1930s, it had this effect only because the new international economic order after World War I was extremely fragile. By October 1929, in fact, production was already declining in all the major Western countries except France.

Certain economic sectors, especially coal mining and agriculture, were already suffering severe problems by the mid-1920s. British coal exports fell partly because oil and hydroelectricity were rapidly developing as alternatives. In agriculture high prices during the war had produced oversupply, leading to a sharp drop in prices once the war was over. The result of low agricultural prices was a diminished demand for industrial goods, which impeded growth in the world economy.

Throughout the 1920s, finance ministers and central bankers had difficulty juggling the economic imbalances created by the war, centering on war debts to the United States and German reparations obligations to France, Britain, and Belgium. The shaky postwar economic system depended on U.S. bank loans to Germany. By 1928, however, U.S. investors were rapidly withdrawing their capital from Germany in search of higher returns in the booming U.S. stock market. This tightened credit in Germany. Then the crash of the overpriced U.S. market in October 1929 suddenly forced strapped American investors to pull still more of their funds out of Germany. This process continued for two years, weakening the major banks in Germany and central Europe.

The Germans seemed to have no choice but to freeze foreign assets—that is, to cease allowing conversion of assets held in German marks to other currencies. In this atmosphere, investors seeking the safest place for their capital tried to cash in currency for gold—or for British pounds, which could then be converted to gold. The flight to gold soon put such pressure on the British currency that Britain was forced to devalue the pound and sever it from the gold standard in September 1931. This proved the definitive end of the worldwide system of economic exchange based on the gold standard that had gradually crystallized during the nineteenth century.

The absence of a single standard of exchange, combined with various currency restrictions, made foreign trade more difficult and uncertain. So did the scramble for tariff protection that proved a widespread response to the developing crisis. Crucial was the U.S. Smoot-Hawley Tariff Act of June 1930, which raised taxes on imports by 50 to 100 percent, forcing other nations to take comparable steps.

The decline of trade spread depression throughout the world economic system. By 1933 most major European countries were able to export no more than two-thirds, and in some cases as little as one-third, of the amount they had sold in 1929. By 1932 the European economies had shrunk to a little over half their 1929 size. With less being produced and sold, the demand for labor declined sharply. Unemployment produced widespread malnutrition, which led, in turn, to sharp increases in such diseases as tuberculosis, scarlet fever, and rickets.

During the first years of the Depression, economic policymakers based their responses on the "classical" economic model, which suggested that a downward turn in the business cycle was a normal and necessary adjustment and that government interference would only upset this self-adjusting mechanism. By 1932, however, it was clear that the conventional response was not working, and governments began seeking to stimulate the economy. Strategies varied widely. In the United States, Franklin D. Roosevelt (1882–1945) defeated the incumbent president, Herbert Hoover, in 1932 with the promise of a New Deal—a commitment to increase government spending to restore purchasing power. In fascist Italy (see pages 638–641), a state agency created to infuse capital into failing companies proved a reasonably effective basis for collaboration between government and business. In Nazi Germany (see pages 644–648), government measures sealed off the German mark from international fluctuations, stimulated public spending, partly on rearmament, and kept wages low.

High unemployment in Norway, Sweden, and Denmark helped social democrats win power in all three countries by the mid-1930s. The new left-leaning governments responded to the crisis by pioneering the "welfare state," providing such benefits as health care, unemployment insurance, and family allowances. To pay for the new welfare safety net, the Scandinavian countries adopted a high level of progressive taxation and pared military expenditures to a minimum. The Scandinavian model attracted much admiration as a "third way" between free-market capitalism and the various dictatorial extremes.

The Depression Worldwide

The Depression had a major impact on the non-Western world and its relations with the West. The radical restriction of international trade meant a sharp decline in demand for the commodities that colonial and other regions exported to the industrialized West. The value of Latin American exports declined by half. With foreign exchange scarce, Latin Americans had to curtail imports and intensify their efforts to industrialize on their own. This enterprise required a greater role for the state—and often entailed political change in an authoritarian direction.

In colonial nations, strains from the Depression further undermined the prestige of the liberal capitalist West and fed nationalist, anti-Western sentiments. In India, the increase in misery among rural villagers spread the movement for national independence from urban elites to the rural masses. In this context Mohandas Gandhi, who had become known by 1920 for advocating non-cooperation with the British, became the first Indian leader to win a mass following throughout the Indian subcontinent. Encouraging villagers to boycott British goods, Gandhi accented simplicity, self-reliance, and an overall strategy of nonviolent civil disobedience based on Indian traditions. (See the box "Encounters with the West: Gandhi on Nonviolence.")

In Japan, the strains of the Great Depression helped produce precisely the turn to imperialist violence that Gandhi sought to counter. Lacking essential raw materials, Japan was dependent on international trade and thus reacted strongly as increasing tariffs elsewhere cut sharply into Japanese exports. Led by young army officers eager for their country to embrace a less subservient form of Westernization, Japan turned to aggressive imperialism. Attacking in 1931, Japanese forces quickly reduced Manchuria to a puppet state, but the Japanese met stubborn resistance when they began seeking to extend this conquest to the rest of China in 1937.

Japanese pressure indirectly furthered the rise of the Chinese communist movement, led by Mao Zedong (1893–1976). Securing a base in the Yanan district in 1936, Mao began seeking to apply Marxism-Leninism to China through land reform and other measures to link the communist elite to the Chinese peasantry. Mao was adapting Western ideas to build an indigenous movement that would overcome Western imperialism and create an alternative to Western capitalism.

The Depression, and the halting responses of the democracies in dealing with it, enhanced the prestige of the new regimes in the Soviet Union, Italy, and Germany, which appeared to be dealing with their economies more effectively. Capitalism seemed to be on trial—and so, increasingly, did parliamentary democracy. In east-central Europe, new democracies seemed to take root after the war, but except in Czechoslovakia and Finland the practice of parliamentary government did not match the promise of the immediate postwar period. Democracy seemed divisive and ineffective, so one country after another adopted a more authoritarian alternative during the 1920s and early 1930s.

Poland offers a dramatic example. Although its democratic constitution of 1921 established a cabinet responsible to parliament, the parliament fragmented into numerous parties. Poland had fourteen different ministries from November 1918 to May 1926, when a coup d'état led by Marshal Josef Pilsudski replaced parliamentary government with an authoritarian regime stressing national unity. The suppression of democracy came as a relief to many Poles—and was even welcomed by the trade unions. The regime held power until Poland was invaded by Nazi Germany in 1939.

THE STALINIST REVOLUTION IN THE SOVIET UNION

In making their revolution in 1917, the Bolsheviks had expected to spark a series of revolutions elsewhere. But a decade later, revolution elsewhere was nowhere in sight, and it seemed that,

ENCOUNTERS WITH THE WEST

Gandhi on Nonviolence

Mohandas Gandhi, a successful English-educated lawyer, emerged as a major force in the movement for Indian independence just after World War I. The following excerpts from articles published in 1935 and 1939—years notable for outbreaks of violence elsewhere—explain the significance of nonviolence to Gandhi's overall strategy.

Non-violence to be a creed has to be all-pervasive. I cannot be non-violent about one activity of mine and violent about others. That would be a policy, not a life-force. That being so, I cannot be indifferent about the war that Italy is now waging against Abyssinia. . . . India had an unbroken tradition of non-violence from times immemorial. But at no time in her ancient history, as far as I know it, has it had complete non-violence in action pervading the whole land. Nevertheless, it is my unshakeable belief that her destiny is to deliver the message of non-violence to mankind. . . .

. . . India as a nation is not non-violent in the full sense of the term. . . . Her non-violence is that of the weak. . . . She lacks the ability to offer physical resistance. She has no consciousness of strength. She is conscious only of her weakness. If she were otherwise, there would be no communal problems, nor political. . . . [I]f we, as Indians, could but for a moment visualize ourselves as a strong people disdaining to strike, we should cease to fear Englishmen whether as soldiers, traders or administrators, and they to distrust us. Therefore if we became truly non-violent . . . we being millions would be the greatest moral force in the world, and Italy would listen to our friendly word. . . .

. . . [W]hen society is deliberately constructed in accordance with the law of non-violence, its structure will be different in material particulars from what it is today. But I cannot say in advance what the government based wholly on non-violence will be like.

What is happening today is disregard of the law of non-violence and enthronement of violence as if it were an eternal law. The democracies, therefore, that we see at work in England, America and France are only so called, because they are no less based on violence than Nazi Germany, Fascist Italy or even Soviet Russia. The only difference is that the violence of the last three is much better organized than that of the three democratic powers. Nevertheless we see today a mad race for outdoing one another in the matter of armaments. . . .

Holding the view that without the recognition of non-violence on a national scale there is no such thing as a constitutional or democratic government, I devote my energy to the propagation of non-violence as the law of our life—individual, social, political, national and international. I fancy that I have seen the light, though dimly. I write cautiously, for I do not profess to know the whole of the Law. If I know the successes of my experiments, I know also my failures. But the successes are enough to fill me with undying hope.

Source: Raghavan Iyer, ed., *The Essential Writings of Mahatma Gandhi* (Delhi: Oxford University Press, 1991), pp. 245–247, 262–263.

for the foreseeable future, the communist regime in Russia would have to go it alone as it sought to transform itself under new leadership.

Seeking to build "socialism in one country," Joseph Stalin led the Soviet Union during the 1930s through one of the most astounding transformations the world had ever seen. It mixed great achievement with brutality and terror in bizarre and often tragic ways. The resulting governmental system, which gave Stalin unprecedented power, proved crucial to the outcome of the great experiment that began with the Russian Revolution of 1917. But whether the fateful turn of the 1930s had been implicit in the Leninist revolutionary model or stemmed mostly from unforeseen circumstances and Stalin's idiosyncratic personality remains uncertain.

Consolidating Communist Power in Russia, 1917–1921

Even after leading the revolution that toppled the provisional government in November 1917, the Bolsheviks could not claim majority support in Russia. When the long-delayed elections to select a constituent assembly were finally held a few weeks after the revolution, the Bolsheviks ended up with fewer than one-quarter of the seats, while the Socialist Revolutionaries won a clear majority. But over the next three years the Communists, as the Bolsheviks renamed themselves, consolidated their power, establishing a centralized and nondemocratic communist regime. Power lay not with the soviets, and not with some coalition of socialist parties, but solely with the Communist party. The Communists also established centralized control of the economy, subjecting workers to more rigorous discipline.

During its first years, the new communist regime encountered a genuine emergency that seemed especially to require a monopoly of power. For over two years the communist Red Army had to fight a brutal civil war against counterrevolutionary "Whites," people who had been dispossessed by the revolution or who had grown disillusioned with the Communist party. The Whites drew support from foreign intervention and from separatist sentiment, as several of the non-Russian nationalities of the old Russian Empire sought to defect.

Although the counterrevolutionary assault seriously threatened the young communist regime, the Whites were unable to rally much popular support. Peasants feared that a White victory would mean the restoration of the old order, including the return of their newly won lands to their former landlords. By the end of active fighting in November 1920, the communist regime had regained most of the territory it had lost early in the civil war.

Many communist initiatives were tabled due to the demands of fighting counterrevolutionaries supported by foreign troops. Nevertheless, the commissar for public welfare, Alexandra Kollontai (1872–1952), established some childcare facilities to aid working parents and began structuring public medical care, though such programs were limited by lack of funds. A disciple of the German Socialist Clara Zetkin (Rosa Luxemburg had introduced them in 1906), Kollontai was the representative of women's concerns in Lenin's regime and as such she promulgated a decree transforming marriage from a religious arrangement legally dominated by the male partner into a civil arrangement between two equals. She also pushed through laws for equal schooling for girls, free hospital maternity care, easy divorce based on equal grounds for men and women, and ready access to birth control and abortion. Kollontai believed that communism could not survive without ensuring women the right to fulfilling work—which required the state to provide for familial domestic chores. She also argued for increased social equality and insisted on an end to double standards in sexual behavior, but these were radical new ideas with little immediate impact, especially under the strains of conterrevolution.

The counterrevolutionary and separatist movements also created a sense that the non-Russian nationalities required close control. Thus, when the Union of Soviet Socialist Republics (U.S.S.R.) was organized in December 1922, it was only nominally a federation of autonomous republics; strong centralization from the Communists' new capital in Moscow was the rule from the start.

Although they had to concentrate on the civil war from 1918 to late 1920, the Russian communists founded the Third, or Communist, International—commonly known as the Comintern—in March 1919. The Russian communists expected to lead the international socialist movement, but the Comintern's aggressive claim to leadership led to a lasting schism in the European socialist movement by early 1921. All over the world socialist parties split between "communists," who chose to affiliate with the Comintern, and "socialists," who rejected Comintern leadership.

At first, many European socialists opted for the Comintern, but as the implications of membership became clearer over the next few years, the balance shifted to favor the socialists. Late in 1923 the Comintern finally concluded that revolution elsewhere could not be expected soon. The immediate enemy was not capitalism or the bourgeoisie but the socialists, communism's rival for working-class support. The communists' incessant criticism of the socialists, whom they dubbed "social fascists," weakened the European left, especially in the face of the growing threat of fascism.

From Lenin to Stalin, 1921–1929

Although it managed to win the civil war, the communist regime was clearly in crisis by the beginning of 1921, partly because of "war communism," the rough-and-ready controlled economy that the war effort seemed to make necessary. With industrial production only about one-fifth the 1913 total, there were strikes in the factories, and peasants were resisting further requisitions of grain. In March 1921, sailors at the Kronstadt naval base mutinied, suffering considerable loss of life as governmental control was re-established.

With the very survival of the revolution in question, Lenin replaced war communism with the New Economic Policy, or NEP, in March 1921. Although transport, banking, heavy industry, and wholesale commerce remained under state control, the NEP restored considerable scope for private enterprise, especially in the retail sector and in agriculture. The economy quickly revived and by 1927 was producing at prewar levels. But what about the longer term? The Marxist understanding of historical progress required industrialization, and so debate focused on industrial development—the scope for it under Soviet conditions and its relationship to the creation of socialism.

This debate about priorities became bound up with questions about the leadership of the new regime. Lenin suffered the first of a series of strokes in May 1922 and died in January 1924, setting off a struggle among his possible successors. Leon Trotsky, a powerful thinker and architect of the Red Army, was by most measures Lenin's heir apparent. Although he favored tighter economic controls to speed industrial development, Trotsky planned for the Soviet Union to concentrate on spreading the revolution to other countries.

But it was Joseph Stalin (1879–1953) who gradually assumed power after Lenin's death. Born Josef Djugashvili into a lower-class family in Georgia, Stalin became party secretary in 1922, enabling him to establish his control of the Soviet system by 1929. Though he lacked Trotsky's charisma and knew little of economics, Stalin proved a master of backstage political maneuvering, playing his rivals against each other and accusing his critics of lack of faith in the Soviet working class. He outmaneuvered Trotsky and his allies, removing them from positions of power, and finally forced Trotsky into exile in 1929. Bitterly critical of Stalin to the end, Trotsky was murdered by Stalin's agents in Mexico in 1940.

Crash Industrialization and Forced Collectivization, 1929–1933

Stalin believed that the Soviet Union had to catch up with the West—and quickly. By 1929, he had instituted a policy of crash industrialization, favoring heavy industry and based on forced agricultural collectivization. This attempt to mobilize and control society was without precedent in Western history, and it affected the whole shape of the regime, including cultural policy. In 1929, Soviet officials began demanding "socialist realism," which portrayed the Soviet revolution in an inspiring, heroic light intended to encourage the intense new productive demands.

Promoting Industrial Growth With the turn to crash industrialization by 1929, the Soviet regime harnessed art to inspire enthusiastic participation in the common effort to build an industrial economy. The mix of images in this poster from about 1932 suggests that, working together, the state and the people were rapidly raising the country's socioeconomic level. *(David King Collection)*

Beginning in 1930, the peasants were forcibly herded into large, government-controlled collective farms. Communist leaders wanted to control agricultural pricing and distribution so that they could squeeze a surplus from agriculture to be sold abroad, earning money to build factories, dams, and power plants. So unpopular was this measure that many peasants killed their livestock or smashed their farm implements rather than let them be collectivized. During the first two months of 1930, as many as 14 million head of cattle were slaughtered, resulting in an orgy of meat eating and a shortage of draft animals. In 1928, there had been 60 million cattle in the Soviet Union; by 1934 there were only 33.5 million.

Collectivization served, as intended, to squeeze from the peasantry the resources needed to finance industrialization. But it was carried out with extreme brutality. What was being squeezed was not merely a surplus—the state's extractions cut into subsistence. So although Soviet agricultural exports went up after 1930, large numbers of peasants starved to death. The great famine of 1932–1933 resulted in between 5 and 6 million deaths, over half of them in Ukraine.

By 1937 almost all Soviet agriculture took place on collective farms, and significant increases in industrial output had established solid foundations in heavy industry, including the bases for military production. But, despite its successes, the forced development program created many inefficiencies and entailed tremendous human costs. The Soviet Union could probably have done at least as well, with much less suffering, through other strategies of industrial development. Moreover, Stalin's program departed from certain socialist principles—egalitarianism in wages, for example—that the regime had taken very seriously in the late 1920s. New labor laws established harsh punishments for absenteeism or tardiness and severely limited the freedom of workers to change jobs. There was no collective bargaining and no right to strike.

From Opposition to Terror, 1932–1939

Stalin's radical course, with its brutality and uncertain economic justification, quickly provoked opposition. During the summer of 1932, a group centered around M. N. Ryutin (1890–1937) circulated among party leaders a two-hundred-page tract calling for a retreat from Stalin's economic program and a return to democracy within the party. Stalin promptly had Ryutin and his associates expelled from the party, then arrested and imprisoned. But as the international situation grew menacing during the 1930s, Stalin became ever more preoccupied with the potential for further opposition.

In 1934 the assassination of Sergei Kirov (1888–1934), party leader of Leningrad (the former Petrograd), gave Stalin an excuse to intensify the crackdown against opponents. Though not conclusive, the evidence suggests that Stalin himself was responsible for killing Kirov. In any case, the event served Stalin's interests by creating a sense of emergency justifying extraordinary measures. The eventual result was a series of bizarre show trials, deadly purges, and, ultimately, a kind of terror, with no one safe from arrest by the secret police.

Between 1936 and 1938, famed Bolshevik veterans confessed to a series of sensational trumped-up charges: that they had been behind the assassination of Kirov, that they would have killed Stalin if given the chance, that they constituted an "anti-Soviet, Trotskyite center," spying for Germany and Japan. Many "confessed" because they thought it would help the regime. Almost all the accused were convicted and executed. Ryutin refused to "confess" and was shot in secret early in 1937.

A purge of the army in 1937 wiped out its top ranks, with 35,000 officers—half the entire officer corps—shot or imprisoned in response to unfounded charges of spying and treason. The Communist party underwent several purges, culminating in the great purge of 1937 and 1938. Of the roughly two thousand delegates to the 1934 congress of the Communist party, over half were shot during the next few years. The purge of the party got rid of the remaining "old Bolsheviks," those who had been involved in the revolution in 1917 and thus retained a certain independence. By 1939, Stalin loyalists constituted the entire party leadership.

The purge process touched virtually everyone as the net widened by 1938. Everybody knew someone who had been implicated, so everyone felt some measure of vulnerability to arrest, which would be followed by execution or exile to forced-labor camps. Moreover, there was a random, arbitrary quality to the purges. Ordinary people were tempted to denounce others, if only to demonstrate their own loyalty. Many believed that there was some treason in their midst: The unending talk of intrigues and plots had affected them deeply. The contrast between propaganda showing heroic achievement and the reality of shortages and hardships further suggested that a vast conspiracy was at work.

Somewhat ironically, Stalin's need to control his population centered on birth as well as death: In 1936 he ended the reproductive freedom that Alexandra Kollontai had put in place after the revolution. Abortion was outlawed, and birth control information became difficult to obtain. Stalin was clearly interested in replacing the depleted population, but these measures also served to regulate women's lives and choices and to make the family reflect the authoritarianism of the state.

The final toll of the purges was staggering. Of the approximately 160 million people in the Soviet Union, something like 8.5 million were arrested in 1937 and 1938, and of these perhaps 1 million were executed. Half the total membership of the Communist party—1.2 million people—was arrested; most were executed or died in forced-labor camps. Altogether, the purges resulted in approximately 8 million deaths. The death toll from Stalin's policies between 1929 and 1939, including forced collectivizations, was perhaps 20 million.

This fateful turn in the development of the communist regime in the Soviet Union proved to be one of the pivotal events of modern history. Some insist that Stalin was pursuing a deliberate policy, seeking to create an all-encompassing system of control. Others argue that though Stalin's ultimate responsibility is undeniable, he was simply responding on an improvised basis to a chaotic situation. Either way, Stalin's personal idiosyncrasies and growing paranoia were crucial to the peculiar development of the Soviet system.

Stalin had won his position based on his backroom political skill, not his popular appeal. Although a special aura came to surround him by the end of the 1930s, his style of leadership remained distinct from that of Mussolini and Hitler, who based their power on a direct relationship with the people.

FASCIST ITALY

Although Soviet communism was something new, it had developed from within the tradition of Marxist socialism. The pedigree of fascism was much less clear. Its leader, Benito Mussolini (1883–1945), had begun as a socialist, but by the end of the war he had left the socialist mainstream behind and was looking for a new constituency. The fascist movement that Mussolini forged in March 1919 proved violent and disturbing, yet it attracted considerable support among those disillusioned with parliamentary politics and hostile to the Marxist left.

The term *fascism* derived from the ancient Roman symbol of power and unity, *fasces,* a bundle of rods surrounding an ax. Stressing national solidarity, the fascists were hostile not only to liberal individualism and parliamentary democracy, but also to Marxist socialism with its emphasis on class struggle. Fascism was not traditionally conservative either. It claimed to be a new alternative to both liberal democracy and Marxist communism, based on values forged in the war.

The Crisis of Liberal Italy and the Creation of Fascism, 1919–1925

The Italian experience of World War I proved especially controversial because the Italians could have avoided it. No one attacked Italy in 1914, and the country could have received significant territorial benefits just by remaining neutral. Still, many Italians felt that participation in this war would be a revitalizing test of the young nation's strength. When Italy finally intervened on the side of the Triple Entente in May 1915, it was because France and Britain had promised specific territorial gains at the secret Treaty of London in April.

Despite the near collapse of the Italian armies in October 1917, Italy lasted out the war and contributed to the victory over Austria-Hungary. Supporters of the war felt that this success could lead to a thoroughgoing renewal of Italian public life, but to many—especially Socialists and Catholics—intervention had been a tragic mistake. Thus, despite Italy's participation in the victory, division over the war's significance immensely complicated the Italian political situation.

The situation became even more volatile when Italy did not reap all the gains expected at the Paris Peace Conference. Italy got most of what it had been promised in the Treaty of London, but appetites increased with the dissolution of the Austro-Hungarian Empire. To some Italians, the disappointing outcome confirmed that the war had been a mistake, its benefits not worth the costs. Others were outraged at what seemed a denigration of the Italian contribution by France, Britain, and the United States. Thus the outcome fanned resentment of Italy's allies, and also of the country's political leaders, who seemed too weak to deliver on their promises.

Amid this tension, Socialist leaders talked of imitating the Bolshevik Revolution. During 1919 and 1920, a wave of quasi-revolutionary labor unrest included several national strikes and a series of factory occupations. Although there was a revolutionary atmosphere in these years, Italian Socialist leaders did not carry out the planning and organization necessary for a Leninist-style takeover.

With the established political system of old liberal politics at an impasse, and the Socialist party too inflexible and too romantic to lead a radical transformation, fascism emerged, claiming to offer a third way. It was bound to oppose the Socialists because of conflict over the meaning of the war and the kind of transformation Italy needed. This antisocialist posture made fascism attractive to reactionary interests. By early 1921 landowners in northern and central Italy were footing the bill as bands of young fascists drove around the countryside beating up workers and burning down socialist meeting halls. But fascist spokesmen claimed to offer something other than mere reaction: a new politics that would prove better than Marxist socialism at pursuing the interests of the working class.

At the same time, important sectors of Italian industry, which had grown rapidly due to government orders during the war, looked with apprehension toward the more competitive postwar international economy. Nationalist thinkers and business spokesmen questioned the capacity of the parliamentary system to provide the vigorous leadership that Italy needed. Prone to bickering and partisanship, politicians lacked the vision to pursue Italy's long-term international economic interests and the will to impose the necessary discipline on the domestic level. Thus, the government had been relatively weak in responding to the labor unrest of 1919 and 1920.

In postwar Italy, then, there was widespread discontent with the established forms of politics, but those discontented were socially disparate, and their aims were not compatible. Some had been socialists before the war; others were nationalists hostile to socialism. While some envisioned a more intense kind of mass politics, others thought the masses already had too much power. Still, these discontented groups agreed on the need for change.

The person who seemed able to translate these discontents and aspirations into a new political force was the one-time socialist Benito Mussolini. From the Romagna region of central Italy, where his father was a blacksmith and a socialist and his mother a teacher, Mussolini became editor of the Socialist party's national newspaper, *Avanti!*, in 1912, when only 29 years old. Many saw him as the fresh face needed to revitalize Italian socialism.

His concern with renewal had made Mussolini an unorthodox socialist even before 1914, and after war broke out, he was prominent among those on the left who called for Italian intervention. The fact that socialists in France, Germany, and elsewhere had rallied to their respective national war efforts caused him to reconsider the old socialism, based on international proletarian solidarity. But the Socialist party refused to follow his call for intervention, remaining neutralist and aloof, so Mussolini found himself cut off from his earlier constituency.

Through his new newspaper, *Il popolo d'Italia* (*The People of Italy*), Mussolini promptly emerged as a leading advocate of Italian participation in the war. He saw military service once Italy intervened, and after the war he aspired to translate the war experience into a new form of politics. But after founding the fascist movement in March 1919, Mussolini became embroiled in periodic disputes with important sectors of his movement. Young fascist militants wanted to replace the existing parliamentary system with a wholly new political order, but Mussolini seemed more prone to use fascism as his personal route to power within the existing system. When his maneuvering finally won him the prime minister's post in October 1922, it was not at all clear that a change of regime was in the offing.

At first, Mussolini emphasized normalization and legality. Fascism had apparently been absorbed within the political system; with Mussolini as prime minister, there would be changes, but not revolutionary changes. Government would become more vigorous and efficient, the swollen Italian bureaucracy would be streamlined, and the trains would run on time. Those

Benito Mussolini The founder of fascism is shown with other fascist leaders in 1922, as he becomes prime minister of Italy. Standing at Mussolini's right (with beard) is Italo Balbo, later a pioneering aviator and fascist Italy's air force minister. *(Corbis-Bettmann)*

who had envisioned more sweeping change were increasingly frustrated.

In June 1924 the murder of Giacomo Matteotti (1885–1924), a moderate socialist parliamentary deputy, sparked a crisis that forced Mussolini's hand. Shortly after a speech denouncing fascist violence, Matteotti was killed by fascist thugs. A great public outcry followed, as Italians questioned whether the government—or Mussolini himself—was responsible for the crime. Many from the establishment who had tolerated Mussolini as the man who could keep order now deserted him. A growing chorus called for his resignation.

Mussolini sought at first to be conciliatory and reassuring, but more radical fascists saw the crisis as an opportunity for fascism to end the compromise with the old order and to create a whole new political system. On December 31, 1924, thirty-three militants called on Mussolini to demand that he make up his mind. The way out of the crisis was not to delimit the scope of fascism but to expand it. Mussolini was the leader of fascism, *Il Duce,* and in that role he would have to implement the fascist revolution.

In a speech to the Chamber of Deputies a few days later, on January 3, 1925, Mussolini finally committed himself to a more radical course. Defiantly claiming the "full political, moral, and historical responsibility for all that has happened," including "all the acts of violence," he promised to accelerate the transformation that he claimed to have initiated with his agitation for intervention in 1914 and 1915.[2]

Innovation and Compromise in Fascist Italy, 1925–1930

Early in 1925, the fascist government imprisoned or exiled opposition leaders and outlawed the other parties and the nonfascist labor unions. But fascism was not seeking simply a conventional monopoly of political power; the new fascist state was to be totalitarian, all-encompassing, limitless in its reach. Under the old liberal regime, the fascists charged, the state had been too weak to promote the national interest, and the society had been too fragmented. So Mussolini's regime expanded the state's sovereignty and mobilized the society to create a deeper sense of national identity. For example, a new system of labor judges settled labor disputes, replacing the right to strike. And the Fascist party fostered new forms of participation in public organizations and clubs.

The centerpiece of the new fascist state was *corporativism*, which entailed mobilizing people as producers by organization of the workplace. Groupings based on occupation or economic function were to replace parliament as the basis for political participation and decision making. Beginning in 1926, corporativist institutions were established in stages until a Chamber of Fasces and Corporations at last replaced the old Chamber of Deputies in 1939.

It was through this corporative state that the fascists claimed to be providing the world with a third way beyond outmoded democracy and misguided communism. The practice of corporativism never lived up to its grandiose rhetoric, but the effort to devise new forms of political participation was central to fascism's self-understanding. The effort attracted much attention abroad, especially during the Great Depression.

The social component of fascism emphasized masculine virility, female subordination, and large families destined to pack the work force and the army. To forcibly change the status of women, the fascists doubled school fees for girls and ordered women to be fired from a range of occupations. In 1927, all women's salaries were reduced by 50 percent. Mussolini's endless praise for war widows and good mothers did strike a chord for many women, hard-pressed by the years of war and the demands of modernity, but overall the strategy was a failure. Fertility did not rise.

In this matter and others, it was difficult to determine whether the fascist regime was really new or actually represented a revival of tradition. In 1929, Mussolini worked out an accord with the Catholic church, formally ending the dispute between the church and the Italian state that had resulted from national unification. The compromise seemed to imply a kind of endorsement of Mussolini's government on the part of the church and the establishment in Italy. But the gesture displeased many fascists, leading to a partial crackdown on Catholic youth organizations in 1931, as Mussolini continued to juggle traditionalist compromise and revolutionary pretension.

GERMANY: FROM THE WEIMAR REPUBLIC TO NATIONAL SOCIALISM

Just as hopes for democratic renewal had met with frustration in Italy, many Germans found their desire for political participation eclipsed by their desire for government stability. With the Weimar Republic of 1918–1933, Germany experienced full-fledged parliamentary democracy for the first time, but this democracy had great difficulty establishing its legitimacy and was unable to address the ills of the Great Depression. As a result, the Nazi leader Adolf Hitler (1889–1945) got a chance to govern early in 1933. He immediately began creating a new regime, the Third Reich, intended as the antithesis of Weimar democracy.

Germany's Cautious Revolution, 1919–1933

The Weimar Republic had two strikes against it from the outset: It was born of national defeat, and it was forced to take responsibility for the harsh and dictated Treaty of Versailles in 1919. During its first years, moreover, the regime encountered severe economic dislocation, culminating in the hyperinflation of 1923, as well as ideological polarization that threatened to tear the country apart.

The initial threat to the new German republic, proclaimed in November 1918, came from the left, stimulated by the Russian example. Spearheaded by Rosa Luxemburg and Karl Liebknecht in Berlin (see page 615), revolutionary unrest reached a peak in December 1918 and January 1919. Even after Luxemburg and Liebknecht were captured and murdered in January, there remained a serious chance of revolution through May 1919, and communist revolutionary agitation continued until the end of 1923.

For this reason, the new government made repression of the extreme left a priority—even though it meant retaining some of the old imperial institutions. New forces of repression were born as well: When the regular army, weakened by war and defeat, proved unable to control radical agitation in Berlin, the government began to organize "Free Corps," irregular volunteer paramilitary groups to be used against the revolutionaries.

During the first five months of 1919, the government unleashed the Free Corps to crush leftist movements all over Germany, often with wanton brutality. In relying on right-wing paramilitary groups, the republic's leaders were playing with fire, but the immediate threat at this point came from the left. In 1920, however, the government faced a right-wing coup attempt, the Kapp Putsch. The army declined to defend the republic, but the government managed to survive thanks largely to a general strike by leftist workers. The republic's early leaders had to juggle both extremes because, as one of them put it, the Weimar Republic was "a candle burning at both ends."

Though sporadic street fighting by paramilitary groups continued, by 1924 the republic had achieved an uneasy stability. But Germany's postwar revolution remained confined to the political level. There was no effort to build a loyal republican army and no attempt to purge the bureaucracy and the judiciary of antidemocratic elements from the old order. When right-wing extremists assassinated prominent leaders, such as the Jewish industrialist Walther Rathenau in 1922, the courts often proved unwilling to prosecute those responsible. In general, those who ran the new government were skeptical of democracy, even hostile to the new regime.

Elections in January 1919 produced a constituent assembly that convened in Weimar, seat of what seemed the best traditions of German culture, to draft a democratic constitution. The elections had taken place before the peace conference produced the widely detested Treaty of Versailles. When the first regular parliamentary elections were finally held in June 1920, the three moderate parties that had led the new government and been forced to accept the treaty suffered a major defeat. Those were the parties most committed to democratic institutions, but they were never again to achieve a parliamentary majority. The 1920 elections, like many of those that followed, revealed an extreme lack of consensus in the German electorate.

The lack of consensus produced a multiparty system and a fragmented Reichstag. No single party ever won an absolute majority during the Weimar years, so governments were always unstable coalitions. Not only was the Weimar party system fragmented and complex, but it encompassed a wide ideological array, including extremes of both left and right bent on sabotaging the new democratic institutions. On the left, the Communists constantly criticized the more moderate Socialists. On the right, the situation was more complex. The extreme right National Socialists, or Nazis, were noisy and often violent, but they did not attract much electoral support until 1930. More damaging to parliamentary democracy for most of the Weimar period was the right-wing Nationalist party (DNVP), which played on nationalist resentments and fears of socialism.

Still, all was not necessarily lost for the republic when the three moderate parties were defeated in 1920. Germans who were unsupportive or hostile at first might be gradually won over. After the death of President Friedrich Ebert in 1925, Paul von Hindenburg, the emperor's field marshal, was elected president. Hindenburg's presidency suggested to skeptics that the new regime was legitimate and a worthy object for German patriotism.

The individual with the best chance of winning converts to the Weimar Republic in the early 1920s was Gustav Stresemann (1878–1929), the leader of the German People's party (DVP), a conservative but relatively flexible party that seemed capable of broadening the republic's base of support. As chancellor, and especially as foreign minister, Stresemann was the republic's leading statesman.

Stresemann became chancellor in August 1923, when inflation was raging out of control. Within months his government had Germany back on its feet, partly because the other powers were becoming more conciliatory. By November 1923 even the French agreed that an international commission should review the reparations question. In the summer of 1924, a commission led by the American financier Charles G. Dawes produced the Dawes Plan, which remained in force until 1929. The plan worked well by lowering payments, providing loans, and securing the stability of the German currency.

Stresemann understood that better relations with the victors had to be a priority if Germany was to overcome the present crisis and return to the councils of the great powers. French foreign minister Aristide Briand (1862–1932) shared Stresemann's desire for improved relations, and together they engineered the more conciliatory spirit in international relations evident by 1924. Its most substantial fruit was the Locarno Agreement of October 1925. France and Germany accepted the postwar border between them, which meant that Germany gave up any claim to Alsace-Lorraine. France, for its part, renounced the sort of direct military intervention in Germany that it had attempted with the Ruhr invasion of 1923 and agreed to begin withdrawing troops from the Rhineland ahead of schedule. Germany accepted France's key advantage, the demilitarization of the Rhineland, and Britain and Italy explicitly guaranteed the measure.

By accepting the status quo in the west, Stresemann freed Germany to concentrate on eastern Europe, where he envisioned gradual but substantial revision in the territorial settlement. Especially with the creation of Poland, that settlement had come partly at Germany's expense. Stresemann, then, was pursuing German interests, not subordinating them to some larger European vision. But he was willing to compromise and, for the most part, to play by the rules.

With the Locarno treaty, the victors accepted Germany as a diplomatic equal for the first time since the war. Germany's return to good graces culminated in its entry into the League of Nations in 1926. Stresemann and Briand were joint winners of the Nobel Peace Prize for 1926.

With the expiration of the Dawes Plan in 1929, the Young Plan, conceived by American businessman Owen D. Young, removed Allied controls over the German economy and specified that Germany pay reparations until 1988. Since the annual amount was less than Germany had been paying, it was expected that this plan would constitute a permanent, and reasonable, settlement. Nevertheless, the Young Plan produced resentment in Germany, leading, yet again, to political gains on the right.

When Stresemann died in October 1929, Weimar Germany was considerably better off than it had been in 1923, but the political consensus remained weak, the party system was still fragmented, and unstable coalition government remained the rule. The onset of the economic depression at the end of 1929 produced problems that Germany's fragile new democracy proved unable to handle. The pivotal issue was unemployment insurance. A Socialist chancellor, Hermann Müller (1876–1931), was leading the government when the Depression began, and as the crisis deepened, his party demanded increases in insurance coverage. When the Socialists failed to convince their coalition partners, the Müller government resigned in March 1930. That proved to be the end of normal parliamentary government in Weimar Germany.

President Hindenburg called on Heinrich Brüning (1885–1970), leader of the moderate Catholic Center party, to replace Müller as chancellor. Brüning promptly proposed an economic program that avoided unemployment insurance and public works projects in favor of directly deflationary measures. Brüning's program encountered opposition not only from socialists but also from conservatives, eager to undermine the republic altogether. As a result, Brüning could get no parliamentary majority. Rather than resigning or seeking a compromise, he invoked Article 48, the emergency provision of the Weimar constitution, which enabled him to govern under presidential decree.

When this expedient provoked strenuous protests, Brüning dissolved the Reichstag and scheduled new elections for September 1930. The outcome was disastrous—for Brüning and ultimately for Germany as well. Two of the democratic, pro-Weimar parties lost heavily, and the two political extremes were the big winners. The Communists gained 23 seats, for a total of 77 deputies in the Reichstag; the National Socialists did even better, climbing from the 12 seats they had garnered in 1928 to 107.

Brüning continued to govern, relying on President Hindenburg and Article 48 rather than majority support in the Reichstag. Meanwhile, the growth of the political extremes helped fuel an intensification of the political violence and street fighting that had bedeviled the Weimar Republic from the beginning. As scuffles between Nazis and Communists sometimes approached pitched battles, the inability of the government to keep order further damaged the prestige of the Republic.

In May 1932, Hindenburg's advisers finally persuaded him to dump Brüning in favor of an antidemocratic conservative. By this point the republic was a mere shell covering the backroom manipulation and dealing in Hindenburg's circle. The results of the July 1932 elections were the republic's death knell. The Nazis won 37.3 percent of the vote (230 seats) and the Communists 14.3 percent (89 seats). Together, the two extremes controlled a majority of the seats in the Reichstag, and each refused to work in coalition with any of the mainstream parties. Although he resisted for months, Hindenburg found it difficult not to give Adolf Hitler, as the leader of the largest party in the Reichstag, a chance to govern.

During the brief and tortured history of the Weimar Republic, there were twenty different cabinets, lasting an average of eight-and-a-half months each. The experience of instability, divisiveness, and finally paralysis reinforced the perception, long prominent in Germany, that parliamentary democracy was petty and ineffective. By 1932, the majority of Germans had lost confidence in the institutions of parliamentary democracy. Even those who voted for the Nazis were not clear what they might be getting, but, in light of economic depression and political impasse, it seemed time to try something else.

THE RISE OF NAZISM, 1919–1933

The National Socialist German Workers' party (NSDAP), or Nazism, emerged from the turbulent situation of Munich just after the war. A center of leftist agitation, the city also became a hotbed of the radical right, nurturing a number of new nationalist, militantly anticommunist political groups. One of them, a right-wing workers' party, attracted the attention of Hitler, who soon gave it his personal stamp.

Adolf Hitler was born in Austria in 1889, the son of a lower government official. By 1913 he had become a German nationalist hostile to the multinational Habsburg empire, and he immigrated to Germany. He volunteered for service in the German army in World War I, and it was during the war, he said later, that he "found himself."

He joined the infant German Workers' party late in 1919, and when his first political speech at a rally in February 1920 proved a resounding success, he began to believe he could play a special political role. But Hitler jumped the gun in November 1923 when, with Erich Ludendorff at his side, he led the Beer Hall Putsch in Munich, an attempt to launch a march on Berlin to overthrow the republic. On trial after this effort failed, Hitler gained greater national visibility as he denounced the Versailles treaty and the Weimar government. Still, *Mein Kampf* (*My*

Battle), the political tract that he wrote while in prison during 1924, sold poorly.

His failure in 1923 convinced Hitler that he should exploit the existing political system, but not challenge it directly, in his quest for power on the national level. Yet Hitler never intended to play by the rules: The Nazi party maintained a paramilitary arm, the Sturmabteilung (SA), which provoked a good deal of antileftist street violence.

In 1928 the Nazis attracted only 2.6 percent of the vote in the Reichstag elections. But, in the elections of September 1930, the first since the onset of the Depression, they increased their share dramatically, and in July 1932 their vote exploded to 37.3 percent, making them the largest party in the Reichstag.

As the crisis of the Weimar Republic deepened in 1932, conservative fears of a Marxist outcome played into Hitler's hands. President Hindenburg was relying heavily on a narrow circle of advisers who wanted to take advantage of the Nazis' mass support for conservative purposes. One of those advisers, Franz von Papen (1878–1969), lined up a new coalition that he proposed to Hindenburg: Hitler would be chancellor, Papen himself vice chancellor, and Alfred Hugenberg (1865–1951), the leader of the Nationalist party, finance minister. Still wary of Hitler, Hindenburg felt this combination might work to establish a parliamentary majority, box out the left, and contain Nazism. Hitler became chancellor on January 30, 1933.

The Consolidation of Hitler's Power, 1933–1934

When Hitler became chancellor, it was not obvious that a change of regime was beginning. Like his predecessors, he could govern only with the president's approval, and governmental institutions like the army, the judiciary, and the diplomatic corps were not in the hands of committed Nazis. But although an element of cultivated ambiguity remained, a revolution quickly began, creating the Third Reich.

On February 23, just weeks after Hitler became chancellor, a fire engulfed the Reichstag building in Berlin. It was set by a young Dutch communist acting on his own, but Hitler used it as an excuse to restrict civil liberties and imprison leftist leaders, including the entire Communist parliamentary delegation. Support from the Nationalists and the Center party enabled the Nazis to win Reichstag approval for an enabling act granting Hitler the power to make laws on his own for the next four years, bypassing both the Reichstag and the president.

Although the Weimar Republic was never formally abolished, the laws that followed fundamentally altered government, politics, and public life in Germany. The other parties were either outlawed or persuaded to dissolve so that in July 1933 the Nazi party was declared the only legal party. When President Hindenburg died in August 1934, the offices of chancellor and president were merged, and Germany had just one leader, Adolf Hitler.

During this period of power consolidation, Hitler generally accented normalization. To be sure, his methods occasionally gave conservatives pause. In an especially dramatic episode, the "blood purge" of June 30, 1934, he had several hundred people murdered. The purge was primarily directed against the SA, led by Ernst Röhm (1887–1934). Because Röhm had had pretensions of controlling the army, his removal seemed evidence that Hitler was taming the radicals in his movement. In fact, this purge led to the ascendancy of the Schutzstaffel, or SS, the Nazi elite, led by Heinrich Himmler (1900–1945), which became the institutional basis for the worst aspects of Nazism.

Nazi Aims and German Society

Hitler acted on the basis of a world-view that had coalesced by about 1924. (See the box "Hitler's World-View: Nature, Race, and Struggle.") The central components of his thinking—geopolitics, biological racism, anti-Semitism, and Social Darwinism—were by no means specifically German. They could be found all over the Western world by the early twentieth century.

Geopolitics claimed to offer a scientific understanding of world power based on geographical determinism. To remain sovereign in the

Hitler's World-View: Nature, Race, and Struggle

Hitler outlined his beliefs and aims in* Mein Kampf, *which he wrote while in prison in 1924. The following passages reveal the racism, the anti-Semitism, and the emphasis on nature and struggle that formed the core of his world-view.

No more than Nature desires the mating of weaker with stronger individuals, even less does she desire the blending of a higher with a lower race, since, if she did, her whole work of higher breeding, over perhaps hundreds of thousands of years, might be ruined with one blow.

Historical experience . . . shows with terrifying clarity that in every mingling of Aryan blood with that of lower peoples the result was the end of the cultured people. . . .

Here, of course, we encounter the objection of the modern pacifist, as truly Jewish in its effrontery as it is stupid! "Man's rôle is to overcome Nature!"

. . . [T]his planet once moved through the ether for millions of years without human beings and it can do so again some day if men forget that they owe their higher existence, not to the ideas of a few crazy ideologists, but to the knowledge and ruthless application of Nature's stern and rigid laws. . . .

In the Jewish people the will to self-sacrifice does not go beyond the individual's naked instinct of self-preservation. . . .

If the Jews were alone in the world, they would stifle in filth and offal; they would try to get ahead of one another in hate-filled struggle and exterminate one another. . . .

Source: Adolf Hitler, *Mein Kampf* (Boston: Houghton Mifflin, Sentry, 1943), trans. Ralph Manheim, pp. 286–289, 299, 301–302.

new era of global superpowers like the United States, Hitler warned, Germany would have to expand its territory. By expanding into Poland and the western part of the Soviet Union, Germany could conquer the living space, or *Lebensraum,* necessary for agricultural-industrial balance—and ultimately for self-sufficiency.

The other strands of Hitler's world-view were much less plausible, though each had become prominent during the nineteenth century. Biological racism insisted that built-in racial characteristics determine what is most important about any individual. Anti-Semitism went beyond racism in claiming that Jews play a special and negative role. Social Darwinism accented the positive role of struggle among racial groups.

The dominant current of racist thinking labeled the "Aryans" as healthy, creative, superior. In much racist thinking, Germanic peoples were somehow especially Aryan, though race mixing had produced impurity—and thus degeneration. For the sake of racial purity and historical progress, it was the duty of superior races to supplant backward races. To Hitler, the Jews were not simply another of the races involved in this endless struggle. Rather, as landless parasites, they had played a special historical role, embodying the principles—from humanitarianism to class struggle—that were antithetical to the healthy natural struggle among unified racial groups.

Although Hitler's world-view provided the underlying momentum for the Nazi regime, it did not specify a consistent program, and the regime often adopted short-term expedients that conflicted with its long-term aims. Thus it was possible for Germans living under Nazi rule in the 1930s to embrace aspects of Nazism without seeing where it was all leading.

Hitler's leadership was based on a charismatic relationship with the German people, a nonrational bond resting on common race. To create a genuine racial community, or *Volksgemeinschaft,* it was necessary to unify society and instill Nazi values, making the individual feel part of the whole—and ultimately an instrument to serve the whole. This entailed more or less forced participation in an array of Nazi organizations, from women's groups to the Hitler Youth, from the Labor Front to the Strength Through Joy leisure-time organization.

The Nazis devised unprecedented ways to stage-manage public life, using rituals like the Hitler salute, symbols like the swastika, new media like radio and film, and carefully orchestrated party rallies. The documentary film of a Nuremberg Nazi party rally, *Triumph of the Will* by Leni Riefenstahl (b. 1902), has long been recognized as one of the most compelling propaganda films ever made. Nazi insistence on a circumscribed role for women could shift markedly when women's labor—in this case the work of a promising young director—was deemed essential.

The constraint that Nazi policy put on the lives of women had several sources, but the government's desire to direct human breeding proved crucial. During the summer of 1933, Hitler's government began offering interest-free loans to help couples set up house if the woman agreed to leave the labor force, and Nazi women's organizations endlessly celebrated motherhood and large families. Yet family size continued to decrease in Germany as elsewhere in the industrialized world during the 1930s.

Efforts to control fertility took horrific form as the regime sought to stop the "unhealthy" from reproducing. Just months after coming to power, Hitler engineered a law mandating the compulsory sterilization of persons suffering from certain allegedly hereditary diseases. Medical personnel sterilized some 400,000, the vast majority of them "Aryan" Germans, during the Nazi years. (Forced sterilization was not limited to Nazi Germany in these years; the United States and other democracies were experimenting with it as well, though not to this degree.)

Hitler and Children Adolf Hitler was often portrayed as the friend of children. This photograph accompanied a story for an elementary school reader that described how Hitler, told it was this young girl's birthday, picked her from a crowd of well-wishers to treat her "to cake and strawberries with thick, sweet cream." *(From Heinrich Hoffman,* Jugend um Hitler. *© "Zeitgeschichte" Verlag und Vertriebs-Gesellschaft Berlin. Reproduced with permission. Photo courtesy Wiener Library, London)*

Despite such extreme measures, Hitler's regime enjoyed considerable popular support, for even after Hitler was well entrenched in power, most Germans did not grasp the regime's deeper dynamic. Certainly some welcomed the feeling of belonging, and Hitler himself was immensely popular as a charismatic and decisive leader after the near paralysis of the Weimar years. Most important, before the coming of war in 1939, he seemed to go from success to success, surmounting the Depression and repudiating the major terms of the hated Versailles treaty.

The skillful work of Hitler's propaganda minister, Joseph Goebbels (1897–1945), played on these successes to create a "Hitler myth," which made Hitler seem at once heroic and a man of the people. This myth became central to the Nazi regime, but it merely provided a façade behind which the real Hitler could pursue deeper, long-term aims. These aims were not publicized directly, because the German people did not seem ready for them. In this sense, then, support for Hitler and his regime was broad but shallow during the 1930s.

Did Germans feel constantly under threat of the Gestapo, the secret police? In principle, the Gestapo could interpret the will of the *Führer,* or leader, and decide whether any individual citizen was "guilty" or not. But the Gestapo's victims were not picked at random. They were generally members of specific groups or people suspected of active opposition. So it cannot be said that the German people were coerced into participation through a general atmosphere of terror.

For Jewish Germans it was a different matter. Within weeks after Hitler became chancellor in 1933, new restrictions limited Jewish participation in the civil service, in the professions, and in German cultural life—and quickly drew censure from the League of Nations. The Nuremberg Laws, announced at a party rally in 1935, included prohibition of sexual relations and marriage between Jews and non-Jewish Germans.

About 11 percent of Germany's 550,000 Jews emigrated during 1933 and 1934, and perhaps 25 percent had gotten out by 1938. The fact that the regime stripped emigrating Jews of their assets made emigration more difficult, because countries were unwilling to take in substantial numbers of penniless Jews.

On November 9, 1938, using the assassination of a German diplomat in Paris as a pretext, the Nazis staged the Kristallnacht (Crystal Night) pogrom, during which almost all the synagogues in Germany and about seven thousand Jewish-owned stores were destroyed. Between 30,000 and 50,000 relatively prosperous Jews were arrested and forced to emigrate.

The systematic physical extermination of the Jews began only during the war, but the killing of others deemed superfluous or threatening to the racial community began earlier, with the euthanasia program initiated under volunteer medical teams in 1939. Its aim was to eliminate chronic mental patients, the incurably ill, and people with severe physical handicaps. Those subject to such treatment were primarily ethnic Germans, not Jews or foreigners. Because a public outcry developed, especially among relatives and church leaders, the program had to be discontinued in 1941, but by then it had claimed 100,000 lives.

The euthanasia program was based on the sense, fundamental to radical Nazism, that readiness for war was the real norm for society. Struggle necessitates selection, which requires overcoming humanitarian scruples—that "weakness" calls for special protection. Thus it was desirable to kill even ethnic Germans who were deemed unfit, as "life unworthy of life."

Preparation for war was the core of Nazism in practice. The conquest of living space in the east would provide not only the self-sufficiency necessary for sovereignty but also the land-rootedness necessary for racial health. Such a war of conquest would strike not only the Slavic peoples of the region but also Soviet communism. Beginning in 1936 the Nazis began to bend the economy to serve their long-term aims of war-making.

The Nazi drive toward war during the 1930s transformed international relations in Europe. The other European powers sought to understand Hitler's Germany in terms of the increasingly polarized political context of the period, betting that Hitler would stop short of engaging Europe in another war.

FASCIST CHALLENGE AND ANTIFASCIST RESPONSE

Communists and adherents of the various forms of fascism were bitterly hostile to each other, and beginning in 1934 communists sought to join with anyone who would work with them to fight the fascists. In France and Spain, this effort led to the formation of antifascist popular front coalition governments that struggled to defend democracy. In both cases, however, the Depression restricted maneuvering room, and these governments ended up furthering the polarization they were seeking to avoid.

The Reorientation of Fascist Italy, 1933–1939

By the mid-1930s, it was clear that Italian businessmen were managing to maintain their autonomy against the fascist effort to subordinate business to the political sphere. The corporative institutions never developed into genuine vehicles of mass participation through the workplace—if anything, in fact, they served to regiment the working class.

Mussolini was increasingly frustrated by the limitations he had encountered on the domestic level. On the international level, however, the new context after Hitler came to power offered him some space for maneuver. So as the fascist revolution in Italy faltered, Mussolini began concentrating on foreign policy.

Though Italy, like Germany, remained dissatisfied with the territorial status quo, it was not obvious that fascist Italy and Nazi Germany had to end up in the same camp. Italy was anxious to preserve an independent Austria as a buffer against Germany. There was considerable sentiment among Germans and Austrians for unification of the two countries, and such a greater Germany might threaten the lands Italy had won from Austria in 1919. When Germany seemed poised to absorb Austria in 1934, Mussolini helped stiffen the resistance of Austria's leaders and played a part in forcing Hitler to back down. Mussolini even warned that Nazism, with its racist orientation, posed a significant threat to the best of European civilization.

As it began to appear that France and Britain might have to work with the Soviet Union to check Germany, French and British conservatives pushed for good relations with Italy to provide ideological balance. So Italy was well positioned to play off both sides as Hitler began shaking things up on the international level after 1933. In 1935, just after Hitler announced significant rearmament measures, unilaterally repudiating provisions of the Versailles treaty for the first time, Mussolini hosted a meeting with the French and British prime ministers at Stresa, in northern Italy. To contain Germany, the three powers agreed to resist "any unilateral repudiation of treaties which may endanger the peace of Europe."

Mussolini was already preparing to extend Italy's possessions in East Africa to encompass Ethiopia (formerly called Abyssinia), assuming that the French and British, who needed his support against Hitler, would not offer significant opposition. Italian troops invaded in October 1935, prompting the League of Nations to announce sanctions against Italy.

The sanctions were applied haphazardly, largely because France and Britain wanted to avoid irreparable damage to their longer-term relations with Italy. In any case, the sanctions did not deter Mussolini, whose forces prevailed through the use of aircraft and poison gas by May 1936. But they did make Italy receptive to German overtures in the aftermath of its victory. And the victory made Mussolini more restless. Rather than continuing to play the role of European balancer, he began sending Italian troops and materiel to aid the antidemocratic Nationalists in the Spanish civil war (see the next section), further alienating democratic opinion elsewhere.

Conservatives in Britain and France continued to hope for a revival of the "Stresa Front" against Hitler. Some even defended Italian imperialism in East Africa. But Italy continued its drift toward Germany. Late in 1936, Mussolini spoke of a new Rome-Berlin axis for the first time. He and Hitler exchanged visits in 1937 and 1938. Finally, in May 1939, Italy joined Germany in an open-ended military alliance, the Pact of Steel, though Mussolini made it clear that Italy could not be ready for a major European war before 1943.

To cement this developing relationship, fascist Italy adopted anti-Semitic racial laws modeled on Germany's, even though Italian fascism had not originally been anti-Semitic and indeed had attracted Jewish Italians to its membership in about the same proportion as non-Jews. The increasing subservience to Nazi Germany displeased even many committed fascists. Such opposition helped keep Mussolini from entering the war until May 1940, eight months after it began.

From Democracy to Civil War in Spain, 1931–1939

By the mid-1930s the threat of fascism was so pressing that the Communists had to begin actively promoting electoral alliances and governing coalitions with Socialists and even liberal democrats to resist its further spread. From 1934 until 1939, Communists everywhere consistently pursued this "popular front" strategy. Nowhere was this strategy more apparent than in Spain.

The Spanish republic was born in April 1931 amid great optimism. In June, elections for a constituent assembly produced a solid victory for a coalition of liberal democrats and Socialists. But the leaders of the new republic dragged their feet on land reform, alienating landowners without satisfying the peasants. Socialists and agricultural workers became increasingly radical, producing upheaval in the countryside. A right-wing coalition (the CEDA) grew in response, becoming the largest party in parliament with elections in November 1933 and joining the government in October 1934. It seemed to the left that the growing role of the CEDA was a prelude to fascism.

The Spanish left may have been too quick to see the right-wing CEDA as fascist, but the German left had been criticized for its passive response to the advent of Hitler and the Spanish left wanted to avoid the same mistake. Thus, during the fall of 1934 the left responded to the opening of the government to the CEDA with quasi-revolutionary uprisings in Catalonia and Asturias, which were crushed.

In February 1936 a popular front coalition of Republicans, Socialists, Syndicalists, and Communists won an absolute majority in parliament. The new government began to implement the land reform that had been promised earlier. But it was too late to undercut the growing radicalization of the masses: A wave of land seizures began in March, followed by a revolutionary strike movement. To many, the government's inability to keep order had become the immediate issue. By the early summer of 1936, the extremes of left and right were each preparing an extralegal solution.

A Nationalist military uprising led by General Francisco Franco (1892–1975) took control of substantial parts of Spain, but elsewhere the Nationalists failed to overcome the resistance of Republican Loyalists determined to defend the republic. Thus began a brutal civil war. Substantial Italian fascist and Nazi German intervention on the Nationalist side intensified the war's ideological ramifications. At the same time, the remarkable, heroic resistance of the Loyalists captured the imagination of the world. Indeed, forty thousand volunteers came from abroad to fight for the Spanish republic.

It proved a war of stunning brutality on both sides. Loyalist anticlericalism led to the murder of perhaps one-eighth of the parish clergy in Spain. On the other side, the German bombing of the Basque town of Guernica on a crowded market day in April 1937—represented unforgettably in Pablo Picasso's painting—came to symbolize the violence and suffering of the whole era.

Although Republican Loyalists assumed that Franco and the Nationalists represented another instance of fascism, Franco was really a traditional military conservative. Nevertheless, Franco's forces did find it expedient to take advantage of the appeal of the Falange, a fascist movement that had emerged under the leadership of the charismatic young José Antonio Primo de Rivera (1903–1936).

They Shall Not Pass! Women were prominent in the citizen militias defending Madrid and other cities during the Spanish civil war. This example of Loyalist poster art celebrates the sacrifices and courage of men and women. Compare this example of propaganda with those shown in the photos on pages 636 and 647. *(Biblioteca Nacional, Madrid)*

Meanwhile, the Republicans had to deal with an anarchist and syndicalist revolution in their own ranks. Ironically, the Communists insisted that this was no time for revolutionary experiments and put down the revolt of anarchist munitions workers in Catalonia. Under these extraordinary circumstances, the Communists gained the ascendancy on the Republican side, partly because they were disciplined and effective, partly because Soviet assistance enhanced their prestige. "They shall not pass," proclaimed the eloquent Spanish communist Dolores Ibarruri (1895–1989), whose impassioned speeches and radio broadcasts captured the attention of the world. But in the end they did pass. Despite considerable heroism, the Loyalists were overwhelmed, and Madrid fell to the Nationalists in March 1939. General Franco's authoritarian regime governed Spain until his death in 1975.

France in the Era of the Popular Front

In France, concern to arrest the spread of fascism also led to a popular front coalition, here including

Socialists, Communists, and Radicals, which governed the country from 1936 to 1938. Although it did not lead to civil war, the popular front experience of the 1930s helped undermine confidence in the Third Republic.

In 1934, the French Communists took the initiative in creating a popular front coalition against fascism. Various nationalist, anticommunist, profascist, and anti-Semitic leagues had gathered momentum in France during the early 1930s, and in defense, the Communists were willing to reach out to the Socialists and even to the Radicals, making no demand for significant economic reforms. But as in Spain, the highly charged ideological climate favored extreme reactions.

In 1936, the popular front won a sizable majority in the Chamber of Deputies, putting Léon Blum (1872–1950) in line to become France's first socialist prime minister. This produced a wave of enthusiasm among workers that escaped the control of popular-front leaders and culminated in a spontaneous strike movement that spread to all major industries nationwide. The major trade union confederation, the Communists, and most Socialists, including Blum himself, saw the strikes as a danger to the popular front, with its more modest aims of defending the republic, and eagerly pursued a settlement, the Matignon Agreement. Workers got collective bargaining, elected shop stewards, and wage increases as a direct result of Matignon, then a forty-hour week and paid vacations in a later reform package.

In the enthusiasm of the summer of 1936, there were other reforms as well, but after that the popular front was forced on the defensive. The left grew disillusioned when a new government under the Radical Edouard Daladier (1884–1970) began dismantling some of the key gains in 1938. Meanwhile, businessmen and conservatives began blaming the workers' gains—like the five-day week—for slowing French rearmament.

As France began to face the possibility of a new war, the popular front was widely blamed for French weakness. When war came at last, resignation and division were prevalent, and when France fell to the Germans, the democratic Third Republic fell with it.

SUMMARY

The 1920s proved a contradictory period of vitality and despair. The era began with bright hopes for democracy, yet the outcome of the democratic experiment in east-central Europe was disappointing. In Germany as well, the new democratic republic remained on the defensive, then failed to weather the economic depression that began in 1929. Even Italy, heir by the 1920s to a respectable tradition of democracy, gave rise to the troubling new phenomenon of fascism. A hopeful new spirit of international conciliation drew France and Germany closer together by the end of 1925, and in early 1929 restabilization seemed to have taken hold in Europe. Germany, Italy, and the Soviet Union, the most volatile and potentially disruptive of the major countries, seemed to be settling down. But it would all come apart over the next decade.

The Depression and the challenges from new political regimes called both capitalism and democracy into question. The most important new political systems of the interwar period—Italian fascism, German Nazism, and Stalinist communism—were not merely authoritarian in the old-fashioned, predemocratic sense. In each of the three regimes, the sovereignty of the state was to become all-encompassing, breaking down the distinction between public and private. Thus Mussolini's boast that there was "nothing outside the state" in fascist Italy and the proclamation of Robert Ley, head of the Nazi Labor Front, that "the private citizen has ceased to exist."

The common totalitarian direction is important, but it glosses over differences, especially in origins and purposes, that are at least as important. Racism and anti-Semitism, fundamental to radical Nazism, were not central to Italian fascism, and Italy's experimentation with ideas of a "corporative state" was not shared by the Nazis.

Communism's philosophical origins distinguish it from fascism. Twisted though it became, the Marxist vision of human liberation, based on long-standing Western values, was still manifest in the ongoing Soviet revolution during the Stalinist 1930s. Committed communists believed that extreme measures were necessary if they were to carry out a transformation that would eventually benefit all humanity. Nazism never claimed a comparably universal aim. Hitler's world-view was the antithesis of the humanistic tradition.

But whatever the differences in values and intentions, the final reckoning must rest on the results. Stalin's way of implementing the Marxist revolution made individual human lives expendable, just as they were for Hitler. The outcome of both Stalinism and Nazism was mass murder on a horrifying scale.

NOTES

1. Virginia Woolf, *A Room of One's Own* (New York: Harcourt, Brace and World, 1975 [1929]), p. 118.
2. Benito Mussolini, speech to the Italian Chamber of Deputies, January 3, 1925, from Charles F. Delzell, ed., *Mediterranean Fascism, 1919–1945* (New York: Harper & Row, 1970), pp. 59–60.

SUGGESTED READING

Bessel, Richard, ed., *Life in the Third Reich.* 1987. Essays on the connections between the Nazi regime and German society. An ideal introductory work.

Bridenthal, Renate, Atina Grossmann, and Marion Kaplan, eds. *When Biology Became Destiny: Women in Weimar and Nazi Germany.* 1984. Excellent studies of Nazi gender ideology, examining issues of work, reproduction, and social organization.

Carr, Raymond. *The Spanish Tragedy: The Civil War in Perspective.* 1977. An accessible account, blending narrative with analysis and commentary. Particularly useful on the politics of the Nationalist zone.

Conquest, Robert. *The Great Terror: A Reassessment.* 1990. An updated edition of an influential work first published in 1968. Offers a gripping account of the Stalinist purges of the 1930s, emphasizing Stalin's personal responsibility.

Eichengreen, Barry. *Golden Fetters: The Gold Standard and the Great Depression, 1919–1939.* 1992. Accents the role of the gold standard both in intensifying the destabilizing process that led to the Depression and in limiting the responses of policymakers.

Fischer, Klaus P. *Nazi Germany: A New History.* 1995. Comprehensive, well researched, and carefully balanced, this is perhaps the best one-volume treatment of Nazism in English.

Fitzpatrick, Sheila. *Stalin's Peasants: Resistance and Survival in the Russian Village after Collectivization.* 1994. A probing study of the peasant response to the forced collectivization that inaugurated Stalin's rule in the Soviet Union.

Fitzpatrick, Sheila, Alexander Rabinowitch, and Richard Stites, eds. *Russia in the Era of NEP: Explorations in Soviet Society and Culture.* 1991. Illuminating scholarly essays accenting the ambiguities of the transitional 1920s, when class identity, economic activity, and gender roles had been radically disrupted but had not yet settled into the forms that came to characterize the Soviet experiment.

Gentile, Emilio. *The Sacralization of Politics in Fascist Italy.* 1996. A masterful account of the cult of political involvement that fed the first overtly totalitarian experiment.

Grossmann, Atina. *Reforming Sex: The German Movement for Birth Control and Abortion Reform, 1920–1950.* 1995. An innovative study tracing German debate and policy across three distinct political regimes.

Jackson, Julian. *The Popular Front in France: Defending Democracy, 1934–1938.* 1988. Combines narrative with thematic chapters on the most controversial issues surrounding the popular front experience.

Kent, Susan Kingsley. *Making Peace: The Reconstruction of Gender in Interwar Britain.* 1993. A concise and accessible work examining the use of traditionalist representations of gender roles in response to the anxieties unleashed in Britain by the war.

Kolb, Eberhard. *The Weimar Republic.* 1988. Provides a good overall survey, then pinpoints the recent trends in research.

Koonz, Claudia. *Mothers in the Fatherland: Women, the Family, and Nazi Politics.* 1987. An influential and accessible study of women in Nazism, accenting their active roles in implementing Nazism on the grassroots level, while ultimately stressing their subordination within the wider Nazi universe.

Noakes, J[eremy], and G[eoffrey] Pridham, eds. *Nazism: A History in Documents and Eyewitness Accounts, 1919–1945.* 2 vols. 1990. An invaluable collection of documents, with running commentary by the editors.

Nolan, Mary. *Visions of Modernity: American Business in the Modernization of Germany.* 1994. Examines the ambiguous impact of Americanism on Germany in the 1920s, when the United States seemed to stand both for economic success and for an impersonal, alienating mass culture.

CHAPTER 25

The Era of the Second World War, 1939–1949

"The effects could well be called unprecedented, magnificent, beautiful, stupendous and terrifying. No man-made phenomenon of such tremendous power had ever occurred before. . . . Thirty seconds after the explosion came first, the air blast pressing hard against the people and things, to be followed almost immediately by the strong, sustained, awesome roar which warned of doomsday and made us feel that we puny things were blasphemous to dare tamper with the forces heretofore reserved to The Almighty."[1]

So wrote Brigadier General Thomas F. Farrell, having just witnessed the birth of the atomic age. On July 16, 1945, watching from a control shelter 10,000 yards away, Farrell saw the first explosion of an atomic bomb at a remote, top-secret testing ground in New Mexico. Within weeks, the United States dropped two other atomic bombs—first on Hiroshima, then on Nagasaki—to force the surrender of Japan. In using the atomic bomb, the Americans not only ended the war but assured that a new set of anxieties would accompany the return to peace.

World War II proved more destructive than World War I and more truly global. Japan's far greater involvement in World War II brought the full brunt of the war to Asia and the Pacific and dramatically changed military strategy. Moreover, because the war expanded as it did, it affected the place of Western civilization in the world, speeding the dissolution of the Western colonial empires.

The ironic outcome of World War II was a cold war between the United States and the Soviet Union, allies in the victorious struggle against Germany, Italy, and Japan. By the end of the 1940s, the United States and the Soviet Union had divided Europe into competing spheres of influence.

Competition between these two superpowers almost immediately became global in scope and world-ending in possible consequence: The nuclear weapons that had ended the war were now being stockpiled, redefining the human condition.

The experience of World War II itself also changed the world forever. Before finally meeting defeat, the Nazis had begun implementing their "new order" in Europe. As part of this effort, in what has become known as the Holocaust, they began systematically murdering Jews in extermination camps, eventually killing as many as 6 million. The most destructive of the camps was at Auschwitz, in Poland. Auschwitz and Hiroshima came to stand for the war's new forms of death and destruction, both of which continued to haunt the world long after the war had ended.

Questions and Ideas to Consider

- Why did the democratic nations of the West allow Hitler to revise Germany's status? Why did Britain and France finally declare war against Germany?
- What was the *Blitzkrieg*? Why was France so quick to surrender? What were the consequences for France and her former allies?
- Why does the Holocaust stand out as a new kind of human brutality? What purpose did it serve?
- Describe the Lend-Lease Act and the Atlantic Charter. Why was the United States reluctant to enter the war, and what made Roosevelt finally commit U.S. troops?
- What were the origins of the cold war? Could it have been avoided?

THE COMING OF WORLD WAR II, 1935–1939

Still under the long shadow of World War I, most Western leaders were determined to preserve the peace during the two ensuing decades. In Germany and eastern Europe, the peace settlement that had followed the war created new problems, and Hitler had consistently trumpeted his intention to overturn that settlement. What scope was there for peaceful revision?

The Germans Strike: Austria, Czechoslovakia, and Appeasement

During his first years in power, Hitler could be understood as merely restoring German sovereignty, revising a postwar settlement that had been misconceived in the first place. However uncouth and abrasive he might seem, it was hard to find a basis for opposing him. Yet in commencing German rearmament in 1935, and especially in remilitarizing the Rhineland in March 1936, Hitler fundamentally reversed the power balance established in France's favor at the peace conference.

France's special advantage had been the demilitarization of the entire German territory west of the Rhine River and a 50-kilometer strip on the east bank. The measure had been reaffirmed at Locarno in 1925, with Germany's free agreement, and it was guaranteed by Britain and Italy. Yet on a Saturday morning in March 1936, German troops moved into the forbidden area. The French and British acquiesced, uncertain what else to do.

But Hitler was not likely to stop there. Three new countries—Austria, Czechoslovakia, and Poland—bordered Germany, and in each the peace settlement had left trouble spots involving the status of ethnic Germans. In 1934, Hitler had moved to absorb his homeland, Austria, but strenuous opposition from Italy led him to back down. The developing understanding with Italy by 1936 enabled Hitler to focus again on Austria—initiating the second, more radical phase of his prewar foreign policy. On a pretext, German troops moved into Austria in March 1938, and it was promptly incorporated into Germany. This time Mussolini was willing to acquiesce, and Hitler was genuinely grateful. The Treaty of Versailles had explicitly prohibited this *Anschluss*, or unity with Germany, but that prohibition violated the principle of self-determination, and

CHAPTER CHRONOLOGY

September 1938	Munich conference ends Sudetenland crisis
August 1939	Nazi-Soviet non-aggression pact
September 1, 1939	Germany invades Poland
May 10, 1940	Germany attacks the Netherlands, Belgium, and France
June 22, 1941	Germany attacks the Soviet Union
August 1941	Churchill and Roosevelt agree to the Atlantic Charter
December 7, 1941	Japanese attack Pearl Harbor
January 1942	Wannsee conference; Nazi plan for the extermination of the Jews
August 1942–February 1943	Battle of Stalingrad
April–May 1943	Warsaw ghetto revolt
July 1943	Allied landings in Sicily; fall of Mussolini
November 1943	Teheran conference
June 6, 1944	D-Day: Allied landings in Normandy
February 1945	Yalta conference
May 7–8, 1945	German surrender
June 1945	Founding of the United Nations
July–August 1945	Potsdam conference
August 6, 1945	U.S. atomic bombing of Hiroshima
March 1947	Truman Doctrine speech
June 1948–May 1949	Berlin Blockade and airlift
August 1949	First Soviet atomic bomb
September 1949	Founding of the Federal Republic in West Germany

it was widely believed in the West that most Austrians favored unity with Germany. The Anschluss could be justified as revising a misconceived aspect of the peace settlement.

Czechoslovakia presented quite a different situation. It included restive minorities of Slovaks, Magyars, Ruthenians, Poles, and—concentrated especially in the Sudetenland—about 3.25 million Germans. After having been part of the dominant nationality in the old Habsburg empire, those Germans were frustrated with their minority status in the new Czechoslovakia. Hitler's agents actively stirred up their resentments.

Leading the West's response, when Hitler began making an issue of Czechoslovakia, was Neville Chamberlain (1869–1940), who had become Britain's prime minister and foreign minister in May 1937. An intelligent, vigorous, and public-spirited man from the progressive wing of the Conservative party, Chamberlain sought to master the difficult international situation through creative bargaining. The excesses of Hitler's policy resulted from the mistakes of Versailles; redo the settlement on a more realistic basis, Chamberlain felt, and Germany would behave responsibly. Moreover, in Britain as elsewhere, there were some who saw Hitler's resurgent Germany as a bulwark against communism.

As the Sudeten Germans escalated their demands for autonomy, tensions between Czechoslovakia and Germany mounted. In September 1938 war appeared imminent—the French and the British began mobilizing. Since 1929, the French had been constructing a fortified line along their border with Germany, from Switzerland to the Ardennes Forest at the border with Belgium. In 1938, troops were sent in to man the "Maginot Line" for the first time.

A 1924 treaty bound France to come to the aid of Czechoslovakia in the event of aggression. The Soviet Union, according to a treaty of 1935, was bound to assist Czechoslovakia if the French did so. Throughout the crisis, the Soviets pushed for a strong stand in defense of Czechoslovakia. But for both ideological and military reasons, the British and French were not anxious for a war on the side of the Soviet Union. The value of the Soviet military was uncertain, at best, at a time when the Soviet officer corps had just been purged.

Hitler seemed eager to smash the Czechs by force, but when Mussolini proposed a four-power conference, he was persuaded to talk again. At Munich late in September, Britain, France, Italy, and Germany settled the matter, with Czechoslovakia—and the Soviet Union—excluded. Determined not to risk war over what seemed to be Czech intransigence, Chamberlain agreed to what Hitler had wanted all along—German annexation of the Sudetenland.

All Sudeten areas with German majorities were to be transferred to Germany; plebiscites would be held in areas with large German minorities, and Hitler pledged to respect the sovereignty of the newly diminished Czechoslovak state. Chamberlain and his French counterpart, Edouard Daladier, returned home to a hero's welcome, having transformed what had seemed certain war to, in Chamberlain's memorable phrase, "peace in our time."

But in March 1939, Germany sent troops into Prague. Slovakia was spun off as a separate nation, while the Czech areas became the Protectorate of Bohemia and Moravia. Less than six months after the Munich conference, most of what had been Czechoslovakia had landed firmly within the Nazi orbit. It was no longer possible to justify Hitler's actions as seeking to unite all Germans in one state.

The Invasion of Poland and the Nazi-Soviet Pact

With Poland, the German grievance was still more serious, for the new Polish state had been created partly at German expense. Especially galling to Germans was the Polish corridor, which cut off East Prussia from the bulk of Germany in order to give Poland access to the sea. The city of Danzig, historically Polish (Gdansk) but part of Germany before World War I, was left a "free city," supervised by the League of Nations.

Disillusioned by Hitler's dismemberment of Czechoslovakia, and angered by the Germans' menacing rhetoric regarding Poland, Chamberlain announced in the House of Commons on March 31, 1939, that Britain and France would intervene militarily in the event of a threat to Poland's independence. Chamberlain was abandoning the policy of appeasement, now possible because Britain was rapidly rearming.

Hitler continued to stress how limited and reasonable German aims were. Germany simply wanted Danzig and German transit across the corridor; it was the Polish stance that was rigid and unreasonable. As the crisis developed, doubts were increasingly expressed, on all sides, on whether the British and French were really prepared to aid Poland—that they were willing "to die for Danzig."

Although they had been lukewarm to Soviet proposals for a military alliance, Britain and France began to negotiate with the Soviet Union more seriously during the spring and summer of 1939. And then, even as negotiations between the Soviet Union and the democracies seemed to continue, the Soviet Union came to an agreement with Nazi Germany on August 22, 1939, in a pact that astonished the world. At this point a nonaggression pact with Germany seemed to serve Soviet interests best. To the Soviets, the democracies seemed no more trustworthy, and potentially no less hostile, than Nazi Germany. So the Soviets and the Germans agreed that each would remain neutral in the event that either became involved in war.

The Nazi-Soviet Pact seemed to have given Hitler the free hand he wanted in Poland. With the dramatic change in alignment, the democracies were surely less likely to intervene. But after Hitler ordered the German invasion of Poland on September 1, the British and French declared war on September 3.

With each step on the path to war, Hitler had alternated between apparent reasonableness and wanton aggressiveness. But he always intended a war of conquest—first against Poland, but ultimately against the Soviet Union. War was essential to the Nazi vision, and only when the assault on Poland became a full-scale war did the underlying purposes of Nazism become clear.

THE VICTORY OF NAZI GERMANY, 1939–1941

Instead of the enthusiasm evident in 1914, the German invasion of Poland on September 1, 1939, produced a grim sense of foreboding, even in Germany. Well-publicized incidents like the German bombing of civilians during the Spanish civil war and the Italian use of poison gas in Ethiopia suggested that the frightening new technologies introduced in World War I would now be used on a far greater scale, making the conflict a much uglier war, involving civilians more directly.

Still, as in 1914, there were hopes that this war could be localized and brief. Hitler did not expect a protracted war with Britain. In light of the Nazi-Soviet Pact, war between Germany and the Soviet Union seemed unlikely. And isolationist sentiment in the United States made U.S. intervention doubtful.

Hitler and the German high command envisioned a *Blitzkrieg*, or "lightning war." At first events seemed to confirm German expectations. When Poland fell after just over a month, Hitler publicly offered peace to Britain and France, seriously thinking that might be the end of it. The British and French refused to call off the war, but from 1939 through 1941 the Nazis won victory after victory, establishing the foundation for their new order in Europe.

Initial Conquests and "Phony War"

The Polish army was large enough to have given the Germans a serious battle. But in adapting the technological innovations of World War I, Germany had developed a new military strategy based on rapid mobility. This Blitzkrieg strategy employed swift, highly concentrated offensives based on mobile tanks covered with concentrated air support, including dive-bombers that struck just ahead of the tanks. The last Polish unit surrendered on October 2, barely a month after the fighting had begun. The speed of the German victory stunned the world.

Meanwhile, the Soviets began cashing in on the pact they had made with Nazi Germany a few weeks before. On September 17, with the German victory in Poland assured, Stalin sent Soviet forces into Poland. Poland was again divided between Germany and Russia. Stalin looked next to the Baltic States, which had been part of the Russian Empire before World War I. Although initially let off with treaties of mutual assistance, Estonia, Latvia, and Lithuania were incorporated as republics within the Soviet Union during the summer of 1940. The Nazi-Soviet agreement had assigned Lithuania to the German orbit, but the Germans agreed to let the Soviets have it in exchange for an additional slice of Poland.

The Soviets invaded Finland in November 1939. In the ensuing "Winter War," the Finns held out bravely and inflicted heavy casualties until the Soviets managed to prevail by March 1940. These difficulties seemed to confirm suspicions that Stalin's purge during the mid-1930s had substantially weakened the Soviet army. Still, by midsummer 1940 the Soviet Union had regained much of the territory it had lost during the upheavals surrounding the revolution of 1917.

In the West, little happened during the strained winter of 1939–1940, known as the "Phony War." Then, on April 9, 1940, the Germans attacked Norway and Denmark to preempt a British and French scheme to cut off the major route for the shipment of Swedish iron ore to Germany. Denmark fell almost at once, while staunch resistance in Norway took a few weeks to overcome. The stage was set for the German assault on France.

The Fall of France, 1940

The war in the West began in earnest on May 10, 1940, when the Germans attacked France and the Low Countries. They launched their assault on France through the Ardennes Forest, above the northern end of the Maginot Line—terrain so difficult the French had discounted the possibility of an enemy strike there. As in 1914, northern France became the focus of a major war pitting French forces and their British allies against invading Germans. But this time, in startling contrast to World War I, the Battle of France was over in less than six weeks, a humiliating defeat for the French. What had happened?

The problem for the French was not lack of men and materiel, but strategy. Germany had no more than a slight numerical advantage in tanks. But it used the tanks to mount rapid, highly concentrated offensives. French strategy, in contrast, was based on the lessons learned in World War I. Anticipating another long, defensive war, France dispersed its tanks among infantry units along a broad front. Once the German tank column broke through the French lines, it quickly cut through northern France toward the North Sea. France's poor showing convinced the British that they should get out and regroup for a longer global war. Finally, 200,000 British troops—as well as 130,000 French—escaped German encirclement and capture through a difficult evacuation at Dunkirk early in June.

As the French military collapsed, the French cabinet resigned, to be replaced by a new government under Marshal Philippe Pétain, the hero of the Battle of Verdun during World War I. Pétain's government asked for an armistice and then engineered a change of regime. The French parliament voted by an overwhelming majority to give Pétain exceptional powers, including the power to draw up a new constitution. So ended the parliamentary democracy of the Third Republic. The republic gave way to the more authoritarian Vichy regime, named after the southern resort city to which the government retreated as the Germans moved into Paris. The end of the fighting in France resulted in a kind of antidemocratic revolution.

According to the armistice agreement, the French government was required to collaborate with the victorious Germans. French resistance began immediately, however. In a radio broadcast from London on June 18, Charles de Gaulle (1890–1970), the youngest general in the French army, called on French forces to rally to him to continue the fight. The military forces stationed in the French colonies, as well as the French troops that had been evacuated at Dunkirk, could form the nucleus of a new French army. Given the circumstances, de Gaulle's appeal seemed quixotic at best, and most French colonies went along with what seemed the legitimate French government at Vichy. To the new Vichy government, de Gaulle was a traitor. Yet a new Free French force grew from de Gaulle's remarkable appeal, and its subsequent role in the war helped overcome the humiliation of France's quick defeat in 1940.

Winston Churchill and the Battle of Britain

With the defeat of France, Hitler seems to have expected that Britain, now apparently vulnerable to German invasion, would come to terms. But the British, having none of it, found a new spokesman and leader in Winston Churchill (1874–1965), who had replaced Neville Chamberlain as prime minister when the German invasion of western Europe began on May 10. Although Churchill had been prominent in British public life for years, his career had not been noteworthy for either judgment or success. He was obstinate, difficult, something of a curmudgeon. Yet he rose to the wartime challenge, becoming one of the notable leaders of the modern era. In speeches to the House of Commons during the remainder of 1940, he uttered perhaps the most memorable words of the war as he sought to inspire the nation. Some Britons, hoping for a negotiated settlement with Germany as the Battle of France ended, objected to Churchill's rhetoric, but his dogged promise of "blood, toil, tears, and sweat" helped rally the British people, so that later he could say, without exaggeration, that "this was their finest hour."

After the fall of France, Britain moved to full mobilization for a protracted war. Churchill consolidated economic policy under a small committee that gave Britain the most thoroughly coordinated war economy of all the belligerents. Between 1940 and 1942, Britain outstripped Germany in the production of tanks, aircraft, and machine guns. In 1941 the National Service Act subjected men aged 18 to 50 and women aged 20 to 30 to military or civilian war service. The upper age limits were subsequently raised to meet the demand for labor.

Hitler weighed his options and decided to attack. In light of British naval superiority, he hoped to rely on aerial bombardment to knock the British out of the war without an actual invasion. The ensuing Battle of Britain culminated in the nightly bombing of London from September 7 through November 2, 1940, killing 15,000 people and destroying thousands of buildings. But the British held. Ordinary people holed up in cellars and subway stations, while the fighter planes of the Royal Air Force fought back effectively, inflicting heavy losses against German aircraft.

Although the bombing continued into 1941, the British had withstood the worst the Germans could deliver, and Hitler began looking to the east, his ultimate objective all along. In December 1940 he ordered preparations for Operation Barbarossa, the assault on the Soviet Union. Rather than continuing the attack on Britain directly, Germany would use submarines to cut off shipping—and thus the supplies the British needed for a long war. Once Germany had defeated the Soviet Union, it would enjoy the geopolitical basis for world power, while Britain, an island nation relying on a dispersed empire, would be forced to come to terms.

Italian Intervention and the Spread of the War

Lacking sufficient domestic support and unready for a major war, Mussolini could only look on as the war began in 1939. But as the Battle of France neared its end, it seemed safe for Italy to intervene and share in the spoils. Thus in June 1940, Italy entered the war, expecting to seize Corsica, Nice, and Tunisia from France. Italy hoped eventually to supplant Britain in the Mediterranean—and even to take the Suez Canal.

Although Hitler and Mussolini got along remarkably well, their relationship was sensitive. When Hitler seemed to be proceeding without Italy during the first year of the war, Mussolini grew determined to show his independence and finally, in October 1940, ordered Italian forces to attack Greece. The Greeks mounted a strong resistance, thanks partly to the help of British forces from North Africa.

Meanwhile, Germany had established its hegemony in much of east-central Europe without military force, often by exploiting grievances over the outcome of the peace conference in 1919. In November 1940, Romania and Hungary joined the Axis camp, and Bulgaria followed a few months later. But in March 1941, just after Yugoslavia had similarly committed to the Axis, a coup overthrew the pro-Axis government in Yugoslavia, and the new Yugoslav government prepared to aid the Allies.

By this point Hitler had decided to push into the Balkans with German troops, both to reinforce the Italians and to consolidate Axis control of the area. By the end of May 1941, Germany had taken Yugoslavia and Greece.

At the same time, the war was spreading to North Africa and the Middle East because of European colonial ties. The native peoples of the area sought to take advantage of the conflict among the Europeans to pursue their own independence. Operating from Syria, Germans aided anti-British Arab nationalists in Iraq. But most important proved to be North Africa, where Libya, an Italian colony since 1912, lay adjacent to Egypt, where the British presence remained strong. In September 1940 the Italian army drove 65 miles into Egypt, initiating almost three years of fighting across the North African desert. A British counteroffensive drove the Italians back into Libya, prompting Germany to send some of its forces from the Balkans into North Africa. Under General Erwin Rommel (1891–1944), the famous "Desert Fox," Axis forces won remarkable successes. But the German forays into the Balkans and North Africa had delayed the crucial attack on the Soviet Union.

THE ASSAULT ON THE SOVIET UNION AND THE NAZI NEW ORDER

The Germans penetrated well into the Soviet Union, reaching the apex of their power in 1942. German conquests by that point enabled Hitler to begin constructing his new European order. Although in western Europe the Nazis generally sought the collaboration of local leaders, in Poland and the Soviet Union the new order meant brutal subjugation of local populations. It was at this point that the Nazis began exterminating the Jews of Europe in specially constructed death camps.

Operation Barbarossa and Hitler's New Order

In ordering preparations for Operation Barbarossa in December 1940, Hitler was betting that the purges of the 1930s had severely weakened the Soviet Union. If Germany were to defeat the Soviet Union, it could gain control of oil and other resources required for a longer war against Britain and, if necessary, the United States.

Attacking the Soviet Union on June 22, 1941, German forces at first achieved notable successes, partly because Stalin was so unprepared for the German betrayal. By late November, German forces were within twenty miles of Moscow. But the Germans were ill equipped for Russian weather, and as an early and severe winter descended, the German offensive bogged down. The Soviets counterattacked near Moscow in December. Although their initial assault had stalled, the Germans still had the advantage, and they reached Stalingrad in November 1942. This proved the deepest penetration of German forces—and the zenith of Nazi power in Europe. Hitler could now begin to put his new order into effect.

By the summer of 1942, Nazi Germany dominated the European continent as no power ever had before (Map 25.1). Satellite states in Slovakia and Croatia and client governments in Romania and Hungary owed their existence to Nazi Germany and readily adapted themselves to the Nazi system. Elsewhere in the Nazi orbit, some countries proved eager collaborators; others did their best to resist; still others were given no opportunity to collaborate but were ruthlessly subjugated instead.

The Nazis' immediate aim was to exploit the conquered territories to serve the continuing war effort. Precisely as envisioned, access to the resources of so much of Europe made Germany considerably less vulnerable to naval blockade than it had been during World War I. France proved a particularly valuable source of raw materials; by 1943, for example, 75 percent of French iron ore went to German factories.

But the deeper purposes of the war were clear in the different way the Nazis treated the territories under their control. In western Europe, there was plenty of brutality, but Nazi victory still led to something like conventional military occupation. However, in Poland and later in the conquered parts of the Soviet Union it at once became clear that the Nazi order would entail something very different.

After the conquest of Poland, Nazi leaders proclaimed a new era of German resettlement in eastern Europe. By mid-1941, 200,000 Germans, carefully selected for their racial characteristics, had been resettled—primarily on farms—in the part of Poland annexed to Germany. Many were ethnic Germans who had been living outside Germany. During the fall of 1942, the Schutzstaffel (SS), under the leadership of Heinrich Himmler, began to expel peasants from the rest of Poland to make way for further German resettlement. By 1943 perhaps 1 million Germans had been moved into what had been Poland.

After the assault on the Soviet Union, Himmler told SS leaders that Germany would have to exterminate 30 million Soviet Slavs to

NORWAY
Oslo
FINLAND
Helsinki
Leningrad
Stockholm
SWEDEN
North Sea
Baltic Sea
DENMARK
Copenhagen
IRELAND
GREAT BRITAIN
London
HOLLAND
Amsterdam
REICHSKOMMISSARIAT OSTLAND
SOVIET UNION
Moscow
Volga
Ural
Don
Stalingrad
Caspian Sea
Elbe
Berlin
Oder
Vistula
Warsaw
Pripyat'
Bug
Kiev
Dnieper
Brussels
BELGIUM
Bonn
Rhine
GREATER GERMANY
Seine
Paris
FRANCE
Loire
Luxembourg
PROTECTORATE OF BOHEMIA & MORAVIA
Prague
GOVERNMENT GENERAL OF POLAND
REICHSKOMMISSARIAT UKRAINE
SLOVAKIA
Danube
Vienna
Budapest
HUNGARY
Vichy
VICHY FRANCE
SWITZ.
Po
ROMANIA
Belgrade
Bucharest
CROATIA
SERBIA
Black Sea
SPAIN
Tagus
Corsica
ITALY
Rome
MONTENEGRO
Sofia
BULGARIA
ALBANIA
Istanbul
Sardinia
TURKEY
GREECE
Athens
Sicily
Malta
Crete
Mediterranean Sea
LIBYA
Area controlled by Axis powers, 1942
Neutral and non-belligerent states
Allies
Boundary of Greater Germany
0 200 400 Km.
0 200 400 Mi.
EXTERMINATION AND CONCENTRATION CAMPS
DENMARK
SWEDEN
Baltic Sea
REICHSKOMMISSARIAT OSTLAND
Elbe
BERGEN-BELSEN
SACHSENHAUSEN
Berlin
Vistula
Oder
TREBLINKA
CHELMNO
Pripyat'
SOBIBOR
REICHSKOM-MISSARIAT UKRAINE
Bug
GREATER GERMANY
MAJDANEK
TREWNIKI
BUCHENWALD
PONIATOWA
BELZEC
PROTECTORATE OF BOHEMIA AND MORAVIA
AUSCHWITZ
GOVERNMENT GENERAL OF POLAND
Danube
SLOVAKIA
DACHAU
MAUTHAUSEN
HUNGARY
Poland before Sept. 1, 1939
Extermination camps
Concentration camps
ITALY
Po
CROATIA
SERBIA
ROMANIA

prepare for German colonization. But there, in contrast to Poland, the program barely got started during the war.

The Holocaust

Conquest of the east gave the Nazis the opportunity for a more radical solution to the "Jewish problem." Under the cover of war, they began the systematic extermination of the Jews that has come to be known as the Holocaust.

When and why this policy was chosen remains controversial. Although prewar Nazi rhetoric suggested the possibility of physical destruction, the "final solution to the Jewish problem" seemed to mean forced emigration. In 1940, the Nazis began confining Polish Jews to ghettos set up in Warsaw and five other cities. Himmler and the SS were making tentative plans to develop a kind of superghetto for perhaps 4 million Jews on the island of Madagascar. However, as the Polish ghettos grew more crowded and difficult to manage, Nazi officials in Poland began pressing for a more definitive policy.

In 1940, Hitler seemed to endorse the Madagascar plan, but he cultivated ambiguity on the operational level—and he left no paper trail—so the precise chain of events remains uncertain. The evidence suggests, however, that Hitler ordered the physical extermination of the Jews in the spring of 1941, before the German assault on the Soviet Union in June. By the fall, the Nazis were actively impeding Jewish emigration from the occupied territories and sending large numbers of German and Austrian Jews to the ghettos in Poland.

Map 25.1 The Nazi New Order in Europe, 1942
At the zenith of its power in 1942, Nazi Germany controlled much of Europe. Concerned most immediately with winning the war, the Nazis sought to coordinate the economies of their satellite states and conquered territories. But they also began establishing what was supposed to be an enduring new order in eastern Europe. The inset shows the location of the major Nazi concentration camps and the six extermination camps the Nazis constructed in what had been Poland.

With the invasion of the Soviet Union, special SS "intervention squads" were assigned to get rid of Jews and Communist party officials. By late November, the Nazis had killed 136,000 Jews, most by shooting, in the invaded Soviet territories. But as it became obvious that mass shooting was impractical, Nazi leaders sought a more systematic and impersonal method of extermination. In late July 1941, Reinhard Heydrich of the SS began developing a detailed plan, which he explained in January 1942 at a conference of high-ranking officials at Wannsee, a suburb of Berlin, though by then the plan was already under way.

The Nazis took advantage of the methods, and especially the deadly Zyklon-B gas, that had proven effective during the earlier euthanasia campaign in Germany. By March 1942 they had constructed several large extermination camps with gas chambers and crematoria, designed for efficient murder and disposal. The first targets of the full-scale mass killing were the Polish Jews already confined to ghettos. The ghettos became mere way stations on the journey to the death camps. The Nazis brutally suppressed attempts at resistance, like the Warsaw ghetto uprising of April and May 1943.

The Nazis constructed six full-scale death camps, although not all were operating at peak capacity at the same time. All six were located in what had been Poland (see inset, Map 25.1). The concentration camps in Germany, such as Dachau, Buchenwald, and Bergen-Belsen, were not extermination camps, although many Jews died in them late in the war.

The largest death camp was the Auschwitz-Birkenau complex, which became the principal extermination center in 1943. The Nazis shipped Jews from all over Europe to Auschwitz, which was killing about twelve thousand people a day in 1944. Auschwitz was one of two extermination camps that included affiliated slave-labor factories, in which Jews most able to work were literally worked to death. Among the companies profiting from the arrangement were two of Germany's best-known, Krupp and IG Farben.

The Jews typically arrived at the camps crammed into cattle cars on special trains. Camp personnel, generally SS medical doctors, subjected new arrivals to "selection," picking some for labor assignments and sending the others, including most women and children, to the gas chambers. Camp personnel made every effort to deceive the Jews who were about to be killed, to lead them to believe they were to be showered and deloused. Even in camps without forced-labor factories, Jews were compelled to do much of the dirty work of the extermination operation. But under the brutal conditions of the camps, those initially assigned to work inevitably weakened; most were then deemed unfit and put to death.

Children at Auschwitz Images from the Nazi camps haunted the decades that followed World War II. The Auschwitz-Birkenau complex proved the largest and most destructive of the camps that the Nazis created specifically for mass killing. The overwhelming majority of those sent to these camps were Jews, most of whom were killed by gassing shortly after their arrival. Those deemed fit for work might be spared, at least for a while, but children were typically killed at once. *(Hulton-Getty/Liaison)*

Himmler constantly sought to accelerate the process, even though it required labor and transport facilities desperately needed for the war effort. He and the other major SS officials, such as Adolf Eichmann, who organized the transport of Jews to the camps, portrayed the extermination of the Jews as a difficult "historical task" that they, the Nazi elite, must do for their racial community. For some camp guards, the extermination process became the occasion to act out sadistic fantasies. But though this dimension is surely horrifying, the bureaucratic, factory-like nature of the extermination process is in some ways more troubling.

Despite an overriding emphasis on secrecy, reports of the genocide reached the West almost immediately in 1942. At first, most tended to discount them as fabricated wartime propaganda. Many people believed that Jews were being interned for the duration of the war, much as Japanese-Americans were interned in camps in the western United States at the same time. But even as the evidence grew, Allied governments, citing military priorities, refused pleas from Jewish leaders in 1944 to bomb the rail line into Auschwitz.

The Nazis' policy of murdering "undesirables" also included communists, homosexuals, Gypsies, and Poles. But the Jews constituted by far the largest group of victims—5.7 to 6 million, almost two-thirds of the Jews in Europe.

Collaboration and Resistance

In rounding up Jews for extermination and in establishing their new order in Europe, the Nazis found willing collaborators in some of the countries within their orbit. Croatia, the most pro-Nazi of the satellite states, was eager to round up Jews and Gypsies as well as to attack Serbs on its own. Romania was happy to deliver foreign-born Jews to the Germans, though it dragged its feet when the Germans began demanding acculturated Romanian Jews. The degree of collaboration varied widely across Europe. Denmark did especially well at resisting the German effort to round up Jews, as did Italy and Bulgaria.

Vichy France was somewhere in the middle, and thus it has remained particularly controversial. When the Vichy regime was launched in the summer of 1940, there was widespread support for Marshal Pétain, its 84-year-old chief of state. Pétain promised to maximize French sovereignty and shield his people from the worst aspects of Nazi occupation. At the same time, the Vichy government claimed to be implementing its own "national revolution," returning France to authority, discipline, and tradition after the shambles of the Third Republic. Vichy's revolution was anti-Semitic and hostile to the left, so it seemed compatible with Nazism. And at first Germany seemed likely to win the war. Thus, Pétain's second-in-command, Pierre Laval (1883–1945), collaborated actively with the Nazis. The Vichy regime did much of the Nazis' dirty work for them—rounding up workers for forced shipment to German factories, hunting down members of the anti-German resistance, and picking up Jews to be sent to the Nazi extermination camps. After the war, Pétain, Laval, and others were found guilty of treason by the new French government. Because of his advanced age, Pétain was merely imprisoned, while Laval and others were executed. But the shame of Vichy collaboration continued to haunt the French.

The great majority of those living under German occupation came to despise the Nazis as their brutality became ever clearer. Nazi rule meant pillage; it meant rounding up workers for forced labor in Germany; it meant randomly killing hostages in reprisal for resistance activity. In one notorious case, the Germans killed everyone in the Czech village of Lidice in retaliation for the assassination of SS security chief Reinhard Heydrich.

Clandestine resistance movements gradually developed all over Europe. Resistance was prominent in France and, beginning in 1943, northern Italy, which was occupied by Germany after the Allies defeated Mussolini's regime. But the strongest anti-German resistance was in Yugoslavia, Poland, and the occupied portions of the Soviet Union, where full-scale guerrilla war against the Germans and their collaborators produced the highest civilian casualties of World War II.

The role of the resistance proved most significant in Yugoslavia, where the Croatian Marxist Josip Broz, taking the pseudonym Tito (1892–1980), forged the opponents of the Axis powers into a broadly based guerrilla army. Its initial foe was the pro-Axis Croatian state that the Germans carved out of Yugoslavia. But Tito's forces soon came up against a rival resistance movement, led by Serb officers, that tended to be pro-Serb, monarchist, and anticommunist. By 1943, Tito led 250,000 men and women in what had become a brutal civil war that deepened ethnic divisions and left a legacy of bitterness. Tito's forces prevailed, enabling him to create a communist-led government in Yugoslavia late in the war.

In France and Italy, communists played a leading role in the resistance movements. As a result, the Communist party in each country overcame the disarray that followed from the Nazi-Soviet Pact of 1939 and after the war enjoyed a level of prestige that would have been unthinkable earlier. In the French case, there could have been conflict between the indigenous resistance, with its significant communist component, and the Free French under Charles de Gaulle, operating outside France until August 1944. But it is striking how well they were able to work together. Still, de Gaulle took pains to cement his own leadership. Among the measures to this end, he decreed women's suffrage for France, partly because women were playing a major role in the resistance.

Some depictions of the resistance, such as those by the French writer Marguerite Duras (b. 1914), detail the extreme difficulty of the movement and the isolation of its members. For the most part, however, western European resistance movements were greatly romanticized, their extent and import overstated. The resistance movements did make some military contribution, especially through sabotage, but in many cases their most significant impact was to create a measure of national self-esteem for countries humiliated by defeat.

Toward the Soviet Triumph

The failure of the Nazi assault on the Soviet Union was the decisive fact of World War II. Although supplies from its new allies—Britain and eventually the United States—helped the Soviet forces to prevail, the most important factor was the unexpected strength of the Soviet military effort.

Although the Germans reached Stalingrad by late 1942, they could not achieve a knockout. Fighting street by street, the Soviets managed to defend their city in what was arguably the pivotal military engagement of World War II. By the end of January 1943, the Soviets had captured what remained of the German force, about 100,000 men. The victory came at an immense price: A million Soviet soldiers and civilians died at Stalingrad.

The war had turned. By February 1944, Soviet troops had pushed the Germans back to the Polish border. The Soviet victory was incredible in light of the upheavals of the 1930s. Stalin was able to rally the Soviet peoples by appealing to patriotism, recalling the heroic defenses mounted against invaders in tsarist times. Moreover, when the Germans invaded in 1941, Soviet leaders dismantled the plants and equipment of 1500 industrial enterprises and shipped them by rail for reassembly farther east, out of reach of German attack. Finally, the earlier purges of the armed forces proved to have done less long-term damage than outside observers had expected. If anything, the removal of so many in the top ranks made it easier for talented young officers to move quickly into major leadership positions.

When the United States entered the war in December 1941, the Soviets were fighting for survival. They immediately began pressuring the United States and Britain to open another front in Europe. But the Allies did not invade northern France until June 1944. By then the Soviets had turned the tide in Europe on their own.

A GLOBAL WAR, 1941–1944

European colonial links spread the war almost at once, most dramatically to North Africa but also to East Asia and the Pacific. The Soviet Union also had interests in Asia and the Pacific, where it had long bumped up against the Japanese. During the 1930s, the United States, too, had become involved in friction with Japan. By 1941, President Franklin Roosevelt was openly favoring the anti-Axis cause, though it took a surprise attack by the Japanese in December 1941 to bring the United States into the war.

Japan and the Origins of the Pacific War

As a densely populated island nation lacking the raw materials essential for industry, Japan had been especially concerned about foreign trade and spheres of economic influence as it modernized after 1868. By the interwar period, the Japanese had become unusually dependent on exports of textiles and other products. During the Great Depression, when countries all over the world adopted protectionist policies, Japan suffered from increasing tariffs against its exports. This situation tilted the balance in Japanese ruling circles from free-trade proponents to those who favored a military-imperialist solution.

To gain economic hegemony by force, Japan could choose either of two directions. The northern strategy, concentrating on China, would risk Soviet opposition as well as strong local resistance. The southern strategy, focusing on southeast Asia and the East Indies, would encounter the imperial presence of Britain, France, the Netherlands, and the United States.

In 1931, Japan opted for the northern strategy, taking control of Manchuria in northeastern China. But the Japanese attempt to conquer the rest of China, beginning in 1937, led to an impasse by 1940. Japanese aggression drew the hostility of the United States, a strong supporter of the Chinese nationalist leader Jiang Jieshi (Chiang Kai-shek, 1887–1975), as well as the active opposition of the Soviet Union. Clashes with Soviet troops along the border between Mongolia and Manchuria led to significant defeats for the Japanese in 1938 and 1939. The combination of China and the Soviet Union seemed more than Japan could handle.

World War II, however, seemed to offer a precious opportunity for Japan to shift to a southern strategy. To keep the Soviets at bay, Japan agreed to a neutrality pact with the Soviet Union in April 1941. Rather than worry about China, the Japanese would seek control of southeast Asia, a region rich in oil, rubber, and tin—precisely what Japan lacked.

Japan had joined Nazi Germany and fascist Italy in an anticommunist agreement in 1936. In September 1940, the three agreed to a formal military alliance. For the Germans, alliance with Japan was useful to help discourage U.S. intervention in the European war. Japan, for its part, could expect the major share of the spoils of the European empires in Asia. However, when Japan assumed control of Indochina, nominally held by Vichy France, the United States imposed sanctions, and the British and Dutch followed, forcing Japan to begin rapidly drawing down its oil reserves. Conquest of the oil fields of the Dutch East Indies now seemed a matter of life and death to the Japanese.

These economic sanctions brought home how vulnerable Japan was and heightened its determination to press forward aggressively now, when its likely enemies were weakened or distracted. The Japanese did not expect to achieve a definitive victory over the United States in a long, drawn-out war. Rather, Japanese policymakers anticipated, first, that their initial successes would enable them to grab the resources to sustain a longer war if necessary, and, second, that Germany would defeat Britain, leading the United States to accept a compromise peace giving the Japanese what they wanted—a secure sphere of economic hegemony in southeast Asia.

The Japanese finally provoked a showdown on December 7, 1941, with a surprise attack on Pearl Harbor, a U.S. naval base in Hawaii. The next day, Japanese forces seized Hong Kong and Malaya, both British colonies, and Wake Island and the Philippines, both under U.S. control. The United States promptly declared war on Japan; in response, Hitler kept an earlier promise to Japan and declared war on the United States. World War II was now unprecedented in its geographical scope (see Map 25.2).

Much like their German counterparts, Japanese forces got off to a remarkably good start. By the summer of 1942, Japan had taken Thailand, the Dutch East Indies, the Philippines, and the Malay Peninsula. Having won much of what it had been seeking, it began devising the Greater East Asia Co-Prosperity Sphere, its own new order in the conquered territories. (See the box "Encounters with the West: Japan's 'Pan-Asian' Mission.")

The United States in Europe and the Pacific

During the first years of the war in Europe, the United States under President Franklin Roosevelt had not been a disinterested bystander. Although the United States did not have armed forces commensurate with its economic strength—in 1940 its army was smaller than Belgium's—it could be a supplier in the short term. And if it chose to intervene, it could become a major player over the longer term. With the Lend-Lease Act of March 1941, intended to provide war materiel without the economic dislocations of World War I, the United States lined up on the side of Britain against the Axis powers. In August 1941, a meeting between Churchill and Roosevelt aboard a cruiser off the coast of Newfoundland produced the Atlantic Charter, the first tentative agreement about the aims and ideals that were to guide the war effort. The Americans extended lend-lease to the Soviet Union the next month.

But though President Roosevelt was deeply committed to the anti-Axis cause, it took the Japanese attack on Pearl Harbor to overcome isolationist sentiment and bring the United States into the war as an active belligerent. By May 1942 the United States had joined with Britain and the Soviet Union in a formal military alliance against the Axis powers.

ENCOUNTERS WITH THE WEST

Japan's "Pan-Asian" Mission

This selection from an essay written just after the bombing of Pearl Harbor by the well-known author Nagayo Yoshio (1888–1961) accents Japan's claim to be freeing Asians from Western imperialism. Although it served Japan's own economic interests and was often applied brutally, Japanese "pan-Asianism" helped fuel the reaction against Western imperialism in Asia and the Pacific, with lasting results after the war.

While desperately fighting with a country which we made our enemy only reluctantly we were trying to find out a principle, an ethic based upon a new view of the world. . . .

. . . We would have nothing to say for ourselves if we were merely to follow the examples of the imperialistic and capitalistic exploitation of Greater East-Asia by Europe and the United States. . . .

. . . It is true that the science of war is one manifestation of a nation's culture. But from this time on we have to realize the increasing responsibility on our part if we are to deserve the respect of the people of East-Asian countries as their leaders, in the sphere of culture in general (not only the mere fusion and continuance of Western and Oriental cultures but something surpassing and elevating them while making the most out of them) such as the formation of national character, refinement, intellect, training to become a world citizen, etc. . . .

The sense of awe and respect with which the Orientals have held the white race, especially the Anglo-Saxons, for three hundred years is deep-rooted almost beyond our imagination. It is our task to realize this fact and deal with this servility at its root, find out why the white people became the objects of such reverence. It goes without saying that we cannot conclude simplemindedly that their shrewdness is the cause. Also we have to be very careful not to impose the *hakko ichiu* [the gathering of the whole world under one roof] spirit arbitrarily upon the Asians. If we make this kind of mistake we might antagonize those who could have become our compatriots and thus might also blaspheme our Imperial rule. . . .

To sum up, we have finally witnessed the dawn of a new principle which we had been searching for over ten years. . . . [T]he phrase "Greater East-Asian Coprosperity Sphere" is no longer a mere abstract idea.

Source: Nagayo Yoshio, "Our Present War and Its Cultural Significance," in William H. McNeill and Mitsuko Iriye, eds., *Modern Asia and Africa* (New York: Oxford University Press, 1971), pp. 232–236. Reprinted by permission of William H. McNeill.

The two democracies had joined with Stalin's Soviet Union in a marriage of expediency, and mutual suspicions marked the relationship from the start. Initially, Britain and the United States feared that the Soviet Union might even seek a separate peace, as Russia had in World War I. The Soviets worried that their newfound allies, with their long-standing anticommunism, might hold back from full commitment or even seek to undermine the Soviet Union.

In response to pressure from Stalin, Britain and the United States agreed to open a second front in Europe as soon as possible. Since the Nazis dominated the Continent, opening such a

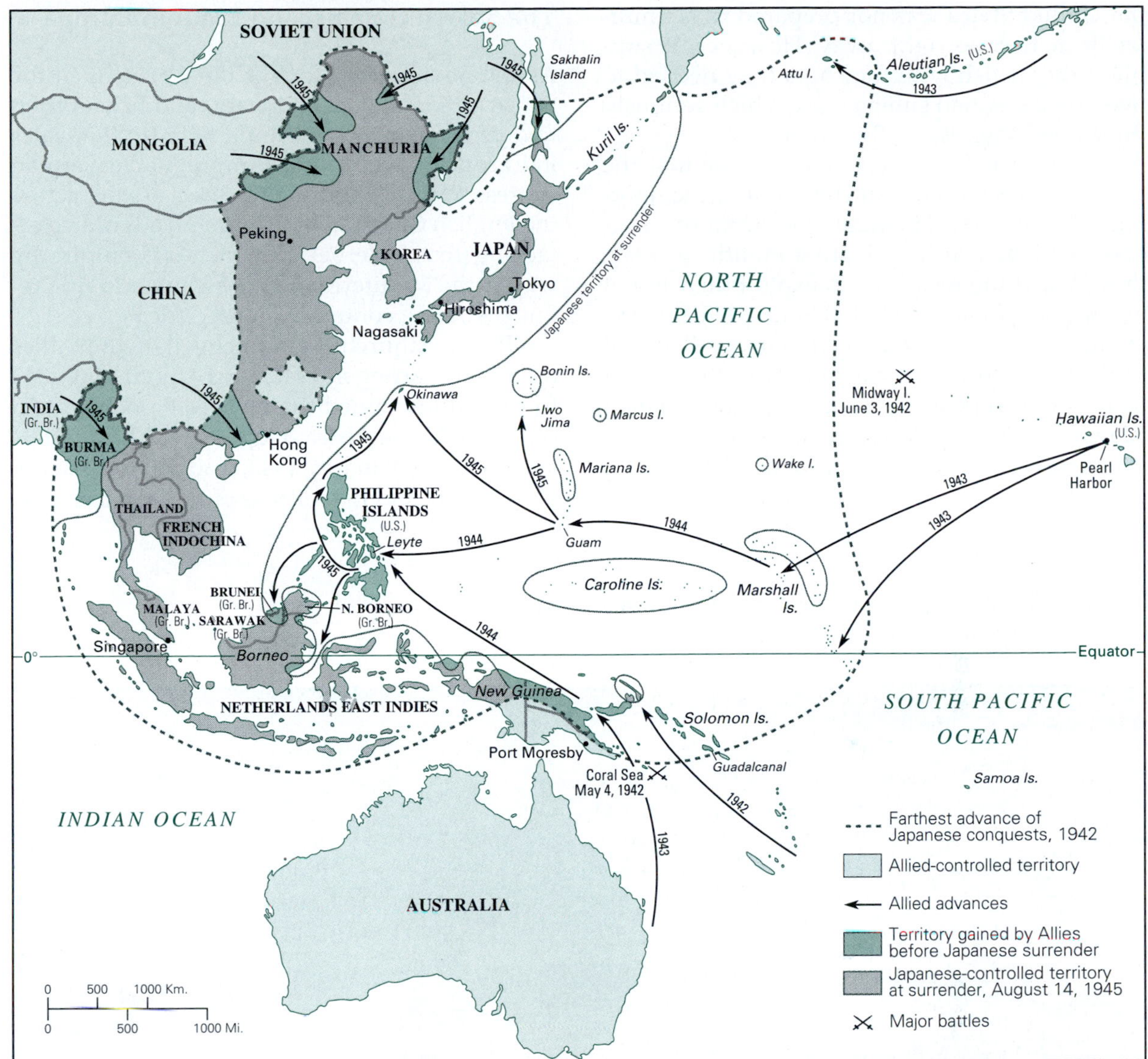

Map 25.2 The War in East Asia and the Pacific After a series of conquests in 1941 and 1942, the Japanese were forced gradually to fall back before U.S. forces. When the war abruptly ended in August 1945, the Japanese still controlled much of the territory they had conquered.

front required landing troops from the outside. It proved far more difficult to mount an assault on Europe than either Churchill or Roosevelt anticipated in 1942. The delays furthered Stalin's suspicions that his allies wanted the Soviet Union to do the bulk of the fighting against Nazi Germany—and weaken itself in the process.

The United States agreed to give priority to the war in Europe. But because it had to respond to the Japanese assault in the Pacific (Map 25.2), the United States was not prepared to act militarily in Europe right away. However, it supplied the British with the ships they needed to overcome German submarines, which seriously threatened shipping to Britain in 1942.

In the Pacific theater, it was clear that the United States would bear the brunt of the fighting. Although the Japanese went from one success to another during the first months of 1942, they lacked the resources to exploit their initial victories. In June, the United States defeated the Japanese navy for the first time in the Battle of Midway, northwest of Hawaii. After the United States stopped Japanese advances in the Solomon Islands and New Guinea early in 1943, U.S. forces began advancing across the islands of the Pacific toward Japan.

The Search for a Second Front in Europe

As the Soviet army fought the Germans in the Soviet Union, the United States and Britain tried to determine how they could help tip the scales in Europe, now an almost impregnable German fortress. Stalin kept urging a direct assault across the English Channel, but Churchill advocated attacking the underbelly of the Axis empire by way of the Mediterranean, which would first require winning control of North Africa.

It was Churchill's strategy that the Allies tried first, starting in 1942. It took until May 1943 for the Allies, joined by the Free French, to win control of North Africa. From there, Allied troops landed in Sicily in July 1943, leading to the arrest of Mussolini and the collapse of the fascist regime.

D-Day, 1944 Allied forces land at Normandy, early in the morning of June 6, 1944, at last opening a major second front in Europe. *(National Archives, Washington)*

Allied forces then moved on to the Italian mainland, but the Germans quickly occupied much of Italy in response. They even managed a rescue of Mussolini and re-established him as puppet leader of a new rump republic in northern Italy. It was a full nine months later before the Allies reached Rome, in June 1944. So Churchill's strategy of assaulting Europe from the south proved less than decisive.

Only when Churchill, Roosevelt, and Stalin met for the first time, at Teheran, Iran, in November 1943, did they agree that the next step would be to invade western Europe from Britain. Preparations had been under way since early 1942. Finally, Allied troops crossed the English Channel to make an amphibious landing on the beaches of Normandy, in northern France, on June 6, 1944, known to history as D-Day.

The D-Day invasion opened the second major front in Europe at last. Now American-led forces from the west and Soviet forces from the east advanced systematically on Germany. The one substantial German counterattack in the west, the Battle of the Bulge in December 1944, slowed the Allies' advance, but on March 7, 1945, Allied troops crossed the Rhine River.

Now, with the defeat of Germany simply a matter of time, Churchill wanted to strike east-central Europe to prevent Soviet domination of the region after the war. But the Americans thought these concerns were misguided. So the Allies concentrated instead on a secondary landing in southern France in August 1944. This assault, in which Free French forces were prominent, led quickly to the liberation of Paris. It was the Soviets alone who drove the Germans from east-central Europe and the Balkans, and this fundamentally affected the postwar order.

THE SHAPE OF THE ALLIED VICTORY, 1944–1945

The leaders of the Soviet Union, Britain, and the United States sought to mold the postwar order at two notable conferences in 1945. They brought different aspirations for the postwar world, but they also had to face the hard military realities that had resulted from the fighting: Each had armies in certain places but not in others. Those military realities led to the informal division of Europe into spheres of influence.

The most serious question the Allies faced concerned Germany. The country was widely held responsible for both world wars, as well as for Nazism with all its atrocities—including the concentration and extermination camps, discovered with shock and horror by the advancing Allied armies in 1945. How should Germany be treated?

In the Pacific theater, as in Europe, the way the war ended had major implications for the postwar world. The United States decided to use the atomic bomb, forcing Japan to surrender in a matter of days. The suddenness of the ending helped determine the fate of the European empires in Asia.

Victory in Europe

Although the tide had turned in 1943, Germany managed to continue the war by exploiting its conquered territories and by more effectively allocating its domestic resources for war production. Germany still had plenty of weapons even as the war was ending, but it was running out of military manpower, and it was running out of oil.

Despite making effective use of synthetics, the Nazi war machine depended heavily on oil from Romania. Late in August 1944, however, Soviet troops crossed into Romania, taking control of the oil fields. In addition, beginning in mid-1944, U.S. and British planes successfully bombed German oil installations.

From the start of the war, some, especially among British military leaders, insisted that bombing could destroy the economic and psychological basis of the enemy's ability to wage war. Beginning in 1942, British-led bombing attacks destroyed an average of half the built-up area of seventy German cities, sometimes producing huge firestorms. The bombing of the historic city of Dresden in February 1945 killed more than 135,000 civilians in the most destructive air

The Soviet Victory in Europe After forcing the Germans back for almost two years, Soviet troops reached Berlin in April 1945. Although it required a day of heavy fighting and bombardment, the Soviets took the Reichstag building, in the heart of the now devastated German capital, on April 30. Here two Soviet sergeants, Yegorov and Kantariya, plant the Soviet flag atop the Reichstag, symbolizing the Soviet victory in the decisive encounter of World War II in Europe. *(ITAR-TAS/Sovfoto)*

assault of the war in Europe. But the widespread destruction did not undermine morale or disrupt production and transport to the extent expected.

The more precise targeting favored by U.S. strategists proved more effective. In May 1944, the United States began bombing the oil fields in Romania and refineries and synthetic oil plants in Germany. Soon Germany lacked enough fuel even to train pilots, so that by 1945 German industry was producing more aircraft than the German air force could use.

Soviet troops moving westward finally met U.S. troops moving eastward at the Elbe River in Germany on April 26, 1945. With his regime thoroughly defeated and much of his country in ruins, Hitler committed suicide in his underground military headquarters in Berlin on April 30, 1945. The war in Europe finally ended with the German surrender to General Dwight D. Eisenhower (1890–1969) at Reims, France, on May 7 and to Marshal Georgi Zhukov (1896–1974) at Berlin on May 8. While the world celebrated the end of the fighting in Europe, East-West differences were already upsetting the anti-German alliance.

The Atomic Bomb and the Capitulation of Japan

In the Pacific, Japan had been forced onto the defensive, but it mounted two major counterattacks in 1944 to challenge American naval supremacy.

The Japanese wanted to prevent American reconquest of the Philippines, which would cut Japan off from its vital raw materials farther south. But the naval battles of 1944 led only to further Japanese defeat.

As the situation grew more desperate, Japanese ground soldiers battled ever more fiercely, often fighting to the death, or taking their own lives, rather than surrendering. Beginning late in 1944, aircraft pilots practiced *kamikaze,* suicidally crashing planes filled with explosives into U.S. targets.

In the spring of 1945, American forces were close enough to be able to launch air raids on the Japanese home islands. But though the United States was now clearly in control, it seemed likely that an invasion of Japan would be necessary to force a Japanese surrender. Some estimated that an invasion might cost the United States as many as 1 million additional casualties, because the Japanese could be expected to fight more desperately to defend their own soil. It was especially for this reason that the Americans decided to try to end the war in an altogether different way, by using an atomic bomb.

In 1939 scientists in several countries, including Germany, had advised their governments that new, immensely destructive weapons based on thermonuclear fission were theoretically possible. The German economics ministry began seeking uranium in 1939, but Hitler favored jet- and rocket-propelled terror weaponry instead. Still, fear that the Nazis were developing atomic weapons lurked behind the Allied effort to produce an atomic bomb as quickly as possible.

Although the British were the first to initiate an atomic weapons program, by late 1941 the Americans were building on what they knew of British findings to develop their own crash program, known as the Manhattan Project. Constructing an atomic bomb was extremely difficult and costly—it was only with great effort that the United States had atomic weapons ready for military use by mid-1945.

The U.S. decision to use the atomic bomb, dropping two of them on Japanese civilians, has been one of the most controversial of modern history. The decision fell to the new president, Harry Truman (1884–1972), who had known nothing of the bomb project when Roosevelt died in April 1945. Over the next few months, Truman listened to spirited disagreement among American policymakers. Was it necessary actually to drop the bomb to force the Japanese to surrender, or would it be enough simply to demonstrate the new weapon to the Japanese in a test firing?

President Truman first warned Japan that if it did not surrender at once, it would be subjected to destruction immeasurably greater than Germany had suffered. The Japanese decided to ignore the American warning, although the United States had begun area-bombing Japanese cities a few months before. The bombing of Tokyo in March produced a firestorm that gutted one-fourth of the city and killed over 80,000 people. Since the Japanese refused to surrender, the use of the atomic bomb could seem the logical next step.

At 8:15 on the morning of August 6, 1945, from a height of 32,000 feet above the Japanese city of Hiroshima, an American pilot released the first atomic bomb to be used against an enemy target. The bomb exploded after 45 seconds, 2000 feet above the ground, killing 80,000 people outright and tens of thousands more in the aftermath. Three days later, on August 9, the Americans exploded a second atomic bomb over Nagasaki. Although sectors of the Japanese military held out for continued resistance, Emperor Hirohito (1901–1989) finally surrendered on August 14.

Death Counts and the Question of Guilt

Between 50 and 60 million people died in World War II—three times as many as in World War I. About that same number were left homeless for some length of time, many of them as refugees. The Soviet Union and Germany suffered by far the highest casualty figures. An appalling 23 million Soviet citizens died, of whom 12 to 13 million were civilians. Germany lost 5 to 6 million, including perhaps 2 million civilians.

In contrast, casualty rates for Italy, Britain, and France were lower than in World War I. Italy suffered 200,000 military and 200,000 civilian deaths. Total British losses, including civilians, numbered 450,000, to which must be added 120,000 Australians, Canadians, Indians, and others from the British Empire. Despite its quick defeat, France lost more lives than Britain because of the ravages of German occupation: The 350,000 deaths among French civilians considerably exceeded the British figure, closer to 100,000.

The United States lost 300,000 servicemen and 5000 civilians. Figures for Japan are problematic, partly because the Japanese claim that 300,000 of those who surrendered to the Soviets in 1945 remain unaccounted for. Apart from this number, 1,740,000 Japanese servicemen died from 1941 to 1945, more from hunger and disease than from combat, and 300,000 civilians died in Japan, most from U.S. bombing.

The great majority of Jews, Poles, and other "undesirables" shipped to Nazi death camps died during the war. Of those Jews who were still alive when the Nazi camps were liberated, almost half died within a few weeks. Even those who managed to return home sometimes faced pogroms when they arrived; forty Jews were killed in the worst of them, at Kielce, in Poland.

The redrawing of Germany's borders contributed to the huge wave of refugees after the war. To guarantee the permanence of the new territorial configurations, the Soviets and Poles began expelling ethnic Germans from historically German areas that were now part of Poland, and the Czechs expelled Germans from the Sudetenland area of Czechoslovakia. So a flood of German refugees was forced to move west after the war, into the shrunken territory of the new Germany. They were among the 16 million Europeans who were permanently uprooted and transplanted between 1939 and 1947.

As the war was ending, Europeans began attempting to assess guilt and punish those responsible for the disasters of the era. In the climate of violence, resistance forces in France, Italy, and elsewhere often subjected fascists and collaborators to summary justice, sometimes through quick trials in ad hoc courts. In Italy, this process led to 15,000 executions; in France, 10,000. After the war, governments sought to dispense justice in a more orderly way, but the results differed widely across Europe. In Belgium, 634,000 of a population of 8 million were prosecuted for collaborating with the Nazis, whereas in Austria, with a comparable population, only 9000 were brought to trial.

In Germany the occupying powers imposed a program of de-Nazification. In the areas occupied by the United States, Britain, and France, German citizens were required to attend lectures on the virtues of democracy and view the corpses of the victims of Nazism. In this context, the Allies determined to identify and bring to justice those responsible for the crimes of the Nazi regime. This effort led to the Nuremberg trials of 1945 to 1946, the most famous of a number of war crimes trials held in Germany and the occupied countries after the war.

Although Hitler, Himmler, and Goebbels had committed suicide, the occupying authorities tried twenty-four individuals who had played important roles in Hitler's Third Reich. All but three were convicted of war crimes and "crimes against humanity." Of the twelve sentenced to death, two committed suicide and the other ten were executed.

TOWARD THE POSTWAR WORLD, 1945–1949

Differences between the Soviets and the Western democracies soon undermined the wartime alliance, producing the division of Germany and a bipolar Europe. Thus the conclusion of World War II led directly to the danger of a nuclear war, threatening the extinction of life on earth. Outside Europe, the war brought to the forefront a new set of issues, from anticolonialism to the Arab-Israeli conflict to the spread of communism to the non-Western world.

The Yalta and Potsdam Conferences

Stalin, Roosevelt, and Churchill met at Yalta, a Soviet Black Sea resort, in February 1945, when

Allied victory was assured but not yet accomplished. The Yalta conference has long been surrounded by controversy. Western critics have charged that the concessions made there to Stalin consigned east-central Europe to communist domination and opened the way to the dangerous cold war of the next forty years. At the time, however, the division of Axis territory was already becoming evident, and, in light of the location of Allied troops, the alignment was probably inevitable. Also, the anticipation of victory produced a relatively cooperative spirit among the Allies. Thus, they firmed up plans for military occupation of Germany in separate zones, for joint occupation of Berlin, and for an Allied Control Council, which would make policy for all of Germany by unanimous agreement.

After Germany fell, the victorious Allies had to decide how to implement their plans. The leaders of the United States, Britain, and the Soviet Union confronted the question at their last wartime conference, at Potsdam, just outside Berlin, from July 17 to August 2, 1945. The circumstances were dramatically different from those at Yalta just months before. With Hitler dead and Germany defeated, there was no longer a common military aim in Europe to provide unity. Of the three Allied leaders who had been at Yalta, only Stalin remained. President Roosevelt had died in April, so his successor, Harry Truman, represented the United States. In Britain, Churchill's Conservatives lost the general election during the first days of the conference, so Clement Attlee (1883–1967), the new Labour prime minister, assumed the leadership of the British delegation.

Germany, devastated by bombing and left without a government, depended on the Allied occupying forces even for its day-to-day survival. The Allies had agreed that Germany was to be forced to surrender unconditionally, but it was not yet clear what would be done with the country over the longer term. U.S. policymakers had even considered destroying Germany's industrial capacity in perpetuity. However, cooler heads understood that the "pastoralization" of

Reconstruction Begins Shortly after the end of the war, women in Berlin pass pails of rubble along a line to a dump. Wartime bombing had severely damaged cities throughout much of Europe, although destruction was greatest in Germany. *(Hulton-Getty/Liaison)*

Germany would not be in anyone's economic interests. Moreover, as the democracies grew increasingly suspicious about Soviet intentions, an economically healthy Germany seemed necessary to help in the balance against the Soviet Union.

The Soviets had reason to take a much harder line against Germany. Having been invaded—and devastated—by German forces twice within living memory, the Soviet Union wanted to weaken Germany both territorially and economically. Of the three victors, the Soviets had suffered a greatly disproportionate share of the wartime destruction and economic loss, so they demanded heavy reparations. The United States and Britain accepted the Soviet proposal that Germany's eastern border with Poland be shifted substantially westward; as a result, the size of Germany was reduced by about 20 percent. Each of the four Allies had responsibility for administering a particular zone of Germany and of Berlin, but they were supposed to coordinate their activities in a common policy toward Germany.

Conflicting Visions and the Coming of the Cold War

To ensure the peace, the Allies agreed to create a new international body—the United Nations. At a conference in San Francisco from April to June 1945, delegates from almost fifty anti-Axis countries created a charter for the new United Nations. The major powers—the United States, Britain, France, the Soviet Union, and China—were given a privileged position in the organization as permanent members of the Security Council, each with veto power. To dramatize its departure from the Geneva-based League of Nations, which the United States had refused to join, the United Nations was headquartered in New York. In July 1945 the American Senate approved U.S. membership.

The cold war soon cast a heavy shadow over the new organization. Whereas the United States envisioned a world order based on the ongoing cooperation of the victors, the Soviet Union gave top priority to creating a buffer zone of friendly states in east-central Europe, especially as a bulwark against Germany. While seeking this sphere of influence in east-central Europe, Stalin gave the British a free hand to settle the civil war in Greece, and he did not push for revolution in western Europe. The strong communist parties that had emerged from the resistance movements in Italy and France were directed to work within broad-based democratic fronts rather than try to take power. Stalin saw this moderate position in western and southern Europe as a tacit exchange with the West for a free hand in east-central Europe.

The United States refused to acquiesce as the Soviets established their sphere of influence in east-central Europe. The American reluctance to abandon the peoples of east-central Europe to Soviet hegemony is understandable. But U.S. policymakers failed to grasp the historical and strategic basis for Soviet priorities and assumed that the Soviets were primarily trying to spread communism. As a result, the cleft between the emerging superpowers widened.

The area of greatest potential stress between the Soviets and the democracies was inevitably Germany. At first, the Western Allies were concerned especially to root out the sources of Germany's antidemocratic, aggressive behavior, but that concern faded as communism, not Nazism, came to seem the immediate menace. At Potsdam, the West had accepted Soviet demands for German reparations, but rather than wait for payment, the Soviets began removing German factories and equipment for reassembly in the Soviet Union. The United States and Britain, in contrast, gave priority to economic reconstruction and quickly began integrating the economies of the western zones for that purpose.

Friction developed after 1945 as the West insisted on reduced reparations and a higher level of industrial production than the Soviets wanted. Finally, as part of their effort to spur economic recovery, the United States and Britain introduced a new currency without Soviet consent. Stalin's response, in June 1948, was to blockade the city of Berlin, cutting its western sectors off from the main Western occupation zones, almost 200 miles west. The Western Allies responded with a massive airlift that kept their sectors of Berlin supplied for almost a year, until May 1949, when the Soviets finally backed down.

The growing split with the Soviet Union reinforced the determination of the United States and Britain to ensure that western Germany would become a viable state—economically, politically, and even militarily. With Allied support, a "parliamentary council" of German leaders met in 1948 and 1949 and produced a document that, when ratified in September 1949, became the "basic law" of a new Federal Republic of Germany. It was intended to be a provisional new state, with a temporary capital in the small city of Bonn, but the Soviets responded by setting up a new state in their zone, in eastern Germany. The Communist-led German Democratic Republic, with its capital in East Berlin, was born in October 1949.

The "Iron Curtain" and the Emergence of a Bipolar World

In east-central Europe, only Yugoslavia and Albania had achieved liberation on their own, and the communist leaders of their resistance movements had a plausible claim to political power. Elsewhere, the Soviet army had provided liberation, and the Soviet military presence remained the decisive political fact as the war ended. To be sure, each country had local political groups that now claimed a governing role, but their standing in relation to the Soviet army was uncertain.

Under these circumstances, the Soviets were able to work with local communists to install new communist-led regimes friendly to the Soviet Union in most of east-central Europe. But though Churchill warned as early as 1946 that "an iron curtain" was descending from the Baltic to the Adriatic, the process of Soviet power consolidation was not easy, and it took place gradually over several years. The Communist-led government of Poland held elections in January 1947—but rigged them to guarantee a favorable outcome. In Czechoslovakia, the communists faced serious losses in upcoming elections and so finally took power outright in 1948. In 1949 there were communist governments relying on Soviet support in Poland, Czechoslovakia, East Germany, Hungary, Romania, and Bulgaria. Yugoslavia and Albania were also communist but were capable of a more independent line.

Communism might have spread still farther in Europe, but the West drew the line at Greece. There, as in Yugoslavia, an indigenous, communist-led resistance movement had become strong enough to contend for political power by late 1944. But when it sought to oust the monarchical government that had returned from exile, the British intervened to help the monarchy. Although Stalin gave the Greek communists little help, communist guerrilla activity continued, thanks partly to support from Tito's Yugoslavia. In 1946 a renewed communist uprising escalated into civil war.

After the financially strapped Labour government in Britain reduced its involvement early in 1947, the United States stepped in. In March, President Truman announced the Truman Doctrine, which committed the United States to the "containment" of communism throughout the world. American advisers began re-equipping the anticommunist forces in Greece. Faced with this determined opposition from the West, Stalin pulled back, but the Greek communists, with their strong indigenous support, were not defeated until 1949.

Thus the wartime marriage of expediency between the Soviet Union and the Western democracies fell apart in the war's aftermath. The antagonism between the two superpowers became more menacing when the Soviets exploded their first atomic bomb in August 1949, intensifying the postwar arms race. By then the United States was on its way to the more destructive hydrogen bomb. The split between these two nations, unmistakable by 1949, established the framework for world affairs for the next forty years. (See the box "The Soviet View of the Cold War.")

The West and the New World Agenda

At the same time, other dramatic changes around the world suggested that, with or without the cold war, the postwar political scene

The Soviet View of the Cold War

The first cold war document the Soviet government made available to Western scholars was a telegram that Nikolai Novikov, the Soviet ambassador to the United States, sent from Washington to Soviet Foreign Minister Vyacheslav Molotov on September 27, 1946. Novikov sought to pinpoint the essential features of the new foreign policy the United States seemed to be pursuing after its victory in World War II. In releasing the document in 1990, Soviet authorities contended it had been of central importance in the Soviet effort to understand postwar American intentions and to formulate their own policy in response.

The foreign policy of the United States, which reflects the imperialist tendencies of American monopolistic capital, is characterized in the postwar period by a striving for world supremacy. This is the real meaning of the many statements by President Truman and other representatives of American ruling circles: that the United States has the right to lead the world. All the forces of American diplomacy—the army, the air force, the navy, industry, and science—are enlisted in the service of this foreign policy. For this purpose broad plans for expansion have been developed and are being implemented through diplomacy and the establishment of a system of naval and air bases stretching far beyond the boundaries of the United States. . . .

. . . [W]e have seen a failure of calculations on the part of U.S. circles which assumed that the Soviet Union would be destroyed in the war or would come out of it so weakened that it would be forced to go begging to the United States for economic assistance. Had that happened, they would have been able to dictate conditions permitting the United States to carry out its expansion in Europe and Asia without hindrance from the USSR. . . .

One of the most important elements in the general policy of the United States, which is directed toward limiting the international role of the USSR in the postwar world, is the policy with regard to Germany. In Germany, the United States is taking measures to strengthen reactionary forces for the purpose of opposing democratic reconstruction. . . .

Careful note should be taken of the fact that the preparation by the United States for a future war is being conducted with the prospect of war against the Soviet Union, which in the eyes of American imperialists is the main obstacle in the path of the United States to world domination. This is indicated by facts such as the tactical training of the American army for war with the Soviet Union as the future opponent, the siting of American strategic bases in regions from which it is possible to launch strikes on Soviet territory, intensified training and strengthening of Arctic regions as close approaches to the USSR, and attempts to prepare Germany and Japan to use those countries in a war against the USSR.

Source: "The Novikov Telegram," *Diplomatic History,* vol. 15, no. 4 (Fall 1991), pp. 527–528, 536–537. Reprinted by permission of Blackwell Publishers.

would be hard to manage. Events in India in 1947, in Israel in 1948, and in China in 1949 epitomized the new hopes and uncertainties that had emerged directly from World War II.

Although the British, under U.S. pressure, had reluctantly promised independence for India in order to elicit Indian support during the war, British authorities and Indian leaders had continued to skirmish. Mohandas Gandhi was twice jailed for resisting British demands and threatening a massive program of nonviolent resistance to British rule. But by 1946 the British lacked the will and the financial resources to maintain their control in India. Britain acquiesced in Indian independence, proclaimed on August 15, 1947.

Questions about the fate of the Jews, who had suffered so grievously during World War II, were inevitable. Almost two-thirds of the Jews of Europe had been killed, and many of the survivors either had no place to go or had concluded that they could never again live as a minority in Europe. Many insisted that they must have a homeland of their own. For decades such Zionist sentiment (see page 617) had centered on the biblical area of Israel, in what had become, after World War I, the British mandate of Palestine. In 1947, pressure from Zionists in Jerusalem and the United States led the British to withdraw from Palestine, leaving its future to the United Nations. The UN voted to partition Palestine, creating both a Jewish and an Arab Palestinian state. Skirmishing between Jews and Arabs became full-scale war in December, and in that context the Jews declared their independence as the new state of Israel on May 14, 1948.

In 1949 the communist insurgency in China under Mao Zedong (Mao Tse-tung) (see page 632) triumphed over the Chinese Nationalists under Jiang Jieshi (Chiang Kai-shek), who were forced to flee to the island of Taiwan. After their victory, the Chinese Communists enjoyed great prestige among other "national liberation" movements struggling against Western colonialists. To many in the West, however, the outcome in China by 1949 intensified fears that communism was poised to spread in the unsettled postwar world.

SUMMARY

World War II brought to a close an era of European history dominated by fascism. As a result of the war, the two major fascist powers collapsed and fascist forms of politics, with their hostility to democracy and their tendencies toward violence and war, stood at least temporarily discredited. But Nazism and fascism continued to haunt the Western mind, especially with the discovery of the Nazi camps.

Because the Soviets bore the brunt of the war in Europe, the Soviet Union—and its communist system—emerged with enhanced prestige. At the same time, an overseas war had again drawn the United States, which was now prepared to play an ongoing leadership role in world affairs.

With the Soviet Union and United States emerging from the war as superpowers, the center of gravity in the West changed dramatically. Weakened and chastened, the once-dominant European countries seemed destined to play a diminished role in world affairs. It quickly became apparent that the costs of the war had left even Britain, a full partner in the Allied victory, too weak to remain a great power. Almost at once, the Europeans began retreating from their long-standing imperial roles, though not without resentment, resistance, and more bloodshed. By 1949 the division of Europe, the advent of nuclear weapons, and the events in India, Israel, and China made it clear that the world's agenda had been radically transformed in the ten years since the beginning of World War II.

Whereas there had been, for a while, some illusion of a "return to normal" after World War I, it was obvious after World War II that the old Europe was gone forever and that the relationship between the West and the rest of the world would never be the same. Indeed, much of Europe's proud culture, on the basis of which it had claimed to lead the world, lay in the ruins of war, apparently exhausted. What role could Europe play in Western civilization, and in the wider world, after all that had happened?

NOTES

1. From Farrell's full account as related by General Leslie Groves in his "Memorandum to the Secretary of War," dated July 18, 1945, in Philip L. Cantelon, Richard G. Hewlett, and Robert C. Williams, eds., *The American Atom: A Documentary History of Nuclear*

Policies from the Discovery of Fission to the Present, 2d ed. (Philadelphia: University of Pennsylvania Press, 1991), pp. 56–57.

SUGGESTED READING

Campbell, John, ed. *The Experience of World War II.* 1989. Focusing on the experience of those touched by the war, this collaborative volume covers everything from prisoners of war to the uses of the arts for propaganda purposes.

Eisenberg, Carolyn Woods. *Drawing the Line: The American Decision to Divide Germany, 1944–1949.* 1996. A detailed, scholarly account that uses newly available sources to accent the American role in the process that culminated in the division of Germany by 1949.

Ellis, John. *On the Front Lines: The Experience of War Through the Eyes of the Allied Soldiers in World War II.* 1991. Based partly on oral testimony, a vivid account of the experiences of those who fought the war on the Allied side in Europe, Africa, and the Pacific.

Gaddis, John Lewis. *We Now Know: Rethinking Cold War History.* 1997. Taking advantage of newly available Russian and Chinese documents, a leading authority reassesses the cold war, from its origins to the Cuban missile crisis of 1962.

Glantz, David M., and Jonathan M. House. *When Titans Clashed: How the Red Army Stopped Hitler.* 1995. A detailed but compelling account of the decisive encounter in World War II, based partly on newly available materials from the former Soviet Union.

Harrison, Mark. *Soviet Planning in Peace and War, 1938–1945.* 1985. Shows how Soviet economic planners responded to invasion in 1941, enabling the Soviet Union to defeat Nazi Germany and emerge from the war as a great power.

Hilberg, Raul. *Perpetrators, Victims, Bystanders: The Jewish Catastrophe, 1933–1945.* 1992. The dean of Holocaust historians offers an accessible, compelling account by weaving capsule portraits delineating the many layers of involvement and responsibility at issue in the Holocaust.

Laqueur, Walter. *A History of Zionism.* 1989. Surveys the five decades of European Zionist activity that helped bring about the establishment of the state of Israel.

Marrus, Michael. *The Holocaust in History.* 1987. An ideal introduction to the major issues. Readable and balanced.

Paxton, Robert O. *Vichy France: Old Guard and New Order.* 1975. A widely admired study that assesses Vichy claims to have shielded the French from the worst features of Nazi occupation.

Pedersen, Susan. *Family, Dependence, and the Origins of the Welfare State: Britain and France, 1914–1945.* 1993. An effective comparative study showing how concerns about gender roles and family relations helped shape discussion and policy as government assumed greater responsibility for social welfare.

Pelling, Henry. *Winston Churchill.* 1974. Among the best single-volume biographies of Churchill. Balanced and readable.

Rhodes, Richard. *The Making of the Atomic Bomb.* 1988. An acclaimed study that combines science, politics, and personality in an especially dramatic way.

Summerfield, Penny. *Women Workers in the Second World War: Production and Patriarchy in Conflict.* 1989. Shows how the disruptions of war affected women's opportunities and self-understanding.

Wright, Gordon. *The Ordeal of Total War, 1939–1945.* 1968. A masterly synthesis of all aspects of the war experience, from the battlefield to the scientific laboratory, from the Nazi "new order" to the coming of the cold war.

Yahil, Leni. *The Holocaust: The Fate of European Jewry.* 1990. A clear and comprehensive account that accents the underlying continuity in Nazi policy and assesses the Jewish response.

CHAPTER 26

An Anxious Stability: The Age of the Cold War, 1949–1985

Sampling an American hotdog at a meatpacking plant in Iowa in 1959, the leader of the Soviet Union, Nikita Khrushchev, wryly observed that "we have beaten you to the moon, but you have beaten us in sausage-making." Khrushchev was in the midst of a two-week visit to the United States at the invitation of President Dwight Eisenhower. The Soviet leader found much to praise in American society, and he took every occasion to stress the possibility of "peaceful coexistence." Still, Khrushchev also took it for granted that vigorous competition would continue between the two countries. It was time to recognize, Khrushchev insisted, that each side fervently believed in its own system; hence, there was no point in trying to convince each other. The two sides would simply compete—and the competition could be peaceful.

But in 1960, less than a year after Khrushchev's visit, the Soviet military shot down a U.S. spy plane over the Soviet Union. The incident wrecked a previously planned summit meeting, and relations between the Soviet Union and the United States cooled. Although they would eventually warm again, this complex postwar era was characterized by ideological competition, mutual suspicion, and a costly and dangerous arms race. It seemed possible that, virtually overnight, the cold war could develop into a hot war that could lead to nuclear annihilation.

Both halves of Europe had to operate within the bipolar framework, but the Western and Soviet blocs each confronted different challenges. Dependent on U.S. leadership, unable to resist the tide of decolonization, the countries of Western Europe adjusted to a diminished international role. The change led many to advocate some form of European union, which might eventually enable the Western Europeans to deal with the superpowers on a more equal basis. On the domestic level, postwar reconstruction rested on a new consensus that government must play a more active role in promoting economic growth and social welfare. By the 1960s the promise of shared prosperity had been realized to a remarkable extent. But changing circumstances by the early 1970s threatened the consensus that postwar prosperity had made possible.

Questions and Ideas to Consider

- Discuss some of the ways in which European intellectuals tried to make sense of human existence in the aftermath of World War II. What were the central questions posed, and what solutions were offered?
- Why did Western governments take on the responsibilities of the "welfare state"? Why did the question of welfare seem to demand a reevaluation of gender roles in the West?
- Why did some colonies manage to gain their independence with relative ease, while others struggled bitterly for years? What factors other than relative military strength influenced these outcomes?
- Discuss the main tenets of Khrushchev's regime. Generally speaking, what was his foreign policy?
- In 1968 much of the West experienced popular protests, often by groups new to the political stage—or long absent from it. How did these new protests differ from earlier political initiatives?

THE SEARCH FOR CULTURAL BEARINGS

The events from World War I to the cold war added up to an unprecedented period of disaster for Europe. Europeans were bound to ask what had gone wrong, and what could be salvaged from the ruins of a culture that had made possible the most destructive wars in history, as well as fascism, totalitarianism, and the Holocaust. The cold war framework inevitably affected the answers. Some embraced the Soviet Union or sought a renewed Marxism. Others returned to religious or classical traditions or embraced new ideas associated with America's recent successes. In Western Europe this effort to take stock led to renewed determination and fresh ideas that helped produce the dramatically successful postwar reconstruction.

Absurdity and Commitment in Existentialism

The postwar mood of exhaustion and despair found classic expression in the work of the Irish-born writer Samuel Beckett (1906–1989), especially in his plays *Waiting for Godot* (1952) and *Endgame* (1957). Through Beckett's characters, we see ourselves going through the motions, with nothing worth saying or doing, ludicrously manipulating the husks of a worn-out culture. The only redeeming element is the comic pathos we feel as we watch ourselves.

The same sense of anxiety and despair led to existentialism, a movement that marked philosophy, the arts, and popular culture from the later 1940s until well into the 1950s. Existentialism developed from the ideas of the German thinker Martin Heidegger (1889–1976), especially from his *Being and Time* (1927), one of the most influential philosophical works of the century. Though it was a philosophy, existentialism was most significant as a broader cultural tendency, finding expression in novels and films. The existentialists explored what it means to be human in a world cast adrift from its cultural moorings.

The most influential postwar existentialists were the Frenchmen Albert Camus (1913–1960) and Jean Paul Sartre (1905–1980), each of whom had been involved in the French resistance. For both, an authentic human response to a world spinning out of control entailed engagement, commitment, responsibility. Camus sought to show how we might go on living in a positive, affirmative spirit, even in an absurd world. Peo-

CHAPTER CHRONOLOGY

1947	Marshall Plan announced
1949	Formation of NATO
1951	Formation of the European Coal and Steel Community
1953	Death of Stalin
	Workers' revolt in East Germany
1954	Defeat of France in Vietnam
1955	Bandung conference of non-Western countries in Indonesia
	West Germany joins NATO
	Warsaw Pact
1956	Khrushchev speech to the twentieth party congress
	Peace terms in Vietnam yield north-south partition
	Suez crisis; defeat for Britain and France in Egypt
	Hungarian reform movement crushed
1957	Treaty of Rome establishes Common Market
1958	Beginning of Fifth Republic under de Gaulle
1961	Berlin Wall erected
1962	Algerian independence from France
	Cuban missile crisis
1964	Ouster of Nikita Khrushchev
1968	Days of May uprising in France
	Prague Spring reform movement crushed
1969	Willy Brandt becomes West German chancellor
1973	First OPEC oil crisis begins
1975	Independence of Mozambique and Angola from Portugal
	Reunification of Vietnam

ple suffer and die, but as we come together to help as best we can, we might at least learn to stop killing one another.

Camus split from Sartre in a disagreement over the ongoing value of Marxism and the communist experiment in the Soviet Union. Though never an orthodox communist, Sartre found potential for human liberation in the working class, in communist parties, even in the Soviet Union itself, which he saw as the strongest alternative to U.S. imperialism. By the 1950s, he was portraying existentialism as fundamentally a way to revitalize Marxism.

By contrast, Camus, who had started as a communist in the 1930s, had grown disillusioned even before the war. Establishing new bases for human happiness and solidarity meant recognizing limits to what human beings could accomplish, limits even to our demands for freedom and justice. These were precisely the limits that the new political movements of the century had so disastrously overstepped. Communism, like fascism, was part of the problem, not the solution.

Marxists and Traditionalists

Sartre was among the many European intellectuals who believed that Marxism had won a new lease on life from the wartime resistance. As they saw it, Marxism could be revamped for the West without the Stalinist excesses of the Soviet Union. Marxism remained a significant strand in the political culture of the West during the cold war era, but it also attracted periodic waves of denunciation.

In Italy, as in France, the communists' major role in the resistance enhanced their prestige, preparing the way for the extraordinary posthumous influence of Antonio Gramsci (1891–1937), a founder of the Italian Communist party who had spent most of the fascist period in prison. His *Prison Notebooks*, published during the late 1940s,

Sartre and de Beauvoir Among the most influential intellectual couples of the century, Jean-Paul Sartre and Simone de Beauvoir emerged as leaders of French existentialism by the later 1940s. See the box on page 689. *(G. Pierre/Sygma)*

helped make Marxism a powerful force in postwar Italian culture. Gramsci pointed Marxists toward a flexible political strategy, attuned to the special historical circumstances of each country.

However, others, like Camus, held that Marxism was inherently flawed and denied that any recasting could overcome its deficiencies. Damaging revelations about the excesses of Stalinism during the 1930s seemed to confirm this view. Such writers as the Hungarian-born Arthur Koestler (1905–1983) and the Italian Ignazio Silone (1900–1978), who had believed in communism during the 1930s, now denounced it as "the God that failed." Whatever its initial promise, Marxism would inevitably lead to the kind of tyranny that had developed in the Soviet Union. In the mid-1970s, the disturbing portrait of the Stalinist *gulag*, or forced-labor-camp system, by the Soviet writer Alexander Solzhenitsyn (b. 1918) stimulated another wave of anticommunist thinking.

Those hostile to Marxism often insisted that the West had to reconnect with older traditions if it were to avoid further horrors like those it had just been through. Especially in the first years after the war, many, like the French Catholic thinker Jacques Maritain (1882–1973), held that only a return to religious traditions would suffice.

The Intellectual Migration and Americanism

The extraordinary migration of European artists and intellectuals to the United States to escape persecution during the 1930s and 1940s profoundly affected the cultural life of the postwar period. An array of luminaries arrived on American shores, from the composer Igor Stravinsky to the theoretical physicist Albert Einstein, from the architect Walter Gropius to the philosopher Hannah Arendt.

Before this cross-fertilization, American culture had remained slightly provincial, sometimes proudly and self-consciously so. All the direct contact with the Europeans by the 1940s helped propel the United States into the Western cultural mainstream. No longer could "Western" culture be identified primarily with Europe. In some spheres—painting, for example—Americans were now confident enough to claim leadership for the first time.

With the abstract expressionism of the later 1940s, American painters began creating visual images the like of which had never been seen in Europe. In comparison with the raw, energetic painting of Jackson Pollock (1912–1956), the work of the Europeans seemed merely "pretty"—and the newly brash Americans were not shy about telling them so. New York began to supplant Paris as the art capital of the Western world.

Some Europeans were eager to embrace what seemed distinctively American, because America had remained relatively free of totalitarian ideologies. By the 1950s there was much talk of "the end of ideology," with America pointing the way to a healthier alternative, combining technology, value-free social science, and scientific management.

Such Americanism fed the notion that Europe needed a clean break based on technological values. If such a break was necessary, however, what was to become of the European tradition? Did anything distinctively European remain, or was Europe doomed to lick its wounds in the shadow of America? These questions lurked in the background, but first Europeans faced the difficult task of economic and political restoration.

THE NEW SOCIAL COMPACT IN WESTERN EUROPE

Democracy quickly revived in Western Europe after World War II, taking root more easily than most had thought possible. The bipolar international framework helped. The United States actively encouraged democracy, and Europeans nervous about communism and the Soviet Union were happy to follow the American lead. Success at economic reconstruction was important as well. Not only was there greater prosperity, but governments could afford to deliver on promises of enhanced security, social welfare, and equality of opportunity.

From Economic Reconstruction to Economic Miracle

It is hard to imagine how desperate the situation in much of Western Europe had been in 1945. Major cities like Rotterdam, Hamburg, and Le Havre lay largely in ruins, and normal routines suffered radical disruption. Production had declined to perhaps 25 percent of the prewar level in Italy, to 20 percent in France, and to a mere 5 percent in southern Germany. Cigarettes, often gained through barter from American soldiers, served widely as a medium of exchange.

Although the U.S. commitment to help reconstruct Europe was not originally a cold war measure, the developing cold war context made it seem all the more necessary. The Marshall Plan, outlined by U.S. secretary of state General George Marshall in 1947, had channeled $13.5 billion in aid to Western Europe by 1951. The need to rebuild gave Europeans a chance to start over, using the most up-to-date methods and technologies. Though rebuilding strategies differed, the Western European countries made remarkable recoveries.

The new German government cut state aid to business and limited the long-standing power of *cartels* (groups of enterprises that worked together to minimize competition through price fixing and production quotas). The state was permitted to intervene in the economy only to assure free competition. In France, by contrast, many were determined to use government to modernize the country, and France adopted a flexible, pragmatic form of government-led economic planning.

In 1946, French economist Jean Monnet (1888–1979) launched the first of the French postwar economic plans, which brought government and business leaders together to agree on production targets. Economic planning enabled France to make especially effective use of the capital that the Marshall Plan provided, and French industrial production returned to its prewar peak by 1951. Strong and sustained rates of economic growth were achieved throughout much of Western Europe through the mid-1960s, with only Britain lagging behind.

During the first years of rapid economic growth, the labor movement remained fairly passive in Western Europe, even though wages stayed relatively low. After an era of depression and war, workers were grateful to have jobs, free trade unions, and at least the promise of greater prosperity in the future. By the 1960s, however, labor began demanding—generally with success—to share more fully in the new prosperity. Now, rather abruptly, much of Western Europe assumed the look of a consumer society, including widespread ownership of automobiles and televisions.

Social Welfare and the Issue of Gender

European governments had begun to adopt social welfare measures on a large scale late in the nineteenth century, and by the 1940s some degree of governmental responsibility for unemployment insurance, workplace safety, and even old-age pensions was widely accepted. Some Europeans found an attractive model in Sweden and Denmark, where the outlines of a welfare state had emerged by the 1930s. Sweden attracted attention as a "middle way" that avoided the extremes of Soviet Marxism, with its coercive statism, and American-style capitalism, with its commercialism and selfish individualism.

Sweden's economy remained fundamentally capitalist, based on private ownership, but the system of social insurance in Sweden was the most extensive in Europe. The government worked with business to promote full employment and steer the economy in directions deemed socially desirable. Moreover, the welfare state came to mean a major role for the Swedish trade unions, which won relatively high wages for workers and even enjoyed a quasi–veto power over legislation.

At the same time, the Swedish government began playing a more active role in spheres of life that had formerly been private, from sexuality to child rearing. Drugstores were required to carry contraceptives beginning in 1946, and Sweden was the first country to provide sex education in the public schools—on an optional basis in 1942, then on a compulsory basis in 1955. By 1979 the Swedes were limiting corporal punishment—the right to spank—and prohibiting the sale of war toys. This deprivatization of the family stemmed from a sense that society is collectively responsible for the well-being of its children.

Britain's decision to move toward the welfare state evidenced its widening appeal. Though Winston Churchill had led his country through the darkest days of the war, Churchill's Conservatives suffered a crushing loss in the 1945 elections. Early in the war most Britons had come to take it for granted that major socioeconomic changes would follow from victory, and the Labour party, led by Clement Attlee (1883–1967), seemed better equipped to deliver on that promise.

The success of government planning and control during the war suggested that government could assume responsibility for the basic needs of the British people in peacetime as well. The welfare state was an alternative to socialism, avoiding large-scale nationalization and concentrating on social welfare measures that significantly affected the lives of ordinary people. These included old-age pensions; insurance against unemployment, sickness, and disability; and allowances for pregnancy, child rearing, widowhood, and burial. The heart of the system was free medical care, provided by the new National Health Service, which was operating by 1948.

In Britain as elsewhere, gender roles were inevitably an issue as government welfare measures were debated. Were married women to have access to the welfare system as individuals or as members of a family unit, dependent on their husbands as breadwinners and responsible for child rearing? Should government seek to enable women to be both mothers and workers, or should it help make it possible for mothers not to have to work outside the home? The answers varied widely.

The percentage of women in the work force had increased significantly during World War II, but in the immediate postwar period traditional domestic patterns seemed to have returned. In

Social Welfare in Sweden With the state playing a major role, Sweden proved a pioneer in responding to the family and children's issues that became increasingly prominent after World War II. Here children play at a day-care center in Stockholm in 1953. *(Roland Janson/ Pressens Bild, Stockholm)*

many cases, women had little choice in the matter as they were fired from their higher-paying war jobs so that men could claim them. For middle-class women this generally meant returning to the solitary and often monotonous world of the home. Often this was welcomed as a return to normality, but many women soon missed the self-sufficiency, creative challenges, and camaraderie that their war jobs had provided. For working-class women, being fired "so a man could have the job" generally meant returning to tedious, low-paid, menial labor.

British feminists at first welcomed provisions of the British welfare state. The government was to ease burdens by providing family allowances, to be paid directly to mothers, for more than one child. This seemed a progressive step beyond the long-standing British trade union demand for a "family wage"—a wage high enough to enable the male breadwinner to support a family so that his wife would not have to work. The new provisions singled out mothers for benefits, enabling them to stay home with their children. But they also reinforced the traditional assumption that marriage meant economic dependence for women and assumed that child care was women's work.

It seemed to some theorists that the relationship between parents, children, and work was going through another monumental shift, comparable to the shift that accompanied the rise of wage labor and the rise of the state. Wage labor demanded that some member of the family work at a distance from the house, and as a result parenting and earning were no longer compatible. Men were able to enter the modern work force and participate in the state because they had a support staff: women. As ideologies of individual freedom progressed, women fought for the opportunity to become full participants in the work force and the state, which would be possible only with a new support system.

France did the best job of responding to these new conditions, and its innovative approach to gender and family issues eventually made France a model for others. After the experience of defeat, collaboration, and resistance, the French were determined to pursue both economic dynamism and individual justice. But they also remained concerned with population growth, so they combined incentives to encourage large families with measures to promote equal opportunity and economic independence for women. Thus, as they expanded the role of government after the war, the French tended to assume that paid employment for women was healthy and desirable. The French also recognized that pregnancy and infant care were demanding tasks and that fathers shared the responsibility for parenting. The challenge was to combine equal treatment and equal employment opportunities with support for child rearing.

New laws gave French women equal access to civil service jobs and guaranteed equal pay for equal work. In addition, the French welfare system treated women as individual citizens, regardless of marital or economic status. Thus they were equally entitled to pensions, health services, and job-related benefits. Yet the French system also provided benefits for women during and after pregnancy. There were also family allowances that treated both parents as equally essential.

Although female participation in the paid labor force in Western Europe declined after the war, it began rising steadily during the 1950s, then accelerated during the 1960s, reaching new highs in the 1970s and 1980s. Thanks partly to the expansion of government, the greatest job growth came in the service sector—in social work, health care, and education, for example—and many of these new jobs went to women. From about 1960 to 1988, the percentage of women aged 25 to 34 in the labor force rose from 38 to 67 in Britain, from 42 to 75 in France, and from 49 to 87 in Germany. But even as their choices expanded in some respects, women became more deeply aware of enduring limits to their opportunities. Their awareness energized a new feminist movement in the 1960s (see page 706). That movement drew intellectual inspiration from *The Second Sex*, a pioneering work published in 1949 by the French existentialist Simone de Beauvoir (1908–1986). Starting with the existentialist emphasis on human freedom, de Beauvoir demonstrated how cultural conventions continued to restrict the range of choices for women. In a profoundly influential phrase, de Beauvoir asserted that "women are made, not born," meaning that so-called "feminine" character traits and abilities are in fact invented and reinforced by the culture and not biologically innate. Men, she argued, had made themselves the standard of humanity, defining women as the "Other" and making them the repository of male fantasies and fears. (See the box "Human Freedom and the Origins of a New Feminism.")

Restoration of Democracy in Germany, France, and Italy

With its turn to a welfare state, Britain was seeking to renew a long-standing democracy after an arduous victory. Much of continental Western Europe faced a deeper challenge—to rebuild democracy after defeat and humiliation. The outcome of the effort to restore democracy was by no means certain in the late 1940s. Communism was weak in the new Federal Republic of Germany, but in France and Italy strong Communist parties had emerged from the wartime resistance and claimed to point the way beyond conventional democracy.

The Federal Republic of Germany held its first election under the Basic Law in 1949, launching what proved a successful democracy. Partly to counter the Soviet Union but also to avoid what seemed the disastrous mistake of the harsh peace settlement after World War I, the victors sought to help get Germany back on its feet as quickly as possible. At the same time, German political leaders, determined to avoid the mistakes of the Weimar years, now better understood the need to compromise. To prevent instability, the Basic Law discouraged splinter parties and allowed the courts to outlaw extremist parties.

Human Freedom and the Origins of a New Feminism

The renewed feminism that became prominent during the later 1960s took inspiration from* The Second Sex, *a pioneering work by the French existentialist Simone de Beauvoir that was first published in 1949. Even while valuing sexual difference, she showed the scope for opening the full range of human choices to women.

[T]he nature of things is no more immutably given, once for all, than is historical reality. If woman seems to be the inessential which never becomes the essential, it is because she herself fails to bring about this change. . . .

To decline to be the Other, to refuse to be a party to the deal—this would be for women to renounce all the advantages conferred upon them by their alliance with the superior caste. Man-the-sovereign will provide woman-the-liege with material protection and will undertake the moral justification of her existence; thus she can evade at once both economic risk and the metaphysical risk of a liberty in which ends and aims must be contrived without assistance. Indeed, along with the ethical urge of each individual to affirm his subjective existence, there is also the temptation to forgo liberty and become a thing. . . .

If a caste is kept in a state of inferiority, no doubt it remains inferior; but liberty can break the circle. Let negroes vote, and they become worthy of having the vote; let woman be given responsibilities and she is able to assume them. . . .

. . . [T]here will be some to object that . . . when woman is "the same" as her male, life will lose its salt and spice. . . .

. . . There is no denying that feminine dependence, inferiority, woe, give women their special character; assuredly woman's autonomy, if it spares men many troubles, will also deny them many conveniences; assuredly there are certain forms of the sexual adventure which will be lost in the world of tomorrow. But this does not mean that love, happiness, poetry, dream, will be banished from it.

. . . New relations of flesh and sentiment of which we have no conception will arise between the sexes; already, indeed, there have appeared between men and women friendships, rivalries, complicities, comradeships—chaste or sensual—which past centuries could not have conceived. . . .

. . . [T]here will always be certain differences between man and woman; her eroticism, and therefore her sexual world, have a special form of their own and therefore cannot fail to engender a sensuality, a sensitivity, of a special nature. . . .

. . . [W]hen we abolish the slavery of half of humanity, together with the whole system of hypocrisy that it implies, then the "division" of humanity will reveal its genuine significance and the human couple will find its true form.

Source: Simone de Beauvoir, *The Second Sex,* trans. H. M. Parshley (New York: Random House, Vintage, 1989), pp. xxv, xxvii, 728–731.

The courts outlawed both the Communist party and a neo-Nazi party during the formative years of the new German democracy. Two mass parties, the Christian Democratic Union (CDU) and the Social Democratic party (SPD), were immediately predominant, although a third, the much smaller Free Democratic party (FDP), proved important in building governing coalitions.

Konrad Adenauer (1876–1967), head of the CDU, the largest party in 1949, emerged as

Germany's leading statesman. Mayor of Cologne during the Weimar Republic, Adenauer had withdrawn from politics during the Nazi period, re-emerging after the war to lead the council that drafted the Basic Law. As chancellor from 1949 until 1963, he oriented German democracy toward Western Europe and the Atlantic bloc led by the United States.

The new bipolar world confronted West Germany with a cruel choice. If it accepted the bipolar framework, the country could become a full partner within the Atlantic bloc. But if it tried to straddle the fence instead, it could keep open the possibility that Germany could be reunified as a neutral and disarmed state. When the outbreak of war in Korea intensified the cold war in the early 1950s, the United States pressured West Germany to rearm and join the Western bloc. Although some West Germans resisted, Adenauer led the Federal Republic into NATO in 1955.

In the late 1950s the West German economy was recovering nicely, and the country was a valued member of the Western alliance. Adenauer's CDU seemed so potent that the other major party, the SPD, appeared to be consigned to permanent opposition. Frustrated, the SPD began to shed its Marxist trappings in an effort to widen its appeal. Prominent among those pushing in this direction was Willy Brandt (1913–1992), who became mayor of West Berlin in 1957 and the party's leader in 1963.

Adenauer stepped down in 1963 at the age of 87, after fourteen years as chancellor. The contrast with Weimar, which had known twenty-one different cabinets in a comparable fourteen-year period, could not be more striking. The Adenauer years proved to Germans that liberal democracy could mean stable and effective government and economic prosperity.

From 1963 to 1969, the CDU proved it could govern without Adenauer, while the SPD came to seem ever more respectable, even joining as junior partner in a government coalition with the CDU in 1966. Finally, in October 1969, Brandt was elected chancellor, and the SPD became responsible for governing West Germany for the first time since the war. Brandt sought to provide a genuine alternative to the CDU without undermining the consensus that had developed since 1949. He wanted to improve relations between West Germany and the Soviet bloc. Under Adenauer, the Federal Republic had refused to deal with East Germany at all. So Brandt's opening to the East, or *Ostpolitik*, was risky, but he pursued it with skill and success.

In treaties with the Soviet Union, Czechoslovakia, and Poland, West Germany accepted the main lines of the postwar settlement. Brandt also improved relations with East Germany. The two countries agreed to mutual diplomatic recognition and were admitted to the United Nations in 1973. Brandt's overtures made possible closer economic ties and broader opportunities for ordinary citizens to interact across the east-west border.

In France and Italy, unlike West Germany, communists emerged powerful from their major roles in wartime resistance movements. Indeed, in either nation they might have made a bid for power as the war was ending. But Moscow, concerned with the larger picture in Europe, called for the moderate route of participation in coalitions. The United States intervened persistently to minimize the communists' role in both countries. When the first parliamentary elections were held in the new Fourth Republic in France in 1946, the Communists won the largest number of seats, and their support continued to rise until 1949. Partly because of pressure from the United States, they were forced out of the coalition government in 1947, and after 1949 their strength began leveling off.

As the leader of the resistance effort, Charles de Gaulle assumed the dominant political role after the liberation of France in August 1944. But he withdrew, disillusioned, from active politics early in 1946, as political life under the new Fourth Republic seemed to return to the patterns of the old Third Republic: multiparty coalitions and constant instability. Governments rose and fell every six months, on the average, over the twelve-year life of the Fourth Republic. This finally ended in 1958, when de Gaulle returned to politics during the Algeria crisis (see page 695).

Although de Gaulle became prime minister within the Fourth Republic, it was clear that his return signified a change of regime. The French legislature gave his government full powers for six months, including a charge to draft a new constitution, which was approved by referendum in the fall of 1958. The result was the Fifth Republic, which featured a stronger executive—and soon a president elected directly by the people and not dependent on the Chamber of Deputies.

Italy's political challenge, after more than twenty years of fascism, was even more dramatic. Shortly after the war, the Italians adopted a new democratic constitution and voted to end the monarchy, making modern Italy a republic for the first time. But much depended on the balance of political forces, which quickly crystallized around the Christian Democratic party (DC) and the Communist and Socialist parties. As the cold war developed, the United States intervened periodically to support the Christian Democrats as a bulwark against the Communists. Many Italian moderates with little attachment to the Roman Catholic church supported the DC for the same reason.

Well into the 1970s, the DC was invariably the largest single party, yet not a majority, so it was forced to work in coalition with smaller parties. Beginning in the early 1960s, with the much-trumpeted "opening to the left," this even included the Socialist party (PSI), which typically won 10 to 15 percent of the vote in national elections. This total fell far behind that of the Communist party, which for decades remained the second largest at 25 to 35 percent. The relative strength of the political parties established the framework for the curious combination of surface instability and deeper stability—or immobility—that came to characterize the new Italian democracy. Domination by the Christian Democrats was the fundamental fact of Italian political life until the early 1990s.

Unlike their counterparts in France, the Italian Communists did not settle for a role of opposition and protest. They organized cooperatives, won regional elections, and garnered the support of intellectuals and journalists. At one time or another, they ran many of Italy's local governments and generally did well at it. Heavily communist Bologna, for example, was one of the best-governed cities in Europe.

As the years after World War II turned to decades, the Italian Communists' successes raised awkward questions. What were the Communists trying to accomplish on the national level, and how long was it supposed to take? Could a communist party function as a governing party within a democratic political system? Meanwhile, the Christian Democrats grew ever more entrenched, arrogant, and corrupt.

WESTERN EUROPE AND THE WORLD

By the early 1950s, the old Europe seemed dwarfed by the two global superpowers. The colonial networks that had symbolized European predominance were unraveling rapidly. One obvious response was some form of European unity. A unified Europe might eventually have the clout to stand as a global superpower in its own right. Although the first steps toward European unity did not go as far as visionaries had hoped, they established lasting foundations by the late 1950s—and they served European prosperity and security well.

NATO and the Atlantic Orientation

As the Soviets tightened their grip on east-central Europe, fears of Soviet expansion into Western Europe led to the creation of the North Atlantic Treaty Organization (NATO) under U.S. leadership in April 1949. In pooling the forces of its member countries under a unified command, NATO went beyond the usual peacetime military alliance. The Atlantic bloc assumed definitive shape in 1955, when it encompassed the newly rearmed West Germany (see Map 26.2 on page 698). Although the prospect of German rearmament made the French nervous at first, by 1954 they had come to agree that this was the best course for French security.

Ban the Bomb As nuclear tension escalated during the 1950s, some people built air-raid shelters, and others took to the streets in antinuclear protest. The protest movement was especially prominent in Britain. Here demonstrators march from Trafalgar Square in London to the Atomic Weapons Research Establishment in Reading to protest the H-bomb. *(Hulton-Getty/Liaison)*

The Soviets had considerable superiority in conventional forces and ready access to Western Europe. U.S. nuclear superiority balanced this and served as the cornerstone of the NATO alliance. As a consequence it seemed crucial for the United States to maintain its superiority in nuclear weapons, a fact that helped fuel the continuing arms race.

When the Soviet Union developed the capacity for a nuclear strike at the United States, Europeans began asking whether the Americans could be counted on to respond to a conventional Soviet attack on Western Europe. Such doubts became especially widespread in France, where President de Gaulle, citing concerns for French sovereignty and security, accelerated the development of a French nuclear force in the 1960s.

The Varieties of Decolonization

World War II had proven a major catalyst for anticolonialist independence movements throughout the world. In southeast Asia and the Pacific, the quick Japanese conquests had revealed the vulnerability of France, the Netherlands, and Britain. Also, the United States took a dim view of European colonialism. Still, the process of decolonization was varied and uneven, partly because the local independence movements differed but also because the interests of Europeans varied. Where there were large numbers of European settlers or their descendants, the remaining colonial powers—Britain, France, Belgium, the Netherlands, and Portugal—were reluctant to yield. But everywhere they were more likely to yield if they could preserve property rights and the possibility of continued influence (Map 26.1).

The effort of the Netherlands to regain control of the Dutch East Indies led to four years of military struggle before Indonesia became independent in 1949. Britain generally sought to avoid such struggles, but policy was inconsistent. Although India, the crown jewel of the empire, had won independence in 1947, many Britons still envisioned extending Commonwealth status to former British colonies as a way of retaining economic ties and political influence. But the Commonwealth became little more than a voluntary cooperative association. Despite illusions and hesitations, however, Britain proved the most realistic of the European colonial powers, grasping the need to compromise and work with emerging national leaders.

Nevertheless, even Britain decided to resist in 1956, when it provoked an international crisis over the status of the Suez Canal in Egypt. Once a British protectorate, Egypt had remained under British influence even after nominally becoming sovereign in 1922. A revolution in 1952 produced a new government of Arab nationalists, led by the able and charismatic Colonel Gamel Abdul Nasser (1918–1970). In 1954, Britain agreed to leave the Suez Canal zone within twenty months, though the zone was to be international, not Egyptian, and Britain was to retain special rights there in the event of war. In 1956, however, Nasser announced the nationalization of the canal, partly so that Egypt could use its revenues to finance public works projects.

Led by the Conservative prime minister Anthony Eden (1897–1977), Britain decided on a showdown. Eden won the support of Israel and France, each of which had reason to fear Nasser's pan-Arab nationalism. Israel had remained at odds with its Arab neighbors since its founding in 1948, and Nasser was helping the Arabs, who were taking up arms against French rule in Algeria. Late in 1956, Britain, Israel, and France orchestrated a surprise attack on Egypt, but the troops met stubborn Egyptian resistance and were defeated. The United States and the Soviet Union both opposed the Anglo-French-Israeli move, as did world opinion. The outcome of the Suez crisis demonstrated the new strength of non-European nations within the new bipolar framework.

Still, the outcome in 1956 did not convince France to abandon its struggle to retain Algeria. And that struggle proved the most dramatic, wrenching experience that any European country was to have with decolonization. However, the process started not in North Africa but in Indochina, in southeast Asia, during World War II.

Led by the communist Ho Chi Minh (1890–1969), the Indochinese anticolonialist movement gained strength resisting the Japanese during the war and established a political base in northern Vietnam in 1945. Although the French re-established control in the south after the war, negotiations between the French and the Vietnamese nationalists seemed at first to be moving toward some form of self-government for Vietnam. There was considerable opposition to this in France, especially within the army, and in 1946 French authorities in Indochina deliberately provoked an incident to start hostilities. Eight years of difficult and expensive guerrilla war followed.

With its strongly anticolonialist posture, the United States was at first unsympathetic to the French cause. But the communist takeover in China in 1949 and the invasion of South Korea by the North in 1950 made the French struggle in Indochina seem a battle in a larger war against communism in Asia. By 1954 the United States was covering 75 percent of the cost of the French effort in Indochina. Nonetheless, when the fall of the fortified area at Dien Bien Phu in May 1954 signaled a decisive French defeat, U.S. President Eisenhower decided to accept a negotiated settlement. Eisenhower had concluded that the Soviet threat in Europe must remain his principal concern.

France worked out the terms of independence for Vietnam in 1955. The country was

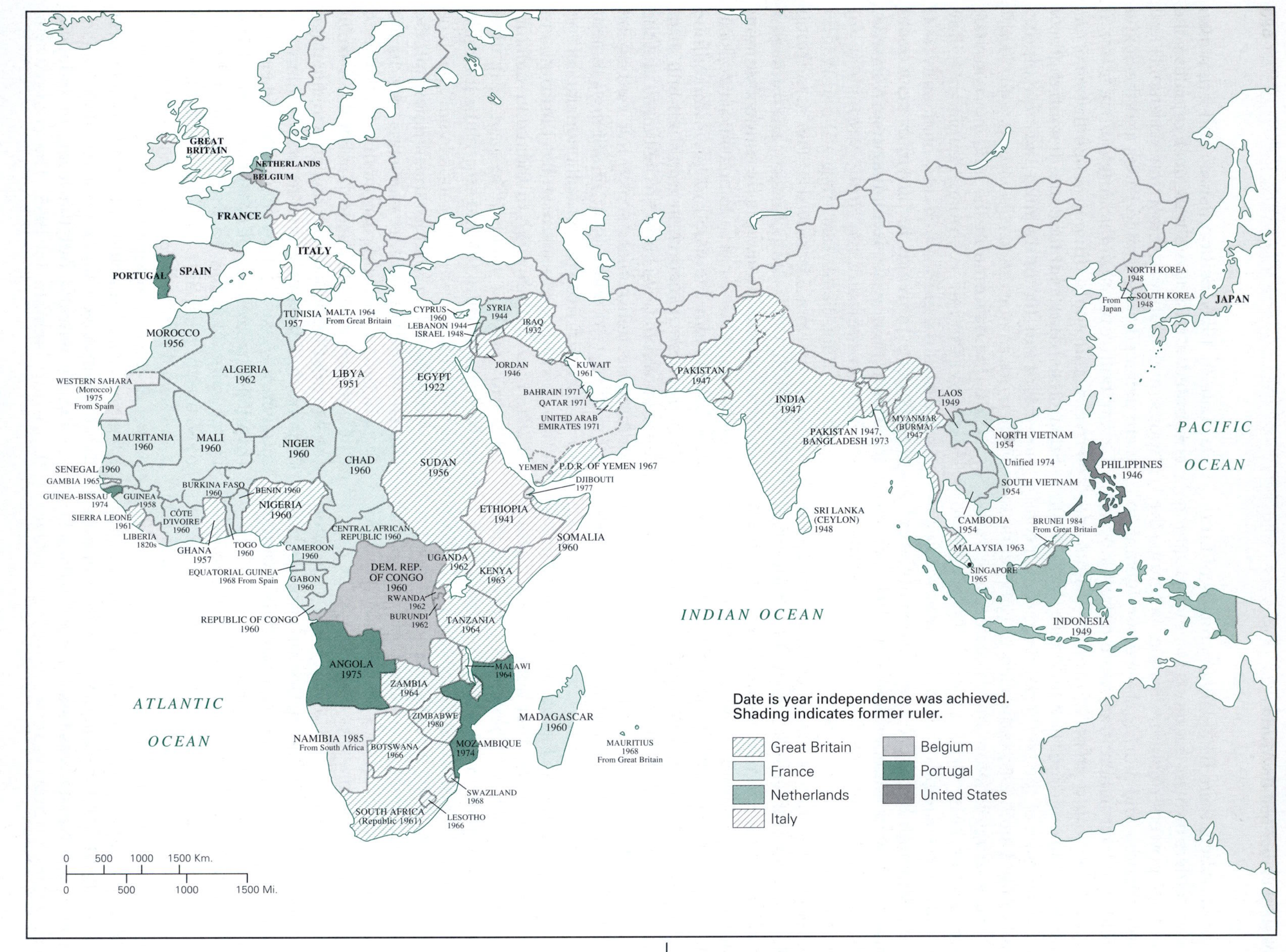

GREAT BRITAIN
NETHERLANDS
BELGIUM
FRANCE
ITALY
PORTUGAL
SPAIN
MOROCCO 1956
TUNISIA 1957
MALTA 1964 From Great Britain
CYPRUS 1960
LEBANON 1944
ISRAEL 1948
SYRIA 1944
IRAQ 1932
JORDAN 1946
KUWAIT 1961
BAHRAIN 1971
QATAR 1971
UNITED ARAB EMIRATES 1971
ALGERIA 1962
LIBYA 1951
EGYPT 1922
WESTERN SAHARA (Morocco) 1975 From Spain
MAURITANIA 1960
MALI 1960
NIGER 1960
CHAD 1960
SUDAN 1956
SENEGAL 1960
GAMBIA 1965
GUINEA-BISSAU 1974
GUINEA 1958
SIERRA LEONE 1961
LIBERIA 1820s
CÔTE D'IVOIRE 1960
BURKINA FASO 1960
GHANA 1957
TOGO 1960
BENIN 1960
NIGERIA 1960
CAMEROON 1960
CENTRAL AFRICAN REPUBLIC 1960
EQUATORIAL GUINEA 1968 From Spain
GABON 1960
REPUBLIC OF CONGO 1960
YEMEN
P.D.R. OF YEMEN 1967
DJIBOUTI 1977
ETHIOPIA 1941
SOMALIA 1960
DEM. REP. OF CONGO 1960
UGANDA 1962
KENYA 1963
RWANDA 1962
BURUNDI 1962
TANZANIA 1964
ANGOLA 1975
MALAWI 1964
ZAMBIA 1964
ZIMBABWE 1980
MOZAMBIQUE 1974
MADAGASCAR 1960
MAURITIUS 1968 From Great Britain
NAMIBIA 1985 From South Africa
BOTSWANA 1966
SWAZILAND 1968
SOUTH AFRICA (Republic 1961)
LESOTHO 1966
ATLANTIC OCEAN
INDIAN OCEAN
PACIFIC OCEAN
PAKISTAN 1947
INDIA 1947
PAKISTAN 1947, BANGLADESH 1973
SRI LANKA (CEYLON) 1948
MYANMAR (BURMA) 1947
LAOS 1949
NORTH VIETNAM 1954
Unified 1974
SOUTH VIETNAM 1954
CAMBODIA 1954
MALAYSIA 1963
SINGAPORE 1965
BRUNEI 1984 From Great Britain
PHILIPPINES 1946
INDONESIA 1949
NORTH KOREA 1948
SOUTH KOREA 1948
From Japan
JAPAN
Date is year independence was achieved.
Shading indicates former ruler.
Great Britain
France
Netherlands
Italy
Belgium
Portugal
United States
0 500 1000 1500 Km.
0 500 1000 1500 Mi.

divided into northern and southern parts to separate the communist and anticommunist forces, pending elections to unify the country. The anticommunist regime the United States sponsored in the south resisted holding the elections, so the country remained divided (see Map 26.1). Only in 1975, after a brutal war with the United States, would the communist heirs of those who had led the fight against the French assume the leadership of a unified Vietnam.

In France, the defeat in Indochina left a legacy of bitterness, especially among army officers, many of whom felt that French forces could have won had they not been undercut by politicians at home. When the outcome in Indochina emboldened Arab nationalists in North Africa to take up arms against the French colonial power, the French army was eager for a second chance. The French government was willing to give it to them and agreed to independence for Tunisia and Morocco by 1956, in order to concentrate on Algeria. Algeria had been under French control since 1830, and it had over a million ethnic Europeans, 10 percent of the population.

France gradually committed 500,000 troops to Algeria, but the war bogged down into a stalemate, with increasing brutality on both sides. The war became a highly volatile political issue in France, finally coming to a head during the spring of 1958. The advent of a new ministry, rumored to favor a compromise settlement, led to violent demonstrations, engineered by the sectors of the French army in Algeria. Military intervention in France itself seemed likely to follow—and with it the danger of civil war.

It was at this moment that Charles de Gaulle returned to lead the change to the Fifth Republic. Those determined to hold Algeria welcomed de Gaulle as their savior. But de Gaulle fooled them, working out a compromise with the rebels that made Algeria independent in 1962. Only de Gaulle could have engineered this outcome without provoking still deeper division in France. As for Algeria, the anticolonial movement there gave rise to a more radical political order than had been the case in Tunisia and Morocco. The new Algerian government's policy of expropriation and nationalization led most of the French settlers to relocate to France.

Map 26.1 From Colonialism to Independence During a thirty-five-year period after World War II, the European empires in Africa, Asia, and the Pacific gradually came apart as the former colonies became independent nations.

As the colonies of sub-Saharan Africa moved toward independence in the decades following World War II (see Map 26.1), the response of the European powers varied considerably. Of the major imperial powers, Britain had done the best at preparing local leaders and proved the most willing to work with indigenous elites. Belgium and Portugal—less certain they could maintain their influence—were the most reluctant to give up imperial status.

The transition was smoothest in British West Africa, where the Gold Coast achieved independence as Ghana, first as a dominion in the Commonwealth in 1957, then as a fully independent republic in 1960. There were few British settlers in that part of Africa, and the small, relatively cohesive African elite favored a moderate transition, not revolution. Where British settlers were relatively numerous, as in Kenya and Rhodesia, the transition to independence was much more difficult. The very presence of Europeans had impeded the development of cohesive local elites, so movements for independence in those areas tended to become more radical, advocating the expropriation of European-held property.

Nowhere was decolonization messier than in the two largest Portuguese colonies in Africa, Mozambique and Angola. Portugal had run the most repressive of the African colonial regimes, with elements of the earlier system of forced labor lingering into the 1960s. Portuguese intransigence radicalized the independence movement, which took advantage of help from the communist world to resist the colonizers militarily. Finally, in 1974, sectors of the Portuguese military, weary of a colonial war they lacked the resources to win, engineered a coup at home. The new government washed its hands of the debilitating struggle, granting independence to both Mozambique and Angola in 1975.

The process of decolonization led to a remarkable transformation in the thirty-five years after World War II. But decolonization hardly offered a neat and definitive solution. In formerly colonial territories, the boundaries often stemmed from the way Europeans had carved things up, rather than from indigenous ethnic or national patterns. Moreover, questions remained about the long-term economic relationships between Europeans and their former colonies.

The leader of Ghana, Kwame Nkrumah (1909–1972), used the term *neocolonialism* in arguing that more subtle forms of Western exploitation had replaced direct rule. But attempts by the former colonies to do without economic ties to the West often proved counterproductive, and in some areas reasonably good relations, compatible with Western economic interests, eventually developed. Generally, postcolonial leaders were highly ambivalent toward the West, where many of them had been educated.

At the same time, the context of superpower rivalry created new challenges and opportunities for the postcolonial world. In April 1955 the leaders of twenty-nine Asian and African nations met at Bandung, Indonesia, in a conference that proved a watershed in the self-understanding of what was coming to be called the "Third World." The most influential, like India's Jawaharlal Nehru, Egypt's Nasser, and Indonesia's Achmed Sukarno (1901–1970), were charismatic nation-builders, at once anti-Western and Westernizing. Along with Tito of Yugoslavia, Nehru was the leading proponent of *nonalignment*, navigating an independent course between the Western and Soviet blocs. Third World leaders often found ways of exploiting the superpower rivalry to their own advantage.

The reaction against Eurocentrism that accompanied the turn from colonialism was not confined to those who had been subjected to European imperialism. It contributed to the vogue of *structuralism*, as developed in anthropology by Claude Lévi-Strauss (b. 1908). While raising deep questions about any notion of Western superiority, Lévi-Strauss expressed a certain nostalgia for a world untouched by Western influence. There was also much interest in the West in the work of Frantz Fanon (1925–1961), a black intellectual from Martinique who became identified with the cause of the Algerian rebels. In *The Wretched of the Earth* (1961), Fanon found the West spiritually exhausted and called on the peoples of the non-Western world to go their own way, based on their own values and traditions. (See the box "Encounters with the West: The Legacy of European Colonialism.")

Economic Integration and the Coming of the European Union

As the old colonialism fell into disrepute, many found in European unity the best prospect for the future. Although hopes for political unity were soon frustrated, the movement for European integration achieved significant fruit in the economic sphere, especially through the European Economic Community (EEC), or Common Market, established in 1957.

The impetus for economic integration came especially from a new breed of "Eurocrats"—technocrats with a supranational, or Pan-European, outlook. Two remarkable French leaders, Jean Monnet and Robert Schuman (1886–1963), set the pattern. As French foreign minister after World War II, Schuman was responsible for a 1950 plan to coordinate French and German production of coal and steel. The Schuman Plan quickly encompassed both Italy and the Benelux countries to become the European Coal and Steel Community (ECSC) in 1951. Monnet served as the ECSC's first president and continued to push for more economic integration. In March 1957, leaders of France, Germany, Italy, Belgium, the Netherlands, and Luxembourg signed the Treaty of Rome, establishing the Common Market, or EEC. Over the next four decades the EEC's membership gradually expanded to include Denmark, Ireland, and Britain (1973), Greece (1981), Spain and Portugal (1986), and Austria, Finland, and Sweden (1995) (Map 26.2).

The immediate aim of the EEC was to facilitate trade by eliminating customs duties within

ENCOUNTERS WITH THE WEST

The Legacy of European Colonialism

In the following passage from* The Wretched of the Earth *(1961), Frantz Fanon probes the negative consequences of colonialism—for both colonizers and colonized—and tries to show why a radical, even violent break from colonialism was necessary.

The violence which has ruled over the ordering of the colonial world, which has ceaselessly drummed the rhythm for the destruction of native social forms and broken up without reserve the systems of reference of the economy, the customs of dress and external life, that same violence will be claimed and taken over by the native at the moment when, deciding to embody history in his own person, he surges into the forbidden quarters. . . .

. . . The colonialist bourgeoisie, in its narcissistic dialogue, expounded by the members of its universities, had in fact deeply implanted in the minds of the colonized intellectual that the essential qualities remain eternal in spite of all the blunders men may make: the essential qualities of the West, of course. . . . Now it so happens that during the struggle for liberation, at the moment that the native intellectual comes into touch again with his people, . . . [a]ll the Mediterranean values—the triumph of the human individual, of clarity, and of beauty— . . . are revealed as worthless, simply because they have nothing to do with the concrete conflict in which the people is engaged.

Individualism is the first to disappear. . . . The colonialist bourgeoisie had hammered into the native's mind the idea of a society of individuals where each person shuts himself up in his own subjectivity, and whose only wealth is individual thought. Now the native who has the opportunity to return to the people during the struggle for freedom will discover the falseness of this theory. The very forms of organization of the struggle will suggest to him a different vocabulary. Brother, sister, friend—these are words outlawed by the colonialist bourgeoisie, because for them my brother is my purse, my friend is part of my scheme for getting on. The native intellectual . . . will . . . discover the substance of village assemblies, the cohesion of people's committees, and the extraordinary fruitfulness of local meetings and groupments. Henceforward, the interests of one will be the interests of all, for in concrete fact *everyone* will be discovered by the troops, *everyone* will be massacred—or *everyone* will be saved.

Source: Frantz Fanon, *The Wretched of the Earth,* trans. Constance Farrington (New York: Grove, 1968), pp. 40–47.

the Common Market and establishing a common tariff on imports from the rest of the world. Tariff reduction entailed the advantage of access to wider markets abroad, but also the risks of new competition in each member country's domestic market. It was hard to be sure who might gain and who might lose. However, the EEC proved advantageous to so many that tariff reduction proceeded well ahead of schedule. Trade among the member countries nearly doubled between 1958 and 1962, and by 1968 the last internal tariffs had been eliminated.

After the merger of the governing institutions of several European supranational organizations in 1967, the term "European Community" (EC) and later "European Union" (EU)

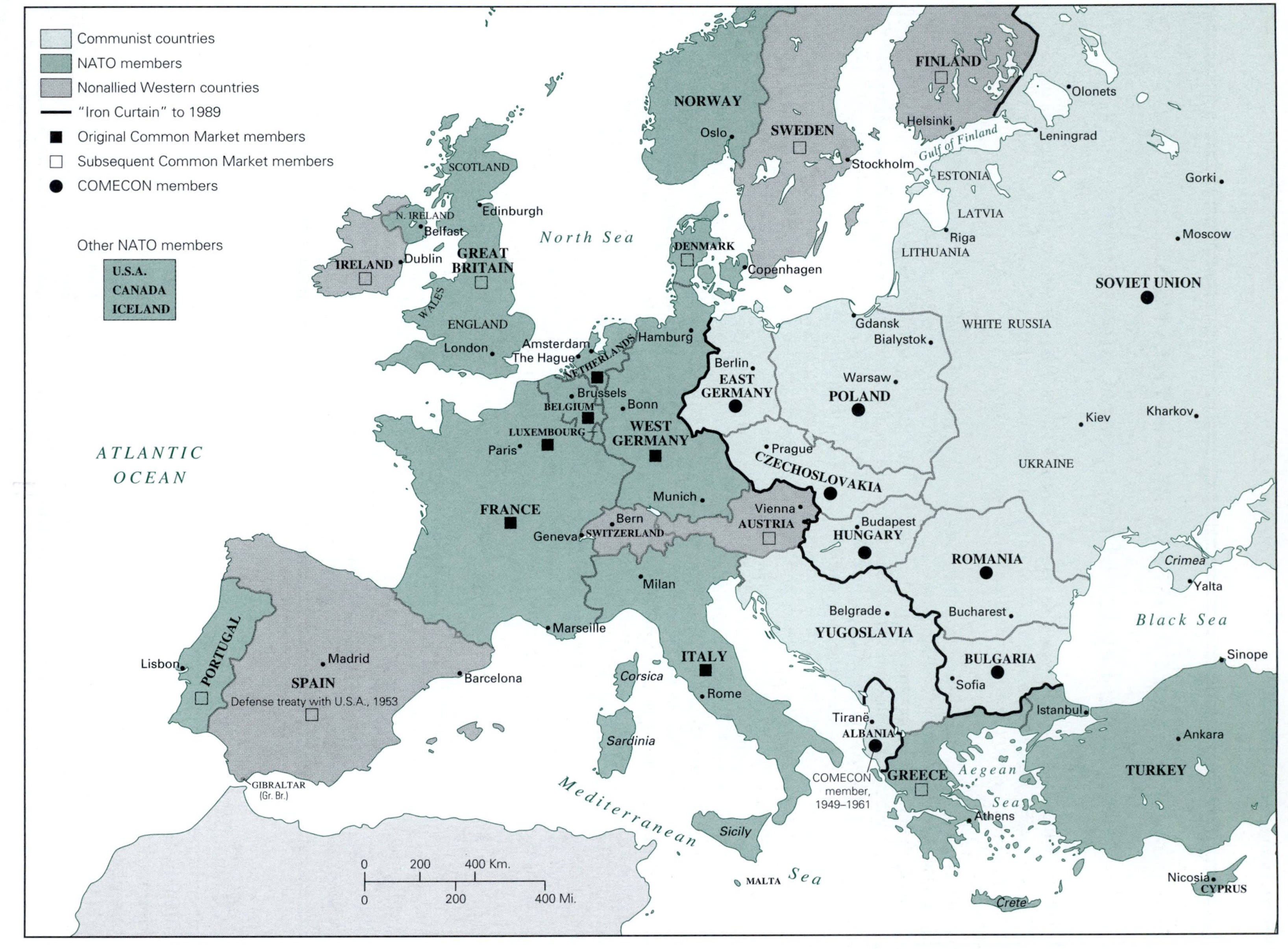

Communist countries
NATO members
Nonallied Western countries
"Iron Curtain" to 1989
Original Common Market members
Subsequent Common Market members
COMECON members
Other NATO members
U.S.A.
CANADA
ICELAND
ATLANTIC OCEAN
North Sea
Mediterranean Sea
Black Sea
Aegean Sea
Gulf of Finland
NORWAY
Oslo
SWEDEN
Stockholm
FINLAND
Helsinki
Leningrad
Olonets
Gorki
Moscow
SOVIET UNION
ESTONIA
LATVIA
Riga
LITHUANIA
WHITE RUSSIA
UKRAINE
Kiev
Kharkov
Crimea
Yalta
Sinope
SCOTLAND
Edinburgh
N. IRELAND
Belfast
IRELAND
Dublin
GREAT BRITAIN
WALES
ENGLAND
London
DENMARK
Copenhagen
Amsterdam
The Hague
NETHERLANDS
Brussels
BELGIUM
LUXEMBOURG
Hamburg
Bonn
WEST GERMANY
Munich
Berlin
EAST GERMANY
Gdansk
Bialystok
Warsaw
POLAND
Prague
CZECHOSLOVAKIA
Vienna
AUSTRIA
Budapest
HUNGARY
ROMANIA
Bucharest
Belgrade
YUGOSLAVIA
BULGARIA
Sofia
Istanbul
Ankara
TURKEY
Nicosia
CYPRUS
Tiranë
ALBANIA
COMECON member, 1949–1961
GREECE
Athens
Crete
Paris
FRANCE
Bern
Geneva
SWITZERLAND
Milan
Marseille
ITALY
Rome
Corsica
Sardinia
Sicily
MALTA
Lisbon
PORTUGAL
Madrid
SPAIN
Defense treaty with U.S.A., 1953
Barcelona
GIBRALTAR (Gr. Br.)
0 200 400 Km.
0 200 400 Mi.

replaced the terms "Common Market" and EEC. This broadening of the EEC did not occur without vigorous debate. The goal of the Common Market—to enable goods, capital, and labor to move freely among the member countries—required some coordination of the social and economic policies of the member states. Thus state sovereignty became an important issue.

In the mid-1960s, President de Gaulle of France forced some of the underlying uncertainties about the Common Market to the fore. De Gaulle was not prepared to compromise French sovereignty, and he was not persuaded that supranational integration offered the best course for postwar Europe. After the Algerian War ended in 1962, de Gaulle's France began playing an assertively independent role in international affairs, developing an independent French nuclear force, curtailing the French role in NATO, and recognizing the communist People's Republic of China.

De Gaulle's stance checked the increasing supranationalism of the Common Market. As the economic context became more difficult in the 1970s, it became harder to maintain the cohesion of the EEC. So though the Common Market proved an important departure, it did not give Western Europe a new world role during the first decades after World War II.

THE SOVIET UNION AND THE COMMUNIST BLOC

By the late 1950s, there was increasing concern in the West that the Soviet Union might have significant advantages in the race with the capitalist democracies. Westerners worried about producing enough scientists and engineers to match the Soviets, and some economists held that central planning might prove as efficient as capitalism. Nonetheless, flaws in the political and economic system that had emerged under Stalin continued in the Soviet Union, and its system of satellites in east-central Europe presented new dilemmas. Efforts to make the Soviet system more flexible after Stalin's death in 1953 proved sporadic at best, and the Soviet suppression of the reform movement in Czechoslovakia during the "Prague Spring" of 1968 confirmed the rigidity of the Soviet system.

Map 26.2 Military Alliances and Multinational Economic Groupings in the Era of the Cold War The cold war split was reflected especially in the two military alliances: NATO, formed in 1949, and the Warsaw Pact, formed in 1955. Each side also had its own multinational economic organization, but the membership of the EEC, or Common Market, was not identical to that of NATO. Although communist, Yugoslavia remained outside Soviet-led organizations, as did Albania for part of the period.

Dilemmas of the Soviet System in Postwar Europe

The Soviet Union had suffered enormously in leading the victory over Nazi Germany. Especially in the more developed western part of the country, thousands of factories and even whole towns lay destroyed, and there were severe shortages of everything from labor to housing. Yet the developing cold war seemed to require that military spending remain high.

At the same time, the Soviet Union faced the challenge of solidifying the system of satellite states it had put together in east-central Europe. Most of the region had no desirable interwar past to try to reclaim, and thus there was widespread sentiment for significant change, including nationalization of industry. The Soviet system seemed to have proven itself in standing up to the Nazis, and many believed that a socialist economic system could work. So a measure of idealism and enthusiasm surrounded postwar reconstruction even in the satellite states.

Partly in response to U.S. initiatives in Western Europe, the Soviets sought to mold the new communist states into a secure, coordinated bloc of allies. The Soviets founded a new organization, COMECON, as part of the effort to lead the economies of the satellite states away from their ties to the West and toward the Soviet Union (see Map 26.2). For example, before the war only

7 percent of Poland's foreign trade had been with the Soviet Union; by 1951 the figure was 58 percent. Through such mechanisms as artificial pricing of imports and exports, these new economic relationships often entailed outright exploitation of the satellite states for the benefit of the Soviet Union.

In the military-diplomatic sphere, the Soviets countered the admission of West Germany to NATO in 1955 by creating the Warsaw Pact, which provided for a joint military command and mutual military assistance in the Soviet bloc. The Warsaw Pact established a new basis for the continuing presence of Soviet troops in the satellite states, but the tensions within the Soviet-dominated system in east-central Europe soon raised questions about what the pact meant.

Yugoslavia had been a point of vulnerability for the Soviet system from the start. Communist-led partisans under Tito had liberated Yugoslavia from the Axis on their own, and they had not needed the Red Army to begin constructing a new communist regime. Tito was willing to work with the Soviets, but he could be considerably more independent than those elsewhere whose power rested on Soviet support. When Soviet demands, including control of the Yugoslav police and army, became intolerably meddlesome from the Yugoslav point of view, Tito broke with the Soviet Union in 1948. Yugoslavia began developing a more flexible socialist economic system, with greater scope for local initiatives.

Stalin's initial response to Tito's defection in 1948 was a crackdown on potential opponents throughout the Soviet bloc. As in the 1930s, Stalin relied on the secret police, who executed those suspected of deviation, inspiring fear even among those closest to him. As the arrest and execution of communist leaders continued in the satellite states, strikes and demonstrations developed as well, reaching a crisis point in East Germany in 1953.

The East German communist leader, Walter Ulbricht (1893–1973), feared that, as the United States pressed West Germany to rearm and join NATO, Soviet leaders would opt for a reunified but strictly neutral and disarmed Germany. German reunification, however, would entail free elections, which the East German Communists could not hope to win. Ulbricht thus intensified the industrial development of East Germany to make his country too valuable an ally for the Soviet Union to sacrifice. The resulting pressure on labor produced strong opposition.

In June 1953, a workers' protest in East Berlin led to political demands, including free elections and the withdrawal of Soviet troops. Disturbances spread quickly to other major East German cities. Though this spontaneous uprising was not well coordinated, Soviet troops had to intervene to save the Ulbricht government. The East German example helped stimulate antigovernment demonstrations elsewhere in the Soviet bloc, convincing Soviet leaders that something had to give. But at this point, shortly after Stalin's death, the leadership of the Soviet Union was still being sorted out.

De-Stalinization Under Khrushchev, 1955–1964

The nature of the struggle for succession after Stalin's death foreshadowed a turn from the extremes of Stalinism. The political infighting involved a reasonable degree of give and take, as opposed to terror and violence. Although one of the eventual losers was sent to Siberia to run a power station and the other was made ambassador to Outer Mongolia, it was a major departure that the winner, Nikita Khrushchev (1894–1971), had neither of them exiled or executed.

Khrushchev had not been Stalin's heir apparent, but he gradually established himself as the new leader by building up patronage networks and playing off factions. Slightly crude, even something of a buffoon, he won out by 1955 partly because his opponents repeatedly underestimated him. Although his period of leadership was brief, it was eventful—and in some ways the Soviet system's best chance for renewal.

At a closed session of the Soviet Communist party's twentieth national congress in February 1956, Khrushchev made a dramatic late-night speech denouncing the criminal excesses of the

Stalinist system and the "cult of personality" that had developed around Stalin. Khrushchev's immediate aim was to undercut his hard-line rivals, but he also insisted that Stalinism had amounted to an unnecessary deviation from Marxism-Leninism. It seemed that Khrushchev might bring liberalization and reform.

At the same time, however, popular discontent in the satellite states placed the whole system in crisis. In the face of the East German uprising of 1953, the Soviets began making room for more moderate communists. Khrushchev even sought to patch things up with Tito, publicly condemning Stalin's treatment of him, exchanging visits in 1955 and 1956, and suggesting that different countries might take different routes to communism.

In Poland beginning in June 1956, strikes against wage cuts took on a political character, finally provoking the intervention of Soviet troops in October. Nonetheless, the Soviets tolerated reform within Poland because it pledged to continue to uphold the Warsaw Pact as a bulwark against Germany. Later that year, however, the Hungarians dismantled their collective farms and moved toward a democratic coalition government. They called for Soviet troops to withdraw, to enable Hungary to leave the Warsaw Pact and become neutral. These were not changes within the system, but changes that would undermine the system itself. So after a democratic government was set up in October, the Soviets used tanks to crush the Hungarian reform movement. Thousands were killed during the fighting or executed and 200,000 Hungarians fled to the West.

The Soviets understood that the system had to become more palatable, but they made it clear

Revolution and Restoration in Hungary Led by students and faculty from the Karl Marx University of Economics, Hungarians march across the Chain Bridge in Budapest on October 23, 1956, initiating the revolutionary phase of the movement for change in communist Hungary. Within two weeks, a Soviet-led crackdown, including shelling by Soviet tanks, had crushed the revolution, inflicting 27,000 casualties on the Hungarians. *(MTI/Eastfoto/Sovfoto)*

that liberalization had to be kept within certain limits. Reformers could not challenge the system itself, especially communist one-party rule and the Warsaw Pact. Hungary's new leader, János Kádár (b. 1912), collectivized agriculture more fully than before, but he also engineered a measure of economic decentralization. There was eventually an amnesty for political prisoners, as well as considerable liberalization in cultural life, so that Hungary came to enjoy freer contact with the West than the other satellites.

East Germany's communist leaders had every reason *not* to distance themselves from the Soviets. Walter Ulbricht, who remained in power until his retirement in 1971, concentrated on central planning and heavy industry in orthodox fashion, and he made the East German economy the most successful in the Soviet bloc.

Still, because that economic growth was built on low wages, East German workers were tempted to immigrate to West Germany as the West German economic miracle gleamed ever brighter during the 1950s. The special position of Berlin, in the heart of East Germany yet still divided among the occupying powers, made emigration relatively easy; 2.6 million East Germans left for the West between 1950 and 1962. With a population of only 17.1 million, East Germany could not afford to let this hemorrhaging continue. Thus, in August 1961 the Ulbricht regime erected the Berlin Wall, a grim reminder that despite periodic thaws in East-West relations, the iron curtain remained in place.

From Liberalization to Stagnation

The most intense phase of the cold war ended with Stalin's death in 1953. In his speech to the twentieth party congress in 1956, Khrushchev repudiated the Soviet tenet that the military showdown between Western capitalist imperialism and the communist world was inevitable. However, despite summit conferences and sporadic efforts at better relations, friction between the Soviet Union and the United States continued.

A new peak of tension was reached in October 1962 when the Soviets placed missiles in Cuba, which had developed close ties with the Soviet Union after the 1959 revolution led by Fidel Castro (b. 1926). Although the United States had its own offensive missiles in Turkey, adjacent to the Soviet Union, the Soviet attempt to base missiles in Cuba seemed an intolerable challenge. For several days, military confrontation appeared a distinct possibility, but President John F. Kennedy (1917–1963) managed an effective combination of resistance and restraint in responding to the Soviet move. The Soviets withdrew their missiles in exchange for a U.S. promise not to seek to overthrow the communist government in Cuba. The outcome was essentially a victory for the United States, which retained its offensive missile capacity adjacent to the Soviet Union. The Cuban missile crisis was the closest the superpowers came to armed confrontation during the cold war period.

Meanwhile, it was becoming clear that international communism was not the monolithic force it had once seemed. The most dramatic indication was the Sino-Soviet split, which developed during the 1950s as the communists under Mao Zedong solidified their regime in China. After taking power in 1949, the Chinese communists pursued their own path to development. The Soviets came to fear that the Chinese might challenge the Soviet leadership of international communism. By the early 1960s, the communist Chinese path had become especially appealing in the non-Western world. The antagonism between China and the Soviet Union added another layer of uncertainty to the cold war era.

As a domestic leader, Khrushchev proved mercurial and erratic, but he was an energetic innovator, willing to experiment. He jettisoned the worst features of the police state apparatus, including some of the infamous Siberian prison camps, and offered amnesties for prisoners. He also liberalized cultural life and gave workers greater freedom to move from one job to another. The government expanded medical and educational facilities and, between 1955 and 1964, doubled the nation's housing stock, alleviating a severe housing shortage.

As part of the domestic thaw in the Soviet Union after Stalin, divorce became easier and abortion was again legalized. Women received liberal provisions for maternity leave, and some measures were taken to assure equal access to higher education and the professions. Still, women were concentrated in lower-paying occupations and rarely rose to the top echelons. Although they were prominent in medicine in the Soviet Union, Soviet doctors did not have the status—or the incomes—that their counterparts enjoyed in the West.

Though living standards remained relatively low, Khrushchev's reforms helped improve the lives of ordinary people by the early 1960s. His claim in 1961 that the Soviet Union would surpass the Western standard of living within twenty years did not seem an idle boast. After all, the Soviets had launched *Sputnik I* in 1957 and put the first human into space in 1961. Such achievements suggested that even ordinary Soviet citizens had reason for optimism. More generally, the communist regimes throughout the Soviet bloc had achieved excellent rates of economic growth during the 1950s. Yet Khrushchev had made enemies with his erratic reform effort, and this led to his forced retirement in October 1964. But not until 1968 did it become clear that the liberalization of the Khrushchev era was over.

By early 1968 a significant reform movement had developed within the Communist party in Czechoslovakia. Determined to avoid the fate of the Hungarian effort in 1956, the reformers emphasized that Czechoslovakia would remain a communist state and a full member of the Warsaw Pact. But within that framework, they felt, it should be possible to invite freer cultural expression and democratize the Communist party's procedures. However, efforts to reassure the Soviets alienated some of the reformers' supporters, who stepped up their demands as a result. Soviet leaders grew concerned, and in August 1968 Soviet tanks moved into the Czech capital, Prague, to crush the reform movement.

The end of the "Prague Spring" closed the era of relative flexibility and cautious innovation in the Soviet bloc that had begun in 1953. A period of relative stagnation followed under Leonid Brezhnev (1906–1982), a careful, consensus-seeking bureaucrat. Now setting the tone was the "Brezhnev doctrine": The Soviet Union would help established communist regimes remain in power against any "counterrevolutionary" threat.

Poland, too, experienced a reform effort in 1968, but it was initiated by students and failed to attract the support of workers. The Polish communist government provided subsidized food, housing, and medical care, but to pay the bill the Polish government had to borrow from foreigners. So even in Poland, where the communist regime seemed to satisfy the workers, its way of doing so was increasingly artificial—and unsustainable.

After the successes of the 1950s and early 1960s, the Soviet Union was finding it ever harder to match the West in economic growth and technological innovation. And despite periodic efforts at economic reform, the satellite states did not do appreciably better. Ordinary people became increasingly frustrated as the communist economic system proved erratic in providing even the most basic consumer goods.

Frustration grew especially among women, who seemed to bear a disproportionate share of the burdens. Women were more likely to be employed outside the home in the Soviet bloc than in the West. Around 90 percent of adult women in the Soviet Union and East Germany had paid jobs outside the home by 1980. Yet not only were women concentrated in jobs with low pay and prestige, but they also still bore the major responsibility for child care, housework, and shopping. They had few of the labor-saving devices available in the West, and they often had to spend hours in line to buy ordinary consumer items. Dissatisfaction among women fed a new underground protest movement that began in the mid-1970s—a further indication of the growing strains in the overall system.

DEMOCRACY AND ITS DISCONTENTS, 1968 AND AFTER

The year 1968, which saw the end of the "Prague Spring," proved a turning point in Western

Europe as well. By this point, a generation after World War II, democracy seemed to have succeeded remarkably. But in the late 1960s it became clear that, despite prosperity and stability, political alienation had been building in Western Europe. The dissatisfactions that began erupting in 1968 fundamentally changed the tone of politics in Europe and the West. Economic difficulties that began in 1973 only added fuel to an already smoldering fire.

Democratic Consolidation and Political Alienation

Observing the success of democracy in the most developed parts of Western Europe, Spain, Portugal, and Greece established workable democracies after periods of dictatorial rule. After the death of Francisco Franco in 1975, democracy returned to Spain more smoothly than most had dared hope. Franco established that a restoration of the monarchy would follow his death, and King Juan Carlos (r. 1975–) served as an effective catalyst in the transition to democracy.

When the first democratic elections in Spain since the civil war were held in 1977, the big winners were a democratic centrist party and a moderate socialist party. The Socialists won a parliamentary majority in the next elections, in 1982, and a moderate Socialist replaced the centrist leader as prime minister. It appeared that Spain had quickly found its way to an effective two-party system. Meanwhile, the new constitution of 1978 dismantled what was left of the Franco system. A comparable transition from military rule to democracy took place in Portugal and Greece. For all three, EEC membership became a pillar of the solidifying democratic consensus.

At the same time, however, political disaffection threatened the consensus in the more established democracies of Europe. The most dramatic eruption of radical protest was the "Days of May" uprising that shook France in May 1968. The movement accused de Gaulle's Fifth Republic of having slighted domestic issues such as housing and education in its preoccupation with raising the international status of the country.

The uprising of 1968 started with university students, who sought to reach out to others, especially industrial workers, by offering a broad critique of the present system. But union activists and workers generally declined to join the movement, and the students ended up settling for relatively limited concessions. Still, the uprising made it clear that the university system needed a complete overhaul—and that students and faculty had to be involved in the changes. Over the next several years, the Education Ministry carried out reforms, breaking existing institutions into smaller units, with more local control over budgets and instructional methods. Student and faculty participation in institutional governance tended to politicize French universities, some of which became communist strongholds, others bastions of the right.

The effort to come to terms with the events of 1968 deepened divisions within the Communist party. Unable to transcend long-standing class categories and embrace the aspirations of those, like the students, who were newly disaffected, French communism increasingly seemed old and stale. In contrast, the French Socialist party gained dramatically during the 1970s. Claiming the mantle of the new left that had emerged in 1968, the Socialists proclaimed that the promise of that year could be translated into substantial change.

The Oil Crisis and the Changing Economic Framework

As the political situation in Western Europe became more volatile, events outside Europe made it clear how interdependent the world had become—and that the West did not hold all the trump cards. In the fall of 1973, Egypt and Syria attacked Israel, seeking to recover the lands they had lost in a brief war in 1967. The assault failed, but the Arab nations of the oil-rich Middle East came together to retaliate against the Western bloc for supporting Israel. By restricting the supply of oil, the Arab-led Organization of Petroleum Exporting Countries (OPEC) produced a sharp increase in oil prices and a severe economic disruption all over the industrialized world. In Western Europe, in January 1975, the price of oil was six times what it had been in 1973, and this increase remained a source of inflationary pressure throughout the West until the early 1980s.

The 1970s proved to be an unprecedented period of *stagflation*—sharply reduced rates of growth combined with inflation and rising unemployment. Increasing global competition, technological change, and high unemployment created new economic strains. The economic miracle was over.

Problems in the Welfare State

A tighter economy made it harder for governments to afford the welfare measures that had helped establish the political consensus since World War II. The Swedish case dramatized the problems of managing a welfare state in conditions of economic stringency.

In the early 1970s, 40 percent of Sweden's national income went for taxes to finance the system—the highest rate of taxation in the world. At the same time, Sweden found itself less competitive because its wages were high and it was not keeping abreast of technological developments. In Sweden, as elsewhere, there were growing doubts that the welfare state could nurture the initiative and productivity needed for success in the increasingly competitive global economy. By 1980 unemployment and efforts to cut government spending led to the most severe labor unrest the country had experienced since the war.

In Britain a dramatic assault on the welfare state developed at the same time. The British economy lagged behind those of the rest of the industrialized West, suffering especially during the 1970s. Between 1968 and 1976, the country lost 1 million manufacturing jobs, and there was no consensus on how to apportion the pain of the necessary austerity measures.

Both of Britain's major political parties made a serious effort to deal with the situation, but neither succeeded. The election of the militantly conservative Margaret Thatcher (b. 1925) as Conservative party leader in 1975 proved the turning point. When she became prime minister in 1979, it was clear that Britain was embarking on a radically different course.

In contrast, during the early 1980s a revitalized socialist party in France marginalized the communists and, for a time, seemed poised to reorient government. François Mitterrand (1916–1996) was elected president in 1981, promising to create the first genuinely democratic socialism. But he gradually abandoned his talk of socialism in the face of economic and political pressures. By the end of the decade, he was questioning the relevance of long-standing socialist tenets and playing up the virtues of entrepreneurship, the profit mechanism, and free-market competition.

The Democratic Consensus and Its Limitations

Discontent with the political consensus after 1968 led to a variety of new political alignments and expedients, some of them violent. In Italy the Communists responded to the economic crisis and political alienation by offering to share power—and responsibility—with the Christian Democrats on the national level for the first time. In 1976, the Communist party's share of the vote in national elections reached an all-time high of 34.4 percent. By the end of the 1970s, however, their efforts had led nowhere; their share of the vote steadily declined, as did their support among younger people and intellectuals. But the Christian Democrats were also losing electoral support. Their message seemed ever less relevant as Italy became more secular. And as the Italian Communists declined, many found it less important to support Christian democracy as a bulwark against communism.

In the 1970s, frustration with political immobility gave rise to a new wave of terrorism, especially in Italy and Germany. Terrorists in such groups as the Red Brigades in Italy and the Baader-Meinhof gang in Germany assassinated a number of prominent public officials and businessmen, including the long-time Italian Christian

Democratic leader Aldo Moro (1916–1978). Left- and right-wing extremism fed on each other, and it was right-wing extremists who were responsible for Italy's most deadly terrorist episode, a bombing in the railway station in Bologna that killed eighty-five people in August 1980.

Political frustration also found productive outlets, as new coalitions developed around newly politicized issues—from abortion to the environment—that had not been associated with the Marxist left. In Germany, the Green movement formed by peace and environmental activists during the late 1970s took pains to avoid acting like a conventional party. Concerned that Germany, with its central location, would end up the devastated battleground in any superpower confrontation, the Greens opposed deployment of additional U.S. missiles on German soil and called for an alternative to the arms race. Socialists and Conservatives held their own, leaving Germany with essentially a two-party system, as the strength of the Green party leveled off at 10 to 15 percent of the vote in the 1980s.

Prominent among the new political currents that emerged after 1968 was a new feminist movement. This new movement arose out of the politically charged atmosphere in Europe and the United States as women found themselves insisting on civil rights for others, only to realize that they, too, represented an oppressed class: Women were officially and unofficially barred from a wide range of educational and employment opportunities. They were denied equal pay for equal work. They were rarely considered for leadership roles in the political or business worlds.

Simone de Beauvoir's *The Second Sex* and Betty Friedan's *The Feminine Mystique* guided women's struggle to redefine themselves within society. These books argued that women were regarded not as human beings but as something inferior and auxiliary, and, as such, they were raised to put the needs and desires of men above their own. Some women struggled against this, explained both de Beauvoir and Friedan, but most were convinced from childhood that they were less capable and less important. They thus concentrated on endearing themselves to men, devoting their time to becoming beautiful, helpful, and noncompetitive.

Feminists forced new issues onto the political stage, working to liberalize divorce and abortion laws throughout the Western world, to obtain some equality in the division of housework and child care, and to address the ways that girls were encouraged to be beautiful and passive. At "consciousness-raising" groups, acting on the notion that "the personal is political," women brought extremely private matters to public attention. These ideas had a tremendous impact in the 1970s, and an even deeper sense of gender issues would become central to public debate and personal choice during the last two decades of the century.

SUMMARY

In the decades that followed World War II, a bipolar framework, dominated by the United States and the Soviet Union, shaped world affairs. The states of Western and central Europe continued to decline in influence and lost their remaining colonial possessions. The new bipolar framework opened certain possibilities but also limited political options in both halves of newly divided Europe. The Western European states had to follow the U.S. lead, especially in matters of national security, though France under de Gaulle grew especially restive. But Western Europe achieved remarkable prosperity and took significant steps toward multinational integration in the European Economic Community (EEC).

In the communist bloc, Stalin's death in 1953 ended the most repressive features of the Soviet regime. Under his successor, Nikita Khrushchev, the Soviet Union seemed able to compete with the United States in areas from education to economic growth to the exploration of outer space. But the experiment with central planning in the Soviet bloc proved ever less successful. At the same time, the fate of a series of opposition and reform efforts, from East Berlin in 1953 to Prague in 1968, made it clear that the Soviets intended to keep their east-central European satellite states on a relatively tight leash.

In Western Europe, the shared experience of wartime led to a new social compact based on greater government responsibility for economic well-being and social welfare. The implicit promise of growing prosperity for all made possible a measure of cooperation between business and labor that eroded earlier assumptions of irreconcilable class struggle. The new consensus provided a foundation for democracy, which became solidly established in Western Europe during the first two decades after the war.

In 1968 strains began to appear in the Western democracies, and slower economic growth during the 1970s jeopardized the postwar settlement. A diffuse discontent developed among many Western Europeans, who felt left out as the most important decisions were made by party leaders, technocratic planners, EEC Eurocrats, or the executives of multinational corporations. A quest for new forms of political participation began in 1968 and continued throughout the 1970s. The Green movement drew attention to the environment. The feminist movement forced Western civilization to extend its principles of human choice and freedom to women. Since women make up more than half of humanity—and the behaviors between the sexes affect all of humanity—this was a deeply significant change.

To a large degree, all these changes had more impact in the West than in the East. In Western Europe there was more room for change in the atmosphere of prosperity and the relative comfort of political legitimacy. Eastern Europe was not as fortunate. There, a persisting sense of social imbalance threatened to undermine the anxious stability that characterized the era from 1949 to 1985.

SUGGESTED READING

Brinkley, Douglas, and Clifford Hackett, eds. *Jean Monnet: The Path to European Unity.* 1991. A collection of essays on Monnet's central role in the movement toward European integration.

Dedman, Martin J. *The Origins and Development of the European Union, 1945–1995: A History of European Integration*. 1996. A concise and accessible introductory work.

Ellwood, David W. *Rebuilding Europe: Western Europe, America and Postwar Reconstruction.* 1992. A readable, well-balanced survey of the course of reconstruction in Western Europe in the decade after World War II.

Hosking, Geoffrey. *The First Socialist Society: A History of the Soviet Union from Within.* Enlarged ed. 1990. Looks at family, religion, nationality, and the experience of factory workers.

Hughes, H. Stuart. *Between Commitment and Disillusion: The Obstructed Path and the Sea Change, 1930–1965.* 1987. An updated edition of two previously published works by an influential intellectual historian. *The Sea Change* covers the intellectual migration from Europe to America.

Kuisel, Richard F. *Capitalism and the State in Modern France: Renovation and Economic Management in the Twentieth Century.* 1981. A thorough study tracing the emergence of economic planning and a technocratic ethos in France.

Laqueur, Walter. *Europe in Our Time: A History, 1945–1992.* 1992. A comprehensive, well-balanced survey by a leading authority on twentieth-century Europe.

Maier, Charles S., ed. *The Cold War in Europe: Era of a Divided Continent.* 3d ed. 1996. A series of essays especially helpful on the implications of the cold war framework for Western European development.

Marks, Elaine, and Isabelle de Courtivon, eds. *New French Feminisms.* 1980. A very strong collection of writings from the French women's movement.

Mommsen, Wolfgang J., and Jürgen Osterhammel, eds. *Imperialism and After: Continuities and Discontinuities.* 1986. A collection of essays by leading scholars. Analyzes the ways European influence continued after the end of formal imperial control.

Morgan, Kenneth O. *The People's Peace: British History, 1945–1990.* 1992. A thorough survey that seeks to avoid overemphasis on decline and pessimism.

Pulzer, Peter. *German Politics, 1945–1995.* 1995. A brief yet probing account of political developments in both East and West Germany.

Rothschild, Joseph. *Return to Diversity: A Political History of East Central Europe Since World War II.* 2d ed. 1993. A straightforward survey that makes sense of the differences as well as the similarities among the Soviet bloc countries during the cold war.

Ruggie, Mary. *The State and Working Women: A Comparative Study of Britain and Sweden.* 1984. A sophisticated comparative study that seeks to explain why women achieved greater economic equality in Sweden than in Britain.

CHAPTER 27

The West and the World in the Late Twentieth Century

During the fall of 1989, three teenaged Muslim girls were suspended from a public school near Paris because they insisted on wearing the headscarves traditional for Islamic women. School authorities cited the law barring religious displays in France's strictly secular school system. The leader of France's largest teachers' union also contended that "this flaunting of a clear symbol of women's subordination negates the teaching of human rights in schools." Thus, when the French minister of education defended the students' right to wear the scarves, he was widely criticized.

In fact, the education minister simply wanted to keep these girls—and the many others like them—in school, to expose them to secular influence and promote their assimilation into French culture. France's prestigious Council of State soon ruled that the scarves did not violate the constitutional separation of church and state, as long as they were not worn in an effort to flaunt religion or to proselytize. But the riddles of multiculturalism at issue in this "affair of the scarves" kept coming up in France and elsewhere by the late twentieth century.

As the population exploded in the less developed world, the prosperous countries of the North were increasingly a magnet for the disadvantaged from around the world. The resulting immigration created new social and political pressures that raised questions about citizenship and assimilation, pluralism and diversity, identity and community.

Such questions came to center stage partly because of the end of the cold war, which had overshadowed all else for decades after World War II. In 1989, dramatic change in the Soviet bloc came to a head, leading to the end of communism and the dissolution of the Soviet Union. The unraveling of the Soviet system brought an abrupt end to the postwar era, which had rested on a tense balance between the communist states and the capitalist democracies. Everywhere, the pace of political, economic, and technological change seemed almost too rapid. Moreover, key decisions seemed to be made increasingly by multinational corporations or supranational organizations beyond democratic control. By the early 1990s, a new set of anxieties and uncertainties had replaced those of the cold war era.

Questions and Ideas to Consider

- Discuss the relationship between greater social equality and traditional social order. In what ways did the changing social role of the French state intersect with the growing feminist movement in France?
- Why did the communist bloc disintegrate when it did? List some of the contributing factors and discuss their relative importance.
- In the late twentieth century, supranational initiatives became increasingly important—and brought new problems and fears. Discuss some of the positive and negative attributes of supranational and global decision making.
- Has democratic capitalism triumphed? What evidence supports this notion, and what evidence suggests a more uncertain future?
- Given the increasing concern for a wider history—one that includes the experiences of women in the West and of all peoples elsewhere—should we continue the "Western Civ" course as it is? Why or why not?

CHALLENGES OF AFFLUENCE IN THE WEST

After the economic dislocations of the 1970s, most of Western Europe again enjoyed strong economic growth in the early 1980s. In Italy a "second economic miracle" enabled the country to surpass Britain and become the world's fifth largest economy. But in Italy and elsewhere in Western Europe, growth was uneven, confined to certain sectors and regions. By the 1990s prosperity mixed with ongoing worries about international competition, unemployment, and environmental constraints in a small and crowded continent.

By the 1980s democracy had become the unchallenged norm in Western Europe. The radical right was largely discredited and the Marxist left seemed to have been domesticated for good. In important respects, conservatives and social democrats sounded more and more alike. But at the same time there was a weakening of the postwar consensus about governmental responsibility for social and economic well-being, as new questions arose about the scope of the public sphere, the reach of the state.

Many of the trends important in Europe were visible in the United States as well. The widening gap between rich and poor, the weakening of organized labor, the increasing awareness of human responsibility for the environment, the growing prominence of women in the work force, the increasing concern about such family issues as child care—all were characteristic of Western civilization in general by the late twentieth century.

The Changing Economies: Prosperity, Imbalance, Limitation

In the early 1980s unemployment in Western Europe reached levels not seen since the Great Depression. Even after solid growth resumed by 1983, unemployment hovered stubbornly at around 10 percent throughout much of the region. This would have seemed unimaginable fifteen years before and was much higher than the rates of 5 to 7 percent in the United States during the same period.

This combination of prosperity and unemployment stemmed in part from the technological changes that produced a "third industrial

CHAPTER CHRONOLOGY

1979	Margaret Thatcher becomes prime minister of Britain
	First direct elections to European parliament
1980	Formation of Solidarity in Poland
1981	Mitterrand elected president of France
1982	Death of Leonid Brezhnev in the Soviet Union
1985	Gorbachev comes to power in the Soviet Union
1986	Explosion at Chernobyl nuclear power plant
1989	Collapse of communism in east-central Europe
1990	Reunification of Germany
	Persian Gulf War begins
1991	Collapse of communism in the Soviet Union; dissolution of the Soviet Union
	Beginning of fighting in Yugoslavia
	Maastricht agreement expands scope of the European Union
1996	Peace in Bosnia
	Yeltsin re-elected as Russian president

revolution" during the late twentieth century. Based most dramatically on the computer, it encompassed everything from robotics to fiber optics. The advent of new technologies in the context of increasing global competition produced new winners, but it also transformed the workplace and patterns of employment in worrisome ways.

Such technologies created opportunities for new firms able to start from scratch, without the problems of redundant workers or outmoded plants and equipment that older competitors faced. Benetton, an Italian clothing firm founded in 1964, quickly made effective use of computer technology in all aspects of its operation. Benetton was successful partly because it needed fewer workers. Manufacturing jobs tended to be lost as competition forced the industrial sector to become more efficient through computers and automation. In the German steel industry over half the jobs disappeared during the 1970s and 1980s.

Changing labor patterns reinforced the decline of organized labor, while the increasing danger of unemployment undercut the leverage of the unions. And as the economy grew more complex, workers were ever less likely to understand themselves as members of a single, unified working class.

Affluence and Secularization

Postwar economic growth had created a secular, consumerist society throughout much of Western Europe by the mid-1960s. Growing prosperity meant not only paid annual vacations of three to four weeks but also the luxury of spending them away from home, often at crowded beach resorts. Television was virtually universal in households across Europe by the early 1980s. Spectator sports grew more popular, with soccer, the undisputed king, drawing rowdy and sometimes violent crowds.

In Western Europe, as in the United States, a remarkable baby boom had followed the end of the war and continued into the early 1960s. The birthrate declined rapidly thereafter, however. In Italy the number of births in 1987 was barely half the number in 1964, when the postwar baby boom reached its peak. By 1995 the population was not sustaining itself in Italy or Spain.

Increasing affluence led to rising expectations and demands for still wider opportunity. Such pressure focused especially on access to higher education, the chief vehicle for upward mobility. As university admissions increased in France, Italy, and West Germany, the development of a mass-based university system produced new dilemmas. In France, the market value of the state diploma declined substantially, as did the prestige of the faculty. In some cases, quality had actually fallen; in others, formerly elite groups simply mourned their past status.

Secularization diminished the once central role of the churches in popular culture, which had long revolved around religious festivals and holy days. Regular church attendance declined steadily. The Catholic church undertook a notable modernization effort under the popular Pope John XXIII (r. 1958–1963), but under his more conservative successors, the church became caught up in controversies such as birth control, abortion, and women's ordination that put it on the defensive.

In France, Italy, and Spain, many people considered themselves "cultural Catholics" and ignored church rulings they found inappropriate, especially those concerning sexuality, marriage, and gender roles. The easier availability of contraception—especially the birth control pill, widely obtainable by the late 1960s—fostered a sexual revolution that was central to the new secular lifestyle. In referenda in 1974 and 1981, two-thirds of Italians defied the Vatican by voting to legalize divorce and approve abortion rights. Even in heavily Catholic Ireland, the electorate narrowly approved the legalization of divorce in 1995.

The Significance of Gender

As the cases of class and religion indicate, long-standing bases of identity and the problems they sometimes gave rise to were becoming less important as an affluent, secular society emerged. At the same time, new questions about identity appeared. By the 1980s a growing consciousness of socially defined gender roles—and the limitations they created—had arisen out of the quest for equality of opportunity and individual self-realization.

As it matured, the feminist movement that had crystallized in the late 1960s found it necessary to expand its focus beyond the quest for equal opportunity. Examining subtle cultural obstacles to equality led feminists to the more general issue of gender—the way societies perceive sexual difference and define social roles. There was much interest in the innovative ideas of the French existentialist Simone de Beauvoir, who had raised in 1949 precisely the issues that came to the fore during the 1980s (see page 688). As the debate expanded from "women's issues" to gender roles, conceptions of masculinity were at issue as well.

Insofar as differentiated gender roles are purposefully "constructed" by particular societies, the notion of gender had been important throughout the long history of the West. Indeed, "gendering" had been central to the socialization process whereby young people learn how to function in their societies. But since most of the gender roles dictated by society were assumed to be natural, gender was only rarely as explicit and controversial an issue as it became in the late twentieth century. By the 1990s the gender issue was central not only to public policy but also to private relationships and to decisions about life choices in much of the Western world.

Male and female feminists fought for government-subsidized day care that would enable both parents to engage in fulfilling, paid employment while raising a family—without saddling women with a double burden. Seeking to enhance both equality of opportunity and long-term economic productivity, governments assumed responsibility for combining productive working parents with effective childhood development.

Setting the pace was France, where the government began making quality day care available to all in the 1980s. Government subsidy kept costs within reach for ordinary working families. In addition, 95 percent of French children aged 3 to 6 were enrolled in the free public nursery schools available by the early 1990s. Comparable figures for Italy (85 percent) and Germany (65 to 70 percent) were also high, although Britain lagged at 35 to 40 percent.

The increasing reliance on child care both reflected and reinforced a decline in the socializing role of the traditional family. This trend prompted concern about the long-term consequences for the socialization of children—and thus for the future of society. At issue was the interaction of family roles, individual self-realization, and the well-being of children.

In any case, the French model seemed to work well. Moreover, in France social services were delivered with less paperwork and intrusiveness

Demonstration for Reproductive Freedom In the late twentieth century, street rallies, marches, and demonstrations became a common and generally peaceful way for groups to make their views public. Here women in Rome, representing a number of organizations, unite in support of women's access to birth control and abortion. *(Gamma-Liaison)*

than elsewhere. In the 1990s, the question was simply whether France could still afford such benefits. And this question reflected a wider set of concerns, becoming central everywhere, about the political order and the role of government.

Re-evaluating the Role of Government

The most dramatic and single-minded assault on the welfare state came in Britain after Margaret Thatcher became prime minister in a new Conservative government in 1979. Thatcher insisted that Britain could reverse its economic decline only by fostering a new "enterprise culture," restoring the individual initiative that had been sapped, as she saw it, by decades of dependence on government. Thatcher took it for granted that the free market, undistorted by government intervention, produced optimum economic efficiency and thus, in the long term, the greatest social benefit.

Abandoning its aristocratic vestiges, the Conservative party now appealed to the upwardly mobile, entrepreneurial middle class. In light of the socioeconomic difficulties Britain had suffered in the 1970s, Thatcher's message had broad appeal across the social spectrum. With Labour increasingly isolated, identified with decaying inner cities and old industrial regions, Thatcher easily won re-election in 1983 and 1987.

Three immediate priorities followed directly from Thatcher's overall strategy. First, her government made substantial cuts in taxes and corresponding cuts in spending for education, national health, and public housing. Second, the government fostered privatization, selling off an array of state-owned firms from Rolls Royce to British Airways. The government even sold public housing to tenants, at as much as 50 percent below market value, a measure that helped Thatcher win considerable working-class support. Third, Thatcher curbed the power of Britain's labor unions.

Several new laws curtailed trade-union power, and Thatcher refused to consult with union leaders as her predecessors had done since the war. A showdown was reached with the yearlong coal miners' strike of 1984 and 1985, one of the most bitter and violent European strikes of the twentieth century. The strike's failure further enhanced Thatcher's prestige among her supporters. Yet the violent encounters between police and picketing strikers, carried nationwide on TV, indicated the cracks in the relative social harmony that Britain had long enjoyed. In addition, riots by unemployed youths broke out in several major industrial cities in 1981 and again in 1985.

In another important conservative move, Thatcher's government sponsored the Nationality Act of 1982, which restricted immigration from the former British colonies. The right-wing tendency to blame immigrants (largely from Britain's former colonies) for unemployment and urban crime gained Thatcher support from the otherwise hostile city dwellers. With her nationalist bent, Thatcher resisted the growing power of the multinational European Union. Her stance on this issue helped provoke opposition within her own party, which finally ousted her as party leader, and thus as prime minister, in 1990.

Controversy over the significance of the Thatcher years mounted after her departure. On the plus side, her efforts helped boost the competitiveness of British industry. Productivity grew at a rate 50 percent above the average of the other industrial democracies. This striking improvement stemmed partly from the attack on the trade unions, which had limited productivity by protecting redundant labor. Privatization found increasing approval, while the number of new businesses reflected a revival of entrepreneurship—apparently the basis for better economic performance over the longer term. Whatever the gains during the Thatcher years, however, the gap between rich and poor widened and the old industrial regions of the north were left ever further behind.

France and Italy prospered as never before but seemed unable to afford all the benefits their governments had gradually come to promise—mostly because of intensifying economic competition. But what the developed countries of the West could afford for education, welfare, or health care could not be established objectively; at issue, rather, were societal priorities, to be worked out through the political process. As the economy became more ruthlessly competitive and the gap in incomes widened, the winners seemed ever more reluctant to pay for those who were less successful. The growing preoccupation with cost reflected an erosion of the sense of community and fairness that had been essential to the postwar consensus—and that had led to the expanded government role in the first place.

ON THE RUINS OF THE COMMUNIST SYSTEM

In the early 1980s, the system hammered out by Stalin and his successors still seemed firmly entrenched in the Soviet Union and its satellites in east-central Europe, despite a lackluster period under the aging leadership of Leonid Brezhnev and his allies. Yet crises were building in both the Soviet Union and the satellite states, producing forces for change that finally engulfed the whole communist bloc. Although the process began in Poland, Hungary, and Czechoslovakia, the ultimate outcome depended on the Soviet response.

So the death of Leonid Brezhnev in 1982 and the beginning of a concerted reform effort in the Soviet Union in 1985 were the decisive moments. By the end of the 1980s the forces for change in the Soviet Union and its satellites had intersected, leading the whole communist system to unravel. The dangerous but stable bipolar world that had emerged from World War II had suddenly vanished, and the countries of the former Soviet bloc began seeking to rejoin the rest of Europe.

Crisis and Innovation in the Soviet Bloc

The impressive rates of economic growth achieved in the Soviet Union and several of its satellite states after World War II continued into the 1960s. However, much of that success came from adding labor—women and underemployed peasants—to the industrial work force. By the end of the 1960s that process was reaching its limits.

Even compared to those elsewhere in the communist bloc, the command economy in the Soviet Union was particularly centralized and inflexible. The persistent shortages of many consumer goods, understandable during the transformation to an industrial society, seemed less and less tolerable. And by the late 1970s the Soviet Union was falling behind in high technology, which required the freedom to experiment and exchange ideas that was notably lacking in the Soviet system. As that system bogged down, the expense of the arms race became increasingly untenable.

For all its terrible excesses, Stalin's regime had continued to inspire a measure of genuine idealism during his lifetime. But by the 1970s the Soviet system had settled into narrow routine or outright corruption. Its major functionaries were a class apart, enjoying access to special shops and other privileges. Brezhnev himself took enormous pleasure in his collection of expensive automobiles.

Brezhnev's death in 1982 made possible the rise of Mikhail Gorbachev (b. 1931), who became party secretary in 1985 and who represented a new generation, beyond those who had been groomed for party careers during the Stalinist 1930s. He quickly charted a reform course—and attracted the admiration of much of the world.

Gorbachev's effort encompassed four intersecting initiatives: arms reduction; liberalization in the satellite states; *glasnost*, or "openness" to discussion and criticism; and *perestroika*, or economic "restructuring." This was to be a reform within the Soviet system. There was no thought of giving up the Communist party's monopoly on power or embracing a free-market economy. The reformers still took it for granted that communism could point the way beyond Western capitalism, with its widespread crime, its illegal drugs, its shallow consumerism. So a measure of idealism guided the reformers' efforts. But they had to make communism work.

Gorbachev understood that "openness" was a prerequisite for "restructuring." The freedom to criticize was necessary to overcome the cynicism of the workers and improve productivity. Openness was also imperative to gain the full participation of the country's most creative people. The main thrust of restructuring was to depart from the rigid economic planning mechanism by giving local managers more autonomy. It did not have to entail privatization or free-market capitalism. It could mean, for example, letting workers elect factory managers.

The Crisis of Communism in the Satellite States

For many intellectuals in the Soviet bloc, the suppression of the Prague Spring in 1968 ended any hope that communism could be made to work. The initial outcome was a sense of hopelessness and resignation, but by the mid-1970s an opposition movement, centering on underground (or *samizdat*) publications, had begun to take shape in Hungary, Poland, and Czechoslovakia.

The first push toward real systemic breakdown came from an international conference in 1975. High-level representatives of thirty-five countries, including all of the Soviet bloc except Albania, came together in Helsinki, Finland. The parties recognized all borders, as the Soviets had wanted, but they also adopted a detailed agreement on human rights, which came to be known as the Helsinki Accords. Through various "Helsinki Watch" groups monitoring civil liberties, opposition intellectuals managed to assume moral leadership.

The most significant such group was Charter 77 in Czechoslovakia. In 1977, protesting against the arrest of an anti-establishment rock group called "The Plastic People of the Universe," 243 individuals signed "Charter 77." In the face of the powerful, heavy-handed communist government, dissidents proposed that change could be won if people simply lived according to their real beliefs. When people used their own names and addresses on the Charter 77 petition, they were carrying out this idea of "living the truth" by acting as if they were free to register such an opinion.

A leader in Charter 77 was the writer Václav Havel (b. 1936), who argued that hope for change depended on people organizing themselves, outside the structures of the party-state, in diverse, independent social groupings. (See the box "Power from Below: Living the Truth.") Havel and a number of his associates were in and out of jail as the government sought to stifle this protest. Despite the efforts of Havel and his colleagues, ordinary people in Czechoslovakia remained relatively passive until the late 1980s. For quite different reasons, Hungary and Poland offered greater scope for change.

Even after the failed reform effort of 1956, Hungary proved the most innovative of the European communist countries. Hungary was relatively prosperous by the late 1970s, though it faced difficulties paying off its foreign debt. The Hungarians responded, as nowhere else, by committing the economy to the discipline of the world market by joining the International Monetary Fund and the World Bank in 1982. This move required economic austerity, and Hungarian living standards declined during the early 1980s. But the country promoted its "second economy"— its autonomous private sector. By the mid-1980s alternative forms of ownership were responsible for one-third of Hungary's economic output.

This openness to experiment in the economy enabled reformers within the Hungarian Communist party to gain the upper hand. Finally, in 1988, the reformers ousted the aging Janós Kádár, who lacked the vision for continued reform. Increasingly open to a variety of viewpoints, the Hungarian communists gradually pulled back from their claim to a monopoly of power.

With growing concern for the Hungarian minority in Romania helping to galvanize political consciousness, new political clubs proliferated in Hungary. In June 1989, popular pressure led to the ceremonial reburial of Imre Nagy, who had led the reform effort in 1956. After having been convicted of treason, executed, and buried in obscurity, Nagy had been derided as a counterrevolutionary traitor in official government pronouncements. His reburial indicated the importance of historical memory—and who controls it.

The reform effort that built gradually in Hungary had stemmed especially from aspirations in the governing elite. More dramatic was the course of change in Poland, where there was already a tradition of labor militancy, especially among shipyard workers on the Baltic coast.

It was crucial that, whereas Polish workers had not supported dissident students and intellectuals in 1968, the two sides managed to come together during the 1970s. An extra ingredient from an unexpected quarter also affected the situation in Poland, perhaps in a decisive way. In 1978 the College of Cardinals of the Roman Catholic church departed from long tradition and, for the first time since 1522, elected a non-Italian pope. But even more startling was the fact that the new pope was from Poland, behind the iron curtain. He was Karol Cardinal Wojtyla (b. 1920), the archbishop of Kracow, who took the name John Paul II.

After World War II, the Polish Catholic church had been unique among the major churches of east-central Europe in maintaining and even enhancing its position. It worked just enough with the ruling communists to be allowed a measure of autonomy. For many Poles, the church remained an institutional alternative to communism and the focus of nationalist feelings. The new pope's visit to Poland in 1979 had an electrifying effect on ordinary Poles, who took to the streets by the millions to greet him—and found they were not alone. This boost in self-confidence provided the catalyst for the founding of a new trade union, Solidarity, in August 1980.

Led by the remarkable shipyard electrician Lech Walesa (b. 1944), Solidarity first emerged in response to labor discontent in the vast Lenin shipyard in Gdansk, on the Baltic Sea (see Map 27.1). Demanding the right to form an independent trade union, seventy thousand workers took over the shipyards, winning support both from

Power from Below: Living the Truth

Considering the scope for change in the communist world by the late 1970s, Václav Havel imagines a conformist grocer who routinely puts a sign in his window with the slogan "Workers of the world, unite!" simply because it is expected. That same grocer, says Havel, has the power to break the stifling sociopolitical system, which ultimately rests on those innumerable acts of everyday compliance.

[T]he real meaning of the greengrocer's slogan has nothing to do with what the text of the slogan actually says. Even so, this real meaning is quite clear and generally comprehensible because the code is so familiar: the greengrocer declares his loyalty . . . in the only way the regime is capable of hearing; that is, by accepting the prescribed *ritual,* by accepting appearances as reality, by accepting the given rules of the game. In doing so, however, he has himself become a player in the game, thus making it possible for the game to go on, for it to exist in the first place. . . .

Let us now imagine that one day something in our greengrocer snaps and he stops putting up the slogans merely to ingratiate himself. He stops voting in elections he knows are a farce. He begins to say what he really thinks at political meetings. . . . He rejects the ritual and breaks the rules of the game. He discovers once more his suppressed identity and dignity. . . .

. . . He has shown everyone that it *is* possible to live within the truth. Living within the lie can constitute the system only if it is universal. The principle must embrace and permeate everything. There are no terms whatsoever on which it can coexist with living within the truth, and therefore everyone who steps out of line *denies it in principle and threatens it in its entirety.* . . .

And since all genuine problems and matters of critical importance are hidden beneath a thick crust of lies, it is never quite clear when the proverbial last straw will fall, or what that straw will be. This . . . is why the regime prosecutes, almost as a reflex action preventively, even the most modest attempts to live within the truth.

. . . [T]he crust presented by the life of lies is made of strange stuff. As long as it seals off hermetically the entire society, it appears to be made of stone. But the moment someone breaks through in one place, when one person cries out, "The emperor is naked!"—when a single person breaks the rules of the game, thus exposing it as a game—everything suddenly appears in another light and the whole crust seems then to be made of a tissue on the point of tearing and disintegrating uncontrollably.

Source: Václav Havel et al., *The Power of the Powerless: Citizens Against the State in Central-Eastern Europe* (Armonk, N.Y.: M. E. Sharpe, 1985), pp. 31, 37, 39–40, 42–43. Reprinted with permission from M. E. Sharpe, Inc., Armonk, NY 10504.

their intellectual allies and from the Catholic church. Support for Solidarity grew partly because, to pay its foreign debts, the government was cutting subsidies and raising food prices. But the new union developed such force because it placed moral demands first—independent labor organizations, the right to strike, and freedom of expression. The tense situation came to a head in December 1981, when the government under General Wojciech Jaruzelski (b. 1923) declared martial law and outlawed Solidarity, imprisoning its leaders.

So much for that, it seemed. Another lost cause, another reform effort colliding with inflexible communist power in east-central Europe, as in 1953, 1956, and 1968. But this time, it was different. The ideas of Solidarity continued to spread underground. Walesa remained a powerfully effective leader, able to keep the heterogeneous movement together. The advent of Gorbachev in 1985 changed the overall framework of the communist bloc, for he was convinced that the restructuring of the Soviet system required reform in the satellites as well. In the spring and summer of 1988, strikes demanding the relegalization of Solidarity alternated with government repression and military force, until eventually, with the economy nearing collapse, the government recognized that it had to negotiate.

When negotiations began early in 1989, Walesa and his advisers sought to secure the legalization of Solidarity within the communist-dominated system. But as the talks proceeded, the government gave ever more in exchange for Solidarity's cooperation, agreeing to make the forthcoming elections free enough for the opposition genuinely to participate.

The elections of June 1989 produced an overwhelming repudiation of Poland's communist government. Even government leaders running unopposed failed to win election as voters crossed out their names. In the aftermath of the elections, President Jaruzelski finally decided to give Solidarity a chance to lead. Tadeusz Mazowiecki (b. 1927), Walesa's choice and one of the movement's most distinguished intellectuals, agreed to form a government.

The chain of events in Poland culminated in one of the extraordinary developments of modern history—the negotiated end of communist rule. It happened partly because the Soviet Union under Gorbachev had become much less likely to intervene militarily. It also mattered that the Polish Catholic church acted as mediator, hosting meetings, reminding both sides of their shared responsibilities in the difficult situation facing their country. But most important was the courage, the persistence, and the vision of Solidarity itself.

The Anticommunist Revolution, 1989–1991

The Polish example suggested that the communist system was open to challenge. During 1989, demands for reform and, increasingly, for an end to communist rule spread through east-central Europe. By the end of that year, the Soviet satellite system was in ruins (Map 27.1).

Though strikes and demonstrations took place throughout the region, the end of the communist order in Hungary, Czechoslovakia, East Germany, Bulgaria, and Albania was more peaceful than anyone would have dreamed possible a few years before. Starting with Hungary, these countries followed the Polish model and negotiated the transfer of power from the communists to opposition leaders. In Czechoslovakia, the transition was so peaceful that it was dubbed the "Velvet Revolution." The signal exception was Romania, where the communist dictator Nicolae Ceausescu's bloody crackdown on the reform movement provoked an armed revolt. The opposition executed Ceausescu and his wife on Christmas Day 1989.

The possibility of violent repression was never far from the surface. In June 1989, the communist leadership in China had crushed a comparable movement for democracy in Tiananmen Square in Beijing. As the opposition movement grew in East Germany early in the fall, with weekly demonstrations in Leipzig attracting 300,000 people, the East German communist leader Erich Honecker (1912–1994) began preparing for a "Chinese solution" in his country. But a dramatic appeal for nonviolence by local opposition leaders in Leipzig helped persuade the police to hold off. Gorbachev, too, called for moderation. Honecker was soon forced to make way for communists favoring reform.

A marked increase in illegal emigration from East Germany to the west had been one manifestation that the whole satellite system was starting to unravel. If the communist reformers in East Germany were to have any chance of turning the situation around, they had to relax restrictions on travel and grant the right to emigrate. They began preparing legislation to both ends, amid a host of reforms intended to save the system. On November 9, 1989, the regime in East Germany did what had long seemed unthinkable: It opened the Berlin Wall, which was promptly dismantled altogether. Germans now

Reykjavík
ICELAND
Faroe Islands
(Den.)
Shetland
Islands
(U.K.)
NORWAY
Oslo
SWEDEN
Stockholm
FINLAND
Helsinki
Tallinn
ESTONIA
Lake
Ladoga
St. Petersburg
(Leningrad)
R U S S I A
Volga
Moscow
KAZAKSTAN
Glasgow
NORTHERN
IRELAND
IRELAND
Dublin
UNITED
KINGDOM
London
North
Sea
DENMARK
Copenhagen
Riga
LATVIA
LITHUANIA
Vilnius
(RUSSIA)
Minsk
BELARUS
The
Hague
NETH.
Amsterdam
Hamburg
Elbe
Gdansk
POLAND
Warsaw
Vistula
Berlin
GERMANY
Brussels
BELGIUM
Bonn
Leipzig
Frankfurt
Luxembourg
LUX.
Stuttgart
Rhine
Munich
LIECH.
Vaduz
Prague
CZECH
REPUBLIC
SLOVAKIA
Bratislava
Vienna
AUSTRIA
Budapest
HUNGARY
ATLANTIC
OCEAN
Paris
Seine
Loire
FRANCE
Zurich
Bern
Geneva
SWITZ.
Lyon
Kiev
Kharkiv
UKRAINE
Dnieper
Dnipropetrovs'k
Donets'k
MOLDOVA
Chisinau
Odessa
Caspian Sea
ROMANIA
Bucharest
Danube
Black Sea
GEORGIA
T'bilisi
Baku
AZERBAIJAN
ARMENIA
Yerevan
AZER.
Porto
PORTUGAL
Lisbon
SPAIN
Madrid
Tagus
ANDORRA
Andorra
la Vella
Barcelona
Monaco
MONACO
Turin
Milan
Po
Ljubljana
SLOVENIA
Zagreb
CROATIA
Belgrade
BOSNIA &
HERZEGOVINA
Sarajevo
YUGOSLAVIA
BULGARIA
Sofia
Skopje
MACEDONIA
ALBANIA
Tiranë
Istanbul
Ankara
TURKEY
SAN
MARINO
San
Marino
ITALY
Rome
Naples
Corsica
(Fr.)
Sardinia
(It.)
Balearic
Islands
(Sp.)
Gibraltar
(U.K.)
Mediterranean Sea
Sicily
(It.)
Valletta
MALTA
GREECE
Athens
Crete
(Gr.)
Nicosia
CYPRUS
0
250
500 Km.
0
250
500 Mi.

traveled freely back and forth between east and west. The liberalization effort proved too late, however. The communist system in the east quickly dissolved, and steps toward reunification followed almost immediately in 1990.

The opening of the Berlin Wall signaled the end of the cold war. The immediate result in the West was euphoria, but few failed to recognize that a still more difficult task lay ahead. To be sure, reformers in the former communist countries claimed to want individual freedom, political democracy, and free-market capitalism. But it would be necessary to build these on the ruins of the now-discredited communist system and its command economy, a task never confronted before.

Meanwhile, in the Soviet Union, Gorbachev sought to avoid alienating hard-line communists, so he compromised, watering down the economic reforms essential to perestroika. The resulting half-measures only made things worse. The structures of the command economy were weakened, but free-market forms of exchange among producers, distributors, and consumers did not emerge to replace them.

In 1986 an accidental explosion at the nuclear power plant at Chernobyl, in Ukraine, released two hundred times as much radiation as the atomic bombs dropped on Hiroshima and Nagasaki combined. The accident contaminated food supplies and forced the abandonment of villages and thousands of square miles of formerly productive land. According to later estimates, the radioactivity released would eventually hasten the death of at least 100,000 Soviet citizens. Despite his commitment to openness, Gorbachev reverted to old-fashioned Soviet secrecy for several weeks after the accident, in an effort to minimize what had happened. As a result, the eventual toll was far greater than it need have been. The accident and its aftermath seemed stark manifestation of all that was wrong with the Soviet system—its arrogance and secrecy, its premium on cutting corners to achieve targets imposed from above.

Map 27.1 Europe After the Cold War The reunification of Germany and the breakup of the Soviet Union, Yugoslavia, and Czechoslovakia fundamentally altered the map of Europe by the early 1990s.

Tearing Down the Wall In 1989 the much-graffitied Berlin Wall was dismantled—in part by ordinary citizens such as this woman. The event marked the end of the cold war. Pieces of the wall itself are now in museums and kept by private individuals as symbols of the times. *(Gamma-Liaison)*

By the end of the 1980s, Soviet citizens felt betrayed by their earlier faith that Soviet communism was leading to a better future. A popular slogan spoke sarcastically of "seventy years on the road to nowhere." While the economic situation was deteriorating, people were free to discuss alternatives as never before. As the discussion came to include once unthinkable possibilities like privatization and a market economy, it became clear that the whole communist system was in jeopardy.

In 1990, the union of Soviet republics itself tottered on the verge of collapse. Lithuania led the way in calling for outright independence. The stakes were raised enormously when the Russian republic, the largest and most important in the U.S.S.R., followed Lithuania's lead.

In June 1990 the newly elected chairman of Russia's parliament, Boris Yeltsin (b. 1931), persuaded the Russian republic to declare its sovereignty. He hoped to force Gorbachev's reform effort beyond the present impasse. As a further challenge to Gorbachev, Yeltsin dramatically resigned from the Communist party during the televised twenty-eighth congress in July 1990. In the free elections of June 1991, the anticommunist Yeltsin was elected the Russian republic's president by a surprising margin.

Gorbachev sought a return to reform after Yeltsin's dramatic election as president of Russia in June 1991. Late in July, Gorbachev prepared a new union treaty that would have given substantial powers, including authority over taxation, to the constituent republics. He also engineered a new party charter that jettisoned much of the Marxist-Leninist doctrine that had guided communist practice since the revolution.

These measures promised the radical undoing of the Soviet system, and now the hard-liners finally struck back, initiating a coup in August 1991. They managed to force Gorbachev from power—but only for a few days. As the world held its breath, Yeltsin, supported by ordinary people in Moscow, stood up to the conspirators. Key units of the secret police, charged to arrest Yeltsin and other opposition leaders, refused to follow orders. The coup quickly fizzled, but the episode galvanized the anticommunist movement and radically accelerated the pace of change.

Although Gorbachev was restored as head of the Soviet Union, the real winner was Yeltsin, who quickly mounted an effort to dismantle the party apparatus before it could regroup. Spontaneous anticommunist demonstrations across much of the Soviet Union toppled statues of Lenin and dissolved local party networks. In a referendum in December 1991, Ukraine, the second most populous Soviet republic, voted overwhelmingly for independence. The Soviet Union was simply disintegrating.

The dissolution of the Soviet empire brought a new set of problems. What was to become of the 27,000 nuclear weapons stationed in four of the Soviet republics? What would be the economic relationship between the new countries? Some new form of coordination and unity seemed essential. Thus in December 1991, the leaders of Russia, Ukraine, and Belarus spearheaded the creation of a new Commonwealth of Independent States, which replaced the Soviet Union with a much looser confederation of eleven of the fifteen former Soviet republics. Late in December, Gorbachev finally resigned. The Soviet Union officially dissolved on January 1, 1992 (see Map 27.1).

Life After Communism

All over the formerly communist part of Europe, calls for Western-style democracy accompanied the end of the old order. But the area had little experience with democratic politics or a free-market economy. Political prospects would rest in large part on the success of the economic transition, but the economies in the former communist countries were close to chaos in the early 1990s. The attempt to construct a market economy brought unemployment, inflation, and widespread corruption. No longer could ordinary people count on the subsidized consumer goods or the welfare safety net that the communist regimes, for all their inadequacies, had provided. While many ordinary citizens suffered great hardship, some former communist functionaries got rich by taking over state-owned companies, provoking widespread resentment. Still, the transition to a market economy seemed to be working by the mid-1990s, though the course of change varied considerably from one country to the next.

Some of the postcommunist governments concentrated on privatizing existing state-owned concerns while others sought to foster entrepreneurship and innovation. Privatization lagged in Poland, but a buoyant new private sector emerged as the Poles proved adept at starting new businesses. Privatization was greatest in the

Czech Republic under the forceful leadership of Václav Klaus, a passionate partisan of market economics. By the end of 1995, the Czechs had achieved a solid annual economic growth rate of 4 percent with low unemployment and relatively low inflation.

Privatization was also rapid in Russia, where two-thirds of state-owned industry had been privatized by 1994. However, the fairness of the process was subject to much dispute. Optimists emphasized that 40 million Russians now owned shares in newly privatized companies. But even they could not deny that in certain sectors the process had included much insider dealing. In Russia, more than anywhere else in the former communist world, privatization benefited former Communist party functionaries, some of whom became instant multimillionaires.

The governmental weakness that accompanied the fall of communism in Russia yielded a chilling increase in lawlessness—from ordinary street crime like auto theft to sophisticated, organized crime with a significant role in the nation's economy. The nostalgia for the stability of communism led many Russians to vote communist in 1995 and 1996.

Communism had far deeper roots in Russia than elsewhere in the former Soviet bloc. Russian communists never dropped the communist label and never fully embraced democratic principles. During the 1996 presidential election, the communists, led by Gennady Zyuganov, exploited economic discontent, winning support especially from workers and older pensioners. The incumbent, Boris Yeltsin, in contrast, enjoyed the support of Russia's powerful new entrepreneurial class, which opposed any retreat from free-market principles; he capped a remarkable uphill struggle by defeating Zyuganov in a runoff election in July 1996. The campaign and election gave Russians their fullest experience of democracy to date.

The end of communism opened up divisive new questions across the former Soviet bloc. It quickly became clear that political freedom did not necessarily bring wider rights and liberties. For example, the eclipse of communism in Poland initially promised a major role for the Roman Catholic church, but angry debate followed when, in 1990, the government ordered that children be taught the Catholic religion in school and the head of the Polish church called for an end to the "communist-inspired" separation of church and state. An effort to pass a strong antiabortion bill in time for a visit by Pope John Paul II in 1991 caused more heated debate; public opinion polls indicated that a majority of Poles favored abortion rights.

Abortion was similarly a major issue when the former East Germany was incorporated into the Federal Republic of Germany in 1990. Abortion law had been more liberal in the communist east than in the west. In the same way, East Germany was considerably more generous than the Federal Republic in providing maternity leave, day care, and other measures to enable mothers to work outside the home. Some East German feminists feared that the transition to capitalism could mean diminished employment opportunities for women. Though a compromise was worked out on the abortion issue, the differences in priorities that surfaced between West and East German feminists made it clear that the end of communism was no panacea.

In the former satellite states, as in several of the republics of the former Soviet Union, autonomy and democracy quickly opened the way to ethnic tensions that occasionally led to outright rebellion. Ethnic repression and conflict were not new to the region, but they had been kept largely submerged within the Soviet bloc.

In Czechoslovakia, the Slovak minority broke away to form an independent republic at the beginning of 1993. By 1995 the government was making Slovak the only official language, angering the large Hungarian minority in Slovakia and drawing protests from Hungary. The status of the Hungarian minority in Romania was an ongoing concern as well. But most dramatic—and tragic—was the situation in Yugoslavia, where ethnic and religious conflict produced not only the disintegration of the country but also a brutal, multisided war among Serbs, Croats, and Bosnian Muslims (see Map 27.2). One of the defining events of the 1990s, this war proved a major challenge for the new international order that had emerged from the cold war.

EUROPE AND THE WEST AFTER THE BIPOLAR PEACE

The dissolution of the Soviet system meant the swift, unexpected end of the cold war framework that had defined the era since World War II. Though it seemed only a balance of terror at the time, the cold war had provided a measure of order and security in the years from 1949 to 1989. What sort of international configuration was to follow? Though it could claim to have won the cold war, the United States had declined in relative strength from the unprecedented preeminence it had enjoyed after World War II.

The new framework seemed to invite Western Europe to become a superpower in its own right, so the movement toward European integration intensified, producing a more integrated union of fifteen members by the mid-1990s. But obstacles remained, stemming especially from traditional concerns about national sovereignty. And fighting in the former Yugoslavia raised questions about the ability of the European Union, or any international body, to assure stability.

The Changing International Framework

As the potential threat from the Soviet Union dissolved, the United States lost some of its leverage in Europe because American support no longer seemed essential for European security, and by the early 1990s, the Americans could no longer claim the same kind of leadership in any case. The role of superpower had taken its toll on the United States, just as it had on the U.S.S.R. The arms race had burdened the budgets of both of the big winners of World War II, while the war's major losers, Germany, Japan, and Italy, pulled back from any great power role and prospered as never before.

The ambiguities of the new international situation came to the fore during the first major international crisis of the post–cold war period, the Persian Gulf War, which the United States led against Iraq in 1990 and 1991. With superpower rivalry no longer an issue, the United States assembled a broad coalition that reversed an Iraqi takeover of oil-rich Kuwait. The United States had to pass the hat among its prosperous allies to pay for the Gulf War, and those called on to contribute seemed unlikely to settle for such arrangements again. This was especially true of Japan and Germany, each of which was engaged in reassessing its international role.

The collapse of communism in east-central Europe had paved the way for German reunification in 1990. Despite some nervousness, the four occupying powers—the United States, Britain, France, and the Soviet Union—gave their blessing as the Federal Republic simply incorporated the five states of the former East Germany. Although some in West Germany were hesitant about immediate reunification, especially because of the economic costs that seemed likely, West German Chancellor Helmut Kohl (b. 1930) sought to complete the process as quickly as possible. By early 1990 emigration of East Germans to the west had become a flood. West German law treated these Germans as citizens, entitled to social benefits, so their arrival in such numbers presented a considerable financial burden.

Reunification prompted anxiety about the role the new Germany, already a major economic power, might seek to play in Europe and the world. Germany, however, remained eager to prove its good intentions by leading the continuing movement toward European integration. Some worried that the European Union would become a vehicle for German domination, but the Germans took care to offer reasoned, cautious leadership, with no hint of bullying.

Reunified Germany also encountered new domestic problems that promoted caution. Because reunification proved far more costly than Kohl had expected, his government found it hard to keep some of the promises it had made to Germans in the east. When his government pulled back from its promise of wage equality between east and west in 1993, workers in the former East Germany mounted the most serious strikes the Federal Republic had experienced since World War II.

The French were particularly restive about the reunification of Germany, which threatened France's leading role in Western Europe. But France was still willing to act independently—and it could be influential in doing so. When the post–cold war international system fell into discredit with the multisided ethnic fighting in the former Yugoslavia, French pressure helped bring the situation to a head. President Jacques Chirac's threat to pull France out of the multinational peacekeeping force in the region influenced U.S. President Bill Clinton to step up the U.S. role. Though the French initiative in this case manifested the new complexity in relations among the Western allies, the outcome confirmed the centrality of U.S. leadership.

The brutality that characterized the fighting in Bosnia, and the halting efforts of the international community in response, brought to an abrupt end the optimism that at first surrounded the end of the cold war. The Serbs were widely accused of "ethnic cleansing"—brutal forced relocation or killing to rid much of Bosnia of its Muslim inhabitants (Map 27.2). Muslim enclaves in Bosnia suffered grievously under Serb fire. In the Bosnian capital, Sarajevo, a culturally diverse city long known for its tolerant, cosmopolitan atmosphere, more than 10,000 civilians, including 1500 children, were killed by shelling and sniper fire during a Serb siege from 1992 to early 1996. Finally, in August 1995, NATO forces responded with air strikes that led to peace accords and the end of four years of fighting by early 1996. The tide turned partly because a Western embargo had devastated the economy of what remained of Yugoslavia, forcing its Serb leader, Slobodan Milosevic, to cooperate with those seeking a peaceful solution.

Although the peace agreement envisioned a unified Bosnian state, the contending Serbs, Croats, and Bosnian Muslims quickly began carving out separate spheres, violating the rights of minorities as they did so. Traditions of statehood were weak in this part of the Balkans, so it remained unclear whether the forces of disintegration at work in the former Yugoslavia were simply an anomaly in the greater scheme of twentieth-century Western history or an indication of potential disintegrative forces at loose in Europe and the West. If every ethnic minority were to claim territorial autonomy, the future would be uncertain indeed.

Although it was a NATO force that imposed peace in the former Yugoslavia, NATO's future was uncertain. The alliance had been formed to check Soviet expansion in Europe and with the end of the Soviet threat, it made sense for members to rethink their military priorities. Some suggested that henceforth each nation ought to look after its own defense. Others envisioned expanding NATO to encompass certain of the former Soviet bloc countries, and this plan prevailed. In the fall of 1996, President Clinton announced that he wanted NATO to add a first round of new nations by 1999. For this to occur, Russia had to be convinced that such expansion would not threaten its security, and at the same time conservatives in the West had to be assured that an expanded NATO could still serve to contain Russia, if necessary. In March 1997, Clinton met with Russian president Boris Yeltsin in Helsinki, and the two established Russian tolerance of the proposed changes in NATO. Two months later, NATO and Russia signed a "Founding Act" of mutual cooperation and security between the alliance and its former adversary. A new Russia-NATO council offered Russia a voice in the alliance, but the North Atlantic Council remained the supreme decision-making body and did not include Russia. In June, NATO leaders invited Poland, the Czech Republic, and Hungary to join the Western alliance.

The European Union

The end of the cold war added urgency to the process of European integration. Although a full customs union had technically been achieved by the late 1960s, national governments continued to compromise the open market, especially by favoring certain companies to give them an advantage in international competition. For domestic political

Ethnic Majority
Ethnic Minority
Albanians AL
Croats CR
Montenegrins ---
Muslims MU
Serbs SB
No majority present
Germans GE
Greeks GK
Hungarians HU
Poles PO
Turks TK
Ukrainians UK
Yugoslavia in 1991
GERMANY
POLAND
UKRAINE
CZECH REPUBLIC
SLOVAKIA
AUSTRIA
HUNGARY
MOLDOVA
ROMANIA
SLOVENIA
CROATIA
BOSNIA AND HERZEGOVINA
YUGOSLAVIA
BULGARIA
MACEDONIA
ALBANIA
GREECE
TURKEY
ITALY
Prague
Bratislava
Budapest
Kishinev
Bucharest
Ljubljana
Zagreb
Belgrade
Sarajevo
Sofia
Skopje
Tiranë
Danube
Dniester
Siret
Tisza
Sava
Lake Balaton
Adriatic Sea
Tyrrhenian Sea
Aegean Sea
Black Sea
0 125 250 Km.
0 100 200 Mi.

The Agony of Bosnia The wars that accompanied the breakup of Yugoslavia during the 1990s made it tragically clear that the end of the cold war was no guarantee of peace in Europe. The Serb shelling of the Bosnian capital, Sarajevo, from 1992 to 1996 caused widespread destruction and forced many to flee the city. Here Bosnian Muslims return to the Dobrinja area of Sarajevo in March 1996, just after the end of the Serb siege. *(Christopher Morris/Time/Black Star)*

reasons, governments sometimes confined their purchases to national firms or granted subsidies to domestic producers, enabling them to offer artificially low prices.

Still, movement toward the full-scale integration of the member economies continued by fits and starts. Amid increasing concern about "Eurosclerosis," or lack of innovation and competitiveness, the EEC's twelve members committed themselves in 1985 to the measures necessary to create a true single market by the end of 1992. Provisions included uniform product standards and equal competition for the government contracts of each country, as well as the free circulation of goods, services, and money among the member countries. By the late 1980s, the thrust toward economic integration increasingly assumed a political dimension. A European Parliament had developed from the assembly of the European Coal and Steel Community by 1962, though it had little importance at first. By the mid-1990s the European Union included a network of interlocking institutions in Brussels, Strasbourg, and Luxembourg. Among them the European Parliament and the European Court of Justice played increasingly important roles.

Map 27.2 Ethnic Conflict in East-Central Europe The Balkans have long been an area of complex ethnic mixture. The end of communist rule opened the way to ethnic conflict, most tragically in what had been Yugoslavia. This map shows ethnic distribution in the region in the early 1990s.

At a meeting in Maastricht, The Netherlands, in 1991, the members of the European Union buttressed the powers of the European Parliament, agreed to move toward a common policy of workers' rights, and committed to a common currency and central banking structure by 1999. But this Maastricht agreement required the approval of the EU members, and in one country after another the ensuing debate over

European integration proved more divisive than expected. In addition to the concern over German domination, some feared entrusting vital decisions to faceless bureaucrats in foreign cities.

Although most of the Maastricht agreements were eventually ratified by the EU's members, implementation was not always smooth. Most controversial was the provision for an Economic and Monetary Union (EMU), based on a common currency, the euro. By eliminating the costs and uncertainties of currency exchange, this measure promised to boost trade among the member countries significantly. To become part of the mechanism, countries had to maintain budget deficits no higher than 3 percent of gross domestic product, requiring most of them to decrease their deficits substantially. Governmental efforts to comply with this provision produced conflict on the domestic level, as the thrust toward European union crashed against the social compact, already under pressure, that had produced high government spending for social welfare. Concerned with these pressures, Britain chose not to commit itself to the EMU, though future involvement was not ruled out.

In a televised speech in 1995, President Chirac emphasized his determination to cut the government's budget deficit to enable France to meet the Maastricht criteria for economic and monetary union. The required austerity would include reducing welfare and pension payments and restructuring the debt-plagued state railways. Chirac's initiative prompted intense popular reaction during the fall of 1995. Railroad workers led the most serious wave of strikes that France had experienced in a decade, including periodic interruptions of public services. Students joined in, insisting that the university system needed more money, not less. For many in France, embracing the EU seemed to jeopardize the egalitarianism that had helped sustain social cohesion among the French.

As of the spring of 1998, the euro was slated to go into circulation on January 1, 2002, with local currencies no longer accepted as of the following July.

Supranational Initiatives and Global Issues

Although less visible than the EU, other supranational entities also wielded increasing clout during the late twentieth century, making decisions that deeply affected the lives of ordinary people. Most obvious were multinational corporations, but the World Bank and the International Monetary Fund also played important roles, helping to keep the industrial economies synchronized and the less developed economies on a free-market path. These organizations could strongly influence domestic policies—by refusing, for example, to lend to countries spending heavily on defense.

At the same time, international cooperation took on greater urgency because of growing concern with the environment. Such problems as global warming, the destruction of rain forests, and the deterioration of the ozone layer were inherently supranational in scope. Yet environmental concerns complicated relations between the industrialized nations and the rest of the world. Countries seeking to industrialize encountered environmental constraints that had not been at issue when the West industrialized. The challenge for the West was to foster protection of the environment in poorer regions of the globe without imposing unfair limitations on economic growth.

Changing demographic and economic patterns suggested that "North-South" tensions between the prosperous countries, concentrated in the northern hemisphere, and the poorer ones, more likely to be found farther south, might replace the East-West tensions of the cold war. World population reached 5.5 billion in 1993, having doubled in forty years. This was the fastest rate of world population growth ever, and virtually all of the growth in the 1990s was in Africa, Asia, and Latin America. The population of Europe was growing at only 0.2 percent per year, and in several countries, including Italy, Germany, and Spain, the population would actually have declined without the boost provided by immigration.

Immigration and Citizenship

As the European Union and other supranational organizations became more prominent, forces in the opposite direction—subnational, religious, ethnic, tribal—simultaneously grew more powerful. Subgroup conflict was most tragic in east-central Europe (see Map 27.2), but it grew in Western Europe as well. In Northern Ireland violent polarization between Protestants and Catholics defied solution even after a 1998 peace compromise. In Spain the restoration of democracy gave the long-restive Basque and Catalan minorities the chance to press openly for autonomy. Even in Belgium, there was growing antagonism between Flemish-speaking Flemings and French-speaking Walloons during the 1990s.

With immigration growing sharply in Western Europe by the 1980s, questions about citizenship became politically central, giving a new twist to the interaction with the non-Western world that had helped define "the West" from the beginning. Demographic pressure in the less developed countries contributed to the rising immigration to Western Europe that made Africans selling jewelry, figurines, and sunglasses familiar in European cities by the early 1990s. In 1995 there were 11 million legal immigrants living in the European Union—including, as the largest contingent, 2.6 million Turks. There were also as many as 4 million illegals. As Europeans faced the problems of an increasingly competitive world economy, such immigration became a divisive political issue. In France the government's expulsion of illegal African immigrants sparked a major protest in 1996.

At issue were not only new immigrants, but long-settled immigrant families. Some of those raising questions were not seeking simply to preserve economic advantages by limiting access. Rather, they were concerned about community, diversity, and national identity—about what it meant to belong. Because of differences in tradition, individual countries tended to conceive the alternatives differently.

Germany had actively recruited foreign workers during the decades of economic boom and labor shortage after the war. In 1973 noncitizens constituted 2.6 million workers, or 11.9 percent of the work force. At first these "guest workers" were viewed as temporary, almost migrant, workers. But as they remained in Germany, their family patterns came to approximate those of the rest of the country, though their birthrates were considerably higher. By the 1980s, Germany had a large and increasingly settled population of non-Germans, many of them born and educated there.

In addition, the German Federal Republic had adopted a generous asylum law in an effort to atone for the crimes of the Nazi period. After the fall of communism, the newly reunified Germany found sixty thousand new arrivals seeking asylum every month by 1993. At that point Germany had a foreign population of 6.4 million.

The 1913 law governing citizenship for immigrants reflected a long-standing assumption that citizenship presupposed German ethnicity. Ethnic Germans—over a million of whom moved to Germany from the Soviet bloc between 1988 and 1991—were immediately accorded German citizenship. But many Turks who had been born in Germany could not become citizens.

As the new wave of immigration from the east swelled the "foreign" population, Germans subject to economic pressures felt that foreigners and asylum-seekers were getting a better deal than ordinary citizens such as themselves. In 1992 there were two thousand attacks on foreigners, some of them fatal. Those responsible were sometimes "skinheads," young people with uncertain economic prospects who claimed to admire Nazism. The violence provoked massive counter-demonstrations, but as reaction against refugees and foreign workers grew, the German parliament voted to restrict the right of asylum in 1993.

Although these issues provoked particular controversy in Germany, the claims of immigrants and refugees confronted all the Western democracies with difficult questions about the meaning of citizenship. In France the right-wing National Front, led by Jean-Marie LePen, forced the issue to center stage in the 1980s. The French accorded citizenship automatically to second-generation immigrants, assuming that the offspring of immigrants would be assimilated into the national community. But as France began to attract rising numbers of immigrants, especially from Algeria and other Islamic countries of North Africa, critics like LePen attacked the French citizenship law as too loose, charging that too many recent immigrants did not want to assimilate. Whereas the French left defended cultural diversity and its compatibility with citizenship, the right complained that citizenship was being devalued as a mere convenience, requiring no real commitment to the national community. This difference in perspective helps explain the controversy over the Muslim girls' headscarves that gripped France in 1989 (see page 708).

As these issues became ever more central in the West, representatives of twenty-seven Mediterranean countries—some European, some Middle Eastern, some African—met in Barcelona in 1995 to seek common ground. The Europeans pledged to help the other Mediterranean economies as a way to limit the flow of immigrants. The need to protect competing EU agriculture made it hard to deliver, however. The Barcelona conference dramatized the web of interlocking difficulties that surrounded Western Europe's relations with its neighbors by the late twentieth century.

IN THE SHADOW OF HISTORY: THE EXPERIMENT CONTINUES

The rapid change at the end of the twentieth century raised new questions for Europeans about the meaning of their history and traditions. Some worried that prosperity necessarily entailed "Americanization," the unwelcome sameness of mass consumer culture. For the formerly communist countries of east-central Europe, the challenge was to find a positive way of reconnecting with their national histories. In some cases, this return of history and memory contributed to the renewed emphasis on ethnic identity, which itself produced conflict and repression.

The collapse of communism in the Soviet bloc seemed to mean the triumph of democratic capitalism. But rapid economic and technological change introduced problems that proved hard to handle within the democratic political sphere. And during the 1990s, divisive issues all over the Western world—from the role of the state to environmental protection to immigration and cultural diversity—threatened to disrupt the political consensus that had crystallized since World War II.

Europe and America, Old and New

Having weakened itself disastrously in the two world wars, Western Europe found itself dependent on the United States, first for its economic recovery, then for its defense. For decades after 1945, Europe seemed to have no choice but to follow the U.S. lead. Such subservience troubled some Europeans, and a kind of love-hate relationship with the United States developed in Western Europe during the later twentieth century.

Even after Europe's recovery, the United States continued to set the pace in high-technology industries, prompting concerns that Europe would become a mere economic satellite of the United States. Europe seemed to be caught in a dilemma: To retain its distinctiveness over the long term, it apparently had to become more like America in the short term. By the 1980s much of Western Europe had caught up with the United States in standard of living, and the Western Europeans set the pace in confronting some of the new problems that resulted from socioeconomic change. The French day-care system was one prominent example (see page 711). Nonetheless, concerns about Americanization deepened at the same time. By the late 1980s consumerism and the widening impact of American popular culture—from blue jeans and American TV to shopping malls—suggested a growing homogenization in the capitalist democracies. A Euro-Disneyland opened in France in 1992 and, after a slow start, proved increasingly popular. Tangible reminders of Europe's distinctive past remained, but the growing "heritage industry" in Britain and elsewhere suggested that they were merely commodities to be packaged like any other.

Postmodern Culture

The sense that history itself had been commodified seemed to put the whole notion of authenticity into question. Many contemporaries felt that truth and reality were no longer useful categories, that the world could be represented from an infinite number of viewpoints and through an endless array of interpretive ideas—and no single representation could encompass all these simultaneous truths. Embracing uncertainty as a fundamental fact was part of what came to be called postmodernism. Whereas the modern styles and theories of the first half of the century had been devoted to the explosion of traditional forms, artists in the postmodern period felt compelled to bear witness to the horrors of World War II and were moved to revive some formal elements from the past in order to communicate effectively. The result was a multitude of innovations that did not have a formal credo in common—the various artists did not comprise a cohesive movement—but rather were joined by their common use of historical references, scientific imagery, and an attempt to depict reality from several vantage points. There was also tremendous interest in selectively borrowing from the techniques of advertising and mass media in an attempt to satirize and undermine the manipulative effects of the dominant culture.

The sometimes playful, sometimes disturbing use of "found images" by Robert Rauschenberg

Sherman: Untitled #92 (1981) Photographs seem to record reality and yet, like paintings, are creative products of a human mind even if they are not staged or altered. Often featuring the artist herself disguised as a film starlet or a figure from a historical painting, Cindy Sherman's work comments on the way in which we look at different images and the way in which these images shape our ideas of gender and class. *(Courtesy of Cindy Sherman and Metro Pictures)*

Holzer: Truisms Installation (1989) Spiraling down the ramp of New York's Guggenheim Museum, Jenny Holzer's "truisms" progressed along LED signs. The odd and constantly changing messages created a heightened version of the postmodern ironic relationship to news, advertisement, historical wisdom, soundbites, and philosophical truth. At the center are more skewed aphorisms, carved into a circle of granite benches. *(Courtesy of Jenny Holzer Studio, New York. © Jenny Holzer. Photo: David Heald)*

(b. 1925) took seriously the visual information of everyday life while substantially transforming the images and conceptually redefining them. The American artist Cindy Sherman (b. 1954) combined performance and painting in her often huge photographic studies. Sherman's subject was the relationship between the human form, mass-produced commodities, and the fantasies that overlay the modern experience of these things—especially in relation to sex and conceptions of femininity. Another important American artist, Jenny Holzer (b. 1950), decorated various sites with sets of phrases, most of which sounded like familiar platitudes but carried strange, disjointed sentiments, especially in relation to one another. Each overall display seemed to close the distance between wisdom and nonsense, and disrupt the notion that the culture could produce valid declarations of any kind. In a more traditional artistic medium, the neoexpressionist German painter Anselm Kiefer (b. 1945) reflected the continuing struggle to represent the unrepresentable: the cataclysms of the recent past.

Though there was considerable eclecticism in arts and letters in the second half of the century, they were guided by some broad theoretical innovations. Philosophy underwent a "linguistic turn" as new works asserted that the age-old attempt to understand existence did not make sense because humans primarily know existence through the imperfect medium of language. Following the lead of the Austrian

Ludwig Wittgenstein (1889–1951), philosophers began to concentrate on how language works, what its limitations are, and to what extent it creates a shared reality. The linguistic focus became a central part of postmodernism. Also essential to postmodernism was the thought of French writer Michel Foucault (1926–1984). In his many historical-philosophical works, Foucault studied the development of modern codes of normality, sickness, madness, criminality, and sexual perversion. Following Nietzsche, Foucault and other postmodern thinkers questioned the legacy of the Enlightenment, most notably the idea that increasing rationality and science would lead to freedom and justice. Events of the twentieth century suggested that new power structures had replaced the more obvious hierarchies of the premodern world and that the rationalist classifications of abnormality had become powerful controlling forces in the lives of ordinary people.

The Uncertain Triumph of Democratic Capitalism

The end of the cold war, the discrediting of communism, and the domestication of socialism all seemed to mean the triumph of political democracy and free-market capitalism. But though there was a good deal of self-congratulation in the West at first, what followed its victory was not a period of untroubled confidence but a deeper questioning of capitalist democracy.

In light of the Western political experience so far, few denied that what worked best, and afforded the only basis for political legitimacy, was representative democracy based on universal suffrage within an open, pluralistic society guaranteeing individual freedom. There must be freedom not only to inquire and criticize but also to pursue individual advantage within a market economy. At the same time, that free-market system had to be bounded by some measure of governmental responsibility—for education, for social welfare, for workplace and product safety, and for the environment. But difficult questions remained about the proper role for government in coordinating or balancing market forces.

As the former communist East struggled to catch up to the West, Western affluence increasingly seemed brittle and uncertain. High unemployment persisted in Western Europe, and although unemployment was considerably lower in the United States, new jobs were often poorly paid, with few health and insurance benefits. Moreover, Americans did not have the security that the European welfare states provided—in health care, most notably. Real wages advanced little between the mid-1970s and the mid-1990s, though by 1998 they were beginning to go up in the United States. Still, for most, the widening gap between the well-off and those barely getting by suggested the emergence of a "winner-take-all" society.[1]

Although the socialist left had won reforms that were now central to the consensus around democratic capitalism, it had abandoned much of what it had stood for—from class struggle and revolution to state ownership and a centrally planned economy. Socialism could apparently serve only as the mildly left-leaning party within the framework of capitalist democracy. Several corruption scandals served to further discredit the Socialist parties. In France such scandals brought the Socialists massive defeat at the polls in 1993 and 1995. In Italy, too, the Socialists were central to a corruption scandal that began in 1992 and quickly spread to discredit the Christian Democrats as well—and indeed the whole entrenched Italian political class.

With the decline of socialism as a political alternative, the new right, which had been associated especially with anti-immigrant sentiment at first, grew in prominence in the 1990s. Although differing considerably in priorities, respectability, and success, right-leaning political leaders from LePen in France and José Maria Aznar in Spain to Jörg Haider in Austria and Gianfranco Fini in Italy tapped into the growing political frustration and economic uncertainty.

What did it mean to be "right wing" or conservative in the late twentieth century? In Italy and Austria, new right politicians criticized the prevailing understanding of the recent past—the era of fascism and World War II—playing up the patriotic, anticommunist thrust of the interwar right. But as far as present priorities were concerned, conservatives sometimes differed sharply among themselves. In Britain the Thatcher government had tamed the labor unions and sold state-owned industries, but it had also expanded centralized control over local government, health care, and education. With its ideological agenda, the Thatcher government had been activist and interventionist, not cautious, gradualist, and pragmatic—not truly conservative. In addressing economic anxieties, the new right sometimes articulated problems that mainstream politicians ignored, but it seemed unable to propose viable solutions.

Extreme though it was, the Italian corruption scandal of the early 1990s dramatized troubling tendencies in the democratic political system of the later twentieth century. The need for money to finance electioneering and political patronage kept the whole system on the edge of corruption. Democracy seemed to place a premium on short-term advantage over vision and principle. By the early 1990s, declining voter turnout suggested growing political cynicism and disillusionment all over the Western world.

At the same time, participation in national politics came to seem less significant partly because key decisions were often made elsewhere, by multinational corporations or supranational organizations not directly subject to democratic control. As global competition intensified, the logic of capitalism seemed increasingly to overwhelm the capacities of democratic politics.

CONCLUSION: WESTERN CIVILIZATION IN A GLOBAL AGE

In the late twentieth century, the West was part of a world that was dramatically less Eurocentric than it had been a century before, when European imperialism was at its peak. Events in the West competed for attention with OPEC meetings, Japanese economic decisions, and the financial crisis in Asia. A planetary culture, a threatened environment, and an interdependent international economy required people to think and react in global terms as never before. All over the world, people were seeing the same films, listening to the same music, chatting over the Internet, and purchasing the same clothing from internationally powerful companies. Yet along with this increasing uniformity, the culture has shown vibrant interest in highlighting human differences based on nationality, ethnicity, religion, gender, and sexual orientation, and this too runs counter to the nineteenth-century notion that there was one correct version of respectable normality and one standard path toward national progress.

One of the defining characteristics of the modern period in the West had been a "master narrative"—a conception of all human development—that took the Europe as a model and assumed that everyone else was trying to catch up. Such developmentalist assumptions were linked to the arrogant sense of superiority that had been used to justify Western imperialism. Even though Westernization continued at the end of the twentieth century, it was increasingly recognized that the West was not necessarily the standard of development.

Since World War II, at least, there was a growing interest in the non-Western world and increasing respect for its diverse traditions. Scholars showed how Western images of the non-Western world had become stereotypes, reinforcing assumptions of Western superiority. Others investigated the long-standing assumptions of masculine superiority. And just as the prejudices of race and gender had reinforced one another, "multiculturalism" and feminism were mutally supportive as each worked to identify and dismantle deeply ingrained mechanisms of oppression. (See the box "Encounters with the West: The Case of 'Orientalism.'")

Such insights led some to deny that Western civilization merited privilege as an object of study. Given the injustices that had long been performed in the name of that civilization, this stance was understandable but not particularly practical. Over the course of several thousand

ENCOUNTERS WITH THE WEST

The Case of "Orientalism"

In his influential book **Orientalism**, *published in 1978, the Palestinian-American scholar Edward Said explored the process through which Westerners had constructed the "Middle East"—as different from the West. Though critical of the West, Said appealed to our common humanity in an effort to overcome the ongoing tendency, which was not confined to the West, to understand oneself as superior by stereotyping others. In the final analysis, he suggested, we all need to learn from one another.*

The Orient is not only adjacent to Europe; it is also the place of Europe's greatest and richest and oldest colonies, the source of its civilizations and languages, its cultural contestant, and one of its deepest and most recurring images of the Other. In addition, the Orient has helped to define Europe (or the West) as its contrasting image, idea, personality, experience. . . .

. . . The relationship between Occident and Orient is a relationship of power, of domination, of varying degrees of a complex hegemony. . . . There is very little consent to be found, for example, in the fact that Flaubert's encounter with an Egyptian courtesan produced a widely influential model of the Oriental woman; she never spoke of herself, she never represented her emotions, presence, or history. *He* spoke for and represented her. He was foreign, comparatively wealthy, male, and these were historical facts of domination that allowed him not only to possess Kuchuk Hanem physically but to speak for her and tell his readers in what way she was "typically Oriental." . . .

. . . [E]nough is being done today in the human sciences to provide the contemporary scholar with insights, methods, and ideas that could dispense with racial, ideological, and imperialist stereotypes of the sort provided during its historical ascendancy by Orientalism. I consider Orientalism's failure to have been a human as much as an intellectual one; for in having to take up a position of irreducible opposition to a region of the world it considered alien to its own, Orientalism failed to identify with human experience, failed also to see it as human experience. . . . I hope to have shown my reader that the answer to Orientalism is not Occidentalism. No former "Oriental" will be comforted by the thought that having been an Oriental himself he is likely—too likely—to study new "Orientals"—or "Occidentals"—of his own making. If the knowledge of Orientalism has any meaning, it is in being a reminder of the seductive degradation of knowledge, of any knowledge, anywhere, at any time. Now perhaps more than before.

Source: Edward W. Said, *Orientalism* (New York: Random House, Vintage, 1979), pp. 1–2, 4–8, 327–328.

years, a civilization had been developing—defining and redefining itself through the writing of history. Poets commented across time to other poets; philosophers interpreted each other's work in the context of a new historical moment. From social theorists to inventors, athletes to cosmologists, the project of human existence continued to refer back through its history. Increasingly the events of that history were seen not as inherently and grandly important, as if part of some preordained narrative, but rather as a series of guideposts, a source of ideas, a catalog of errors, and a reminder of heroic responses to a difficult world.

Though debate continues regarding the importance of Western civilization as a category of study, some consensus seems to be forming that knowledge of Western history is crucial—if only because that history continues to shape the West and, less directly, the world. Many people believe that the Western narrative is terribly flawed as a model for humanity: Its assumptions of ascending progress seem questionable at best. But understanding had to come first. The invitation to think freely about the Western tradition, to criticize it, and to build a better future on it rested on precisely that tradition—and remained perhaps its most fundamental legacy.

The effort to make a better civilization begins in knowledge of the civilization that has been inherited. Fortunately, that civilization—wretchedly unfair as it has often been to many of its members—is still one that offers extraordinary intellectual and cultural pleasures. Many voices have been silenced, but the conversation across centuries is still incalculably rich. The many voices that *can* be heard, whether part of the dominant culture or at its fringes, whether long canonized or even now half-hidden in its shadows—these voices can still provide insight, strength, and passion as the new millennium begins to unfold.

NOTES

1. Robert H. Frank and Philip J. Cook, *The Winner-Take-All Society* (New York: Free Press, 1995).

SUGGESTED READING

Barkan, Joanne. *Visions of Emancipation: The Italian Workers' Movement Since 1945.* 1984. A sympathetic account of the postwar Italian labor movement.

Best, Steven, and Douglas Kellner. *Postmodern Theory: Critical Interrogations.* 1991. A difficult but extremely interesting introduction to postmodern theory emphasizing its social and political ramifications.

Bridenthal, Renate, et al., eds. *Becoming Visible: Women in European History.* 1987. A major collection of essays on women's history, including seven that deal with twentieth-century topics.

Brubaker, Rogers. *Citizenship and Nationhood in France and Germany.* 1992. A lucid comparative study showing how very different conceptions of citizenship emerged in the two countries as a result of their contrasting historical experiences.

Cheles, Luciano, et al., eds. *The Far Right in Western and Eastern Europe.* 2d ed. 1995. A superior collection of essays on the revival of the extreme right in the 1980s and 1990s.

Funk, Nanette, and Magda Mueller, eds. *Gender Politics and Post-Communism: Reflections from Eastern Europe and the Former Soviet Union.* 1993. A country-by-country analysis and critique by feminist scholars from the region, with an effective mixture of outside perspectives.

Garton Ash, Timothy. *The Magic Lantern: The Revolution of '89 Witnessed in Warsaw, Budapest, Berlin, and Prague.* 1990. Firsthand testimony on the fall of communism by a British intellectual with close contacts among anticommunists in east-central Europe.

Glenny, Misha. *The Fall of Yugoslavia: The Third Balkan War.* 3d rev. ed. 1996. An influential account of the disintegration of Yugoslavia, combining historical analysis with dramatic treatment of the fighting.

Havel, Václav. *Disturbing the Peace: A Conversation with Karel Hvífizfidala.* 1991. Part autobiography, part history, part philosophy. Demonstrates the moral vision that made Havel so effective as a leader in the Czech opposition to communism.

Kuisel, Richard F. *Seducing the French: The Dilemmas of Americanization.* 1993. An illuminating study of the French response to all things American in the half-century that followed World War II.

Laba, Roman. *The Roots of Solidarity.* 1991. Seeks to show that workers, not the Polish intelligentsia, were the driving force behind Solidarity.

Mosse, George L. *The Image of Man: The Creation of Modern Masculinity.* 1996. Traces the idea and image of the masculine from the advent of nineteenth century bourgeois society to the late twentieth century.

Remnick, David. *Lenin's Tomb: The Last Days of the Soviet Empire.* 1994. An acclaimed and compelling account of the fall of the communist regime. Makes effective use of oral testimony.

Stokes, Gale. *The Walls Came Tumbling Down: The Collapse of Communism in Eastern Europe.* 1993. Dramatic and comprehensive, the first standard account of the dissolution of communism in east-central Europe.

Index

The Pains of Mass Imprisonment

The purpose of this book is to convey the magnitude of mass imprisonment in the United States, especially of people of color, not by objective statistics and trends, but by presenting to readers the voices and lived experiences of individuals who live these harsh conditions on a daily basis. From this reading, the authors seek to foster among readers a more critical awareness of the challenges faced by disproportionately oppressed groups, and perhaps through this critical engagement, some may elect to become involved in one of the organizations detailed in the book's appendix.

Benjamin Fleury-Steiner is Associate Professor of Sociology and Criminal Justice at the University of Delaware. For more than a decade, he has taught graduate and undergraduate courses on inequality, mass imprisonment, and the death penalty. Fleury-Steiner's recent books include, *Jury Stories of Death: How America's Death Penalty Invests in Inequality* and *Dying Inside: The HIV/AIDS Ward at Limestone Prison* (both published by the University of Michigan Press).

Jamie Longazel is an Assistant Professor in the Department of Sociology, Anthropology, and Social Work at the University of Dayton. He teaches and conducts research in the areas of crime and punishment, law and inequality, and immigration. His recent publications have appeared in *Punishment & Society, Sociology Compass, Chicana/o Latina/o Law Review*, and *Race & Justice.*

Framing 21st Century Social Issues

The goal of this new, unique Series is to offer readable, teachable "thinking frames" on today's social problems and social issues by leading scholars. These are available for view on http://routledge.customgateway.com/routledge-social-issues.html.

For instructors teaching a wide range of courses in the social sciences, the Routledge *Social Issues Collection* now offers the best of both worlds: originally written short texts that provide "overviews" to important social issues *as well as* teachable excerpts from larger works previously published by Routledge and other presses.

As an instructor, click to the website to view the library and decide how to build your custom anthology and which thinking frames to assign. Students can choose to receive the assigned materials in print and/or electronic formats at an affordable price.

Available

Body Problems
Running and Living Long in a Fast-Food Society
Ben Agger

Sex, Drugs, and Death
Addressing Youth Problems in American Society
Tammy Anderson

The Stupidity Epidemic
Worrying About Students, Schools, and America's Future
Joel Best

Empire Versus Democracy
The Triumph of Corporate and Military Power
Carl Boggs

Contentious Identities
Ethnic, Religious, and Nationalist Conflicts in Today's World
Daniel Chirot

The Future of Higher Education
Dan Clawson and Max Page

Waste and Consumption
Capitalism, the Environment, and the Life of Things
Simonetta Falasca-Zamponi

Rapid Climate Change
Causes, Consequences, and Solutions
Scott G. McNall

The Problem of Emotions in Societies
Jonathan H. Turner

Outsourcing the Womb
Race, Class, and Gestational Surrogacy in a Global Market
France Winddance Twine

Changing Times for Black Professionals
Adia Harvey Wingfield

Why Nations Go to War
A Sociology of Military Conflict
Mark P. Worrell

How Ethical Systems Change
Eugenics, the Final Solution, Bioethics
Sheldon Ekland-Olson and Julie Beicken

How Ethical Systems Change
Abortion and Neonatal Care
Sheldon Ekland-Olson and Elyshia Aseltine

How Ethical Systems Change
Tolerable Suffering and Assisted Dying
Sheldon Ekland-Olson and Elyshia Aseltine

How Ethical Systems Change
Lynching and Capital Punishment
Sheldon Ekland-Olson and Danielle Dirks

Nuclear Family Values, Extended Family Lives
The Power of Race, Class, and Gender
Natalia Sarkisian and Naomi Gerstel

Disposable Youth
Racialized Memories, and the Culture of Cruelty
Henry Giroux

Due Process Denied
Detentions and Deportations in the United States
Tanya Golash-Boza

Oversharing
Presentation of Self in the Internet Age
Ben Agger

Foreign Remedies
What the Experience of Other Nations Can Tell Us about Next Steps in Reforming U.S. Health Care
David A. Rochefort and Kevin P. Donnelly

DIY
The Search for Control and Self-Reliance in the 21st Century
Kevin Wehr

Torture
A Sociology of Violence and Human Rights
Lisa Hajjar

Terror
Social, Political, and Economic Perspectives
Mark Worrell

Girls With Guns
Firearms, Feminism, and Militarism
France Winddance Twine

Beyond the Prison Industrial Complex
Crime and Incarceration in the 21st Century
Kevin Wehr and Elyshia Aseltine

Unequal Prospects
Is Working Longer the Answer?
Tay McNamara and John Williamson

Forthcoming

From Trafficking to Terror
Pardis Mahdavi

Color Line?
Race and Sport in America
Krystal Beamon

Identity Problems in the Facebook Era
Daniel Trottier

The Pains of Mass Imprisonment

Benjamin Fleury-Steiner
University of Delaware

Jamie Longazel
University of Dayton

NEW YORK AND LONDON

First published 2014
by Routledge
711 Third Avenue, New York, NY 10017

Simultaneously published in the UK
by Routledge
2 Park Square, Milton Park, Abingdon, Oxon OX14 4RN

Routledge is an imprint of the Taylor & Francis Group, an informa business

Library of Congress Cataloging-in-Publication Data
Fleury-Steiner, Benjamin, 1970-
The pains of mass imprisonment / by Benjamin Fleury-Steiner, University of Delaware, Jamie Longazel, University of Dayton.
pages cm. — (Framing 21st century social issues)
Includes bibliographical references and index.
1. Prisoners—United States—Social conditions. 2. Prisons—United States.
3. Corrections—United States. 4. Criminal justice, Administration of—United States.
I. Longazel, Jamie. II. Title.
HV9469.F62 2014
365'.60973—dc23 2013008036

ISBN: 978-0-415-51883-3 (pbk)
ISBN: 978-0-203-79510-1 (ebk)

Typeset in Garamond and Gill sans
by Cenveo Publisher Services

Contents

Series Foreword

The early years of the 21st century have been a time of paradoxes. Growing prosperity and the growth of the middle classes in countries such as Brazil, China, India, Russia, and South Africa have been accompanied by climate change, environmental degradation, labor exploitation, gender inequalities, state censorship of social media, governmental corruption, and human rights abuses. Sociologists offer theories, concepts, and analytical frames that enable us to better understand the challenges and cultural transformations of the 21st century. How can we generate new forms of collective knowledge that can help solve some of our local, global, and transnational problems?

We live in a world in which new communication technologies and products such as cell phones, iPads, and new social media such as Facebook, Google, and Skype have transformed online education, global communication networks, local and transnational economies, facilitated revolutions such as the "Arab Spring," and generated new forms of entertainment, employment, protest, and pleasure. These social media have been utilized by social justice activists, political dissidents, educators, entrepreneurs, and multinational corporations. They have also been a source of corporate deviance and government corruption used as a form of surveillance that threatens democracy, privacy, creative expression, and political freedoms.

The goal of this series is to provide accessible and innovative analytical frames that examine a wide range of social issues including social media whose impact is local, global, and transnational. Sociologists are ideally poised to contribute to a global conversation about a range of issues such as the impact of mass incarceration on local economies, medical technologies, health disparities, violence, torture, transnational migration, militarism, and the AIDS epidemic.

The books in this series introduce a wide range of analytical frames that dissect and discuss social problems and social pleasures. These books also engage and intervene directly with current debates within the social sciences over how best to define, rethink, and respond to the social issues that characterize the early 21st century. The contributors to this series bring together the works of classical sociology into dialogue with contemporary social theorists from diverse theoretical traditions including but not limited to feminist, Marxist, and European social theory.

Readers do not need an extensive background in academic sociology to benefit from these books. Each book is student-friendly in that we provide glossaries of terms for the uninitiated that appear in bold in the text. Each chapter ends with questions for further thought and discussion. The books are the ideal level for undergraduates because they are accessible without sacrificing a theoretically sophisticated and innovative analysis.

This is the fourth year of our Routledge Social Issues book series. Ben Agger was the former editor of this series during its first three years. These books explore contemporary social problems in ways that introduce basic sociological concepts in the social sciences, cover key literature in the field, and offer original diagnoses. Our series includes books on a broad range of topics including climate change, consumption, eugenics, torture, surrogacy, gun violence, the Internet, and youth culture.

This book on mass imprisonment by Benjamin Fleury-Steiner and Jamie Longazel offers a much needed and compelling analysis of the contemporary prison system in the United States. Sociologists have been central to social justice movements and social change intended to make the world a more humane place. Fleury-Steiner and Longazel provide a beautifully written and powerful analysis of the U.S. penal system that points to changes needed if we are to care ethically for the incarcerated. It illuminates forms of social suffering that characterize the prison industrial complex today. This book should be required reading for all sociology students because this is a growth industry which employs a significant segment of the labor force in states such as California. This book is ideal for courses in criminology, human rights, social justice, and sociology of law.

France Winddance Twine
Series Editor

Preface

We have taught undergraduate courses on prisons for many years and are always struck by the pedagogical challenges. Many students hold strong beliefs of crime and deviance as the problems of individuals in the absence of broader societal and institutional failings (e.g., "You do the crime, you do the time") and punishment as a matter of course (e.g., "You made your bed, and now you have to sleep in it"). Such preconceptions make it difficult to facilitate critical thinking in the classroom. How can we get students to think about these issues in a broader social context? To address this challenge, we have used a variety of readings in our classes, many of which document in rich empirical detail the United States' harmful embrace of decades of mass imprisonment. One might then expect that challenging students to question their conventional wisdom would not be difficult. Yet even in the face of the evidence many, if not most, students struggle to see beyond their deeply held beliefs. And even students that come to see the problem of mass imprisonment as beyond individuals view it as a kind of hopeless tragedy of individuals who have been dealt a bad hand in life.

One approach that we have found effective in the classroom—although, until now it has been loosely organized and largely anecdotal—is to supplement empirical data on relevant imprisonment trends with the detailed experiences of actual prisoners. In this way, the observation of a leading sociologist of race relations, Joe R. Feagin, has been especially germane to us: "There is a tendency in sociological theory to see human beings as determined by social forces and restrictions, yet people work in many individual and collective ways to try to bring change in the structures and institutions that oppress them" (Feagin 2006: 31). It is from this perspective that we present prisoners' experiences as first documented by advocacy organizations that have long fought to expose their often-needless pain and suffering behind bars. We situate prisoners' experiences in the context of broader conditions of penal oppression. In this way, we hope the material presented here fosters a more critical awareness of the challenges faced by disproportionately oppressed groups on the inside who confront these harsh conditions on a daily basis. We also hope this book will allow readers to see life behind bars as far more complex than individuals facing the consequences of their actions. Perhaps through this critical engagement some readers may even become involved in one of the organizations we detail in the book's appendix.

Introduction: Penal Oppression

Gresham Sykes's classic book *The Society of Captives*—published more than a half-century ago—remains one of the most influential in the canon of sociological studies of prisons. This **prison ethnography** endures for the critical insight it provides on the inner workings of the prison and its key actors. Despite the maximum security prison's volatility in which the captives clearly outnumber the captors, Sykes shows how the prison manages to maintain some semblance of order. According to his **functionalist** account, the glue that holds the prison together is the deprivations prisoners must endure on the inside. Because the experience of confinement is by its nature harsh, prisoners must find ways to adapt to this experience. At the same time, guards seeking to maintain order are confronted with the challenge of not making deprivations too severe if they are to prevent prison riots and rebellions. In short, contrary to the popular wisdom of the time, Sykes argued that the interior life of the prison is a kind of balancing act between the captives and the captors.[1]

Our task in this book is to revisit Sykes's classic work in light of profound changes that the prison has undergone since he was writing in 1954. Drawing on the visceral and increasingly painful experiences of today's captives as well as recent research that

1 Our reference throughout is the 50th anniversary edition of Sykes's 1958 original: *The Society of Captives: A Study of a Maximum Security Prison, Princeton Classics Edition*. Princeton, NJ: Princeton University Press, 2007. *The Society of Captives*, however, did not escape critique. For perhaps the earliest and most detailed, see Irwin and Cressey (1962: 142–55). Irwin and Cressey challenged both premises of Sykes's argument—namely, that the pains of imprisonment that structure a kind of order between captors and captives are not a function of a unique "prison society." Alternatively, Irwin and Cressey argue that prisons are much more disorderly institutions than Sykes imagines precisely because the overwhelming majority of the imprisoned bring with them into the prison experiences of deprivation and deviant norms learned on the outside—what Irwin and Cressey term an "importation model" of prison subculture. For Irwin and Cressey, the prison is an organization that is always plagued by conflict as opposed to a struggle for order. In contrast to Sykes's functionalist perspective, the argument here is that prisons endure only because guards learn to pit prisoners against one another by manipulating rules that are brought inside by prisoners. Beyond this "importation model," Irwin's later work documents how growing prison populations and growing perceived threat of the prisoner subculture lead guards routinely to resort to harsh and dehumanizing treatment of prisoners. See John Irwin (1980).

grounds these individual accounts in a broader empirical context, we argue that the give-and-take nature of the prison has been replaced by a much harsher regime of what we call **penal oppression**. Specifically, our analysis is grounded in what sociologists refer to as the "radical" or **conflict perspective**. From this theoretical viewpoint, life behind bars cannot be understood as a self-contained society with its own indigenous norms and values. In contrast to the functionalist perspective, the prison is seen as an institution impacting historically oppressed groups in ways that above all else oppress them further. Yet as criminologist Michael Welch observes in *Corrections: A Critical Approach*, the conflict or critical perspective of crime and punishment is viewed as far less "radical" than in previous eras: "Economic, political, and historical considerations that generally were associated with radicalism have emerged as significant elements of mainstream criminology" (Welch 2011).

In the present book, we take our greatest inspiration from the late criminologist John Irwin. In his classic ethnography *The Jail: Managing the Underclass in American Society*, Irwin illuminates how attention to oppressive conditions within a penal institution sheds important light on conditions of social marginality on the outside. In contrast to Sykes's account of penal institutions compromising their own internal functionalist logic, Irwin shows how the jail serves as a veritable dumping ground for the poor who are subjected to various forms of oppression on the inside. Rather than a struggle for order between captives and captors, Irwin shows how incarceration in the lives of the poor serves "to unravel their few social ties [and] reduces their capacity and their resolve to make the journey back into society" (Irwin 1985: 66).

The Rise of Penal Oppression

The first and most glaring difference between prisons today and those in 1954 is the sheer size of the confined population. At the time of Sykes's research, there were approximately 250,000 prisoners in the U.S. (state and federal) prisons and jails. As of 2010, there are more than 2.2 million (Sentencing Project n/d)—that is, just about *nine* times as many prisoners (see Figure 1)[2]. Indeed, when it comes to recognizing crucial differences between confinement in the 1950s and prisons today, the numbers speak for themselves:

> Adding up all probationers and parolees, prisoners and jail inmates, you'll find the United States now has more than 7.3 million adults under some form of

2 Although we should note that these figures include numbers for both jail and prison population in the U.S. they are thus indicative of rates of mass *incarceration* rather than mass imprisonment. Nevertheless, the U.S. prison population alone has skyrocketed from 1950 to the present (from approximately 200,000 to 1.6 million).

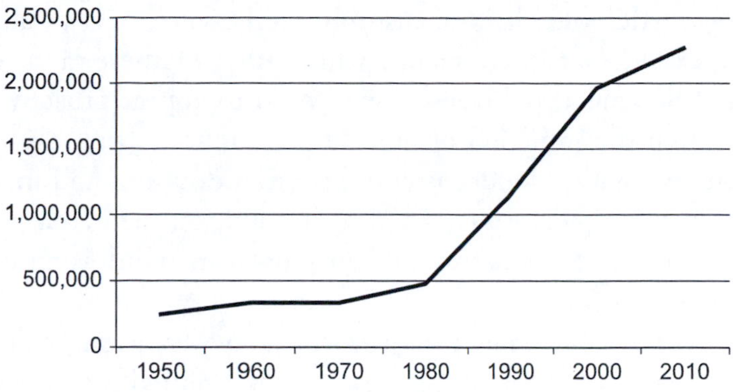

Figure 1 Number of Prisoners in U.S. Prisons and Jails (1950–2010).
Source: 1950–2000, Justice Policy Institute analysis of U.S. Department of Justice data. Available online at http://www.justicepolicy.org/images/upload/00-05_rep_punishingdecade_ac.pdf; 2010, Bureau of Justice Statistics.

> correctional control. That whopping figure is more than the populations of Chicago, Philadelphia, San Diego and Dallas put together, and larger than the populations of 38 states and the District of Columbia. During Ronald Reagan's first term as president, 1 in every 77 adults was under the control of the correctional system in the United States. Now, 25 years later, it is 1 in 31, or 3.2 percent of all adults.
>
> (Pew Center 2009: 5)

But numbers are only part of the story. In order to understand life behind bars today, we must also confront the broader social and ideological changes that have occurred outside of prison walls that brought us to this point of **mass imprisonment.** Sykes was writing just a little over a decade after the prosecution of the Nazi regime in the Nuremburg trials. During this time countries all across the globe were questioning governmental power in general and the inhumanity of prisons in particular. How could an institution that was fundamental to carrying out the genocide of the Jews remain in societies committed to the preservation of human dignity?

In contrast, we revisit this classic work at a historical moment when the dominant approach to crime and punishment is very different. Beginning in the late 1960s, the United States launched a "war on crime" that persists into the present day. In addition to filling our nation's prisons beyond capacity, this proverbial "war" has prompted a sea change in the dominant U.S. ideology regarding crime and punishment. Since passage of the Safe Streets Act of 1968, politicians have sought to portray themselves as tougher on crime than their political opponents, thus engendering public punitiveness and support for harsh penal sanctions (Beckett 1997). In the decades that followed, what emerged was a narrow focus on "getting tough" on crime. Laws and policies of the era such as California's infamous "Three Strikes" law and New York's "Rockefeller Drug Laws" are two poignant examples. Both imposed often extremely harsh sentences under the dubious claim of ensuring public safety.[3] As a leading sociologist of punishment David Garland explains, while most of these laws were passed in response to what became a "politically urgent need to appear proactive on crime the end result was often the infliction of punishment alone… [the] capacity to control future crime, though always loudly asserted, is often doubtful and in any case is less important than their immediate ability to enact public sentiment, to provide an instant response, to function as a retaliatory measure that can stand as an achievement in itself" (Garland 2002: 133).

Reverberations of this increasingly punitive ideology were unsurprisingly felt behind bars as well and have had an enduring legacy in the United States. After traditional penological goals such as rehabilitation were deemed "soft on crime," a central objective has been what criminologist Todd Clear aptly calls **penal harm.** Rather than imprisonment serving only retributive ends, a movement to make prison *more* painful has gained traction in recent years. As Craig Haney cogently observes:

> Policies of mass imprisonment and the widespread use of "warehouse" prisons have shifted the terms of the debate over the effects of incarceration from whether and how prisons can achieve the elusive goal of rehabilitation to how much debilitation they bringabout. As the "nothing works" movement of the 1970s gave way to the era of "penal harm" in the decades that followed, the severe pains of imprisonment were not only taken for granted but explicitly welcomed in many circles.
>
> (Haney 2012)

An additional key to understanding changes in the treatment of prisoners in contemporary penal institutions in the United States is the increasingly common use of the prison as a site of oppression. It is important to keep in mind that the rise of a harsh punitive ideology took place alongside a divisive politics of racial backlash in the United States (Gottschalk 2006). The war on crime was launched at the end of the **Civil Rights Movement** when the Republican Party began courting disillusioned Southern Whites, channeling their open racial hostility into a racially coded rhetoric of quelling "inner city" "street crime" and protecting "suburban" "public safety." George H.W. Bush's infamous "Willie Horton ad," which depicted his presidential opponent, Michael Dukakis, as "soft on crime" juxtaposed with the scowling face of Horton, a Black male, alongside the words "rape," "kidnap," and "murder" is perhaps the most infamous example in recent decades. What one commentator has called the

3 For two compelling journalistic accounts of how otherwise petty offenders were subject to extremely harsh punishments as a result of the wars on crime and drugs, see Gonnerman (2004) and Abramsky (2002).

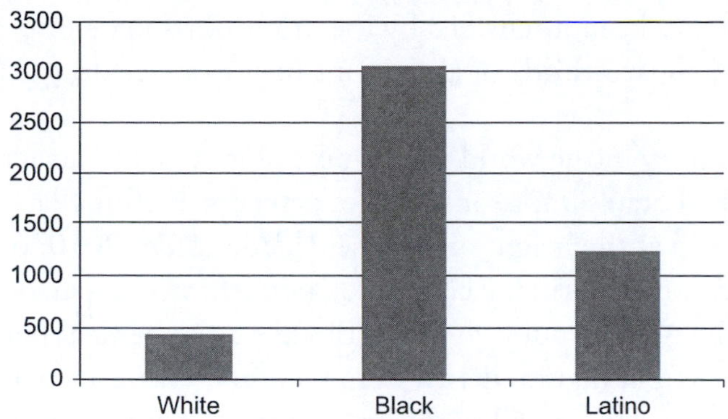

Figure 2 U.S. Male Rate of Incarceration per 100,000 Residents by Race/Ethnicity, in 2010.
Source: Guerino, Harrison, and Sabol (2011). For more information on racial disparities in sentencing, see the Sentencing Project's Race and Justice Clearinghouse: http://www.sentencingproject.org/clearinghouse.

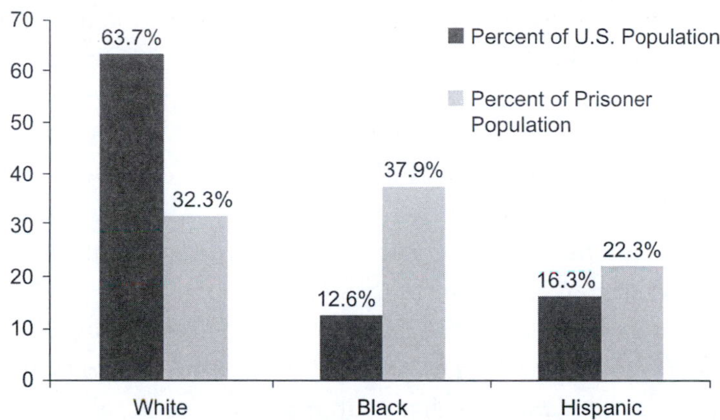

Figure 3 Total U.S. Population and Total Prison Population Percentages by Race/Ethnicity (Males and Females Included), 2010.
Source: U.S. Census Briefs (2010) and Guerino, Harrison, and Sabol (2011). "White" refers specifically to non-Hispanic Whites in both sets of data. Those identifying with groups other than White, Black, and Hispanic are excluded here because such data was unavailable in the Bureau of Justice Statistics report upon which we relied.

"Hortonization" of the U.S. criminal justice system has grossly impacted impoverished people of color (Anderson 1995). Here again, the numbers speak for themselves (see also Figures 2 and 3):

- "More young (20 to 34-year-old) Black men without a high school diploma or GED are currently behind bars (37 percent) than employed (26 percent)" (Pew Center 2010: 4).
- "More than 60 percent of the people in prison are now racial and ethnic minorities. For Black males in their thirties, 1 in every 10 is in prison or jail on any given day.

These trends have been intensified by the disproportionate impact of the "war on drugs," in which two-thirds of all persons in prison for drug offenses are people of color."[4]

- "No other country in the world imprisons so many of its racial or ethnic minorities. The United States imprisons a larger percentage of its Black population than South Africa did at the height of apartheid" (Alexander 2010: 6).
- There are far more Blacks in the U.S. prison population compared to Whites, despite (non-Hispanic) Whites outnumbering Blacks in the general population by more than a 5 to 1 margin (figures drawn from Guerino, Harrison, and Sabol 2011).
- "1 in 3 young Black men will serve time in prison if current trends continue, and in some cities more than half of all young adult Black men are currently under correctional control—in prison or jail, on probation or parole" (Alexander 2010: 9).
- "1 in 9 Black children (11.4 percent), 1 in 28 Hispanic children (3.5 percent) and 1 in 57 white children (1.8 percent) have an incarcerated parent" (Pew Center 2010: 4). This is especially significant because "Children with fathers who have been incarcerated are significantly more likely than other children to be expelled or suspended from school (23 percent compared with 4 percent)" (ibid., p. 5).

Yet these numbers also reflect something much deeper: The ideological shift toward law and order was not just about controlling "criminals." The "war on crime" was also *a war on poor Blacks*. Describing contemporary U.S. prisons as "surrogate ghettos," sociologist Loïc Wacquant persuasively argues that a primary objective of penal institutions today is to create an "organizational means for the capture and management of a population considered contemptible and expendable" (Wacquant 2009: 195). In her important book *The New Jim Crow: Mass Incarceration in the Age of Colorblindness*, Michelle Alexander similarly argues that contemporary penal policy can be seen as the latest link in a historical chain of racial oppression in the United States. For Alexander, this chain is comprised of the transition from slavery to Jim Crow segregation to what she refers to as "The New Jim Crow" of the present era. Under the New Jim Crow racial oppression has moved beyond public view into our nation's prisons and jails. From this perspective, Alexander argues that mass incarceration is more than indicative of a biased criminal justice system; it represents the re-emergence of **racial caste**:

> In ghetto communities, nearly everyone is either directly or indirectly subject to the new caste system. The system serves to redefine the terms of the relationship of poor people of color and their communities to mainstream, white society, ensuring their subordinate and marginal status. The criminal and civil sanctions that were once

4 For an informative overview of racial disparity and sentencing policy in the United States, see the Sentencing Project's website here: http://www.sentencingproject.org/template/page.cfm?id=122.

> reserved for a tiny minority are now used to control and oppress a racially defined majority in many communities, and the systemic manner in which the control is achieved reflects not just a difference in scale. The nature of the criminal justice system has changed. It is no longer concerned primarily with the prevention and punishment of crime, but rather with the management and control of the dispossessed. Prior drug wars were ancillary to the prevailing caste system. This time the drug war *is* the system of control (Alexander 2010: 183, emphasis in original).

We concur with Alexander that mass imprisonment is a system built upon racial oppression. Coupling this insight with the realization that the prison is a site where differential power relationships are especially pronounced serves as the starting point for our exploration into contemporary conditions of confinement. While Sykes ended his book with a call for prison reform, declaring that the "authoritarian community of the prison does not need to be a harshly repressive one" (Sykes 2007: 133), we argue that in the context of the rise of penal harm and the emergence of the criminal justice system as a tool of oppression, precisely the *opposite* has occurred. In stark contrast to a negotiated order between officers and prisoners that Sykes documented in his classic account, we contend that prison life today can more accurately be understood as a form of *penal oppression*. In other words, prison life today is characterized by the assertion of dominance over marginalized groups in a setting where imbalances of power are especially pronounced and opportunities for meaningful resistance are dramatically curtailed.

We should note that while Blacks have borne the brunt of mass incarceration, oppression takes place along multiple, intersecting axes such as gender, class, nationality, and ability. To that end, our conception of penal oppression encompasses oppression as it manifests in various forms. Accordingly, many of the examples we present depict power being asserted by prison guards and staff against subordinate prisoners, many of whom have social identities that reflect their multiple and overlapping positions of marginality. For example, although representing a small percentage of the prison population, women—especially poor women of color—have increasingly been ensnared by the wars on crime and drugs and find themselves often violently oppressed in the hyper-masculine environment of the prison (see Chapter IV, and see e.g., Levi and Waldman 2011). Immigrants, especially Latinos/as, have likewise been detained at alarming rates in recent years and thus subjected to many of the harsh conditions we describe throughout this book (see e.g., Dow 2005). Opportunities for upward mobility for impoverished members of the U.S. population have also been thwarted (Pew Center 2010). Indeed, under mass imprisonment many are now part of a system of exploited prison labor that has exploded behind bars (see Chapter III). It is also important to understand how mass imprisonment in the United States has been exported into military prisons in Afghanistan and Iraq (Huq and Muller 2008: 215–29). We explore this line of inquiry in Chapter V to show how normal the brutalization of prisoners in the United States has become.

Plan of the Book: Revisiting Sykes's "*Pains of Imprisonment*"

In revisiting Sykes's account, we use as a jumping off point his inventory of the "**pains of imprisonment**"—those "deprivations or frustrations of the modern prison... [that] can be just as painful as the physical maltreatment which they have replaced" (Sykes 2007: 64). Sykes identified five pains in particular which a consensus of prisoners he interviewed declared were especially troubling and posed "profound threats to the inmate's personality or sense of personal worth." The first is the **deprivation of liberty**, in which the prisoner experiences limitations on the "freedom of movement" and loses contact with those in the outside world. The second is the **deprivation of goods and services**, where the experience of the prison's "harshly Spartan environment... [is defined as] painfully depriving." The third and fourth "pains" on Sykes's list were the **deprivation of heterosexual relationships** and the **deprivation of autonomy.** He described how heterosexual male prisoners lose their sense of self-concept by identifying only with men and how the rigidity of prison life "reduce[s] the prisoner to the weak, helpless, dependent status of childhood." Finally, when Sykes discusses the **deprivation of security**, he is referring to the inherent dangerousness of the prison environment, captured well by the line of one of his interviewees: "the worst thing about prison is you have to live with other prisoners."

In considering some of the most disturbing changes the system has undergone in this era of penal harm, we quickly realized that Sykes's original inventory remains relevant, but that the specific pains he identified have clearly been exacerbated. To that end, we have developed a new inventory that is both a complement to and a departure from Sykes. These ***pains of mass imprisonment*** include: **containment**, **exploitation**, **coercion**, **isolation**, and **brutality** (see Table 1 to see how this conception contrasts with Sykes's classic "pains of imprisonment"). We arrive at our new inventory based on the following developments:

- As opposed to focusing on more traditional penological goals such as rehabilitation, the prerogative of prisons today is aggressive **incapacitation**. In this way, the deprivation of liberty has been exacerbated in the contemporary era, amounting to what can more accurately be described as *containment.*
- Beyond having to endure what amounts to forced poverty (i.e., the deprivation of goods and services), today's prisoners must cope with a massive for-profit prison industry that routinely *exploits* them for financial profits by, for example, making them engage in low-wage labor under often dangerous conditions.
- Sykes's extensive observations of the New Jersey State Prison and interviews with those imprisoned there illustrate a lack of access to sexual relationships; yet today with the recent explosion of the number of women behind bars, we have witnessed a crisis of prisoner sexual abuse as female prisoners find themselves subjected to widespread sexualized *coercion* by their male captors.

Table 1 The Pains of Imprisonment: Then and Now

Sykes's "Pains of Imprisonment"	*"The Pains of Mass Imprisonment"*
The Deprivation of Liberty—the prisoner is confronted with limited mobility and an inability to keep in contact with family and friends	**Containment**—prisoners are treated as objects in a warehouse; basic human needs (e.g., health care, contact with friends and relatives) become secondary to incapacitation
The Deprivation of Goods and Services—the self-image of the prisoner is harmed by conditions of forced poverty	**Exploitation**—prisoners are used for the financial benefit of their captors; this includes forced prison labor, charging exuberant rates for basic goods and services, and the commodification of prisoners
The Deprivation of Heterosexual Relationships—heterosexual male prisoners are forced into involuntary celibacy	**Coercion**—female prisoners are forced to engage in sexual relations with male guards through the use of force or intimidation
The Deprivation of Autonomy—guards treat prisoners like children, denying them the ability to make their own choices and subjecting them to arbitrary decisions	**Isolation**—often arbitrary decisions made by prison staff commonly force prisoners into conditions where they are deprived of all human contact and sensory stimuli
The Deprivation of Security—prisoners live in constant fear of being the victims of violence committed by other prisoners	**Brutality**—prisoners live with the potential of being the victims of violence committed by their captors and risk retaliation for exposing such violence

- Whereas being deprived of autonomy once entailed being reduced to the "weak, helpless, dependent status of childhood" (ibid., p. 75), mass imprisonment has wrought a far more aggressive focus on the *isolation* of exorbitant numbers of prisoners in the brutal conditions of solitary confinement, utterly stripping away the humanity of many prisoners.
- The potentially violent behavior of other prisoners once encompassed the deprivation of security, but today is compounded as prisoners are subjected to numerous forms of prison guard *brutality*.

Subsequent chapters are organized around our updated inventory as presented in Table 1. We also include a concluding chapter entitled "Desperation" that reflects upon the fleeting ability of prisoners to endure such brutal confinement. We explore each of these pains through the experiences of actual prisoners, and include in each chapter graphic vignettes that capture prisoners' experiences in vivid and often disturbing detail. We do this by drawing from various reports and legal briefs assembled by prisoner rights and prison legal aid groups such as the *Center for Constitutional Rights, Equal Justice Initiative, Florida Justice Institute, Human Rights Coalition, Human Rights Watch, Juvenile Law Center, Prison Activist Resource Center, Prison Law Office,* the *Sentencing Project,* and the *Southern Center for Human Rights.* We also turn to a number of important pieces of investigative journalism that have exposed widespread atrocities behind bars.

What follows is by no means a "replication" of Sykes's empirical study of a single maximum security prison in New Jersey in the early 1950s. Alternatively, we draw on an admittedly small sampling from an imposing body of secondary materials collected in the more than half-century since the publication of *The Society of Captives*. Such materials paint a disturbing picture of what life behind bars is like today, an observation that is further bolstered by relevant empirical literature we draw on throughout. The combination of these materials enables the reader to see that the stories we present are more than "war stories." Indeed, we believe each chapter illuminates prisons today as both viscerally and systemically more painful institutions.

DISCUSSION QUESTIONS

1. What are some of the major changes the U.S. prison system has undergone in this era of mass imprisonment?
2. How are broader social inequalities relevant for understanding what the authors call "penal oppression"?
3. How does the authors' conflict approach (e.g., a focus on penal oppression) differ from Sykes's functionalist analysis of life behind bars?
4. How do the classic pains of imprisonment differ from what the authors call the pains of mass imprisonment? In what ways are they similar?

I: Containment

For Sykes, how prisoners experience the deprivation of liberty involves two fundamental aspects. The first is restricted mobility. Not only is the prisoner unable to travel beyond the confines of the institution, but "his freedom of movement is further confined by a strict system of passes, the military formations in moving from one point within the institution to another, and the demand that he remain in his cell until given permission to do otherwise" (Sykes 2007: 65). In other words, "the prisoner's loss of liberty is a double one—first, by confinement to the institution and second, by confinement within the institution" (ibid.).

Yet Sykes believed the restriction of movement was ultimately less painful than the *social* isolation that prisoners endure. Obviously, prisoners are separated from their friends and family, "but what makes this pain of imprisonment bite most deeply is the fact that the confinement of the criminal represents a deliberate, moral rejection of the criminal from the free community" (ibid.). However, one of the limitations of Sykes's observation is a rather narrow conception of "community." As he later recognized in a rejoinder to the 50th anniversary edition of the *Society of Captives*:

> First, sociologists writing about the prison in the 1950s were almost exclusively white, and I suspect this helped to shape not only the range of their concerns but also their ability to establish relationships of trust with black inmates. And second, there was an assumption that the social systems of black and white inmates—and their relationship with the power structure of the prison—were essentially the same. (ibid., p. 144)

Despite these obvious limitations, we believe Sykes's fundamental insight of the especially painful separation of prisoners from family and their communities remains important in the current era. This is especially pronounced in the lives of poor, urban prisoners of color. Such prisoners not only may be barred from seeing their children as a matter of more restrictive visitation policies (as we examine below), but are isolated by the very fact that they are confined disproportionately in inaccessible rural penal institutions (Hulling 2002).

Both the restriction of movement and the severing of social ties are essential for understanding the deprivation of liberty as it is manifest in U.S. prisons today. In the decades since *The Society of Captives* was published, the restriction of movement is found to be a *very* serious problem in the nation's prisons.[1] The sheer number of prisoners incarcerated has led to a movement away from a proactive approach to corrections that, at least in theory, attends to the well-being of prisoners (e.g., a rehabilitation model) and toward a reactive model that focuses narrowly on *containment*. As legal scholar and political scientist Jonathan Simon describes it, the underlying penological goal in the era of mass imprisonment is *social waste management*:

> The distinctive new form and function of the prison today is a space of pure custody, a human warehouse or even a kind of social waste management facility, where adults and some juveniles distinctive only for their dangerousness are concentrated for purposes of protecting the wider community. The waste management prison promises no transformation of the prisoner through penitence, discipline, intimidation, or therapy.
>
> (Simon 2007: 142)

Penal oppression is apparent in the sense that disproportionately Black and Latino/a prisoners, many of whom are aging, mentally ill, or suffering from life-threatening illnesses, are warehoused and denied movement in unprecedented ways. Their ability to remain connected to friends, family, and society more generally is also inhibited and may have serious repercussions (e.g., the separation of a prisoner who is a mother from her child). In this chapter, we investigate both of these consequences of containment. We begin with investigation of prison health care and then turn to the impact of increasingly restrictive family visitation policies.

Prisoner First, Patient Second

In late November of 1997, Marciano Plata took a horrible fall in the kitchen. The tumble was so bad that he tore ligaments in his right knee. As he writhed in pain on the cold floor, others in the kitchen helped him up. But the pain was so intense he felt dizzy. Given the seriousness of his injury, one would have expected that Marciano would have been rushed to a hospital emergency room. Indeed, even people without health insurance can receive treatment, and Medicaid will cover much, if not all, of the hospital bills. As a prisoner at the massively overcrowded, disproportionately Black and Hispanic Salinas Valley State Prison at Soledad, California, however, Marciano Plata did not receive emergency care. And to confound his struggle, Marciano, who speaks little English, was not provided with a translator.

Several hours had gone by before Marciano was seen by a prison Medical Technical Assistant (MTA) who conducted only a very superficial examination of

1 For an analysis of a case involving the brutal segregation of HIV+ prisoners in Alabama and its implications for mass imprisonment in the United States more broadly, see Fleury-Steiner (2008).

Marciano, and still did not provide him with treatment nor refer him to a physician. The prison did not even provide Marciana Plata with transportation back to his cell. In what must have been a dreadfully painful slog, he walked across the prison without assistance. Back at work a month later, his damaged knee buckled again, and he crashed brutally to the floor, landing this time with an audible thud on his back and head.

Repeated injuries of this sort will eventually get you an appointment with a physician, even in prison. Marciano's X-rays revealed an injury to the meniscus, a ball of cartilage in the knee that acts as a literal shock absorber. The physician gave Marciano a low dose of Motrin and ordered him to bed rest for two weeks. But lying around did no good, and the over-the-counter medication did little to relieve his pain. Marciano finally could take no more and hobbled desperately to the prison medical clinic where an MTA subsequently denied him treatment, telling him frankly, "there's nothing we can do."

Despite having weeks to go before his reexamination, Marciano was ordered back to work by a correctional officer. Barely able to stand, a predictably dreadful chain of events occurred. After making just a slight movement, a searing back spasm caused Marciano to double over in pain as his knee buckled and he once again crashed violently onto the floor. This time fellow prisoners took Marciano in a wheelchair to the prison medical clinic. But upon arrival, rather than seeing a physician, he was met by a correctional officer who informed him that no doctor was on duty. The officer summarily ordered Marciano to return to his cell.

It is difficult to comprehend the pain he must have endured, but Marciano went another full month without seeing a physician again. During this time, his condition did not improve. A victim of the prison's grossly understaffed medical system, Marciano was cast adrift without any treatment. Finally, a doctor agreed to see him after several months and he was sent to a local community hospital for arthroscopic surgery.

Such a procedure requires post-operative care to heal properly. Yet 24 hours later, prison staff transported Marciano back to the prison infirmary where corrections officers, unaware of the extent of his injury, required him to walk on his surgically repaired knee. This predictably caused him extreme pain and more swelling. Ultimately, despite filing numerous formal grievances with the prison, Marciano went several years without post-operative care.

Otis Shaw's experience with prison health care has been similarly painful. In April of 2000, approximately two weeks after he had a procedure to have a plastic tube surgically implanted in his arm, not a single physician attended to Otis. Suffering from a debilitating kidney disease called end-stage renal failure that requires dialysis, Otis, like Marciano Plata, would go weeks without receiving meaningful post-operative care. As a prisoner at California's infamous San Quentin Prison, prison staff instead left him for days in an unsanitary cell in the prison's infirmary. Shaw filed a formal grievance charging the prison with the failure to provide adequate medical care. Several weeks later, Otis Shaw learned that the prison had formally rejected his complaint. Shaw then did the only thing he could do: he cleaned his wound and changed the bandages himself, but because of the wound's location on his upper arm, it was impossible for him to use both hands to perform the dressing competently.

The infected wound continued to ooze and Otis continued to file formal complaints against the prison. Prison authorities rendered no decision. Instead, guards placed Otis Shaw in San Quentin's notoriously brutal Administrative Segregation Unit. In an act of brazen retaliation, Otis went without dialysis treatment as prison officials virtually left him to waste away. His condition worsened and he nearly lost his life. Fortunately, after many months of neglect, Otis Shaw finally received post-operative care for his wound and underwent dialysis treatment. (The source material used to construct this vignette comes from the Prison Law Office's original complaint in the *Brown v. Plata* case, which also named Otis Shaw and other prisoner plaintiffs. Accessed online at http://www.prisonlaw.com/pdfs/Medcomplaint.pdf).

****

Containing Prisoners in Pain

A primary reason for the dangerously reactive model of prison health care illustrated by the cases above and characteristic of prisons across the country (Fleury-Steiner 2008: 177–80) is a gross lack of staffing and resources. In this way, sick prisoners are left to the mercy of untrained correctional officers whose job is not to care for patients but to keep prisoners contained. This is so because the correctional officer is part of an organization whose primary mission is one of security of the captive institution above all else. Such a dangerously narrow approach has profoundly inhumane consequences for prisoners with serious medical conditions. As Nancy Stoller, a sociologist who has conducted extensive empirical research on contemporary prison health care settings, poignantly observes:

> Where humanistic health practice requires an acknowledgment of interconnectedness, prisons are based on principles of exclusion, separation, and confinement. Where physicians and nurses provide care and comfort to those in pain and those who are disabled, a prison system demands discipline and the stripping of identity, possessions, affection, and touch. And where medicine attempts to provide cure and management of disease, the primary goal of 21st century corrections (despite the implications of training and rehabilitation in the word "correction") is typically detention and punishment.
>
> (Stoller 2003: 2265)

In the case of Marciano Plata, he must obey the orders of the correctional officer in order to move, even if that movement means putting immensely *painful* weight on a surgically repaired knee. His status as prisoner outstrips his needs as patient. Otis Shaw is likewise denied critical care for a serious kidney disease. With the prison's narrow focus on containment, he finds himself initially abandoned in a woefully deficient and unsanitary prison medical infirmary where he must struggle to care for himself. And then this man with a life-threatening illness is literally trapped in administrative segregation (a condition we explore in more detail in Chapter IV "Isolation"), is forced to endure a horribly infected wound on his arm, and is denied dialysis treatment.

Marciano Plata's and Otis Shaw's experiences illuminate how restricted movement has become a disturbingly *normal* pain of contemporary imprisonment. In California, the cases of Plata and Shaw represented the plight of prisoners throughout the system as they were named plaintiffs in perhaps the most sweeping prisoner rights lawsuit ever to appear before the U.S. Supreme Court. The decision rendered in *Brown v. Plata* (2011) provides a graphic view into how the restriction of movement is a crisis indicative of the entire California prison system. These examples are precisely what we mean when we talk about containment as one of the most extreme and pervasive pains of imprisonment:

- A shortage of treatment beds led to the confinement of seriously mentally ill prisoners in "telephone-booth sized cages" that do not have sinks or toilets.
- California's prisons were designed to meet the medical needs of a population at 100 percent of design capacity and so have only half the clinical space needed to treat the current population. One correctional officer testified that up to 50 sick inmates may be held together in a 12 × 20ft cage for up to five hours awaiting treatment.
- In many instances, prisoners with life-threatening ailments in captive institutions across the state would go *more than a year* without seeing a physician.
- A survey of prisoner deaths by an outside physician concluded that extreme departures from the standard of care were "widespread" and that the proportion of "possibly preventable or preventable" deaths was "extremely high" in California's prisons.

Each of these horrifying findings highlights how a focus on containment leads to dangerous and sometimes deadly consequences for prisoners with serious health problems. And when we consider the extent to which the prison population is aging and suffering from mental illness, we see more clearly the extent of this problem. According to a recent Human Rights Watch report entitled *Old Behind Bars*, "[b]etween 1995 and 2010, the number of state and federal prisoners age 55 or older nearly quadrupled (increasing 282 percent), while the number of all prisoners grew by less than half (increasing 42 percent)." There are now 124,400 state and federal prisoners age 55 and older; 26,200 are over 65 (Human Rights Watch 2012). In short:

> Prisons in the United States contain an ever growing number of aging men and women who cannot readily climb stairs, haul themselves to the top bunk, or walk

long distances to meals or the pill line; whose old bones suffer from thin mattresses and winter's cold; who need wheelchairs, walkers, canes, portable oxygen, and hearing aids; who cannot get dressed, go to the bathroom, or bathe without help; and who are incontinent, forgetful, suffering chronic illnesses, extremely ill, and dying.

(ibid.)

A reactive containment model also raises serious questions in light of **deinstitutionalization**, the process whereby severely mentally ill people are moved from state institutions. Many such persons have found themselves in reactive prisons or jails as opposed to institutions that are focused primarily on their care. Recent estimates suggest that "approximately 10 percent of all jail and prison inmates appear to meet [the] diagnostic criteria" of mental illness. In fact, many prisons and jails now house more people who are mentally ill than mental institutions themselves. Los Angeles County Jail, for instance, "where approximately 3,300 of the 21,000 inmates require mental health services on a daily basis," is now de facto "the largest mental institution in the country" (Torrey 1997).

In light of such changes spurred by mass incarceration, the response has been a shift to the human warehousing model characterized by the containment of more people in smaller cages. In this way, the profound loss of the freedom of movement has become more than what Sykes described as a "frustration" of the individual prisoner; containment may literally mean a slow and painful death.

"It's Crucial that a Prisoner has Contact with Loved Ones"

When the Michigan Department of Corrections (MDOC) decided to restrict family visitation rights for prisoners, attorneys preparing a lawsuit brought in Dr Terry Kupers, a seasoned psychiatrist with extensive background in prisoner mental health, for consultation purposes. It was clear to Dr Kupers that dramatically restricting prisoner social relations could lead to very severe mental illnesses, including psychosis and suicide. Dr Kupers also knew that limiting prisoners' options for socialization to letters and phone calls was an unrealistic alternative to in-person visitation. For one, some 40 percent of prisoners are illiterate, and in this case, Dr Kupers suspected a more accurate illiteracy rate was more like 60 or 80 percent. From his many years of experience in the system, he believed only a very small fraction of prisoners were capable of writing a comprehensible letter to anyone. Second, he knew even functionally literate prisoners would have their letters read by prison authorities and would censor what they wrote at the risk of losing their letter-writing privileges altogether. Dr Kupers also knew from first-hand experience that there were invariably long delays in getting mail in and out of the prison.

Phone calls in prison are even more problematic. Not only is phone time very constricted behind bars, but collect calls are expensive, especially for prisoners' disproportionately low-income family members. He knew from his own observation that prisoner families would often have their phones disconnected because they could no longer afford to pay the bill. Given his knowledge and skepticism, Dr Kupers was not surprisingly emphatic in his testimony on behalf of the family visitation rights of Michigan's prisoners:

> *Separation from family is part of the function of incarceration. It's part of the function of quarantining people. Their contact with family and loved ones and friends and community is severed. The idea, then, is to restore some unity and some continuity of close bonds by having visitation. That's why, in almost every arena, visitation is required, whether it's the Department of Corrections in Michigan [or elsewhere], and their policies state that. It's crucial that a prisoner has contact with loved ones in order to maintain their stability while they're in prison, to do their program without falling apart, and then to prepare and then succeed at post release, becoming part of the community again.*

Despite this compelling testimony, the Department of Corrections put into place restrictions on visitors under the age of 18 that had enormous negative consequences for prisoners and their families. Prisoners' siblings, nieces, and nephews who had been visiting without incident could no longer see their imprisoned brothers, sisters, aunts, and uncles. Another consequence of this regulation is that prisoners' adult siblings are far less likely to visit because they cannot bring their kids. Furthermore, far fewer parents of prisoners are able to visit because they cannot bring their young grandchildren for whom they are caring—namely, the child of the prisoner. That is to say, if prisoners cannot see their parents, many of their sons and daughters are denied visitation as well.

The MDOC implemented these strict regulations in the early nineties. Only six years later, the number of family visits to prisoners in Michigan decreased by a full 50 percent. Several prisoners were also permanently *banned from family visitations under MDOC's "two strikes and you're out" ban for substance abuse violations. In practice, however, the prison implemented this draconian rule for conduct that was either relatively minor or occurred in the context of extenuating circumstances. Consider the following Michigan prisoners and the violation that resulted in the permanent loss of their family visitation rights:*

Marcos Martinez:	*Received an alcohol ticket for making homemade liquor to share with friends on New Year's Eve*
Gerald Gaines:	*Used marijuana because his mother recently died and he "was looking for escape"*

Merion Johnson:	*Used marijuana to "ease the hurt" after his mother died*
Jerold Terrell:	*Accepted an offer of drugs from another prisoner the day after a very painful cancer operation*
Andre Fountain:	*Failed to tell staff that his roommate had alcohol*
William Irby:	*Received a second misconduct for "refusing" to complete a urine screening within the allotted one hour, even though prisoner was on medication for a serious prostate condition*
Jeffrey Carey:	*Mentally ill prisoner found guilty of possessing restricted medication for spitting out prescribed medication he was authorized to refuse*
Stacy Barker:	*Prisoner had a single Motrin tablet and an expired prescription*

In defending the policy, MDOC officials admitted that while there were very few serious prisoner violations of the earlier version of the family visitation policy, large increases in Michigan's prison population coupled with insufficient staffing drove the change. As Dan Bolden, Michigan's Deputy Commissioner of Corrections, testified:

> *One of the things that we did is reduce the number [of visitors]. By reducing the number, you can better supervise those that are there. Before, we had visiting rooms that were packed elbow to elbow, and often out our front door, which made it very difficult to supervise children or anybody else. By reducing the number to a manageable number, our front desk staff can properly supervise and monitor what's going on.*

Despite Bolden's concerns, the District Court judge was not persuaded:

> *The evidence presented in this case provides an intimate look at the psychological, emotional, and physical constraints of incarceration. Visits from family and friends are one of the slender reeds sustaining prisoners during their confinement; prisoners and prison administrators rely upon the stabilizing and rehabilitative effects promoted by supportive visits. For all the reasons stated above, the visitation restrictions challenged by Plaintiffs violate the constitutional rights of Michigan's prisoners. Even under the most deferential review, these restrictions are not reasonably related to legitimate penological interests. The Court finds in favor of Plaintiffs on all claims.* (The source material used to construct this vignette comes from the U.S. District Court of Michigan 2001).

****

Containment and the Loss of Contact with Family

Only a year later, MDOC's restrictions on prisoner family visitation became the basis of the U.S. Supreme Court case, *Overton v. Bazetta* (2002), an enormous class-action lawsuit filed on behalf of Michigan's prisoners and their family members. The plaintiffs challenged the strict visitation rules as an infringement on their First Amendment freedom of association and the permanent visitation ban for substance abuse as a violation of the Eighth Amendment's prohibition on cruel and unusual punishment. In a unanimous and very brief decision, the Court overruled the lower court's opinion upholding both parts of MDOC's revised family visitation policy as constitutional:

> The very object of imprisonment is confinement. Many of the liberties and privileges enjoyed by other citizens must be surrendered by the prisoner. An inmate does not retain rights inconsistent with proper incarceration ... And, as our cases have established, freedom of association is among the rights least compatible with incarceration. Some curtailment of that freedom must be expected in the prison context.

Nowhere in the Court's opinion do they evaluate Dr Kupers's testimony nor any of the arbitrarily imposed permanent bans described above. This is all the more distressing when one considers that the experience of Michigan's prisoners is not unique. The sheer amount of children who have incarcerated parents is staggering. According to a Bureau of Justice Statistics (BJS) report, "Incarcerated Parents and their Children," "[i]n 2007, 1.7 million children had a parent in prison, more than 70 percent of whom were children of color" (Mumola 2000). This translates to one in 43 children having a parent in prison and one in 15 Black children having an incarcerated parent. It also represents an 82 percent increase in children with incarcerated parents since 1991. Despite the glaring numbers, the report adds that:

- Fewer than half of incarcerated parents in state prisons *ever* see their children in person.
- Of those who do see their children, approximately 20 percent have visits at least once a month.
- Approximately half of incarcerated mothers and 40 percent of fathers in state prisons make monthly phone calls.

An imposing body of research demonstrates the detrimental consequences of the above findings. Studies of state prisoners show that children who are separated from their parents are more likely to suffer negative consequences. (For a comprehensive overview, see Eddy and Poehlmann 2010). As Nell Bernstein observes in *All Alone in the World: Children of the Incarcerated*:

> The children of prisoners are likely to bounce from one caregiver to another; to have and to cause trouble in school. Often poor to begin with, they get poorer once a

> parent is arrested. As many as half of all boys whose parents do time will wind up behind bars themselves—a formula that virtually guarantees one generation's prison boom will feed and fuel the next.
>
> (Bernstein 2007: x)

While Sykes may be correct in his observation that what makes separation from family and friends "bite most deeply is the fact that the confinement of the criminal represents a deliberate moral rejection of the criminal by the free community" (Sykes 2007: 65), it is clear that in this age of mass imprisonment the impact goes far beyond individual prisoners. When considering the enormity of these consequences as Bernstein does above, it also becomes clear that prisoners surrender their liberty not because of any "penological goal" related to transforming the prisoner. Harsh restrictions on family visitation only inflame an already painful situation. In other words, the systemic embrace of the unprovoked containment of prisoners—a bloodless waste management strategy—is obvious in the approaches to custody in both California and Michigan. Indeed, containment is one of the most insidious characteristics of contemporary imprisonment that is not easily separated from the other pains of mass imprisonment we describe throughout this book. In today's human warehouses, the aggressive containment of prisoners results in needless physical suffering, social strain, and family dissolution.

Conclusion

In this era of mass imprisonment, prison systems hyper-focus on warehousing and containment of huge prison populations. These prerogatives, we have shown, have come to override the basic humanitarian principle of treating those who are sick.[2] The consequence of this is needless suffering and death. In the case of prisoners who are parents, a sweeping focus on containment has meant protracted or permanent loss of contact with family members—a policy that has serious consequences, especially in communities of color, not only for the well-being of prisoners but also for their loved ones, including young children who desperately need their contact. In the next chapter, we explore prison labor and other profit-motivated strategies employed in prisons today, revealing how, in a slight twist on the human warehouse concept, prisons also serve as "factories with fences"[3] that exploit human bodies for profit in a system that amounts to de facto slavery.

2 For an analysis of how prison health care in an era of penal harm violates medical ethics, in particular the Hippocratic Oath, see Vaughn and Smith (1999).

3 This phrase was first used in a government publication promoting prison labor. The report may be accessed online at http://www.unicor.gov/information/publications/pdfs/corporate/CATMC1101_C.pdf.

DISCUSSION QUESTIONS

1. What do the authors mean by human warehousing?
2. How does the prison-as-human-warehouse model limit prisoner mobility and access to social relationships?
3. Do you think prisoner rehabilitation is possible in institutions that practice human warehousing? For that matter, do you think rehabilitation is possible under mass imprisonment?
4. Prisons are constructed in such a way that prisoners are "sealed off" from society. Yet it is hard to deny that the treatment of prisoners has effects beyond prison walls. In light of the discussion in this chapter, can you identify some of the other "collateral costs" of human warehousing?

II: Exploitation

Sykes's second "pain of imprisonment," the deprivation of goods and services, refers to how the material conditions of imprisonment adversely affect the self-image of the prisoner. He acknowledged that prisoners' *basic* needs are often met. However, Sykes was also well aware that the prisoner "wants—needs, if you will—not just the so-called necessities of life but also the amenities: cigarettes and liquor as well as calories, interesting foods as well as sheer bulk, individual clothing as well as adequate clothing, individual furnishings for his living quarters as well as shelter, privacy as well as space" (Sykes 2007: 68). In a culture which places such a high value on material possessions, "to be stripped of them is [thus] to be attacked at the deepest layers of personality," he wrote (ibid., p. 69), because these items play an essential role in defining who we are. The logo on your shirt, the picture on your wall, the pedestal resting in your living room: all of these items contribute to your sense of identity. Without them, you feel worthless. And this worthlessness is exacerbated, Sykes said, when the prisoner is told that his or her own inadequacy is the reason for such deprivation.

Today, while impoverishment may indeed "[remain] as one of the most bitter attacks on the individual's self-image that our society has to offer" (ibid., p. 70), Sykes could not have possibly predicted that "as prisons proliferate in U.S. society, private capital [would] become enmeshed in the punishment industry" (Davis 1998). In other words, with the emergence of what has been termed a **prison industrial complex**—a network of companies, politicians, and bureaucrats who benefit financially and otherwise from mass imprisonment and, as a result, play a key role in maintaining it by influencing policy—prisoners today are not merely deprived of goods and services but *exploited* for the financial gain of others. At the time Sykes was writing, forced prison labor was more or less in remission and prison privatization had not yet begun (Sentencing Project 2012). It was not until the recent prison boom began about three decades ago that sweeping prison policy would be driven by the primary goal of financial profit. As scholar and anti-prison activist Angela Davis describes it:

> When prisons disappear human beings in order to convey the illusion of solving social problems, penal infrastructures must be created to accommodate a rapidly swelling population of caged people.... All this work, which used to be the primary province of government, is now also performed by private corporations, whose links to government in the field of what is euphemistically called "corrections" resonate

dangerously with the military industrial complex. The dividends that accrue from investment in the punishment industry, like those that accrue from investment in weapons production, only amount to social destruction. Taking into account the structural similarities and profitability of business–government linkages in the realms of military production and public punishment, the expanding penal system can now be characterized as a "prison industrial complex."

(Davis 1998)

Prisoners today suffer more than the severe boredom that accompanies a non-voluntary minimalistic lifestyle. The modern-day iteration of the deprivation of goods and services amounts to penal oppression in that wealth is literally extracted from often already-impoverished prisoners as they toil in dangerous jobs for minimal pay, are charged exorbitant rates for basic services, and, perhaps most disturbingly of all, traded as commodities in the private prison market. All of this happens as prisoners are told that their own inadequacy is the reason for their suffering. After examining two case studies on the exploitation of prison labor, we will explore each of these aspects of the prison industrial complex, in turn.

"A Cocktail of Hazardous Chemicals"

Adam[1] *is a prisoner employed by UNICOR, a government-owned corporation created in the 1930s with the intent of reducing prison idleness. He works in its e-waste recycling program. Every day, thousands of electronic devices—computers, televisions, stereos, cell phones—become obsolete and are discarded. Each contains many recyclable precious materials as well as a "cocktail of hazardous chemicals" (Center for Environmental Health et al. 2006: 4), such as mercury, cadmium, PVC, and lead. Cognizant of these chemical hazards, many states have banned electronics from landfills. Lead in particular makes up about one-fifth of the glass in many computer and television monitors and can have devastating effects on the nervous system, the cardiovascular system, and the kidneys. Adam, in short, works a dangerous and highly toxic job.*

Yet he is often left in the dark about the specific dangers posed by the materials he deals with on a daily basis, and requests for such information often provoke threats from prison staff. "I and other inmates asked for [Material Safety Data Sheet information]," Adam explains, "but each time we did we were given the implied threat that, 'This job is a voluntary one. If you are not happy here, you can quit,' meaning, 'Shut up. Don't ask us for anything. Do your job or we'll replace you by pushing you out or forcibly retiring you.'" In one instance, Adam's co-workers were posting information they received about the hazards of their job on a bulletin board, only to have the information ripped down by prison staff who threatened to sanction anyone posting educational literature.

1 This is a pseudonym.

Information is not the only thing withheld from Adam and his co-workers. Prison e-waste recyclers also find themselves deprived of the proper tools and protections necessary to conduct this hazardous work safely. Improper tools increase the risk of exposure to dangerous chemicals and improper protection has resulted in a multitude of injuries. Adam explains how prisoners dangerously adapt to the problem of having inadequate tools as he describes the process of opening a monitor case:

> *To get around this problem, we must do one or two things: hit the [monitor] case with the small, ineffective hammer in the general area of where the screw holds the case to the inner screw stanchions, or misuse the air-gun to 'drill' the plastic away from the screw/stanchion area to free the case. This can/does cause MANY problems: the plastic can break and/or shatter, which releases dust/particles into the air, or we can accidently break the lead-encased glass CRT. NOT good. If we 'drill' the case, fumes are caused by the heat/friction; thus we smell the toxic fumes as we try to open up each monitor case.*

UNICOR employees have nothing to protect themselves from these dangerous particles released into the air. The long-term health implications of this are undoubtedly serious, and many prisoners are already experiencing adverse health effects. As Adam explains further:

> *Even when I wear the paper mask, I blow out black mucus from my nose every day… The black particles in my nose and throat look as if I am a heavy smoker who works uncovered in a coal mine and who just made it through a house fire inhalation… Cuts and bruises happen all the time. Of these, the open wounds are exposed to the dirt and dust, and many do not heal as quickly as normal wounds. I and other inmates have noticed increased sinus problems, scratchy throats, headaches, unexplained fatigue, and burning skin, eyes, noses, and throats… We can get bandages, but all we get to clean an injured area with is cold water and 20 mule team Boraxo soap.*

Because he is a prisoner, the many government regulations that assure fair treatment and safe working conditions do not apply to prison e-waste recyclers such as Adam. They are exempt, for example, from the Fair Labor Standards Act of 1938 (FLSA), which, among other things, promises workers a minimum wage. UNICOR employees can expect to earn only between $0.23 and $1.15 per hour. Granted, this is higher than the $0.12 and $0.40 per hour usually made in prison maintenance jobs, but that is the point: prisoners who owe restitution fees and need to buy basic items from the ***prison commissary*** *have little choice but to chase these slightly higher wages. The same tactic is used by sweatshops all over the world. UNICOR as a result profits greatly and is able to offer products at prices against which companies not* *relying on captive labor and abiding by safety regulations cannot compete. David,*[2] *a fellow prison e-waste recycler explains:*

> *You might be asking why I would continue to work in this glass department knowing I had been poisoned. The reasons are simple. UNICOR pays the best you can get here… Also I have restitution the court has ordered me to pay. So you see for every dollar UNICOR pays me they automatically take a dollar. I earn $100 they take $50. I live on $50 a month, soap, shampoo, toothpaste… wham, and it's gone. Prison is not a good place to be without even a modest amount of [money and] UNICOR exploits this; they always tell us you want to complain about the work conditions, quit, it's an all-volunteer workforce, nobody is forced to work in UNICOR* (The source material used to construct this vignette comes from the report entitled Toxic Sweatshops compiled by the Center for Environmental Health in collaboration with other organizations. Accessed online at http://www.ceh.org/storage/documents/toxicsweatshops.pdf.)

****

"New Slavery" on the Shores of Louisiana

In April of 2010, BP's Deepwater Horizon wellhead gushed an estimated 17 to 39 million gallons of oil into the Gulf of Mexico. Wildlife became drenched in petroleum and oil spattered miles upon miles of Louisiana's sandy shore. In the days following the disaster, cleanup workers were spotted on the beaches wearing garb identifying them as "Inmate Labor;" a group of prisoners whose identities are hidden under a company-imposed gag rule.

Deference to the demands of private industry seeking to profit off mass imprisonment in Louisiana has become a ubiquitous feature of the state's penal landscape (Chang 2012). These prison clean-up workers are nearly all Black. Indeed, in Louisiana nearly one in seven Blacks are under criminal justice supervision in the state (ibid.). Of those fortunate enough to receive work release, they are aggressively driven into unforgiving, punishing employment routines that involve 72-hour workweeks for what amounts to slave wages.

The BP contract is perhaps the crown jewel of Louisiana's robust for-profit prison industry. Despite the fact that oil cleanup might arguably be the most dangerous job in the United States—indeed, "the chemicals in crude oil can damage every system in the body, as well as cell structure and DNA" (Young 2010)—Louisiana's captive cleanup crews get paid practically nothing. They also have no right to unionize, and complaining or refusing to accept a work assignment only puts them in jeopardy of losing "good time" credits or facing additional penal sanctions. At the same time, as the new slavery in Louisiana plunders

2 This is a pseudonym.

onward in its oil-contaminated sands, little has been done to help massive unemployment among fishermen and shrimpers, a group of workers whose livelihoods have taken a major hit as the result of what appears to be BP's catastrophic negligence. (The source material used to construct this vignette comes from Young 2010).

****

Exploiting Prison Labor

Prison labor is often defended on the grounds that it is rehabilitative (e.g., "a little work might actually do prisoners some good"). Or it is framed as an instance of state generosity and unearned privilege (e.g., "prisoners are fortunate to be working outside prison walls while so many law-abiding U.S. citizens are out of work"). However, when we consider the rise of an enormous prison industrial complex, such claims only serve to divert our attention from the extent to which enormous profits are being made on the backs of exploited prisoners. Employment in prison industries does not make one less likely to commit a post-release offense (Maguire, Flanagan, and Thornberry 1988: 3–18) and "most states have given up rehabilitation as even a stated goal" (Erlich 1995). Rather, it is purely profit that drives the employment of prisoners. Consider this very brief list of some of the more well-known companies that, like UNICOR and BP, have reportedly at one time hired prison labor or at least have had a stake in the prison labor market: Starbucks, Nintendo, Microsoft, Costco, JanSport, Dell, Boeing, Victoria's Secret, JCPenney, Wal-Mart, IBM, AT&T Wireless, Compaq, Motorola, Texas Instruments, Hewlett-Packard, Lucent Technologies, TWA, Nordstrom's, Revlon, Macy's, Pierre Cardin, and Target Stores (Winter 2008; also see Khalek 2011).

Not only is prison labor cheap—as the cases above demonstrate, prisoner wages are "competitive with the wages paid to illegal immigrant sweatshop workers here in the United States and wages paid to garment workers in the Far East and Central America" (Wright 1994: 105)—it is also easily exploited. Prisoners lack labor rights, they cannot unionize, they receive no workers' compensation, and they are excluded from all vital government protections (ibid., p. 104). On top of all that, their freedom constantly hangs in the balance. Refusing a job, complaining about unhealthy or dangerous conditions, or not working hard enough leaves prisoners susceptible to retaliation. This often comes in the form of delays in release or being subjected to needlessly harsher conditions of confinement. As one UNICOR e-waste recycling employee pointed out, he and his co-workers always found themselves taking orders from the factory manager even if that meant exposing themselves to dangerous toxins because they "knew that [the factory manager] could make prison life better or worse with a few key strokes, or spoken words" (Center for Environmental Health et al. 2006: 12).

The "High Cost" of Life Behind Bars

Beyond cheap, expendable labor, corporations also extract wealth from prisoners by charging them exorbitant prices for basic goods and services. As we have already briefly discussed, telephone companies charging prisoners high rates for collect phone calls is a clear example of this. This has occurred because restructured communication laws enable telephone companies to create profit sharing schemes with correctional facilities. Already in a fiscal crisis, state correctional departments commonly take advantage of this setup by contracting the phone companies who charge prisoners the *highest* rates. The result is that the often already impoverished families of prisoners find themselves between a rock and a hard place: pay extremely high rates on one hand or lose contact altogether on the other. Expanding on Dr Terry Kupers's testimony concerning how collect calls cause hardships to exploited prisoners and their families (Chapter I), Stephen Jackson documents the following nationwide trends:

> Family members...[forego] medical operations or prescription drugs in order to meet payments on their MCI, AT&T, or other phone bills. For some, telephone service surpassed rent as the largest household monthly bill. Many more had had their numbers blocked, suspended, or permanently disconnected over unpaid prison bills, thus losing telephone service altogether. Some had seen their credit ratings permanently ruined.
>
> (Jackson 2007: 241)

Perhaps the most blatant form of prisoner exploitation is recent proposals to treat prisons as "hotels." Under such arrangements, prisoners would be forced to pay for their "stay" as well as any other "expenses" such as drug testing (Miles 2011). Yet even when prisoners are not targeted directly as consumers, companies still manage to reap enormous profits in overcrowded correctional institutions that provide desperate prisoners with few options. The food prisoners eat, the means by which they are transported, the products they use for hygiene, and even the devices that harshen their confinement (e.g., Tasers, restraining chairs, and chemical agents) are hot commodities behind bars. As Joel Dyer documents in his important book *The Perpetual Prisoner Machine*:

> [T]he variety of corporations making money from prisons is truly dizzying, ranging from Dial Soap to Famous Amos cookies, from AT&T to health-care providers to companies that manufacture everything from prefab cells, leather restraints, cooking utensils, food, leg bracelets for home monitoring, security systems, razor wire, computer programs, knife-proof vests, laundry detergent, and so on. To give you an idea of what a small exclusive contract on a captive audience of prisoners can be

worth, consider that in 1995 Dial Soap sold $100,000 worth of its product to the New York City jail system alone—one jail system.

(Dyer 2000: 14)

From Exploitation to Commodification

Extracting wealth from prisoners by forcing them to consume expensive products and produce goods and services for slave wages draws attention to disturbing features embedded in our modern penal landscape. Yet perhaps the most dehumanizing aspect of the prison industrial complex is the **commodification** of imprisoned human beings. In recent years, the reliance on private prisons has exploded and the result is the treating of rising prison populations "not as a social problem but as a business opportunity" (Selman and Leighton 2010: 91). In the words of Norwegian criminologist Nils Christie, "the raw material is prisoners, and the industry will do what is necessary to guarantee a steady supply" (cited in Selman and Leighton 2010: 93).

The embodiment of this trend is publicly traded companies and private prison firms such as the Corrections Corporation of America (CCA). CCA operates more than 60 correctional, detention, and juvenile facilities in nearly a third of all U.S. states and has over 100,000 prisoners locked inside its imprisonment empire. The company does not hide the fact that its primary motivation is satisfying its investors by increasing its profits, and it accomplishes this by engaging in aggressive lobbying campaigns, which work to assure that prison populations remain high (Selman and Leighton 2010). One group who now find themselves detained at increasingly alarming rates thanks in large part to such efforts are undocumented immigrants. As former CCA Board Chairman William Andrews blithely stated, "The policy in this country has changed from catch and release to more detention … that means we'll be incarcerating more illegal aliens" (Kirkham 2012). In fact, expanding into the realm of immigration helped save the private prison industry from financial peril in the late 1990s. Currently, the number of immigrants detained in the United States is at an all-time high; about 400,000 immigrants are detained a year with nearly half confined in private facilities. The financial bottom-line of these companies has been more than achieved: between 2005 to 2012, both CCA and fellow corrections giant GEO Group, Inc. have more than doubled their revenues (ibid.).

The private prison boom has also affected children. As Tara Herivel explains, "Despite an indisputable current decline in crime committed by youth, the private youth detention industry nevertheless managed to carve out its niche… Nationally, about 92,000 children are held in juvenile detention facilities, 30,000 of whom are confined in private detention facilities" (Herivel 2007: 164). A recent scandal in Luzerne County, Pennsylvania vividly highlights how children convicted of crimes find themselves turned into commodities that are bought and sold. After illegally cutting a deal with the developer of a newly constructed juvenile detention facility, two judges were indicted for trading "kids for cash": handing down sentences at rates that far exceeded state averages and often going against the advice of probation officers in order to assure the newly constructed facilities would turn a profit for the developer.[3]

Conclusion

The indifference to human life revealed in the case of e-waste recycling and BP's cleanup efforts thus sheds light on a much larger trend of exploitation that intensifies the frustrations associated with forced poverty that Sykes had described. Corporations in the prison industry have put their own financial interests ahead of prisoners' basic human dignity, never mind rehabilitation or any other penological goal. While numerous entities seek to make a buck from the prison boom, the health, safety, finances, and freedom of those who are detained are severely compromised. In this context, it should not be surprising to learn that private prisons have been far less effective at reducing recidivism (Spivak and Sharp 2008). Plagued by scandals, many of which involve gruesome incidents such as sexual and physical assaults against children (Herivel 2007) and requiring severely injured prisoners to work (*Minneci et al. v. Pollard et al. 565 U.S.* 2012), these companies continue to prosper in the second decade of the 21st century. In the next chapter, we turn to another disturbing, yet ever common feature of mass imprisonment: the widespread sexual coercion of female prisoners perpetrated by their male captors.

DISCUSSION QUESTIONS

1. What is the prison industrial complex and how has it contributed to making prison life more painful?
2. With corporations now having such a high financial stake in imprisonment, how has the purpose of imprisonment changed?
3. In what ways is prison labor harmful to those seeking work outside of prison walls?
4. If we as a society were to get serious about reducing our prison population, what sort of impediments would the prison industrial complex pose?

3 Materials from the class-action lawsuit *H.T. et al. v. Mark A. Ciavarella, Jr. et al.* filed in part by the Juvenile Law Center can be accessed online at http://www.jlc.org/legal-docket/ht-et-al-v-mark-ciavarella-jr-et-al.

III: Coercion

This chapter provides an alternative to what Sykes called "the deprivation of heterosexual relationships." Writing in an era where homosexuality was considered deviant behavior, Sykes chose to focus on the experience of confined heterosexual men. Specifically, he attends to the psychological effects of the deprivation of sexual intimacy, which caused "an essential component of a man's self-conception—his status as male—[to be] called into question" (Sykes 2007: 71).

There are many ways to approach this issue in the context of contemporary conditions of mass imprisonment. For one, Sykes's study downplayed the seriousness of **sexual violence** behind bars as perpetrated by "aggressive prisoners who have turned to homosexuality as a temporary means of relieving their frustration" (ibid.). In the decades since Sykes's work was published, numerous studies of male prisoner rape demonstrate that the problem is far more serious than he observed in the late fifties. (For a powerful overview of the crisis of male prisoner rape in the words of social scientists and prisoners, see Sabo, Kupers, and London 2001).

However, we have chosen to focus instead on female prisoners, considering that one of the most notable changes in prisoner demographics that has occurred since the publication of *The Society of Captives* has been the dramatic rise in the number of women behind bars. According to the Sentencing Project, "The number of women in prison has increased at nearly *double* the rate of men since 1985, 404% vs. 209%" (Sentencing Project 2007). We explore the most disturbing consequence of the dramatic increases in female prisoners—namely, a campaign of sexual brutality and enduring coercion perpetrated by correctional officers and administrators.

This development differs from Sykes's observation in two important ways. First, the perpetrators of sexual abuse against women prisoners are not other prisoners, but nearly always male correctional officers and administrators. Second, rather than being understood as a *deprivation* where one's masculinity is called into question, attending to experiences of women prisoners reveals the violent *assertion* of masculine dominance inflicted upon female prisoners by male guards.

At the same time, the experiences of female prisoners are in many ways strikingly similar to what Sykes described. Of particular relevance to us is his acknowledgment that the psychological and social pains associated with the deprivation of sexuality are more pressing than the physical ones. At times, as we will explain, sexual encounters involving male guards and female prisoners are forceful, amounting to sexual assault.

Alternatively, there are instances where such encounters are "consensual," but are based on extremely unequal power relationships that exist between female captives and their male captors. In this context, usage of the term "consent" is obviously problematic. In either case, penal oppression is realized in the explicit coercion and control of women prisoners through systematic psychological pain and suffering. In this way, we contend that both sorts of encounters align squarely with what Evan Stark has called **coercive control**:

> Coercive control entails a malevolent course of conduct that subordinates women to an alien will by violating their physical integrity (violence), denying them respect and autonomy (intimidation), depriving them of social connectedness (isolation), and appropriating or denying them access to the resources required for personhood and citizenship (control) … The combination of these big and little indignities best explains why women suffer and respond as they do in abusive relationships, including why so many women become entrapped … [And] why they are prone to develop a range of psychosocial problems and exhibit behaviors or commit a range of acts that are contrary to their nature.
>
> (Stark 2007: 15–16)

We begin by recounting a number of horrifying tales of prison rape committed against women prisoners by male guards. Once again an ever-present climate of retaliation makes such experiences psychologically painful in the extreme. After reviewing relevant empirical research on the topic and exploring efforts undertaken to reduce instances of prison rape, we turn our attention to the plight of pregnant women behind bars. Specifically, we show how this issue is not necessarily separate from sexual coercion, as women prisoners may be impregnated against their will by their male captors. Yet even for those women who come into prison pregnant, extreme power differentials leave them at the mercy of often unforgiving custodial regimes.

Rape and Retaliation

Ronesha Williams is a young Black woman in Michigan's largest women's prison, Scott Correctional Facility. While imprisoned she experienced a disturbingly common trend in the experience of women behind bars in general and Black women in particular: she was violently raped by a male corrections officer. The aftermath of Ronesha's horrifying experience is also all too common: prison investigators made no attempt to protect her identity and she was summarily stigmatized as a "problem prisoner" for daring to report her victimization. Even after she was finally granted a transfer to a new facility, upon arrival she was met with the menacing words of corrections officers who "didn't want her here." These words marked the beginning of an aggressive campaign of retaliation against Ronesha.

The retaliation began with a succession of absurd disciplinary infractions: Prison staff wrote her up for insubordination after arriving early to breakfast, even though as a kitchen worker that was a requirement of her job. They also subjected her to numerous painful pat-frisk searches followed by threatening comments. In one such incident, an officer told Williams that he frisked her so aggressively in order "to teach her to keep her mouth shut." This threat became even less subtle, as another officer warned that she "better not show up in relation to the lawsuit." She asked to be transferred from the prison numerous times but was denied, issued more erroneous disciplinary infractions, and subsequently denied parole.

Another Michigan prisoner from the Scott Facility, Jackie Myrick, was raped by a corrections officer while in administrative segregation. After Myrick went public with her allegations, the officer committed suicide. She was subsequently paroled and then imprisoned again. However, at sentencing the court specifically recommended that prison staff place Myrick in a facility to guarantee her safety. The Michigan Department of Corrections summarily ignored the court's recommendation. From her first day at Scott, Jackie was subjected to verbal harassments and threats by guards who blamed her for the officer's death. The constant threats led Myrick to become suicidal and she ended up being placed in administrative segregation. Since the time of the rape, doctors diagnosed Jackie with numerous psychological problems, including chronic post-traumatic stress. After several months, she was finally transferred to another institution, but within months she was informed that she would be sent back to Scott. When she returned to the institution, Jackie Myrick was so distraught that she was immediately placed on suicide watch. Three days later she was transferred again to another prison where she sits in her cell in constant fear of retaliation.

Another Michigan prisoner, "Jane Doe 1," after being sexually abused by an officer, informed a prison chaplain. The chaplain informed prison authorities, but charges against the officer were dropped, and in a pattern all too disturbingly predictable, she was issued a major misconduct ticket for "interference with the administration of rules by making a false charge against a corrections officer." Like Ronesha Williams, "Jane Doe 1" was subsequently denied parole for misconduct. (The source material used to construct this vignette comes from Human Rights Watch 1998).

Women imprisoned in California are subjected to the most extreme forms of overcrowding in the nation. They routinely live in facilities in which women are double or even triple-bunked in a space that is more than 100 percent over capacity. This overcrowding exacerbates problems with women's privacy behind bars. They are forced to shower and change out in the open and prison officers have ready access to their cells. Some women even find themselves subjected to violent cell invasions. As "Uma M." described: "I felt fear real quick. I knew something was wrong and I didn't want to look. [Officer G] pulled the blanket. I sat up and tugged at the blanket.

The other guard had the garbage can in the door and then the whole blanket came off ... He just tore my whole shirt. That's when he assaulted me sexually. [Officer H] yelled at [Officer G] to calm down and left. I was screaming, yelling and crying. Martha across the hall was banging on her window. While he was still in the room, I went into the shower. I felt dirty." (The source material used to construct this vignette comes from Human Rights Watch 1996).

****

Prisons of Coercion and Sexual Violence

According to a 1999 report issued by the U.S. General Accountability Office (GAO), "Women in Prison: Sexual Misconduct by Correctional Staff," correctional administrations from 23 correctional institutions from across the United States had been named as defendants in class-action or individual lawsuits alleging sexual misconduct against women prisoners (GAO 1999). And given the climate of retaliation which drives underreporting, it is probably safe to conclude that sexual brutality against women prisoners is even more commonplace than these disturbingly high numbers already suggest. The experiences of Ronesha Williams, Jane Doe 1, Jackie Myrick, and Uma M. are thus not atypical of extensively documented abuses of women prisoners:

> Women in prisons across the United States are subjected to diverse and systematic forms of sexual abuse: vaginal and anal rape; forced oral sex and forced digital penetration; quid pro quo coercion of sex for drugs, favors, or protection; abusive pat searches and strip searches; observation by male guards while naked or toileting; groping; verbal harassment; and sexual threats ... Women prisoners become pregnant when the only men they have had contact with are guards and prison employees; often they are sent to solitary confinement—known as "the hole"—as punishment for having sexual contact with guards or for getting pregnant.
>
> (Buchanan 2007: 46)

Clearly, the threat of sexual violence and violent retaliation is an ever-present threat behind bars. However, it is important to understand that such threats encompass both physical *and* psychological harm. Sexual violence and the threat thereof as perpetrated against female prisoners by their captors inflicts psychological pain that often lasts over the course of their entire sentence (and beyond). This is especially evident in the case of Jackie Myrick. Empirical studies provide a more concise picture of how women prisoners experience coercive control behind bars and of how such coercion needs to be understood not as an act committed by a few "bad apples" but rather as a practice endemic to overcrowded, hyper-masculine institutions that dehumanize prisoners and use the threat of retaliation to constantly deny prisoner agency:

- Drawing on numerous interviews with women prisoners over a two-year period (2000–2002), investigative journalist Cristina Rathbone describes a widespread and routinized coercive system of daily intimidation in which corrections officers raped, groped, verbally harassed, and demanded sex under threat of retaliation (Rathbone 2005).
- Officers often inform victims that if they report abuse, no one will believe them. This is a warning that women prisoners are likely to heed to avoid being "stereotyped as liars and trouble makers" (Majury 2003: 8).
- Women prisoners cannot trust that their reports will remain confidential and concerns about retaliation are very real.[1]
- Women prisoners are part of a coercive prison culture that "frowns upon disclosure as weakness and betrayal" (Majury 2003: 10).
- Guards and prison officials notoriously disregard institutional rules and procedures, often refusing to provide women prisoners with the required means for filing formal grievances.[2]

The sexual abuse of women prisoners extends to so-called "consensual" relations between captor and captive—relationships that are not criminalized in most states. Avery J. Calhoun and Heather D. Coleman's study of 100 female prisoners in Hawaii provides important insight into the phenomenon. Specifically, they find that unequal power relations create the illusion of "consent":

> [S]ome of the situations described by participants suggest a certain amount of mutual agreement in the "trading" form of staff–inmate sexual contact. Labeling the sexual contact as "trading" or even "pseudo consensual" is troubling because it obscures power relationships within prison…"trading" would more appropriately be labeled "sexualextortion" because it arises out of indebtedness. The correctional officer has the resources to create the debt. An example of the limits to female inmates' ability to negotiate "trading" occurs when the inmate wants to stop the sexual contact with a prison employee. In the words of one participant, this is when "we don't want to play any more." The inmate then faces the threat of retaliation by being "written up."
>
> (Calhoun and Coleman 2002: 108)

1 For a detailed documentation of this abuse in state prisons from across the United States, see Human Rights Watch (1996).

2 Ibid.

Ending Sexual Violence and Coercion Behind Bars?

Until very recently, the pleas of women prisoners who are courageous enough to go public with their grievances have received little sympathy from courts or legislatures. Given the federal government's embrace of mass imprisonment policies, it is not surprising that it has been reluctant to involve itself in the crisis of prisoner sexual abuse. However, by 2000, the national scandal of sexual abuse in the nation's prisons created such public outrage that both House and Senate Judiciary committees convened investigative hearings. To be sure, the outrage was driven by a publicized case of brutal male prisoner rape. However, sexual violence against women prisoners was also addressed. The result of these hearings was the passage of a sweeping bipartisan bill, the **Prison Rape Elimination Act of 2003** (PREA). Subsequently signed into law by President George W. Bush, PREA creates a "zero tolerance" policy for prison rape by requiring the creation of "best practices" for training correctional officers to prevent sexual abuse in prisons. Moreover, the Bureau of Justice Statistics (BJS) is now required to carry out comprehensive reports that detail the incidence of sexual victimization in both male and female prisons.

BJS's most recent PREA report was issued on August 26, 2010. The report found that Alabama's Julia Tutwiler Prison for Women had the highest incidence of sexual abuse in the nation. Following up on BJS's statistical findings, investigators from Alabama's Equal Justice Initiative (EJI) conducted numerous interviews with Tutwiler's prisoners and concluded:

> The most visible and striking evidence of Tutwiler staff members' illegal sexual contact with incarcerated women is the resulting pregnancies. In 2010, a woman in custody gave birth to a baby after being raped by a correctional officer at Tutwiler Prison. Over the past five years, EJI has received numerous complaints from women who have become pregnant after being raped by male correctional staff.
>
> (EJI 2012)

Despite the passage of PREA, women prisoners at Tutwiler continue to be subjected to a brutal regime of coercive control by prison officials. Consider these additional findings from EJI's report:

- "Women who report sexual abuse at Tutwiler are routinely placed in segregation by the warden. While in segregation, these women are treated no differently from women held there for punitive reasons: they are deprived of telephone, mail, and visit privileges and have no access to recreation, programs, or work assignments" (EJI 2012).
- "Incarcerated women who are sexually abused by correctional officers are not informed of the results of investigations conducted by the Department of Corrections, even when the claims of sexual abuse are substantiated and formal action is taken to terminate the officer" (EJI 2012).

The sexual coercion of women prisoners indeed continues to be characterized by systematic forms of sexual abuse and violent threats that are perversely routinized. And as the number of women behind bars continues to grow, this population of prisoners find themselves entrapped by their male captors in numerous forms of coercive control, including, as we will see, the denial of humane prenatal care. In contrast to Sykes's description of male prisoners as being "figuratively castrated by … involuntary celibacy" (2007: 70), female prisoners are more ruthlessly denied their own sexuality.

Pregnancy Policies as Coercive Control Behind Bars

Sheriff Joe Arpaio of Maricopa County, Arizona has long denied women imprisoned in his infamous "tent city" jails access to adequate prenatal care. Ambrett Spencer was one of Maricopa County's prisoners who paid a high price for the jail's brazenly inhumane conditions. Ambrett was not a typical prisoner: she was pregnant. She filed numerous grievances against the vermin-infested, unsanitary jail. She was also not provided prenatal vitamins or healthy food—indeed, all prisoners of the Maricopa County jail system are fed three, often spoiled, baloney sandwiches a day.

While the jail steadfastly denies its lack of attention was driven out of retaliation for Ambrett Spencer's history of filing grievances, the subsequent events seem to suggest otherwise. By the time she was nine months pregnant and ready to give birth, Ambrett awoke from her bunk with an extreme pain in her stomach. Her desperate cries for help initially fell on deaf ears. When she finally got the attention of an officer who contacted the jail infirmary's nurse and the severity of her pain was confirmed, she was ordered to be immediately transferred to the jail infirmary.

An hour would pass and Ambrett still lay in her bed writhing in pain. When she finally arrived at the infirmary, the nurse on duty—who had no prenatal training—determined that Ambrett Spencer's pain was not an emergency. Left another hour without treatment, Ambrett passed out. By the time the ambulance arrived at the Maricopa County Hospital, she had been in severe pain and without a doctor's care for a full four hours. When she finally was admitted into the hospital, a doctor delivered her daughter, Ambria, stillborn. It was later determined that Ambrett's daughter's death was preventable as she was suffering from placental abruption, a condition that is not all that rare among pregnant women, but that does require the immediate delivery of the baby so as to prevent death from blood loss. (The source material used to construct this vignette comes from Dickerson 2008; Stolberg and Pear 2010).

****

The gross mistreatment of pregnant prisoners such as Ambrett Spencer is not uncommon. Pregnant women in jails and prisons routinely go without proper care and miscarry at wildly disproportionate rates (Parker 2004–5: 259–95). Perhaps most egregiously, many states keep women prisoners shackled throughout their pregnancies, including on the delivery table while giving birth. In fact, as of this writing only six U.S. states ban the practice (National Organization for Women 2010). What is all the more remarkable is that both the *American Public Health Association* and the *American College of Obstetricians and Gynecologists* have long condemned the practice as extraordinarily dangerous (American Public Health Association 2003: 108).[3] During labor and postpartum recovery, shackling can interfere with appropriate medical care and can be detrimental to the health of the woman and her newborn child. Restraints on a pregnant woman can, moreover, interfere with the medical staff's ability to appropriately assist in childbirth or to conduct emergency procedures.

Conclusion

Sexual coercion is both physically and emotionally devastating to women prisoners. The abuse of pregnant prisoners testifies to yet another profoundly inhumane aspect of the United States' human warehouses that is both common and dangerously routinized. Many women prisoners are literally shackled on the delivery table. Prisoners suffer brutal miscarriages or, as in Ambrett Spencer's case, stillbirths that could have been prevented. We have also documented how corrections officers rape, sexually harass, and retaliate against female prisoners with impunity. Despite these women having experienced prior, often long-term sexual abuse, their captors coerce them into sexual submission by preying on their double vulnerability as prisoner and victim. If they are not compliant, many corrections officers and administrators have retaliated against them with myriad coercive and arbitrary sanctions. One of the more painful of these sanctions is transfer into solitary confinement. It is there where women prisoners are sentenced, in effect, to a prison within a prison for daring to confront their victimizers. The consequences of this practice are often dire, and, as was the case with Jackie Myrick, may lead to repeated attempts to take one's life. How isolation in solitary confinement has been transformed from a rare sanction to an all-too-common practice involving vast numbers of prisoners confined for extended periods is the topic of the next chapter.

3 On June 12, 2007, the American College of Obstetricians and Gynecologists (ACOG) stated on its website in a "Letter in Opposition to Shackling":

> The practice of shackling an incarcerated woman in labor may not only compromise her health care but is demeaning and unnecessary.... Women [who have been shackled during labor] describe the inability to move to allay the pains of labor, the bruising caused by chain belts across the abdomen, and the deeply felt loss of dignity.

The letter can be accessed online at http://www.acog.org/departments/underserved/20070612saarLTR.pdf.

DISCUSSION QUESTIONS

1. What is unique about the experience of women prisoners?
2. What is coercive control? How is it employed in the context of women prisoners?
3. Although the focus of this chapter is women prisoners, the authors acknowledge that there are many ways to approach this issue in the context of contemporary conditions of mass imprisonment. How is the prison experience of gay men in prison relevant? How is the issue of male prison rape relevant?
4. The medical field has decried the shackling of pregnant prisoners yet it remains an accepted practice in almost all states. Use what you learned in previous chapters about "human warehousing" to explain this apparent dilemma.

IV: Isolation

Imprisonment takes away the ability to do what you want to do when you want to do it. The prisoners Sykes interviewed were especially frustrated with this deprivation of autonomy. Being told when to wake up, where to stand, and what to eat—that is, having one's life subject to a "vast body of rules and commands which are designed to control… behavior in minute detail" (Sykes 2007: 73)—is severely painful for people behind bars. The fact is, "the nominal objectives of the custodian are not, in general, the objectives of the prisoners" (Sykes 2007: 73–74). Having a sandwich for lunch, taking a walk, or visiting a friend—seemingly mundane acts—are not, for the prisoner, things that can be done when one feels like it.

Prisoners' frustrations are, moreover, often compounded when they are not given sufficient explanation for why decisions are made. In other words, the arbitrariness of guards' decisions leaves already restricted prisoners wondering why they were denied parole, why their mail was not delivered, and why they are unable to bring food with them back from the mess hall. In combination, these restrictions on autonomy, like the previous pains Sykes had articulated, "involved a profound threat to the prisoner's self image because they reduce the prisoner to the weak, helpless, dependent status of childhood" (Sykes 2007: 75).

The deprivation of autonomy always has been a hallmark of imprisonment, but in the contemporary era of extreme prison overcrowding where guards and other prison officials have become willing to take aggressive measures to maintain control, many prisoners are now denied any semblance of normalcy. When Sykes describes prisoners as reduced to the "dependent status of childhood," he is implicitly acknowledging that institutions permit prisoners to retain at least some of their humanity. But with the advent of the **supermax** facility and the re-emergence of **solitary confinement**—a mode of punishment that as early as 1838 was acknowledged as having "little influence in decreasing the amount of crime committed" (Sykes 2007: 7) and decried as being torturous and "too severe" in 1890[1]—the humanity of many prisoners today has

1 Referring to failed experiments with solitary confinement in Philadelphia and elsewhere in the late 18th century, the Supreme Court noted in *In re Medley* (1890): "Experience demonstrated that there were serious objections to [solitary confinement]. A considerable number of prisoners fell, after even a short confinement, into a semifatuous condition, from which it was next to impossible to arrounse

been utterly stripped away. As many as 25,000 prisoners in 44 states across the country now sit alone in isolation in a tiny concrete cell in a state of extreme sensory deprivation.[2] Under these circumstances, the deprivation of autonomy becomes so severe that not only are prisoners *not permitted* to make their own decisions, they eventually *lose the ability* to control their own behavior. As Craig Haney, a leading expert on the psychological effects of imprisonment and solitary confinement, specifically describes it:

> The unprecedented totality of control in supermax units forces prisoners to become entirely dependent on the institution to organize their existence... Thus, many prisoners gradually lose the ability to initiate or to control their own behavior, or to organize their own lives. The two separate components of this reaction—problems with the self-control and self-initiation of behavior—both stem from the extreme over-control of supermax. That is, all prisoners in these units are forced to adapt to an institutional regime that limits virtually all aspects of their behavior. Indeed, one of the defining characteristics of supermax confinement is the extent to which it accomplishes precisely that. But because almost every aspect of the prisoners' day-to-day existence is so carefully and completely circumscribed in these units, some of them lose the ability to set limits for themselves or to control their own behavior through internal mechanisms.
>
> (Haney 2003: 138-39)

A close look at the experience of one prisoner in one of the country's most notorious supermax facilities, Pelican Bay State Prison in California, will shed further light on how the deprivation of autonomy has been taken to the extreme under mass incarceration. Prisoners literally stripped of their humanity often arbitrarily by guards working in a regime obsessed with maintaining control reflects penal oppression in one of its most revolting forms. This can be seen vividly in the psychologically harmful effects of solitary confinement, a practice that is used ever more frequently in this era of mass imprisonment.

them, and others became violently insane; others still, committed suicide; while those who stood the ordeal better were not generally reformed, and in most cases did not recover sufficient mental activity to be of any subsequent service to the community. It became evident that some changes must be made in the system ... It is within the memory of many persons interested in prison discipline that some 30 or 40 years ago the whole subject attracted the general public attention, and its main feature of solitary confinement was found to be too severe." For a comprehensive review of the history of solitary confinement, see Haney and Lynch (1997).

2 There seems to be no consensus on the actual number of prisoners currently in solitary confinement, although the most commonly used figure is 25,000; yet when one considers those being held in other forms of isolation (i.e., restricted housing), that number elevates to 80,000. For a review of these statistics, see Casella and Ridgeway (2012).

Not Even a Hug

At 69 years old, many would consider George Ruiz an "old man." For more than half of his adult life—a full 28 years—he has been confined in a tiny 8ft by 10ft, windowless cell for about 23 hours a day. The cell is made of poured grey concrete and contains only a concrete bed, two concrete slabs that serve as a desk and stool, a sink, and a toilet. The door of his cell is solid steel, has a few small holes that allow a partial view into the hallway, and a food slot through which a guard slides him substandard meals twice a day.

A resident of California's Pelican Bay State Prison since it opened in 1989, George has endured nearly three full decades of extremely limited recreation, almost no contact with loved ones, and constant surveillance and control. Under court order, the prison must provide people detained in the Security Housing Unit (SHU) with five hours of recreation per week; as such, barring staff shortages, inclement weather, or arbitrary staff decisions, George is occasionally released from his proverbial cage into what is referred to as a "dog run"—a cement yard that is still unequivocally small (about the size of three cells) but represents a rare opportunity for at least some mobility. The partial opening to the sky in the dog run is the only means by which George ever sees the light of day. That opening also happens to permit rain to pour into the exercise pen, however, causing water to frequently pool onto the floor and mildew or mold to form on the walls. Prior to a 2011 hunger strike, prison officials did not permit the use of any exercise equipment. They are now given a measly handball.

Only in the case of an emergency like a death in the family is George permitted to make a telephone call. And even these calls come at the guards' discretion. Visits are even rarer. Pelican Bay's remote location makes it a difficult and expensive place for friends and family to visit. It is 355 miles from San Francisco, 728 miles from Los Angeles. For many families it is not even worth the hassle; visits are "no contact," ruling out the possibility of even a hug. All interactions on visits take place over a telephone behind a Plexiglas wall and prison staff monitor, record, and review everything. Before and after each visit, prisoners must endure the humiliation of a strip search.

George used to pass the time by reading. Those held captive in Pelican Bay are permitted 10 books or magazines in their cell. But the psychological toll of solitary confinement has made this, too, almost impossible for him. Years of extreme sensory deprivation have left George unable to concentrate long enough to read more than a few sentences and he has developed severe memory problems that impede him from comprehending what he has just read.

George also has a host of other mounting health concerns. He suffers from glaucoma, had to have a corneal transplant in one eye, and may soon need one in the other. He also has diabetes, pneumonia, kidney failure, and shortness of breath. The conditions of his confinement have undoubtedly contributed to these ailments, and, to confound matters, the delays in getting medical attention are especially bad in solitary.

But what is perhaps most painful of all about George's experience is the solitude he is forced to endure. George must eat, sleep, and recreate alone. Normal human conversation is impossible. The only way he can communicate with other prisoners is by shouting loud enough for the prisoner in the next cell to hear; that is, if a guard does not punish him for doing so, as this is technically a rule violation. Outside of "pinky shakes" with guards, which prisoners accomplish by sticking their pinky finger through one of the tiny holes in the cell door, physical contact with another human being almost never occurs. One of George's fellow SHU prisoners has gone 13 years without even shaking another person's hand. Another has not hugged his now adult daughter since she was in preschool nearly two decades ago. (The source material used to construct this vignette comes from the Center for Constitutional Rights' original complaint in the case of *Ruiz v. Brown.* Available online at http://www.georgiagreenparty.org/system/files/5-31-12%20Ruiz%20Amended%20Complaint.pdf).

****

The Psychological Toll of Solitary Confinement

Many would argue that prisoners like George Ruiz "deserve" to be where they are. As Pelican Bay Associate Warden Larry Williams argues, "Prison is a deterrent. We don't want them to like being in prison" (Sullivan 2006). But such statements overlook the devastating psychological damages caused by this sort of confinement, damages which are on par with those experienced by concentration camp survivors and victims of torture (Haney and Lynch 1997). Consider this list of negative psychological outcomes and problematic behaviors that multiple research studies have confirmed regarding the effects of solitary confinement: negative attitudes and affect, insomnia, anxiety, panic, withdrawal, hypersensitivity, **ruminations**, cognitive dysfunction, hallucinations, loss of control, irritability, aggression, rage, paranoia, hopelessness, depression, a sense of impending emotional breakdown, self-mutilation, **suicidal ideation** and behavior, deteriorating mental and physical health, other-directed violence, and post-traumatic stress disorder (Haney and Lynch 1997).

How many confined in solitary actually experience these conditions? According to one of the most comprehensive studies on the subject, almost all. In his extensive interviews of prisoners in solitary at Pelican Bay, Craig Haney concludes:

> More than four out of five of those evaluated suffered from feelings of anxiety and nervousness, headaches, troubled sleep, and lethargy or chronic tiredness, and over

> half complained of nightmares, heart palpitations, and fear of impending nervous breakdowns. In addition, equally high numbers reported specific psychopathological effects of social isolation. That is, more than four out of five of solitary confinement prisoners suffered from ruminations, confused thought processes, an over-sensitivity to stimuli, irrational anger, and social withdrawal. In addition, well over half reported violent fantasies, emotional flatness, mood swings, chronic depression, and feelings of overall deterioration, nearly half suffered hallucinations and perceptual distortions, and a quarter experienced suicidal ideation.
>
> (Haney 2003: 124–56)

Amidst such extreme psychological pain, prisoners continue to crave human interaction. Scholar and activist Stephen F. Eisenman provides two particularly poignant examples of prisoners in solitary confinement at Illinois' notorious Tamms Correctional Center. One prisoner, in his 20s, "became so desperate for physical contact that he often refused to return his food tray through the slot in his door so that the 'tag team'—a squad of masked and helmeted officers—would come to his cell to tackle and extract him" (Eisenman 2009). Another victim of solitary confinement, Eisenman explains, "plotted with a fellow prisoner he met in the hospital to seriously cut themselves on a given date in the future, so that they might have a chance to meet again" (Eisenman 2009).

Are We Isolating the "Worst of the Worst"?

Others will dismiss the seriousness of solitary confinement by pointing out that only the "worst of the worst" are susceptible to these conditions or that some "new breed" of prisoner has emerged that requires extreme isolation. Indeed, Pelican Bay was built for this explicit purpose and was conceived as a "state-of-the-art" facility that would become a "model for the rest of the nation" (Haney and Lynch 1997: 566). Yet as Haney writes: "There is no evidence that the rise of supermax prisons was driven by the threat of some new breed of criminal prisoner" (Haney 2003: 129). Likewise, "there is no evidence that these allegedly 'worst' prisoners are any worse than those who had been adequately managed by less dramatic measures in the past" (ibid).

From this perspective, solitary confinement emerges not as a "suitable punishment" for those who pose a "real threat," but rather as a zero-tolerance approach to prison overcrowding that disregards the humanity of those held captive. In other words, rather than confronting prison overcrowding as a social problem, correctional officials responded by harshening the conditions of prisoners' confinement (ibid).

As is by this point a recurring theme in our discussions of the pains of contemporary imprisonment, rather than housing perpetually violent "monsters," this psychologically brutal means of imprisonment is instead more commonly employed by prison officials for the purpose of retaliation. As Daniel Burton-Rose explains, one group that is at a particularly high risk of being isolated in solitary is "activist prisoners who have made themselves unpopular with staff as a result of attempts to try to check the brutal excess that frequently occurs in prisons" (Burton-Rose 1998: 187). Solitary is also commonly used as a way to deal with the crisis of mental illness in prisons, which has followed deinstitutionalization. Mentally ill prisoners are often "dumped" into these cages as an alternative to treatment and the result is often an exacerbation of their original illness (ibid). In fact, the "percentage [of mentally ill prisoners in supermax facilities] may be as much as twice as high as in the general prisoner population" (Haney 2003: 142).

There is also a disturbing irony at work here. As Burton-Rose (1998: 187) explains further, "even for those for whom the units are supposedly intended—the uncontrollably violent—the extreme isolation and lack of positive outlets make them more violent and self-destructive" Haney 2003: 142). Consider again the list of psychological harms long-term solitary confinement may cause prisoners. It is thus easy to understand how such brutal conditions of confinement foster violent behavior in many prisoners. Feelings of anger, rage, and aggression are fueled when one lacks an outlet for emotional expressions (Haney and Lynch 1997). This explains the conclusions from a multitude of studies on the subject:[3]

- More than half of all self-mutilation incidents in a Virginia prison had occurred in isolation units (Jones 1986: 286–96).
- Nationally, isolation has been found to correlate with jail suicide (Hayes 1989: 7–29).
- Both self-inflicted and staff-directed violence was found to be more common when the violator was in disciplinary or restricted housing (Steinke 1991: 111–32).
- 71 percent of all staff assaults in one federal institution occurred in an isolation unit where just 10 percent of all prisoners were housed (Kratcoski 1988: 27–32).

In short, how solitary confinement is actually used and the consequences it generates are often starkly different from the stated intent and purpose. This inconsistency between policy and action is even more glaring when we consider how long people are being detained under such conditions. Recognizing the potential for profound psychological harm, the original intent in constructing Pelican Bay was to keep prisoners secluded for a maximum of 18 months. Yet the facility, like others in the state of California, quickly filled beyond capacity, prompting an embrace of the "waste management" philosophy (see Chapter I) and a frighteningly aggressive reliance on solitary.

3 For a comprehensive review of the empirical literature on solitary confinement, see Haney and Lynch (1997).

Of Pelican Bay's 1,106 prisoners in SHU, 513 have been there for *more than 10 years*, 222 for *more than 15 years*, and 78 for *more than 20 years* (*Ruiz v. Brown*).

"Debrief or Die"

George Ruiz has been eligible for parole for almost two decades. But parole rules forbid the release of SHU inmates, and because the prison has "validated" George as a gang member, he is perpetually forced to remain in "the hole" unless he "debriefs." Pelican Bay staff claim that debriefing entails simply declaring one's intent to walk away from the gang; yet in practice prisoners find themselves forced to "snitch" on fellow prisoners. As one Pelican Bay detainee put it, "They literally say that those of you in the [SHU] will die in the [SHU] unless you debrief and tell us what we want to know… the debriefer is encouraged to fabricate lies against the non-debriefer, which is what allows the [prison gang investigators] to retain prisoners in SHU indefinitely." Debriefing is thus extremely dangerous as it puts the prisoner and his family at significant risk. Yet at the same time, gang-involvement is often an arbitrary designation. George faces no allegations of actual gang activity nor has he committed any gang-related rule violations. His designation as being involved with the Mexican Mafia comes only from uncorroborated accusations—namely, some questions about drawings that hang on his cell wall and the alleged appearance of his name on a list of active gang members maintained by another prisoner. In fact, for almost three decades, George's behavior inside Pelican Bay suggests he is a far cry from one of the institution's "worst of the worst" prisoners. During the entire length of his imprisonment, George has committed only four minor rules violations: missing court in 1981, possession of wine in 1983, possession of unlabeled medication in 1986, and a seemingly ambiguous charge labeled "Mail Violation With No Security Threat" in 2007 (Ruiz v. Brown).

****

Isolation as Arbitrary Control

Keep in mind: *no one gets sentenced to solitary confinement.* This is a punishment handed down without a judge, without a jury, out of the public's view, and, in many cases, completely at the discretion of prison staff. As noted by Human Rights Watch, prisoners often find themselves "sentenced twice: once by the court, to a certain period of imprisonment, and the second time by the prison administration, to particularly harsh conditions" (Human Rights Watch 1993).

This arbitrariness led prisoners at Pelican Bay to hunger strike in 2011 (see Conclusion). The questionable placement of prisoners in solitary confinement also led to a sweeping class-action lawsuit in which George Ruiz is a named plaintiff. Prisoners in Pelican Bay's SHU frequently find themselves in solitary confinement without adequate justification, are not entitled to fair hearings once there, and are, for all intents and purposes, being held hostage as their release is contingent upon providing information to prison staff. Specifically, the prison's policy dictates that Pelican Bay's prisoners are re-sentenced to solitary confinement once they are recognized by prison staff as gang members. They are then entitled to a review every 180 days to determine the appropriateness of their sentence. These reviews feature no actual assessment regarding the efficacy of prisoners' placement in SHU and as such do not result in the release of any prisoners who are unwilling to debrief. A more thorough assessment then occurs every six years, "yet even this six-year interactive review is meaningless for most prisoners housed in the SHU" (*Ruiz v. Brown*) as prison staff routinely dismiss prisoner claims of gang inactivity despite collecting no evidence to the contrary. Added to the psychological devastation of solitary is thus the frustration of being trapped endlessly in the prison's bureaucratic maze. Consider the arbitrary reasons given to other prisoners named in the Ruiz class-action suit that prevented them from leaving SHU:

- Todd Ashker is confined to SHU until he "either debriefs or dies." Pelican Bay Warden Joe McGrath was quoted as saying Ashker must "formally renounce his membership [with the Aryan Brotherhood] and divulge all of their secrets to the authorities. The alternative is remaining where extremely dangerous inmates belong: the SHU."
- Gabriel Reyes was initially denied inactive status because he was seen exercising in a group yard with other prisoners who had validated gang status. The prison subsequently denied him inactive status because of drawings that officials found in his cell. One of these drawings was for a tattoo with his name that allegedly also contained a gang symbol. Yet this exact symbol already appears on a tattoo Reyes has on his left pectoral that officials declared to be non-gang-related on multiple prior reviews.
- Jeffrey Franklin, like George Ruiz, had his name turn up on a gang roster that was confiscated from another prisoner. Later he was accused of "communicat[ing] by talking" with a validated member from another gang.
- Ronnie Dewberry also had his name show up on a roster and was denied inactive status in 2011 because he possessed political and historical writings, a pamphlet written in Swahili, and because a confidential memo stated that Dewberry is an "enforcer" in a group known as the Black Guerilla Family. Dewberry is thus currently spending six more years in SHU despite no evidence that he was involved in any violent gang-related activity (*Ruiz v. Brown*).

The arbitrary decisions that keep prisoners trapped in SHU are not limited to Pelican Bay. Lawsuits such as this are a growing trend across the country. Disturbingly, some of these cases involve the prolonged segregation of prisoners as retaliation for filing complaints that protest prison conditions. Such was the case for Alex Pearson who was just days away from being transferred out of Tamms when he was issued a ticket alleging sexual misconduct. Pearson testified that his long-term re-commitment to isolation came in retaliation for his refusal to act as a confidential gang informant once in the general population and in response to his involvement in a legal grievance filed against prison officials (*Pearson v. Wellborn*).

Conclusion

Protracted solitary confinement is profoundly dehumanizing. It strips prisoners of their autonomy and subjects them to horrifying psychological violence. Throughout this chapter and others, we have learned that prisoners may be placed in solitary confinement as, in effect, an "extra punishment." It is imposed on prisoners by their captors as part of a pervasive and arbitrary system of retaliation. In this era of mass imprisonment, where the overriding goal is waste management, retaliation against prisoners by their captors has become widespread. In the next chapter, we explore another form of retaliation, revealing that what Sykes described as the deprivation of security is today part of a pervasive regime of brutality.

DISCUSSION QUESTIONS

1. If solitary confinement was declared inhumane as early as 1890, why do you think it has reemerged to the extent that it has today?
2. Many supporters of solitary confinement will claim that it is a necessary tactic designed to keep guards and other prisoners safe. What are some of the problems with this argument?
3. Many prisoners who find themselves in solitary confinement will eventually be released. Given the psychological consequences of solitary confinement discussed in this chapter, what type of difficulties would you envision a former prisoner who had experienced long-term solitary confinement encountering when he or she returns to society?

V: Brutality

For Sykes, the deprivation of security referred to the constant threat of prisoner-on-prisoner violence. Consistent with his articulation of the other deprivations associated with the pains of imprisonment Sykes, moreover, calls our attention not simply to physical violence experienced by prisoners, but to the psychological trauma of having to live with a constant threat of victimization: "The prisoner's loss of security arouses acute anxiety… not just because violent acts of aggression and exploitation occur but also because such behavior constantly calls into question the individual's ability to cope with it, in terms of his own inner resources, his courage, his 'nerve.'" (Sykes 2007: 78).

Under mass imprisonment, the deprivation of security no longer adequately captures the situation in which numerous prisoners find themselves. In addition to being confronted with the threat of violence by other captives, prisoners today are increasingly brutalized by their captors. Although this observation is not a new one, we contend that the scale and form of guard brutality in the age of mass imprisonment is unprecedented.

To understand the widespread use of brutality in contemporary U.S. prisons, it is first important to attend to the present historical moment. Just as Sykes was writing during the Cold War in the 1950s where prison populations were comparatively very low but scholarly interest in the prison as a totalitarian institution was on the rise, both of the recent U.S. wars on crime and terror serve as a critical backdrop for understanding what we believe is a dramatic rise in brutal custodial regimes.

A recent volume *The Violence of Incarceration* (2009) edited by Phil Scraton and Jude McCulloch presents important insight into why this is so. Reflecting on the "normalization of legitimate violence," especially in U.S. prisons, Scraton and McCulloch challenge the notion that the international scandal at Abu Ghraib prison was an extraordinary incident. Indeed, Scraton and McCulloch's volume documents widespread prison-guard brutality in North American and European penal institutions. Calling attention to Angela Davis's recent writing on violence in U.S. prisons, they argue: "The torture, degradation, and sexual coercion captured in the photographs and video footage from Abu Ghraib have foundations laid deep in [quoting Davis] 'routine, quotidian violence that is justified as the everyday means of controlling prison populations in the United States'" (Scraton and McCulloch 2009: 3).

In a remarkable chapter in this volume, "The United States Military Prison: The Normalcy of Exceptional Brutality," sociologist Avery F. Gordon documents how the brutalization of prisoners at Abu Ghraib has direct connections to punishment regimes in U.S. prisons. Gordon illuminates the role of U.S. military organizations such as the International Criminal Investigative Training Assistance Program (ICITAP) in enlisting high-level civilian prison personnel—including the former directors of supermax prisons in Connecticut, Virginia, and Utah—to create military prisons in Afghanistan and Iraq, including Abu Ghraib. That is to say, the crisis of mass imprisonment catalyzed by the domestic war on crime has become a model for brutal U.S. military prisons abroad. At the operational level, Gordon shows how the National Guardsmen at Abu Ghraib—many of whom were also employed as prison guards in notoriously brutal U.S. prisons—described their actions to the FBI as quite normal. Drawing extensively on documents detailing the FBI interrogations that were obtained by the American Civil Liberties Union under the Freedom of Information Act, Gordon observes:

> [N]o one interviewed reported observing any "misconduct" or "mistreatment" of those detained at Abu Ghraib. The guards described what they saw and often what they did: Prisoners handcuffed to the wall with nylon bags over their heads being deprived of sleep; prisoners spread-eagled on the floor yelling and flailing; men ordered to strip, placed in isolation and then subjected to deafening music and/or extreme temperatures; the punitive use of electric shock and stun guns; ritual humiliation and sexual assault; police guards repetitively kicking prisoners in the stomach; intimidation and threats to harm or kill family members; burning and branding. None of it "rose to the level of mistreatment" in the minds of their observers because they were, to quote the respondents in the report, "*no different from … procedures we observed by guards in U.S. jails*."
>
> (Gordon 2009: 172–73; emphasis in original)

We begin this chapter with a vignette from Georgia that provides an example of this brutal yet increasingly normal behavior. We then review research that documents recent trends in prison brutality, including the widespread use of "goon squads" and the link between guard violence and retaliation.

"Do What the Warden Says or Get your Ass Beat Every Day"

October 20, 2003 was a day no different from most for Thomas Clark. He was working in the kitchen of Georgia's Hays State Prison (Trion, Georgia). Seemingly out of nowhere, officers summoned Thomas to the prison's administrative office where he was met by several corrections officers and two officers from Georgia's Correctional Emergency Response Team or CERT, a special operations unit that responds to emergencies involving any of the state's prisons. One of the Hays officers confronted Clark stating that he was insubordinate and "refused to turn back on the tray machine." CERT officers then inexplicably handcuffed Clark and threw him violently face-first onto the concrete floor. The officers proceeded to literally drag Thomas Clark by his cuffed wrists to the prison's medical unit where CERT officers handcuffed him extremely tightly to a bed pole. Helpless at this point, Thomas was violently beaten again. Although what happened next may seem as though it comes out of a horror movie, it actually occurred; and, even more disturbingly so, turns out to be one of three forms of goon squad brutality used routinely against Georgia's prisoners.

Somewhere in the time after briefly seeing a nurse for his injuries, at least six Hays correctional officers attacked Thomas Clark, punching and kicking him repeatedly. The officers then subjected Clark to what they callously call a "Georgia Motorcycle." First, Clark was stripped completely naked. He was then strapped down to an iron bed where guards left him to writhe in pain for a full 24 hours. In order to prevent any visible wounds to his head, officers strapped a football helmet to Thomas's head. The following morning Clark woke up in Hays' Special Management Unit (SMU)—an isolation cell—where he was summarily awakened by two members of the CERT team who informed the on-duty officer that "this is the bad ass." The officer then punched Clark in the chin and eye and chillingly stated, "Welcome to SMU."

Another Georgia prisoner, Lebert Francis, had just completed his detail, cleaning the F-1 dorm at the Calhoun State Prison (Morgan, Georgia), when the prison's Deputy Warden Mathis summoned him. Francis must have been surprised when the Deputy Warden's request was to clean the lid of a trashcan. Francis refused and the warden sent him to solitary confinement.

As he packed up his clothes in his cell, two CERT officers barged in and put Lebert in handcuffs. They then threw him to the ground and as one officer choked Lebert the other repeatedly landed blows to his ribs. Both officers were overheard yelling, "This is not GSP [Georgia State Prison] … we run this prison … you was going to do what the warden says or get your ass beat every day." The CERT officers then dragged Lebert down a long flight of stairs, through the prison gym area, and directly to the solitary lockdown unit. Once in lockdown, CERT officers stripped Francis naked, placed him in an empty shower stall, and beat him until he literally pleaded for his life.

Unfortunately, Lebert Francis's nightmare had only just begun. CERT officers then extracted him from the shower and threw him into an empty office. Once inside, Lebert was subjected to the "Georgia G-String"—chains were run between his backside squeezing his testicles and then the chain was locked to his waist to induce agonizing pain. Lebert Francis was left in this torturous position for over three hours. When a CERT officer finally returned, he refused to release Lebert until he called him "daddy." Despite his serious injuries, corrections staff summarily denied Lebert medical care. Still in great pain and spitting up blood, an entire week would pass before Lebert was given permission by the Deputy Warden to seek treatment at the prison's medical clinic. (The source material used to construct this vignette comes from the following two separate civil actions filed against Hays State Prison and

Calhoun State Prison respectively: *Thomas E. Clark v. Steve Upton, et al.*, Civil Action No. 4:05-CV-00210-HLM and *Lebert W. Francis v. Steve Upton, et al.*, Civil Action No. 1:04-CV-191-WLS. These cases of guard brutality and numerous others filed by Georgia prisoners can be accessed online here: http://www.clearinghouse.net/chDocs/public/PC-GA-0014-0001.pdf.)

****

The Normalcy of Brutality in U.S. Prisons

A regime of prison-guard brutality in domestic prisons has been extensively documented by both human rights organizations and social scientists (Scraton and McCulloch 2009). One of the most illuminating empirical analyses is criminologist James Marquart's participant observation study of the Texas Department of Corrections (TDOC) at "Johnson Prison" (a pseudonym) in the mid-1980s. For over 19 months, Marquart documented various forms of guard brutality, including "ass whippings," "tap dances," and severe beatings in which prisoners required hospitalization. Perhaps most strikingly, Marquart's study reveals how white rural guards brutally targeted urban Black prisoners:

> The inmates at Johnson were mostly urban blacks while the guards were primarily rural whites who viewed the black inmates as basically antiauthority, inferior, disrespectful, aggressive, and, most of all, nondeferential... For the white guards, black prisoners represented troublesome, hostile, and rebellious prisoners ... Racial prejudice was common, and this factor helped facilitate the belief on the part of the guards that black inmates were impolite and troublesome.
>
> (Marquart 1986: 358)

Beyond this single institution, Marquart learned from the Court monitor that brutality was seen as legitimate by guards and occurred routinely in prisons throughout the entire state of Texas:

> The use of unofficial force was so common in the institution under study that the guards viewed it as an everyday operating procedure and legitimized its use. Further, Johnson was not an anomaly with regard to punitive force. Although this researcher did not observe the use of force in other Texas prisons, the trial proceedings from a prison reform case documented numerous (and quite similar) incidences of guard coercion in seven other state prisons. The Court found that the guards' use of punitive force was not an isolated phenomenon but constituted a routine (and rampant) guard activity.
>
> (Marquart 1986: 358)

An increasingly common form of prison guard brutality is the use of teams of guards trained to suppress disorder by any means necessary. While the threat of prison riots may unsurprisingly be very real in the United States' overcrowded prisons, a widespread pattern in both state and federal prisons, as documented above, has been the excessive use of force by such teams or what prisoners refer to as "goon squads." These Special Operations Response Teams (SORTs) or some variation thereof (e.g., Correctional Emergency Response Teams (CERTs)) are used throughout federal and state prisons in the United States. One of the chief objectives of SORTs is to capture and secure confessions from prison gang members or other prisoners who refuse to work (such as Thomas Clark) or are perceived as a broader threat to the prison's security. As an alternative to solitary confinement as detailed in the previous chapter, SORT raids typically involve dozens and sometimes hundreds of prisoners who are not gang members. Goon squad methodology is invariably a one-size-fits-all approach in which all prisoners in a particular cell block or institution are stripped naked and subjected to various forms of brutality, including the use of vicious dogs, painful restraint techniques, and weapons such as stun guns and Tasers to gain intelligence or confessions. In the most extreme instance, goon squads in California prisons have engaged in a sadistic campaign of brutality, including the use of lethal firearms, that resulted in the deaths of 175 prisoners over a five-year period between 1989 and 1994. Despite an FBI probe of one institution, Corcoran State Prison, where a prisoner was shot to death by a guard in his cell, Christian Parenti in *Lockdown United States: Police and Prisons in an Age of Crisis* reports:

> [B]rutality continued unabated. During the summer of 1995—even as FBI agents were gathering evidence from Corcoran's files—a gang of guards beat and tortured a busload of thirty-six newly arrived African–U.S. prisoners … Two years later one of the worst Corcoran COs had turned state's evidence … His specialty had been strangling inmates while other guards crushed and yanked the victims' testicles.
>
> (Parenti 2000: 174)

While the aggressive use of *lethal* force against prisoners in California may be less common in prisons in other states, the excessive prison-guard brutality documented in Georgia and Texas is not anomalous, nor is such behavior restricted to prisons in particular regions of the country. Consider the multitude of brutality that has been documented all across the United States:

Pennsylvania: *Prisoners are routinely subjected to unprovoked beatings and other forms of brutality by groups of prison guards. Four years of prisoner abuse logs (2007–2011) documenting the experiences of 900 prisoners from prisons across the state obtained by the Pennsylvania and Pittsburgh chapters of the Human Rights Coalition reveal* *horrifying beatings, aggressive use of pepper spray, unprovoked use of Tasers, and the deliberate starvation of prisoners.*[1]

Arizona: *Maricopa County Sheriff Joe Arpaio openly describes his desert tent city prison as a "concentration camp."*[2] *In addition to being fed rancid baloney three times a day and other inhumane conditions of confinement, prisoners are subjected by Arpaio's goon squads to excessive use of Tasers, shooting with stun guns, and vicious attacks by prison dogs.*[3]

Florida: *Officers excessively utilize dangerous chemical agents (e.g., pepper ball guns, pepper spray, and CS gas) on prisoners throughout the system. A class-action lawsuit filed by the Florida Justice Institute in February 2006 revealed that, among other serious injuries, prisoners suffered brutal flesh burns. Such burns were found to leave large blisters and open wounds all over the body and permanent scarring.*[4]

New Jersey, Colorado, Texas, Oklahoma, etc.: *These and many other state systems have aggressively turned to using restraining or "devil" chairs in which prisoners are tightly bound. Class-action lawsuits filed in numerous states show how prisoners are strapped down for many hours at a time. These cases reveal that prisoners are often beaten or pepper-sprayed while in restraints. The use of restraining chairs by multiple prison guards against prisoners has thus resulted in numerous serious injuries and at least 20 deaths.* (For a concise overview of the widespread use of restraining chairs to torture prisoners, see Cusac 2009: 230–43).

****

1 The entire database of prisoner abuse logs may be accessed from the Human Rights Coalition (HRC) website at http://hrcoalition.org/node/147. See also HRC's recent report, *Institutionalized Cruelty: Torture at SCI Dallas and in Prisons Throughout Pennsylvania.*

2 Sheriff Arpaio openly acknowledges that his tent city jails are concentration camps at approximately the 2min 50sec mark of the following video: http://www.upworthy.com/American-sheriff-says-and-i-quote-i-already-have-a-concentration-camp-its-call?rc=ifbc. For a disturbing documentary of the brutal treatment suffered by tent city prisoners go to: http://www.youtube.com/watch?v=_1tfIKUZ0fY.

3 Since 2008, the ACLU's National Prison Project has built an enormous class action lawsuit against Sheriff Arpaio. In addition to numerous prisoner abuses, the lawsuit documents a number of senseless prisoner deaths, including Earnest "Marty" Atencio whose brutal beating was videotaped by jail surveillance cameras and can be viewed here: http://www.youtube.com/watch?feature=player_embedded&v=YRgoNOMnUo#!

4 The original complaint, *Thomas v. Butler* (2011), filed by the Florida Justice Institute (FJI) provides extensive details into the torture of state prisoners with chemical agents—including the death of an asthmatic prisoner. These materials can be accessed from FJI's website at http://www.floridajusticeinstitute.org/Images/ButlerCompl.pdf.

The Nexus of Prison-Guard Brutality and Violent Retaliation

Beyond these egregious examples of brutality representing one of the most pervasive pains of mass imprisonment, recent empirical work has revealed that retaliation on the part of correctional officers has become an accepted norm in prisons today. Vincent S. Nathan's survey of prisoners and correctional officers finds that 70.1 percent of prisoners reported suffering retaliation after filing a formal grievance (Nathan 2001). An overwhelming 92 percent of prisoners, moreover, agreed with the statement, "I believe staff will retaliate or get back at me if I use the grievance process." Even among senior-level prison staff, a full 79 percent believed that retaliation by officers occurred. One warden Nathan interviewed tellingly characterized official retaliation as "commonplace," especially when prisoners file grievances against their captors. And 60 percent of prisoners in Nathan's study stated that a "substantial number of inmates" do not file grievances, despite suffering serious harms (Nathan 2001: 26–27).

In addition to survey research, James Robertson's comprehensive overview of legal cases involving official retaliation behind bars and contemporary correctional officer codes of conduct substantiates the pervasive way retaliation is legitimized under mass imprisonment. This occurs from the corrections officer's perspective because discretionary rules "readily mask retaliatory intent. As illustrated by rules sanctioning 'insubordination' and 'disrespect,' the frequent vagueness of disciplinary rules provides correctional officers ample leeway in deciding when and where to enforce these rules" (Robertson 2009: 616). Given the rise of the highly bureaucratized human warehouse model and its highly formulaic grievance procedures, it is then not surprising that Robertson observes that:

> The grievance process is emblematic of how the bureaucratic style of prison administration attempts to rationalize guard power within a rule-bound framework that accords inmates the opportunity to challenge guard power, especially their rule enforcement power … [And] correctional officers 'abhor' responding to inmate grievances presumably because they are an exercise in scrutinizing officer conduct.
>
> (Robertson 2009: 616)

Conclusion

Understanding widespread brutality behind bars cannot be separated from the broader total institutional context of the prison. Throughout this chapter we see how the brutalization of prisoners by their captors has become commonplace. One of the most insidious catalysts is grievances that prisoners file against prison staff. Here, we can see that the harsh conditions of confinement in this era of mass imprisonment are nearly always tied to brutal acts of officer retaliation and cover-ups. In a cruel irony—one that differs substantially from the "society of captives" described by Sykes—the very system designed to make prisoners safer and more secure leads prison officials to falsify reports, disable surveillance video cameras, and use excessive force to make prisoners far less safe. What happens then when the prison system has crossed the threshold from painful to systemically dehumanizing? What recourse do prisoners have when their lives are deemed largely expendable by the state? In the concluding chapter, we explore these questions from the prisoner's perspective.

DISCUSSION QUESTIONS

1. How have U.S. prisons served as a model for prisons in Iraq and Afghanistan, including Abu Ghraib?
2. Beyond the gruesome stories of brutality that have taken place in U.S. prisons today, why do the authors believe this state of affairs has become normalized in this era of mass imprisonment?
3. How do the authors believe brutality in contemporary U.S. prisons breaks from Sykes's classic conception of the pains of imprisonment?
4. How does this chapter illustrate the ways that guard brutality may be linked to retaliation?

Conclusion: Desperation

On July 1, 2011, 1,035 of the 1,111 prisoners trapped in Pelican Bay's SHU refused food. With no means of escape and no other available mode of resisting the cruel treatment they have endured, the prisoners opted for the most desperate of measures. "We have decided to put our fate in our own hands," Mutope DuGuma, one of the hunger strikers, explained. "Some of us have already suffered a slow, agonizing death in which the state has shown no compassion toward these dying prisoners. No one wants to die. Yet under this current system of what amounts to immense torture, what choice do we have? If one is to die, it will be on our own terms." The strikers put forth a list of five demands to the California Department of Corrections and Rehabilitation (CDRC):

1. *Eliminate group punishments for individual rule violations.*
2. *Abolish the debriefing policy and modify active/inactive gang status criteria.*
3. *Comply with the recommendations of the 2006 U.S. Commission on Safety and Abuse in Prisons regarding an end to long-term solitary confinement.*
4. *Provide adequate food.*
5. *Expand and provide constructive programs and privileges for indefinite SHU inmates.*

Reflective of a broader pattern of abuse we have documented throughout this book, the hunger strikers found themselves victim to official retaliation. Hunger strikers were written-up for "leading a riot or strike or causing others to commit acts of force and violence." The CDRC also threatened the strikers with additional criminal charges that would subject them to outside prosecution. Prison staff also removed family visitation rights and raided prisoner cells while the strike was in progress.

In the wake of the strike, three prisoners committed suicide: two from Pelican Bay, Johnny Owens Vick and Alex Machado, and a third, Hozel Blanchard, who was confined in the Administrative Segregation Unit at Calipatria, an institution whose prisoners joined the Pelican Bay detainees in solidarity. Although details of each of these men's deaths are shrouded in secrecy, many report that the decision to take their own lives was intimately linked to the torturous conditions they had endured and to the threat of retaliation they faced because of their involvement in the hunger strike. As Pelican Bay prisoner Todd Ashker said of Vick and Machado: "Obviously these men could not stand it anymore and preferred to die by their own hand rather than be subject to another minute of torture" (Law 2012). The mother of Hozel Blanchard's daughter wrote the following in the San Francisco Bay View newspaper:

> *We received a phone call advising us of his passing, but no information letting us know what happened. Hozel had explained to us in his letters that he was a part of the hunger strike, and his reasons for doing such was because of false accusations, resulting in two recent additional charges that were recently filed against him ... Hozel feared for his life and made sure that he got word to us that he no longer felt safe (Revolution 2011).*

(The following source materials were used to construct this vignette: Law (2012); Crowford and DuGuya (2011); de la Paz (2011); *Revolution*, November 17, 2011).

****

The experiences of the confined men and women we have described throughout this book reveal the many atrocious forms of penal oppression associated with life behind bars today. Building on Gresham Sykes's original articulation of the "pains of imprisonment," we have shown a distinctive rise in *barbarism* that is not separate from unprecedented increases in the number of U.S. men and women behind bars and an ideological commitment to getting "tough" on criminals no matter the cost. We have shown how, beyond being merely deprived of their liberty, today's warehoused prisoner experiences often unprovoked *containment* within prison walls. More than grappling with the pains of forced poverty, the prison industrial complex subjects the prisoner to harsh *exploitation*. Sexual *coercion* as experienced by women, the largest growing demographic of prisoners, emerges in our articulation of the pains of mass imprisonment as a far more serious threat to the prisoner than the deprival of sexual relationships. Prisoners today, moreover, face having their humanity stripped away in total *isolation*, often with minimal justification. And the threat of violence once posed by other prisoners is now compounded as brutal regimes of official *brutality* have become commonplace in U.S. prisons both at home and abroad.

For Sykes, the pains of imprisonment were indeed difficult, although throughout the remainder of his classic book he described a situation in which prison guards struggled to maintain control: "Unable to depend on a sense of duty among their prisoners as a basis for obedience, barred from the habitual use of force, and lacking an adequate stock of rewards and punishments, the custodians find themselves engaged in a constant struggle to achieve even the semblance of dominance" (Sykes 2007: 130–31). Sykes understood this not as a problem, but as a sort of natural outgrowth of his conception of the prison as a "society of captives." Whether guards or prisoners, what Sykes observed involved real people with real emotions, real concerns, and real interests that needed to be reconciled. Although the "pains of imprisonment" were real, for Sykes there remained a *give-and-take* relationship between captors and captives.

As the United States' prison population has exploded and far-reaching pains of confinement have become increasingly the norm, such a give-and-take relationship appears to have substantially eroded. The experiences of prisoners presented throughout this book indeed depict prison not as a "society" or as an "authoritarian community" in the way Sykes described it, but rather as a system needlessly inflicting what we have termed *penal oppression.* Corrections officers and officials today wield near-total power. No longer resistant to the use of force, they dangle the constant threat of retaliation over prisoners' heads. Captives are seen not as human beings with legitimate concerns but instead largely as *non-beings*. In contrast to the less repressive, more democratic prison Sykes envisioned, prisons today are ruled with an iron fist.

The desperation that characterizes prisons can be seen perhaps most profoundly in the recent hunger strikes at California's Pelican Bay and Calipatria prisons as well as prisons in several other U.S. states. As of this writing, in addition to California, hunger strikes are also underway in prisons all across the states of Georgia and North Carolina. For information regarding the Georgia strike, see Bright (2012). For more information on the North Carolina strike, see Infoshop News (2012).

Although the refusal to eat is by no means a new form of prisoner resistance,[1] the scale of recent hunger strikes in the United States is unprecedented. Indeed, in early 2010 Georgia prisoners in 11 of the state's 12 prisons organized one of the largest hunger strikes in U.S. history.[2] These acts of desperation testify to the widespread regime of inhumane treatment. In such an environment, prisoners willingly risk their own lives rather than continue to endure the pains of mass imprisonment. Stripped down to their bare existence and unable to take any more abuse, these prisoners are not asking to be "coddled" as some would claim. Far from it. As one hunger striker explains: "Our struggle is not about making prison more comfortable. It's about being treated humanely and with the hope of a positive future" (Law 2012).

Whereas Sykes concluded *The Society of Captives* with a rather hopeful call for prison reform, as we reflect back on how his classic work pertains to the contemporary era, questions of "reform" seem far off at best. What we have described in these chapters is not a system in need of reform in the penological sense. It is instead a humanitarian crisis on the grandest of scales: More than 1,600,000 prisoners, the majority of whom are people of color, are locked in a system that disregards their human dignity by subjecting them to containment, exploitation, coercion, isolation, and brutality. At the very least, we have captured in vivid detail the United States' crisis behind bars.

1 For a powerful account of hunger strikes and other acts of visceral prisoner resistance, see Perkinson (2010: 177–214).

2 realnews.com is one of the few media outlets to provide extensive coverage of the origins and subsequent events of the Georgia prison hunger strike of 2010: http://therealnews.com/t2/index.php?option=com_content&task=view&id=31&Itemid=74&jumival=8631.

Perhaps we have inspired some readers to become engaged in the struggle for the more humane treatment of prisoners (see Appendix). Despite the enormous challenges the current crisis presents, the efforts of prisoner rights groups and the prisoners they represent have been nothing short of remarkable. We can only hope that this movement will grow and that the crisis of mass imprisonment will end sooner rather than later.

DISCUSSION QUESTIONS

1. Why is it important for prisoners and their captors to have a "give-and-take relationship."?
2. With approximately 1,600,000 people behind bars in the United States today, is a "give-and-take relationship" even possible? Why or why not?

Appendix: Prisoner Rights Activism

Given the climate of retaliation that exists in prisons today, it is admittedly surprising that much of the material presented in this book was even available to the authors. As we have mentioned, the stories described are not anomalous prison horror stories and may not even represent the worst of what goes on behind prison walls today. Because today's prisoner is put at risk by making even the slightest attempt to expose grossly painful prison conditions, getting the word out about such injustices poses an extreme challenge. To that end, we would be remiss not to acknowledge the prisoners who were brave enough to report these injustices and the activist groups who helped make their reports visible to the public eye. Without their collective efforts, a book like this would not be possible. This appendix provides a list of the activist groups whose materials we drew on. By acknowledging their important work, we hope readers will learn more about these organizations and join this important struggle.

Center for Constitutional Rights (CCR)

Description: "Dedicated to advancing and protecting the rights guaranteed by the U.S. Constitution and the Universal Declaration of Human Rights," CCR is a non-profit legal and educational organization that works on a number of human rights-related issues, mass imprisonment among them. This is the group responsible for filing the lawsuit to protect prisoners in solitary confinement at Pelican Bay.
Website: http://ccrjustice.org

Equal Justice Initiative (EJI)

Description: This group provides legal representation to "indigent defendants and prisoners who have been denied fair and just treatment in the legal system." They also prepare reports that expose problems in the administration of criminal justice. One such report exposed widespread sexual abuse at the Julia Tutwiler Prison for Women in Alabama.
Website: http://www.eji.org/about

Florida Justice Institute (FJI)

Description: This not-for-profit public-interest litigation law firm represents "prisoners in civil lawsuits challenging the conditions of their confinement in state prisons and jails, and has done so for over 30 years." Among other cases challenging brutal prison conditions, FJI has recently filed a lawsuit to vindicate the death of Rommell Johnson who suffered a deadly asthma attack after being sprayed in his cell by prison officials with deadly chemical agents that attack the respiratory system.
Website: http://www.floridajusticeinstitute.org/default.aspx

Human Rights Coalition (HRC)

Description: This is a group composed primarily of ex-prisoners and prisoners' families. Their ultimate goal is the abolition of prisons, and immediate goal "to make visible to the public the injustice and abuse that are common practice throughout our judicial and prison systems across the country, and eventually end those abuses." HRC is responsible for exposing the widespread abuse—beatings, aggressive use of pepper spray and Tasers, and deliberate starvation of prisoners—which occurred in Pennsylvania.
Website: http://hrcoalition.org

Human Rights Watch (HRW)

Description: HRW is widely regarded as one of the world's leading organizations in defending and protecting human rights. While their focus is on human rights abuses as they occur in a variety of contexts, Human Rights Watch has done some vitally important work on improving prison conditions. An example of this is their sweeping 1993 report, *The Human Rights Watch Global Report on Prisons,* that we make reference to in Chapter IV.
Website: http://www.hrw.org

Juvenile Law Center (JLC)

Description: "The oldest non-profit, public-interest law firm for children in the United States," the Juvenile Law Center has been a tireless legal advocate for children who come into contact with the justice system for more than 30 years. JLC played a central role in exposing the "kids for cash" scandal mentioned in Chapter II.
Website: http://www.jlc.org

Prison Activist Resource Center (PARC)

Description: Describing itself as an "abolitionist group committed to exposing and challenging all forms of institutionalized racism, sexism, able-ism, heterosexism, and classism, specifically within the prison industrial complex," PARC is a clearinghouse of information for prisoners and their advocates. The organization publishes and distributes, for example, a highly regarded and expansive *Jailhouse Lawyers Manual*. PARC also publishes important reports, one of which we drew from to describe the toxic conditions to which prisoners working in UNICOR's e-waste recycling program were exposed.
Website: http://www.prisonactivist.org

Prison Law Office

Description: This California-based public-interest law firm has worked for more than 30 years "to enforce the Constitution and other laws inside the walls of California's prisons." Lawyers from the Prison Law Office successfully litigated the landmark *Brown v. Plata*, the case presented in Chapter I, in front of the Supreme Court, which resulted in a court order to reduce the size of California's prison population.
Website: http://www.prisonlaw.com

Sentencing Project (SP)

Description: "The Sentencing Project is dedicated to changing the way Americans think about crime and punishment." Since its inception in 1986, SP has been a leader in helping to distribute widely information about inequalities in the U.S. criminal justice system. We relied on Sentencing Project reports on numerous occasions in writing this book, as we often do when studying the criminal justice system.
Website: http://www.sentencingproject.org/template/index.cfm

Southern Center for Human Rights (SCHR)

Description: This group is responsible for exposing the disturbing and graphic instances of torture you read about in Chapter V. In addition to doing the important work of challenging human rights violations as they occur in prisons and jails in the southern United States, SCHR also represents death row prisoners, seeks to improve legal representation for poor people accused of committing crimes, and advocates for criminal justice reform more generally.
Website: http://www.schr.org

Bibliography

Abramsky, Sasha. 2002. *Hard Time Blues: How Politics Built a Prison Nation.* New York: St. Martin's Press.

Alexander, Michelle. 2010. *The New Jim Crow: Mass Incarceration in the Age of Colorblindness*. New York: The New Press.

American Public Health Association (APHA). 2003. *Standards for Health Services in Correctional Institutions*, 3rd edition. Washington, DC: APHA, Task Force on Correctional Health Care.

Anderson, David C. 1995. *Crime and the Politics of Hysteria*. New York: Times Books.

Beckett, Katherine. 1997. *Making Crime Pay: Law and Order in Contemporary American Politics.* New York: Oxford University Press.

Bernstein, Nell. 2007. *All Alone in the World: Children of the Incarcerated.* New York: The New Press, 2007.

Bright, Marcus. 2012. "Georgia Prison Hunger Strike Highlights an Invisible Population." *Huffington Post* (June 16). Accessed online at http://www.huffingtonpost.com/marcus-bright/hunger-strike-georgia-prison_b_1623052.html

Brown v. Plata. 131 U.S. 1910 (2011).

Buchanan, Kim Shayo. 2007. "Impunity: Sexual Abuse in Women's Prisons." *Harvard Civil Rights and Civil Liberties Law Review 42*(1): 46.

Burton-Rose, Daniel. 1998. "Permanent Lockdown: Control Unit Prisons and the Proliferation of the Isolation Model." P. 187 in *The Celling of America.* Monroe, ME: Common Courage Press.

Calhoun, Avery J. and Coleman, Heather D. 2002. "Female Inmates' Perspectives on Sexual Abuse by Correctional Personnel." *Women & Criminal Justice 13*(2/3): 108.

Casella, Jean and Ridgeway, James. 2012. "How Many Prisoners are in Solitary Confinement in the United States?" (February 1). Accessed online at http://solitarywatch.com/2012/02/01/how-many-prisoners-are-in-solitary-confinement-in-the-united-states

Center for Environmental Health, Prison Activist Resource Center, Silicon Valley Toxics Coalition, and the Computer TakeBack Campaign. 2006. *Toxic Sweatshops: How UNICOR Prison Recycling Harms Workers, Communities, the Environment, and the Recycling Industry*. Accessed online at http://www.ceh.org/storage/documents/toxicsweatshops.pdf

Chang, Cindy. 2012. "Louisiana is the World's Prison Capital." *The Times-Picayune* (May 13). Accessed online at http://www.nola.com/crime/index.ssf/2012/05/louisiana_is_the_worlds_prison.html

Crowford, James and DuGuya, Mutop. 2011. "Pelican Bay State Prison Security Housing Units Peaceful Protest Hunger Strike Starting July 1, 2011." *Prisoner Hunger Strike Solidarity.* Accessed online at http://prisonerhungerstrikesolidarity.wordpress.com/voices-from-inside/why-prisoners-are-protesting

Cusac, Anne-Marie. 2009. *Cruel and Unusual: The Culture of American Punishment.* New Haven, CT: Yale University Press.

Davis, Angela. 1998. "Masked Racism: Reflections on the Prison Industrial Complex." Accessed online at http://www.thirdworldtraveler.com/Prison_System/Masked_Racism_ADavis.html

Dickerson, John. 2008. "Arpaio's Jail Staff Cost Ambrett Spencer Her Baby, and She's Not the Only One." *Phoenix New Times* (October 30). Accessed online at http://www.phoenixnewtimes.com/2008-10-30/news/arpaio-s-jail-staff-cost-ambrett-spencer-her-baby-and-she-s-not-the-only-one

Dow, Mark. 2005. *American Gulag: Inside U.S. Immigration Prisons*. Berkeley: University of California Press.

Dyer, Joel. 2000. *The Perpetual Prisoner Machine: How America Profits from Crime.* Boulder, CO: Westview Press.

Eddy, J. Mark and Poehlmann, Julie. 2010. *Children of Incarcerated Parents: A Handbook for Researchers and Practitioners.* Washington, DC: Urban Institute Press.

Eisenman, Stephen F. 2009. "The Resistible Rise and Predictable Fall of the U.S. Supermax." *Monthly Review* (November). Accessed online at http://monthlyreview.org/2009/11/01/the-resistable-rise-and-predictable-fall-of-the-u-s-supermax

Equal Justice Initiative (EJI). 2012. *Investigation Into Sexual Violence at Tutwiler Prison.* Accessed online at http://eji.org/eji/files/EJI%20Findings_from_Tutwiler_Investigation.pdf

Erlich, Reese. 1995. "Prison Labor: Workin' for the Man." Accessed online at http://people.umass.edu/kastor/private/prison-labor.html

Feagin, Joe R. 2006. *Systemic Racism: A Theory of Oppression*. New York: Routledge.

Fleury-Steiner, Benjamin. 2008. *Dying Inside: The HIV/AIDS Ward at Limestone Prison.* Ann Arbor, MI: University of Michigan Press.

Garland, David. 2002. *The Culture of Control: Crime and Social Order in Contemporary Society*. Chicago: University of Chicago Press.

General Accountability Office. 1999. Accessed online at http://www.gao.gov/archive/1999/gg99104.pdf

Gonnerman, Jennifer. 2004. *Life on the Outside: The Prison Odyssey of Elaine Bartlett.* New York: Farrar, Straus and Giroux.

Gordon, Avery F. 2009. "The America Military Prison: The Normalcy of Exceptional Brutality." Pp. 164–86 in *The Violence of Incarceration*, Phil Scraton and Jude McCulloch, eds. New York: Routledge.

Gottschalk, Marie. 2006. *The Prison and the Gallows: The Politics of Mass Incarceration in America.* Cambridge Studies in Criminology.

Guerino, Paul, Harrison, Paige M., and Sabol, William. 2011. *Prisoners in 2010.* Washington, DC: Bureau of Justice Statistics.

Haney, Craig. 2003. "Mental Health Issues in Long-Term Solitary and 'Supermax' Confinement." *Crime & Delinquency 49*(1): 138–39.

———. 2012. "Prison Effects in the Age of Mass Incarceration." *The Prison Journal*, 92(4): 1. Accessed online at http://tpj.sagepub.com/content/early/2012/07/02/0032885512448604.abstract

Haney, Craig and Lynch, Mona. 1997. "Regulating Prisons of the Future: A Psychological Analysis of Supermax and Solitary Confinement." *New York University Review of Law and Social Change 23*: 477–95.

Hayes, Lindsay M. 1989. "National Study of Jail Suicides: Seven Years Later." *Psychiatric Quarterly 60*(1): 7–29.

Herivel, Tara. 2007. "Behind Closed Doors: Privatized Prisons for Youth." In *Prison Profiteers: Who Makes Money From Mass Incarceration*, eds. Tara Herivel and Paul Wright. New York: The New Press.

Hulling, Tracy. 2002. "Building a Prison Economy in Rural America." Pp. 197–213 in *Invisible Punishment: The Collateral Consequences of Mass Imprisonment*, eds. Marc Mauer and Meda-Chesney Lind. New York: The New Press.

Human Rights Coalition (HRC). 2012. *Institutionalized Cruelty: Torture at SCI Dallas and in Prisons Throughout Pennsylvania.* Accessed online at http://hrcoalition.org/sites/default/files/Institutionalized%20Cruelty.pdf

Human Rights Watch. 1993. *The Human Rights Watch Global Report on Prisons.* Accessed online at http://dmitrijus.home.mruni.eu/wp-content/uploads/2009/12/Human-Rights-Watch-Global-Report-on-Prisons.pdf

———. 1996. *All Too Familiar: Sexual Abuse of Women in U.S. State Prisons.* Accessed online at http://www.aclu.org/hrc/PrisonsStates.pdf

———. 1998. *Nowhere to Hide: Retaliation Against Women Prisoners in Michigan State Prisons.* Accessed online at http://www.hrw.org/legacy/reports/reports98/women

———. 2012. *Old Behind Bars.* Accessed online at http://www.hrw.org/node/104747/section/2

Huq, Aziz Z. and Muller, Christopher. 2008. "The War on Crime as Precursor to the War on Terror." *International Journal of Law, Crime and Justice 38*: 215–29.

Infoshop News. 2012. "North Carolina Prisoners on Hunger Strike." *San Francisco Bay View* (July 25). Accessed online at http://sfbayview.com/2012/north-carolina-prisoners-on-hunger-strike

Irwin, John. 1980. *Prisons in Turmoil.* Boston: Little, Brown.

——. 1985. *The Jail: Managing the Underclass in American Society.* Berkeley, CA: University of California Press.

Irwin, John and Cressey, Donald R. 1962. "Thieves, Convicts and the Inmate Culture." *Social Problems 10*(2): 142–55.

Jackson, Steven J. 2007. "Mapping the Prison Telephone Industry." In *Prison Profiteers: Who Makes Money From Mass Incarceration*, eds. Tara Herivel and Paul Wright. New York: The New Press.

Jones, Anne. 1986. "Self-Mutilation in Prison: A Comparison of Mutilators and Nonmutilators." *Criminal Justice and Behavior 13*(3): 286–96.

Khalek, Rania. 2011. "21st-Century Slaves: How Corporations Exploit Prison Labor." *AlterNet* (July 21). Accessed online at http://www.alternet.org/world/151732/21st-century_slaves%3A_how_corporations_exploit_prison_labor

Kirkham, Chris. 2012. "Private Prisons Profit From Immigration Crackdown, Federal and Local Law Enforcement Partnerships." *The Huffington Post* (June 7). Accessed online at http://www.huffingtonpost.com/2012/06/07/private-prisons-immigration-federal-law-enforcement_n_1569219.html

Kratcoski, Peter. 1988. "The Implications of Research Explaining Prison Violence and Disruption." *Federal Probation 52*: 27–32.

Law, Victoria. 2012. "Pelican Bay Prison: One Year Later, Policy Remains 'Debrief or Die.'" *Truthout* (June 30). Accessed online at http://truth-out.org/news/item/10011-pelican-bay-prison-one-year-later-policy-remains-debrief-or-die?newsletter

Levi, Robin and Waldman, Ayelet, eds. 2011. *Inside this Place, Not of It: Narratives from Women's Prisons.* San Francisco, CA: McSweeney's Press.

Maguire, Kathleen E., Flanagan, Timothy J., and Thornberry, Terence P. 1988. "Prison Labor and Recidivism." *Journal of Quantitative Criminology 4*(1): 3–18.

Majury, Diana. 2003. *The Tip of the Discrimination Iceberg: Barriers to Disclosure of the Abuse and Mistreatment of Federally Sentenced Women.* Women's Legal Education and Action Fund (LEAF). Accessed online at http://www.elizabethfry.ca/submissn/leaf/leaf.pdf

Marquart, James W. 1986. "Prison Guards and the Use of Physical Coercion as Mechanism of Prisoner Control." *Criminology 24*(3): 358.

Miles, Kathleen. 2011. "Riverside Charges Inmates for Stays in 'Prison Hotels.'" *The Huffington Post* (November 3). Accessed online at http://www.huffingtonpost.com/2011/11/03/riverside-charges-inmates_n_1075129.html

Minneci et al. v. Pollard et al. 565 U.S. (2012). Syllabus available online at http://www.supremecourt.gov/opinions/11pdf/10-1104.pdf

Mumola, Christopher J. 2000. *Incarcerated Parents and their Children.* Washington, DC: Bureau of Justice Statistics (BJS). Accessed online at http://www.bjs.gov/content/pub/pdf/iptc.pdf

Nathan, Vincent S. 2001. *Evaluation of the Ohio Inmate Grievance System.* Yale Law School. Accessed online at http://www.law.yale.edu/documents/pdf/Nathan_Evaluation_of_the_Ohio_Grievance_System.pdf

National Organization for Women (NOW). 2010. *End Shackling Now!* Accessed online at www.now.org/issues/violence/AntiShacklingKit.pdf

Overton v. Bazzetta. 539 U.S. 126 (2002).

Parenti, Christian. 2000. *Lockdown America: Police and Prisons in an Age of Crisis*. New York: Verso.

Parker, Kelly. 2004–5. "Pregnant Women Inmates: Evaluating Their Rights and Identifying Opportunities for Improvements in Their Treatment." *Journal of Law and Health 19*: 259–95.

de la Paz, Noelle. 2011. "Guards Retaliate Against Inmates in Growing Prison Hunger Strikes." *ColorLines* (October 5). Accessed online at http://colorlines.com/archives/2011/10/california_department_of_corrections_cracks_down_on_prisoner_hunger_strike.html

Pearson v. Wellborn. Decision available here: http://bulk.resource.org/courts.gov/c/F3/471/471.F3d.732.05-1241.05-1068.html

Perkinson, Robert. 2010. *Texas Tough: The Rise of America's Prison Empire*. New York: Picador.

Pew Center on the States. 2009. *One in 31: The Long Reach of American Corrections.* Accessed online at http://www.pewstates.org/research/reports/one-in-31-85899371887

———. 2010. *Collateral Costs: Incarceration's Effect on Economic Mobility.* Available online at http://www.pewstates.org/uploadedFiles/PCS_Assets/2010/Collateral_Costs%281%29.pdf

Rathbone, Cristina. 2005. *A World Apart: Women, Prison, and Life Behind Bars*. New York: Random House.

Revolution. 2011. "Three Prisoners from Hunger Strike Die—Prison Officials Withhold Information" (November 17). Accessed online at http://revcom.us/a/251/prisoners-from-hunger-strike-die-en.html

Robertson, James E. 2009. "'One of the Dirty Secrets of American Corrections': Retaliation, Surplus Power, and Whistleblowing Inmates." *University of Michigan Journal of Law Reform 42*(3): 616.

Ruiz v. Brown. Available online at http://www.georgiagreenparty.org/system/files/5-31-12%20Ruiz%20Amended%20Complaint.pdf

Sabo, Don, Kupers, Terry A., and London, Willie. 2001. *Prison Masculinities.* Philadelphia, PA: Temple University Press.

Scraton, Phil and McCulloch, Jude, eds. 2009. *The Violence of Incarceration.* New York: Routledge.

Selman, Donna and Leighton, Paul. 2010. *Punishment for Sale: Private Prisons, Big Business, and the Incarceration Binge*. Lanham, MD: Rowman and Littlefield.

Sentencing Project. n/d. Accessed online at http://www.sentencingproject.org/template/page.cfm?id=107

———. 2007. "Women in the Criminal Justice System: Briefing Sheets, May 2007." Accessed online at http://www.sentencingproject.org/doc/publications/womenincj_total.pdf

———. 2012. "Too Good to be True: Private Prisons in America." Accessed online at http://sentencingproject.org/doc/publications/inc_Too_Good_to_be_True.pdf

Simon, Jonathan. 2007. *Governing Through Crime: How the War on Crime Transformed Democracy and Created a Culture of Fear.* New York: Oxford University Press.

Spivak, Andrew L. and Sharp, Susan F. 2008. "Inmate Recidivism as a Measure of Private Prison Performance." *Crime & Delinquency 54(*3): 482–508.

Stark, Evan. 2007. *Coercive Control: How Men Entrap Women in Personal Life*. New York: Oxford University Press.

Steinke, Pamela. 1991. "Using Situational Factors to Predict Types of Prison Violence." *Journal of Offender Rehabilitation 17*(1–2): 111–32.

Stolberg, Sheryl Gay and Pear, Robert. 2010. "Wary Centrists Posing Challenge in Health Care Vote." *New York Times* (February 27). Accessed online at http://www.nytimes.com/2010/02/28/us/politics/28health.html

Stoller, Nancy. 2003. "Space, Place and Movement as Aspects of Health Care in Three Women's Prisons." *Social Science and Medicine 56*(11): 2265.

Sullivan, Laura. 2006. "At Pelican Bay Prison, a Life in Solitary." *NPR* (July 26). Accessed online at http://www.npr.org/templates/story/story.php?storyId=5584254

Sykes, Gresham. 2007. *The Society of Captives: A Study of a Maximum Security Prison, Princeton Classics Edition*. Princeton, NJ: Princeton University Press.

Torrey, E. Fuller. 1997. *Out of the Shadows: Confronting America's Mental Illness Crisis*- New York: John Wiley and Sons. An excerpt is available online at http://www.pbs.org/wgbh/pages/frontline/shows/asylums/special/excerpt.html#ret10

U.S. Census Briefs. 2010. "Overview of Race and Hispanic Origin: 2010." Available online at http://www.census.gov/prod/cen2010/briefs/c2010br-02.pdf

U.S. District Court of Michigan. 2001. Accessed online at http://www.mied.uscourts.gov/judges/archive/Edmundspdf/NGE95cv73540.pdf

Vaughn, Michael S. and Smith, Linda G. 1999. "Practicing Penal Harm Medicine in the United States: Prisoners' Voices from Jail." *Justice Quarterly 16*(1): 175–231.

Wacquant, Loïc. 2009. *Punishing the Poor: The Neoliberal Government of Social Insecurity*. Durham, NC: Duke University Press.

Welch, Michael. 2011. *Corrections: A Critical Approach.* New York: Routledge.

Winter, Caroline. 2008. "What Do Prisoners Make for Victoria's Secret?" *Mother Jones* (July/August). Accessed online at http://www.motherjones.com/politics/2008/07/what-do-prisoners-make-victorias-secret

Wright, Paul. 1994. "Slaves of the State." P. 105 in *The Celling of America,* ed. Daniel Burton-Rose. Monroe, ME: Common Courage Press. Accessed online at http://www.thirdworldtraveler.com/Prison_System/Slaves_State.html

Young, Abe Louise. 2010. "BP Hires Prison Labor to Clean Up Spill While Coastal Residents Struggle." *The Nation* (July 21). Accessed online at http://www.thenation.com/article/37828/bp-hires-prison-labor-clean-spill-while-coastal-residents-struggle

Index

Page numbers followed by 'f' refer to figures and followed by 't' refer to tables.

D

H

I

J

K

L

S